Policing America

Policing America

Methods, Issues, Challenges

FIFTH EDITION

KENNETH J. PEAK

University of Nevada, Reno

PEARSON
Prentice Hall

Upper Saddle River, New Jersey 07458

Library of Congress Cataloging-in-Publication Data

Peak, Kenneth J.,
Policing America: methods, issues, challenges / Kenneth J. Peak—5th ed.
p. cm.
Includes bibliographical references.
ISBN 0-13-118864-X
1. Police–United States. 2. Law enforcement–United States. I. Title.
HV8141.P33 2005
363.2'0973–dc22

2004065338

Executive Editor: Frank Mortimer, Jr.
Associate Editor: Sarah Holle
Executive Marketing Manager: Tim Peyton
Managing Editor: Mary Carnis
Production Liaison: Brian Hyland
Production Editor: Janet Bolton
Director of Manufacturing and Production: Bruce Johnson
Manufacturing Manager: Ilene Sanford
Manufacturing Buyer: Cathleen Petersen
Senior Design Coordinator: Miguel Ortiz
Cover Design: Joseph DePinho Design
Cover Image: Corbis
Electronic Art Creation: Carlisle Communication
Printing and Binding: Hamilton Printing
Proofreader: Maine Proofreading Services
Copy Editor: Judith Mara Riotto

Pearson Education LTD.
Pearson Education Australia PTY, Limited
Pearson Education Singapore, Pte. Ltd.
Pearson Education North Asia Ltd.
Pearson Education Canada, Ltd.
Pearson Educacion de Mexico, S.A. de C.V.
Pearson Education—Japan
Pearson Education Malaysia, Pte. Ltd.
Pearson Education, Upper Saddle River, New Jersey

PEARSON
Prentice
Hall

10 9 8 7 6
ISBN 0-13-118864-X

Dedication

Bullfight critics ranked in rows
Crowd the enormous stadium full.
But only one there *really* knows.
And that is the one who fought the bull.

I was quite taken by this quotation when I heard it for the first time; President John F. Kennedy is supposed to have carried it in his wallet. It speaks, of course, to the human tendency to criticize others in whose shoes we've not walked. While the field of law enforcement has been accorded relatively high public esteem since the terrorist attacks of September 11, 2001, history has shown the cyclic and fickle nature of community support for its protectors. Given that, I wish to dedicate this edition to all law enforcement officers who "fight the bull" and are still too often maligned for their efforts.

During a recent trip to our nation's capital, I visited the Law Enforcement Officers Memorial, where I traced from the wall the engraved names of four very good friends, two of whom were murdered while on duty. Hence I especially wish to dedicate this edition to all those officers who have lost their lives while performing their duties.

Contents in Brief

CHAPTER 1 HISTORICAL DEVELOPMENT 1

CHAPTER 2 LAW ENFORCEMENT LEVELS AND FUNCTIONS: DEFENDING OUR HOMELAND 41

CHAPTER 3 POLICE SUBCULTURE: THE MAKING OF A COP 68

CHAPTER 4 ORGANIZATION AND ADMINISTRATION 99

CHAPTER 5 ON PATROL: METHODS AND MENACES 130

CHAPTER 6 COMMUNITY-ORIENTED POLICING AND PROBLEM SOLVING 160

CHAPTER 7 CRIMINAL INVESTIGATION: THE SCIENCE OF DETECTION 185

CHAPTER 8 EXTRAORDINARY PROBLEMS AND METHODS 224

CHAPTER 9 THE RULE OF LAW 257

CHAPTER 10 ACCOUNTABILITY: ETHICS, FORCE AND CORRUPTION, AND DISCIPLINE 287

CHAPTER 11 CIVIL LIABILITY: FAILING THE PUBLIC TRUST 328

CHAPTER 12 ISSUES AND TRENDS 347

CHAPTER 13 COMPARATIVE PERSPECTIVES: POLICING IN FOREIGN COUNTRIES 386

CHAPTER 14 TECHNOLOGY REVIEW 419

CHAPTER 15 FOCUS ON THE FUTURE 445

Contents

Foreword, by Edward A. Flynn, Secretary of Public Safety, Commonwealth of Massachusetts xix
Preface xxiii
Acknowledgments xxv
About the Author xxvii

CHAPTER 1 **HISTORICAL DEVELOPMENT 1**

English and Colonial Officers of the Law 2
Sheriff 2 • Constable 3 • Coroner 5 • Justice of the Peace 6
The Old English System of Policing 7
Policing in Colonial America 8 • Legacies of the Colonial Period 10
Police Reform in England and America, 1829–1860 12
Full-Time Policing Comes to the United States 16
Imitating Peel 16 • Early Issues and New Traditions 18 • Attempts at Reform in Difficult Times 19 • Increased Politics and Corruption 20 • Meanwhile, on the American Frontier... 22
PRACTITIONER'S PERSPECTIVE WHAT SCIENCE HAS DONE FOR THE POLICE, CHIEF FRANCIS O'NEILL, CHICAGO, 1903 23
The Entrenchment of Political Influence 25
The Movement toward Professionalization 25
Attempts to Thwart Political Patronage 25 • The Era of August Vollmer 26 • The Crime Fighter Image 28 • The Wickersham Commission 28
EXHIBIT 1-1 THE CRIB OF MODERN LAW ENFORCEMENT 29
Police as the "Thin Blue Line": William H. Parker 30
A Retreat from the Professional Model 32
Coming Full Circle to Peel: The President's Crime Commission 32
Community-Oriented Policing and Problem-Solving Era 33
The Three Generations of COPPS 35
SUMMARY 36
REVIEW QUESTIONS 36

INDEPENDENT STUDENT ACTIVITIES 36
RELATED WEB SITES 37
NOTES 37

CHAPTER 2 LAW ENFORCEMENT LEVELS AND FUNCTIONS: DEFENDING OUR HOMELAND 41

Federal Agencies 42

The Department of Homeland Security 42 • The Department of Justice 48 • Other Related Federal Agencies 59

State and Local Agencies 61

State Police 61 • Local (Municipal Police and County Sheriff) Agencies 62

SUMMARY 63
REVIEW QUESTIONS 63
INDEPENDENT STUDENT ACTIVITIES 63
RELATED WEB SITES 64
NOTES 65

CHAPTER 3 POLICE SUBCULTURE: THE MAKING OF A COP 68

First Things First: Recruiting Qualified Applicants 69

Wanted: Those Who Walk on Water 69 • Recruiting Problems and Successes 71

Testing: The Hurdle Process for New Personnel 73

Written Examinations: General Knowledge and Psychological Tests 73 • Physical Agility Test 74 • Oral Interview 75 • Character Investigation 76 • Polygraph Examination 76 • Medical Examination and Drug Screening 77

The Recruit's Formal Entry into Policing: Academy Training 78

Types of Academies 78 • The Curriculum: Status and Ongoing Need for Revision 78 • A New Uniform and Demeanor 80 • A Sixth Sense 81

Postacademy Field Training 85

The Field Training Officer Concept 85 • New Technology 85

Having the "Right Stuff": A Working Personality 86

Developing and Using a Police Personality 86 • What Traits Make a Good Cop? 88

Roles, Functions, and Styles of Policing 89

Defining and Understanding the Police Role 89 • Role Conflicts 90 • Policing Functions and Styles 91 • Which Role, Function, and Style Are Typically Employed? 93

SUMMARY 93
REVIEW QUESTIONS 93
INDEPENDENT STUDENT ACTIVITIES 94
RELATED WEB SITES 94
NOTES 94

CHAPTER 4 **ORGANIZATION AND ADMINISTRATION 99**

Organizations and the Police 100

What Are Organizations? 100 • Organizations as Bureaucracies 101

Organizational Communication 101

Definition and Characteristics 101 • Communication within Police Organizations 103 • The Grapevine 103 • Written Communication 104 • Barriers to Effective Communication 104

Police Agencies as Organizations 105

Chain of Command 105 • Organizational Structure 106 • Unity of Command and Span of Control 107 • Organizational Policies and Procedures 109

Contemporary Police Chiefs and Sheriffs 110

Police Chief 110 • The Sheriff 112

The Chief Executive Officer: A Model 114

Applying the Mintzberg Model of CEOs 114 • The Interpersonal Role 114 • The Informational Role 115 • The Decision-Maker Role 115 • An Example of Mintzberg in Action: NYPD's Compstat 116

PRACTITIONER'S PERSPECTIVE POLICE INGENUITY AND ENTREPRENEURSHIP, DENNIS D. RICHARDS 118

Middle Managers: Captains and Lieutenants 118

The First-Line Supervisor 120

Ten Tasks 121 • Types of Supervisors 121

EXHIBIT 4-1 GOOD, BETTER, BEST: WHAT MAKE SOME SERGEANTS A CUT ABOVE THE REST? 122

Police and Politics 123

Political Exploitation of the Police 124 • Police Executive Relations and Expectations 124

SUMMARY 125
REVIEW QUESTIONS 126
INDEPENDENT STUDENT ACTIVITIES 126
RELATED WEB SITES 127
NOTES 127

CHAPTER 5 **ON PATROL: METHODS AND MENACES 130**

Patrol as Work: Culture of the Beat 131

Purposes and Nature of Patrol 131

EXHIBIT 5-1 POLICE PATROL: A JOB DESCRIPTION 134

Filling Occasional Hours of Boredom 137 • Patrol Work as a Function of Shift Assignment 137 • Influences of One's Assigned Beat 139 • Where Danger Lurks: The Hazards of Beat Patrol 140

An Unappreciated American Icon: The Patrol Vehicle 143

A Sanctuary and a Place for Vital Gear 143 • Evolution of the Patrol Vehicle 144 • Today's Accoutrements 145

Studies of the Patrol Function 145

Discretionary Use of Police Authority 148

The Link between Patrol and Discretion 148 • An Exercise in Discretion 148 • Attempts to Define Discretion 149 • Determinants of Discretionary Actions 150 • Pros, Cons, and Politics of Discretionary Authority 151

A Related Function: Traffic 152

Policing Today's Motorized Society 152 • Traffic Accident Investigation 153 • In Pursuit of the "Phantom Driver" 154

Summary 155
Review Questions 156
Independent Student Activities 156
Related Web Sites 156
Notes 157

CHAPTER 6 **Community-Oriented Policing and Problem Solving 160**

Basic Principles of Community Policing 161

A Major Step Forward: Problem-Oriented Policing 162

The Problem-Solving Process: SARA 164

A Collaborative Approach: Basic Principles of COPPS 169

Exhibit 6-1 The Home Page of the Tempe, Arizona, Police Department's Crime Analysis Unit 170

Implementing COPPS 171

Principal Components of Successful Implementation 172

A Broader Role for the Street Officer 173

Did It Succeed? Evaluating COPPS 174

Crime Prevention 175

Crime Prevention through Environmental Design 176 • Studying Prey: Repeat Victimization 177 • Drug Abuse Resistance and Education 177

COPPS Case Studies 178

Addressing Domestic Violence in Charlotte-Mecklenburg 178 • Ameliorating Juvenile Problems in Tulsa 179

Summary 181
Review Questions 181
Independent Student Activities 182
Related Web Sites 182
Notes 182

CHAPTER 7 **Criminal Investigation: The Science of Detection 185**

The Scope of Forensic Science and Criminalistics 186

Exhibit 7-1 Making His Bones: Famed Sculptor Is a Secret Weapon in Missing–Person Cases 188

Origins of Criminalistics 189

Personal Identification: Anthropometry and Dactylography 189 • Firearms Identification 192 • Contributions of August Vollmer and Others 194

The Evolution of Criminal Investigation 195

Investigative Beginnings: The English Contribution 195 • Investigative Techniques Come to America 196 • State and Federal Developments 197

Forensic Science and the Criminal Justice System 197

Investigative Stages and Activities 197 • Arrest and Case Preparation 199

Detectives: Qualities, Myths, and Attributes 200

Officers Who "Disappear": Working Undercover 201

Problems with the Role 201 • Returning to Patrol Duties 202

Uses of the Polygraph 202

DNA Analysis 203

Methods 203 • Methods and Standards for Testing 205

EXHIBIT 7-2 DNA AND THE GREEN RIVER KILLER 206

Recent Developments: Mitochondrial DNA and National Databases 206

Behavioral Science in Criminal Investigation 208

Criminal Profiling 208 • Psychics and Hypnosis 209

Recent Developments in Forensic Science and Investigation 210

Interrogations of a Different Sort: Terrorism Suspects 210 • Forensic Entomology: Using "Insect Detectives" 211

EXHIBIT 7-3 A NEW CRIME SCENE ACADEMY 213

Stalking Investigations 213 • Investigating "Cybercrooks" 214 • Protecting the Innocents: Investigating Crimes against Juveniles and Missing Youths 215

EXHIBIT 7-4 LOOKING AT "COLD" CASES 216

No Stone Unturned: Handling Cold Cases 216

SUMMARY 217

REVIEW QUESTIONS 217

INDEPENDENT STUDENT ACTIVITIES 218

RELATED WEB SITES 218

NOTES 219

CHAPTER 8 **EXTRAORDINARY PROBLEMS AND METHODS 224**

Terrorism and Homeland Security 225

A Nation Changed and Challenged 225 • Definitions and Types 225 • Greater Law Enforcement Powers: The USA PATRIOT Act 227 • Spiking Resources 229 • An Intelligence Overhaul 230 • A Companion Threat: Bioterrorism 230

EXHIBIT 8-1 WITH BIOCHEM TERROR NO LONGER "UNTHINKABLE," NYPD GETS READY 231

PRACTITIONER'S PERSPECTIVE BIOTERRORISM: THE CHALLENGES FOR LOCAL LAW ENFORCEMENT, KENNETH W. HUNTER JR., SC.D. 232

Policing Hate 236

Policing the Mafia 238

Origin and Organization 238 • Successful Police Offensives 239

Practitioner's Perspective Going Undercover: An FBI Agent's Two-Year Experience, George Togliatti 240

Policing Street Gangs 243

Definition and Extent of the Problem 243 • Organization and Revenues 243 • Ethnic and Racial Gangs 244 • Graffiti and Hand Signals 245 • New Threats 247 • Gangs and Terrorism 248

Policing America's Borders 249

A New Terrorist Watch Program 249 • The Southwestern Border 250 • New Technologies: Border Drones 251

Summary 251

Review Questions 252

Independent Student Activities 252

Related Web Sites 252

Notes 253

CHAPTER 9 **The Rule of Law 257**

The Rule of Law 258

The Fourth Amendment 258 • The Fifth Amendment 275 • The Sixth Amendment 278

Juvenile Rights 280

Summary 282

Review Questions 282

Independent Student Activities 283

Related Web Sites 283

Notes 283

CHAPTER 10 **Accountability: Ethics, Force and Corruption, and Discipline 287**

In the Beginning: Problems Greet the New Millennium 288

Troubles in Cities Large and Small 288 • A New Tool: Federal Investigations 289

Police Ethics 290

A Scenario 290

Exhibit 10-1 Measuring a Police Department's "Culture of Integrity" 291

Exhibit 10-2 Law Enforcement Code of Ethics 292

Definition and Types 294 • Ethics and Community Policing 294

Use of Violence and Force 295

A Tradition of Problems 295 • The Prerogative to Use Force 296 • Police Brutality 297

Exhibit 10-3 Good News, Better News on Use of Force 298

Exhibit 10-4 Study Links Use of Force to Suspect's Back Talk 299

Use and Control of Lethal Force 301 • Further Sources of Tension: Bias-Based Policing and Other Field Tactics 302

Exhibit 10-5 Sacramento Searches for Biased Policing 303

A Related Issue: Domestic Violence 304

Police Corruption 305

A Long-Standing "Plague" on Policing 305 • Types and Causes 306 • The Code of Silence 308 • Investigation and Prosecution 309 • Possible Solutions 309

Limitations on Officers' Constitutional Rights 310

Free Speech 310 • Searches and Seizures 311 • Self-Incrimination 312 • Religious Practices 312 • Sexual Misconduct 312 • Residency Requirements 313 • Moonlighting 314 • Misuse of Firearms 314 • Alcohol and Drug Abuse 315

Disciplinary Policies and Practices 316

Maintaining the Public Trust 316 • Due Process Requirements 316 • Dealing with Complaints 317 • Determining the Level and Nature of Sanctions 321

Summary 322
Review Questions 322
Independent Student Activities 322
Related Web Sites 323
Notes 323

CHAPTER 11 **Civil Liability: Failing the Public Trust 328**

A Legal Foundation 329

History and Growth of Section 1983 Litigation 332 • Police Actions Leading to Section 1983 Liability 334 • Criminal Prosecutions for Police Misconduct 337

Liability of Police Supervisors 338

New Areas of Potential Liability 339

Police Vehicle Pursuits: A High-Stakes Operation 339

Practitioner's Perspective Police and Civil Liability, Samuel G. Chapman 340

Computer Evidence 342 • Disseminating Public Information 342

Summary 343
Review Questions 343
Independent Student Activities 343
Related Web Sites 344
Notes 344

CHAPTER 12 **Issues and Trends 347**

Contemporary Policing Trends 348

Labor Relations: Officers' Rights, Unionization, and Collective Bargaining 348 • Women Who Wear the Badge 355

Practitioner's Perspective Women in Policing: Past, Present, and Future, Chief Penny Harrington 358

Minorities as Police Officers 363 • On Guard: The Private Police 365 • Accreditation 368

Contemporary Policing Issues 369

Higher Education for Police 369

Exhibit 12-1 For Florida Police, Higher Education Means Lower Risk of Disciplinary Action 371

A Related Program: The Police Corps 372 • Stress: Sources, Effects, and Management 373

Exhibit 12-2 The Blue Plague of American Policing 378

Summary 379

Review Questions 379

Independent Student Activities 380

Related Web Sites 380

Notes 380

CHAPTER 13 **Comparative Perspectives: Policing in Foreign Countries 386**

Iraq 387

A History of Dictators and Disorder 387 • Policing the World's Most Perilous Place 388 • Since Saddam's Fall: A Poorly Trained and Equipped Force 388 • The Future 389

Saudi Arabia 389

An Exodus over Terrorism 389

Exhibit 13-1 Changing Bad Cops to Good 390

Social Behavior in a Patriarchal Land 390 • Religious Underpinnings 391 • Laws and Prohibitions 392 • Guardians of Religious Purity 393

China 395

Policing a Vast Land 395 • Reform under Police Law 1995 395

Northern Ireland 399

Recent Developments and Violence in a Long Civil War 399 • A Divided Land 400 • Political Factions 400 • Policing the Terrorist War 401 • A New Source of Terror: Paramilitary Groups 403

Mexico 405

A New President and Unfulfilled Promises 406 • Police Organization 406 • Recruitment and Training 407 • Criminal Codes and the Legal System 408 • Jail Atrocities 408

Toward Democratizing the Police Abroad: Lessons Learned 409

Interpol 410

Tracking International Criminals 410 • A Formula for Success 412

Exhibit 13-2 Needs of Police Training and Education Transcend International Boundaries 413

Summary 413
Review Questions 414
Independent Student Activities 414
Related Web Sites 415
Notes 415

CHAPTER 14 **Technology Review 419**

Police and Technology of the Future: Problems and Prospects 420
Exhibit 14-1 The Power of Information, in a Palm-Sized Package 421
Technology versus Terrorists 422
The Development of Less-Lethal Weapons 422
A Historical Overview 422
Exhibit 14-2 Reducing the Death Toll from Nonlethal Weapons 425
The Quest Continues 426
The Use of Wireless Technology 428
Instant Access to Information 428 • Integrated Databases 428 • Crime Mapping 429 • Locating Serial Offenders 430
Exhibit 14-3 Interactive Crime Mapping on the Internet 431
Exhibit 14-4 Twenty-First-Century Police Department 432
Gunshot Locator System 432 • Dogs and Searches for Lost Persons 433
Electronics in Traffic Functions 434
Accident Investigation 434 • Arresting Impaired Drivers 435 • Preventing High-Speed Pursuits 435
DNA 436
Fingerprints and Mug Shots 437
Crime Scenes: Computers to Explore and Draft Evidence 438
Developments Relevant to Firearms 439
Computer-Assisted Training 439 • Using Gun "Fingerprints" to Solve Cases 439
Gang Intelligence Systems 440
Summary 440
Review Questions 441
Independent Student Activities 441
Related Web Sites 441
Notes 442

CHAPTER 15 **Focus on the Future 445**

Taking Futures Seriously: A Working Group and a Futurists' Society 446
What the Future Might Hold for the Police 446
Exhibit 15-1 Police Futurists International 447
Futures Research 447 • High Technology: Coming Attractions 447 • Nanotechnology 449 • Community-Oriented Policing and Problem Solving 450 • The Role of the Beat Officer 452 • Other Personnel Issues 453

Crime, Violence, and the Influence of Drugs and Guns 453
SUMMARY 455
REVIEW QUESTIONS 456
INDEPENDENT STUDENT ACTIVITIES 456
RELATED WEB SITES 456
NOTES 456

APPENDIX A CAREER INFORMATION 459
Preparing for Job Hunting 459
Careers in Federal Law Enforcement 460
Careers with the State Police 460
Careers in Local Policing 461

APPENDIX B THE POLICE CORPS 462

Index 465

Foreword

The subtitle to the fifth edition of *Policing America* sums up in the words "Methods, Issues, Challenges" what law enforcement practitioners must be prepared to learn, to understand, and to confront. As I write these words, I am struck by the notion that I am addressing the future leaders of American law enforcement. I feel not unlike a parent whose teenage children cannot conceive of the fact that Dad or Mom ever experienced adolescence with all its attendant thrills, temptations, and anxieties. At the same time, that harried parent can't believe how fast the time went from youth to middle age and yearns to release that inner young rebel who's in there somewhere. Meanwhile, hope persists that the young will be open to the message of experience. In my case, it's my "inner patrolman" that's struggling to break free, who is shocked at how far away that cruiser is now, and who is amazed by the progress and improvements that have occurred in law enforcement over the course of one career.

This textbook ably demonstrates that policing as a profession has moved far beyond the admonition I heard from more than one "old salt" when I started out: "All you need for this job is common sense." Common sense will always be a tool in the successful practitioner's bag, but in my experience there are fewer things less common than common sense. Furthermore, if one sees *common sense* as another term for *good judgment,* then it becomes clear that education, as well as experience, is an essential component of its development.

I hope that those of you reading this book, whether as part of a promotional study course or an introductory college course, in an academy setting or for professional improvement, aspire to be a leader. Make no mistake about it: If you choose a career in law enforcement, you are choosing to become a leader, with all of its attendant responsibilities. You cannot opt to fade into the background or to be a follower. Law enforcement demands leadership at every rank, in every assignment, at every level of experience. The public demands leadership from every police officer, sergeant, lieutenant, captain, deputy chief, or chief—whether on the street or in city council chambers. If you aspire to serve your country in law enforcement, you must be prepared to lead the public and your peers and, if you are promoted, those for whom you are responsible.

The fulfillment of professional responsibility in law enforcement entails, therefore, a leadership requirement. Neighborhoods need leadership to overcome problems of crime and disorder. Colleagues need leadership that models honorable police behavior in the use of authority, the use of force, and the exercise of discretion. Subordinates require leadership that guides, supports, and inspires them. And political figures need leadership from their police officials, who must be willing to "speak truth to power" and be able to translate the police experience in all its complexity and nuance into sound public policy. Such leadership demands moral courage and the responsibility to always put the needs of those you would lead first.

Leadership is an act of will dependent upon a commitment to self-improvement. No one can claim to be a professional and to provide leadership without becoming a student—a student of the profession and a student of leadership. *Policing America* addresses the needs of the emerging police practitioner/leader by focusing on what kind of person one must be, what one must know, and what one must be able to do. Success demands that those who would police America, and by definition lead it, must be people of integrity who understand the complexity of their society and the sweep of their profession's history. In short, they must have character and perspective.

But character and perspective, essential as they are, are not a guarantee of effectiveness. Our police professionals must be able to do certain things, do them well, and do them in ambiguous and sometimes dangerous circumstances. This requires professional competence. Competence requires a firm basis of study, reinforced by practice and solidified by experience.

This textbook provides a solid and generous foundation upon which you, the future of American law enforcement, can prepare yourself for the challenges of today and tomorrow. No one can aspire to the term *professional* without an understanding of their profession's history. *Policing America* ably traces the evolution of American policing. Just as important, the student is exposed to the police subculture. Every profession has a subculture, and every subculture is an adaptation to the professional environment with healthy and unhealthy attributes. Then the book addresses all of the things an officer must be, know, and do by thoroughly covering administrative issues, patrol techniques, and methods of investigation. What is signal about this work is its attention to the ethical and legal underpinnings of law enforcement. Many texts cover the "know" and "do" aspects of policing. Few general texts so thoughtfully cover the "be."

As has been true throughout history, America, and by extension its police establishment, is beset by internal and external challenges. My generation grappled with urban riots, the explosion of street crime, the heroin and crack epidemics, strained relations with minority groups, a frequently unhelpful "war on crime" policy debate, and the frustrations of being misunderstood by a public that wanted frequently contradictory things from their police.

But we were also privileged to participate in the evolution of policing from a military model to a community-based, problem-oriented model. We witnessed our ranks diversify and strengthen as barriers to the recruitment of women and racial and ethnic minorities were removed. We participated in the reclamation of our nation's cities as crime and disorder were, finally, successfully confronted and contained.

You, the reader, are confronting a new array of issues, many of which derive directly from the recent past. If history teaches us anything, it is that nothing is ever truly settled and that the judgment of history is at best provisional and always open to deconstruction. For the police profession, that means that today's successes frequently breed tomorrow's problems.

Yes, the United States experienced a dramatic decrease in crime in the last decade. But in many jurisdictions, there are indications of an increase, fueled in part by an increase in the youth demographic but also by an enormous returning offender population. This is the "reentry" problem. That part of the crime decrease resulting from the incapacitation of repeat offenders for mandatory sentences is now vulnerable.

Yes, the most profound decreases in crime were experienced in our most vulnerable urban neighborhoods, which were often populated by racial or ethnic minorities. But many of those same populations experienced the increased police attention as "racial profiling." Those concerns have been heard politically, and in many places they have strained police-community relations, which had only just begun to improve. This challenges police assumptions about effective tactics and causes frustration and cynicism among officers who feel unjustly maligned.

The community-policing movement brought a dramatic change in how the police interact with the neighborhoods and how they solve problems before they become crimes. But new homeland security responsibilities are creating burdens on police departments at a time of declining financial and personnel resources. Furthermore, there are pressures on police to "militarize" to confront the terrorist threat. This threatens to separate police from their communities at a time when the building of relations with new ethnic groups may be the most important antiterror campaign the police can wage.

All this is to say that you face a career full of great responsibilities and great challenges. This has been and always will be the lot of law enforcement. I hope you are not daunted by what lies before you. Understand, always, that what makes policing a vocation and not a mere job is precisely the enormity of the task assigned to it. We have the responsibility to support and make possible the grand experiment that is America. It is policing, more than any other function, that guarantees an environment in which the most diverse, prosperous, dynamic society on earth is capable of governing itself in a manner that relies on democratic processes but guarantees minority rights. Our nation's character is defined not merely by its laws, but in the manner in which those laws are enforced.

The future depends on the decisions you will make, understanding that you protect a society deeply ambivalent about police power even as its cohesion depends on its judicious use. Be proud of what you have chosen to become. Take to heart the lessons contained on these pages. And never stop improving your ability to be worthy of the trust your nation places in you.

Edward A. Flynn,

Secretary of Public Safety,
*Commonwealth of Massachusetts**

*Edward A. Flynn was appointed secretary of public safety by Governor Mitt Romney in January 2003. Secretary Flynn is responsible for the Massachusetts State Police, the Department of Correction, the National Guard, the Department of Fire Services, the Massachusetts Emergency Management Agency, and other organizations. He also serves as the chief adviser to the governor on homeland security. He is responsible for administering a budget of more than $1 billion and more than ten thousand people. Secretary Flynn comes to this position with over thirty-two years of law enforcement experience, including five years as the chief of police in Arlington County, Virginia, where he was instrumental in the recovery effort at the Pentagon after the September 11 terrorist attack; fifteen years in the Jersey City Police Department, where he rose to the rank of inspector; and chief of police in Braintree, Massachusetts, and Chelsea, Massachusetts. In 2003, he participated in the investigation into the sniper shootings in the Washington, D.C., area.

Secretary Flynn is a past member of the board of directors for the Police Executive Research Forum and is a recipient of the prestigious Gary Hayes Memorial Award for Police Leadership. He holds a bachelor's degree in history from LaSalle University in Philadelphia and a master's degree in criminal justice from John Jay College of Criminal Justice in New York, and he has completed all course work in the Ph.D. program in criminal justice at the City University in New York. Chief Flynn is a graduate of the FBI National Academy and the National Executive Institute and was a National Institute of Justice Pickett Fellow at Harvard's Kennedy School of Government.

Preface

This fifth edition of *Policing America,* more than its predecessors, reflects the changing times in which we live and the tremendous challenges facing law enforcement officers each day. The specter of terrorism and our resulting emphasis on homeland security loom large throughout this edition, as well as what the police are doing to prevent—and react to—any future attacks.

Like its forerunners, however, this edition is my best attempt to inform the reader, to the fullest extent possible, of what it is like to wear a police uniform. Because I bring more than 35 years of both scholarly and policing experience to this effort, the chapters contain a real-world flavor not found in most policing textbooks. This text provides a highly practical yet comprehensive view of the largely misunderstood, often obscure world of policing. New materials have been added throughout, including discussions on terrorism, the three eras of community policing, mitochondrial DNA, crimes against children, cold cases, policing in Iraq, developing technologies, and recent court decisions. At the same time, this edition continues to provide updated information and in-depth coverage of such topics as patrol, the police subculture, accountability, civil liability, extraordinary problems and practices, the rule of law, investigations, organization and administration, policing in selected foreign countries, and the future of policing. Throughout the book are several Practitioner's Perspectives—short essays written by selected individuals who have expertise in selected areas of policing.

There are other pedagogical attributes as well. To continue my attempt to make this textbook more reader-friendly, each chapter begins with a list of key terms and an overview of the topic. Each key term is bolded in the chapter. There are review questions, independent student activities, and related Web sites at the end of each chapter. I recommend that you examine the review questions after reading each chapter to get a feel for how well you understand the chapter's contents. The independent activities and Web sites are intended to enhance your understanding of the applied aspects of policing. Other instructional aids include the aforementioned Practitioner's Perspectives, tables and figures, and exhibit boxes with recent news items. Finally, a detailed index at the end of the book makes it easy for you to find information on specific topics quickly. An instructor's manual/test bank is also available for classroom instructors using this textbook.

From the foreword by Edward A. Flynn through the final chapter, this book provides a penetrating view of what is certainly one of the most difficult and challenging occupations in America.

Chapter Organization and Overview

Chapter 1 discusses the history of policing, and Chapter 2 examines the contemporary status of federal, state, and local law enforcement agencies; here the focus is on the federal agencies, which have been reorganized in major fashion since the creation of the Department of Homeland Security. Chapter 3 examines the police subculture and how ordinary citizens are socialized to the role. The next chapter considers how police agencies are organized and administered, and how administrators, middle managers, and supervisors perform their functions. Chapter 5 explores the very important function of patrolling, including its methods and menaces.

Chapter 6 focuses on a form of policing that is being embraced by thousands of police agencies across the United States and around the world: community-oriented policing and problem solving (COPPS). Chapter 7 focuses on criminal investigation, including the highly progressive fields of forensic science and criminalistics, and Chapter 8 looks at several extraordinary problems and methods with regard to policing, including terrorism, hate crimes, the Mafia, gangs, and the nation's borders. The rule of law is discussed in Chapter 9, which delineates the constitutional guidelines that direct and constrain police actions. Chapter 10 looks at police accountability to the public, including the issues of police ethics, use of force, and corruption.

Police civil liability is examined in Chapter 11. Chapter 12 describes a number of issues and trends, including the rights of police officers, unionization, women and minorities in policing, the private police, the accreditation of police agencies, higher education for police, and police stress. Then, to better understand policing in this country, Chapter 13 analyzes policing in five international venues: Iraq, Saudi Arabia, China, Northern Ireland, and Mexico. Interpol, the international crime-fighting organization, is also discussed.

Chapter 14 examines contemporary police technology, including the myriad uses of computers, electronics, and imaging and communications systems. The development of less-lethal weapons, innovations in firearms training, and other technologies are discussed. Finally, Chapter 15 looks at the future of policing, with emphasis on new technologies that could dramatically affect police operations and training. Two appendices follow concerning careers in policing and the federal Office of the Police Corps and Law Enforcement Education. The book's Index serves as its ending point.

Acknowledgments

This edition, like its four predecessors, is the result of the professional assistance of several practitioners and publishing people at Prentice Hall. First, I continue to benefit from my friendships and professional associations with Frank Mortimer, executive editor; Sarah Holle, associate editor; and project manager, Janet Bolton. I also wish to acknowledge the invaluable assistance of the following reviewers: Michael Grabowski, Santa Rosa Junior College, Santa Rosa, CA; William Kelly, Auburn University, Auburn, AL; and Ronald Swan, Lincoln College, Normal, IL. Their reviews of this fifth edition resulted in many beneficial changes. Also, Michael Goo, Washoe County (Nevada) Sheriff's Office, provided assistance with photographs.

About the Author

Ken Peak is a full professor and former chairman of the Department of Criminal Justice, University of Nevada, Reno, where he was named teacher of the year by the university's honor society. He entered municipal policing in Kansas in 1970 and subsequently held positions as a nine-county criminal justice planner in Kansas; director of a four-state Technical Assistance Institute for the Law Enforcement Assistance Administration; director of university police at Pittsburg State University in Kansas; acting director of public safety at the University of Nevada, Reno; and assistant professor of criminal justice at Wichita State University. He has authored or coauthored sixteen other textbooks, including *Women in Law Enforcement Careers: A Guide for Preparing and Succeeding* (with V. Lord); *Justice Administration: Police, Courts, and Corrections Management* (4th ed.); *Community Policing and Problem Solving: Strategies and Practices* (4th ed., with Ronald W. Glensor); *Police Supervision and Management: In an Era of Community Policing* (2nd ed., with Ronald W. Glensor and Larry K. Gaines); and *Policing Communities: Understanding Crime and Solving Problems* (an anthology, with R. Glensor and M. Correia). He has also published two historical books—*Kansas Temperance: Much Ado about Booze, 1870–1920* (with P. Peak) and *Kansas Bootleggers* (with Patrick G. O'Brien)—as well as more than fifty journal articles and book chapters. He has served as chairman of the Police Section of the Academy of Criminal Justice Sciences and as president of the Western and Pacific Association of Criminal Justice Educators. His teaching interests include policing, administration, victimology, and comparative justice systems. He received two gubernatorial appointments to statewide criminal justice committees while residing in Kansas and holds a doctorate from the University of Kansas.

Policing America

CHAPTER 1

Historical Development

The farther back you can look, the farther forward you are likely to see.

—*Winston Churchill*

Human history becomes more and more a race between education and catastrophe.

—*H. G. Wells*

Fellow citizens, we cannot escape history.

—*Abraham Lincoln*

Key Terms

August Vollmer
community policing
constable
coroner
justice of the peace (JP)
modus operandi
President's Crime Commission
professional era of policing
republicanism
sheriff
team policing
Wickersham Commission
William H. Parker

To understand contemporary policing in America, it is necessary to understand its antecedents. The police, it has been said, are "to a great extent, the prisoners of the past. Day-to-day practices are influenced by deeply ingrained traditions."[1] Another reason for analyzing historical developments and trends is that several discrete legacies have been transmitted to modern police agencies. In view of the significant historical impact on modern policing, it is necessary to turn back the clock to about A.D. 900.

Therefore, we begin with a brief history of the evolution of four primary criminal justice officers—sheriff, constable, coroner, and justice of the peace—from early England to the twentieth century in America. We then examine policing from its early beginnings in England to the American colonial period, when volunteers watched over their "human flock." The concepts of patrol, crime prevention, authority, professionalism, and discretion can be traced to the colonial period. We move on to the adoption of full-time policing in American cities (with their predominant issues, political influences, and other problems) and on the western frontier. Then we consider the movement to professionalize the police by removing them from politics (and, at the same time, the citizenry) and casting them as crime fighters. Next, we discuss the movement away from the professional model, centering on the influence of the President's Crime Commission. Then the chapter presents an overview of the current community-oriented policing and problem solving (COPPS) approach, including its three eras. A chapter summary, review questions, independent student activities, and related Web sites conclude the chapter.

English and Colonial Officers of the Law

All four of the primary criminal justice officials of early England—the sheriff, constable, coroner, and justice of the peace—either still exist or existed until recently in the United States. Accordingly, it is important to grasp a basic understanding of these offices, including their early functions in England and, later, in America. Following is a brief discussion of each.

Sheriff

The word **sheriff** is derived from *shire reeve—shire* meaning "county" and *reeve* meaning "agent of the king." The shire reeve appeared in England before the Norman Conquest of 1066. His job was to maintain law and order in the tithings. (Tithings are discussed further in the next section.) The office survives in England, but since the nineteenth century, the sheriff has had no police powers. When the office began, however, the sheriff exercised the powers of a virtual viceroy in his county. He assisted the king in fiscal, military, and judicial affairs and was referred to as the "king's steward," but the sheriff was never a popular officer in England. As men could buy their appointment from the Crown, the office was often held by nonresidents of the county who seemed intent only upon fattening their purses and abusing the public. In addition, English sheriffs were often charged with being lazy in the pursuit of criminals. Indeed, by the late thirteenth century, sheriffs were forbidden to act as justices. The position of coroner was created to act as a monitor over the sheriff. Thereafter, the status and responsibility of the position began to diminish. Coroners were locally elected officials, and their existence prompted the public to seek similar selection and control over sheriffs. In response, just before his death, Edward I granted to the counties the right to select their sheriffs. With the subsequent appearance of the justice of the peace, the sheriff's office declined in power even further. At the present time in England, a sheriff's only duties are to act as officer of the court, summon juries, and enforce civil judgments.[2]

The first sheriffs in America appeared in the early colonial period. By contrast to the status of the office in England, control over sheriffs has rested with the county electorate since 1886. Today, the American sheriff remains the basic source of rural crime control. When the office appeared in the colonies, it was little changed from the English model. However, the power of appointment was originally vested in the governor, and the sheriff's duties included apprehending criminals, caring for prisoners, executing civil process, conducting elections, and collecting taxes. In keeping with English tradition, and fearing oppression and extortion by the sheriff, colonists generally limited the sheriff's term of office; sometimes the term was as short as a single year. The duties of collecting taxes and conducting elections alone accorded the sheriffs tremendous power and influence.[3]

In the late nineteenth century, the sheriff became a popular figure in the legendary Wild West (discussed later in this chapter). The frontier sheriffs often used the concept of *posse comitatus,* an important part of the criminal justice machine that allowed the sheriff to deputize common citizens to assist in the capture of outlaws, among other tasks. The use of the posse declined after 1900 because the enlistment of untrained people did not meet the requirements of a more complex society. Overall, by the turn of the twentieth century, the powers and duties of the sheriff in America had changed very little in status or function. In fact, the office has not changed much today; the sheriff continues to enjoy the authorization to use police powers.

Constable

Like the sheriff, the **constable** can be traced back to Anglo-Saxon times. The office began during the reign of Edward I, when every parish or township had a constable. As the county militia turned more and more to matters of defense, the constable alone pursued felons. Hence the ancient custom of citizens raising a loud "hue and cry" and joining in pursuit of criminals lapsed into disuse. During the Middle Ages, there was as yet no high degree of specialization. The constable had a variety of duties, including collecting taxes, supervising highways, and serving as magistrate. The office soon became subject to election and was conferred upon local men of prominence. However, the creation of the office of justice of the peace around 1200 quickly changed this trend forever; soon the constable was limited to making arrests only with warrants issued by a justice of the peace. As a result, the office, deprived of social and civic prestige, was no longer attractive. It carried no salary, and the duties were often dangerous. Additionally, there was heavy attrition in the office, and so its term was limited to one year in an attempt to attract officeholders. Patrick Colquhoun, a London magistrate and noted police author, disposed of the parish constables altogether, and in 1856 Parliament completely discarded the office.[4]

The office of constable experienced a similar process of disintegration in the colonies. As elected officials, American constables had a variety of duties similar to those of their counterparts in England. However, the American constables, usually two in each town, were given control over the night watch. By the 1930s, state constitutions in twenty-one states provided for the office of constable. However, constables still received no pay in the early part of the twentieth century, and again like their British colleagues, they enjoyed little prestige or popularity the early 1900s. The position fell into disfavor largely because most constables were untrained and were believed to be wholly inadequate as officials of the law.[5]

A leatherhead and his sentry box. Called "leatherheads" because of their distinctive leather helmets, constables patrolled New York City from scattered sentry boxes in the early decades of the nineteenth century. They wore helmets for protection against falling debris from fires—a constant danger in cities with many wooden buildings.

(*Courtesy City of New York Police Department Photo Unit*)

Coroner

The office of **coroner** is more difficult to describe. It has been used to fulfill many different roles throughout its history and has steadily changed over the centuries. There is no agreement concerning the date when the coroner first appeared in England, but there is general consensus that the office was functioning by the end of the twelfth century. The reason is that both the Crown and the property holders were anxious to increase the prestige of this office at the expense of the sheriff. From the beginning, the coroner was elected; his duties included oversight of the interests of the Crown, not only in criminal matters but in fiscal matters as well. In felony cases, the coroner could conduct a preliminary hearing, and the sheriff often came to the coroner's court to preside over the coroner's jury. The coroner's inquest provided another means of power and prestige. The inquest determined the cause of death and the party responsible for it. Initially, coroners were given no compensation, yet they were elected for life. Soon, however, it became apparent that officials holding this office were unhappy with the burdensome tasks and the absence of compensation. Therefore, they were given the right to charge fees for their work.[6]

As was true of sheriffs and constables, at first the office of the coroner in America was only slightly different than what it had been in England. The office was slow in gaining recognition in America, as many of the coroners' duties were already being performed by the sheriffs and justices of the peace. By 1933, the coroner was recognized as a separate office in two-thirds of the states. Tenure was generally limited to two years. By then, however, the office had been stripped of many of its original functions, especially its fiscal roles. Today, in many states, the coroner legally serves as sheriff when the elected sheriff is disabled or disqualified. However, since the early part of the twentieth century, the coroner has basically performed a single function: determining the causes of all deaths by violence or under suspicious circumstances. The coroner or his or her assistant is expected to determine the causes and effects of wounds, lesions, contusions, fractures, poisons, and more. The coroner's inquest resembles a grand jury at which the coroner serves as a kind of presiding magistrate. If the inquest determines that the deceased came to his or her death through criminal means, the coroner may issue a warrant for the arrest of the accused party.[7]

The primary debate regarding the office of coroner has centered on the qualifications needed to hold the office. Many states have traditionally allowed laypeople, as opposed to physicians, to be coroners. Thus people of all backgrounds—ranging from butchers to musicians—have occupied this powerful office. America still clings to the old English philosophy that the chief qualifications for the position of coroner are "the possession of tact, sound discretion, practical sense, sympathy, quick perception and a knowledge of human nature."[8]

Justice of the Peace

The **justice of the peace (JP)** can be traced back as far as 1195 in England. By 1264 the *custos pacis,* or conservator of the peace, nominated by the king for each county, presided over criminal trials. Soon, in recognition of its new status, the term *custos* was dropped and *justice* substituted for it. Early JPs were wealthy landholders. They allowed constables to make arrests by issuing them warrants. Over time, this practice removed power from constables and sheriffs. The duties of JPs eventually included the granting of bail to felons, which led to corruption and criticism as the justices bailed people who clearly should not have been released into the community. By the sixteenth century, the office came under criticism again because of the caliber of the people holding it. Officeholders were often referred to as "boobies" and "scum of the earth."[9] The only qualification necessary was being a wealthy landowner who was able to buy his way into office.

By the early twentieth century, England had abolished the property-holding requirement, and many of the medieval functions of the JP's office were removed. Thereafter, the office possessed extensive criminal jurisdiction but no jurisdiction whatsoever in civil cases. This contrasts with the American system, which gives JPs limited jurisdiction in both criminal and civil cases. Interestingly, even today relatively few English JPs have been trained in the law.

The JP's office in the colonies was a distinct change from the position as it existed in England. Justices of the peace were elected to office and given jurisdiction in both civil and criminal cases. By 1930, the office had constitutional status in all of the states. JPs have long been allowed to collect fees for their services. For example, in the 1930s the JP typically received 10¢ for administering an oath, 50¢ for preparing information, 50¢ for issuing a warrant for arrest, $1.00 per day for attendance in court, 25¢ for issuing a subpoena, and 5¢ for filing each paper required by law. As in England, it is typically not necessary to hold a law degree or to have pursued legal studies in order to be a JP in the United States. Thus tradespeople and laborers have long held the position, and American JPs come from all walks of life. In the past, they held court in their saddle shops, kitchens, and flour mills.[10]

Perhaps the most colorful justice of the peace was Roy Bean, popularized in the movies as the sole peace officer in a 35,000-square-mile area west of the Pecos River, near Langtry, Texas. Bean was known to hold court in his shack, where three signs hung on the front porch. One read "Justice Roy Bean, Notary Public," another read "Law West of the Pecos," and the third read "Beer Saloon." Cold beer and the law undoubtedly shared many quarters on the western frontier.

A familiar complaint about modern-day JPs has been that they often operate in collusion with police officers, who set up speed traps to collect and share the fines. Indeed, many JPs have been known to complain when the

Justice of the Peace Roy Bean, Langtry, Texas, circa 1900.

(Courtesy Library of Congress)

police bring them too few cases, or none at all, or when the police take their "business" to other JPs, thereby reducing their incomes. This reputation, coupled with the complaints about their qualifications, has caused the office of justice of the peace to be ridiculed. JPs are today what they perhaps were intended to be—lay and inexpert upholders of the law. On the whole, the office has declined from dignity to obscurity and ridicule. As one observer noted, this loss of prestige can never be recovered.[11]

The Old English System of Policing

Like much of the American criminal justice system, modern American policing can be traced directly to its English heritage. Ideas concerning community policing, crime prevention, the posse, constables, and sheriffs were developed from English policing. Beginning about A.D. 900, the role of law enforcement was placed in the hands of common citizens. Each citizen was responsible for aiding neighbors who might be victimized by outlaws.[12] No formal mechanism existed with which to police the villages, and the voluntary, informal model that developed was referred to as "kin police."[13] Slowly this model developed into a more formalized, community-based system.

After the Norman Conquest of 1066, a community-based system called "frankpledge" was established. This system required that every male above the age of 12 form a group with nine of his neighbors. This group, called a "tithing," was sworn to help protect fellow citizens and to apprehend and deliver to justice any of its members who committed a crime. Tithingmen were not paid salaries for their work, and they were required to perform certain duties under penalty of law.[14] Ten tithings were grouped into a hundred, directed by a constable who was appointed by a nobleman. The constable was the first police official with law enforcement responsibility greater than simply protecting his neighbors. As the tithings were grouped into hundreds, the hundreds were grouped into shires, which are similar to today's counties.

By the late seventeenth century, however, wealthier merchants and farmers became reluctant to take their turn in the rotating job of constable. The office was still unpaid, and the duties were numerous. Wealthier men paid the less fortunate to serve in their place until there came a point at which no one but the otherwise unemployable would serve as constable. Thus from about 1689 on, the demise of the once-powerful office was swift. All who could afford to pay their way out of service as constable to King George I did so. Daniel Defoe, the noted author, spoke for many when he wrote in 1714 that the office of constable represented "an unsupportable hardship; it takes up so much of a man's time that his own affairs are frequently totally neglected, too often to his ruin."[15]

Another cause of the decline of the old system, as mentioned earlier, was the corruption of the justices of the peace. Following the Glorious Revolution in 1688, many families whose members had once filled the office became disaffected with the Crown and began to refuse the position. Soon, the people who did become justices of the peace were inspired primarily by the office's potential for profit. The unsavory magistrates became known as the "justices of mean degree," and the "trading justice" of the first half of the eighteenth century emerged in a criminal justice system where anything was possible for a fee.

The potential for corruption in this system is obvious. The justice of the peace was rewarded in proportion to the number of people he convicted, so extortion was rampant. Ingenious criminals were able to exploit this state of affairs to great advantage. One such criminal was Jonathan Wild, who, for seven years before his execution in 1725, obtained single-handed control over most of London's criminals. Wild's system was simple: After ordering his men to commit a burglary, he would meet the victim and courteously offer to return the stolen goods for a commission. Wild was so successful in fencing stolen property that he found it necessary to transport his booty to warehouses abroad. That he could have operated such a business for so long is a testimony to the corrupt nature of the magistrates of the "trading justice" period.[16]

This early English system, in large measure voluntary and informal, continued with some success well into the eighteenth century. By 1800, however, the collapse of its two primary offices and the growth of large cities, crime, and civil disobedience required that the system be changed. The British Parliament was soon forced to consider and adopt a more dependable system.

Policing in Colonial America

The first colonists transplanted the English policing system, with all of its virtues and faults, to seventeenth- and eighteenth-century America. Most of the time, the colonies were free of crime as the settlers busied themselves carving out a farm and a living. Occasionally colonists ran afoul of the law by violating or neglecting some moral obligation. They then found themselves in court for working on the Sabbath, cursing in public, failing to pen animals properly, or begetting children out of wedlock. Only two "crime waves" of note occurred during the seventeenth century, both in Massachusetts. In one case, between 1656 and 1665, Quakers who dared challenge the religion of the Puritan colony were whipped, banished, and, in three instances, hanged. The second "crime wave" involved witchcraft. Several alleged witches were hanged in 1692 in Salem; dozens more languished in prison before the hysteria abated.[17]

Once colonists settled into villages, including Boston (1630), Charleston (1680), and Philadelphia (1682), local ordinances provided for the appointment of constables, whose duties were much like those of their English predecessors. County governments, again drawing on English precedent, appointed sheriffs as well. The county sheriff, appointed by a governor, became the most important law enforcement official, particularly when the colonies were small and rural. The sheriff apprehended criminals, served subpoenas, appeared in court, and collected taxes. The sheriff was also paid a fixed amount for each task performed; the more taxes he collected, for example, the higher his pay.[18]

Criminal acts were so infrequent as to be largely ignored; in fact, law enforcement was given low priority. Service as a constable or watchman was obligatory, and for a few years citizens did not seem to mind this duty. But as towns grew and the task of enforcing the laws became more difficult and time-consuming, the colonists, like their English counterparts, began to evade the duty when possible. The "watch-and-ward" responsibility of citizens became more of a comical "snooze-and-snore" system. In Boston, the citizens were so evasive about performing police services that in 1650 the government threatened citizens who refused to serve with heavy fines. New Amsterdam's Dutch officials introduced a paid watch in 1658, and Boston tried the concept in 1663, but the expense quickly forced both cities to discontinue the practice.[19] Apparently, paid policing might have been a good substitute for halfhearted voluntary service, but only if the citizens did not have to pay for it.

Unfortunately for these eighteenth-century colonists, their refusal to provide a dependable voluntary policing system came at a time when economic, population, and crime growth required a reliable police force. But the most reliable citizens continued to refuse the duty, and watchmen were hardly able to stay awake at night. The citizen-participation model of policing was breaking down, and something had to be done, especially in the larger colonies. Philadelphia devised a plan, enacted into law, that restructured the way the watch was performed. City officials hoped that it would solve the problem of enforcing the laws. The law empowered officials, called "wardens," to hire as many watchmen as needed; the powers of the watch were increased; and the legislature levied a tax to pay for it. Instead of requiring all males to participate, only male citizens interested in making money needed to join the watch. Philadelphia's plan was moderately successful; other cities were soon inspired to follow its example and offer tax-supported wages for watches.[20]

From the middle to the late eighteenth century, massive social and political unrest caused police problems to increase even more. From 1754 to 1763, the French and Indian War disrupted colonial society. When the war ended, a major depression impoverished many citizens. That depression ended with the American Revolution. In 1783, after the revolution ended, another depression struck; this one lasted until about 1790. Property and street crime continued to flourish, and the constabulary and the watches were unable to cope with it. Soon it became evident that, like the English, the American people needed a more dependable, formal system of policing.

Legacies of the Colonial Period

As uncomplicated and sedate as colonial law enforcement seems, especially when compared to contemporary police problems, the colonial period is very important to the history of policing because many of the basic ideas that influence modern policing were developed during that era. Specifically, the colonial period transmitted three legacies to contemporary policing.[21]

First, as just discussed, the colonists committed themselves to local (as opposed to centralized) policing. Second, the colonists reinforced that commitment by creating a theory of government called **republicanism**. Republicanism asserted that power can be divided, and it relied on local interests to promote the general welfare. Police chiefs and sheriffs might believe that they alone know how to address crime and disorder, but under republicanism, neighborhood groups and local interest blocs have input with respect to crime-control policy. Republicanism thus established the controversial political framework within which the police would develop during the next two hundred years.[22]

Finally, the colonial period witnessed the onset of the theory of crime prevention. This legacy would alter the shape of policing after 1800 and would eventually lead to the emergence of modern police agencies. The population of England doubled between 1700 and 1800. Parliament, however, did nothing to solve the problems that arose from social change. Each municipality or county, therefore, was left to solve its problems in piecemeal fashion. After 1750, practically every English city increased the number of watchmen and constables, hoping to address the problem of crime and disorder but not giving any thought to whether this ancient system of policing still worked. However, the cities did adopt paid, rather than voluntary, watches.[23]

London probably suffered the most from this general inattention to social problems; awash in crime, whole districts had become criminal haunts that no watchmen visited and no honest citizens frequented. Thieves became very bold, robbing their victims in broad daylight on busy streets.

In the face of this situation, English officials still continued to prefer the existing policing arrangements over any new ideas. However, three men—Henry Fielding, his half brother John Fielding, and Patrick Colquhoun—began to experiment with possible solutions. And although their efforts would have no major effect in the short term in England, they laid the foundation on which later reformers would build new ideas.

Henry Fielding's acute interest in, and knowledge of, policing led to his 1748 appointment as chief magistrate of Bow Street in London. He soon became one of England's most acclaimed theorists in the area of crime and punishment. Fielding's primary argument was that the severity of the English penal code, which provided for the death penalty for a large number of offenses, including the theft of a handkerchief, did not work in controlling criminals. He believed the country should reform the criminal code to deal more with the origins of crime. In 1750, Fielding made the pursuit of criminals more systematic by creating a small group of "thief takers." Victims of crime paid handsome rewards for the capture of their assailants, so these volunteers stood to profit nicely by pursuing criminals.[24]

When Henry Fielding died in 1754, John Fielding succeeded him as Bow Street magistrate. By 1785, his thief takers had evolved into the Bow Street Runners—some of the most famous policemen in English history. While the Fieldings were considering how to create a police force that could deal with changing English society, horrible punishments and incompetent policing continued throughout England.

Henry Fielding.

(Courtesy Library of Congress)

Patrick Colquhoun was a wealthy man who was sincerely interested in improving social conditions in England. In 1792, Colquhoun was appointed London magistrate, and for the next quarter of a century he focused on police reform. Like the Fieldings, he wrote lengthy treatises on the police, and he soon established himself as an authority on police reform. Colquhoun believed that government could, and should, regulate people's behavior. This notion contradicted tradition and even constitutional ideals, undermining the old principle that the residents of local communities, through voluntary watchmen and constables, should police the conduct of their neighbors. Colquhoun also endorsed three ideas originally set forth by the Fieldings: (1) the police should have an intelligence service for gathering information about offenders; (2) a register of known criminals and unlawful groups should be maintained; and (3) a police gazette should be published to assist in the apprehension of criminals and to promote the moral education of the public by publicizing punishments such as whipping, the pillory, and public execution. To justify these reforms, Colquhoun estimated that in 1800 London had ten thousand thieves, prostitutes, and other criminals who stole goods valued at more than a half million pounds from the riverside docks alone.[25]

Colquhoun also believed that policing should maintain the public order, prevent and detect crime, and correct bad manners and morals. He did not agree with the centuries-old notion that watchmen—who, after all, were amateurs—could adequately police the communities. Thus Colquhoun favored a system of paid professional police officers who would be recruited and maintained by a centralized governmental authority. Colquhoun believed that potential criminals could be identified before they did their unlawful deeds.[26] Thus began the notion of proactive policing—that is, preventing the crime before it occurs. Colquhoun died before his proposals were adopted, and as the eighteenth century ended in England and America, the structure of policing was largely unchanged. However, both nations had experienced the inadequacies of the older form of policing. Although new ideas had emerged, loyalties to the old system of policing would remain for some time.

Police Reform in England and America, 1829–1860

Two powerful trends in England and America brought about changes in policing in both countries in the early and mid-nineteenth century. The first was urbanization, and the second was industrialization. These developments generally increased the standard of living for both Americans and western Europeans. Suddenly, factories needed sober, dependable people who could be trusted with machines. To create a reliable workforce, factory owners began advocating temperance. Although many workers resented this attempt at social control and reform, clearly a new age, a new way of thinking, had begun. Crime also increased during this period. Thus social change, crime, and unrest made the old system of policing obsolete. A new policing system was needed, one that could deal effectively with criminals, maintain order, and prevent crime.[27]

In England, after the end of the Napoleonic Wars in 1815, workers protested against new machines, food shortages, and an ongoing increase in crime. The British army, traditionally used to disperse rioters, was becoming less effective as people began resisting its commands. In 1822, England's ruling party, the Tories, moved to consider new alternatives. The prime minister appointed Sir Robert Peel to establish a police force to combat the problems. Peel, a wealthy member of Parliament who was familiar with the reforms suggested by the Fieldings and Colquhoun, found that many English people objected to the idea of a professional police force, thinking it a possible restraint on their liberty. They also feared a stronger police organization because the criminal law was already quite harsh, as it had been for many years. By the early nineteenth century, there were 223 crimes in England for which a person could be hanged. Because of these two obstacles, Peel's efforts to gain support for full-time, paid police officers failed for seven years.[28]

Sir Robert Peel.

(Courtesy Library of Congress)

Peel finally succeeded in 1829. He had established a base of support in Parliament and had focused on reforming only the metropolitan police of London rather than trying to create policing for the entire country. Peel submitted a bill to Parliament. This bill, which was very vague about details, was called "An Act for Improving the Police In and Near the Metropolis." Parliament passed the Metropolitan Police Act of 1829. The general instructions of the new force stressed its preventive nature, saying that "the principal object to be attained is 'the prevention of crime.' The security of person and property will thus be better effected, than by the detection and punishment of the offender after he has succeeded in committing the crime."[29] The act called on the home secretary to appoint two police commissioners to command the new organization. These two men were to recruit "a sufficient number of fit and able men" as constables.[30] Peel chose a former military colonel, Charles Rowan, as one commissioner, and a barrister (attorney), Richard Mayne, as the other. Both turned out to be excellent choices. They divided London into seventeen divisions, using crime data as the primary basis for creating the boundaries. Each division had a commander called a "superintendent"; each superintendent had a force of 4 inspectors, 16 sergeants, and 165 constables. Thus London's Metropolitan Police immediately consisted of nearly 3,000 officers. The commissioners decided to put their constables in a uniform (blue coat, blue pants, and a black top hat) and to arm them with a short baton (known as a "truncheon") and a rattle for raising an alarm. Each constable was to wear his own identifying number on his collar, where it could be easily seen.[31]

Interestingly, the London police (nicknamed "bobbies" after Sir Robert Peel) quickly met with tremendous public hostility. Wealthy people resented their very existence and became particularly incensed at their attempts to control the movements of their horse-drawn coaches. Several aristocrats ordered their coachmen to whip the officers or simply drive over them. Juries and judges refused to punish those who assaulted the police. Defendants acquitted by a hostile judge would often sue the officer for false arrest. Policing London's streets in the early 1830s proved to be a very dangerous and lonely business. The two commissioners, Rowan and Mayne, fearing that public hostility might kill off the police force, moved to counter it. The bobbies were continually told to be respectful yet firm when dealing with the public. Citizens were invited to lodge complaints if their officers were truly unprofessional. This policy of creating public support gradually worked; as the police became more moderate in their conduct, public hostility also declined.[32]

Peel, too, proved to be very farsighted and keenly aware of the needs of both a professional police force and the public that would be asked to maintain it. Indeed, Peel saw that the poor quality of policing contributed to social disorder. Accordingly, he drafted several guidelines for the force, many of which focused on community relations. He wrote that the power of the police to fulfill their duties depended on public approval of their actions; that as public cooperation increased, the need for physical force

A "Peeler," circa 1829. "Peeler," "Robert," and "bobby" were all early names for a police officer, the latter remaining as a nickname today. All are memorials to Sir Robert Peel.

(Courtesy City of New York Police Department Photo Unit)

by the police would decrease; that officers needed to display absolutely impartial service to law; and that force should be employed by the police only when attempts at persuasion and warning had failed, and then they should use only the minimal degree of force possible. Peel's remark that "the police are the public, and the public are the police" emphasized his belief that the police are first and foremost members of the larger society.[33]

Peel's attempts to appease the public were necessary; during the first three years of his reform effort, he encountered strong opposition. He was denounced as a potential dictator, the *London Times* urged revolt, and *Blackwood's* magazine referred to the bobbies as "general spies" and "finished tools of corruption." A secret national group, the Blue Devils and the

Raw Lobsters, was organized to combat the police. During this initial five-year period, Peel endured the largest police turnover rate in history. Estimates vary widely, but this is thought to be fairly accurate: 1,341 constables resigned from London's Metropolitan Police from 1829 to 1834; that's roughly half of the constables on the force. The pay of three shillings a day was meager, and probably few of the officers ever considered the position as a career. In fact, many of the men, who had been laborers, took jobs as bobbies to tide them through the "stress of weather," waiting until the inclement weather passed and they could resume their trades.[34] Peel drafted what have become known as "Peel's principles of policing." Most, if not all, are relevant to today's police community:

1. The police must be stable, efficient, and organized along military lines.
2. The police must be under governmental control.
3. The absence of crime will best prove the efficiency of the police.
4. The distribution of crime news is absolutely essential.
5. The deployment of police strength both by time and area is essential.
6. No quality is more indispensable to a policeman than a perfect command of temper; a quiet, determined manner has more effect than violent action.
7. Good appearance commands respect.
8. The securing and training of proper persons is at the root of efficiency.
9. Public security demands that every police officer be given a number.
10. Police headquarters should be centrally located and easily accessible to the people.
11. Policemen should be hired on a probationary basis.
12. Police records are necessary to the correct distribution of police strength.[35]

London's experiment in full-time policing did not bring about the instant expansion of the model across England. It would take many years for other English communities to replace their stubborn reliance on the watchman system.

Full-Time Policing Comes to the United States

Imitating Peel

Americans, meanwhile, were observing Peel's successful experiment with the bobbies on the patrol beat. However, industrialization and social upheaval had not reached the proportions here that they had in England, so there was not the same urgent need for full-time policing. Yet by the 1840s, when industrialization began in earnest in America, U.S. officials began to watch the police reform movement in England more closely.

When the movement to improve policing did begin in America in the 1840s, it occurred in New York City. (Philadelphia, with a private bequest of $33,000, actually began a paid daytime police force in 1833; however, it was disbanded three years later.) The police reform movement had actually begun in New York in 1836, when the mayor advocated a new police organization that could deal with civil disorders. The city council denied the mayor's request, saying that the doctrine of republicanism prevented it and that, instead, citizens should simply aid one another in combating crime.

Efforts at police reform thus fell dormant until 1841, when a highly publicized murder case resurrected the issue, showing again the incompetence of the officers under the old system of policing. Mary Cecilia Rogers left her New York home one day and disappeared; three days later, her body was discovered in the Hudson River. The public and newspapers clamored for the police to solve the crime. The police appeared unwilling to investigate until an adequate reward was offered.[36] Edgar Allan Poe's 1850 short story "The Mystery of Marie Roget" was based on this case. The Rogers case and the police response did more to encourage police reorganization than all of the previous cries for change.

In 1844, the New York State legislature passed a law establishing a full-time preventive police force for New York City. However, this new body came into being in a very different form than in Europe. The American version, as begun in New York City, was deliberately placed under the control of the city government and city politicians. The American plan required that each ward in the city be a separate patrol district, unlike the European model, which divided the districts along the lines of criminal activity. The process for selecting officers was also different. The mayor chose the recruits from a list of names submitted by the aldermen and tax assessors of each ward; the mayor then submitted his choices to the city council for approval. This system adhered to the principles of republicanism and resulted in most of the power over the police going to the ward aldermen, who were seldom concerned about selecting the best people for the job. Instead, the system allowed and even encouraged political patronage and rewards for friends.[37]

The law also provided for the hiring of eight hundred officers—not nearly enough to cover the city—and for the hiring of a chief of police, who had no power to hire officers, assign them to duties, or fire them. Furthermore, the law did not require the officers to wear uniforms; instead, they were to carry a badge or other emblem for identification. Citizens would be hard-pressed to recognize an officer when they needed one. As a result of the law, New York's officers would be patrolling a beat around the clock, and pay scales were high enough to attract good applicants. At the same time, the position of constable was dissolved. Overall, these were important reforms over the old system and provided the basis for continued improvements that the public supported.[38]

It did not take long for other cities to adopt the general model of the New York City police force. New Orleans and Cincinnati adopted plans for a new police force in 1852, Boston and Philadelphia followed in 1854, Chicago in 1855, and Baltimore and Newark in 1857.[39] By 1880, virtually every major American city had a police force based on Peel's model.

Early Issues and New Traditions

Three important issues confronted these early American police officers as they took to the streets between 1845 and 1869: whether the police should be in uniform, whether they should be armed, and whether they should use force.

The issue of a police uniform was important for several reasons. First, the lack of a uniform negated one of the basic principles of crime prevention—that police officers be visible. Crime victims wanted to find a police officer in a hurry. Further, uniforms would make it difficult for officers to avoid their duties, since it would strip them of their anonymity. Interestingly, police officers themselves tended to prefer not to wear a uniform. They contended that the uniform would hinder their work because criminals would recognize them and flee and that the uniform was demeaning and would destroy their sense of manliness and democracy. One officer went so far as to argue that the sun reflecting off his badge would warn criminals of his approach; another officer hired an attorney and threatened to sue if he were compelled to don a uniform. To remedy the problem, New York City officials took advantage of the fact that their officers served four-year terms of office; when those terms expired in 1853, the city's police commissioners announced they would not rehire any officer who refused to wear a uniform. Thus New York became the first American city with a uniformed police force. In 1860, it was followed by Philadelphia, where there was also strong police objection to the policy. In Boston (1858) and Chicago (1861), police accepted the adoption of uniforms more easily.[40]

A more serious issue confronting politicians and the new police officers was the carrying of arms. At stake was the personal safety of the officers and the citizens they served. Nearly everyone viewed an armed police force with considerable suspicion. However, after some surprisingly calm objections by members of the public, who noted that the London police had no need to bear arms, it was agreed that an armed police force was unavoidable. Of course, America had a long tradition that citizens had the right—sometimes even the duty—to own firearms. And armed only with nightsticks, the new police could hardly withstand attacks by armed assailants. The public allowed officers to carry arms simply because there was no alternative, which was a significant change in American policing and a major point of departure from the English model. Practically from the first day, then, the American police have been much more open to the idea of carrying weapons.[41]

Eventually, the use of force, the third issue, would become necessary and commonplace for American officers. Indeed, the uncertainty about whether an offender was armed perpetuated the need for an officer to rely on physical prowess for survival on the streets. The issue of use of force will be discussed further in Chapter 10.

Attempts at Reform in Difficult Times

By 1850, American police officers still faced a difficult task. In addition to maintaining order and coping with vice and crime, they would, soon after putting on the uniform, be separated from their old associates and viewed with suspicion by most citizens. With few exceptions, the work was steady, and layoffs were uncommon. The nature of the work and the possibility of a retirement pension tied officers closely to their jobs and their colleagues. By 1850, there was a surplus of unskilled labor, particularly in the major eastern cities. The desire for economic security was reason enough for many able-bodied men to try to enter police service. New York City, for example, paid its police officers about twice as much as unskilled laborers could earn. Police departments had about twice as many applicants as positions. The system of political patronage prevailed in most cities, even after civil service laws attempted to introduce merit systems for hiring police.[42]

In New York, the police reform board was headed by Theodore Roosevelt, who sought applications for the department from residents in upstate areas. When these officers, later called "bushwhackers," were appointed, they were criticized by disgruntled Tammanyites (corrupt New York City politicians) who favored the political patronage system. The Tammanyites complained that the bushwhackers "could not find their way to a single station house."[43] Roosevelt's approach violated the American tradition of hiring local boys for local jobs. In England, meanwhile, police officials

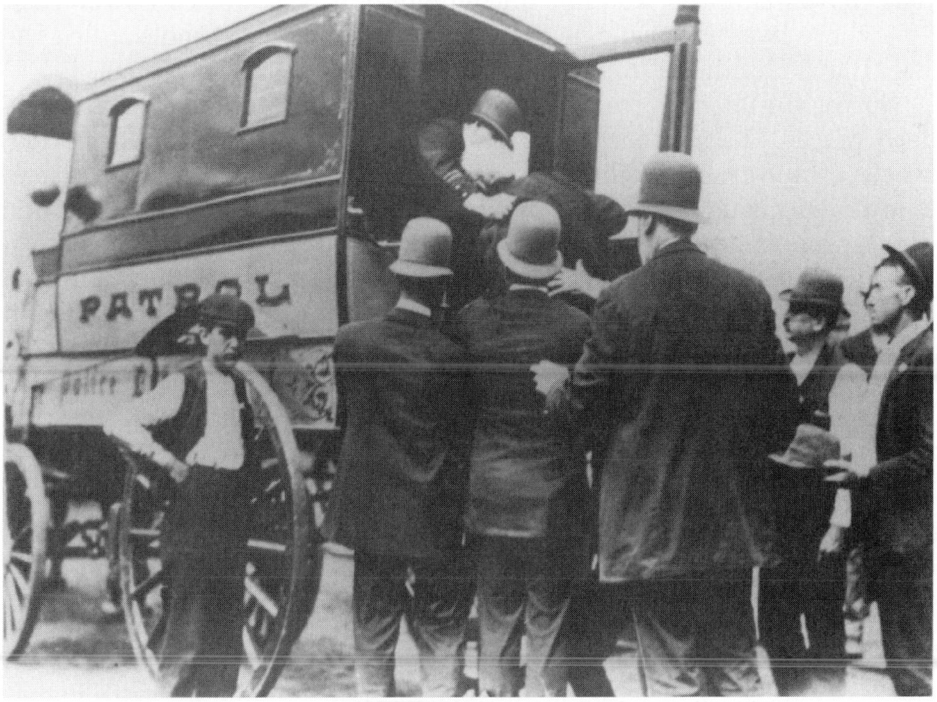

A horse-drawn paddy wagon like those in use in many cities at the turn of the twentieth century.

(Courtesy International Association of Chiefs of Police)

purposely sought applicants from outside the London area, believing that it was advantageous to hire young men who were not wise to the local ways or involved with local people.[44]

Citizens saw these new uniformed anomalies as people who wanted to spoil their fun or close their saloons on Sunday. In addition to police officers' geographic and social isolation, they became isolated in other ways, some of which still exist today. For example, from the onset of professional American policing, there was little or no lateral movement from one department to another; the officer typically spent his entire career in one city, unable to transfer seniority or knowledge for use in a promotion in another city. Consequently, police departments soon became very inbred; new blood entered only at the lowest level. Tradition became the most important determinant of police behavior: A major teaching tool was the endless string of war stories the recruit heard, and the emphasis in most departments was on doing things as they had always been done. Innovation was frowned upon, and the veterans impressed on the rookies the reasons why things had to remain the same.[45]

The police officers of the late nineteenth century kept busy with riots, strikes, parades, and fires. These events often made for hostile interaction between citizens and the police. Labor disputes often meant long hours of extra duty for the officers, for which no extra pay was received. This, coupled with the fact that the police did not engage in collective bargaining, resulted in the police having little empathy or identification with strikers or strikebreakers. Therefore the use of the baton to put down riots, known as the "baton charge," was not uncommon. On New York's Lower East Side—where labor conflict was frequent—Jewish spokespeople called the police "Black Hundreds" in memory of conditions in czarist Russia.[46]

During the late nineteenth century, large cities gradually became more orderly places. The number of riots dropped. In the post–Civil War period, however, ethnic group conflict sometimes resulted in individual and group acts of violence and disorder. Hatred of Catholics and Irish Protestants led to the killing and wounding of over one hundred people in large eastern cities. Still, American cities were more orderly in 1900 than they had been in 1850. The possibility of violence involving labor disputes remained, and race riots increased in number and intensity after 1900, but daily urban life became more predictable and controlled. American cities absorbed millions of newcomers after 1900 without the social strains that attended the Irish immigration of the 1830s to 1850s.[47]

Increased Politics and Corruption

A more developed urban life also promoted order. Work groups and social clusters provided a sense of integration and belonging. Immigrants established benefit societies, churches, synagogues, and social clubs. At the same time, the police had acquired experience in dealing with potential sources of violence. Police in northern and western cities reflected the

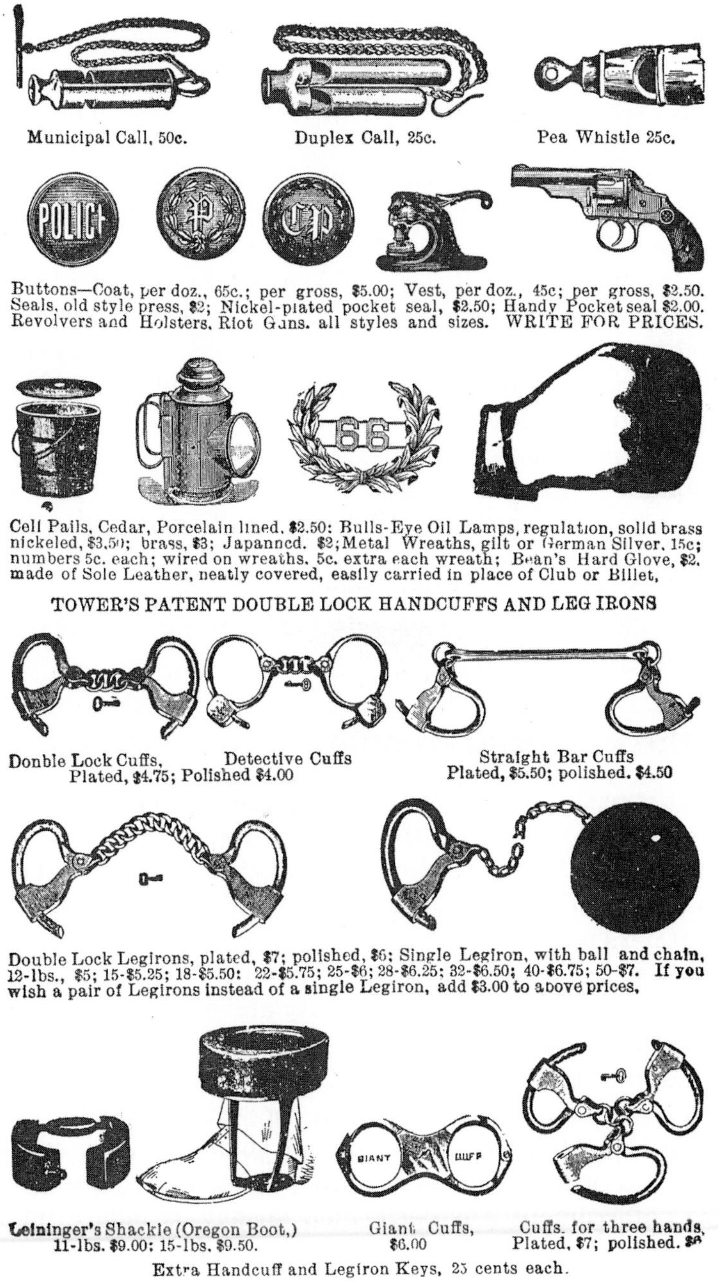
Municipal Call, 50c.
Duplex Call, 25c.
Pea Whistle 25c.
POLICE
Buttons—Coat, per doz., 65c.; per gross, $5.00; Vest, per doz., 45c; per gross, $2.50. Seals, old style press, $2; Nickel-plated pocket seal, $2.50; Handy Pocket seal $2.00. Revolvers and Holsters, Riot Guns, all styles and sizes. WRITE FOR PRICES.
66
Cell Pails, Cedar, Porcelain lined, $2.50: Bulls-Eye Oil Lamps, regulation, solid brass nickeled, $3.50; brass, $3; Japanned. $2; Metal Wreaths, gilt or German Silver, 15c; numbers 5c. each; wired on wreaths, 5c. extra each wreath; Bean's Hard Glove, $2. made of Sole Leather, neatly covered, easily carried in place of Club or Billet,
TOWER'S PATENT DOUBLE LOCK HANDCUFFS AND LEG IRONS
Donble Lock Cuffs, Detective Cuffs
Plated, $4.75; Polished $4.00
Straight Bar Cuffs
Plated, $5.50; polished. $4.50
Double Lock Legirons, plated, $7; polished, $6; Single Legiron, with ball and chain, 12-lbs., $5; 15-$5.25; 18-$5.50: 22-$5.75; 25-$6; 28-$6.25; 32-$6.50; 40-$6.75; 50-$7. If you wish a pair of Legirons instead of a single Legiron, add $3.00 to above prices,
GIANT CUFF
Leininger's Shackle (Oregon Boot,)
11-lbs. $9.00: 15-lbs. $9.50.
Giant Cuffs,
$6.00
Cuffs. for three hands,
Plated, $7; polished.
Extra Handcuff and Legiron Keys, 25 cents each.

Early-twentieth-century police equipment.

(Courtesy City of New York Police Department Photo Unit)

times. Irish-Americans constituted a heavy proportion of the police departments by the 1890s; they made up more than one-fourth of the New York police force as early as the 1850s. Huge proportions of Irish officers were also found in Boston, Chicago, Cleveland, and San Francisco.[48]

Ethnic and religious disputes were found in many police departments. In Cleveland, for example, Catholics and Masons distrusted one another, while in New York, the Irish officers controlled many hirings and promotions.

And there were still strong political influences at work. George Walling, a New York Police Department superintendent for eleven years, lamented after his retirement that he had largely been just a figurehead. Politics were played to such an extent that even nonranking patrol officers used political backers to obtain promotions, desired assignments, and transfers.

Police corruption also surfaced at this time. Corrupt officers wanted beats close to the gamblers, saloonkeepers, madams, and pimps—people who could not operate if the officers were "untouchable" or "100 percent coppers."[49] Political pull for corrupt officers could work for or against them; the officer who incurred the wrath of his superiors could be transferred to the outposts, where he would have no chance for financial advancement.

While police departments often had strong rivalries and political and religious factions, the officers banded together against outside attack. In New York, officers routinely committed perjury to protect one another against civilian complaints. An early form of "internal affairs" thus developed in the 1890s: the "shoofly," a plainclothes officer who checked on the performance of the patrol officers. When Theodore Roosevelt served as police commissioner in New York, he frequently made clandestine trips to the beats to check his officers; any malingerers found in the saloons were summoned to headquarters in the morning.[50]

Meanwhile, on the American Frontier . . .

While large cities in the east were struggling to overcome social problems and establish preventive police forces, the western half of America was anything but passive. Many historians believe that the true character of Americans developed on the frontier. Rugged individualism, independence, and simplicity of manners and behavior lent dignity to American life.

Most Americans are fascinated by this period of police history, a time when heroic marshals had gunfights in Dodge City and other wild cowboy towns. But this period is also riddled with exaggerated legends and half-truths. During the second half of the nineteenth century, the absence of government created a confusing variety of forms of policing in the West. Large parts of the West were under federal control, some had been organized into states, and still others were under Native American control, at least on paper. Law enforcement was performed largely by federal marshals and their deputies. Once a state was created within a territory, its state legislature had the power to attempt to deal with crime by appointing county sheriffs. Otherwise, there was no uniform method for attempting to control the problems of the West.

When the people left the wagon trains and their relatively law-abiding ways, they attempted to live together in communities. Many different ethnic groups—Anglo-Americans, Mexicans, Chinese, Native Americans, freed blacks, Australians, Scandinavians, and others—competed for often scarce resources and fought one another violently, often with mob attacks. Economic conflicts were frequent between cattlemen and sheepherders,

PRACTITIONER'S PERSPECTIVE

What Science Has Done for the Police

CHIEF FRANCIS O'NEILL, CHICAGO, 1903

The watchman of a century ago with his lantern and staff who called out the passing hours in stentorian tones during the night is now but a tradition. He has been succeeded by a uniformed constabulary and police who carry arms and operate under semimilitary discipline. The introduction of electricity as a means of communication between stations was the first notable advance in the improvement of police methods. I remember the time when the manipulation of the dial telegraph by the station keeper while sending messages excited the greatest wonder and admiration. The adoption of the Morse system of telegraphy was a long step forward and proved of great advantage. In 1876, all desk sergeants were required to take up the immediate study of the Morse system of telegraphy. Scarcely one-fourth of them became proficient before modern science, advancing in leaps and bounds, brought forth that still more modern miracle—the telephone. Less than one-quarter century ago the policeman on post had no aid from science in communicating with his station or in securing assistance in case of need. When required by duty to care for the sick and injured or to remove a dead body, an appeal to the owner of some suitable vehicle was his only resource. These were desperate times for policemen in a hostile country with unpaved streets. The patrol wagon and signal service have effected a revolution in police methods. The forward stride from the lanterned night watch, with staff, to the uniformed and disciplined police officer of the present, equipped with telegraph, telephone, signal service, and the Bertillon system of identification,* is indeed an interesting one to contemplate.

*Alphonse Bertillon (1853–1914) developed a system for criminal identification based on precise measurements of the human body. The system was used in Paris in 1882 and was officially adopted for all of France in 1888.

Source: Proceedings of the International Chiefs of Police, tenth annual convention, May 12–14, 1903, p. 67.

and they often led to major range wars. There was constant labor strife in the mines. The bitterness of slavery remained, and many men with firearms skills learned during the Civil War turned to outlawry after leaving the service. (Jesse James was one such person.) In spite of these difficulties, westerners did manage to establish peace by relying on a combination of four groups who assumed responsibility for law enforcement: private citizens, U.S. marshals, businessmen, and town police officers.[51]

Private citizens usually helped to enforce the law by joining a posse or through individual efforts. Such was the case with the infamous Dalton Gang in Coffeyville, Kansas. The five gang members attempted to rob a bank in Coffeyville in 1892. However, private citizens, seeing what was occurring, armed themselves and shot at the Daltons as they attempted to escape, killing four of the five. Another example of citizen policing was the formation of vigilante committees. Between 1849 and 1902, there were 210 vigilante movements in the United States, most of them in California.[52] While it is true that they occasionally hung outlaws, they also performed valuable work by ridding their communities of dangerous criminals.

Federal marshals were created by congressional legislation in 1789. As marshals began to appear on the frontier, the vigilantes tended to disappear. The marshals enforced federal laws, so they had no jurisdiction over matters not involving a federal offense. They could act only in cases involving theft of mail, crimes against railroad property, murder on federal lands (much of the West was federal property for many decades), and a few other crimes. Their primary responsibility was in civil matters arising from federal court decisions. Federal marshals obtained their office through political appointment; therefore they did not need any prior experience and were politically indebted. Initially, they received no salary but were instead compensated with fees and rewards. Because chasing outlaws did not pay as much as serving civil process papers, the marshals tended to prefer the more lucrative, less dangerous task of serving court paperwork. Congress saw the folly in this system and, in 1896, enacted legislation providing regular salaries for marshals.[53]

When a territory became a state, the primary law enforcement functions usually fell to local sheriffs and marshals. Train robbers like Jesse James and the Dalton Gang were among the most famous outlaws to violate federal laws. Many train robbers became legendary for having the courage to steal from the despised railroad owners. What is often overlooked in the tales of these legendary outlaws is their often total disregard for the safety and lives of their victims. To combat these criminals, federal marshals found their hideouts, and railroad companies and other businesses often offered rewards for information leading to their capture. Occasionally, as in the case of Jesse James and the Daltons, the marshals' work was done for them—outlaws were often killed by friends (usually for a reward) or by private citizens.[54]

Gunfights in the West actually occurred very rarely; few individuals on either side of the law actually welcomed stand-up gunfights. It was infinitely more sensible to find cover from which to have a shootout. Further, handguns were not the preferred weapon; a double-barreled shotgun could do far more damage than a handgun at close range. Local law enforcement occurred as people settled into communities. Town meetings were held where a government was established and local officials were elected. Sheriffs quickly became important officials, but they spent more time collecting taxes, inspecting cattle brands, maintaining jails, and serving civil papers than they did actually dealing with outlaws. In fact, "Wild Bill" Hickok only killed two men while marshal of Abilene, Kansas; William "Bat" Masterson killed no one while living near Dodge City; and Wyatt Earp, who was never actually a marshal, may have killed one.[55]

Only forty-five violent deaths from all causes can be found in western cow towns from 1870 to 1885, when they were thriving. This low figure reflects the real nature of the cow towns. Businessmen had a vested interest in preventing crime from occurring and in not hiring a trigger-happy sheriff or marshal. They tended to avoid hiring individuals like John Slaughter, sheriff of Cochise County, Arizona, for eight years, who never brought a prisoner back alive. Too much violence ruined a town's reputation and harmed the local economy.[56]

The Entrenchment of Political Influence

Partly because of their closeness to politicians, police during the early twentieth century began providing a wide array of services to citizens. Many police departments were involved in the prevention of crime and the maintenance of order as well as a variety of social services. In some cities, they operated soup lines, helped find lost children, and found jobs and temporary lodging in station houses for newly arrived immigrants.[57] Police organizations were typically quite decentralized, with cities being divided into precincts and run like small-scale departments, hiring, firing, managing, and assigning personnel as necessary. Officers were often recruited from the same ethnic stock as the dominant groups in the neighborhoods and lived in the beats they patrolled, and they were allowed considerable discretion in handling their individual beats. Detectives operated from a caseload of: "persons" rather than offenses, relying on their charges to inform on other criminals.[58]

The strength of the local political influence over the police was that officers were integrated into neighborhoods. This strategy proved useful; it helped contain riots, and the police helped immigrants establish themselves in communities and find jobs. There were weaknesses as well: The intimacy with the community, closeness to politicians, and decentralized organizational structure (and its inability to provide supervision of officers) also led to police corruption. The close identification of police with neighborhoods also resulted in discrimination against strangers, especially ethnic and racial minorities. Police officers often ruled their beats with the "end of their nightsticks" and practiced "curbside justice."[59] The lack of organizational control over officers also caused some inefficiencies and disorganization; thus the image of the bungling Keystone Kops was widespread.

The Movement toward Professionalization

Attempts to Thwart Political Patronage

During the early nineteenth century, reformers sought to reject political involvement by the police, and civil service systems were created to eliminate patronage and ward influences in hiring and firing police officers. In some cities, officers were not permitted to live in the same beat they patrolled in order to isolate them as completely as possible from political influences. Police departments became one of the most autonomous agencies in urban government.[60] However, policing also became a matter viewed as best left to the discretion of police executives. Police organizations became law enforcement agencies with the sole goal of controlling crime. Any noncrime activities they were required to do were considered "social work." The **professional era of policing** would soon be in full bloom.

The scientific theory of administration was adopted, as advocated by Frederick Taylor during the early twentieth century. Taylor first studied the work process, breaking down jobs to their basic steps and emphasizing time and motion studies, all with the goal of maximizing production. From this emphasis on production and unity of control flowed the notion that police officers were best managed by a hierarchical pyramid of control. Police leaders routinized and standardized police work; officers were to enforce laws and make arrests whenever they could. Discretion was limited as much as possible. When special problems arose, special units (for example, vice, juvenile, drugs, tactical) were created rather than assigning problems to patrol officers.

The Era of August Vollmer

August Vollmer's career in policing has been established as one of the most important periods in the development of police professionalism. In April 1905 at age 29, Vollmer became the town marshal in Berkeley, California. At that time, policing had become a major issue all across America. Big-city police departments had become notorious for their corruption, and politics rather than professional principles dominated most police departments.[61]

Vollmer commanded a force of only three deputies; his first act as town marshal was to request an increase in his force from three to twelve deputies in order to form day and night patrols. Obtaining that, he soon won national publicity for being the first chief to order his men to patrol on bicycles. Time checks he had run demonstrated that officers on bicycles would be able to respond three times more quickly to calls than men on

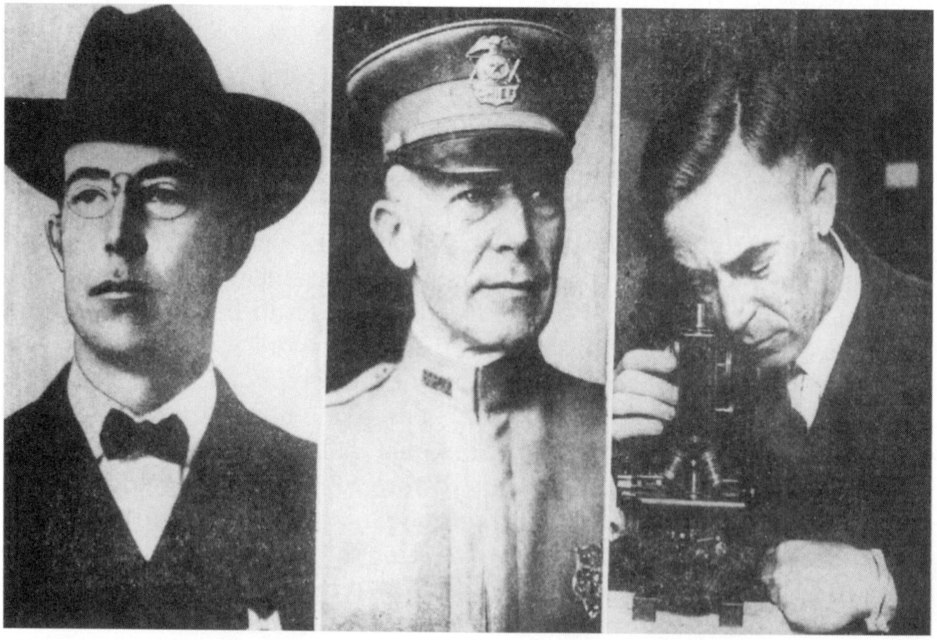

August Vollmer as town marshal, police chief, and criminalist.

(Courtesy Samuel G. Chapman)

foot possibly could. His confidence growing, Vollmer next persuaded the Berkeley City Council to purchase a system of red lights. The lights, hung at each street intersection, served as an emergency notification system for police officers—the first such signal system in the country.[62]

In 1906, Vollmer, curious about the methods criminals used to commit their crimes, began to question the suspects he arrested. He found that nearly all criminals used their own peculiar method of operation, or *modus operandi*. In 1907, following an apparent suicide case that Vollmer suspected of being murder, Vollmer sought the advice of a professor of biology at the University of California. He became convinced of the value of scientific knowledge in criminal investigation.[63]

Vollmer's most daring innovation came in 1908: the idea of a police school. The first formal training program for police officers in the country drew on the expertise of university professors as well as police officers. The school included courses on police methods and procedures, fingerprinting, first aid, criminal law, anthropometry, photography, public health, and sanitation. In 1917, the curriculum was expanded from one to three years.[64]

In 1916, Vollmer persuaded a professor of pharmacology and bacteriology to become a full-time criminalist in charge of the department's criminal investigation laboratory. By 1917, Vollmer had his entire patrol force operating out of automobiles; it was the first completely mobile patrol force in the country. And in 1918, to improve the quality of police recruits in his department, he began to hire college students as part-time officers and to administer a set of intelligence, psychiatric, and neurological tests to all applicants. Out of this group of "college cops" came several outstanding and influential police leaders, including O. W. Wilson, who served as police chief in Wichita and Chicago and as the first dean of the school of criminology at the University of California. Then, in 1921, in addition to experimenting with the lie detector, two of Vollmer's officers installed a crystal set and earphones in a Model T touring car, thus creating the first radio car.

These and other innovations at Berkeley had begun to attract attention from municipal police departments across the nation, including Los Angeles, which persuaded Vollmer to serve a short term as chief of police beginning in August 1923. Gambling, the illicit sale of liquor (Prohibition was then in effect), and police corruption were major problems in Los Angeles. Vollmer hired ex-criminals to gather intelligence information on the criminal network. He also promoted honest officers, required three thousand patrol officers to take an intelligence test, and, using those tests, reassigned personnel.[65] These personnel actions made Vollmer, already unpopular with crooks and corrupt politicians, very unpopular within the department as well. When he returned to Berkeley in 1924, he had made many enemies, and his attempts at reform had met with too much opposition to have any lasting effect. It would not be until the 1950s, under Chief William H. Parker, that the Los Angeles Police Department (LAPD) would become a leader in the professional era of policing.[66]

Vollmer, although a leading proponent of police professionalism, also advocated the idea that the police should function as social workers. He believed the police should do more than merely arrest offenders; they should also seek to prevent crime by "saving" offenders.[67] He suggested that police work closely with existing social welfare agencies, inform voters about overcrowded schools, and support the expansion of recreational facilities, community social centers, and antidelinquency agencies. Basically, he was suggesting that the police play an active part in the life of the community. These views were very prescient; today, his ideas are being implemented in the contemporary movement toward **community policing** and problem-oriented policing (discussed in Chapter 6). Yet the major thrust of police professionalization had been to insulate the police from politics. This contradiction illustrated one of the fundamental ambiguities of the whole notion of professionalism.[68]

In the late 1920s, Vollmer was appointed the first professor of police administration in the country at the University of Chicago. Upon returning to Berkeley in 1931, he received a similar appointment at the University of California, a position he held concurrently with the office of chief of police until his retirement from the force in 1932. He continued to serve as a university professor until 1938.[69]

The Crime Fighter Image

The 1930s marked an important turning point in the history of police reform. O. W. Wilson emerged as the leading authority on police administration, the police role was redefined, and the crime fighter image gained popularity.

Wilson, who learned from J. Edgar Hoover's transformation of the Federal Bureau of Investigation (FBI) into a highly prestigious agency, became the principal architect of the police reform strategy.[70] Hoover, appointed FBI director in 1924, had raised the eligibility and training standards of recruits and had developed an incorruptible crime-fighting organization. Municipal police found Hoover's path a compelling one.

Professionalism came to mean a combination of managerial efficiency and technological sophistication and an emphasis on crime fighting. The social work aspects of the policing movement fell into almost total eclipse. In sum, under the professional model of policing, officers were to remain in their "rolling fortresses," going from one call to the next with all due haste. As Mark Moore and George Kelling observed, "In professionalizing crime fighting . . . citizens on whom so much used to depend [were] removed from the fight."[71]

The Wickersham Commission

Another important development in policing, one that was strongly influenced by August Vollmer, was the creation of the Wickersham Commission. President

EXHIBIT 1-1

The Crib of Modern Law Enforcement

A Chronology of August Vollmer and the Berkeley Police Department

1905	Vollmer is elected Berkeley town marshal. Town trustees appoint six police officers at a salary of $70 per month.
1906	Trustees create detective rank. Vollmer initiates a red light signal system to reach beat officers from headquarters; telephones are installed in boxes. A police records system is created.
1908	Two motorcycles are added to the department. Vollmer begins a police school.
1909	Vollmer is appointed Berkeley chief of police under new charter form of government. Trustees approve appointment of Bertillon expert and purchase of fingerprinting equipment. A "modus operandi" file is created, modeled on British system.
1911	All patrol officers are using bicycles.
1914	Three privately owned autos are authorized for patrol use.
1915	A central office is established for police reports.
1916	Vollmer urges Congress to establish a national fingerprint bureau (later created by the FBI in Washington, D.C.), begins annual lectures on police procedures, and persuades biochemist Albert Schneider to install and direct a crime laboratory at headquarters.
1917	Vollmer has first completely motorized force; officers furnish own automobiles. Vollmer recruits college students for part-time police jobs. He begins consulting with police, reorganizing departments around the country.
1918	Entrance examinations are initiated to measure mental, physical, and emotional fitness of recruits; a part-time police psychiatrist is employed.
1919	Vollmer begins testing delinquents and using psychology to anticipate criminal behavior. He implements juvenile program to reduce child delinquency.
1921	Vollmer guides development of first lie detector and begins developing radio communications between patrol cars, handwriting analysis, and use of business machine equipment (a Hollerith tabulator).

Following his retirement from active law enforcement in 1932, Vollmer traveled around the world to study police methods. He continued serving as professor of police administration at the University of California, Berkeley, until 1938 and authored or coauthored four books on police and crime from 1935 to 1949. He died in Berkeley in 1955.

Coolidge had appointed the first National Crime Commission in 1925, in an admission that crime control had become a national problem. This commission was criticized for working neither through the states nor with professionals in criminal justice, psychiatry, social work, or the like. Nevertheless, coming on the heels of World War I, the crime commission took advantage of FBI Director J. Edgar Hoover's popular "war on crime" slogan to enlist public support. Political leaders and police officials also loudly proclaimed the "war on crime" concept; it continued the push for police professionalism.

Coolidge's successor, President Herbert Hoover, became concerned about the lax enforcement of Prohibition, which took effect in 1920. It was common knowledge that an alarming number of American police chiefs and sheriffs were accepting bribes in exchange for overlooking moonshiners; other types of police corruption were occurring as well.

Hoover replaced the National Crime Commission with the National Commission on Law Observance and Enforcement—popularly known as the **Wickersham Commission** after its chairman, former U.S. Attorney General George W. Wickersham. This presidential commission completed the first national study of crime and criminal justice, issuing fourteen reports. Two of those reports, the "Report on Lawlessness in Law Enforcement" and the "Report on Police," represented a call by the national government for increased police professionalism.

The "Report on Police" was written in part by August Vollmer, and his imprint on this and other reports is evident. The second, "Report on Lawlessness in Law Enforcement," concerned itself with police misconduct and has received the greatest public attention, both then and today. The report indicated that the use of third-degree interrogation methods of suspects by the police (including the infliction of physical or mental pain to extract confessions) was widespread in America. This report, through its recommendations, mapped out a path of professionalism in policing for the next two generations. The Wickersham Commission recommended, for example, that the corrupting influence of politics should be removed from policing. Police chief executives should be selected on merit, and patrol officers should be tested and should meet minimal physical standards. Police salaries, working conditions, and benefits should be decent, the commission stated, and there should be adequate training for both preservice and in-service officers. The commission also called for the use of policewomen (in cases involving juveniles and females), crime-prevention units, and bureaus of criminal investigation.

Many of these recommendations represented what progressive police reformers had been wanting for the previous forty years; unfortunately, President Hoover and his administration could do little more than report the Wickersham Commission's recommendations before leaving office. Franklin Roosevelt's administration provided the funding and leadership necessary for implementing Wickersham's suggestions in the states.

Police as the "Thin Blue Line": William H. Parker

The movement to transform the police into professional crime fighters found perhaps its staunchest champion in **William H. Parker**, who began as a patrol officer with the Los Angeles Police Department in 1927. Parker used his law degree to advance his career, and by 1934 he was the LAPD's trial prosecutor and an assistant to the chief.[72]

Parker became police chief in 1950. Following an uproar over charges of police brutality in 1951, he conducted an extensive investigation that resulted in the dismissal or punishment of over forty officers. Following this incident, he launched a campaign to transform the LAPD. His greatest success, typical of the new professionalism, came in administrative reorganization. The command structure was simplified as Parker aggressively sought ways to free every possible officer for duty on the streets, including forcing the county sheriff's office to guard prisoners and adopting one-person patrol cars. Parker also made the rigorous selection and training of personnel a major characteristic of the LAPD. Higher standards of physical fitness, intelligence, and scholastic achievement weeded out many applicants, while others failed the psychiatric examinations.

Once accepted, recruits attended a thirteen-week academy that included a rigorous physical program, rigid discipline, and intensive study. Parker thus molded an image of a tough, competent, polite, and effective crime fighter by controlling recruitment. During the 1950s, this image made the LAPD the model for reform across the nation; thus the 1950s marked a turning point in the history of professionalism.[73]

But Parker's impact on the police shows the very real limitations of the professional style of policing. Parker conceived of the police as a thin blue line, protecting society from barbarism and Communist subversion. He viewed urban society as a jungle, needing the restraining hand of the police; only the law and law enforcement saved society from the horrors of anarchy. The police had to enforce the law without fear or favor. Parker opposed any restrictions on police methods. The law, he believed, should give the police wide latitude to use wiretaps and to conduct search and seizure. For him, the Bill of Rights was not absolute but relative. Any conflict between effective police operation and individual rights should be resolved in favor of the police, he believed, and the rights of society took precedence over the rights of the individual. He thought that evidence obtained illegally should still be admitted in court and that the police could not do their jobs if the courts and other civilians were continually second-guessing them.

Basically, Parker believed that some "wicked men with evil hearts" preyed on society and that the police must protect society from attack by them. But Parker's brand of professional police performance lacked total public support. Voters often supported political machines that controlled and manipulated the police in anything but a professional manner; the public demanded a police department that was subject to political influence and manipulation and then condemned the force for its crookedness. The professional police officer was in the uncomfortable position of offering a service that society required for its very survival but that many people did not want at all.[74]

Still, Parker's influence over police administration has not perished altogether. And to the extent that his influence remains today, it may hinder the spread of the concepts of community policing and problem-oriented policing, which are discussed more thoroughly in Chapter 6.

A Retreat from the Professional Model

Coming Full Circle to Peel: The President's Crime Commission

The 1960s were a time of explosion and turbulence. Inner-city residents rioted in several major cities, protestors denounced military involvement in Vietnam, and assassins ended the lives of President John F. Kennedy and Dr. Martin Luther King Jr. The country was witnessing tremendous upheaval, and incidents like the so-called police riot at the 1968 Democratic National Convention in Chicago raised many questions about the police and their function and role.

To this point, there had been few inquiries concerning police functions and methods[75] for two reasons. First was a tendency on the part of the police to resist outside scrutiny. Functioning in a bureaucratic environment, they, like other bureaucrats, were sensitive to outside research. Many police administrators perceived a threat to their career and to the image of the organization, as well as a concern about the legitimacy of the research itself. There was a natural reluctance to invite trouble. Second, few people in policing perceived a need to challenge traditional methods of operation. The "if it ain't broke, don't fix it" attitude prevailed, particularly among old-school administrators. Some ideas were etched in stone, such as the belief that more police personnel and vehicles equalled more patrolling and, therefore, less crime, a quicker response rate, and a happier citizenry. A corollary belief was that the more officers riding in the patrol car, the better. The methods and effectiveness of detectives and their investigative techniques were not even open to debate. As Herman Goldstein has stated, however, "Crises stimulate progress. The police came under enormous pressure in the late 1960s and early 1970s, confronted with concern about crime, civil rights demonstrations, racial conflicts, riots and political protests."[76]

Five national studies looked into police practices during the 1960s and 1970s, each with a different focus: the President's Commission on Law Enforcement and the Administration of Justice (1967), the National Advisory Commission on Civil Disorders (1968), the National Commission on the Causes and Prevention of Violence (1968), the President's Commission on Campus Unrest (1970), and the National Advisory Commission on Criminal Justice Standards and Goals (1973).

Of particular note was a commission whose findings are still widely cited today and that provided the impetus to return the police to the community: the President's Commission on Law Enforcement and the Administration of Justice. Termed the **President's Crime Commission**, this body was charged by President Lyndon Johnson to find solutions to America's internal crime problems, including the root causes of crime, the workings of the justice system, and the hostile, antagonistic relations between the police and civilians. Among the commission's recommendations for the police were hiring more minority members as officers to improve police-community relations, upgrading the quality of police officers through hiring better educated officers, promoting to supervisory positions college-educated individuals, screening applicants more rigorously, and providing intensive preservice training for new recruits. It was believed that a higher caliber of recruits would raise police service delivery, promote tranquility within the community, and relegate police corruption to a thing of the past.[77]

The President's Crime Commission brought policing full circle, restating several of the same principles that were laid out by Sir Robert Peel in 1829: that the police should be close to the public, that poor quality of policing contributed to social disorder, and that the police should focus on community relations. Thus by 1970, there had been what was termed a systematic demolition of the assumptions underlying the professional era of policing.[78] Few authorities on policing today could endorse the basic approaches to police management that were propounded by O. W. Wilson or William Parker. We now know much that was still unknown by the staff of the President's Crime Commission in 1967. For example, as will be seen in Chapter 5, we have learned that adding more police or intensifying patrol coverage does not reduce crime and that neither faster response time nor additional detectives will improve clearance rates.

Community-Oriented Policing and Problem-Solving Era

In the early 1970s, it was suggested that the performance of patrol officers would improve by redesigning their job based on motivators.[79] This suggestion later evolved into a concept known as **team policing**, which sought to restructure police departments, improve police-community relations, enhance police officer morale, and facilitate change within the police organization. Its primary element was a decentralized neighborhood focus for the delivery of police services. Officers were to be generalists, trained to investigate crimes and basically attend to all of the problems in their area; a team of officers would be assigned to a particular neighborhood and would be responsible for all police services in that area.

In the end, however, team policing failed for several reasons. Most of the experiments were poorly planned and hastily implemented, resulting in street officers who did not understand what they were supposed to do. Many mid-management personnel felt threatened by team policing and did not support the experiment.

There were other developments for the police during the late 1970s and early 1980s. Foot patrol became more popular, and many jurisdictions (such as Newark, New Jersey; Boston; and Flint, Michigan) even demanded it. In Newark, an evaluation found that officers on foot patrol were easily seen by residents, produced a significant increase in the level of satisfaction with police service, led to a significant reduction of perceived crime problems, and resulted in a significant increase in the perceived level of neighborhood safety.[80]

These findings and others discussed later shattered several long-held myths about measures of police effectiveness. In addition, research conducted during the 1970s suggested that information could help police improve their ability to deal with crime. These studies, along with studies of foot patrol and fear reduction, created new opportunities for police to understand the increasing concerns of citizens' groups about problems (e.g., gangs, prostitutes) and to work with citizens to do something about them. Police discovered that when they asked citizens about their priorities, citizens appreciated their asking and often provided useful information.

Simultaneously, the problem-oriented approach to policing was being tested in Madison, Wisconsin; Baltimore County, Maryland; and Newport News, Virginia. Studies there found that police officers have the capacity to do problem solving successfully and can work well with citizens and other agencies. Also, citizens seemed to appreciate working with police. Moreover, this approach gave officers more autonomy to analyze the underlying causes of problems and to find creative solutions. Crime control remained an important function, but equal emphasis was given to prevention.

In sum, following are some of the factors that set the stage for the emergence of the community-oriented policing and problem-solving (COPPS) era:

- The narrowing of the police mission to crime fighting
- Increased cultural diversity in our society
- The detachment of patrol officers in patrol vehicles
- Increased violence in our society
- A scientific view of management, stressing efficiency more than effectiveness, quantitative policing more than qualitative policing
- A downturn in the economy and, subsequently, a "do more with less" philosophy toward the police
- Increased dependence on high-technology equipment rather than contact with the public
- The emphasis on organizational change, including decentralization and greater officer discretion
- Isolation of police administration from community and officer input
- Concern about police violation of the civil rights of minorities
- A yearning for personalization of government services
- Burgeoning attempts by the police to adequately reach the community through crime prevention, team policing, and police-community relations

Most of these elements contain a common theme: the isolation of the police from the public.

COPPS is now recognized as being on the cutting edge of what is new in policing.[81] Indeed, the Violent Crime Control and Law Enforcement Act of 1994 authorized $8.8 billion over six years to create the Office of Community Oriented Policing Services (COPS) within the U.S. Department of Justice, to add one hundred thousand more police officers to communities across the country, and to create thirty-one regional community policing institutes (RCPIs) to provide training and technical assistance for implementation and technology throughout the nation (educating police personnel on the proper approach to implementing the strategy and the technologies that are available for enhancing COPPS, discussed in Chapter 14).

The Three Generations of COPPS

COPPS is the established paradigm of contemporary policing, both at home and abroad; it enjoys a large degree of public acceptance.[82] According to Willard M. Oliver, it has now moved through three generations: innovation, diffusion, and institutionalization.[83]

The first generation of COPPS, *innovation,* spans the period from 1979 through 1986. It began with the seminal work of Herman Goldstein concerning needed improvement of policing[84] and with the "broken windows" theory of James Q. Wilson and George L. Kelling.[85] Early trials of community policing during this period—called "experiments," "test sites," and "demonstration projects"—were usually restricted to larger metropolitan cities. The style of policing that was employed was predominantly narrow in focus, such as foot patrols, problem-solving methods, or community substations. These small-scale experiments provided a source of innovative ideas for others to consider.

The second generation, *diffusion,* covers the period from 1987 through 1994. The concepts and philosophy of community policing and problem solving spread rapidly among police agencies through various forms of communication within the police subculture. Community policing was adopted quickly during this period. In 1985, slightly more than three hundred police agencies employed some form of community policing,[86] whereas by 1994 it had spread to more than eight thousand agencies.[87] The practice of community policing during this generation was still generally limited to large and medium-sized cities, and the strategies normally targeted drugs and fear-of-crime issues while improving police-community relations. Much more emphasis was placed on evaluating outcomes through the use of appropriate research methodologies.

The third generation, *institutionalization,* began in 1995 and continues to the present. Today we see widespread implementation of community policing and problem solving across the United States. Nearly seven in ten (68 percent) of the nation's 17,000 local police agencies, employing 90 percent of all officers, have adopted this strategy.[88] This generation has seen COPPS become deeply entrenched within the political process, funded by federal grant money through the Violent Crime Control and Law Enforcement Act of 1994. Community policing today has extended to such programs as youth firearm violence, gangs, and domestic violence, while extending into geomapping software and crime prevention through environmental design.

SUMMARY

This chapter has presented the evolution of policing and some of the individuals, events, and national commissions that were instrumental in taking policing through several eras. It has also shown how the history of policing may be said to have come full circle to its roots, wherein it was intended to operate with the consent and assistance of the public. Policing is now attempting to throw off the shackles of tradition and become more community oriented.

This historical overview also reveals that many of today's policing issues and problems actually began surfacing many centuries ago: graft and corruption, negative community relations, police use of force, public unrest and rioting, general police accountability, the struggle to establish the proper roles and functions of the police, the police subculture, and the tendency to withdraw from the public, cling to tradition, and be inbred.

REVIEW QUESTIONS

1. What were the major police-related offices and their functions during the early English and colonial periods?
2. What legacies of colonial policing remained intact after the American Revolution?
3. List the three early issues of American policing, and describe their present status.
4. What unique characteristics of law enforcement existed in the Wild West? What myths concerning early western law enforcement continue today?
5. What were some of the advantages of the political and professional eras of policing?
6. What led to the development of the contemporary community-oriented policing and problem-solving era, and what are some of its main features?
7. Explain how it can be said that policing has come full circle, returning to its origins.
8. Describe the three generations of community-oriented policing and problem solving.

INDEPENDENT STUDENT ACTIVITIES

1. Interview retired or long-time police officers about the kinds of changes they have witnessed in policing from their earliest years in the field to the present.
2. Through these interviews and your own independent research of police operations of the past, explore the ways in which the traditional model of policing differs from today's community policing and problem solving.

3. Looking at some of the early police offices described in this chapter (such as coroner, justice of the police, and constable), determine through interviews and research whether such positions ever existed in your home jurisdiction and, if so, their duties and functions.

RELATED WEB SITES

Library of Congres
http://loc.gov/library

National Archive of Criminal Justice Data
http://www.icpsr.unmich.edu/NACJD/index.html

Office of Community Oriented Policing Services (COPS)
http://www.usdoj.gov/cops

NOTES

The author is indebted to Professor Samuel G. Chapman for contributing much of the information for this chapter and for sharing photographs from his personal files and correspondence.

1. SAMUEL WALKER, *The Police in America: An Introduction* (New York: McGraw-Hill, 1983), p. 2.
2. BRUCE SMITH, *Rural Crime Control* (New York: Columbia University, 1933), p. 40.
3. Ibid., pp. 42–44.
4. Ibid.
5. Ibid.
6. Ibid., pp. 182–84.
7. Ibid., pp. 188–89.
8. Ibid., p. 192.
9. Ibid., pp. 218–22.
10. Ibid., pp. 245–46.
11. Ibid.
12. CRAIG UCHIDA, "The Development of American Police: An Historical Overview," in *Critical Issues in Policing: Contemporary Readings,* ed. ROGER G. DUNHAM and GEOFFREY P. ALPERT (Prospect Heights, IL: Waveland Press, 1989), p. 14.
13. CHARLES REITH, *A New Study of Police History* (London: Oliver and Boyd, 1956).
14. CARL KLOCKARS, *The Idea of Police* (Beverly Hills: Sage, 1985).
15. Ibid., pp. 45–46.
16. Ibid., p. 46.

17. DAVID R. JOHNSON, *American Law Enforcement History* (St. Louis: Forum Press, 1981), p. 4.
18. Ibid., p. 5.
19. Ibid.
20. Ibid., p. 6.
21. Ibid., p. 1.
22. Ibid., pp. 8–10.
23. Ibid., p. 11.
24. Ibid., p. 13.
25. DAVID A. JONES, *History of Criminology: A Philosophical Perspective* (Westport, CT: Greenwood Press, 1986), p. 64.
26. JOHNSON, *American Law Enforcement History,* pp. 14–15.
27. Ibid., pp. 17–18.
28. Ibid., pp. 18–19.
29. LEON RADZINOWICZ, *A History of English Criminal Law and Its Administration from 1750,* vol. IV: *Grappling for Control* (London: Stevens and Son, 1968), p. 163.
30. JOHNSON, *American Law Enforcement History,* p. 19.
31. Ibid., pp. 19–20.
32. Ibid., pp. 20–21.
33. A. C. GERMANN, FRANK D. DAY, and ROBERT R. J. GALLATI, *Introduction to Law Enforcement and Criminal Justice* (Springfield, IL: Charles C. Thomas, 1962), p. 63.
34. CLIVE EMSLEY, *Policing and Its Context, 1750–1870* (New York: Schocken, 1983), p. 37.
35. PAMELA D. MAYHALL, *Police-Community Relations and the Administration of Justice,* 3rd ed. (New York: John Wiley and Sons, 1985), p. 425.
36. JOHNSON, *American Law Enforcement History,* p. 26.
37. Ibid., pp. 26–27.
38. Ibid., p. 27.
39. Ibid.
40. Ibid., pp. 28–29.
41. Ibid., pp. 30–31.
42. JAMES F. RICHARDSON, *Urban Policing in the United States* (London: Kennikat Press, 1974), pp. 47–48.
43. JAMES F. RICHARDSON, *The New York Police: Colonial Times to 1901* (New York: Oxford Press, 1970), p. 259.
44. RICHARDSON, *Urban Policing in the United States,* p. 48.
45. RICHARDSON, *The New York Police,* pp. 195–201.
46. RICHARDSON, *Urban Policing in the United States,* p. 51.
47. Ibid.
48. Ibid., pp. 53–54.
49. Ibid., pp. 55–56.
50. Ibid., pp. 59–60.

51. JOHNSON, *American Law Enforcement History,* p. 92.
52. Ibid.
53. Ibid., pp. 96–97.
54. Ibid., p. 98.
55. Ibid.
56. Ibid., pp. 100–101.
57. ERIC H. MONKKONEN, *Police in Urban America, 1860–1920* (New York: Cambridge University Press, 1981), p. 158.
58. JOHN E. ECK, *The Investigation of Burglary and Robbery* (Washington, DC: Police Executive Research Forum, 1984).
59. GEORGE L. KELLING, "Juveniles and Police: The End of the Nightstick," in *From Children to Citizens,* Vol. II: *The Role of the Juvenile Court,* ed. FRANCIS X. HARTMANN (New York: Springer-Verlag, 1987).
60. HERMAN GOLDSTEIN, *Policing a Free Society* (Cambridge, MA: Ballinger, 1977).
61. AUGUST VOLLMER, "Police Progress in the Past Twenty-five Years," *Journal of Criminal Law and Criminology* 24 (1933): 161–75.
62. ALFRED E. PARKER, *Crime Fighter: August Vollmer* (New York: Macmillan, 1961).
63. DOUTHIT, "August Vollmer," in *Thinking about Police: Contemporary Readings,* ed. CARL B. KLOCKARS (New York: McGraw-Hill, 1983), p. 102.
64. Ibid.
65. PAUL JACOBS, *Prelude to Riot: A View of Urban America from the Bottom* (New York: Random House, 1966), pp. 13–60.
66. Ibid.
67. SAMUEL WALKER, *A Critical History of Police Reform: The Emergence of Professionalism* (Lexington, MA: Lexington Books, 1977), p. 81.
68. Ibid., pp. 80–83.
69. See GENE E. CARTE and ELAINE H. CARTE, *Police Reform in the United States: The Era of August Vollmer, 1905–1932* (Berkeley: University of California Press, 1975), for a chronology of Vollmer's career and a listing of his publications.
70. ORLANDO W. WILSON, *Police Administration* (New York: McGraw-Hill, 1950).
71. MARK H. MOORE and GEORGE L. KELLING, "'To Serve and Protect': Learning from Police History," *The Public Interest* 70 (Winter 1983): 49–65.
72. JOHNSON, *American Law Enforcement History,* pp. 119–20.
73. Ibid., pp. 120–21.
74. RICHARDSON, *Urban Police in the United States,* pp. 139–43.
75. PETER K. MANNING, "The Researcher: An Alien in the Police World," in *The Ambivalent Force: Perspectives on the Police,* 2nd ed. (Hinsdale, IL: Dryden Press, 1976), pp. 103–21.
76. HERMAN GOLDSTEIN, *Problem-Oriented Policing* (New York: McGraw-Hill, 1990), p. 9.
77. WILLIAM G. DOERNER, *Introduction to Law Enforcement: An Insider's View* (Englewood Cliffs, NJ: Prentice Hall, 1992), pp. 21–23.

78. Samuel Walker, "'Broken Windows' and Fractured History: The Use and Misuse of History in Recent Police Patrol Analysis," in *Classics in Policing,* ed. Steven G. Brandl and David E. Barlow (Cincinnati: Anderson, 1996), pp. 97–110.
79. Thomas J. Baker, "Designing the Job to Motivate," *FBI Law Enforcement Bulletin* 45 (1976): 3–7.
80. Police Foundation, *The Newark Foot Patrol Experiment* (Washington, DC: Author, 1981).
81. Ibid., p. 71.
82. George Gallup, *Community Policing Survey* (Wilmington, NY: Scholarly Resources, 1996).
83. Willard M. Oliver, "The Third Generation of Community Policing: Moving through Innovation, Diffusion, and Institutionalization," *Police Quarterly* 3 (December 2000): 367–88.
84. Herman Goldstein, "Improving Policing: A Problem-Oriented Approach," *Crime and Delinquency* 25 (1979): 236–58.
85. James Q. Wilson and George L. Kelling, "Broken Windows: The Police and Neighborhood Safety," *Atlantic Monthly* (March 1982): 29–38.
86. Samuel Walker, *The Police in America: An Introduction* (New York: McGraw-Hill, 1985).
87. T. McEwen, *National Assessment Program: 1994 Survey Results* (Washington, DC: National Institute of Justice, 1995).
88. Department of Justice, Bureau of Justice Statistics, *Law Enforcement Management and Administrative Statistics: Local Police Departments 2000* (Washington, DC: Author, January 2003), p. iii.

CHAPTER 2

Law Enforcement Levels and Functions: Defending Our Homeland

Blessed are the peacemakers.

—Matthew 5:8

Key Terms

Department of Homeland Security (DHS)
Department of Justice
directorate
federal law enforcement agencies
Federal Law Enforcement Training Center (FLETC)
municipal police department
National Crime Information Center (NCIC)
sheriff's office
state police
Uniform Crime Reports (UCR)

Perhaps more than any other chapter in this textbook, this one reflects the impact of the events of September 11, 2001, when foreign terrorists attacked us on our own soil. No segment of our society was altered more than the structure and functions of our nation's police organizations, particularly the **federal law enforcement agencies**.

Our state and local law enforcement agencies were also compelled to change. They have become much more strategic in their approach to their work, adopting a long-term view, and much better trained at responding to terrorist attack. This nation's seventeen thousand law enforcement agencies received a mandate to cooperate, coordinate, and communicate.

In sum, this chapter demonstrates how law enforcement agencies function in a democratic society, particularly one in which the nation's very existence depends on the ability to be proactive to prevent further terrorist attacks. The chapter begins with an examination of the newly formed U.S. Department of Homeland Security. It looks at the roles and functions of its five directorates and their organizations, including the U.S. Secret Service. Next is a discussion of the retooled U.S. Department of Justice and its four primary law enforcement organizations: the Federal Bureau of Investigation (FBI); the Bureau of Alcohol, Tobacco, Firearms, and Explosives (ATF); the Drug Enforcement Administration (DEA); and the U.S. Marshals Service (USMS). Then the chapter reviews the functions of three related organizations: the Central Intelligence Agency (CIA), the Criminal Investigation Division of the Internal Revenue Service (IRS), and the Federal Law Enforcement Training Center (FLETC). Next is an overview of state and local agencies (that is, municipal police and county sheriff's offices). A chapter summary, review questions, independent student activities, and related Web sites conclude the chapter.

Appendix I provides information for those wishing to pursue a career in federal, state, or local law enforcement agencies. Another significant, burgeoning level of policing—the private security industry—is examined in Chapter 12. The general problem of terrorism is discussed in Chapter 8.

Federal Agencies

This section describes the major law enforcement arms of the federal government, most of which are found within the Department of Homeland Security and the Department of Justice.

The Department of Homeland Security

The new **Department of Homeland Security (DHS)** was created by H.R. 5005, the Homeland Security Act of 2002. This legislation put 180,000 new federal employees to work and committed $14 billion in new funds for securing the nation. Of that amount, $5.6 billion was for developing vaccines to protect against biological or chemical threats, $4 billion was for first responders (ensuring that local police, firefighters, and medical personnel received the necessary training and equipment), and about $1 billion went for science and technology projects to counter the use of biological weapons and to assess vulnerabilities.[1]

The primary enforcement arm of DHS is the newly established Bureau of Immigration and Customs Enforcement (ICE). The mission of ICE includes a vast investigative authority over terrorist financing, money laundering, illegal arms dealing, immigration fraud, and migrant smuggling.

With a workforce of fourteen thousand, ICE's investigative and intelligence resources equip it to address the complex criminal enterprises that threaten the United States.[2]

The Five Directorates. DHS's twenty-three federal agencies fall under five major divisions, or **directorates**:

- Border and Transportation Security (BTS)
- Emergency Preparedness and Response
- Science and Technology (S & T)
- Information Analysis and Infrastructure Protection (IAIP)
- Management

Besides these five directorates, which are discussed below, other critical agencies have been folded into DHS or newly created, including the U.S. Coast Guard, the U.S. Secret Service, and the Bureau of Citizenship and Immigration Services. Figure 2-1 shows the DHS organizational structure and includes all of its key components.

Border and Transportation Security. Border and Transportation Security (BTS), the largest directorate, is responsible for maintaining the security of our nation's 7,500 miles of border with Canada and Mexico, and our 95,000 miles of shoreline.[3] To carry out its mission, it houses the new office of Customs and Border Protection, as well as the Federal Law Enforcement Training Center; the Federal Protective Service, which protects government buildings; and the newly created Transportation Security Administration, which is responsible for the security of all of the airports.

The new office of Customs and Border Protection (CBP) was formed in March 2003. It has a workforce of more than forty thousand employees, including some employees brought over from the Department of Agriculture, the former U.S. Customs Service, the U.S. Border Patrol, and the Immigration and Naturalization Service. The rationale for forming CBP is simple: one agency, one goal. Four agencies were combined to work as one to better coordinate information and to stem the illegal export of equipment, technology, and munitions to unauthorized destinations. A major aim of CBP is to modernize its automated systems and information technology to better enhance border security and commercial trade information.[4]

Figure 2-2 shows the CBP's organizational structure. Chapter 8 discusses a new federal program, initiated in early 2004, under which twenty-four million foreigners are expected to be checked at the nation's airports each year.

The new Transportation Security Administration (TSA) assumed responsibility for aviation security in November 2001. TSA protects the nation's transportation systems to ensure freedom of movement for people

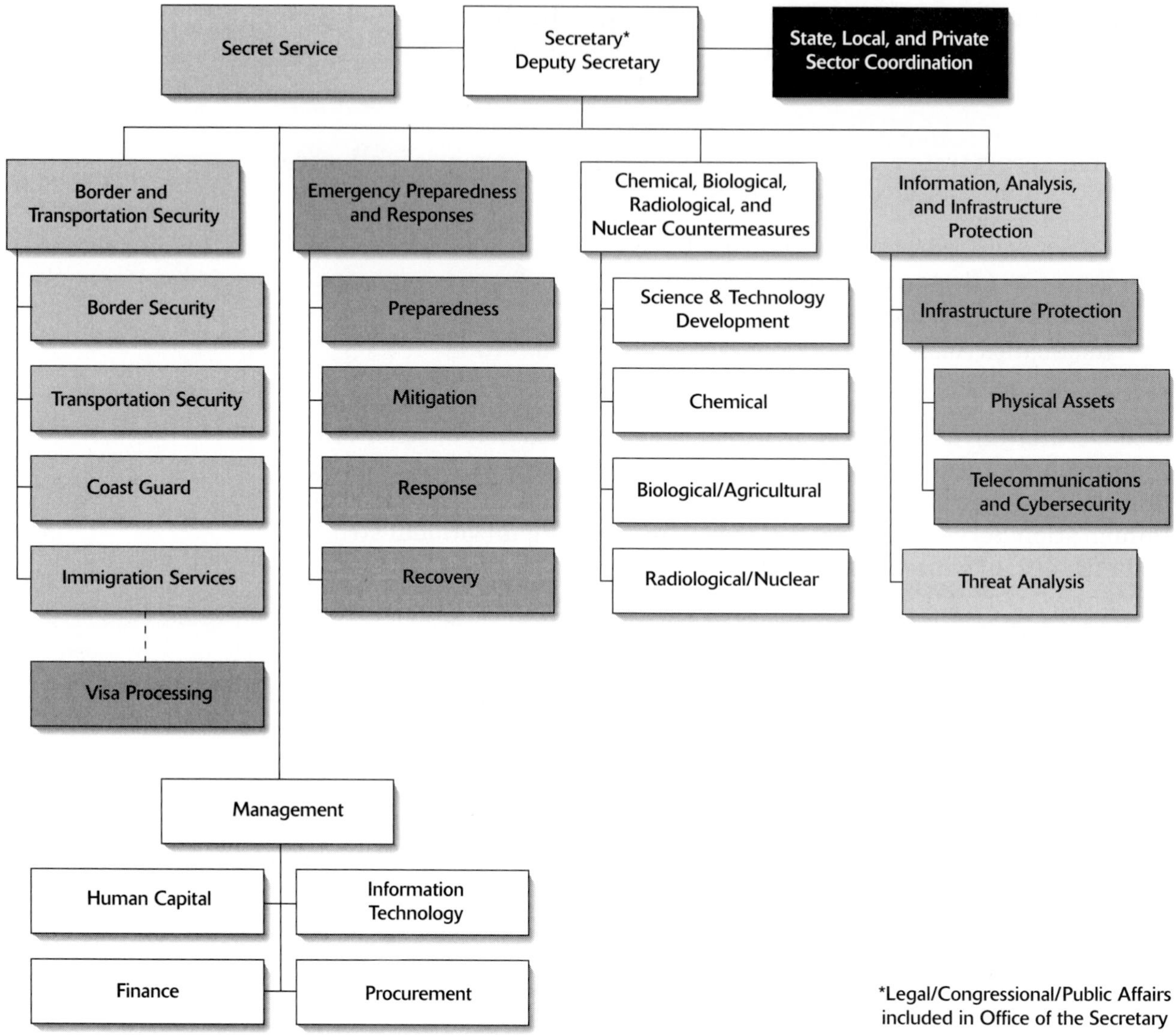

FIGURE 2-1 The organizational structure of the Department of Homeland Security.

Source: Department of Homeland Security

and commerce. Although its Web site provides relatively scant information and is guarded for security purposes, it states that TSA's annual budget request is about $5 billion.

TSA initially supervised the federal Air Marshal Service, which provides about five thousand specially trained, armed agents who are deployed worldwide on antihijacking missions. However, under a reorganization in December 2003, the air marshals were moved from TSA to the Bureau of Immigration and Customs Enforcement.

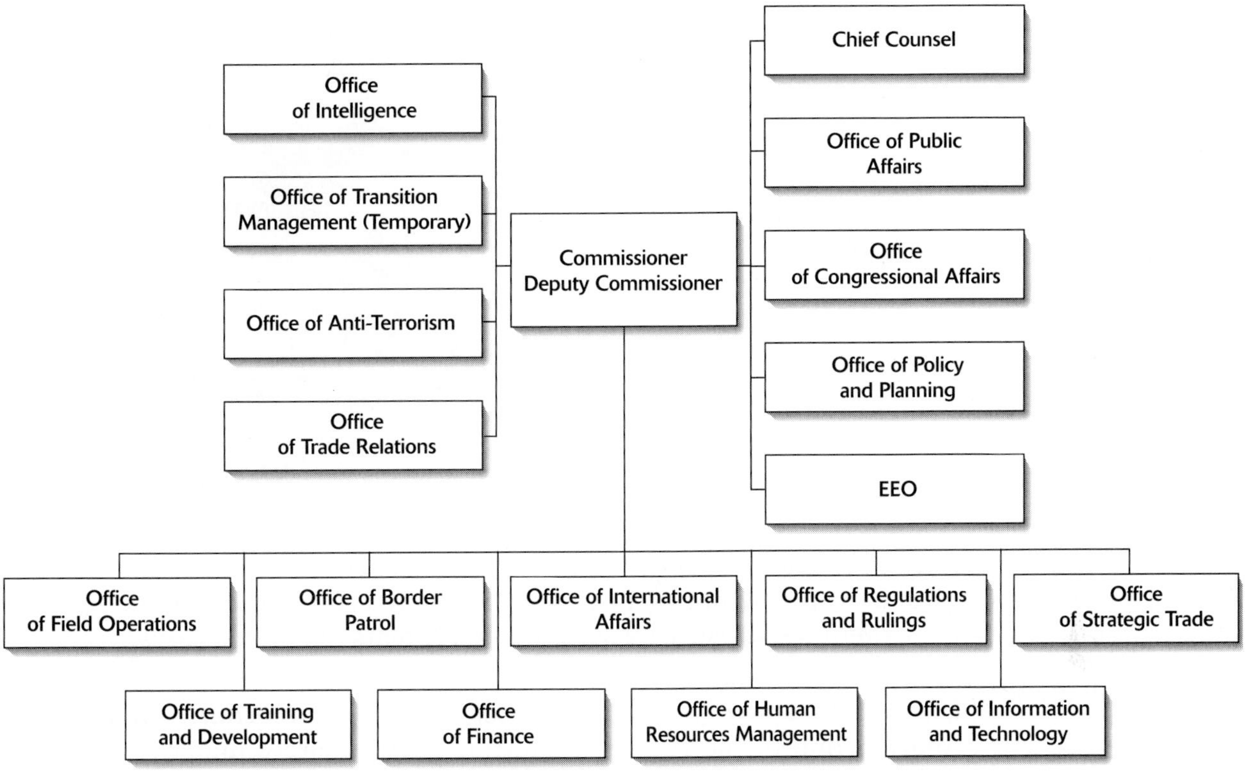

FIGURE 2-2 The organizational structure of the Bureau of Customs and Border Protection.

Source: Bureau of Customs and Border Protection

Emergency Preparedness and Response. The Emergency Preparedness and Response directorate ensures that the nation is prepared for, and able to recover from, terrorist attacks and natural disasters. It builds on the very successful history of the Federal Emergency Management Agency (FEMA) and continues FEMA's efforts to reduce the loss of life and property through preparedness, prevention, response, and recovery. The directorate develops and manages a national system to design curriculums, set standards, and evaluate and reward performance in training efforts. It focuses on risk mitigation by promoting disaster-resistant communities, leads the DHS response to any sort of biological or radiological attack, and coordinates the involvement of National Guard and other federal efforts.[5]

Science and Technology. This directorate is the primary research and development (R & D) arm of DHS, organizing the nation's vast scientific and technological resources to mitigate the effects of terrorism. It unifies and coordinates the federal efforts to develop scientific and technological countermeasures and sponsors R & D to invent new vaccines, antidotes, and therapies

(Courtesy of the Department of Homeland Security)

against biological and chemical warfare agents. Science and Technology's (S & T) responsibilities include a constant examination of the nation's vulnerabilities, its security systems, and threats and weaknesses.[6]

Information Analysis and Infrastructure Protection. Information Analysis and Infrastructure Protection (IAIP) merges under one roof the ability to identify and assess a broad range of intelligence information from other agencies (such as the CIA and the FBI) concerning threats to the homeland. When necessary, it issues timely warnings and encourages citizens to take appropriate preventive or protective action. It coordinates the federal government's lines of communication with state and local public-safety agencies and protects our critical infrastructure (for example, food and water supplies; health, safety, and emergency services; transportation, finance, and postal systems); a high priority is placed on protecting our cyber infrastructure.[7]

Management. The Management directorate is responsible for budget, appropriations, accounting and finance, procurement, human resources, information technology systems, facilities, property, equipment, and other resources relating to the responsibilities of DHS. Key to the success of DHS is the success of its 180,000 employees, and Management ensures that the employees have the resources, means of communication, and clear responsibilities that they need.[8]

The Secret Service. On March 1, 2003, the U.S. Secret Service (USSS) was formally moved from the Department of Treasury to DHS. This organization originated in 1865 to fight counterfeiting. In 1908, the division was transferred to the Department of Justice. Presidential security became a permanent function of the office in 1951.[9]

Secret Service agents are authorized to carry firearms and to make arrests for violations of any federal law. The U.S. Code also authorizes them to investigate credit and debit card frauds and frauds relating to electronic fund transfers, such as automated teller machines (ATMs).[10]

But clearly, the Secret Service's primary responsibility is to protect the lives of top government officials and their families, both at their homes and as they travel. This task has never been easy, but it has become more difficult since the terrorist attacks of September 11. How to best guarantee the safety of the president, the vice president, and their families is just one element of debate among its undercover agents and its uniformed officers (known as the Uniformed Division, or UD, who form the front line of defense at the White House and at foreign missions). Traditionally, the Secret Service has relied on a guarantee of 360-degree coverage of its protectees. The approach calls for a team of agents enveloping the person under protection in a kind of moving box, covering him or her from all angles. A new protective methodology being tested is based on an evaluation of threat assessments, calculating different levels of risk for the person protected. For instance, using current intelligence information and historic precedents like past assassination attempts, executives determine how many agents and what kinds of special teams need to be assigned. Some agents fear that this approach is dangerously flawed, especially in light of the intelligence failures that occurred before September 11.[11]

Recently, the Secret Service has had to endure other forms of criticism as well. Although its budget has increased 75 percent since 1999 (to more than $1 billion today), it suffered a debilitating loss of manpower to about three thousand agents and roughly one thousand Uniformed Division officers. In 2002 alone, 265 UD officers and more than a hundred plainclothes agents resigned or retired, many saying that they were fed up and wanted better pay and better working conditions (they were averaging eighty-one hours per month of overtime). The Secret Service has also had long-standing management difficulties with its UD officers, many of whom complain that an agency "caste system" of UD officers and undercover special agents causes large disparities in pay, promotion, and rules regarding use of weapons. UD officers also complain that only special agents have been named to be the agency's directors, that UD officers are seldom allowed to join the coveted plainclothes ranks, and that they must even fight for parking around the White House. The resulting morale problem has led to wholesale desertions from UD into the new Transportation Security Administration, the federal Air Marshal Service, and other agencies. In turn, the loss of experienced personnel in 2002 and 2003 caused a troubling need for the Secret Service to engage in fast-track hiring of new agents, which resulted in rookie recruits being assigned to security posts at the White House and in other sensitive areas.[12]

These personnel losses and morale problems, some of which are long-standing, must be addressed if the agents' jobs are to be made more attractive to prospective hires, to those already working in the trenches, and for the protectees in their charge.

The Department of Justice

The **Department of Justice** is headed by the attorney general, who is appointed by the president and approved by the Senate. The president also appoints the attorney general's assistants and the U.S. attorneys for each of the judicial districts. The U.S. attorneys in each judicial district control and supervise all federal criminal prosecutions and represent the government in legal suits in which it is a party. These attorneys may appoint committees to investigate other governmental agencies or offices when questions of wrongdoing are raised or when possible violations of federal law are suspected or detected.

The Department of Justice is the official legal arm of the government of the United States. Within this department are several law enforcement organizations that investigate violations of federal laws (Figure 2-3). We will discuss the Federal Bureau of Investigation; the Bureau of Alcohol, Tobacco, Firearms, and Explosives; the Drug Enforcement Administration; and the U.S. Marshals Service. (The Community Oriented Policing Services office will be discussed in Chapter 6.)

The Federal Bureau of Investigation

Beginnings. The Federal Bureau of Investigation (FBI) was created and funded through the Department of Justice Appropriation Act of 1908. The FBI was first known as the Bureau of Investigation. With thirty-five agents, it originally had no specific duties other than the "prosecution of crimes," focusing on bankruptcy frauds, antitrust crimes, neutrality violations, and crimes on Native American reservations. Espionage and sabotage incidents during World War I, coupled with charges of political corruption reaching into the Department of Justice and the bureau itself, prompted angry demands for drastic changes.

A new era was begun for the FBI in 1924 with the appointment of J. Edgar Hoover as director; he served in that capacity until his death in 1972. Hoover was determined that the organization would become a career service in which appointments would be made strictly on personal qualifications and abilities, and promotions would be based on merit. Special agents had to be college graduates with degrees in law or accounting. A rigorous course of training had to be completed, and agents had to be available for assignment wherever their services might be needed. Hoover also coordinated development of the Uniform Crime Reporting system and supervised the pursuit of many notorious criminals, such as Bonnie Parker, Clyde Barrow, and John Dillinger. The building housing the FBI Headquarters in Washington, D.C., bears his name.

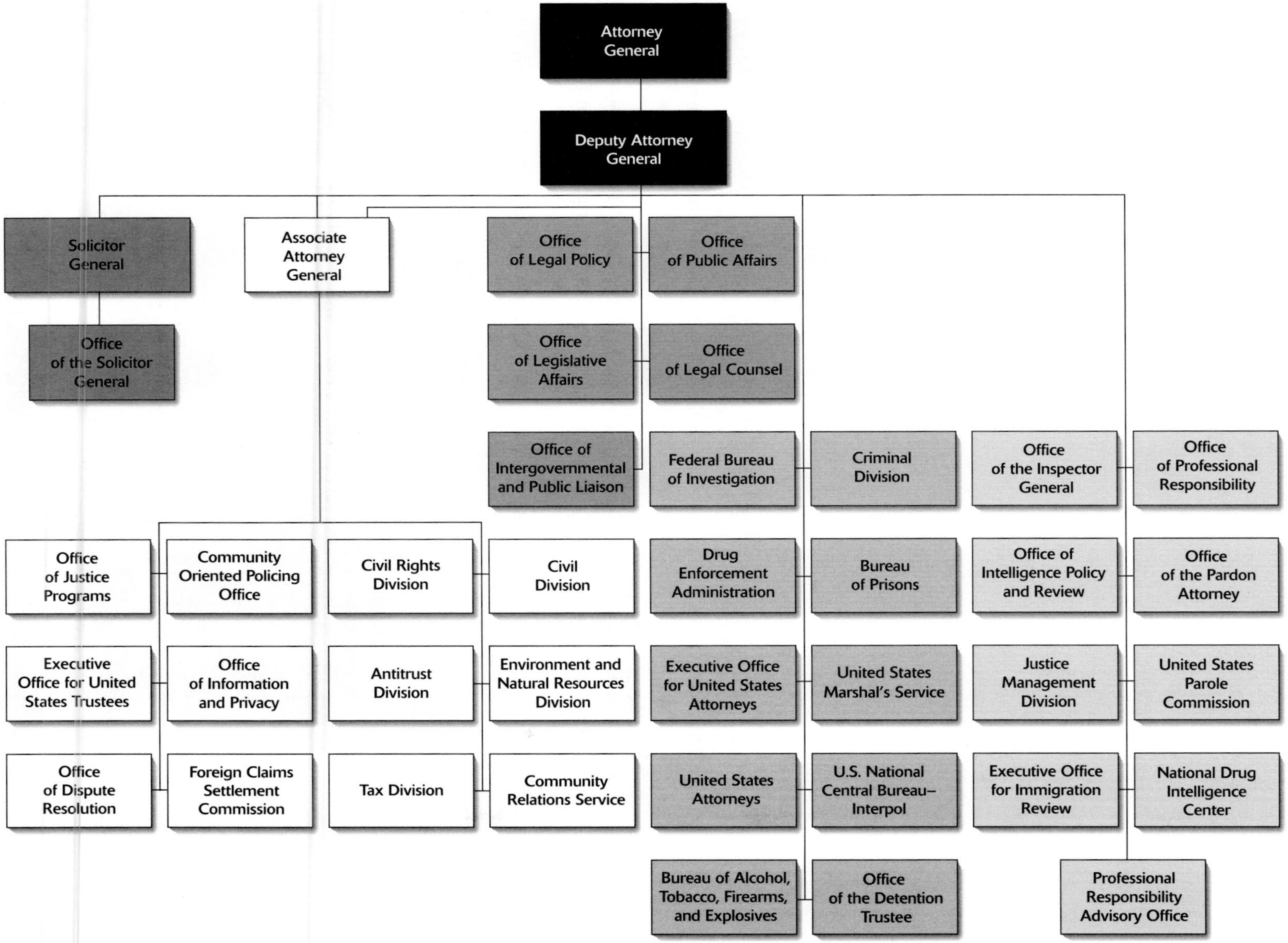

FIGURE 2-3 The organizational structure of the Department of Justice.

Source: Department of Justice

J. Edgar Hoover.

(Courtesy Federal Bureau of Investigation)

The bureau's Identification Division was created on July 1, 1924, and its laboratory opened in 1932. Then, in 1933, all of the bureau's functions were consolidated and transferred to a Division of Investigation, which became the Federal Bureau of Investigation on March 22, 1935.

Contemporary Priorities and Roles. Today the FBI has fifty-six field offices and approximately four hundred resident agencies and more than

The FBI's headquarters: the J. Edgar Hoover building, Washington, D.C.

(Courtesy Federal Bureau of Investigation)

forty foreign liaison posts. There are about 11,400 special agents and more than 16,400 other employees who perform professional, administrative, technical, clerical, or trade operations.[13]

The national priorities of the FBI have been modified in major fashion since September 11. Today, the agency's top three priorities are

- To protect the United States from terrorist attack
- To protect the United States against foreign intelligence operations and espionage
- To protect the United States against cyber-based attacks and high-technology crimes

Beyond these, the FBI's priorities include combating public corruption, transnational and national criminal organizations, white-collar crime, and significant violent crime and protecting civil rights.[14]

These priorities have certainly changed since the twin towers fell in New York City; before September 11, the FBI focused on merely "catching bad guys and putting them behind bars." Sweeping structural and philosophical changes have come as well, transforming an investigative agency into an intelligence-gathering service. And the FBI has been successful in its new role, identifying "sleeper cells" of terrorists in the United States and disrupting al Qaeda operations in places such as Michigan and New York. Ultimately, the bureau will have 1,200 special agents and analysts assigned to counterterrorism work, coordinating all terrorism investigations, sifting and analyzing strands of information. About 22,000 new computers and a new $596 million software package have been added to the FBI field offices to aid agents in doing complex searches, e-mailing color photos of suspects, and searching for trends. This upgrade includes a 40-million-page database of evidence dating back to the 1993 bombing of the World Trade Center, documents seized from Afghanistan, and two million pages of cable traffic.[15]

Recently, the FBI was given new powers to aid its reform efforts to battle terrorism. The bureau can now monitor Internet sites, libraries, churches, and political organizations. In addition, under revamped guidelines, agents can attend public meetings for the purpose of preventing terrorism.[16] The bureau also participates with local police in dozens of task forces nationwide that target fugitives and violent gangs.

But counterterrorism still constitutes only a fraction of the bureau's workload; Congress has not reduced the number of laws the FBI must enforce. The FBI continues to investigate bank robberies, white-collar crimes, and organized crime and drug syndicates—the staples of the agency's workload for a long time—while it combats radical Islamic fundamentalism and global terrorism with a workforce in which only seventy-six agents speak Arabic.[17]

Ancillary Investigative, Training, and Reporting Services. Today, the FBI's laboratory examines blood, hair, firearms, paint, handwriting, typewriters, and other types of evidence. Highly specialized techniques are now performed—at no charge to state and local police agencies—with DNA, explosives, hairs and fibers, tool marks, drugs, plastics, and bloodstains.

Another feature of the bureau is its National Academy, which graduated its first class in 1935. Today, thousands of local police managers from across the country have received training at the National Academy in Quantico, Virginia, which has twenty-one buildings on 385 acres. The FBI also provides extensive professional training to national supervisory-level police officers at the National Academy. (More information on local police training is provided in Chapter 3.)

A very successful function of the FBI, inaugurated in 1950, is its "Ten Most Wanted Fugitives" list, which over the years has contained many notable fugitives. As of 2000, the bureau had caught about 460 top ten fugitives; the Internet has helped to invigorate the program, with the "Ten Most Wanted" Web page receiving about 25 million hits per month.[18]

The FBI also operates the **National Crime Information Center (NCIC)**, through which millions of records relating to stolen property and missing persons and fugitives are instantaneously available to local, state, and federal authorities across the United States and Canada. In a related vein, one of the FBI's several annual publications is the **Uniform Crime**

(Courtesy Federal Bureau of Investigation)

Reports (UCR), which includes crime data reported from more than fifteen thousand state and local police agencies concerning twenty-nine types of offenses: eight Part I, or index, offenses (criminal homicide, forcible rape, robbery, aggravated assault, burglary, larceny-theft, motor vehicle theft, and arson) and twenty-one Part II offenses. The UCR also includes a so-called crime clock, shown in Figure 2-4.

There are several shortcomings in the UCR data, however. First, many crime victims do not report their victimization to the police; the local police, therefore, are unaware of these "hidden" offenses. Also, the entire reporting system is voluntary, and there is no penalty for police agencies that do not report to the FBI. Furthermore, the reporting system is not uniform. Crimes may be reported incorrectly or inaccurately. At best, the UCRs have limitations and must be used cautiously.

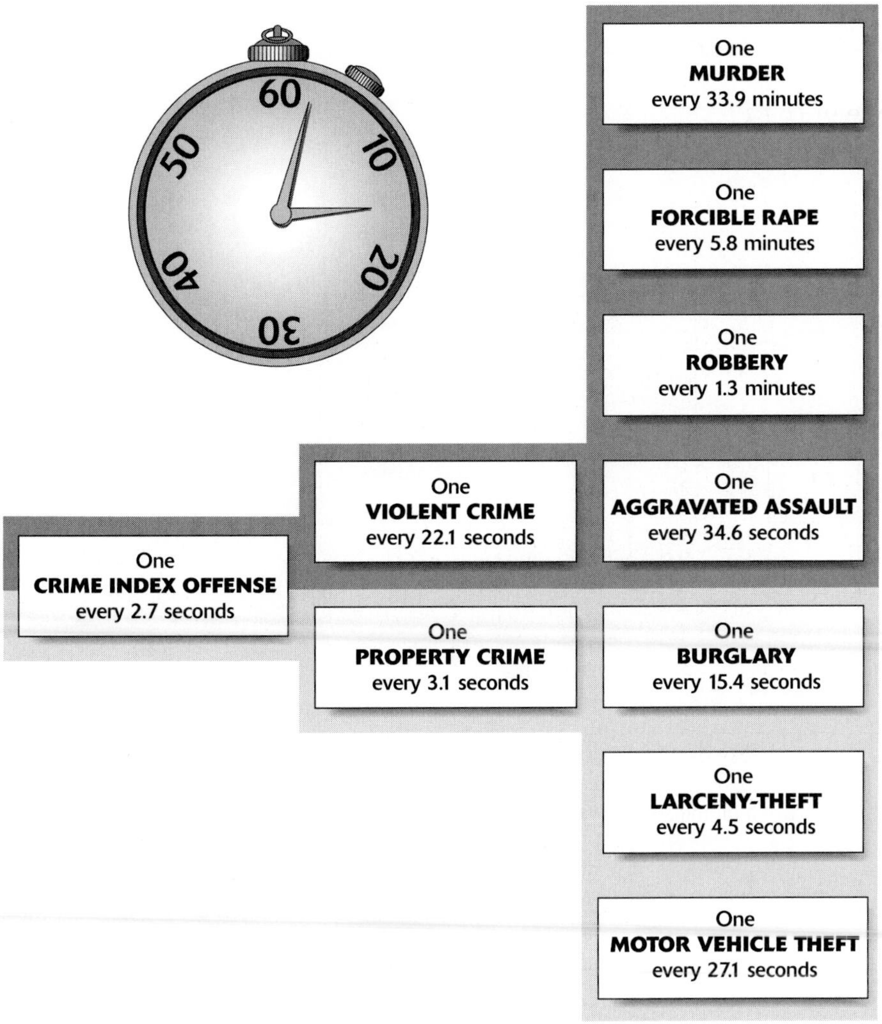

FIGURE 2-4 The UCR crime clock.

Source: Federal Bureau of Investigation, Uniform Crime Reports

A large amount of information concerning the FBI's application and hiring process—including its minimum requirements and the kinds of knowledge, skills, and abilities it now seeks for its new special agents—is available on the agency's Web site. Figure 2-5 depicts the FBI's organizational structure.

The Bureau of Alcohol, Tobacco, Firearms, and Explosives. The Bureau of Alcohol, Tobacco, Firearms, and Explosives (ATF) originated as a unit within the Internal Revenue Service (IRS) in 1862, when certain alcohol and tobacco tax statutes were created. The next year, Congress authorized the hiring of three "detectives" to aid in the prevention, detection, and punishment of tax evaders. Originally called the Alcohol, Tobacco, Tax Unit, it eventually became the Alcohol, Tobacco, and Firearms Division within the IRS. In 1972 it became the Bureau of Alcohol, Tobacco, and

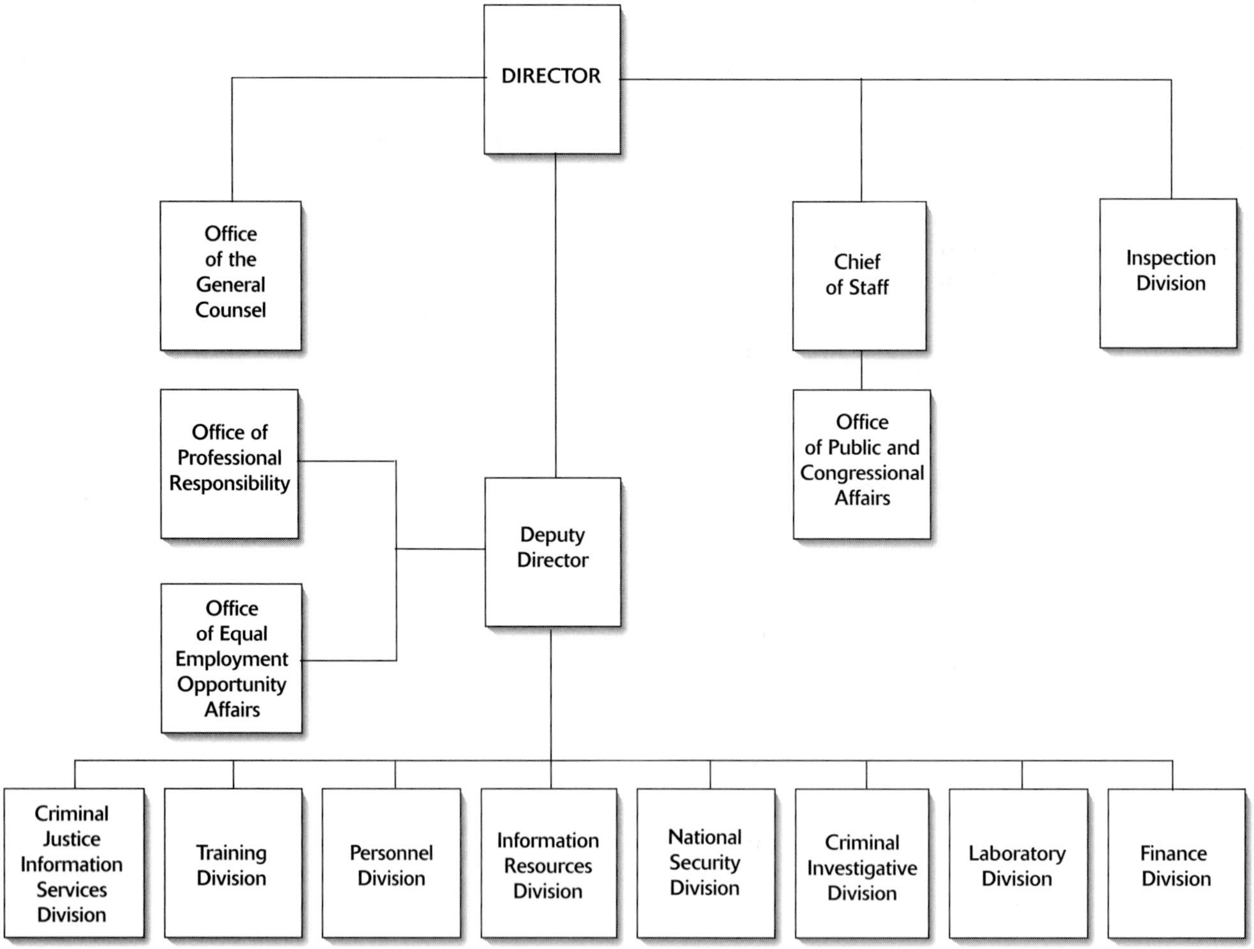

FIGURE 2-5 The organizational structure of the Federal Bureau of Investigation.

Source: Federal Bureau of Investigation

Firearms, under the direct control of the Treasury Department, and in January 2003, it was moved to the Justice Department and renamed the Bureau of Alcohol, Tobacco, Firearms, and Explosives.[19]

Like the FBI and several of the other federal agencies, ATF has a rich and colorful history, much of which has involved capturing "bootleggers" and disposing of illegal whiskey stills during Prohibition.[20] From 1920 to 1933, congressional legislation made it illegal to manufacture, possess, or sell intoxicating liquors in the United States (with a few exceptions). Still, America was awash with liquor. History is replete with accounts of violations of Prohibition laws; much has been written and portrayed in movies of that era, when the moonshiners tried to outsmart and outrun the law.[21] "Speakeasies" (secret bars) proliferated across America to satisfy the American yearning for liquor. This era bolstered the popularity of such G-men as Eliot Ness; the 1960s television program *The Untouchables* was based on his career.

ATF administers the U.S. Criminal Code provisions concerning alcohol and tobacco smuggling and diversion. ATF is responsible for enforcing all the federal laws relating to firearms, explosives, and arson. ATF works with federal, state, and local law enforcement organizations and seeks to battle terrorism, prevent crime, conduct fair and effective industry regulation, and provide training and expertise to federal, state, local, and international law enforcement partners. The Homeland Security Act of 2002 transferred these enforcement activities of the ATF, along with certain other functions, to the Department of Justice from the Department of the Treasury. ATF's approximately forty-eight hundred special agents, inspectors, regulatory specialists, forensic auditors, laboratory technicians, and other personnel work primarily in twenty-three field divisions across the fifty states, with offices as well in Guam, the U.S. Virgin Islands, Puerto Rico, Mexico, Canada, Columbia, and France.[22]

In fiscal year 2003, ATF initiated about 30,000 firearms investigations, resulting in more than 6,000 defendants being convicted of firearms-related offenses.[23] ATF also investigated nearly 400 bombings, 750 incidents involving recovered explosives or explosive devices, and more than 60 thefts of explosives;[24] performed about 15,000 firearms-related inspections; and completed more than 2,700 explosives-compliance and 5,000 explosives-application inspections.[25] ATF also maintains a Bomb and Arson Tracking System, which allows state, local, and other federal agencies to share information about bomb and arson cases;[26] four National Response Teams of highly trained agents that can be deployed to major explosion and fire scenes in the United States; an International Response Team that provides assistance in other countries; thirty-two explosives-detection canine teams; and three national laboratory facilities.[27]

The Drug Enforcement Administration. The Drug Enforcement Administration (DEA) began with the passage of the Harrison Narcotic

(Courtesy Bureau of Alcohol, Tobacco, Firearms, and Explosives)

Act, signed into law on December 17, 1914, by President Woodrow Wilson. The act made it unlawful for any "nonregistered" person to possess heroin, cocaine, opium, morphine, or any of their by-products. Drug enforcement began in 1915, and during that first year, agents seized forty-four pounds of heroin and achieved 106 convictions (mostly a result of illicit activities of physicians).[28]

In the 1920s, federal narcotics agents focused on organized gangs of Chinese immigrants suspected of importing opium. In 1920, the Volstead Act ("Prohibition") was enacted; the Narcotics Division of the Prohibition Unit of the Revenue Bureau consisted of 170 agents working out of seventeen offices around the country. New authority was granted to agents by the Narcotic Drugs Import and Export Act of 1922.

(Courtesy Drug Enforcement Administration)

Today's DEA is also an outgrowth of the former Bureau of Narcotics, which was established in 1930 under the direct control of the Treasury Department. In 1968, the Bureau of Narcotics was transferred from the Treasury to the Department of Justice and was renamed the Bureau of Narcotics and Dangerous Drugs. In 1973, the DEA was established under a plan that combined the functions of several agencies. In January 1982, the DEA was given primary responsibility for drug and narcotics enforcement, sharing this jurisdiction with the FBI.

The major responsibilities of the DEA, under the U.S. Code, include the following:

- The development of an overall federal drug-enforcement strategy, including programs, planning, and evaluation
- Full investigation of and preparation for the prosecution of suspects for violations under all federal drug-trafficking laws
- Full investigation and preparation for the prosecution of suspects connected with illicit drugs seized at U.S. ports of entry and international borders
- Conduct of all relations with drug-enforcement officials of foreign governments
- Full coordination and cooperation with state and local police officials on joint drug-enforcement efforts
- Regulation of the legal manufacture of drugs and other controlled substances[29]

Overseas, the DEA maintains seventy-one offices in fifty foreign countries.[30] Figure 2-6 depicts DEA's various programs and operations.

DEA
Programs and Operations

Asset Forfeiture	Marijuana Eradication
Aviation	Mobile Enforcement Teams (MET)
Computer Forensics Program	Money Laundering
DEA Museum	Ombudsman
Demand Reduction	Operations Pipeline and Convoy
Diversion Control	Organized Crime Drug Enforcement Forces
Foreign Cooperative Investigations	Regional Enforcement Teams
Forensic Sciences	Southwest Border Initiative
High Intensity Drug Trafficking Areas	State and Local Task Forces
Integrated Drug Enforcement Assistance (IDEA)	Training

Intelligence

El Paso Intelligence Center	National Drug Pointer Index (NDPI)*

*The NDPI allows law enforcement agencies to determine if other such organizations are investigating the same subject/suspect.

FIGURE 2-6 Programs and operations of the Drug Enforcement Administration.

Source: Drug Enforcement Administration

The U.S. Marshals Service. The U.S. Marshals Service (USMS) is one of the oldest federal law enforcement agencies, established under the Judiciary Act of 1789; George Washington appointed thirteen marshals, one for each of the original thirteen states. The USMS was established in 1969 and formally became a bureau in 1974. Today it has about 2,650 officers with arrest powers. Each district headquarters office is managed by a politically appointed U.S. marshal and a chief deputy U.S. marshal, who direct a staff of supervisors, investigators, deputy marshals, and administrative personnel. As in the Wild West, the backbone of the USMS is the deputy U.S. marshals, who pursue and arrest DEA fugitives—suspects wanted for federal drug violations—and escaped federal prisoners and who provide a secure environment for the federal courts and judges.[31]

Virtually every federal law enforcement initiative involves the USMS. Its agents produce prisoners for trial; protect the courts, judges, attorneys, and witnesses; track and arrest fugitives; and manage and dispose of seized drug assets.

In 1971, the USMS created the Special Operations Group (SOG), consisting of an elite, well-trained group of deputy marshals. The group provides support in priority or dangerous situations, such as the movement of a large group of high-risk prisoners, and at trials involving alleged drug traffickers or members of subversive groups.

Another important function of the USMS is the operation of the Witness Protection Program. Federal witnesses are sometimes threatened by defendants or their associates (for example, they sometimes testify against organized crime figures). If certain criteria are met, the USMS will provide

(Courtesy U.S. Marshals Service)

a complete change of identity for witnesses and their families, including new Social Security numbers, residences, and employment. This protection program was established in 1970.

Other Related Federal Agencies

The Central Intelligence Agency. The National Security Act of 1947 established the National Security Council, which in 1949 created a subordinate organization, the Central Intelligence Agency (CIA). Considered the most clandestine government service, the CIA participates in undercover and covert operations around the world for the purposes of managing crises and providing intelligence during the conduct of war.[32]

To accomplish its mission, the CIA engages in research and development and deploys high technology for intelligence purposes. After the terrorist attacks in this country, the CIA created special centers to address such issues as counterterrorism, counterintelligence, international organized crime and narcotics trafficking, and arms control intelligence.[33]

The CIA is an independent agency responsible to the president through its director. The different kinds of intelligence information it collects and disseminates are shown in Figure 2-7.

The Internal Revenue Service. The Internal Revenue Service (IRS) has as its main function the monitoring and collection of federal income taxes from American individuals and businesses. Since 1919, the IRS has had a Criminal Investigation (CI) Division employing "accountants with a

Different Kinds of Intelligence

COMINT: Communications intelligence is derived from the intercept of foreign communications.

ELINT (ee-lint): Electronic Intelligence is the technical and intelligence information derived from foreign electromagnetic noncommunications transmissions by other than the intended recipients.

HUMINT (h-you-mint): Human intelligence is information acquired by human sources through covert and overt collection techniques.

IMINT: Imagery intelligence includes satellite photography or other imagery that is then analyzed and processed for intelligence use.

MASINT (maze-int): Measurement and Signature intelligence is technically derived intelligence data, such as nuclear, optical, radiofrequency, acoustics, seismic, and materials sciences data.

SIGINT: Signals intelligence is information derived from signals intercept, comprising all COMINT, ELINT, and MASINT, however transmitted.

OPEN SOURCE: Information that is in the public domain, such as periodicals, news broadcasts, and information on the Internet.

FIGURE 2-7 Types of CIA intelligence.

Source: Central Intelligence Agency

badge." The CI Division investigates possible criminal violations of income tax laws and recommends appropriate criminal prosecution whenever warranted.[34]

The first chief of the Special Intelligence Unit, Inspector Elmer I. Irey, gained notoriety by participating in investigations that included income tax evasion charges against Mafia kingpin Alphonse ("Al") Capone and the kidnapping of Charles Lindbergh's baby in 1932.[35] Since then, the list of celebrated, prosecuted CI "clients" has been impressive, including federal judges and prominent politicians and athletes. Indeed, today there is a much greater appreciation for what a financial investigator can do for almost any type of criminal investigation.[36]

IRS agents are armed; the U.S. Code authorizes them to execute search warrants, make arrests without warrants for tax-related offenses, and seize property related to violations of the tax laws. Agents engage in money-laundering investigations under Title 18 of the U.S. Code and investigate for tax and currency violations any individuals who organize, direct, and finance high-level criminal enterprises.[37]

CI enforces nearly all of the provisions of the Bank Secrecy Act, requiring financial institutions or individuals to report certain domestic and foreign currency transactions to the federal government. CI also enforces the wagering tax laws and conducts investigations related to the pornography industry. Another important area of CI is the Questionable

(Courtesy Internal Revenue Service)

Refund Program, which attempts to detect and stop fictitious claims for tax refunds.

The Federal Law Enforcement Training Center. The **Federal Law Enforcement Training Center (FLETC)**, which was established in 1970 and remains part of the Treasury Department, offers law enforcement training for personnel from many federal agencies. In 1975, the center was located in Glynco, Georgia, where it occupies a 1,500-acre campus with state-of-the-art classrooms and provides training for about seventy-five U.S. federal law enforcement organizations.[38] Other domestic campuses are located in Artesia, New Mexico, and Charleston, South Carolina, and a fourth training facility is being built in Maryland.

Like most of the federal agencies discussed in this chapter, FLETC has been struggling to meet new demands placed on it since September 11. A significant surge in hiring by federal agencies (particularly in the new Federal Air Marshal Service and Transportation Security Administration) resulted in an influx of a large number of law enforcement personnel at FLETC's campuses around the country.

In the fiscal year preceding the terrorist attacks, more than 21,000 students spent over 101,000 student weeks of training at FLETC's campuses; in the fiscal year following the attacks, more than 28,000 students spent about 157,000 weeks in training at these campuses. This latter figure represented a 72 percent increase in weeks of training since fiscal year 1999.[39]

To help address the demands placed on FLETC, its budget of about $146 million includes 754 full-time staff members.

State and Local Agencies

Today, Sir Robert Peel would be amazed; there are now about 17,000 general-purpose local police departments and sheriff's offices in the United States:[40] about 441,000 sworn, full-time municipal police officers,[41] 165,000 sworn sheriff's personnel,[42] and 56,000 full-time sworn **state police** agents.[43]

State Police

As noted above, today there are about 56,000 full-time sworn personnel in the forty-nine state law enforcement agencies (Hawaii has no state agency).[44] Most states also have a bureau of investigation or identification, many of which serve as the repository for state crime data, collecting, analyzing, and publishing state crime information. Agents of these state bureaus perform routine criminal investigation functions as well as specialized operations, such as investigations of organized crime or livestock brand theft. State investigators often assist local police agencies in investigative matters, such as performing background checks on police applicants.[45]

Local (Municipal Police and County Sheriff) Agencies

Because the remaining chapters of this book focus on municipal and county agencies operating at the local level, only a brief description is provided here.

Municipal police departments have general police responsibilities, including such functions as traffic enforcement, accident investigation, patrol and first response to incidents, property and violent crime investigation, and death investigation.

Fifteen percent of local police departments require recruits to have completed at least some college. Field and classroom training requirements for new recruits average about 1,600 hours combined in cities with more than 100,000 population, and 800 hours in cities serving fewer than 2,500. Two-thirds of all departments have full-time sworn personnel engaged in community policing activities.(Community policing is examined in Chapter 6.) Three-fourths of all municipal police officers work in agencies using in-field computers or terminals.[46]

Eleven percent of all sheriff's offices require recruits to have completed at least some college. Field and classroom training requirements for

More than 80 percent of all sheriffs operate a jail.

(Courtesy Washoe County, Nevada, Sheriff's Office)

new recruits in jurisdictions serving more than 100,000 residents average about 1,400 hours combined, compared to about 780 hours in those service a population of less than 10,000. About 62 percent of all sheriff's offices have deputies engaged in community policing activities. Sixty-one percent of sheriff's deputies work in an agency using in-field computers or terminals. Most (about 80 percent) of the nation's sheriff's departments are responsible for operating a jail.[47]

SUMMARY

This chapter described the major federal law enforcement agencies of the new Department of Homeland Security and the Department of Justice and provided an overview of state and local police agencies.

It is clear that, more than any other time in this nation's history, "business as usual" cannot be the order of the day. Our federal, state, and local law enforcement agencies must take a more farsighted approach to their work, while learning new methods for preventing and responding to potential terrorist attacks. This chapter has demonstrated law enforcement's ability to be flexible as the need arises, and this ability is most pronounced with the federal government's massive reorganization.

REVIEW QUESTIONS

1. What are the five directorates of the Department of Homeland Security? Describe the primary functions of the directorates and the U.S. Secret Service.
2. What are the major functions of the four agencies of the Department of Justice that are described in this chapter?
3. Where and how are federal agents trained?
4. What functions do the CIA and the IRS perform?
5. What are the primary differences between federal, state, and local law enforcement agencies?
6. Describe some of the characteristics of local agencies.

INDEPENDENT STUDENT ACTIVITIES

1. Select two federal, state, or local law enforcement agencies in which you have a particular interest. Using information obtained from agency Web sites or interviews, determine how the selected agencies differ with respect

to origin, jurisdiction, mission, and functions. Also compare them in terms of salaries, benefits, and overall working conditions. Learn about each agency's budget, policies and procedures, recruitment and training, and so forth.

2. In your interviews, ask about the measures each agency has taken for homeland defense, any specialized training that has been provided in the event of a terrorist attack or other critical incident, how the agency will cooperate with other agencies, and so on.

RELATED WEB SITES

Bureau of Alcohol, Tobacco, Firearms, and Explosives
http://www.atf.gov/

Bureau of Immigration and Customs Enforcement
http://www.customs.gov/

Bureau of Justice Assistance
askncjrs@ncjrs.org
http://www.ncjrs.org

Bureau of Justice Statistics
http://www.ncjrs.org
http://www.ojp.usdoj.bjs

Department of Homeland Security
http://www.dhs.gov/dhspublic/

Department of Justice
http://www.usdoj.gov

Drug Enforcement Administration
http://www.dea.gov/

Federal Bureau of Investigation
http://www.fbi.gov

National Commission on Terrorist Attacks upon the United States (also known as the 9–11 Commission)
http://www.gpoaccess.gov/911/

U.S. Marshals Service
http://www.usdoj.gov/marshals/

U.S. Secret Service
http://www.ustreas.gov/usss/protection/shtml

NOTES

1. WHITE HOUSE NEWS RELEASE, http://www.whitehouse.gov/news/releases/2003/10/20031001–4.html (accessed January 4, 2004).
2. DEPARTMENT OF HOMELAND SECURITY, Bureau of Immigration and Customs Enforcement, http://uscis.gov/graphics/publicaffairs/statements/032003_ICE.htm (accessed January 4, 2004).
3. DEPARTMENT OF HOMELAND SECURITY, "DHS Organization," http://www.dhs.gov/dhspublic/interapp/editorial/editorial_0089.xml (accessed January 4, 2004).
4. BUREAU OF CUSTOMS AND BORDER PROTECTION, "Welcome to Customs and Border Protection," http://www.customs.ustreas.gov/xp/cgov/toolbox/about/missions.cbp.xml (accessed January 4, 2004).
5. DEPARTMENT OF HOMELAND SECURITY, "DHS Organization: Emergency Preparedness and Response, Preparing America," http://www.dhs/gov/dhspublic/interapp/editorial/editorial_0093.xml (accessed January 4, 2004).
6. DEPARTMENT OF HOMELAND SECURITY, "DHS Organization: Science and Technology, Developing Technology," http://www.dhs/gov/dhspublic/interapp/editorial/editorial_0095.xml (accessed January 4, 2004).
7. DEPARTMENT OF HOMELAND SECURITY, "DHS Organization: Information Analysis and Infrastructure Protection," http://www.dhs.gov.dhspublic/interapp/editorial/editorial_0094.xml (accessed January 4, 2004).
8. DEPARTMENT OF HOMELAND SECURITY, "DHS Organization: Management," http://www.dhs.gov/dhspublic/interapp/editorial/editorial_0096.xml (accessed January 4, 2004).
9. CHITRA RAGAVAN, "Under Cloudy Skies," *U.S. News and World Report*, December 9, 2002, p. 18.
10. DEPARTMENT OF JUSTICE, Bureau of Justice Statistics Bulletin, "Federal Law Enforcement Officers, 1996," December 1997, p. 3.
11. RAGAVAN, "Under Cloudy Skies," p. 19.
12. Ibid., pp. 20–23.
13. FEDERAL BUREAU OF INVESTIGATION, http://www.fbi.gov/aboutus/htm (accessed March 11, 2003).
14. PERSONAL COMMUNICATION, Edward Duffer, September 23, 2003.
15. CHITRA RAGAVAN, "Muller's Mandate," *U.S. News and World Report*, May 26, 2003, pp. 19–29.
16. ASSOCIATED PRESS, "FBI Agents Get Sweeping New Powers," May 31, 2002.
17. Ibid.
18. JEFF GLASSER, "In Demand for Fifty Years: The FBI's 'Most Wanted' List—Good Publicity, and a History of Success," *U.S. News and World Report*, March 20, 2000, p. 60.
19. BUREAU OF ALCOHOL, TOBACCO, FIREARMS, AND EXPLOSIVES, PRESS RELEASE, "Changes in ATF Resulting from the Signing of the Homeland Security Bill; Two Separate Bureaus Created," http://www.atf/gov/press/fy03press/ 112702homelandatf.htm (accessed September 7, 2004).
20. For an excellent overview of the duties of federal law enforcement agents as well as other state and local personnel, see for example DEPARTMENT OF

LABOR, BUREAU OF LABOR STATISTICS, "Occupational Outlook Handbook, "Police and Detectives" (http://www.bls.gov/oco/ocos160.htm (accessed January 13, 2005); JAMES STINCHCOMB, *Opportunities in Law Enforcement and Criminal Justice Careers (Rev. Ed.)* (New York: Mc-Graw-Hill, 2003).

21. See, for example, PATRICK G. O'BRIEN and KENNETH J. PEAK, *Kansas Bootleggers* (Manhattan, KS: Sunflower University Press, 1991); JOSEPH E. DABNEY, *Mountain Spirits* (New York: Charles Scribner's Sons, 1974); and JESS CARR, *The Second Oldest Profession: An Informal History of Moonshining in America* (Englewood Cliffs, NJ: Prentice-Hall, 1972).
22. BUREAU OF ALCOHOL, TOBACCO, FIREARMS, and EXPLOSIVES, "ATF Snapshot 2004," http://www.atf.gov/about/snap2004.htm (accessed September 13, 2004).
23. Ibid.
24. Ibid.
25. Ibid.
26. Ibid.
27. Ibid.
28. DEPARTMENT OF JUSTICE, Drug Enforcement Administration, "DEA Mission Statement," http://www.usdoj.gov.dea/agency/mission.htm (accessed January 6, 2004).
29. DEPARTMENT OF JUSTICE, Drug Enforcement Administration, "Factsheet: DEA Data," July 1995, pp. 1–2.
30. DEPARTMENT OF JUSTICE, Bureau of Justice Statistics Bulletin, "Federal Law Enforcement Officers, 1996," December 1997, p. 3.
31. DEPARTMENT OF JUSTICE, U.S. Marshals Office, *The FY 1993 Report to the U.S. Marshals* (Washington, DC: Author, 1994), pp. 188–89.
32. CENTRAL INTELLIGENCE AGENCY, "CIA Vision, Mission, and Values," http://www. cia.gov/cia/information/mission.html (accessed January 4, 2005).
33. CENTRAL INTELLIGENCE AGENCY, "About the CIA," http://www.cia/gov/cia/information/info.html (accessed January 5, 2005).
34. DEPARTMENT OF JUSTICE, "Federal Law Enforcement Officers, 1996," p. 3.
35. LUDOVIC KENNEDY, "The Airman and the Carpenter: The Lindbergh Kidnapping and the Framing of Richard Hauptmann," *Seton Hall Law Review* 14, 574–98.
36. DON VOGEL, quoted in Department of the Treasury, Internal Revenue Service, *CI Digest*, pub. no. 1827, June 1994, p. 12.
37. See the Internal Revenue Service Web site, "Criminal Investigation Special Agent," http://www.jobs.irs.gov/mn-LawEnforcement.html (accessed January 4, 2004).
38. DEPARTMENT OF THE TREASURY, Federal Law Enforcement Training Center, *Catalog of Training Programs* (Washington, DC: Author, 1995), p. 1.
39. GENERAL ACCOUNTING OFFICE, *Federal Law Enforcement Training Center: Capacity Planning and Management Oversight Need Improvement,* Report to Congressional Requesters (Washington, DC: Author, July 2003), p. 7.
40. DEPARTMENT OF JUSTICE, Bureau of Justice Statistics Bulletin, "Census of State and Local Law Enforcement Agencies, 1996," June 1998, p. 1.

41. Department of Justice, Bureau of Justice Statistics, "State and Local Law Enforcement Statistics," http://www.ojp.usdoj.gov/bjs/sandlle.htm (accessed January 12, 2005), p. 1.
42. Ibid.
43. Department of Justice, Bureau of Justice Statistics, *Sheriff's Offices 2000* (Washington, DC: Office of Justice Programs, 2003), p. 1.
44. Ibid.
45. Kenneth J. Peak, *Policing America: Methods, Issues, Challenges,* 4th ed. (Upper Saddle River, NJ: Prentice Hall, 2003), p. 53.
46. Department of Justice, Bureau of Justice Statistics, "State and Local Law Enforcement Statistics," http://www.ojp.usdoj.gov/bjs/sandlle.htm (accessed January 12, 2005), pp. 1–2.
47. Department of Justice, Bureau of Justice Statistics, *Sheriff's Offices 2000* (Washington, DC: Office of Justice Programs, 2003), p. 3.

CHAPTER 3

Police Subculture: The Making of a Cop

I think the necessity of being ready increases. Look to it.

—Abraham Lincoln

Make thy Model before thou buildest; and go not too far in it without due Preparation.

—Thomas Fuller

Learn how to be a policeman, because that cannot be improvised.

—Pope John XXIII

Key Terms

academy training
computer-based training (CBT)
field training
hurdle process
police cynicism
police subculture
policing functions
policing styles
recruiting
"sixth sense"
traits of good officers
working personality

This chapter focuses on the **police subculture**. It describes how an officer's career begins and, to a large extent, how his or her occupational personality is formed. Studying the subculture of the police helps us define the "cop's world" and the officer's role in it; this subculture shapes the officer's attitudes, values, and beliefs.

The idea of a police subculture was first proposed by William Westley in his 1950 study of the Gary, Indiana, Police Department, where he found, among many other things, a high degree of group cohesion, secrecy, and violence.[1] It is now widely accepted that the police develop traditions, skills, and attitudes that are unique to their occupation because of their duties and responsibilities.[2]

We begin at the threshold, looking at some of the methods, challenges, and problems connected with the recruitment of qualified individuals. Then we track the typical police applicant's progression through the various types of tests that may be employed: written, psychological, physical, oral, character, and medical.

Then we examine formal police training at the academy; this is where the initiation of the officer-to-be into the police subculture commences in earnest. The chapter discusses types of academies, their general curriculum, and some of the informal learning that takes place. We then look at postacademy training—the field training officer concept. Following that is a look at how officers adopt their working personality: the formal and informal rules, customs, and beliefs of the occupation. This portion of the chapter includes an assessment of the traits that make a good officer. Finally, we examine the roles, functions, and styles of policing. It is important to define and understand how these aspects of policing may differ and conflict; even though in these difficult times it is easy to believe that our society has a unified view of the purposes and operations of its police agencies, there actually can be a good deal of disagreement in these areas.

A chapter summary, review questions, independent student activities, and related Web sites conclude the chapter.

First Things First: Recruiting Qualified Applicants

Wanted: Those Who Walk on Water

Recruiting an adequate pool of applicants is an extremely important facet of the police hiring process. August Vollmer said that law enforcement candidates should

> have the wisdom of Solomon, the courage of David, the patience of Job and leadership of Moses, the kindness of the Good Samaritan, the diplomacy of Lincoln, the tolerance of the Carpenter of Nazareth, and, finally, an intimate knowledge of every branch of the natural, biological and social sciences.[3]

Many people believe that the police officer has the most difficult job in America. Police officers are solitary workers, spending most of their time on the job unsupervised. Also, people who are hired today will become the supervisors of the future. For all of these reasons, police agencies must attempt to attract the best individuals possible.

Police applicants typically come from lower-middle-class or working-class backgrounds;[4] they generally have a high school education and a history of employment. They also tend, at the application stage, to be enthusiastic, idealistic, uninformed about the reality of police work, and very different from the stereotype of the police officer as authoritarian, suspicious, and insensitive.[5]

Some studies indicate that police applicants are primarily motivated by the need for job security.[6] Other researchers have found that both males and females listed the same six factors—helping people, job security, fighting crime, job excitement, prestige, and a lifetime interest—as strong positive influences in their career choices.[7] Joel Lefkowitz concluded that police candidates were lower than average in their desire to do autonomous work,[8] and other studies have indicated that applicants tend to favor a more directive leadership style. Such findings are not unusual, given that most police agencies are highly structured and paramilitary in nature. Studies do not establish that police candidates fit the stereotypes of harsh, controlling people who wish to dominate others. Leadership, or the ability to take charge of situations, is a desirable attribute, however. Some researchers have found that the typical police applicant is very similar to the average college student.[9]

Bruce Carpenter and Susan Raza, using the Minnesota Multiphasic Personality Inventory (MMPI), found that police applicants differed from the general population in several important ways.[10] Police applicants, they learned, are somewhat more psychologically healthy, are generally less depressed and anxious, and are more assertive and interested in making and maintaining social contacts. Furthermore, few police aspirants have emotional difficulties, and they have a greater tendency to present a good impression of themselves than the general population. They are a more homogeneous group.

Female police applicants tend to be more assertive and nonconforming and to have a higher energy level than male applicants. They are also less likely to identify with traditional sex roles than male applicants. Older police applicants tend to be less satisfied, have more physical complaints, and are more likely to develop physical symptoms under stress than younger applicants. Applicants to large city police forces are generally less likely to have physical complaints and have a higher energy level than applicants to small or medium-size agencies. (This is probably explained by the fact that applicants in large cities are significantly younger.[11]) Some departments are under a mandate to recruit special groups of people, such as women, African-Americans, and Hispanics; several cities have also recruited homosexuals.

What psychological qualities should agencies seek? According to psychologist Lawrence Wrightsman,[12] it is important that police applicants be incorruptible and have high moral character. They should be well adjusted, able to carry out the hazardous and stressful tasks of policing without "cracking up," and thick-skinned enough to operate without defensiveness.

They should have a genuine interest in people and a compassionate sense of the innate dignity of others. Applicants should also be free of emotional reactions, they should not be impulsive or overly aggressive, and they should be able to exercise restraint. This is especially important given their active role in crime detection.

Finally, they need logical skills to assist in their investigative work. An interesting example of some of the logical skills needed for police work is provided by Al Seedman, former chief of detectives in the New York Police Department:

> In the woods just outside of town they found the skeleton of a man who'd been dead for three months or so. I asked whether this skeleton showed signs of any dental work. But the local cops said no, although the skeleton had crummy teeth. No dental work at all. Now, if he'd been wealthy, he could have afforded to have his teeth fixed. If he'd been poor, welfare would have paid. If he was a union member, their medical plan would have covered it. So this fellow was probably working at a low-paying non-unionized job, but making enough to keep off public assistance. Also, since he didn't match up to any family's missing-person report, he was probably single, living alone in an apartment or hotel. His landlord never reported him missing, either, so most likely he was also behind on his rent and the landlord probably figured he had just skipped. But even if he had escaped his landlord, he would never have escaped the tax man. The rest was simple. I told these cops to wait until the year is up. Then they can go to the IRS and get a printout of all single males making less than $10,000 a year but more than the welfare ceiling who paid withholding tax in the first three quarters but not in the fourth. Chances are the name of their skeleton will be on that printout.[13]

Other desirable traits of entry-level officers are discussed later in this chapter.

Recruiting Problems and Successes

Whether one blames the national economy, higher educational requirements, or noncompetitive wages and benefits, police and sheriff's department officials in virtually every region of the country agree that the generous pool of applicants from which they once sought qualified candidates is becoming increasingly shallow.[14] In fact, the National Association of Police Organizations (NAPO) recently named recruitment one of the top problems facing police agencies.[15]

The state of the economy can also have a strong influence on recruitment. The recent boom in California's economy caused problems for recruiters in that state's police agencies. With the unemployment rate running below 5 percent, police departments found it hard to compete with the private sector, despite offering relatively high pay, full benefits, and generous retirement plans. The Los Angeles Police Department saw its applications decline by about half in three years.[16] Chicago, which tested 25,000 applicants in 1993, had only 1,900 testees in the year 2000.

The requirement that applicants possess college credits is believed to make recruitment problems more acute. Several agencies that now require two years of college credits believe that this standard has reduced their applicant pool significantly. (The benefits of higher education for police officers are discussed in Chapter 12.) At the same time, a Census Bureau report put the average salary of a nonsupervisory police officer at $34,700; this compares to the average $40,546 that a technical support worker can expect to make and the average $51,351 that managers or executives earn. According to NAPO, add to that the media attention given to corrupt officers, police shootings, and department scandals, and it may be understandable why people are shying away from police careers. To counter this declining interest, departments are accentuating the occupation's positive aspects: solid insurance, excellent retirement plans, long vacations, and opportunities to advance.[17]

Recruiting and retaining women in police service remains particularly problematic. Gender bias (reflected in the absence of women being hired and promoted to policy-making positions) and sexual harassment concerns prevent many women from applying and cause many female officers to leave, and quickly: About 60 percent of female officers who leave their agency do so during their second to fifth years on the job.[18] (Problems associated with bringing women into policing—and retaining them—are discussed more fully in Chapter 12.)

But some agencies have successfully addressed the recruitment dilemma. For example, the New York State Police (NYSP) recently swore in its largest class in thirty years. Using an academic survey developed by a high-ranking trooper with a doctorate, the agency asked people what would make them consider joining the state police. (Their answer: job enrichment or more interesting work.) The survey also revealed that the two factors playing a key role in a person's decision to enter police work were the ability to help others and the opportunity to serve the community—two factors that the NYSP stresses in its mission and values statements and in its recruitment drives. Also emphasized in recruitment literature and television announcements are how female troopers can balance family and career and the various specialized jobs—scuba diving, for example—that are available within the NYSP. The organization also enlisted the entire force as recruiters and sought applicants at nontraditional locations, such as women's road races and health clubs.[19]

Other methods employed by police agencies in their attempts to develop a bigger pool of applicants include seeking applicants far from home (for example, Los Angeles recruits in Chicago, and Chicago recruits in Wisconsin), having downloadable application forms on the Web, lowering the minimum age from twenty-two to twenty-one, and allowing some applicants to substitute work experience for college credits.[20]

TESTING: THE HURDLE PROCESS FOR NEW PERSONNEL

Once the recruit is allowed in the door, much work still remains to be done before he or she is ready to work as a police officer. The new recruit must successfully complete what is known as the **hurdle process**. In this section, we consider some of the kinds of tests that are used to weed out undesirable candidates.

Not all of the types of tests shown in Figure 3-1 are employed by the seventeen thousand police agencies in America; nor are these tests necessarily given in the sequence shown. However, nearly all local police agencies (99 percent) use criminal record checks, background investigations (98 percent), driving record checks (98 percent), and medical exams (97 percent) to screen applicants. Psychological (91 percent), aptitude (84 percent), and physical agility (78 percent) tests are also commonly used.[21] Under affirmative action laws and court decisions, a burden rests with police administrators to demonstrate that the tests used are job related. The hiring sequence shown in Figure 3-1, called the "multiple hurdle procedure,"[22] may take longer than three months to complete, depending on the number and types of tests used and the ease of scheduling and performing them.

Written Examinations: General Knowledge and Psychological Tests

Measures of general intelligence and reading skills are the best means a police agency can use for predicting who will do well in the police academy.[23] Of course, any such test must be reliable and valid. To achieve reliability and validity, many if not most police agencies purchase and use "canned" test instruments—those prepared by professional individuals or companies.

Larger police departments and state police agencies use four types of written tests: cognitive tests (measuring aptitudes in verbal skills and mathematics, reasoning, and related perceptual abilities), personality-type tests (predominantly the MMPI), interest inventories (the Strong-Campbell, the Kuder, and the Minnesota Interest tests), and biographical data inventories.[24]

A study of deputy sheriffs found that candidates with written test scores above the 97th percentile were most apt to be successful.[25] However, a study of the Tucson, Arizona, Police Department determined that the IQ scores of officers who dropped out of the force were significantly higher than

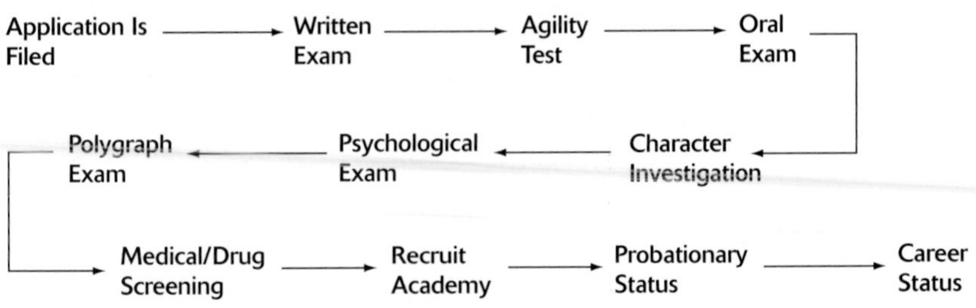

FIGURE 3-1
Major elements of the police hiring process.

those of a norm group. The study concluded that one can be too bright to be a cop, unless an alternate career development program can be developed to challenge and use highly intelligent people.[26] Of course, there is much more to police work than reading skills.

General intelligence tests are often administered and scored by the civil service or the central personnel office. Most frequently, those who fail the entrance examination, that is do not make the minimum score (usually set at 70 percent), will go on to other careers, although most jurisdictions allow for a retest after a specified period of time. The names of those who pass are forwarded to the police agency for any further in-house testing and screening.[27]

Another form of written examination for police applicants is the psychological screening test. There are two major concerns in using such tests to screen out applicants: stability and suitability. Candidates must be carefully screened in order to exclude those who are emotionally unstable, overly aggressive, or suffering from some personality disorder. The two primary tests of suitability of police candidates are the MMPI and the California Personality Inventory (CPI).[28] Stability is a major legal concern. If an officer commits a serious, harmful, and inappropriate act, the question of his or her stability will be raised. The police agency may be asked to provide documentation about why the officer was deemed stable at the time of employment. It has been found that 2 to 5 percent of the police applicant pool may be eliminated due to severe emotional or mental problems.[29]

Physical Agility Test

Entry-level physical examinations range from a minimally acceptable number of push-ups to timed running and jumping tests to tests of strength and agility, such as dragging weights, pushing cars, leaping over six-foot walls, walking on horizontal ladders, crawling through tunnels, and negotiating monkey bars. The problem is that very few of these activities are actually performed by police officers on the job.

The challenge for police executives, and an area of lawsuit vulnerability, is selecting a truly job-related physical agility examination. Police agencies must determine the nature and extent of physical work performed

Physical agility testing is an important part of the police recruitment process.

(Courtesy Washoe County, Nevada, Sheriff's Office)

by police officers and must use that information to develop an instrument to measure applicants' ability to perform that work. One such test is based on the theory that police officers must perform three basic physical functions: getting to the problem (possibly needing to run, climb, vault, and so forth), resolving the problem (perhaps needing to fight or wrestle with an offender), and removing the problem (often requiring that the officer carry heavy weights). To establish the testing protocol for a given jurisdiction, the officers fill out written forms concerning the kinds of physical work that they performed each workday for one month. Information from the forms is then analyzed by computer and used to develop a physical agility test that accurately measures the recruit's ability to do the kinds of work performed by police officers in that specific locale.[30] If challenged in court, agencies that use such tests can show that they test for the actual job requirements of their jurisdiction and do not discriminate on the basis of gender, race, height, age, and physical condition.

Oral Interview

The oral interview is used by more than 90 percent of all police agencies as part of the selection process.[31] Candidates appear individually before one or more boards that are composed of members of the police agency and often the community. Candidates may also be asked to participate in a clinical interview with a psychologist; studies have indicated that the clinical interview complements the written psychological test.[32]

The purpose of the oral interview is to assess aspects of the candidate that cannot be measured on other tests, such as appearance, the ability to communicate and reason (often using situational questions), and general poise and bearing. The interview is not normally well suited for judging character, dependability, initiative, or other such factors.

A primary advantage of the interview is that evaluators can ask applicants to explain how they would behave and use force in given situations. Any number of possible scenarios exist; following are examples of the kinds of situations that might be posed to police applicants to see how well they think on their feet, develop appropriate responses, and prioritize their actions.

1. You are dispatched to a neighborhood park to check out a young man who is acting strangely. Upon arrival, you see the youth standing near a group of children playing on a merry-go-round. He is holding a .22-caliber rifle. What is your next action?
2. You are in the men's locker room at the end of your shift. You hear another male officer talking about a female officer's body. What do you do?
3. You are at home on a weekend, watching a football game. Your neighbor comes to your door and frantically claims that his door has been kicked in and that he believes someone is inside. What do you do? What if the neighbor tells you that his daughter is upstairs in his house. How would you proceed?
4. You are in a downtown area making an arrest. A crowd gathers and you begin to hear comments about "police harassment." Soon the crowd becomes more angry. How do you react?

5. You and another officer are responding to a burglary call at an office building. While searching the scene, you observe the other officer remove an expensive fountain pen from a desktop and put it in his pocket. What do you do?

Character Investigation

As indicated earlier, nearly all local police departments use background checks or character investigations—probably the most important element of the selection process. If properly done, the character investigation can be one of the most time-consuming and costly elements as well.

Character is one of the most subjective yet most important factors an applicant brings to the job; it cannot be measured with data and interviews. A character investigation involves talking to the candidate's past and current friends, coworkers, teachers, neighbors, and employers. The applicant should be informed that references will be checked—and, in the course of reviewing them, the investigation may spread to other references and others who are known to the applicant. No expense should be spared in talking with anyone who has personal knowledge of the candidate and can provide crucial information; if the job is done properly, the investigator will not only have a complete knowledge of the person's character but will also know where any skeletons may be buried in the applicant's background.

Polygraph Examination

A survey of the nation's 626 largest police agencies found that 62 percent conducted polygraph examinations as part of their selection process. The agencies indicated that the primary benefits of polygraph screening are that applicants are more honest and that it produces higher-quality employees; 90 percent of these agencies automatically reject applicants who refuse to undergo polygraph testing.[33]

A survey of the benefits of polygraph examinations for police applicants by Richard Arther, director of the National Center of Lie Detection, supported the need for the polygraph for police recruitment:

- An applicant for a police position in Lower Merion, Pennsylvania, came to that agency highly recommended by a police lieutenant and his employer at a home for blind, retarded children. During the polygraph examination, however, the applicant admitted to at least fifty instances of sexually abusing the children under his care.
- An applicant with the Wichita, Kansas, Police Department admitted to the polygrapher that he had been involved in many burglaries. The detective division was able to clear eight unsolved crimes as a result of the applicant's confession.
- A police officer in one California police department applied for employment in the Salinas, California, Police Department. He appeared to be a model police

officer, was in excellent physical condition, and was familiar with state codes. His previous experience made him a potentially ideal candidate. However, during the polygraph exam, he admitted to having committed over a dozen burglaries while on duty and to having used his patrol car to haul away the stolen property. He also admitted to planting stolen narcotics on innocent suspects in order to make arrests and to having had sexual intercourse with girls as young as 16 in his patrol car.

- An applicant for the San Diego Sheriff's Department admitted to that agency's polygrapher that on weekends he would go from bar to bar pretending to be drunk. He would then seek out people to pick fights with, since he could only have an erection and orgasm while inflicting pain on others. In addition to these sadistic tendencies, he also admitted that he got rid of his frustrations by savagely beating "niggers, Chicanos, and long-haired pukes who cause all the trouble."[34]

These are but a few examples of how the investment of time and money for polygraph examinations can spare the public and the police agency a tremendous amount of trouble and expense later on. It is doubtful that few if any of these behaviors would have surfaced during the course of an oral interview or a background investigation. Polygraph testing is discussed in greater detail in Chapter 7 in connection with criminal investigations.

Medical Examination and Drug Screening

Someone once said that some police medical examinations are often of the "Can you hear thunder/see lightning?" variety—meaning that they are cursory at best. It is also widely believed that policing is only for those young people who are in peak physical condition. Whether these statements are facetious or not, it is certainly true that policing is no place for the physically unfit. Such officers would be a hazard not only to themselves but also to their coworkers. The job, with its stress, shift work, many hours of inactivity during patrol time, and other factors, can be physically debilitating enough for veteran officers, especially those who fail to exercise and eat properly. Police administrators certainly do not want applicants who are unfit. The Federal Bureau of Investigation (FBI), for example, will not consider applicants whose weight exceeds the norm for their height and body type. Unfit personnel are thought to have lower energy levels, to give less attention to duty, and to take more sick days. Early retirements and disability often result, as well as increased operating expenses for replacing ill officers and hiring and training new permanent replacements.

More and more, police agencies, like private-sector businesses, the military, and other sensitive government agencies, are compelling prospective employees to submit to a drug test. Substance abuse remains a very real problem in the workplace, resulting in poor productivity, lowered agency morale, and increased accidents and injuries.

THE RECRUIT'S FORMAL ENTRY INTO POLICING: ACADEMY TRAINING

Types of Academies

Today, with the concern for employing well-trained officers and avoiding civil liability lawsuits, **academy training** is regarded as a vital part of the hiring process, or, as W. Clinton Terry puts it, as "another filter through which the candidate must successfully pass."[35] The recruit academy marks a major point in the career of the officer-to-be; for many police agencies, academy training provides the bulk of the formal training that officers will acquire during their career. The academy also plays a significant role in shaping the officer's attitudes and is the beginning point for the officer's occupational socialization.

With in-house police academies, the department is authorized by some certifying body to train its own officers; there are also state and regional academies. Some police academies are operated by community colleges and universities. In a relatively new concept, civilians attend police academies at their own cost, hoping to gain employment as a free agent with a police agency after graduating and becoming formally certified. This preservice model is becoming more and more popular; police administrators are realizing tremendous savings by not paying salaries, registration fees, living expenses, and the other costs that normally accrue while their employees receive academy training.

The length of academy training varies by state; the norm is about four hundred hours. Many metropolitan police agencies, some federal organizations (such as the FBI), and many state agencies operate their own basic training academies. Several federal agencies send their personnel to the Federal Law Enforcement Training Center in Glynco, Georgia.

The Curriculum: Status and Ongoing Need for Revision

Recruit training curricula vary from state to state, but most are heavily weighted toward the technical aspects of police work. Typically, today's basic recruit academy provides training in the following general areas: the criminal justice system, the law, human values and problems, patrol and investigation procedures, police proficiency (including armed and unarmed defense, riot and prisoner control, physical conditioning, and driver training), and administration (including departmental rules and regulations, policies, and organization).[36] More specifically, the modern training academy environment includes presentations about diverse cultural groups, resolving disputes, victim and witness assistance, conducting field sobriety tests, and using computers. Modern recruits can expect to learn about proper radio procedures, the recognition and management of stress, courtroom demeanor, and accurate report writing. Training may also be provided on such diverse topics as organized crime, state alcoholic beverage control, and wildlife and game laws.

John Broderick contended that there are essentially three types of police academies: the plebe system (or stress academy), the technical training model, and the college system.[37] The stress academy has been described as "a cross between Paris Island marine boot camp and college."[38]

Stress academies are intended to emphasize physical, mental, and emotional activities that transform the recruit into a disciplined police officer. Typically, many recruits drop out or lose their self-esteem.[39]

The technical training model, adopted by many departments, is like advanced military training in that it teaches useful operational skills and the use of equipment. The graduate of this program has technical competence. Officers who graduate are good at report writing, can cite many of the laws they are to enforce, know the radio code, have qualified with their weapons, and are able to testify in court. Critics of this model, however, contend that it requires only that recruits be receptive to the "pour it in with a funnel" approach of instructors and be able to recite what has been taught.

The third type of academy training often occurs in a college setting and stresses professionalism. The college system of academy training, which recognizes that recruits are intelligent and capable of reason and decision making, has gotten a good deal of attention in recent years. Less emphasis is put on stress, discipline, and technical training, and more is placed on discussion and problem analysis.

Studies indicate that upon entry into the academy, recruits are normally confident and believe that their success is all but guaranteed. John Van Maanen wrote that this level of confidence is not always justified, however:

> The individual usually feels upon swearing allegiance to the department, city, state and nation that "he's finally made it." However, the department instantaneously and somewhat rudely informs him that until he has served his probationary period he may be severed from the membership rolls at any time without warning, explanation or appeal. It is perhaps ironic that in a period of a few minutes, a person's position vis-a-vis the organization can be altered so dramatically.[40]

An analysis of the curricula of basic training academies in thirty states by David Bradford and Joan Pynes revealed that little has changed since 1986. Less than 3 percent of basic training academy time is spent in the cognitive and decision-making domain; the remaining time is spent in task-oriented activities. The exception is the Commonwealth of Massachusetts, which recently revised its basic curriculum so that now nearly all of its training is cognitive. According to the Massachusetts Criminal Justice Training Council, the objective of the cognitive training is to get the officer to "understand how to speak to, reason with, and listen to people and learn to use communication skills to manage a wide range of problematic situations.

Physical tactics and tools, though readily available, are secondary to the primary response of communication."[41]

Bradford and Pynes assert that community-oriented policing and problem solving (COPPS, discussed in Chapter 6) requires the utilization of extensive cognitive and reasoning aptitudes and effective interpersonal skills and judgment. However, their examination of current basic training curricula found that problem solving and interpersonal skills development are low priorities of administrators and training directors.[42] Bradford and Pynes conclude that there is a lack of congruence between the curriculum taught in many police academies and the job responsibilities of COPPS officers; given the rapid spread of the COPPS approach, as well as the availability of related textbooks, they ask, "Why, then, are training academy curricula not changing?"[43]

A New Uniform and Demeanor

As the academy training begins, recruits adopt a new identity and a system of discipline in which they learn to take orders and not to question authority. They learn that loyalty to fellow officers, a professional demeanor and bearing, and respect for authority are highly valued in this occupation. The classroom teaches the recruit how to approach situations. Outside the classroom, as they share war stories discussed with academy staff, they informally transmit the proper attitudes to one another. Thus the recruits begin to form a collective understanding of policing and how they are supposed to function, and they gradually develop a common language and demeanor. Many people also believe that the police develop a swagger, or a confident, authoritarian way of walking and presenting themselves. This is the beginning of the police officer's working personality.[44]

Recruits may wear a uniform for the first time during academy training; this is typically an awe-inspiring experience for them. The uniform sets them apart from society at large and conveys a sense of authority and responsibility to the recruit and to the public. "Image is everything," according to a popular saying, and the choice of agency uniform can go a long way toward setting the image and tone of the department. Police uniforms come in various colors, styles, and fabrics. Some agencies even have their officers wearing blue jeans or shorts and T-shirts (for beach patrol, for example).

The belt is one of the most important components of the patrol uniform; it is certainly one of the heaviest. It often exceeds twenty pounds when laden with weapon, cuffs, baton, radio, flashlight, extra ammunition, Mace, and so on. The uniform hat comes in several styles and is probably the piece of equipment that most readily identifies the officer and the department's image; each type of hat makes a certain statement to the public about the officer and his or her authority. The officer's badge also conveys a tremendous sense of authority. The most popular are customized shields, incorporating everything from the state motto and seal to symbols that convey the agency's

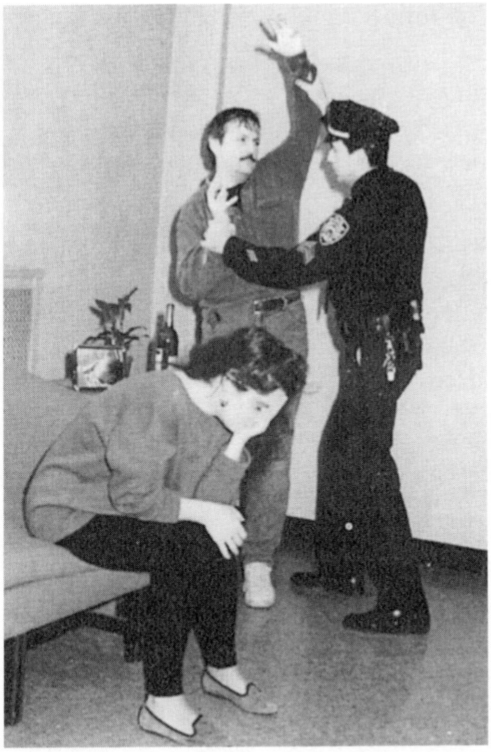

Role-playing scenarios are also effective for teaching academy recruits to handle difficult situations.

(Courtesy City of New York Police Department Photo Unit)

image and philosophy. When designing its badge, a police department considers its tradition and history as well as those of the community.[45]

A Sixth Sense

Police recruits are taught to nurture a "**sixth sense**": suspicion. A suspicious nature is as important to the street officer as a fine touch is to a surgeon. The officer should not only be able to visually recognize but also be able to physically sense when something is wrong or out of the ordinary. As a Chicago Police Department bulletin stated,

> Actions, dress, or location of a person often classify him as suspicious in the mind of a police officer. Men loitering near schools, public toilets, playgrounds and swimming pools may be sex perverts. Men loitering near . . . any business at closing time may be robbery suspects. Men or youths walking along looking into cars may be car thieves or looking for something to steal. Persons showing evidence of recent injury, or whose clothing is disheveled, may be victims or participants in an assault or strong-arm robbery.[46]

Officers are trained to be observant, to develop an intimate knowledge of the territory and people, and to "notice the normal. . . . Only then can [they] decide what persons or cars under what circumstances warrant the appellation 'suspicious.'"[47] They must recognize when someone or something needs to be checked out. The following observations often warrant a field investigation:

- People who do not "belong" where they are observed
- Automobiles that do not "look right" (such as dirty cars with clean license plates or a vehicle with plates attached with wire or in another unusual fashion)
- Businesses open at odd hours or not according to routine or custom
- People exhibiting exaggerated unconcern over contact with the officer or being visibly "rattled" when near the officer
- Solicitors or peddlers in a residential neighborhood
- A lone male sitting in a car near a shopping center or near a school paying unusual attention to women or children
- Hitchhikers
- A person wearing a coat on a hot day[48]

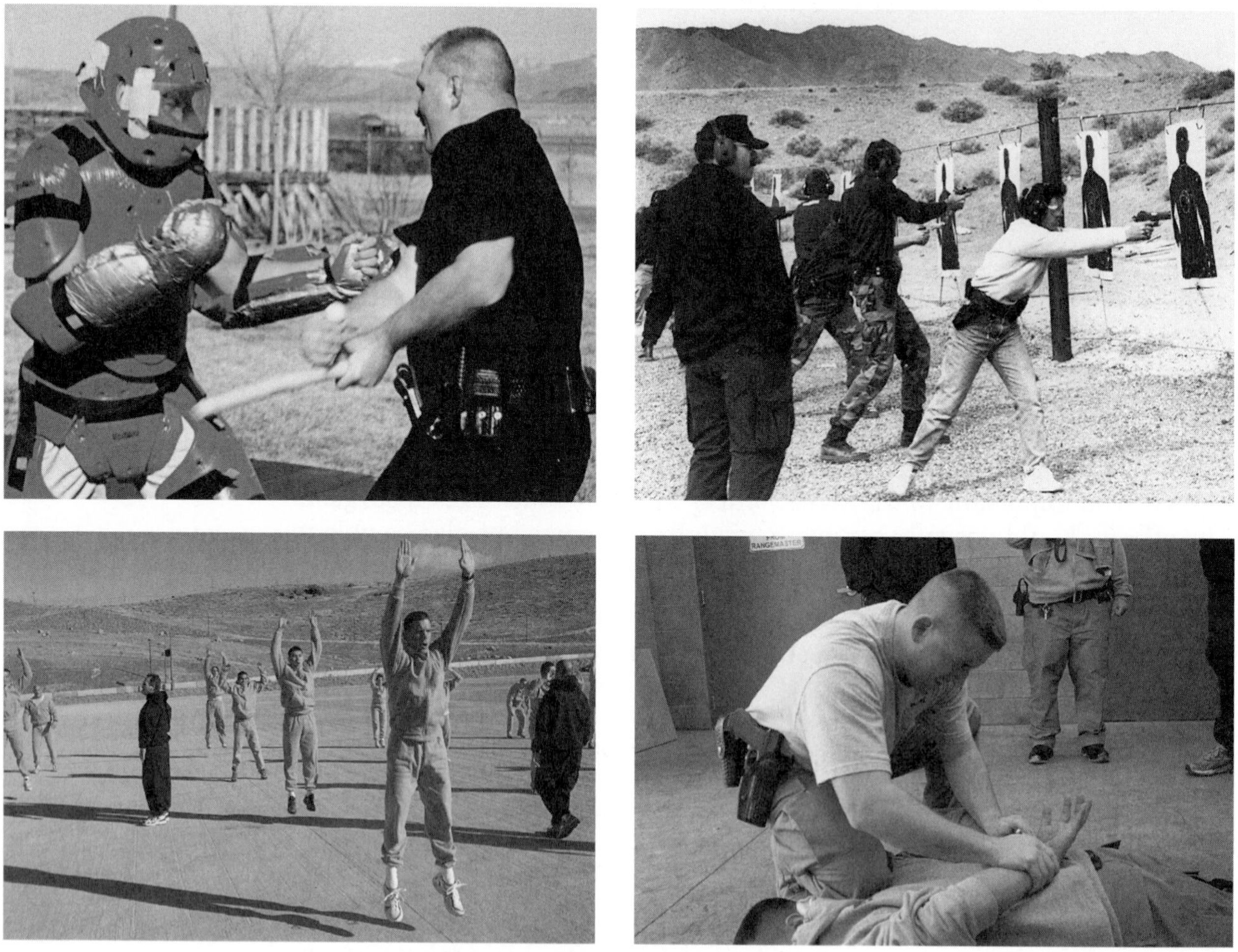

Police academy recruits engage in a variety of training activities.

(Courtesy City of New York Police Department Photo Unit [top left]; R. Brand [top right]; and Washoe County, Nevada, Sheriff's Office [bottom photos])

The academy also teaches neophyte officers that their major tool is their body; like mountain climbers, acrobats, or athletes, their body is an essential tool for the performance of their trade. The gun and nightstick initially fascinate the recruits, but until they are adequately trained, officers using them would be more a menace to society than a protector. Proper handling and safety measures are drilled into the recruits; the message is unequivocal that recruits will not be trusted with these potentially lethal weapons until they become proficient in their use. The new officers must be taught to measure their capacity to do the job, to assess carefully the physical capabilities of people they confront on the street, and to determine whether someone can be subdued without assistance or the risk of injury if a physical altercation should develop.[49]

The officers are also told, however, that they cannot approach every situation with holster unsnapped or baton raised or twirling; they must demonstrate poise and not be eager to use force. It is constantly instilled in them that the days of the club-swinging cop are gone. Thus, knowing that the body is a tool, the recruits are taught how to unobtrusively position themselves, whether at a vehicle stop or while engaged in a discussion on the street, in order to gain a physical advantage should trouble arise. They are taught when to use force and when to relent, to always keep control of the situation, and to feel that they would emerge victorious should force be required. Thus in addition to weapons training, they may be given some weaponless defense training, including some holds that can be applied to subjects to bring them into compliance.

Recruits are taught some aspects of human nature and are encouraged not to be prejudicial in their actions or speech. They learn to deal with criminal suspects, offenders, victims, and witnesses and to be suspicious of "eyewitness" accounts. (For example, twenty-five "witnesses" claimed that they helped carry Abraham Lincoln from Ford Theater into the little house where he died; eight different people said they held his head, and eighty-four people said they were in the room that night.[50])

Recruits often participate in hands-on training, practicing their new techniques in the field in simulated situations. Quite possibly the ultimate in hands-on training occurs at the Hogan's Alley complex at the FBI Academy in Quantico, Virginia, which opened in 1987 and covers almost thirty-five acres. This facility combines training, office, and classroom space on one site, increasing training effectiveness. Hogan's Alley (the name given to many turn-of-the-century training facilities, apparently after an old comic strip about mischievous Irish kids) resembles a fully developed urban area. The set includes a business area and a residential street with townhouses and apartments. The use of movie-set techniques gives the illusion of depth and space. All furnishings—including a fleet of cars, furniture, desks, and even a pool table—were forfeited by convicted criminals. Federal agents are trained in the practical skills of crime-scene investigation and photography, surveillance techniques, the mechanics of

A segment of Hogan's Alley.

(Courtesy Federal Bureau of Investigation)

arrest, and investigative skills. Trainees use only deactivated weapons that fire blanks.

Other methods of police training that are currently used include **computer-based training (CBT)**, electronic bulletin boards, satellite training and teleconferencing, online computer forums, and correspondence courses. With computer costs declining, CBT is becoming increasingly popular and has been shown to be very effective. As CBT simulates real-life situations through the use of computer-modeled problems, it closely duplicates the way we think. One study found that police officers who learned about the exclusionary rule (discussed in Chapter 9) through CBT understood the material significantly better than the non-CBT control group.[51]

Virtual reality is another available (although very costly) form of police training. Trainees wear a head-mounted device that restricts their vision to two monitors and projects a computer-generated, three-dimensional illusion that engulfs the senses of sight, sound, and touch. Virtual reality may one day be commonly used for training police officers in such areas as pursuit driving, firearms training, critical incident management, and crime-scene processing.

Finally, graduation day arrives, and the academy experience becomes a rite of passage. Graduation also means new uniforms, associates, and responsibilities and a raise in pay and status. As Arthur Niederhoffer observed, for many officers academy graduation is a worthy substitute for a college education. But "the very next morning the graduate is rudely dumped into a strange precinct where he must prove himself."[52]

POSTACADEMY FIELD TRAINING

The Field Training Officer Concept

Once the recruits leave the academy, their knowledge of and acceptance into the police subculture is not yet complete. Another very important part of this acquisition process is being assigned to a veteran officer for initial field instruction and observation. This veteran is sometimes called a "field training officer" (FTO). The oldest formal **field training** program began in the San Jose, California, Police Department in 1972.[53] This training program provides recruits with an opportunity to make the transition from the academy to the streets under the protective arm of a veteran officer. Recruits are on probationary status, normally ranging from six months to one year; they understand that they may be immediately terminated if their overall performance is unsatisfactory during that period.

Most FTO programs consist of four identifiable phases: an introductory phase (the recruit learns agency policies and local laws); training and evaluation phases (the recruit is introduced to more complicated tasks that patrol officers confront); and a final phase (the FTO acts strictly as an observer and evaluator while the recruit performs all the functions of a patrol officer).[54] The National Institute of Justice (NIJ), surveying nearly six hundred police agencies, found that 64 percent had a field training program and that such programs had reduced the number of civil liability suits filed against their officers and against standardized training programs.[55] The length of time rookies are assigned to FTOs will vary. A formal FTO program might require close supervision for a range of one to twelve weeks.

Although some police officers end their formal training with the conclusion of academy and field training, most police officers receive in-service training throughout their careers. Most states require a minimum number of hours of in-service training for police officers, and many departments exceed the minimum requirement. News items, court decisions, and other relevant information can be covered at roll call before the beginning of each shift. Short courses ranging from a few hours to several weeks are available for in-service officers through several such means as videos and nationally televised training programs.

With the ever-changing laws and methods of policing and the constant specter of liability, such ongoing training is essential; police officers must keep abreast of current changes in their field. As Geoffrey Alpert and Roger Dunham put it, "Whether an officer is overweight or out-of-shape, a poor shot, uses poor judgment, or is too socialized into the police subculture to provide good community policing, in-service training can be used to restore the officer's skills or to improve his attitude."[56]

New Technology

New technology in the training function includes software known as ADORE, for Automated Daily Observation Report and Evaluation. FTOs in several agencies now field testing the software find that it saves them time because they do not have to write reports for each recruit by hand. ADORE, which can be accessed through either a laptop or a Palm Pilot, allows FTOs to take computerized notes while watching trainees at work; it also reduces paperwork by allowing trainers to easily compile numbers for evaluating performance in dozens of categories. The software is credited with reducing FTO burnout, which is often a part of the paper-intensive evaluation process.[57]

Another new form of technology for police training that is being tested involves pursuit simulation. The training simulator is thought to be an effective means to determine how and when a vehicle pursuit should be halted. In one scenario, trainees in a simulated pursuit swerve around computerized images of a transit bus, a produce truck, a minivan, and a child on a skateboard before the chased vehicle enters a school zone, where the officer should end the hot pursuit. These simulated pursuits also allow supervisors to see how well trainees conduct themselves in accordance with their agency's pursuit policy, which is often several pages long.[58]

Having the "Right Stuff": A Working Personality

Developing and Using a Police Personality

Since William Westley first wrote about the police subculture in 1950, the notion of a police personality has become a popular area of study. In 1966, Jerome Skolnick described what he termed the **working personality** of the police. He determined that the police role contained two important variables: danger and authority. Danger is a constant feature of police work. Police officers, constantly facing potential violence, are warned at the academy to be cautious. They are told many war stories of officers shot and killed at domestic disturbances or traffic stops. Consequently, they develop a "perceptual shorthand," Skolnick said, that they use to identify certain kinds of people as "symbolic assailants"—individuals whom the officer has come to recognize as potentially violent based on their gestures, language, and attire.

The police, as Skolnick stated, represent authority. But unlike doctors, ministers, and the like, they must establish their authority. The symbols of that authority—the gun, the badge, and the baton—assist them, but officers' behavior and confidence are more important in social situations. As William Westley said, an officer "expects rage from the underprivileged and the criminal but understanding from the middle classes: the professionals, the merchants and the white-collar workers. They, however, define him as a servant, not as a colleague, and the rejection is hard to take."[59] Thus officers cannot even depend on their symbols and position of authority in dealing with the public; they are often confused when the public does not automatically observe and accept their authority.

Considerable research has compared the personality characteristics of the police with those of the general public,[60] and a number of differences have been discovered. One study found the average officer to be more intelligent, assertive, dependable, straightforward, and conscientious than civilians.[61] Other researchers who recently studied state traffic officers and deputy sheriffs using the MMPI and CPI scales reported that the officers scored high on the values of achievement, a strong work ethic, ambition, leadership potential, and organizational skills.[62] Studies have also found conservatism and a high degree of cynicism among officers, although those traits are found to be present in much of the society at large. The late Los Angeles Police Department (LAPD) Chief William Parker asserted that police were "conservative, ultraconservative, and very right wing."[63]

Niederhoffer reported his classic study of **police cynicism** in 1967, using the New York Police Department as the site of a longitudinal study.[64] He found that although a typical recruit begins his or her career without a trace of cynicism, police cynicism spikes most dramatically immediately after recruits leave the basic academy. This is probably because they confront the reality of the streets—the pain and criminality of society—and perhaps lose friends. Cynical veteran peers frequently reinforce the worst aspects of the job. From about two to six years of service, the cynicism level continues to increase but at a slower rate. The recruit has begun to adapt to the occupation and the people to be dealt with every day. At about mid-career (about eight to thirteen years of service), the cynicism level actually begins to decline, possibly because the officer has accepted the job and has been promoted, earns a decent salary and benefits, and realizes that he or she is about halfway to retirement. Toward the end of the career, the degree of cynicism levels off; for many officers, this is a period of coasting toward retirement.

A police officer's view of humanity may become distorted and cynical because many of the people the police deal with are offenders. They see what they feel are miscarriages of justice (for example, improper or lenient court decisions, perjury on the witness stand, plea bargaining—where defendants are allowed to plead guilty for a less serious offense[s] than charged or to fewer counts than charged—and so on) and observe fellow officers who do not live up to their code of ethics. Cynicism does have a protective feature, however. It can help to make the officer callous, allowing him or her to observe things that would sicken or horrify the average citizen without becoming mentally debilitated.

John Broderick presented another view of the working personality of the police. He believed that there are actually four types of police personalities: enforcers, idealists, realists, and optimists. Enforcers are officers who believe that the job of the police consists primarily of keeping their beats clean, making good arrests, and sometimes helping people. These officers have sympathy for vagrants, the elderly, the working poor, and others whom they see as basically good people. However, drug users, cop haters, and others frustrate the efforts of enforcers to make them "good." This makes the enforcers very unhappy. Thus they have high job dissatisfaction and an attitude of resentment, feeling that a lot of people are hostile toward them.

Idealists, according to Broderick, are officers who put high value on individual rights and due process. They also believe that it is their duty to keep the peace, protect citizens from criminals, and generally preserve the social order. As a group with a high percentage of college graduates, their commitment to the job is the lowest of the four groups, and they are less likely to recommend the job to a son or daughter.

Realists place relatively little emphasis on either social order or individual rights, Broderick says. They seem less frustrated, having found a way to come to terms with a difficult job. For them, the reality of the job consists of manila envelopes and properly completed forms. Realists see many problems in policing, such as special privileges given to politicians. Reality is not warm bodies to be dealt with but rather the paperwork that the bodies leave behind. They work well in the ordered, predictable environment of a police records room.

Broderick's last group, the optimists, also place a relatively high value on individual rights. Like idealists, they see their job as people oriented instead of crime oriented. They see policing as providing opportunities to help people; they view the television version of policing as totally unrealistic and find it rewarding to spend the majority of their time in service activities. Optimists have the lowest amount of job resentment, are committed to the job, and would choose policing as a career all over again. They enjoy the mental challenge of problem solving.

What Traits Make a Good Cop?

It is not too difficult to identify a bad cop through his or her unethical or criminal behavior. It is probably more difficult for the average person to identify the **traits of good officers**. How can a quantitative measure assess the work of police? Is it possible to judge the quality of an officer's work? These are challenging questions for police supervisors.

A major obstacle to assessing police performance rests with the nature of police work generally and the variation in kinds of work performed between shifts. The police role varies according to whether the officer is assigned to the day shift, evening (swing) shift, or night (graveyard) shift. (See Chapter 5 for a description of how police work varies by shift.)

Dennis Nowicki acknowledged that while certain characteristics form the foundation of a police officer—honesty, ethics, and moral character—no scientific formula can be used to create a highly effective officer. However, he compiled twelve qualities that he believes are imperative for entry-level police officers:

> *Enthusiasm:* Believing in what one is doing and going about even routine duties with a certain vigor that is almost contagious.
>
> *Good communications skills:* Having highly developed speaking and listening skills and the ability to interact equally well with a wealthy person or someone lower on the socioeconomic ladder.

Good judgment: Having wisdom and the ability to make good analytic decisions based on an understanding of the problem.

Sense of humor: Being able to laugh and smile, to help oneself cope with regular exposure to human pain and suffering.

Creativity: Using creative techniques to place oneself in the mind of the criminal and accomplish legal arrests.

Self-motivation: Making things happen, proactively solving difficult cases, and creating one's own luck.

Knowing the job and the system: Understanding the role of a police officer, the intricacies of the justice system, and what the administration requires; using both formal and informal channels to be effective.

Ego: Believing one is a good officer; having self-confidence that enables one to solve difficult crimes.

Courage: Being able to meet physical and psychological challenges; thinking clearly during times of high stress; admitting when one is wrong; standing up for what is right.

Understanding discretion: Enforcing the spirit of the law, not the letter of the law; not being hard-nosed, hardheaded, or hard-hearted; giving people a break; and showing empathy.

Tenacity: Staying focused; seeing challenges, not obstacles; viewing failure not as a setback but as an experience.

A thirst for knowledge: Being aware of new laws and court decisions; always learning (from the classroom but also via informal discussions with other officers).[65]

Roles, Functions, and Styles of Policing

Defining and Understanding the Police Role

Why do the police exist? What are they supposed to do? Often these questions are given oversimplified answers, such as "They enforce the law" or "They 'serve and protect.' "[66]

But policing is much more complex. As Herman Goldstein put it, "Anyone attempting to construct a workable definition of the police role will typically come away with old images shattered and with a newfound appreciation for the intricacies of police work."[67] Even with all of the movies and television series depicting police in action, most Americans probably still do not have an accurate idea of what the police really do. This confusion is quite understandable because the police are called on to perform an almost countless number of tasks. Police are even used as prosecutors in some states, such as New Hampshire.

Who defines the police role? There are several groups and individuals who do so:

- Private citizens influence the nature of the role through their contacts with the police, by participating in community-oriented policing and problem-solving groups (discussed in Chapter 6), and through the election of public officials who set policy and appoint police administrators.

- Legislative bodies influence the role of the police by enacting statutes, both those that govern the police and those that the police use to govern others. In addition, legislative bodies determine police department budgets.
- The courts actively police the police by handing down decisions that regulate police conduct.
- Executives such as city managers and prosecutors help to define the police role by determining the types of cooperative agreements and evidence necessary for a prosecutable case.
- Police officers themselves define their roles by choosing to intervene in some incidents while ignoring others.[68]

One of the greatest obstacles to understanding the American police is the crime fighter image. Many people believe that the role of the police is confined to law enforcement: the prevention and detection of crime and the apprehension of criminals. This is not an accurate view of contemporary policing.[69] It does not describe what the police do on a daily basis. First, only about 20 percent of the police officer's typical day is devoted to fighting crime per se.[70] And, as Jerome Skolnick and David Bayley point out, the crimes that terrify Americans the most—robbery, rape, burglary, and homicide—are rarely encountered by police on patrol: "Only 'Dirty Harry' has his lunch disturbed by a bank robbery in progress. Patrol officers individually make few important arrests. The 'good collar' is a rare event. Cops spend most of their time passively patrolling and providing emergency services."[71]

The crime fighter image persists, although it is extremely harmful to the public, police departments, and individual officers.[72] The public suffers from this image because it gives rise to unrealistic expectations about the ability of the police to catch criminals. The image harms individual officers, who believe that rewards and promotions are tied only to success in capturing criminals. Also, many individuals enter policing expecting it to be exciting and rewarding, as depicted on television and in the movies. Later they learn that much of their time is spent with boring, mundane tasks that are anything but glamorous. Much of the work is trivial, and paperwork is seldom stimulating.

Role Conflicts

Role conflicts may develop with officers and their departments. A family disturbance is a good example. Assume that Jane Smith reports to the police that her husband, John, is assaulting her. Police officers must respond to the disturbance, and the law empowers them to intervene, to enforce the law, and to maintain order. For the combatants, it is a very trying experience, not only because of their family dysfunction but also because the police have been summoned to their home. Veteran officers might view the domestic call as trivial and inconvenient, leaving the scene as quickly as possible to go perform "real" police duties.

By the same token, the role of the police is often in the eye of the beholder. For example, the domestic argument just described might best seem to fit in the category of maintaining order. However, if the responding officers are trained in crisis intervention or if they refer the couple to counseling, they are providing a social service. On the other hand, if John is found to have assaulted Jane, it is likely a criminal matter. If the police make an arrest or even just assist Jane in swearing out a warrant, the matter becomes a law enforcement issue. The category to which this incident is assigned will vary greatly from agency to agency, officer to officer, and researcher to researcher, making it difficult to draw any solid conclusions about the police role.

Still, it is important to be as explicit as possible about the police role for several reasons. First, we can recruit and select competent police personnel only when we have a clear vision of what the police are supposed to accomplish. Second, evaluation for retention and promotion is useful only to the extent that we evaluate in terms of what the police are supposed to do. Third, budgetary decisions should be based on an accurate analysis of police roles. Fourth, efficiency and effectiveness in police organizations depend on accurate task description. And finally, public cooperation with the police depends on developing reasonable expectations of the roles of the police and the public.[73]

The police must identify those crimes on which police resources should be concentrated, focusing on the crimes that generate the most public fear and economic loss. The chief executive should have written policies to ensure that the police mission and the objectives used to achieve that mission are maintained by the police department. In other words, it is not enough for the police to "maintain order" or "provide justice." A police department may use many methods to maintain order and provide justice. In China or Saudi Arabia, those methods would be far different from those generally employed in the United States. But would "justice" result? In America, the police must maintain order without resorting to extralegal means or violating human rights.

Policing Functions and Styles

Officers may be said to perform four basic **policing functions**: (1) enforcing the laws; (2) performing services (such as maintaining or assisting animal control units, reporting burned-out street lights or damaged traffic signs, delivering death messages, checking the welfare of people in their homes, or delivering blood); (3) preventing crime (patrolling, providing the public with information on crime prevention); and (4) protecting the innocent (by investigating crimes, police are systematically removing innocent people from consideration as crime suspects).

James Q. Wilson looked at the functions of the police differently, determining that the police perform two basic functions: maintaining order (peacekeeping) and enforcing the law. Maintaining order constitutes most of the activities of the police; as noted earlier, less than 20 percent of the calls answered by police are directly related to crime control or law enforcement. Much of an officer's time is spent with such service activities as traffic control and routine patrol. Indeed, in some cases the police deliberately avoid enforcing the law in an attempt to maintain order. For example, if the police know of a busy street where many drivers speed, they may desist from setting up a speed trap during rush hours so as not to impede the flow of traffic and possibly cause accidents.

The law enforcement function means upholding the statutes, but this is not as simple and straightforward a function as it might seem. First, the police are really not very good at performing the law enforcement function. They have not traditionally been successful at preventing crime or providing long-term solutions to neighborhood disorder (although the relatively new community-policing and problem-solving concepts are addressing this shortcoming). Second, there are several types of crime—such as white-collar crime—with which the local police seldom deal. Third, the police, representing only about 2.3 officers per 1,000 population in the United States, cannot effectively control the public alone. Finally, the police are successful in solving only a fraction of the property and personal crimes that occur.[74]

Wilson also maintained that there are three distinctive **policing styles**: the watchman style, the legalistic style, and the service style.[75]

- The watchman style involves the officer as a "neighbor." Here, officers act as if order maintenance (rather than law enforcement) is their primary function. The emphasis is on using the law as a means of maintaining order rather than regulating conduct through arrests. Police ignore many common minor violations, such as traffic and juvenile offenses. These violations and so-called victimless crimes, such as gambling and prostitution, are tolerated; they will often be handled informally. Thus the individual officer has wide latitude concerning whether to enforce the letter or the spirit of the law; the emphasis is on using the law to give people what they "deserve." It assumes that some people, such as juveniles, are occasionally going to "act up."
- The legalistic style casts the officer as a "soldier." This style takes a much harsher view of law violations. Police officers issue large numbers of traffic citations, detain a high volume of juvenile offenders, and act vigorously against illicit activities. Large numbers of other kinds of arrests occur as well. Chief administrators want high arrest and ticketing rates not only because violators should be punished but also because it reduces the opportunity for their officers to engage in corrupt behavior. This style of policing assumes that the purpose of the law is to punish.
- The service style views the officer as a "teacher." This style falls in between the watchman and legalistic styles. The police take seriously all requests for either law enforcement or order maintenance (unlike in the watchman-style department) but are less likely to respond by making an arrest or otherwise imposing formal sanctions. Police officers see their primary responsibility as protecting public order against the minor and occasional threats posed by unruly teenagers and "outsiders" (tramps, derelicts, out-of-town visitors). The

citizenry expects its service-style officers to display the same qualities as its department store salespeople: They should be courteous, neat, and deferential. The police will frequently use informal sanctions instead of making arrests.

Which Role, Function, and Style Are Typically Employed?

As we have seen, the role, function, and style of the police will differ by time and place. They will also be fluid within the agency, changing with the times, the political climate, and the problems of the day. Most police agencies do not determine which problems they address; rather, they respond to the problems that citizens believe are important and depend on the goals set by the community, the chief executive, and the individual officers. Sometimes roles, functions, and styles overlap, but most of the time they are distinct.

SUMMARY

This chapter examined how ordinary citizens are recruited, tested, and trained for their role as police officers. It demonstrated how recruits are socialized into the cop's world—how they are brought into the police subculture and transformed psychologically, physically, and emotionally in order to become competent to perform this very challenging occupation.

A working personality develops in police officers, and both formal training and informal peer relations are helpful in teaching the novice officer how to act and how to think on the job. Police officers develop a sense of cynicism by virtue of their having to deal every day with the pain and problems of our society.

This chapter also examined the roles, functions, and styles of the local police in America. More than a century and a half after the adoption of the early British model of policing (discussed in Chapter 1), there is still widespread disagreement, conflict, and debate concerning what we truly want our police to do, represent, and become.

REVIEW QUESTIONS

1. Describe some of the problems confronting today's police recruiters as well as some of the unique measures being tried to obtain a viable applicant pool.
2. Explain in general the hiring process of new police officers. List the kinds of tests that are commonly given to applicants.
3. Relate in general terms the kinds of skills and knowledge that are imparted to police trainees during their academy training. Describe the typical subjects that are found in a police academy curriculum, and explore its strengths and weaknesses.

4. Discuss the methods and purposes of the FTO concept.
5. Describe what is meant by the term *working personality*. Explain how the working personality is developed and how it functions.
6. Define police cynicism, and discuss how it operates, according to Niederhoffer.
7. Review the ideal traits of police officers.
8. Explain why the crime fighter image is the greatest obstacle in accepting a realistic view of the police role.
9. Describe the primary functions and styles of policing.

INDEPENDENT STUDENT ACTIVITIES

1. Visit your city or county human resources office to learn about police recruitment and hiring methods, including the desired qualities of candidates, the various kinds of tests that are given, the length of academy training, and so on.
2. Interview local police officers to learn about their socialization into the police subculture, including the academy experience, their adjustment to being "set apart" from society by wearing a police uniform, their development of a "sixth sense," and their general development of a working personality.
3. Ask local police executives whether they believe that police officers should possess a college degree (and why or why not). Learn about any educational incentive programs that local agencies offer. Ask the interviewees what constitutes a "good" police officer.
4. Meet with female and minority officers to learn of the unique challenges they encountered upon entering law enforcement.

RELATED WEB SITES

Equal Employment Opportunity Commission
http://www.eeoc.gov/

National Association of Police Organizations
http://www.napo.org/

National Law Enforcement Trainers Association
http://www.nleta.com/

NOTES

1. William A. Westley, *Violence and the Police* (Cambridge, MA: MIT Press, 1970).
2. Geoffrey P. Alpert and Roger G. Dunham, *Policing Urban America*, 2nd ed. (Prospect Heights, IL: Waveland Press, 1992), p. 80.

3. Quoted in V. A. LEONARD and HARRY W. MORE, *Police Organization and Management*, 3rd ed. (Mineola, NY: Foundation Press, 1971), p. 128.
4. JOEL LEFKOWITZ, "Industrial-Organizational Psychology and the Police," *American Psychologist* (May 1977): 346–64.
5. R. B. MILLS, "Use of Diagnostic Small Groups in Police Recruit Selection and Training," *Journal of Criminal Law, Criminology and Police Science* 60 (1969): 238–41; and JOHN VAN MAANEN, "Police Socialization: A Longitudinal Examination of Job Attitudes in an Urban Police Department," *Administrative Science Quarterly* 20 (1975): 207–28.
6. C. GORER, "Modification of National Character: The Role of the Police in England," *Journal of Social Issues* 11 (1955): 24–32; and ARTHUR NIEDERHOFFER, *Behind the Shield: The Police in Urban Society* (New York: Anchor, 1967), p. 140.
7. M. STEVEN MEAGHER and NANCY A. YENTES, "Choosing a Career in Policing: A Comparison of Male and Female Perceptions," *Journal of Police Science and Administration* 14 (1986): 320–27.
8. LEFKOWITZ, "Industrial-Organizational Psychology and the Police."
9. J. D. MATARAZZO, B. V. ALLEN, G. SASLOW, and A. N. WIENS, "Characteristics of Successful Policemen and Firemen Applicants," *Journal of Applied Psychology* 48 (1964): 123–33.
10. BRUCE N. CARPENTER and SUSAN M. RAZA, "Personality Characteristics of Police Applicants: Comparisons across Subgroups and with Other Populations," *Journal of Police Science and Administration* 15 (1987): 10–17.
11. CARPENTER and RAZA also compared police applicants with other similar occupational groups and found that police applicants appear to be most like nuclear submariners and least like air force trainees and security guards.
12. LAWRENCE S. WRIGHTSMAN, *Psychology and the Legal System* (Monterey, CA: Brooks/Cole, 1987), pp. 85–86.
13. AL SEEDMAN and P. HELLMAN, *Chief!* (New York: Arthur Fields, 1974), pp. 4–5.
14. JENNIFER NISLOW, "Is Anyone Out There?" *Law Enforcement News*, October 31, 1999, p. 1.
15. NICOLE ZIEGLER DIZON, "Searching for Police," Associated Press, June 3, 2000.
16. MARC LIFSHER, "State Strains to Recruit New Police," *Wall Street Journal*, November 10, 1999, p. CA1.
17. DIZON, "Searching for Police."
18. "Plenty of Talk, Not Much Action," *Law Enforcement News*, January 15/31, 1999, p. 1.
19. "Hiring Problem? What Hiring Problem? NYSP Has Answers to Recruiting Slump," *Law Enforcement News*, November 30, 2000, p. 1.
20. "Police Chiefs Try Many Recruiting Strategies to Boost Applicant Pool," *Crime Control Digest*, February 2, 2001, pp. 1–2.
21. DEPARTMENT OF JUSTICE, Bureau of Justice Statistics Executive Summary, *Local Police Departments, 1997* (Washington, DC: Author, October 1999).
22. ALFRED STONE and STUART DELUCA, *Police Administration* (New York: John Wiley and Sons, 1985).

23. Hans Toch, *Psychology of Crime and Criminal Justice* (Prospect Heights, IL: Waveland Press, 1999), p. 44.
24. Philip Ash, Karen B. Slora, and Cynthia F. Britton, "Police Agency Officer Selection Practices," *Journal of Police Science and Administration* 17 (December 1990): 259–64.
25. S. H. Marsh, "Validating the Selection of Deputy Sheriffs," *Public Personnel Review* 23 (1962): 41–44.
26. William H. Thweatt, "A Vocational Counseling Approach to Police Selection" (unpublished dissertation, University of Arizona).
27. W. Clinton Terry III, *Policing Society* (New York: John Wiley and Sons, 1985), p. 194.
28. George E. Hargrave, "Using the MMPI and CPI to Screen Law Enforcement Applicants: A Study of Reliability and Validity of Clinicians' Decisions," *Journal of Police Science and Administration* 13 (1985): 221–24.
29. Roger G. Dunham and Geoffrey P. Alpert, *Critical Issues in Policing: Contemporary Readings* (Prospect Heights, IL: Waveland Press, 1989), p. 80.
30. For a complete discussion of the Sparks Police Officers Physical Abilities Test (POPAT), see Ken Peak, Douglas Farenholtz, and George Coxey, "Physical Abilities Testing for Police Officers: A Flexible, Job Related Approach," *Police Chief* (January 1992): 51–56.
31. Terry Eisenberg, D. A. Kent, and C. R. Wall, *Police Personnel Practices in State and Local Governments* (Gaithersburg, MD: International Association of Chiefs of Police, 1973), p. 15.
32. George E. Hargrave and Deirdre Hiatt, "Law Enforcement Selection with the Interview, MMPI, and CPI: A Study of Reliability and Validity," *Journal of Police Science and Administration* (1987): 110–17.
33. Frank Horvath, "Polygraphic Screening of Candidates for Police Work in Large Police Agencies in the United States: A Survey of Practices, Policies, and Evaluative Comments," *American Journal of Police* 12 (1993): 67–86.
34. Quoted in Charles R. Swanson, Leonard Territo, and Robert W. Taylor, *Police Administration*, 2nd ed. (New York: Macmillan, 1988), pp. 202–3.
35. Terry, *Policing Society*, p. 196.
36. See, for example, David Bradford and Joan E. Pynes, "Police Academy Training: Why Hasn't It Kept Up with Practice?" *Police Quarterly* 2 (September 1999): 283–301; N. Marion, "Police Academy Training: Are We Teaching Recruits What They Need to Know?" *Policing: An International Journal of Police Strategies and Management* 21 (1998): 54–79; Richard F. Brand and Ken Peak, "Assessing Police Training Curriculums: 'Consumer Reports,' " *Justice Professional* 9, no. 1 (winter 1995): 45–58.
37. John J. Broderick, *Police in a Time of Change*, 2nd ed. (Prospect Heights, IL: Waveland Press, 1987), p. 215.
38. Quoted in John M. Violanti, "What Does High Stress Police Training Teach Recruits? An Analysis of Coping," *Journal of Criminal Justice* 21 (1993): 411–17.
39. Ibid., p. 416.
40. John Van Maanen, "On the Making of Policemen," in *Thinking about Police*, ed. Carl Klockars (New York: McGraw-Hill, 1983), pp. 388–400.

41. Quoted in BRADFORD and PYNES, "Police Academy Training," p. 289.
42. Ibid., pp. 292, 297.
43. Ibid., p. 298.
44. ALPERT and DUNHAM, *Policing Urban America*, p. 50.
45. LOIS PILANT, "Enhancing the Patrol Image," *Police Chief* (August 1992): 55–61.
46. WRIGHTSMAN, *Psychology and the Legal System*, p. 86.
47. Quoted in JEROME SKOLNICK, "A Sketch of the Policeman's Working Personality," in *The Police Community*, ed. Jack Goldsmith and Sharon S. Goldsmith (Pacific Palisades, CA: Palisades Publishers, 1974), p. 106.
48. THOMAS F. ADAMS, "Field Interrogation," *Police* (March–April 1963): 1–8.
49. JONATHAN RUBENSTEIN, "Cop's Rules," in *Police Behavior: A Sociological Perspective*, ed. Richard J. Lundman (New York: Oxford University Press, 1980), pp. 68–78.
50. BRUCE CATTON, "Eyewitness Reports on the Assassination of Abraham Lincoln," in *Criminal Justice: Allies and Adversaries*, ed. John R. Snortum and Ilana Hader (Pacific Palisades, CA: Palisades Publishing, 1978), pp. 155–57.
51. TOM WILKENSON and JOHN CHATTIN-MCNICHOLS, "The Effectiveness of Computer-Assisted Instruction for Police Officers," *Journal of Police Science and Administration* 13 (1985): 230–35.
52. NIEDERHOFFER, *Behind the Shield*, p. 51.
53. DUNHAM and ALPERT, *Critical Issues in Policing*, p. 112.
54. Ibid., p. 111.
55. Ibid., pp. 112–15.
56. ALPERT and DUNHAM, *Policing Urban America*, p. 58.
57. "Field Trainers Have Reports Well in Hand," *Law Enforcement News*, November 15, 2000, p. 5.
58. "Pursuit Simulation Training Is No Ordinary Crash Course," *Law Enforcement News*, November 15, 2000, p. 6.
59. WILLIAM WESTLEY, *Violence and the Police* (Cambridge, MA: MIT Press, 1970), p. 56.
60. ELIZABETH BURBECK and ADRIAN FURNHAM, "Police Officer Selection: A Critical Review of the Literature," *Journal of Police Science and Administration* 13 (1985): 58–69.
61. J. MATARAZZO, B. V. ALLEN, G. SASLOW, and A. N. WIENS, "Characteristics of Successful Policemen and Firemen Applicants," *Journal of Applied Psychology* 48 (1964): 123–33.
62. GEORGE E. HARGRAVE, DEIRDRE HIATT, and TIM W. GAFFNEY, "A Comparison of MMPI and CPI Profiles for Traffic Officers," *Journal of Police Science and Administration* 14 (1986): 250–58.
63. Quoted in SEYMOUR M. LIPSET, "Why Cops Hate Liberals—and Vice Versa," *Atlantic Monthly* 223 (March 1969): 76.
64. NIEDERHOFFER, *Behind the Shield,* p. 140.
65. BRODERICK, *Police in a Time of Change*, pp. 22–116. Adapted from DENNIS NOWICKI, "Twelve Traits of Highly Effective Police Officers," *Law and Order*, October 1999, pp. 45–46.

66. Samuel Walker, *The Police in America: An Introduction*, 2nd ed. (New York: McGraw-Hill, 1992), p. 61.
67. Herman Goldstein, *Policing a Free Society* (Cambridge, MA: Ballinger, 1977), p. 21.
68. Steven M. Cox, *Police: Practices, Perspectives, Problems* (Boston: Allyn and Bacon, 1996), pp. 18–19.
69. Ibid., p. 61.
70. See Albert Reiss, *The Police and the Public* (New Haven: Yale University Press, 1971), p. 96.
71. Jerome H. Skolnick and David H. Bayley, *The New Blue Line: Police Innovation in Six American Cities* (New York: Free Press, 1986), p. 4.
72. Patrick V. Murphy and Thomas Plate, *Commissioner: A View from the Top of American Law Enforcement* (New York: Simon and Schuster, 1977). Also see Samuel Walker, *The Police in America*, pp. 55–56.
73. Cox, *Police*, pp. 18–19.
74. Ibid.
75. James Q. Wilson, *Varieties of Police Behavior* (Cambridge, MA: Harvard University Press, 1968), pp. 140–226.

CHAPTER

4

Organization and Administration

Uneasy lies the head that wears the crown.

—*Shakespeare,* Henry IV

Leadership is like the Abominable Snowman, whose footprints are everywhere but who is nowhere to be seen.

—*Warren Bennis*

Key Terms

bureaucracy
chain of command
communication
Compstat
first-line supervisor
middle manager
Mintzberg model of CEOs
organizational structure
organization
police chief
policies and procedures
rules and regulations
sheriff

Imagine yourself as a police chief or sheriff in San Diego County, California—an area that has embraced community policing (discussed in Chapter 6) since the 1970s and that remains one of the safest in the country. Still, envision yourself confronting such disasters as a gunman's shooting spree at a McDonald's, killing twenty-one people; the suicide of thirty-nine members of a doomsday cult who take a poisonous mixture of applesauce, vodka, and barbiturates; and a school yard shooting in which a fifteen-year-old boy opens fire, killing two students and wounding thirteen other people.[1] Critical incidents of this nature—many of which are related to San Diego County's problems with illegal immigration—would challenge even the most seasoned police chief executive.

This chapter examines this very challenging aspect of policing: its organization and administration. After first looking at organizations and bureaucracies generally, we discuss organizational communication, including that which occurs within police organizations. Next we examine police agencies as organizations, including their structure, command principles, and use of policies and procedures. Then we review the positions of chief of police and sheriff, including their qualifications, selection, and tenure. Following that, we use a management model to better understand the general functions of police administrators in their interpersonal, informational, and decision-maker roles, including a brief illustration of good police administration: the Compstat process in New York City. We will briefly consider the roles and functions of middle managers and examine more thoroughly the complex role of first-line supervisors. Next we address the tenuous historical relationship between police administrators and politicians. A chapter summary, review questions, independent student activities, and related Web sites conclude the chapter.

Later chapters deal with additional police organization and administration issues. For example, disciplinary policies and practices are examined in Chapter 10, and labor relations (which includes unionization and collective bargaining) is discussed in Chapter 12. Also see Chapter 10 for a discussion of police accountability.

Organizations and the Police

What Are Organizations?

Organizations are entities of two or more people who cooperate to accomplish an objective. In that sense, undoubtedly the first organizations were primitive hunting parties. Organization and a high degree of cooperation were required to bring down large animals. Organizations were also used to build pyramids and other monuments.[2] *Organization* can be defined as arranging and utilizing resources of personnel and materiel in such a way as to attain specified objectives.

Every organization is unique. Larry Gaines, Mittie Southerland, and John Angell provided an excellent analogy that helps us understand organizations:

> Organization corresponds to the bones which structure or give form to the body. Imagine that the fingers were a single mass of bone rather than four separate fingers and a thumb made up of bones. The mass of bones could not, because of its structure, play musical instruments, hold a pencil, or grip a baseball bat. A police department's organization is analogous. It must be structured properly if it is to be effective in

> fulfilling its many diverse goals. Organization may not be important in a police department consisting of three officers, but it is extremely important in [larger] cities.[3]

As Gaines, Southerland, and Angell also noted, the development of an organization should be done with careful evaluation, or the agency may become unable to respond efficiently to community needs. For example, the implementation of too many specialized units in a police agency (such as community relations, crime analysis, or media relations units) may leave too few people to do the general grassroots work of the organization. (As a rule of thumb, at least 55 percent of all sworn police personnel should be assigned to patrol.)[4]

Formal organizational structures, which spell out areas of responsibility, lines of communication, and the chain of command, are discussed later in this chapter.

Organizations as Bureaucracies

Organizations can be **bureaucracies**. Large organizations are more complex than smaller ones, with much more specialization, a more hierarchical structure, and a more authoritarian style of command.[5] Bureaucracies share several traits: People perform many different tasks toward a common goal, specialized tasks are placed in separate departments or bureaus with a hierarchical structure and a division of labor between personnel, and there is a clear **chain of command** through which information flows upward and commands flow downward. To ensure consistency and uniformity, there are normally an abundance of written rules for the performance of duties. Career paths up the organization allow employees to progress in an orderly fashion.[6]

Organizational Communication

Definition and Characteristics

Communication is one of the most important dynamics of an organization. Indeed, a major role of today's administrators and other leaders is that of communication. Managers of all types of organizations spend an overwhelming amount of their time engaged in the process of—and coping with problems in—communication.

Today we communicate via electronic mail, Web sites, facsimile machines, video camcorders, cellular telephones, satellite dishes, and other high-tech means. We converse orally, in written letters and memos, through our body language, via television and radio programs, and through newspapers and meetings. Even private thoughts—which take place four times faster than the spoken word—are communication. Every waking hour our minds are full of ideas and thoughts. Psychologists say that nearly one hundred thousand thoughts pass through our minds every day, conveyed by a multitude of media.[7] Communication becomes exceedingly important and sensitive in nature in a police organization because of the nature of the information that is processed by officers—who often see people at their worst and when they are in their most embarrassing and compromising situations. To "communicate" what is known about these kinds of behaviors could be devastating to the parties concerned.

Studies have long shown that communication is the primary problem in administration, however, and lack of communication is the primary complaint of employees about their immediate supervisors.[8] Managers are in the communications business. It has been said that

> of all skills needed to be an effective manager/leader/supervisor, skill in communicating is the most vital. In fact, more than 50 percent of a [criminal justice] manager's time is spent communicating. First-line supervisors usually spend about 15 percent of their time with superiors, 50 percent of their time with subordinates, and 35 percent with other managers and duties. These estimates emphasize the importance of communications in everyday . . . operations.[9]

Several elements constitute the communication process: encoding, transmission, the medium, reception, decoding, and feedback.[10] Following are brief descriptions of these elements:

Encoding: To convey an experience or idea to someone, we translate, or encode, that experience into symbols. We use words or other verbal behaviors and gestures or other nonverbal behaviors to convey the experience or idea.

Transmission: This element involves the translation of the encoded symbols into some behavior that another person can observe. The actual articulation (moving our lips, tongue, and so on) of the symbol into verbal or nonverbal observable behavior is transmission.

Medium: Communication must be conveyed through some channel, or medium. Media for communication may include our sight, hearing, taste, touch, or smell. Some other media are the television, the telephone, paper and pencil, and the radio. The choice of the medium is very important. For example, a message that is tranmitted via a formal letter from the chief executive officer will carry more weight than if the same message is conveyed via a secretary's memo.

Reception: The stimuli, the verbal and nonverbal symbols, reach the senses of the receiver and are conveyed to the brain for interpretation.

Decoding: The individual who receives the stimuli develops some meaning for the verbal and nonverbal symbols and decodes the stimuli. These symbols are translated into some concept or experience of the receiver.

Feedback: When the receiver decodes the transmitted symbols, he or she usually provides some response or feedback to the sender. If somone appears puzzled, we repeat the message or we encode the concept differently and transmit some different symbols to express the same concept. Feedback acts as a guide or steering device and lets us know whether the receiver has interpreted our symbols as we intended.

Communication within Police Organizations

Communication within police organizations may be downward, upward, or horizontal. There are five types of downward communication within such an organization:

Job instruction: Communication relating to the performance of a certain task.

Job rationale: Communication relating a certain task to organizational tasks.

Procedures and practice: Communication about organizational policies, procedures, rules, and regulations.

Feedback: Communication about how an individual performs an assigned task.

Indoctrination: Communication designed to motivate the employee.[11]

Upward communication in a police organization may encounter several obstacles. First, the physical distance between superior and subordinate impedes upward communication. Communication is often difficult and infrequent when superiors are isolated. In large police organizations, the administration may be located in headquarters that are removed from the operations personnel. The complexity of the organization may also cause prolonged delays in communication. For example, if a patrol officer observes a problem that needs to be taken to the highest level, normally this information must first be taken to the sergeant, then to the lieutenant, the captain, the deputy chief or the chief, and so on. At each level, the superiors reflect on the problem, put their own interpretation on it (possibly including how the problem might affect them professionally or even personally), and may even dilute or distort the problem. Thus delays in communication are inherent in a bureaucracy.

Horizontal communication thrives in an organization when formal communication channels are not open.[12] The disadvantage of horizontal communication is that it is much easier and more natural to achieve than vertical communication, and therefore it often replaces vertical channels. Horizontal channels are usually of an informal nature, including the grapevine, which is discussed next. The advantage is that horizontal communication is essential if the subsystems within a police organization are to function in an effective and coordinated manner. Horizontal communication among peers may also provide emotional and social bonds that build morale and feelings of teamwork among employees.

The Grapevine

Something "heard through the grapevine" is a rumor from an anonymous source. The expression "grapevine telegraph" is also sometimes used, referring to the speed with which rumors spread. Rumors are another type of communication, and police agencies certainly have their share of scuttlebutt. Departments even establish rumor control centers during major riots.

Compounding the usual barriers to communication is the fact that policing is a twenty-four-hour, seven-day occupation, so that rumors are easily carried from one shift to the next.

The grapevine's most effective characteristics are that it is fast, it operates mostly at the place of work, and it supplements regular, formal communication. On the positive side, it can be a tool management can use to get a feel for employees' attitudes, to spread useful information, and to help employees vent their frustrations. The grapevine, however, can also carry untruths and be malicious. Without a doubt, the grapevine is a force for administrators to reckon with every day.

Written Communication

Within complex organizations, confidence is generally placed in the written word. It establishes a permanent record, but transmitting information in this way does not necessarily ensure that the message will be clear to the receiver, despite the writer's best efforts. This may be due in large measure to shortcomings with the writer's skills. Nonetheless, police organizations rely heavily on written communication, as evidenced by the proliferation of written directives and reports found in most of these agencies.

In the same vein, written communication is also preferred as a medium for dealing with citizens or groups outside the police agency. This means of communication provides the greatest protection against the growing number of legal actions taken against agencies by activists, citizens, and interest groups. In recent years, e-mail has also proliferated as a communication medium in criminal justice organizations. E-mail can provide an easy-to-use and almost instantaneous communication through a computer—in upward, downward, or horizontal directions. For all its advantages, however, e-mail messages can lack security and be ambiguous not only with respect to the meaning of the content but also with regard to what it represents. Are such messages, in fact, mail that should be given the full weight of an office letter or memo, or should they be treated more as offhand comments?[13]

Barriers to Effective Communication

In addition to the inaccurate nature of the grapevine and the preponderance of poor writing skills, several other potential barriers to effective communication exist. Some people, for example, are not good listeners. Unfortunately, listening is one of the most neglected and the least understood of the communication arts.[14] We allow other things to obstruct our communication, including time, too little or too much information, the tendency to say what we think others want to hear, failure to select the best word, prejudices, and strained sender-receiver relationships.[15] Also, subordinates do not always have the same "big picture" viewpoint that superiors possess and may not communicate well with more fluent and persuasive superiors.

POLICE AGENCIES AS ORGANIZATIONS

Chain of Command

The administration of most police organizations is based on a traditional, pyramidal, quasi-military organizational structure that contains the elements of an organization and a bureaucracy. First, these agencies are organized into a number of specialized units. Figure 4-1 shows the hierarchy of managers within the typical police organization and the inverse relationship between rank and numbers of personnel; in other words, as rank increases, the number of people occupying that rank decreases. Some larger agencies have additional ranks, such as corporal and major, but this can lead to concerns about becoming too top-heavy. The rank hierarchy allows an organization to designate authority and responsibility at each level and to maintain a chain of command.

Administrators (chiefs and assistant chiefs), mid-level managers (captains and lieutenants), and first-line supervisors (sergeants) ensure that these units work together toward a common goal. If each unit worked independently, fragmentation, conflict, and competition would result, subverting the goals and purposes of the entire organization. Police agencies consist of people who interact within the organization and with external groups, and they exist to serve the public.

Police departments are different from most other kinds of organizations for the simple reason that policing is significantly different from most other kinds of work. A special organizational structure has evolved to help carry out the complex responsibilities of policing. The highly decentralized nature and the varying size of American police departments, however, compel police agencies to vary in organization.

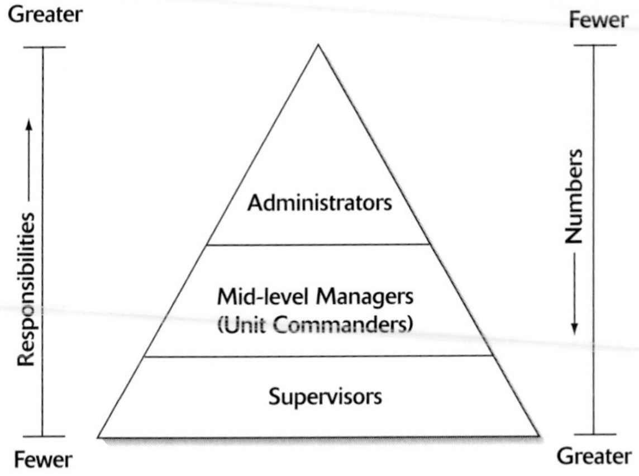

FIGURE 4-1 Hierarchy of managers within the typical police organization.

Source: Larry K. Gaines, Mittie D. Southerland, and John E. Angell, Police Administration *(New York: McGraw-Hill, 1991), p. 11. Used with permission of the McGraw-Hill Companies.*

Organizational Structure

Every police agency, no matter what its size, has an **organizational structure**, which is often prominently displayed for all to see in the agency's facility. Even a community with only a town marshal has an organizational structure, although the structure will be very horizontal, with the marshal performing all of the functions displayed in Figure 4-2, the basic organizational chart for a small agency.[16]

Operations, or line-element, personnel are engaged in active police functions in the field. They may be subdivided into primary and secondary operations elements. The patrol function—often called the backbone of policing—is the primary operational element because of its major responsibility for policing. (The patrol function is examined in Chapter 5.) In most small police agencies, patrol forces are responsible for all operational activities: providing routine patrols, conducting traffic and criminal investigations, making arrests, and functioning as generalists.[17] The investigative and youth functions are the secondary operations elements. (We discuss the investigative function thoroughly in Chapter 7 and the police role with juveniles in Chapter 9.)

The support (or nonline) functions and activities can become quite numerous, especially in a large agency. These functions fall within two broad categories: staff (or administrative) services and auxiliary (or technical) services. The staff services usually involve personnel and include such matters as recruitment, training, promotion, planning and research, community relations, and public information services. Auxiliary services are the kinds of functions that civilians rarely see. They include jail management, property and evidence, crime laboratory services, communications, and records and identification. Many career opportunities exist for those who are interested in police-related work but who cannot or do not want to be a field officer.

Obviously, the larger the agency, the greater the need for specialization and the more vertical the organizational chart will become. With greater specialization comes the need and opportunity for officers to be

FIGURE 4-2 A basic police organizational structure.

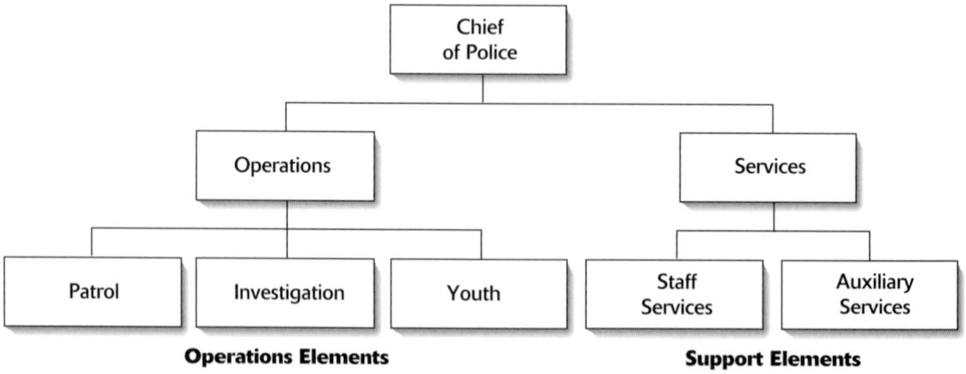

assigned to different tasks, often rotating from one assignment to another after a fixed interval. For example, in a medium-sized department serving a community of one hundred thousand or more, it would be possible for a police officer with ten years of police experience to have been a dog handler, a motorcycle officer, a detective, and a traffic officer while simultaneously holding a slot on the special-weapons or hostage-negotiation team.

The organizational structure of the Portland, Oregon, Police Bureau (PPB) is shown in Figure 4-3. The City of Portland has a population of about 530,000, and the PPB has about thirteen hundred total personnel, a thousand of whom are sworn. The police budget is about $121 million.[18] Some of the boxes shown in the structure are parochial in nature and demand further explanation: DPSST is the Department of Public Safety Standards and Training, to which the PPB loans officers; PPA is the Portland Police Association, the bureau's collective bargaining agent; the Management Services Division manages the bureau's facilities, liability, and loss control; the Sunshine Division includes personnel who work to provide food, clothing, and toys to needy families; the HAP liaisons and Safety Action Team include officers assigned to the Housing Authority of Portland; the Douglas and Parkrose liaisons are officers working in school districts; the APP liaison is a downtown officer position funded by a private association of businesses; the Public Utility Commission has grant-funded positions for conducting traffic enforcement along interstate corridors; ROCN is the Regional Organized Crime and Narcotics task force; and Womenstrength is a program to teach women self-defense tactics.[19]

This organizational structure is designed to fulfill five functions: (1) It apportions the workload among members and units according to a logical plan; (2) it ensures that lines of authority and responsibility are as definite and direct as possible; (3) it specifies a unity of command throughout, so there is no question about which orders should be followed; (4) it places responsibility and authority, and if responsibility is delegated, the delegator is held responsible; and (5) it coordinates the efforts of members so that all will work harmoniously to accomplish the mission.[20] In sum, this structure establishes the chain of command and determines lines of communication and responsibility.

In addition to these generally well-known and visible areas of specialization, there are other lesser known areas of policing, such as community crime prevention, child abuse, drug education, and missing children units.[21]

Unity of Command and Span of Control

A related principle is unity of command, an organizational principle dictating that every officer should report to one and only one superior (following the chain of command) until that superior officer is relieved. Ambiguity about authority can and does occur in police organizations—who should handle calls, who is in charge at a crime scene, and so on. Nevertheless, the unity-of-command principle ensures that multiple and/or

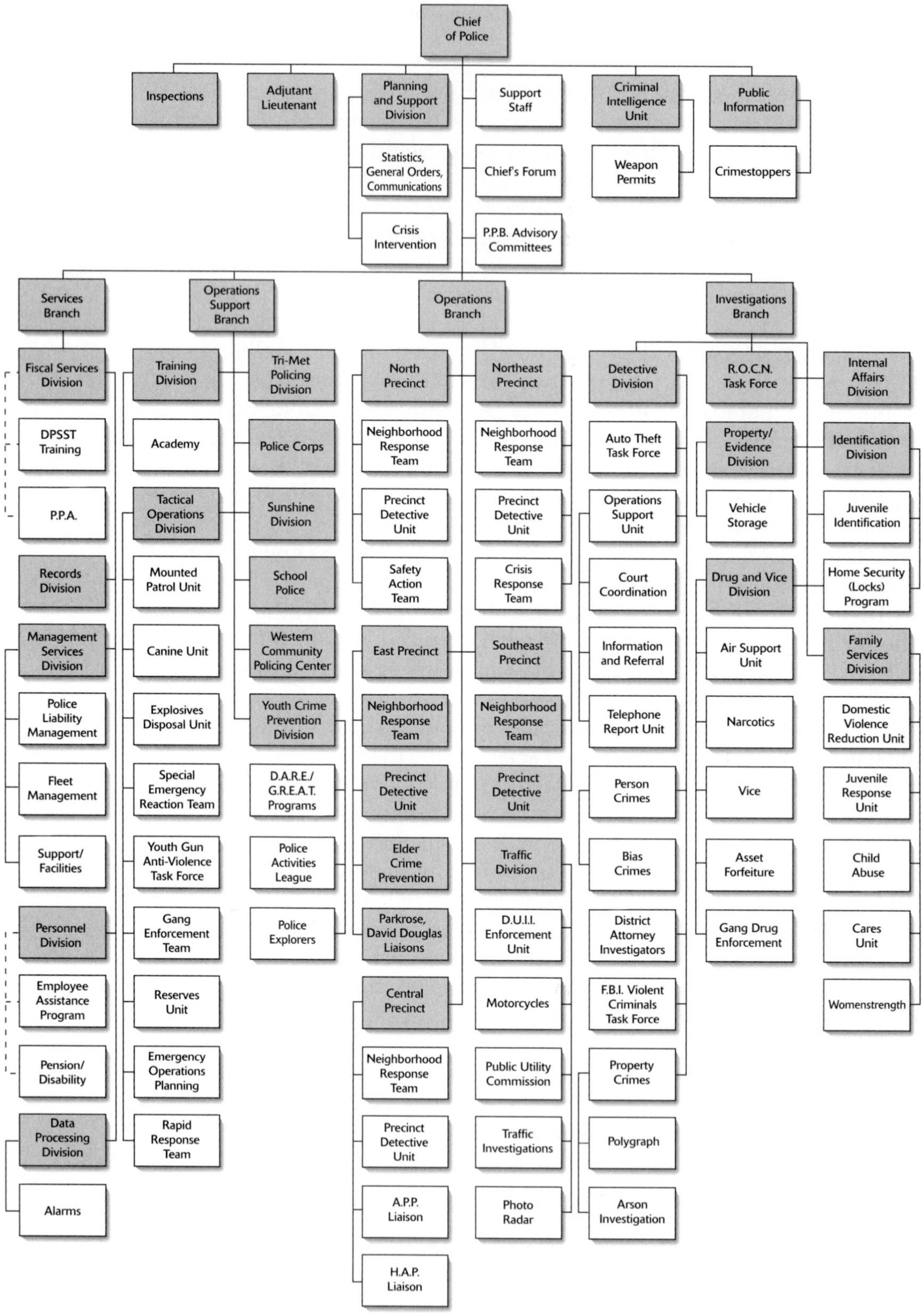

FIGURE 4-3 Organizational structure of the Portland, Oregon, Police Department.

Courtesy of the Portland, Oregon, Police Department

conflicting orders are not issued to the same officers by several supervisors. It is important that all officers know and follow the chain of command at critical incidents.

The term *span of control* refers to the number of subordinates one individual can effectively supervise. The limit is small; it is normally three to five at the top level of the organization and is often broader at the lower levels.[22] The tendency in modern police operations is to have supervisors spread too thinly.

Organizational Policies and Procedures

It has been said that a well-written policy and procedure manual serves as the foundation of a professional law enforcement agency.[23] In policing, **policies and procedures** and **rules and regulations** are also important for defining role expectations for officers. Police leaders rely on these directives to guide officers' behavior and performance. Because police agencies are intended to be service oriented in nature, they must work within well-defined, specific guidelines designed to ensure that all officers conform consistently to behavior that will enhance public protection.[24]

This tendency for organizations to promulgate rules, policies, and procedures has been caused by three contemporary developments. First is the requirement for administrative due process in employee disciplinary matters, encouraged by federal court rulings, police officer bill of rights legislation, and labor contracts. Another development is the threat of civil litigation. Lawsuits against local governments and their criminal justice agencies and administrators have become commonplace; written guidelines by law enforcement agency prohibiting certain acts provide a hedge against successful civil litigation.[25] Finally, a third stimulus is the trend toward the accreditation of police agencies. Agencies that are either pursuing accreditation or that have become accredited must follow policies and practice procedures.[26]

Policies are quite general and serve basically as guides to thinking rather than action. Policies reflect the purpose and philosophy of the organization and help interpret them for the officers. An example of a policy might be that everyone found to be driving while under the influence of drugs or alcohol must be arrested or that all juveniles who are to be detained must be taken to a specified facility.

Procedures are more detailed than policies and provide the preferred methods for handling matters pertaining to investigation, patrol, booking, radio procedures, filing reports, roll call, use of force, arrest, sick leave, evidence handling, promotion, and many other elements of the job. Most police agencies are awash in procedures. Methods for accomplishing certain tasks are also found in myriad city or county administrative regulations and police agency general orders (such as when a new federal court decision relating to search and seizure is announced or a new state or local law regarding the use of force takes effect).

Rules and regulations are specific guidelines that leave little or no latitude for individual discretion. Some examples are requirements that police officers not smoke in public, that they check the operation of their vehicle and equipment before going on patrol, that they not consume alcoholic beverages within a specified number of hours before going on duty, or that they arrive in court or at roll call early. Rules and regulations are not always popular, especially if they are perceived as unfair or unrelated to the job. Nonetheless, it is the supervisor's responsibility to ensure that officers perform these tasks with the same degree of professional demeanor as they do other job duties.

Contemporary Police Chiefs and Sheriffs

Having analyzed police organizations, we now look at the two primary chief executive officers: the police chief (also known as the police superintendent, commissioner, or director) and the county sheriff. After looking at the qualifications for and functions of these positions, we consider their roles in more detail with the Mintzberg model of chief executive officers.

The chief or sheriff of a ten-person agency faces many of the same problems and expectations as his or her big-city counterpart. The difference between managing large and small departments is a matter of scale. Executives of large departments face a larger volume of many of the same problems that executives of small departments face. The leader of a small department must not only deal with all these managerial concerns, but in many cases must also perform the duties of a working officer.

Furthermore, the police manager's style must be flexible. Management style is always contingent on the situation and the people being managed.[27] The police manager would behave one way at the scene of a hostage situation and another way at the scene of a shoplifting. A less experienced employee will require a more authoritarian style of management than a more experienced employee.

Police Chief

Qualifications, Selection, and Tenure. The required qualifications for the position of **police chief** vary widely, depending on the size of the agency and the region of the country. Smaller agencies, especially those in rural areas, may not have any minimum educational requirement for the job. Large agencies, on the other hand, may require college education plus several years of progressively responsible police management experience.[28]

Although it is certainly cheaper to select a police chief from within the organization than to recruit an outsider, the value of doing so is open to debate. There are obvious advantages and disadvantages to both practices. One study of police chiefs promoted from within and hired from outside in the West found significant differences in only one area: educational attainment. The outsiders were more highly educated, but the two groups did not differ in other areas, including background, attitudes, salary, tenure in current position or policing, or size of agency, community, or current budget.[29] Some states have made it nearly impossible for nonresidents to be hired as police chiefs. For example, California has mandated that the chief be a graduate of its full Peace Officers Standards and Training (POST) academy; New Jersey and New York also encourage "homegrown" chiefs.[30]

A recent survey by the Police Executive Research Forum of 358 police chiefs in larger jurisdictions (fifty thousand or more residents) found that these chiefs were more educated than ever before (87 percent held a bachelor's degree and 47 percent had a master's degree) and were more likely to have been chosen from outside the agencies they head. Even so, most chiefs spent less than five years in the position.[31]

To obtain the most capable people for executive positions in policing—and to avoid personnel, liability, and other kinds of problems that can arise from poor personnel choices—many agencies have adopted the assessment center method, an elaborate yet efficacious means of hiring and promoting personnel. Although more costly and time-consuming than conventional testing methods (for example, candidates' resumes are examined and oral interviews are held), the assessment center method is well worth the extra investment. Money invested at the early stages of hiring or promotion can save untold dollars and problems for many years to come. The process may include interviews; psychological tests; "in-basket" exercises; management tasks; group discussions; simulations of interviews with subordinates, the public, and the news media; fact-finding exercises; oral presentation exercises; and written communications exercises.[32]

Individual and group role-playing provides a hands-on atmosphere during the selection process. For example, candidates may be required to perform in simulated police-community problems (such as having candidates conduct a "meeting" to hear concerns of local minority groups), react to a major incident (such as having candidates explain what they will do and in what order in a simulated shooting or riot situation), hold a news briefing, or participate in other such exercises. They may be given an "in-basket" situation in which they take the role of the new chief or captain who receives an abundance of paperwork, policies, and problems to be prioritized and dealt with in a prescribed amount of time. Writing abilities may also be evaluated by having candidates provide specific written products, such as a policy or a procedure.

During each exercise, several assessors analyze the candidate's behavior and perform some type of evaluation. When the assessment center process ends, they submit their individual rating information to the person making the hiring or promotional decision. Typically selected because they have held the position for which candidates are now vying, assessors must not only know the types of problems and duties incumbent in the position but also should be keen observers of human behavior.

Job security for police chiefs ranges from full civil service protection in a small percentage of agencies to appointment and removal at the discretion of the mayor or city manager. There is a growing trend for a fixed term of office, such as a four- or five-year contract. Traditionally, however, the tenure of police chiefs has been short. A federal study in the mid-1970s found that the average term in office by chiefs of police was 5.4 years.[33] Another study by the Police Executive Research Forum (PERF) a decade later found the average to be practically unchanged: 5.5 years. That figure has not changed in more recent times.[34] Those who are appointed from within the agency tend to have longer tenure than those appointed from outside. This lack of job tenure has several negative consequences, including the difficulty of long-range planning, the possible negative effect of frequently having new policies and administrative styles, the inability of the short-term chief to develop a political power base and local influence, and the time and expense involved in hiring a new chief.

The Sheriff

Contemporary Nature and Functions. The stereotypical image of the county **sheriff**, derived from old movies like *Smokey and the Bandit* and television programs like *The Dukes of Hazzard*, is often that of a corrupt character with a Southern drawl, wearing a Stetson, sunglasses, and a five-point star. Although we will see later that the sheriff's office, being largely elective, has the potential for problems, this is an overly simplistic and negative image of the American sheriff.

As discussed in Chapter 1, the position of sheriff has a long tradition. Sheriffs today tend to be elected; thus most candidates are aligned with a political party, and it is possible that the only qualification a person brings to the office is the ability to get votes.

In some areas of the country, the sheriff's term of office is limited to two years, and the sheriff is prohibited from serving successive terms (thus the office is sometimes "rotated" between the sheriff and the undersheriff). In most counties, however, the sheriff has a four-year term and can be reelected. Sheriffs enjoy no guarantee of tenure in office, although a federal study found that sheriffs (who average 6.7 years in office) had longer tenure in office than police chiefs.[35] The politicization of the office of sheriff can obviously result in high turnover rates of personnel who do not have civil service protection as well as a lack of long-range (strategic) planning.

Also, largely due to the political nature of the office, sheriffs tend to be older, are less likely to have been promoted through the ranks of the agency, have less specialized training, and are less likely to be college graduates compared to police chiefs. Research has also found that sheriffs in small agencies have more difficulty with organizational problems (field activities and budget management, for example), whereas sheriffs in large agencies find dealing with local officials and planning and evaluation to be more troublesome.

Because of the diversity of sheriff's offices throughout the country, it is difficult to describe a "typical" sheriff's department; those offices run the gamut from the traditional, highly political, limited-service office to the modern, fairly nonpolitical, full-service police organization.[36] It is possible, however, to list functions commonly associated with the sheriff's office:

- Maintaining and operating the county correctional institutions
- Serving civil processes (protective orders, liens, evictions, garnishments, and attachments) and other civil duties, such as extradition and transportation of prisoners
- Collecting certain taxes and conducting real estate sales (usually for nonpayment of taxes) for the county
- Performing routine order-maintenance duties by enforcing state statutes and county ordinances, arresting offenders, and performing traffic and criminal investigations
- Serving as bailiff of the courts

Other general duties vary from one region to another.

Regional Role Differences. The status and operations of sheriff's offices have been studied in four regions of the country: the East, the South, the Midwest, and the West.[37] In most parts of the East, the sheriff has lost all law enforcement authority and has been reduced to functions such as court security and civil process serving. Even the traditional jail management function is declining with the increasing use of independent jail management boards. The eastern sheriff's office is often quite small and has a tight budget. The office has become increasingly political, and legislation is regularly introduced to abolish the office altogether.

In the South, the sheriff continues to be a strong law enforcement figure; larger agencies provide a full range of police services and have eliminated the need for state police forces. These sheriffs have maintained enough political clout to survive challenges to their existence and authority and have developed strong formal lobbying efforts and sheriff's associations. The political power of southern sheriffs has led to some abuse and corruption; nonetheless, these sheriff's offices tend to be efficient, effective, and secure, just like the historical model described in Chapter 1.

Midwestern sheriff's offices can be categorized into two types: one that is similar to the eastern model, and the other that is similar to the southern. Vast geographic distances, relatively low population density, and a general lack of demand for law enforcement services have created a unique situation. In many areas, the sheriff's staff is small, with little specialization. These sheriffs provide services to unincorporated areas of the county, operate jails, and generally provide all the civil processes found in the East. Midwestern sheriffs tend to have more professional status and more basic qualifications and receive a somewhat higher salary than those in the other two regions. The office is generally secure.

The western sheriff still carries many of the vestiges of the Wild West, with vast, wide-open territories of responsibility. In many respects, these sheriffs resemble the midwestern sheriffs, remaining as the chief law enforcement officer in the county.

THE CHIEF EXECUTIVE OFFICER: A MODEL

Applying the Mintzberg Model of CEOs

What do contemporary police executives really do? Ronald Lynch described in simple terms their primary tasks:

> They listen, talk, write, confer, think, decide—about men, money, materials, methods, facilities—in order to plan, organize, direct, coordinate, and control their research service, production, public relations, employee relations, and all other activities so that they may more effectively serve the citizens to whom they are responsible.[38]

A police executive actually has many roles. Some chief executive officers (CEOs) openly endorse and subscribe to the philosophy of Henry Mintzberg, who described a set of behaviors and tasks of CEOs in any organization.[39] Following is an overview of the roles of the police agency CEO—that is, the chief of police or sheriff—using the **Mintzberg model** and its interpersonal, informational, and decision-maker roles as an analytic framework.

The Interpersonal Role

First we will consider the interpersonal role, which includes figurehead, leadership, and liaison duties. As a figurehead, the CEO performs various ceremonial functions. Examples include riding in parades and attending other civic events; speaking before school and university classes and civic organizations; meeting with visiting officials and dignitaries; attending academy graduation and swearing-in ceremonies and some weddings and funerals; and visiting injured officers in the hospital. Like the mayor who cuts ribbons and kisses babies, the CEO performs these duties simply because of his or her position within the organization; the duties come with being a figurehead. While police chiefs and sheriffs cannot realistically be expected to attend every committee meeting, speaking engagement, and other event to which they are invited, they are obligated from a professional standpoint to attend as many as they can.

The leadership function requires the CEO to motivate and coordinate workers while resolving different goals and needs within the department and the community. A chief or sheriff may have to urge the governing board to enact a code or ordinance that, whether popular or not, is in the best interest of the jurisdiction. For example, a police chief recently led a drive to pass an ordinance that prohibited parking by university students in residential neighborhoods surrounding the campus. This was a highly unpopular undertaking, but the chief pursued it because of the hardships suffered by the area residents. CEOs also provide leadership in such matters as bond issues (to raise money for more officers or new buildings) and should advise the governing body on the effects of proposed ordinances.

The role as liaison is performed when the CEO of a police organization interacts with other organizations and coordinates work flows. It is not uncommon for police executives from one geographic area—the police chief, the sheriff, the ranking officer of the local highway patrol office, the district attorney, the campus police chief, and so forth—to meet informally each month to discuss common problems and strategies. Also, the chief executives serve as liaisons between their agencies and others in forming regional police councils, narcotics units, crime labs, dispatching centers, and so forth. They also meet with representatives of the courts, the juvenile system, and other criminal justice agencies.

The Informational Role

The second major role of CEOs under the Mintzberg model is the informational role. This role involves the CEO in monitoring/inspecting and disseminating information and acting as spokesperson. In the monitoring/inspecting function, the CEO constantly looks at the workings of the department to ensure that things are operating smoothly (or as smoothly as a police agency can be expected to run). This function is often referred to as "roaming the ship," and many CEOs who have isolated themselves from their personnel and from the daily operations of the agency can speak from sad experience of the need to be alert and to create a presence. Many police executives use daily staff meetings to discuss any information about the past twenty-four hours that might affect the department.

The dissemination tasks involve getting information to members of the department. This may include memorandums, special orders, general orders, and policies. The spokesperson function is related, but it is more focused on getting information to the news media. This is another very difficult task for the chief executive; news organizations are in a competitive field in which scoops and deadlines and the public's right to know are omnipotent. Still, the media must understand those occasions when a criminal investigation can be seriously affected by premature or overblown coverage. The police executive would do well to remember the power of the pen and not alienate the media; a wise person once said, "Never argue with someone who buys his ink by the barrel."

The Decision-Maker Role

Finally, as a decision maker, the CEO of a police organization serves as an entrepreneur, a disturbance handler, a resource allocator, and a negotiator. As entrepreneur, the CEO must sell ideas to the governing board or the department. Ideas might include new computers or a new communications system, a policing strategy (such as community-oriented policing and problem solving), or different work methods, all of which are intended to improve the organization. Sometimes there is a blending of roles, as when several police executives band together (functioning as liaisons) and go to the state attorney general and the legislature to lobby (in an entrepreneurial capacity) for new crime-fighting laws.

As a disturbance handler, the executive's tasks range from the minor (perhaps resolving trivial disputes between staff members) to the major (such as handling riots or muggings in a local park or cleaning up the city's downtown). Sometimes the intradepartmental disputes can reach major proportions; for example, if the patrol commander tells the street officers to arrest more public drunks, it might create a severe strain on the jail division commander's resources, causing enmity between the two commanders and forcing the chief executive to intervene.

As a resource allocator, the CEO must be able to say no to subordinates. However, subordinates should not be faulted for trying to obtain more resources or for trying to improve their unit as best they can. The CEO must have a clear idea of the budget and what the priorities are and must listen to citizen complaints and act accordingly. For example, ongoing complaints of motorists speeding in a specific area will result in a shifting of patrol resources to that area or neighborhood.

As a negotiator, the police manager resolves employee grievances and sits as a member of the negotiating team for labor relations. A survey by the Police Executive Research Forum found that seven out of ten municipal police departments with more than 75 employees have some form of union representation.[40]

Collective bargaining puts the CEO in a difficult position. As a member of management, the CEO is often compelled to argue against salaries and benefits that would assist the rank and file. As mentioned earlier, however, as long as a limited supply of funds is available to the jurisdiction, managers will have to draw the line at some point and say no to subordinates. Again, the collective-bargaining unit and individual officers cannot be faulted for trying to improve salaries, benefits, and working conditions, but sometimes these associations go outside the boundary of reasonableness and reach an impasse or deadlock in contract negotiations with management. These situations can become uncomfortable and even disastrous, leading to work stoppages, work speedups, work slowdowns, or other such tactics (discussed further in Chapter 12).

An Example of Mintzberg in Action: NYPD's Compstat

New York City's **Compstat** process is a relatively new approach to crime analysis and prevention that employs several aspects of the Mintzberg model for chief executive officers—including the interpersonal, informational, and decision-maker roles and several of their subcategories.

Because of the massive size and bureaucracy of the New York Police Department (NYPD), New York City is probably the last city in which one would expect to find a major innovation in police administration and -operations—one that has been described as having the "potential to become the dominant mode of policing in America."[41] But that situation changed with the election of Mayor Rudolph Giuliani in November 1993 and his appointment of Police Commissioner William Bratton in January 1994.

Before 1993, the city's daily crime statistics were almost useless for crime analysis: At least two months' time was required for commanders to even obtain the figures. Meanwhile, crime was at a very high level, and the NYPD, by its own admission, had gotten out of the habit of being held accountable for the crime problem. Bratton established three clear-cut goals for the NYPD: Reduce crime significantly, reduce the fear of crime, and work on improving the quality of life.[42] What quickly evolved in the NYPD was a computer file to compare statistics—hence the acronym *Compstat*.

Computerization changed everything in the NYPD, enabling the organization to change from being reactive to being proactive and goal specific. A four-step process became the essence of Compstat: collecting information in a timely and accurate manner, using effective tactics to respond to problems, deploying personnel and resources rapidly, and following up and assessing relentlessly. With these four steps, Compstat enables the NYPD to pinpoint and analyze crime patterns almost instantly and to respond in the most appropriate manner. A side benefit is that with Compstat, the organization is able to identify emerging leaders from deep within the ranks.[43]

Compstat is best known for its semi-weekly, high-stress 7:00 A.M. brainstorming sessions at police headquarters, where field commanders are grilled about crime in their areas. The results have been impressive: From 1993 to 1996, New York City experienced the most dramatic decline in crime in the nation. As an example, according to Federal Bureau of Information statistics, New York accounted for 61 percent of the nationwide decline in felonies during the first six months of 1995. The most unanticipated result of Compstat was that the decline in crime occurred in every police precinct in the city, debunking the theory that police can only displace crime from one area to another.[44] Because of its successes, by late 1996, the National Institute of Justice was attempting to replicate Compstat in two other jurisdictions.

According to one observer, "Compstat and the re-engineered NYPD are pointing the way to a new perspective on community policing, and demonstrating that a community orientation is not incompatible with aggressive, focused law enforcement."[45]

PRACTITIONER'S PERSPECTIVE

Police Ingenuity and Entrepreneurship

DENNIS D. RICHARDS

Dennis D. Richards served as deputy, sergeant, and lieutenant with the Los Angeles County Sheriff's Office (LACSO) from 1965 to 1986. He holds an associate's degree in police science from Pierre County Community College. He was a helicopter pilot with the LACSO, which was the first agency to deploy helicopters for regular patrol. As a member of the LACSO administrative division, he was also head of the employee relations division (the sheriff's department was among the first to have a full-time unit as liaison between the administration and the labor union).

The thirty-odd miles of California shore loosely known as Malibu is arguably one of the most famous stretches of beach in the world. In the early 1970s, it was a composite of public recreation and expensive private homes that coexisted in a fragile and uneasy truce. The Malibu coast was also a part of the more than 240 square miles policed by the Malibu Station of the Los Angeles County Sheriff's Department. The public beaches generated great seasonal surges of transient population. Predictably, the police problems of the nearby expensive real estate were exacerbated by the summer influx. Patrol officers, driving conventional vehicles, made what reasonable observations they could from highways or parking lots and ventured onto the sand only in response to a call for service. Although it was generally agreed there was a need for increased police presence on the beach side, the question remained how best to provide that presence. I was asked to study the feasibility of routine beach patrol at Malibu and, if such an operation was practicable, to suggest a proposal.

The first patrol vehicle under consideration was a three-wheel all-terrain vehicle known as an ATC. The ATC, equipped with soft, oversized tires, was light and maneuverable enough to travel over both dry sand and the wet areas where tides rendered previous patrol activities marginal. However, it was not enough

DLE MANAGERS: CAPTAINS AND LIEUTENANTS

Few police administration books discuss the **middle managers** of a police department: captains and lieutenants. This is unfortunate because they are too numerous and too powerful within police organizations to ignore. Opinions vary about these mid-management personnel, however, as will be seen later.

Normally, captains and lieutenants are commissioned officers, with the position of captain second in rank to the executive managers. Captains have authority over all officers of the agency below the chief or sheriff and are responsible only to them. Lieutenants are in charge of sergeants and all officers and report to captains. Captains and lieutenants may perform the following functions:[46]

- Inspecting assigned operations
- Reviewing and making recommendations on reports
- Helping to develop plans

that the vehicle be practicable for sand navigation. The ATC would be unable to transport prisoners, underpowered, unable to carry extra equipment in a secure manner, and would need significant renovation to carry and power a police radio.

We launched a search for a better patrol vehicle. Previous experiments with traditional four-wheel drive vehicles had been less than inspiring. Visibility of objects on the ground was poor, making it somewhat tricky for an officer to wend his way through a crowd of sunbathers without running over someone's arm or leg. The big four-wheelers were comparatively heavy and tended to bog down. Moreover, the beachgoers found these vehicles offensive because of their military, tanklike appearance. I then discovered that the lifeguards were experimenting with a dune buggy and were extremely enthusiastic regarding the buggy's performance. I tested it and was convinced that a dune buggy was the best mode of patrol, but the department's executives still had to be convinced of its efficacy.

I borrowed the lifeguard buggy, positioned it on a scenic stretch of beach, and photographed it with a uniformed deputy standing on either side. A department staff artist used this photograph as a basis for conceptual drawings, changing the bright lifeguard yellow to black and white and overlaying the department's radio car logo on the buggy's blunt shovel nose. The artist also attached a traditional light bar and siren to the crash bar and, in various drawings, dressed the deputies in standard patrol uniform and presented them in a softer image wearing shorts and baseball caps.

Armed with these visual aids, we made our presentation. The concept captured the administration's imagination, and the dune buggy beach patrol was approved. The patrol was launched with considerable attention from the media. The sheriff personally chauffeured individual members of the press along Malibu Beach in a patrol buggy, and a grand time was had by all. More importantly, the stubby little cars were an instant hit with the public. Even the most die-hard libertarians found them more amusing than threatening. Beachgoers frequently flagged them down to be photographed with the vehicle. The positive public relations achieved by this operation was one of its most valuable aspects.

- Preparing work schedules
- Overseeing records and equipment
- Overseeing recovered or confiscated property
- Enforcing all laws and orders

Too often, middle managers become glorified paper pushers, especially in the present climate of myriad reports, budgets, grants, and so on. Police agencies should take a hard look at what managerial services are essential and whether lieutenants are needed to perform such services. Recently, some communities, such as Kansas City, Missouri, eliminated the rank of lieutenant, finding that this move had no negative consequences and some positive effects.[47]

Obviously, when a multilayered bureaucracy is created, a feudal kingdom and several fiefdoms will occupy the building. As Richard Holden observed, however, "If feudalism was so practical, it would not have died out in the Middle Ages."[48] It is important to remember that the two crucial elements to organizational effectiveness are top administrators and operational personnel. Middle management can pose a threat to the agency by acting as a barrier between these two primary elements. As has often been noted, the Roman Catholic Church serves many millions and employs many thousands of people with only five levels in the hierarchy.[49] Research has shown an inverse relationship between the size of the hierarchy in an organization and its effectiveness.[50] Normally, the closer the administrator is to the operations, the more effective the agency.

The First-Line Supervisor

At some point during the career of a patrol officer who has acquired the minimum years of experience, he or she has the opportunity to test for promotion to **first-line supervisor**, or sergeant. Competition for this position is quite keen in most departments. To compete well, officers are often advised to rotate into different agency assignments to gain exposure to a variety of police functions and supervisors before testing for the sergeant's position. The promotional system, then, favors not only those officers who are skilled at test taking but also those who have experience outside the patrol division.[51]

The supervisor's role, put simply, is to get his or her subordinates to do their very best. This task involves a host of activities, including communicating, motivating, mediating, mentoring, leading, team building, training, developing, appraising, counseling, and disciplining. As a result, no other rank in the police hierarchy exerts more direct influence over the working environment, morale, and performance of employees.

Getting that first promotion.

(Courtesy Sparks, Nevada, Police Department)

Adding to the complexity of the supervisor's role is the fact that the supervisor is generally in his or her first leadership position. A new supervisor must learn how to exercise command and be responsible for the behavior of several other employees. Long-standing relationships are put under stress when one party suddenly has official authority over former equals. Expectations of leniency or preferential treatment may have to be dealt with.

The supervisor is caught in the middle, working with rank-and-file employees—labor—on the one hand and middle or upper management on the other. While it is management's job to squeeze as much productivity out of workers as possible, labor's motivation often seems to be to avoid work as much as possible. Supervisors find themselves right in the middle of this contest.

Ten Tasks

For all of these reasons, the first-line supervisor has one of the most complex roles in the organization. If the supervisor fails to make sure that employees perform correctly, the unit will not be very successful, causing difficulties for mid-level managers and administrators. Ten tasks are most important for sergeants; they are listed in order of importance:[52]

1. Supervising subordinate officers in the performance of their duties (including such tasks as maintaining inventory of equipment, training subordinates, preparing monthly activity reports, scheduling vacation leave)
2. Disseminating information to subordinates
3. Ensuring that general and special orders are followed
4. Observing subordinates in handling calls and other duties (including securing major crime scenes)
5. Reviewing and approving various departmental reports
6. Listening to problems voiced by officers
7. Answering backup calls
8. Keeping superiors apprised of ongoing situations
9. Providing direct supervision on potential high-risk calls or situations
10. Interpreting policies and informing subordinates

Types of Supervisors

Four distinct types of first-line supervisors have been identified: traditional, innovative, supportive, and active.[53] These types of supervisors can be found in any police department, depending on the individual's experiences on the job, his or her training, and the department's organizational climate.

The traditional supervisor is law enforcement oriented. These supervisors expect their subordinates to produce high levels of measurable

EXHIBIT 4-1

Good, Better, Best: What Makes Some Sergeants a Cut above the Rest?

What is it that separates an excellent sergeant from one who is merely good? The ability to devise creative solutions that take into account life's moral ambiguities is a key ingredient, and a more prudent use of sick leave doesn't hurt.

Those were the surprising findings of a National Institute of Justice study that attempted to tease out those differences by examining the work habits and backgrounds of a small sample of Baltimore's first-line supervisors.

In the report, "Identifying Characteristics of Exemplary Baltimore Police Department First Line Supervisors," researchers from Johns Hopkins University and the College of Notre Dame of Maryland used a focus group of commanders, police officers and supervisors to develop a set of characteristics that could be used by peers to identify sergeants they considered exemplary, and those who were less so.

Participants in the study were asked to think about supervisors they had known since 1985 and name the one they felt best met the criteria for leadership identified by a focus group of commanders, officers and sergeants. They were also asked to choose a second-best, and explain what it was that placed those supervisors in the second ranking.

Among the traits identified as vital by the focus group were character and integrity; knowledge of the job; management skills; communication skills; interpersonal skills; ability to develop entry-level officers; problem-solving and critical thinking skills; effectiveness as role model and as disciplinarian, and the ability to be proactive.

In all, 24 exemplary sergeants were nominated, and 26 of their less-effective peers, who were used as controls. Of 38 variables, the two groups rated the same on 14 of them, including parents with strong work ethics; education levels; achievement and power as motivating factors, and "tough mindedness" as a personality characteristic.

Where the groups differed significantly, however, was on tests given by researchers which rated moral reasoning; their tendency to select friends, relatives and authority figures in their lives as examples of moral excellence, as compared to the well-known historical or religious figures selected by the controls, and their use of non-line of duty sick days.

Those three factors were cited by the study as being the most distinguishing characteristics between the two groups.

"The most important difference was the moral reasoning," said Phyllis P. McDonald, director of research for Johns Hopkins University's School of Professional Studies in Business and Education, who was the NIJ program manager for the study. "They could solve police-related moral issues far better than their peers. They came up with more solutions, they were more complete and they were just better quality solutions."...

"They are better at problem solving and their sick leave pattern is different because they may have a higher investment in the job," she told *Law Enforcement News*...

"It's the kind of person who thinks about it 24-hours a day, and gathers information, interrelates with subordinates, that kind of thing," she said.

Another factor that separated the exemplary from the less so was the confidence that their supervisors had in them. When lieutenants were asked whom they would choose in a crisis situation, McDonald said, most often it was the exemplary sergeant.

"We know they're better at decision-making, organizing, handling issues, somehow," she said. "Those three areas are significant."

Source: "Good, Better, Best: What Makes Some Sergeants a Cut above the Rest?" *Law Enforcement News,* March 15/31, 2003, pp. 1, 6. John Jay College of Criminal Justice, CUNY, 555 West 57th St., New York, NY 10019.

activities, such as traffic citations and arrests, to respond efficiently to calls for service, and to accurately complete reports and other paperwork. Traditional supervisors provide officers with a substantial amount of instruction and oversight, and they tend to place greater emphasis on punishment than rewards. They see their primary role as controlling subordinates, and they often have morale and motivational problems with them.

The *innovative* supervisor is most closely associated with community policing. Innovative supervisors may be the opposite of traditional supervisors. They do not generally place a great deal of emphasis on citations or arrests, and they depend more on developing relationships with subordinates than on using power to control or motivate them. Innovative supervisors usually are good mentors, tending to coach rather than order. They are open to new ideas and innovations. Their ultimate goal is to develop officers so that they can solve problems and have good relations with citizens.

The third type of supervisor is the *supportive* supervisor, who, like the innovative supervisor, is concerned with developing good relations with subordinates. The primary difference is that the supportive supervisor is concerned with protecting officers from what they view as unfair management practices, seeing themselves as a buffer between management and officers. They attempt to develop strong work teams and motivate officers by inspiring them. Their shortcoming is that they tend to see themselves as "one of the troops" and sometimes fail to emphasize departmental goals and responsibilities.

The final category of supervisor is the *active* supervisor. These supervisors tend to be active in the field. They sometimes act like police officers, but with stripes or rank (not afraid to "get their hands dirty"), and they often become involved with field situations rather than supervising them. They are able to develop good relations with subordinates because they are perceived as being hardworking and competent. Their shortcoming is that by being overly involved in some field situations, they may not give their subordinates the opportunity to develop.

Overall, the most effective form of supervision may be the active supervisor. Subordinates working for active supervisors perform better in a number of areas, including problem solving and community policing. Active supervisors are able to develop a more productive work unit because they lead by example.

Police and Politics

Another long-standing problem permeating police administration is that of political influence, which ranges from major policy and budgetary decisions to the overzealous city manager or city council member who appears unexpectedly at night to "help" officers at a burglary in progress and barely avoids being shot.

Political Exploitation of the Police

Politics is the art or science of government. One definition of policing is very similar to that of politics: "the internal control and regulation of a political unit [such as a state or community] through exercise of governmental powers."[54] Both words derive from the Greek terms for "citizen" and "citizenship," and *police* also comes from the Greek work for "city": *polis*.

Historically, police departments in the United States have been political bodies, extensions of the municipal political authority.[55] Because of the close relationship between police departments and the political leadership of the community, political power has often been abused. From the beginning of the twentieth century, when the journalist Lincoln Steffens exposed corruption in American cities, to more recent times, when police scandals have rocked departments in New York City, Chicago, and Miami, politics has been shown to be entwined in the relationships that often bind criminals and police officers. Partisan politics has often been the cause of police corruption.[56]

Even in the nineteenth century, police forces were not autonomous; political figures outside the departments began to make key decisions regarding promotions, assignments, and disciplinary matters. For their own part, police officers often sought promotions, soft jobs, or particular beats. Some officers wanted a beat close to their homes. Corrupt officers wanted a beat with many saloons and brothels to raise their income. In the late nineteenth century, promotion depended on political influence and money, and some officers had to borrow the means for career advancement. Impartial police administration was the last thing politicians in large cities wanted. Their interests were best served by a policing system that was easily manipulated.[57]

Police Executive Relations and Expectations

The chief of police is generally considered to be one of the most influential and prestigious people in local government. However, much of the power of the office has eroded because of the high attrition rate, the increased power of local personnel departments, and the strong influence of police unions. Furthermore, mayors, city managers and administrators, members of the agency, citizens, special-interest groups, and the media all have differing, often conflicting, expectations of the role of chief of police.

The mayor or city manager is likely to believe that the chief of police should be an enlightened administrator whose responsibility is to promote departmental efficiency, reduce crime, improve service, and so on. Other mayors and managers will appreciate the chief who simply "keeps the lid on" and manages to keep the morale high and the number of citizen complaints low.[58] However, the mayor or city manager may also properly expect the chief to be part of the city management team, communicate city management's policies to police personnel, establish agency goals and objectives, select and effectively manage people, and be a responsible steward of the budget.[59]

The relationship between the police chief and the mayor is difficult to articulate. However, Richard Brzeczek contends that several points are indispensable in the relationship. First, the mayor is boss. Indeed, the mayor possesses the legal or political power to fire or force the police chief out of office almost at whim. Second, the mayor has the responsibility for assuring the public that the police are doing the best they can with available resources. Third, the police executive, if chosen on merit, has considerable knowledge about the problems of the community and a wide array of possible solutions—expertise that will serve city hall well. The mayor should come to rely on the chief's pragmatism and take-charge approach as well. Finally, the mayor must give the chief the authority to run his department day to day; without this autonomy, perhaps guided by the mayor's input, the chief's authority will be eroded.[60]

Members of the police agency may have different expectations of the chief executive. They may be less concerned with cost effectiveness and more concerned with good salaries, benefits, and equipment. The officers expect the chief to be their advocate, backing them up when necessary and representing the agency well in dealings with judges and prosecutors who may be indifferent or hostile to their interests. Citizens, for their part, expect the chief of police to provide efficient and cost-effective police services while keeping crime and tax rates down and eliminating corruption and illegal use of force.

Special-interest groups expect the chief to advocate desirable policy positions; for example, Mothers Against Drunk Driving (MADD) insists on strong police measures combating driving under the influence. Finally, the media expect the chief to cooperate fully with their efforts to obtain fast and complete crime information.

SUMMARY

This chapter has discussed police agencies as organizations and bureaucracies and has explored the roles and functions of police executives, middle managers, and first-line supervisors. A management model was employed to clarify the general roles and functions of police administrators; included was a brief illustration of good police administration—the Compstat process in New York City, which is believed by many observers to be the dominant mode of policing in the future. Also addressed was the problem of politics and the police administrator.

The difficulties of leadership in policing were implied, as was the fact that all of the elements and issues of administration revolve around one very important component of the workplace: people. To be an effective administrator in this labor-intensive field, one should learn all that can be learned about human resources in addition to learning all one can about police methods.

REVIEW QUESTIONS

1. Diagram and explain the elements of the basic organizational structure of a police agency.
2. Describe the basic elements of the communications process.
3. Explain the processes of upward, downward, horizontal, and grapevine communication, applying these processes to a police organization.
4. Discuss the roles of the police executive, using the Mintzberg model of chief executive officers.
5. Review the advantages and possible component parts of an assessment for hiring and promoting police chief executives.
6. Contrast the roles and functions of contemporary chiefs of police and county sheriffs.
7. Discuss the roles and functions of middle-level managers and first-line supervisors.
8. Explain how New York City's Compstat process functions, and describe its potential promise in other jurisdictions.
9. Describe the historical relationship and major problems between the police and politicians.

INDEPENDENT STUDENT ACTIVITIES

1. Examine the contemporary nature of the police chief's and sheriff's duties in your area; determine what qualifications they possessed in order to attain their present positions.

2. Determine how the roles and functions of police chiefs and sheriffs differ—and, by extension, those of their employees (e.g., what seems to be the public's role expectations of the officers on the street who do the work of law enforcement and order maintenance).

3. Interview a first-line supervisor to better ascertain why the role and functions of that position are considered to be among the most complex in the police hierarchy.

4. Determine, to the extent possible, the priorities, budgets, management philosophies, and major contemporary challenges and problems that confront police executives in your area.

RELATED WEB SITES

International Association of Chiefs of Police
http://www.theiacp.org/

National Sheriffs Association
http://www.sheriffs.org/

Police Executive Research Forum (PERF)
http://www.policeforum.org

NOTES

1. BEN FOX, "Shootings Haunt San Diego Sheriff," Associated Press, March 11, 2001.
2. DAVID A. TANSIK and JAMES F. ELLIOTT, *Managing Police Organizations* (Monterey, CA: Duxbury, 1981), p. 1.
3. LARRY K. GAINES, MITTIE D. SOUTHERLAND, and JOHN E. ANGELL, *Police Administration* (New York: McGraw-Hill, 1991), p. 9.
4. Ibid.
5. SAMUEL WALKER, *The Police in America: An Introduction*, 2nd ed. (New York: McGraw-Hill, 1992), pp. 356–59.
6. Ibid., p. 77.
7. Ibid., p. 86.
8. *Interpersonal Communication: A Guide for Staff Development*, Institute of Government, University of Georgia, (Athens, GA: August 1974), p. 15.
9. WAYNE W. BENNETT and KAREN HESS, *Management and Supervision in Law Enforcement*, 2nd ed. (St. Paul, MN: West, 1996), p. 85.
10. See R. C. HUSEMAN, quoted in Bennett and Hess, *Management and Supervision in Law Enforcement*, pp. 21–27. Material for this section was also drawn from CHARLES R. SWANSON, LEONARD TERRITO, and ROBERT W. TAYLOR, *Police Administration: Structures, Processes, and Behavior*, 6th ed. (Upper Saddle River, NJ: Prentice Hall, 2005), pp. 309–11.
11. D. KATZ and R. L. KAHN, *The Social Psychology of Organizations* (New York: John Wiley and Sons, 1966), p. 239. As cited in P. V. LEWIS, *Organizational Communication: The Essence of Effective Management* (Columbus, OH: Grid, 1975), p. 36.
12. See R. K. ALLEN, *Organizational Management through Communication* (New York: Harper and Row, 1977), pp. 77–79.
13. ALEX MARKELS, "Managers Aren't Always Able to Get the Right Message Across with E-mail," *Wall Street Journal*, August 6, 1996, p. 2.
14. ROBERT L. MONTGOMERY, "Are You a Good Listener?" *Nation's Business* (October 1981): 65–68.
15. BENNETT and HESS, *Management and Supervision in Law Enforcement*, p. 101.

16. See George D. Eastman and Esther M. Eastman, eds., *Municipal Police Administration*, 7th ed. (Washington, DC: International City Management Association, 1971), p. 17.
17. Ibid., p. 18.
18. Personal communication, Marsha R. Palmer, Planning and Support Division, City of Portland, Oregon, Bureau of Police, July 20, 2001.
19. Ibid., June 4, 2001.
20. President's Commission on Law Enforcement and Administration of Justice, *Task Force Report: The Police* (Washington, DC: Government Printing Office, 1967), p. 46.
21. Department of Justice, Bureau of Justice Statistics, *Police Departments in Large Cities, 1987*, Special Report NCJ-119220 (Washington, DC: Author, 1989), p. 5, Table 10.
22. M. D. Iannone and Nathan F. Iannone, *Supervision of Police Personnel*, 6th ed. (Upper Saddle River, NJ: Prentice Hall, 2000).
23. Michael Carpenter, "Put It in Writing: The Police Policy Manual," *FBI Law Enforcement Bulletin*, October 2000, p. 1.
24. Robert Sheehan and Gary W. Cordner, *Introduction to Police Administration*, 2nd ed. (Cincinnati, OH: Anderson, 1989), pp. 446–47.
25. Charles R. Swanson, Leonard Territo, and Robert W. Taylor, *Police Administration: Structures, Processes, and Behavior*, 5th ed. (Upper Saddle River, NJ: Prentice Hall, 2001), p. 248.
26. Stephen W. Mastrofski, "Police Agency Accreditation: The Prospects of Reform," *American Journal of Police* 5, no. 3 (1986): 45–81.
27. Gaines, Southerland, and Angell, *Police Administration*, pp. 10–11.
28. Ibid., p. 42.
29. Janice Penegor and Ken Peak, "Police Chief Acquisitions: A Comparison of Internal and External Selections," *American Journal of Police* 11, no. 1 (1992): 17–32.
30. Richard B. Weinblatt, "The Shifting Landscape of Chiefs' Jobs," *Law and Order*, October 1999, p. 50.
31. "Survey Says Big-City Chiefs Are Better-Educated Outsiders," *Law Enforcement News*, April 30, 1998, p. 7.
32. R. J. Filer, "Assessment Centers in Police Selection," in *Proceedings of the National Working Conference on the Selection of Law Enforcement Officers*, ed. C. D. Spielberger and H. C. Spaulding (Tampa, FL: University of South Florida, March 1977), p. 103.
33. National Advisory Commission on Criminal Justice Standards and Goals, *Police Chief Executive* (Washington, DC: U.S. Government Printing Office, 1976), p. 7.
34. Weinblatt, "The Shifting Landscape of Chiefs' Jobs," p. 51.
35. National Advisory Commission on Criminal Justice Standards and Goals, *Police Chief Executive*, p. 7.
36. Clemens Bartollas, Stuart J. Miller, and Paul B. Wice, *Participants in American Criminal Justice: The Promise and the Performance* (Englewood Cliffs, NJ: Prentice Hall, 1983), pp. 51–52.

37. Ibid., pp. 53–59.
38. RONALD G. LYNCH, *The Police Manager: Professional Leadership Skills*, 3rd ed. (New York: Random House, 1986), p. 1.
39. HENRY MINTZBERG, "The Manager's Job: Folklore and Fact," *Harvard Business Review* 53 (July–August 1975): 49–61.
40. DONALD C. WITHAM, *The American Law Enforcement Chief Executive: A Management Profile*, (Washington, DC: Police Executive Research Forum, 1985) p. xii.
41. PETER C. DODENHOFF, "LEN Salutes Its 1996 People of the Year, the NYPD and Its Compstat Process," *Law Enforcement News*, December 31, 1996, pp. 1, 4–5.
42. Ibid., p. 4.
43. Ibid.
44. ELI B. SILVERMAN, "Mapping Change: How the New York City Police Department Re-engineered Itself to Drive Down Crime," *Law Enforcement News*, December 15, 1996, p. 10.
45. DODENHOFF, "LEN Salutes Its 1996 People of the Year, the NYPD and Its Compstat Process," p. 4.
46. BENNETT and HESS, *Management and Supervision in Law Enforcement*, pp. 44–45.
47. RICHARD N. HOLDEN, *Modern Police Management* (Englewood Cliffs, NJ: Prentice Hall, 1986), pp. 294–95.
48. Ibid., p. 295.
49. Ibid., p. 117.
50. THOMAS J. PETERS and ROBERT H. WATERMAN Jr., *In Search of Excellence* (New York: Warner, 1982), pp. 306–17.
51. JOHN VAN MAANEN, "Making Rank: Becoming an American Police Sergeant," in *Critical Issues in Policing: Contemporary Readings*, ed. Roger G. Dunham and Geoffrey P. Alpert (Prospect Heights, IL: Waveland Press, 1989), pp. 146–61.
52. KENNETH J. PEAK, LARRY K. GAINES, and RONALD W. GLENSOR, *Police Supervision and Management: In an Era of Community Policing*, 2nd ed. (Upper Saddle River, NJ: Prentice Hall, 2004), pp. 33–34.
53. R. S. ENGEL, "Supervisory Styles of Patrol Sergeants and Lieutenants, *Journal of Criminal Justice* 29 (2001): 341–55.
54. *Webster's Ninth New Collegiate Dictionary* (Springfield, MA: Merriam-Webster, 1983), p. 910.
55. RICHARD BRZECZEK, "Chief-Mayor Relations: The View from the Chief's Chair," in *Police Leadership in America: Crisis and Opportunity*, ed. William A. Geller (New York: Praeger, 1985), pp. 48–55.
56. GEORGE F. COLE and CHRISTOPHER SMITH, *The American System of Criminal Justice*, 9th ed. (Belmont, CA: West/Wadsworth, 2001), p. 237.
57. JAMES F. RICHARDSON, *Urban Police in the United States* (Port Washington, NY: Kennikat Press, 1974), pp. 55–58.
58. BARTOLLAS, MILLER, and WICE, *Participants in American Criminal Justice*, p. 35.
59. Ibid., pp. 39–40.
60. Ibid., pp. 49–50.

CHAPTER 5

On Patrol: Methods and Menaces

The wicked flee when no man pursueth, but the righteous are bold as a lion.

—Proverbs 28:1 (inscribed on the National Law Enforcement Officers Memorial in Washington, D.C.)

For some must watch while some must sleep; so runs the world away.

—Shakespeare, Hamlet

You can observe a lot by watching.

—Yogi Berra

Key Terms

beat culture
deployment
discretionary use of police authority
shift assignment
Tennessee v. *Garner*
traffic control

The patrol function has long been viewed as the backbone of policing. Since the founding of professional policing by Sir Robert Peel (discussed in Chapter 1), patrol has been considered the most important and visible part of police work. Indeed, this chapter serves as a prologue to many police activities described in later chapters, all of which branch off from the patrol function. Because patrol duties normally involve 60 to 70 percent of a police agency's workforce, this task has been a topic of considerable interest and analysis.

In addition to the patrol function, the work of policing revolves around the discretionary use of authority. Officers possess a wide range of options as they go about the business of patrolling, including whether or not to stop, whether or not to arrest, whether or not to use force, whether or not to shoot, and so on. From the relatively innocuous traffic stop to the use of lethal force, many choices are involved, including some with serious consequences.

This chapter begins by describing the culture of the beat: the purposes and nature of patrol, patrol work as a function of shift and beat assignment, and the kinds of dangers that are inherent in this aspect of police work. Next is an overview of what research has revealed concerning the patrol function. Then we consider an often overlooked yet extremely important aspect of patrol: the patrol vehicle. Following that is an examination of the discretionary use of police authority. An exercise is presented in the use of police discretion, followed by a review of the factors and political considerations that can enter into an officer's decision-making process and the advantages and disadvantages of such discretionary authority. After an examination of another function that is closely related to patrol—traffic—the chapter concludes with a summary, review questions, independent student activities, and related Web sites.

Two closely related topics that are at the heart of the patrol function are discussed in later chapters: community-oriented policing and problem solving (Chapter 6) and the tools and high technology used by patrol officers in the performance of their duties, including less-lethal weapons (Chapter 14).

PATROL AS WORK: CULTURE OF THE BEAT

Purposes and Nature of Patrol

In Chapter 3, we discussed the role and functions of the police, including the four basic tasks of policing: preventing crime, enforcing the laws, protecting the innocent, and providing services. In this section, we expand that discussion by looking at the beat culture, or some of the methods and problems that are connected with the patrol function.

Police work has certainly changed since 1910, when Leonard Fuld observed that "the policeman's life is a lazy life in as much as his time is spent doing nothing."[1] Today there are myriad duties for the patrol officer to perform, and danger is a constant adversary. (Danger as an element of patrol is discussed later.)

When not handling calls for service, today's officers frequently engage in problem-solving activities (discussed in Chapter 6) and in random preventive patrol, hoping to deter crime with a police presence. There are several forms of preventive patrol, including automobile, foot, bicycle, horse, motorcycle, marine, helicopter, and even snowmobile patrols. During all of these, the officer is alert for activities and people who seem out of the ordinary. The traditional method of **deployment** of patrol officers should take into account the where and when of crime, attempting to distribute available personnel at the places and the times of day and days of week when trouble and crime seem to occur with greatest frequency. Unfortunately, many departments still deploy their patrol officers in their jurisdictions by using convenient beat dividers, such as streets or bodies of water, instead of analyzing when and where crime and other disturbances are taking place. (We discuss methods for determining patrol deployment later.)

Patrol officers also attempt to effect good relations with the people on their beat, realizing that they cannot apprehend criminals or even maintain a quiet sector without public assistance. In many ways, the success of the entire police agency depends on the skill and work of the patrol officers. For example, upon arriving at a crime scene, they must protect and collect evidence, treat and interview victims, locate and interview suspects and witnesses, and make important discretionary decisions, such as whether to arrest someone and even perhaps whether to use their weapons.

The American Bar Association offered the following major purposes of police patrol:

- To deter crime by maintaining a visible police presence
- To maintain public order
- To enable the police department to respond quickly to law violations or other emergencies
- To identify and apprehend law violators
- To aid individuals and care for those who cannot help themselves
- To facilitate the movement of traffic and people
- To create a sense of security in the community[2]

Today's police patrol function involves many methods of transportation aside from the automobile.

(Courtesy Ft. Lauderdale, Florida, Police Department)

Officers must become very knowledgeable about their beats: They must be familiar with such details as where the doors and windows of buildings are, where the alleys are, where smaller businesses are located, and how the residential areas they patrol are laid out. Officers must learn what is normal on their beats and thus be able to discern people or things that are abnormal; in short, they should develop a kind of sixth sense that is grounded on suspicion—an awareness of something bad, wrong, harmful, without solid evidence; this is often termed "JDLR"—things "just don't look right."

Patrol officers may also develop certain informal rules pertaining to their beats. For example, they may adopt the belief that "after midnight, these alleys belong to me." In other words, an officer may take the position that any person who is observed in "his" or "her" alley after midnight must be checked out—especially if that person is wearing dark clothing or is acting in a furtive or surreptitious manner.

Several authors have described, often in colorful but realistic terms, the kinds of situations encountered by officers on patrol. For example, as W. Clinton Terry III put it:

> Patrol officers respond to calls about overflowing sewers, reports of attempted suicides, domestic disputes, fights between neighbors, barking dogs and quarrelsome cats, reports of people banging their heads against brick walls until they are bloody, requests to check people out who have seemingly passed out in public parks, requests for more police protection from elderly ladies afraid of entering their residence, and requests for information and general assistance of every sort.[3]

A former police chief described patrol duties as follows:

> Cops on the street hurry from call to call, bound to their crackling radios, which offer no relief—especially on summer weekend nights. That is the time when the [city] throbs with noise, booze, violence, drugs, illness, blaring TVs, and human misery. The cops jump from crisis to crisis, rarely having time to do more than tamp one down sufficiently and leave for the next. Gaps of boredom and inactivity fill the interims, although there aren't many of these in the hot months.[4]

Indeed, patrolling officers will encounter all manner of things while engaged in routine patrol—things they discover as well as problems phoned in by citizens. They are assigned "attempt to locate" calls (usually involving missing persons, ranging from juveniles who have not returned home on time to elderly people who have wandered away from nursing homes); "attempt to contact" and "be on the lookout" calls (requested by an out-of-town individual who needs police to try to locate someone in order to deliver a message, for example); and "check the welfare of" calls (involving a person who has not been seen or heard from for some time).

One type of call is said to have broken the back of many police agencies: nonemergency calls to 911. Several hundred thousand 911 calls are made each day across the nation—and 90 percent of them are for nonemergencies. Departments must find ways to free patrol officers from what

EXHIBIT 5-1

Police Patrol: A Job Description

This behavioral analysis of a patrol officer's job provides one of the few empirical descriptions of the complex and varied demands of patrol work. Based on extensive field observations, the findings are reported as a list of the attributes that are required for successful performance in the field. Although completed over three decades ago, the findings appear to conform well to the patrol activities of today. The researchers concluded that patrol officers must do the following:

1. Endure long periods of monotony in routine patrol, yet react quickly (almost instantaneously) and effectively to problem situations observed on the street or to orders issued by the radio dispatcher.
2. Gain knowledge of the patrol area, not only of its physical characteristics, but also of its normal routine of events and the usual behavior patterns of its residents.
3. Exhibit initiative, problem-solving capacity, effective judgment, and imagination in coping with the numerous complex situations they are called on to face, such as a family disturbance, a potential suicide, a robbery in progress, an accident, or a disaster.
4. Make prompt and effective decisions, sometimes in life-and-death situations, and be able to size up a situation quickly and take appropriate action.
5. Demonstrate mature judgment—for example, when deciding whether an arrest is warranted by the circumstances or whether a warning is sufficient or when facing a situation in which the use of force may be needed.
6. Demonstrate critical awareness in discerning signs of out-of-the-ordinary conditions or circumstances that indicate trouble or a crime in progress.
7. Exhibit a number of complex psychomotor skills, such as driving a vehicle in normal and emergency situations; firing a weapon accurately under extremely varied conditions; maintaining agility, endurance, and strength; and showing facility in self-defense and apprehension (for example, taking a person into custody with a minimum of force).
8. Adequately perform the communication and record-keeping functions of the job, including oral reports, formal case reports, and departmental and court forms.

has been called the "tyranny of 911": nonstop calls that send officers bouncing from one nonemergency call for service to the next. (The author witnessed one such call to a 911 dispatcher in the Midwest. The caller was reporting a goat standing on the front porch.) Indeed, the range of "emergencies" 911 callers report boggles the mind: Some people call because they want to know when the National Football League game begins that day, some people want to know the weather report, and some want help to exorcise the alien who entered their kitchen through the refrigerator's electrical cord. Nonemergency 911 calls leave officers little time for community-oriented policing and problem-solving activities.[5]

Exhibit 5-1 describes the complex nature of a patrol officer's work. Table 5-1 shows the difference in patrol allocation in selected large police

9. Have the facility to act effectively in extremely divergent interpersonal situations. Police officers constantly confront people who are violating the law, ranging from curfew violators to felons. They constantly confront people who are in trouble or who are victims of crimes. At the same time, officers must relate to law-abiding citizens on their beat—businessmen, residents, school officials, visitors. Their interpersonal relations must range up and down a continuum defined by friendliness and persuasion on one end and by firmness and force at the other.
10. Endure verbal and physical abuse from citizens and offenders (as when placing a person under arrest or facing day-in and day-out race prejudice) while using only necessary force in the performance of their job.
11. Exhibit a professional, self-assured presence and a self-confident manner when dealing with offenders, the public, and the courts.
12. Be capable of restoring equilibrium to social groups—for example, restoring order in a family fight, in a disagreement between neighbors, or in a clash between rival youth groups.
13. Be skillful in questioning suspected offenders, victims, and witnesses of crimes.
14. Take charge of situations, such as a crime or accident scene, yet not unduly alienate participants or bystanders.
15. Be flexible enough to work under loose supervision in most day-to-day patrol activities and also under direct supervision in situations where large numbers of officers are required.
16. Tolerate stress in a multitude of forms, such as meeting the violent behavior of a mob, coping with the pressures of a high-speed chase or a weapon being fired, or assisting a woman bearing a child.
17. Exhibit personal courage in the face of dangerous situations that may result in serious injury or death.
18. Maintain objectivity while dealing with a host of special-interest groups, ranging from relatives of offenders to members of the press.
19. Maintain a balanced perspective in the face of constant exposure to the worst side of human nature.
20. Exhibit a high level of personal integrity and ethical conduct—for example, refraining from accepting bribes or "favors" and providing impartial law enforcement.

Source: Adapted from M. E. Baehr, J. E. Furcon, and E. C. Froemel, *Psychological Assessment of Patrolman Qualifications in Relation to Field Performance* (Washington, DC: Department of Justice, 1968), pp. 11–3 to 11–5.

departments. The table shows departments' diverse attempts to meet various needs (such as those created by streets, freeways, downtown areas, parks, and lakes) with different patrol staffing levels and types of patrol. For example, Detroit and Los Angeles staff over 60 percent of their patrol units with two officers, while Atlanta and Baltimore have no two-officer units. Furthermore, Atlanta, Chicago, and Houston commit over 25 percent of their officers to patrol on a 24-hour basis, while the remaining cities commit less than 20 percent of their officers to this task. There are also vast differences with respect to how agencies use the various types of patrol. For example, while most of the agencies assign 77 to 95 percent of their patrol resources to automobiles, Los Angeles, New York, and Seattle assign 64 percent or less to automobiles.

TABLE 5-1

Patrol Allocation in Selected Large Police Departments

	Departments Using Patrol Type and Percentage of all Patrol Units Accounted For							
Department	Auto	Motorcycle	Foot	Bicycle	Horse	Marine	Percentage of Officers on Patrol per 24 Hours	Percentage of Units with Two Officers
Atlanta	R 77%	R 1%	R 14%	R 3%	R 1%	M 0%	31%	0%
Baltimore	R 96	R 1	R 2	S 0	R 1	R 0	16	0
Chicago	R 82	R 1	R 15	R 1	R 0	R 0	26	52
Detroit	R 84	R 1	R 7	R 3	R 1	R 4	16	68
Houston	R 95	R 1	R 1	R 1	R 1	R 0	27	11
Los Angeles	R 64	R 6	R 5	R 15	S 0	S 0	19	63
New York City	R 54	R 1	R 39	R 5	R 1	R 0	19	57
Seattle	R 42	R 14	R 8	R 16	R 4	R 3	16	31

Note: The codes for patrol use are as follows:

R = Patrol type is used on a routine basis

S = Patrol type is used for special events only

M = Patrol type is not used

Source: Adapted from B. A. Reaves and A. L. Goldberg. 1999 *Law Enforcement Management and Administrative Statistics,* 1997. Washington, DC: Department of Justice, pp. 71–80.

Filling Occasional Hours of Boredom

As indicated earlier, contrary to the image that is portrayed on television, some (or even much) of the time officers devote to patrolling consists of gaps of inactivity. During those periods of time (particularly on the graveyard shift, when even late-night people and party-goers submit to fatigue and go home to sleep), patrol officers engage in a variety of activities to pass the time:

- They create "private places" for themselves—fire stations, hospitals, and other places where they can wash up, have a cup of coffee, make a phone call, or simply relax for a few moments.
- They engage in police-related activities, such as completing reports, checking license plates of vehicles that are parked at motels (to locate stolen vehicles or wanted persons), or meeting with other officers. Other more relaxing activities might include exercising in the station house workout room.
- Even while engaged in routine patrol, the officer is often encouraged during recruit training to make good use of this slack time by engaging in "what if" mental exercises: "What if an armed robbery occurred at (location)? How would I get there most rapidly? What would I do after arrival? Where would I find available cover?" Of course, officers can concoct any number of scenarios and types of calls for service to keep themselves mentally honed and ready to respond in the most efficacious manner.
- An often overlooked part of policing is that patrol officers must also spend a lot of time—especially during the earlier part of their careers—memorizing many things: the "Ten Code," for example, and the numbering systems of streets and highways within their jurisdiction. (Indeed, new recruits can and do "wash out" during the field-training phase of their careers because of their inability to read an in-car map of the city, thus being unable to arrive at their destination promptly.)

Patrol Work as a Function of Shift Assignment

Although the following analysis does not apply to all jurisdictions, the nature of patrol work is very closely related to the officer's particular **shift assignment**. Following are general descriptions of the nature of work on each of the three daily shifts.

Officers working the day shift (approximately 8 A.M. to 4 P.M.) probably have the greatest contact with citizens. Officers may start their day by watching school crossings and unsnarling traffic jams. Speeding and traffic accidents are more common as people hurry to work in the morning. Officers also participate in school and civic presentations and other such programs. Most errands and nonpolice duties assigned to the police are performed by day shift officers, such as unlocking parking lots, escorting people, delivering agendas to city council members, transporting evidence to court, and seeing that maintenance is performed on patrol vehicles. Day shift officers are more likely to be summoned to such major crimes as armed robberies and bomb threats. This shift often has lull periods, as most people are at work or in school. Usually, the officers with the most seniority work the day shift.

Officers of the swing, or evening, shift (4 P.M. to 12 A.M.) come on duty in time to untangle evening traffic jams and respond to a variety of complaints from the public. Youths are out of school, shops are beginning to close, and, as darkness falls, officers must begin checking commercial doors and windows on their beat; new officers are amazed at the frequency with which businesspeople leave their buildings unsecured. Warm weather brings increased drinking and partying, along with noise complaints. Domestic disturbances begin to occur, and the action at bars and nightclubs is beginning to pick up; soon fights will break out. Many major events, such as athletic events and concerts, occur in the evenings, so officers often perform crowd and traffic control duties. Toward the end of the shift, fast food and other businesses begin complaining about loitering and littering by teenagers. Arrests are much more frequent than during the day shift, and officers must attempt to take one last look at the businesses on the beat before ending their shift to ensure that none have been burglarized during the evening and night hours. That done, arrest and incident reports must be completed before officers may leave the station house for home.

The night shift (12 A.M. to 8 A.M.), known throughout history as the graveyard shift, is an entirely different world. Because of its adverse effects on the officer's sleeping and eating habits, this shift is usually worked by newer officers (who also, because of low seniority, work most weekends and holidays), but only long enough for the officer to build enough seniority to transfer to another shift. Few officers actually like the shift enough to want to devote much of their career working it. (Many agencies also have shift rotation, transferring their officers from one shift to another at fixed intervals.)

Officers on this shift come on duty fresh and ready for action. From about midnight to 3 A.M., the night shift is quite busy as bars and taverns close. Traffic is relatively heavy for several hours, and then it normally drops off to a trickle. The "night people" begin to come out—those who sleep in the daytime and prowl at night, including the burglars. The nightly cat-and-mouse game begins between the cops and the robbers. Night shift officers come to know who these people are and what vehicles they drive, what crimes they prefer, what their habits are, and where they hang out. Night shift officers spend much of the night patrolling alleys and businesses, working their spotlight as they seek signs of suspicious activity, open doors and windows in businesses, and unlawful entry. They also watch the residential areas, performing courtesy checks of homes in general or with greater scrutiny when people are away on vacation and have asked the police for a periodic check of their property.

Such patrol work is inevitably eerie in nature. Officers typically work alone under cover of darkness, often without hope of rapid backup units, although where possible, greater attention is given to providing backup to night shift officers, even during traffic stops. The police never know who or what awaits them around the next dark corner. The protective shroud of darkness given to the offenders makes the night shift officers more wary. As mentioned earlier, after midnight, graveyard officers view alleys as theirs alone; anyone violating the peace of "their" alleys—especially one of the known "night people" or anyone wearing dark clothing or engaging in other suspicious activity—should be prepared to explain their actions and presence. Such individuals may also be compelled to undergo a stop-and-frisk (pat-down) search.

Once the alleys and buildings have been checked, the officers begin rechecking them, avoiding any routine pattern that burglars may discern. Some burglars can tell which beats are "open"—that is, wide open for burglarizing—by observing which patrol vehicles are parked at the station or at restaurants; therefore, officers should vary their patrol routine each night. At two or three in the morning, boredom can set in. Some officers welcome this change of pace, while others loathe it and look for ways to fight the monotony of the "dog watch." For them, the occasional high-speed chase may bring a welcome adrenaline rush, as does a crime in progress. Other means of staying alert include meeting and chatting with other officers who are also bored with patrol and stopping for coffee. But these officers must be mentally prepared for action; they know that while this is normally a quiet shift after the initial activity, when something does occur on the night shift, it is often a major incident or crime.

Influences of One's Assigned Beat

Just as the work of the patrol officer is influenced by his or her shift assignment, the nature of that work is determined by the beat assignment. Each beat has its own personality, which may be quite different from other contiguous beats in terms of its structure and demographic character, as seen in the following hypothetical examples:

- Beat A contains a university with many large crowds that attend athletic and concert events; it also contains a number of taverns and bars where students congregate, resulting in an occasional need for police presence. A large hospital is located in this sector. Residents here are predominantly middle class. A large number of shopping malls and retail businesses occupy the area. The crime rate is quite low here, as are the numbers of calls for service. The university commands a considerable amount of officer overtime for major events as well as general officer attention for parking problems. During university homecoming week and other major events, officers in this beat will be going from call to call, while officers assigned to other beats may find themselves completely bored. One portion of the beat contains several bars that attract working-class individuals and generate several calls for service each week due to fights, traffic problems, and so forth.

- Beat B is almost totally residential in nature and is composed of the "old money" people of the community: upper- and upper-middle classes who "encourage" routine patrols by the police. Some of the community's banks, retail businesses, and industrial complexes are also located in this area. Most people have their homes wired for security, either to a private security firm or to the local police department. The crime rate and calls for service are relatively low in this beat, but there is a large amount of territory to patrol, and a major thoroughfare runs along the beat's perimeter, generating some serious traffic accidents.
- Beat C is composed primarily of blue-collar, working-class people. It generates a low to medium number of calls for service relative to the other beats, and much of its geographic area is consumed by a small airport and a large public park with a baseball diamond/golf course complex.
- Beat D is the worst in the city in terms of quality of life, residents' income levels, and police problems. Though smaller in size than the other beats, it generates a very high number of calls for service. It contains a large number of residents living on the margins of the economy, lower-income housing complexes, taverns, barely surviving retail businesses, older mobile home parks and motels, and a major railroad switching yard. Officers are constantly driving from call to call, especially during summer weekend nights. At night, officers who are engaged in calls for service—even traffic stops—are given backup by fellow officers whenever possible.

Of course, even the normal ebb and flow of beat activity is greatly altered when a critical incident occurs; for example, an act of nature (such as a tornado, an earthquake, or a fire) or a major criminal event (such as a bank robbery or a kidnapping) can wreak havoc on a beat that is normally the most placid in nature.

Three "cops' rules" are part of the **beat culture**:

1. Don't get involved in another officer's sector; "butt out" unless asked to come to a beat to assist. Each officer is accountable for his or her territory, and each officer must live with the consequences of decisions that pertain to his or her beat.
2. Don't leave work for the next duty shift; take care of such practical matters as putting gas in the patrol car and taking all necessary complaints before leaving the station house.
3. Hold up your end of the work: don't slack off.[6]

Where Danger Lurks: The Hazards of Beat Patrol

It is well known that police officers have a very dangerous job. Although several other occupations outrank that of policing in terms of the yearly rate of employee deaths, officers face an omnipresent peril; they never know if the citizen they are about to confront is armed, high on drugs or alcohol, or planning to engage in a recent phenomenon known as "suicide by cop."

During 2003, 132 police officers lost their lives in the line of duty (including both felonious killings and accidental means); the annual average in the 1990s was 153, compared to 187 during the 1980s and 222 during the 1970s.[7] This is still a dangerous nation, notwithstanding the highly publicized decrease in violent crime during the past several years. An adverse omen is the fact that the number of murders committed in the nation's thirty largest cities seems to have leveled off, after dropping 37 percent from 1991 to 1999.[8] We discuss the dangers of police work at greater length in Chapter 12, when we examine police stress.

Jerome Skolnick and David Bayley describe how officers prepare to face the beat's dangers on their tour of duty:

> Policing in the United States is very much like going to war. Three times a day in countless locker rooms, large men and a growing number of women carefully arm and armor themselves for the day's events. They

The patrol function often takes officers to places that are "brutish" and dangerous.

(Vivan Lord [top] and Washoe County, Nevada, Sheriff's Office [bottom])

> begin by strapping on flak jackets. Then they pick up a wide, heavy, black leather belt and hang around it the tools of their trade: gun, mace, handcuffs, bullets. When it is fully loaded they swing the belt around their hips with the same practiced motion of the gunfighter in Western movies, slugging it down and buckling it in front. Inspecting themselves in a full-length mirror, officers thread their night sticks into a metal ring on the side of their belt.[9]

As John Crank states, "This is not a picture of American youth dressing for public servitude. These are warriors going to battle, the New Centurions, as Wambaugh calls them. In their dress and demeanor lies the future of American policing."[10] As Crank also observes, police recognize many citizens for what they are: "Dangerous, unpredictable, violent, savagely cunning . . . in a world of capable and talented reptilian, mammalian . . . predators."[11]

This depiction of the people officers confront on the beat may seem overly contrived, exaggerated, or brusque. Most patrol officers with any length of service, however, can attest to the fact that there are certain members of our society who, as one officer put it, are "irretrievable predators that just get off . . . on people's pain and on people's crying and begging and pleading. They don't have any sense of morality, they don't have any sense of right and wrong."[12] During their careers, most patrol officers are verbally threatened by such individuals; they take the great majority of such threats with a grain of salt. Occasionally, however, the "irretrievable predator" who possesses no sense of morality will issue such a threat, which the officer will (and must) take quite seriously; this is a very disconcerting part of the job.

The importance of patrol officers' providing backup to one another—especially during the hours of darkness—cannot be overstated, as shown by Anthony Bouza:

> The sense of "us vs. them" that develops between cops and the outside world forges a bond between cops whose strength is fabled. It is widened by the dependence cops have on each other for safety and backup. The

Patrol vehicles are used for a variety of purposes.

(Courtesy Washoe County, Nevada, Sheriff's Office)

> response to help is a cop's life-line. An "assist police officer" is every cop's first priority. The ultimate betrayal is for one cop to fail to back up another.[13]

In this same vein, patrol officers quickly come to know whom they can count on when everything "hits the fan"—which officers will race to assist another officer at a barroom brawl, a felony in progress, and so on—and which will not.

An Unappreciated American Icon: The Patrol Vehicle

A Sanctuary and a Place for Vital Gear

Long before the *Blues Brothers* movie provided notoriety for police vehicles (the main characters adopted as their "Blues Mobile" a retired 1974 Dodge Monoco police car, with a powerful 440-cubic-inch engine), vehicles used by the police for patrolling and chasing offenders were being viewed with some degree of awe by most Americans. Conversely, the patrol vehicle is perhaps the most underappreciated and ignored aspect of police work—by both scholars and officers themselves. The patrol vehicle warrants greater attention because it is not only a place where officers on patrol spend a great deal of their time, but also their sanctuary; it contains the myriad vital tools for accomplishing their work and to a great extent represents their authority.

The patrol vehicle is generally safe and comfortable, containing several essential accoutrements (e.g., a radio, spotlight, and weapons, such as a shotgun or rifle) that contribute to the officer's safety. It is a mobile haven, providing comfort from the extreme climates that exist in much of the nation, as well as against humans who would hurt the officer. Because the officer's world can be cruel and dangerous (an average of 60 police officers have been feloniously killed each year in this millennium)[14] the patrol car affords one access to the tools of defense. The vehicle is also a safe place to deposit combative prisoners for transport, and many models are constructed to be hosed out in case a prisoner vomits or urinates in the vehicle.

Vital tools can also be stored in or mounted on the vehicle, which serves as a virtual office: the radio (for summoning assistance), warning lights and siren, defensive weapons (for example, a shotgun or other firearm; a Taser, baton, or other less-lethal tool), possibly an onboard computer and video recorder, flares, cameras and other evidence-gathering equipment, and so forth. On the graveyard shift, the spotlight can be the officer's greatest asset.

Finally, the police vehicle is a rolling symbol of authority. For this reason, few people enjoy seeing a police vehicle appear in their rearview mirror; indeed, for some, it is a prelude to being issued a traffic citation or, worse, being taken to jail. Still, it can be stated that since the first police car appeared, citizens have been fascinated with the speed and imposing appearance of these automobiles.

Input from patrol officers is often used to create the console setup; here, microphones are placed on the passenger side, at an angle and height that are easy for the officer to reach.

(Courtesy Woodcrest Vehicle Center)

Evolution of the Patrol Vehicle

At one time or another, police departments have placed decals and emergency equipment on all sorts of cars. In 1950, Ford Motor Company introduced the first "police package,"—a vehicle with a 110-horsepower (hp) engine, heavy-duty suspension components, a larger radiator, extra transmission and power steering cooling, a larger battery, and a more powerful electrical system. Soon Buick produced a police package as well, and the early 1960s saw the Dodge Dart following suit. The late 1960s brought Plymouth's twin offerings, the Belvedere and the Fury, and Dodge introduced its 440 CI Magnum engine, with 375 hp.[15]

In the early 1970s, the AMC Matador was widely used, but durability problems caused it to reign for only a few years. The energy crisis of the mid-1970s brought the Chevrolet Nova 9C1, which was developed through a collaboration between Chevrolet, the Los Angeles County Sheriff's Office, and *Motor Trend* magazine; it and the highly recognizable Dodge Monaco dominated the market in the late 1970s.[16]

The drive for fuel efficiency and stricter emissions standards continued into the 1980s, which has been termed the "Dark Ages" of police vehicle history.[17] The creation of the underpowered Dodge R-body police package was a result, as well as the Aries K; with a mere 84-hp engine, the Aries required 17 seconds to reach 60 mph. The only bright spot of this decade was the California Highway Patrol's unveiling of the 157-hp Ford Mustang GT pursuit vehicle, which was used in thirty-five states by 1991.[18]

During the early 1990s, both Dodge and Chrysler announced that they were dropping out of the police car market, shocking police departments everywhere and leaving only the Chevrolet Caprice and the Ford Crown Victoria as heavy-duty models.[19] By the late 1990s, and continuing into the early 2000s, the Crown Victoria assumed the mantle as the nation's most popular police cruiser, with three-fourths of the market. The Crown Victoria came under a cloud, however, because of fires that killed as many as eleven officers when their cars were struck at the rear, causing the fuel tanks to explode. Over several years' time, a recall, many lawsuits and investigations, and a task force created by Ford were initiated with regard to the problem.[20]

Today's Accoutrements

Henry Ford would be amazed with today's police cruisers, in which high technology and utility still trump luxury. In addition to the traditional beefed-up engines, heavy suspension, and upgraded electrical systems, some also contain several features that mean a lot to the officers on patrol. For example, some new models come with plates in the driver's seatback to protect against assault from the rear, cutouts in the driver's seat for a holster, extra-long safety belts, reinforced front steel beams and higher rated tires for high-speed pursuits, a voice-recognition system for accessing onboard computers, a camera mounted in the overhead light bar with output to a laptop computer, an aircraft-style "blue box" accident data recorder, and crush-resistant bumpers.[21]

In sum, it is clear that the value of the patrol vehicle cannot be overstated in terms of helping the police to fulfill their mission to serve and protect. In addition, the vehicle will continue to become even more important to officers and citizens alike, as new technological advances are included in its design and functionality.

Studies of the Patrol Function

Because of the vast resources devoted to the patrol function and a desire to make patrolling more productive and pleasant for the officers, many patrol studies have been conducted. Several have uncovered deficiencies and exposed myths about preventive patrol. These studies have helped us understand how the professional policing model put up walls between the public and the police, whom many people began to view as an occupying force.[22] As the Police Foundation said, "Isolated in their rolling fortresses, police seem[ed] unable to communicate with the citizens they presumably served."[23]

The best-known study of patrol efficiency was conducted in Kansas City, Missouri, in 1973, by George Kelling and a research team at the Police Foundation. The researchers divided the city into fifteen beats, which were then categorized into five groups of three matched beats each. Each group consisted of neighborhoods that were similar in terms of population, crime characteristics, and calls for police services. Patrolling techniques used in the three beats varied; there was no preventive patrol in one (police only responded to calls for service), there was increased patrol activity in another (two or three times the usual amount of patrolling), and there was the usual level of service in the third beat. Citizens were interviewed and crime rates were measured during the year the experiment was conducted. This experiment challenged several traditional assumptions about routine police patrol. The study found that the deterrent effect of policing was not weakened by the elimination of routine patrolling. Citizens' fear of crime and their attitudes toward the police were not affected, nor was the ability of the police to respond to calls.

This experiment—known as the Kansas City Preventive Patrol Experiment (depicted in Figure 5-1)—indicated that the old sacrosanct patrol methods were subject to question. As one of the study's authors stated, it "show[ed] that the traditional assumptions of 'Give me more cars and more money and we'll get there faster and fight crime' is probably not a very viable argument."[24]

In the mid-1970s, it was suggested that the performance of patrol officers would improve by redesigning the job based on motivators rather than by attempting to change the individual officer selected for the job (by such means as increasing education requirements).[25] This suggestion later evolved into a concept known as "team policing," which differed from conventional patrol in several areas. Officers were divided into small teams

FIGURE 5-1 Schematic representation of fifteen-beat area, Kansas City Preventive Patrol Experiment.

Source: George L. Kelling et al., The Kansas City Preventive Patrol Experiment: Final Report. *(Washington, DC: Police Foundation, 1974), p. 9. Used with permission.*

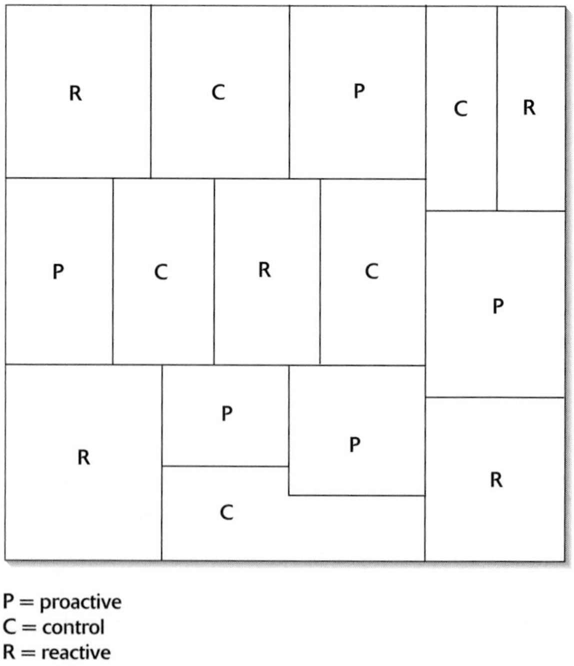

that were assigned permanently to small geographic areas or neighborhoods. Officers were to be generalists, trained to investigate crimes and attend to all of the problems in their area. Communication and coordination between team members and the community were to be maximized; team involvement in administrative decision making was emphasized as well. This concept, later abandoned by many departments, apparently because of its strain on resources, was the beginning of the 1980s' movement to return to community-oriented policing.

Two more attempts to increase patrol productivity, generally referred to as "directed patrol," occurred in 1975. The New Haven, Connecticut, Police Department used computer data of crime locations and times to set up deterrent runs (D-runs) to instruct officers how to patrol. For example, the officer might be told to patrol around a certain block slowly, park, walk, get back in the car, and cruise down another street. A D-run took up to an hour, with each officer doing two or three of them per shift. Support for patrol officers was generally low, and the program did not reduce crime but rather displaced it. After a year, the experiment quietly died.[26] Wilmington, Delaware, instituted a split-force program, whereby three-fourths of the 250 patrol officers were assigned to a basic patrol unit to answer prioritized calls. The remainder of the officers were assigned to the structured unit; they were deployed in high-crime areas, usually in plainclothes, to perform surveillances, stakeouts, and other tactical assignments. An evaluation of the project found that police productivity increased 20 percent and crime decreased 18 percent in the program's first year.[27]

In the late 1970s, a renewed interest in foot patrol—in keeping with Peel's view that police officers should walk the beat—compelled the Police Foundation to evaluate the effectiveness of foot patrol in selected New Jersey cities between 1977 and 1979. It was found that, for the most part, crime levels were not affected by foot patrol, but it did have a significant effect on the attitudes of area residents. Specifically, residents felt safer, thinking that the severity of crimes in their neighborhoods had diminished. Furthermore, evaluations of the Neighborhood Foot Patrol Program in Flint, Michigan, in 1985 found that foot officers had a higher level of job satisfaction[28] and felt safer on the job than motor officers.[29]

Other studies have illuminated the patrol function as well. First, a long-standing assumption was that as police response time increased, the ability to arrest perpetrators proportionately decreased. Thus, conventional wisdom held, more police were needed on patrol in order to get to the crime scene more quickly and catch the criminals. In 1977, a study examined police response time in Kansas City, Missouri, finding that response time was unrelated to the probability of making an arrest or locating a witness. Furthermore, neither dispatch nor travel time was strongly associated with citizen satisfaction. The time it takes to report a crime, the study found, is the major determining factor of whether an on-scene arrest takes place and whether witnesses are located.[30] It is also known that two-person patrol cars are no more effective than one-person cars in reducing crime or catching criminals. Furthermore, injuries to police officers are not more likely to occur in one-person cars. Finally, most officers on patrol do not stumble across felony crimes in progress.[31]

While these studies should not be viewed as conclusive—different results could be obtained in different communities—they do demonstrate that old police methods should be viewed very cautiously. Many police executives have had to rethink the sacred cows of patrol functions.

Discretionary Use of Police Authority

The Link between Patrol and Discretion

George Kelling, coauthor with James Q. Wilson of the well-known "Broken Windows" article, described a Newark, New Jersey, street cop with whom he spent many hours walking a beat:

> As he saw his job, he was to keep an eye on strangers, and make certain that the disreputable regulars observed some informal but widely understood rules. Drunks and addicts could sit on the stoops, but could not lie down. People could drink on side streets, but not at the main intersection. Bottles had to be in paper bags. Talking to, bothering or begging from people waiting at the bus stop was strictly forbidden. Persons who broke the informal rules, especially [the latter], were arrested for vagrancy. Noisy teenagers were told to keep quiet.[32]

This quote points out the inextricable link between the patrol function and **discretionary use of police authority**. We cannot discuss one without the other. A hypothetical exercise begins our discussion of police discretion.

An Exercise in Discretion

Imagine this scenario. You are a graveyard shift police officer alone on duty in a town of three thousand people. It is about 1 A.M., and it is quiet; nothing is moving except for the local wildlife. You are parked on a two-lane highway that runs adjacent to your community, enjoying the solitude and peacefulness while indulging in your favorite summertime drink. Eventually, headlights appear in the distance and approach you on the highway. The vehicle, a pickup truck, passes by, and as it does, you notice that the vehicle is weaving perceptibly, crossing the center line of the highway several times. Your training indicates that alcohol may be a factor, and thus spurred to action, you pursue the pickup for about a half mile and then pull it over with your red lights and siren.

The driver exits his truck, and you notice a slight stagger in his gait and then detect the telltale odor of alcohol on his breath. He is wearing a gray denim work shirt that says "Acme Heating and Cooling" on the back and "Bob" on the front. You ask Bob how much he has had to drink, and the answer (one that is given to police officers probably 90 percent of the time) is "A couple of beers." You conduct a field sobriety test, and Bob's performance is poor. Your experience and training indicate that his blood alcohol content is approximately .15 (.10 being legally intoxicated).

Your mission is to list all of the possible legitimate and lawful measures that you as a police officer can employ to deal with this police matter. Do not concern yourself with trying to determine which options may be better or worse at this point; however, do discuss the obvious ramifications, advantages, and disadvantages of each. A hint—there are at least a half dozen options available to you. Some possible answers and further discussion are provided at the end of the chapter.

Attempts to Define Discretion

Scholarly knowledge about the way police make decisions is limited. What is known, however, is that when police observe something of a "JDLR" nature, two important decisions must be made: (1) whether to intervene in the situation and (2) how to intervene. The kinds, number, and possible combinations of interventions are virtually limitless. What kinds of decisions are available for an officer who makes a routine traffic stop (as in the hypothetical situation just described)? David Bayley and Egon Bittner observed long ago that officers have as many as ten actions to select from at the initial stop (for example, order the driver out of the car), seven strategies appropriate during the stop (such as a roadside sobriety test), and eleven exit strategies (for instance, releasing the driver with a warning), representing a total of 770 different combinations of actions that might be taken![33]

Criminal law has two sides—the formality and the reality. The formality is found in the statute books and opinions of appellate courts. The reality is found in the practices of enforcement officers. In some circumstances, the choice of action to be taken is relatively easy, such as arresting a bank robbery suspect. In other situations, such as quelling a dispute between neighbors, the choice is more difficult. Drinking in the park is a crime according to many local ordinances, but quietly drinking at a family picnic without disturbing others is not a crime according to the reality of the law because officers uniformly refuse to enforce the ordinance in such circumstances. When the formality and the reality differ, the reality prevails.[34]

These examples demonstrate why the use of discretion is one of the major challenges facing U.S. police today. Our system tends to treat people as individuals. One person who commits a robbery is not the same as another person who commits a robbery. Our system takes into account why and how a person committed a crime (his or her intent, or *mens rea*). Under our judicial process, when A shoots B, a variety of possible outcomes can occur. The most important decisions take place on the streets, day or night, generally without the opportunity for the officer to consult with others or to carefully consider all the facts.

Determinants of Discretionary Actions

Ours is supposed to be a government of laws and not of people. That axiom is simply a myth, at least in the manner by which the law is applied. Official discretion pervades all levels and most agencies of government. The discretionary power of the police is awesome. Kenneth Culp Davis, an authority on police discretion, writes, "The police are among the most important policy makers of our entire society. And they make far more discretionary determinations in individual cases than does any other class of administrators; I know of no close second."[35]

What determines whether the officer will take a stern approach (enforcing the letter of the law with an arrest) or will be lenient (issuing a verbal warning or some other outcome short of arrest)? Several variables enter into the officer's decision. First, the officer's attitude is a consideration. Police, being human, bring to work either a happy or an unhappy disposition. If, on that same day, the officer received an IRS notice saying back taxes were owed, had a nasty spat with his or her spouse, was severely bitten on the leg by the family dog when leaving for work, and was stranded on the way to work because of car trouble, he or she may be more inclined to exercise an arrest in the scenario presented earlier. Conversely, if on that day the officer received an IRS check for overpayment of taxes, had a particularly amorous evening with his or her significant other, was licked affectionately by the dog when leaving for work, and can now afford to purchase a new car, he or she may be more likely to give Bob a break. Personal views toward specific types of crimes also play a role; perhaps the officer in our scenario is especially fed up with the lives taken by intoxicated drivers (likely outcome: arrest) but is not especially outraged about kids who drag race on the highway (likely outcome: verbal or written warning).

Another major consideration in the officer's choice among various options is the citizen's attitude. If the offender is rude and condescending, denies having done anything wrong, or uses some of the standard clichés that are almost guaranteed to rankle the police ("You don't know who I am" or "I'll have your job" or "I know the chief of police" or "As a taxpayer, I pay your salary"), the probable outcome is obvious. On the other hand, the person who is honest with the officer, avoids attempts at intimidation and sarcasm, and does not try to "beat the rap" will normally fare better.

Several studies have found that not only a citizen's demeanor, but also his or her social class, sex, age, and race influence the decisions made by patrol officers.[36] This possible discrimination on the part of the officers points out that the police—like other citizens—are subject to stereotypes and biases that will affect their behavior.

Pros, Cons, and Politics of Discretionary Authority

Several ironies are connected with the way in which the police apply discretion. First is the inverse relationship between the officers' rank and the amount of discretion that is available. In other words, as the rank of the officer increases, the amount of discretion that he or she can employ normally decreases. The street officer makes discretionary decisions all the time—decisions about whether to arrest, shoot, and so forth. But the chief of police, who does very little actual police work, may be very constrained by department, union, affirmative-action, or governing board guidelines and policies. Furthermore, the chief of police knows that there are neither the resources nor the desire to enforce all the laws that are broken.

The police executive knows that the exercise of discretion is an essential part of police work. However, he or she cannot broadcast that fact to the rank and file or to the public. There is a myth of full enforcement of the laws—that all of the laws should be, and are, enforced all of the time and with impartiality. It is a delicate matter to tell police officers which laws they will enforce and which they will not. And when the chief is asked at a civic club luncheon which laws are not enforced, it is normally neither prudent nor politically wise to list the offenses for which the police look the other way. Police agencies are also pressured to support the status quo. There are legal concerns as well. For example, releasing drunk drivers cannot be the official policy of the agency.

Finally, the issue of police discretion is shrouded in controversy. There are several arguments both for and against discretion. Advantages include that it allows the officer to treat different situations in accordance with humanitarian and practical goals. For example, take an officer who pulls over a speeding motorist, only to learn that the car is en route to the hospital with a woman who is about to deliver a baby. While the agitated driver is endangering everyone in the vehicle as well as other motorists on the roadway, discretion allows the officer to be compassionate and empathetic, giving the car a safe escort to the hospital rather than issuing a citation for speeding. In short, discretionary use of authority allows the police to employ a philosophy of justice tempered with mercy.

Conversely, discretion smacks of partiality. In the scenario discussed earlier, the officer may arrest Bob for driving under the influence on a Tuesday but, in an identical situation, may allow Jack to sleep it off on Friday. Also, critics of discretion in policing can argue that such wide latitude in decision making may serve as a breeding ground for police corruption; for example, an officer may be bribed to exercise his or her discretion and overlook a traffic violation or an even more serious offense. And as Lawrence Sherman observed, another problem is that the police do not know the consequences of their discretionary decisions. The police mission, Sherman wrote, is defined as answering calls and being available to answer more calls; therefore, police managers have created only an input information system. Sherman contrasted the police to artisans and navigators who receive feedback on the effects of their decisions. The police, however, have failed to create a feedback information system that tells them what happens after they leave a call or even after they make an arrest. Thus police lack knowledge about the effects of their discretionary actions on suspects, victims, witnesses, and potential criminals.[37]

A large number of people in the nation would probably support greater control over police discretion. Incidents of abuse of discretion certainly lend weight to their argument. Control means guidelines, and even the National Advisory Commission on Criminal Justice Standards and Goals (1973) recommended a greater reliance on guidelines and policy over police discretion.[38] Certain aspects of policing will never be completely free of discretion, however; to a large extent, the work of a police officer is unsupervised and unsupervisable. And as the police strive to achieve professionalism, they will remember that discretion is a key element of a profession.

Police discretion is also part of the American political process.[39] As Kenneth Culp Davis observed, a major contributing factor to police discretion is that state legislative commands are ambiguous. Legislatures speak with three voices: (1) They enact state statutes that seemingly require full enforcement of the laws, (2) they provide only enough resources for limited enforcement of them, and (3) they consent to such limited enforcement.[40] Some observers have even questioned the legality and morality of police discretion.[41] And, finally, it might be added, the statute books are often treated as society's "trash bins." A particular behavior is viewed negatively, and a law is passed against it. The police are stuck with the dilemma of having to enforce or ignore what may be an unpopular law.

There are other aspects of politics in police discretion. For example, several state and local governments restricted police use of deadly force long before the Supreme Court did away with the common law "fleeing felon" doctrine in ***Tennessee* v. *Garner*** (1985).[42]

A Related Function: Traffic

O. W. Wilson reportedly said that "the police traffic function overshadows every other function." That may be an overstatement today, but a strong link still exists between the patrol function and **traffic control**. Traffic stops account for about half (52 percent) of the contact Americans have with the police. Nearly twenty million Americans will be subjected to such stops in a given year; more than half of them (54 percent) will be cited.[43] Therefore, the importance of a seemingly trivial traffic stop cannot be overstated, because the manner in which the officer conducts the stop may in large measure determine the citizen's view of the police for many years to come.

Policing Today's Motorized Society

Police endeavor to reduce traffic deaths and injuries through the enforcement of motor vehicle laws. Indeed, many citizens have had their only contact with a police officer by virtue of a traffic-related matter.

There are, of course, various levels of traffic enforcement policy. Some departments are relatively lenient, while others have ticket quotas and pressure officers to have a "ticket blizzard" to bring in revenues. The stricter policies normally do not help police-community relations. Even with departmental policies, traffic enforcement carries wide discretion for patrol officers, who must decide whether to cite individuals.[44] It is an area in which many citizens think the police should practice discretion that is skewed toward leniency. Citizen perceptions of the police mission (or "Why aren't you out catching bank robbers?") and the perceived lack of seriousness of the offense often contribute to the citizen's unhappiness when cited for a traffic offense. As a result, traffic stops are a major source of friction between police officers and citizens.[45]

Notwithstanding the weight that many police agencies put on traffic enforcement, studies have found that crackdowns on speeding have no impact on fatality rates[46] and little influence on traffic violations or accident rates.[47] In fact, it has been shown that paying a small traffic fine and receiving a warning citation from an officer had a greater effect on future driving than appearance in a tough traffic court.[48]

Despite citizen disgruntlement with traffic enforcement, traffic stops and citations generally remain an integral part of police work. Police administrators find such work to be easily verifiable evidence that their officers are working.[49] Traffic enforcement has even gone high tech with the advent of the traffic camera, which has been nicknamed "the photocop." Traffic cameras, either mounted on a mobile tripod or permanently fixed on a pole, emit a narrow beam of radar that triggers a flash camera when the targeted vehicle is exceeding the speed limit by a certain amount, usually 10 miles per hour.

Police in Berkeley, California, have applied a new twist to the traffic function. Drivers who are "caught" driving safely and courteously are stopped and issued coupons good for movies or free nonalcoholic beverages at a local cafe. This Good Driver Recognition Program, which began with officers' donations, now receives city funding.[50]

Traffic Accident Investigation

Patrol officers have long been required to engage in traffic accident investigation (TAI). In this era of accountability and litigation, and considering the vast damage done to people and property each year as a result of traffic accidents, it is essential that officers understand this process of investigation and cite the guilty party—not only from a law enforcement standpoint but also in the event that the matter is taken to civil court. Until officers receive formal training in this complex field, they are in a very precarious position.

In addition to basic TAI training normally provided at the police academy, several agencies offer good in-service courses, and Northwestern University has a renowned traffic accident investigation program. The process of analyzing road and damage evidence, estimating speeds, reconstructing what occurred and why, issuing citations properly, drawing a diagram of the

The traffic function is a major part of the police role.

(Courtesy Washoe County, Nevada, Sheriff's Department)

scene, and explaining what happened in court is too important to be left to untrained officers. The public demands skilled accident investigations.

In Pursuit of the "Phantom Driver"

One of the traffic-related areas in which the police enjoy wide public support is in their efforts to identify, apprehend, and convict the hit-and-run (or so-called phantom) driver. No one thinks highly of drivers who collide with another vehicle or person and leave the scene. These drivers are often intoxicated. This matter is more of a criminal investigation than an accident investigation for the police. In some states, the killing of a human being while driving under the influence (DUI) is a felony. Physical evidence and witness statements must be collected in the same fashion as in a conventional criminal investigation; paint samples and automobile parts left at the scene are sent to crime laboratories for examination. The problem for the police is that unless the driver of the vehicle is identified—by physical evidence, an eyewitness, or a confession—the case can be lost. If the phantom vehicle is located, the owner can simply tell the police his or her vehicle was stolen or on loan. Thus, the police often must resort to psychology to get a confession by convincing the suspect that incriminating evidence exists.

Chapter 14, dealing with police technology, contains information on the use of the Global Positioning System (GPS) for investigating traffic accidents.

SUMMARY

This chapter has examined several issues related to the backbone of policing: patrol. It discussed the influences of an officer's shift, beat, and vehicle; some hazards of the job; the discretionary authority of patrol officers; and the traffic function.

Possible solutions to the discretion exercise presented in this chapter are offered next.

Possible Solutions to the Discretion Exercise

Following are some options available to the officer in the hypothetical discretion exercise on pages 148–149. Clearly, some options are not as good as others, and none are specifically recommended over others in all cases. Rather, the point is that officers in America's seventeen thousand police agencies can—and do—exercise daily all of the following alternatives in this kind of situation. Note that in each situation where Bob is separated from his vehicle, you should consider impounding it so it will not pose a safety hazard on the highway or be burglarized during the night.

1. Arrest the driver. This is obviously the formal, hard-line approach, certainly within the officer's power in order to remove Bob from the highway. Bob would be incarcerated for several hours, subjected to a blood alcohol test, and compelled to stay in jail until bond is posted. The officer would need to impound Bob's truck as well. In addition to towing and impound fees, other possible repercussions for Bob include an increase in his insurance premiums, and he may lose his driver's license (as well as his job). His expenses for fines and attorney's fees may be considerable. He may also be compelled to attend a driving or DUI school.
2. Issue a verbal warning and release. This is not a good choice unless the driver is clearly able to drive responsibly and the officer is certain that he will not injure others.
3. Issue a written warning and release. Again, this can be a poor choice, especially if Bob leaves and injures or kills others on the highway. If he does, the officer would certainly be morally if not legally responsible for those injuries.
4. Book Bob for protective custody, and let him sleep it off in the local jail.
5. Let Bob ride around in the patrol car until he is able to drive. This option is probably employed more often than the public realizes, especially in smaller jurisdictions where most residents are known to the police. This option helps to break the officer's monotony on patrol.
6. Tell Bob to sleep it off in his truck. Remove his vehicle keys to ensure he doesn't leave; then give him the keys and release him when he is able to drive.
7. Call his employer or a friend or relative to come and get him.

What is the common thread of these options? Note that for all options except 2 and 3, the officer is getting Bob off the highway. This exercise demonstrates the nature of police discretion. You should now understand that several means are often available to police officers—both formal (arrest) and informal—for dealing with problems. Some offenses (for example, driving under the influence, serious crimes, or citizen calls for service for noise complaints) allow the officer little discretion, but most situations (especially order-maintenance tasks, such as disorderly conduct, trespassing, and public intoxication) allow for considerable latitude as to whether to arrest the offender.

REVIEW QUESTIONS

1. Explain how the patrol function is affected by the officer's shift assignment and the nature of the beat to which he or she is assigned.
2. Describe some of the hazards that are inherent in beat patrol.
3. Review some of the major studies of the patrol function.
4. Define police discretion, list some of its advantages and disadvantages, and describe the factors that enter into the officer's decision-making process.
5. Describe the importance of the traffic function in patrol work.

INDEPENDENT STUDENT ACTIVITIES

1. If possible, participate in a ride-along program with local police officers. Try to determine the primary differences in police work from shift to shift and from officer to officer. Observe the patrol methods that the officers use, and note the patrol vehicle and the various "tools"—including the lethal and less-lethal weapons—they carry. Also explore the priority and methodologies of traffic enforcement.
2. Examine the use of police discretion in a local law enforcement agency. Which offenses allow officers little or no discretionary use of authority? Which offenses provide the greatest amount of freedom in terms of options? What do officers see as the advantages and disadvantages of this discretion, generally?

RELATED WEB SITES

COPNET (links to law enforcement agencies nationwide)
http://police.sas.ab.ca

Northwestern University Traffic Institute
http://server.traffic.northwestern.edu/

Police Foundation
pfinfo@policefoundation.org

NOTES

1. Quoted in JOHN A. WEBSTER, "Patrol Tasks," in *Policing Society: An Occupational View*, ed. W. CLINTON TERRY III (New York: John Wiley and Sons, 1985), pp. 263–313.
2. AMERICAN BAR ASSOCIATION, *Standards Relating to Urban Police Function* (New York: Institute of Judicial Administration, 1974), Standard 2.2.
3. TERRY, ed., *Policing Society*, pp. 259–60.
4. ANTHONY V. BOUZA, *The Police Mystique: An Insider's Look at Cops, Crime, and the Criminal Justice System* (New York: Plenum, 1990), p. 27.
5. DEPARTMENT OF JUSTICE, Office of Community Oriented Policing Services, *COPS Facts: 3–1–1 National Non-Emergency Number* (October/November 1996), p. 1.
6. ELIZABETH REUSS-IANNI, *Two Cultures of Policing: Street Cops and Management Cops* (New Brunswick, NJ: Transaction Books, 1983).
7. "More Police Killed This Year Than Last," Associated Press, December 29, 2000.
8. KIT R. ROANE, "Deadly Numbers: Cops Fear New Surge," *U.S. News and World Report*, February 26, 2001, p. 29.
9. JEROME H. SKOLNICK and DAVID H. BAYLEY, *The New Blue Line: Police Innovation in Six American Cities* (New York: Free Press, 1986), pp. 141–42.
10. JOHN P. CRANK, *Understanding Police Culture* (Cincinnati: Anderson, 1998), p. 83.
11. Ibid., p. 254.
12. Quoted in MARK BAKER, *Cops: Their Lives in Their Own Words* (New York: Pocket Books, 1985), p. 298.
13. BOUZA, *The Police Mystique*, p. 74.
14. DEPARTMENT OF JUSTICE, Federal Bureau of Investigation, *Law Enforcement Officers Killed and Assaulted, 2003* (Washington, DC: Author, November 2004), p. 15
15. LUKE DAWSON, "The Evolution of the Cop Car," *GEAR (nd)*, p. 70.
16. Ibid.
17. Ibid., p. 71.
18. Ibid.
19. Ibid.
20. GEORGE P. BLUMBERG, "Detroit's High-Speed Pursuit of the Police Car Market," *New York Times*, July 7, 2002, p. 12–1.
21. DAWSON, "The Evolution of the Cop Car," p. 72.
22. JOEL SAMAHA, *Criminal Justice*, 2nd ed. (St. Paul, MN: West, 1991), pp. 163–64.
23. POLICE FOUNDATION, *The Newark Foot Patrol Experiment* (Washington, DC: Author, 1981), p. 9.
24. Quoted in KEVIN KRAJICK, "Does Patrol Prevent Crime?" *Police Magazine* 1 (September 1978): 4–16.
25. T. J. BAKER, "Designing the Job to Motivate," *FBI Law Enforcement Bulletin* 45 (1976): 3–7.
26. KRAJICK, "Does Patrol Prevent Crime?" p. 10.

27. Ibid., pp. 11–13.
28. ROBERT C. TROJANOWICZ and DENNIS W. BANAS, *Job Satisfaction: A Comparison of Foot Patrol versus Motor Patrol Officers* (East Lansing: Michigan State University, 1985).
29. ROBERT C. TROJANOWICZ and DENNIS W. BANAS, *Perceptions of Safety: A Comparison of Foot Patrol versus Motor Patrol Officers* (East Lansing: Michigan State University, 1985).
30. Ibid., p. 235.
31. SKOLNICK and BAYLEY, *The New Blue Line*, p. 4.
32. JAMES Q. WILSON and GEORGE L. KELLING, "'Broken Windows': The Police and Neighborhood Safety," *Atlantic Monthly*, March 1982, pp. 28–29.
33. DAVID H. BAYLEY and EGON BITTNER, "Learning the Skills of Policing," in *Critical Issues in Policing: Contemporary Readings*, ed. ROGER G. DUNHAM and GEOFFREY P. ALPERT (Prospect Heights, IL: Waveland, 1989), pp. 87–110.
34. KENNETH CULP DAVIS, *Police Discretion* (St. Paul, MN: West, 1975), p. 73.
35. KENNETH CULP DAVIS, *Discretionary Justice* (Urbana: University of Illinois Press, 1969), p. 222.
36. RICHARD J. LUNDMAN, "Routine Police Arrest Practices: A Commonweal Perspective," *Social Problems* 22 (1974): 127–41; and DONALD PETERSEN, "Informal Norms and Police Practices: The Traffic Quota System," *Sociology and Social Research* 55 (1971): 354–61.
37. LAWRENCE W. SHERMAN, "Experiments in Police Discretion: Scientific Boon or Dangerous Knowledge?" *Law and Contemporary Problems* 47 (1984): 61–82.
38. NATIONAL ADVISORY COMMISSION ON CRIMINAL JUSTICE STANDARDS AND GOALS, *Police* (Washington, DC: U.S. Government Printing Office, 1973), pp. 21–33.
39. For a thorough discussion, see GREGORY HOWARD WILLIAMS, "The Politics of Police Discretion," in *Discretion, Justice and Democracy: A Public Policy Perspective*, ed. CARL F. PINKELE and WILLIAM C. LOUTHAU (Ames: Iowa State University, 1985), pp. 19–30.
40. DAVIS, *Police Discretion*, p. 22.
41. See JAMES F. DOYLE, "Police Discretion, Legality, and Morality," in *Police Ethics: Hard Choices in Law Enforcement*, ed. WILLIAM C. HEFFERNAN and TIMOTHY STROUP (New York: John Jay Press, 1985), pp. 47–68.
42. *TENNESSEE* v. *GARNER*, 471 U.S. 1 (1985).
43. PATRICK A. LANGAN, LAWRENCE A. GREENFIELD, STEVEN K. SMITH, MATTHEW R. DUROSE, and DAVID J. LEVIN, *Contacts between Police and the Public: Findings from the 1999 National Survey* (Washington, DC: Department of Justice, Bureau of Justice Statistics, February 2001), p. 2.
44. JAMES F. RICHARDSON, *Urban Police in the United States* (Port Washington, NY: Kennikat, 1974), pp. 111–12.
45. Ibid., p. 55; see also JONATHAN RUBENSTEIN, *City Police* (New York: Ballantine, 1973), pp. 153–55.
46. DONALD CAMPBELL and HAROLD L. ROSS, "The Connecticut Crackdown on Speeding," *Law and Society Review* 3 (1968): 33–53.

47. JOHN A. GARDINER, "Police Enforcement of Traffic Laws: A Comparative Analysis," in *City Politics and Public Policy*, ed. J. WILSON (New York: John Wiley and Sons, 1968), pp. 171–85.
48. HAROLD ROSS, "Folk Crime Revisited," *Criminology* 11 (1973): 71–85.
49. RICHARD J. LUNDMAN, "Working Traffic Violations," in *Policing Society*, ed. TERRY, pp. 327–33.
50. "The Right to Remain Foamy," *Newsweek*, July 17, 2000, p. 8.

CHAPTER

6

Community-Oriented Policing and Problem Solving

No problem can be solved by the same consciousness that created it. We must learn to see the world anew.

—Albert Einstein

If people are informed, they will do the right thing. It's when they are not informed that they become hostages to prejudice.

—Charlayne Hunter-Gault

None of us know all the potentialities that slumber in the spirit of the people, or all the ways in which people can surprise us when there is the right interplay of events.

—Vaclav Havel

Key Terms

community-oriented policing
crime prevention through environmental design (CPTED)
evaluation
implementation
problem-analysis triangle
repeat victimization (RV)
SARA

This is a uniquely challenging time to be entering police work. As mentioned in Chapter 1, a strategy that runs counter to the professional model of policing is spreading across the country: community-oriented policing and problem solving. This chapter examines the rationale for, and methods of, that strategy, which represents a return to the philosophy and practices of policing of the early nineteenth century.

For the past several decades, the dominant police strategy emphasized motorized patrol, rapid response time, and retrospective investigation of crimes. Those strategies have some merit for police operations, but they were not designed to address root community problems. They were instead designed to detect crime and apprehend criminals—hence the image of the "crime fighter" cop. Current wisdom holds that the police cannot unilaterally attack the burgeoning crime, drug, and gang problems that beset our society, draining our federal, state, and local resources. Communities must police themselves. We also understand that it is time now for new police methods and measures of effectiveness.

This chapter begins by examining community-oriented policing (COP), and then it reviews a more recent development, which extends COP by using the community to address crime and disorder: problem-oriented policing (POP). Included is an overview of the scanning, analysis, response and assessment (SARA) problem-solving process. Following that, we look at how these two interrelated and complementary concepts work to engage the community in crime fighting through what has been termed *community-oriented policing and problem solving (COPPS)*. We review how COPPS should be implemented and evaluated and how it relates to two elements of crime prevention: environmental design and repeat victimization. Next are two case studies of problem-solving efforts by police in Charlotte-Mecklenburg, North Carolina, and Tulsa, Oklahoma. A chapter summary, review questions, independent student activities, and related Web sites conclude the chapter.

Basic Principles of Community Policing

There is a growing awareness that the community can and must play a vital role in problem solving and crime fighting. A fundamental aspect of **community-oriented policing** has always been that the public must be engaged in the fight against crime and disorder. And as we noted in Chapter 1, Robert Peel emphasized in the 1820s in his principles of policing that the police and community should work together.[1]

In the early 1980s, the notion of community policing emerged as the dominant model for thinking about policing. It was designed to reunite the police with the community.[2] No single program describes community policing. Community policing has been applied in various forms by police agencies in the United States and abroad and differs according to community needs, local politics, and available resources.

COP is much more than a police-community relations program; it attempts to address crime control through a working partnership with the

Citizen input is crucial to the police for crime detection and prevention.

(Courtesy Hayward Police Department)

community. Community institutions such as families, schools, and neighborhood and merchants' associations are seen as key partners with the police in creating safer, more secure communities. The views of community members have greater status under community policing than under the traditional policing model.[3]

COP is a long-term process that involves fundamental institutional change. This concept redefines the role of the officer on the street, from crime fighter to problem solver and neighborhood ombudsman. It forces a cultural transformation of the entire department, including a decentralized organizational structure and changes in recruiting, training, awards systems, evaluation, and promotions. Furthermore, this philosophy asks officers to break away from the binds of incident-driven policing and to seek proactive and creative resolution to the problems of crime and disorder.

The major points at which COP departs from traditional policing are shown in Table 6-1.

A Major Step Forward: Problem-Oriented Policing

Problem solving is not new; police officers have always tried to solve problems. The difference is that in the past, officers received little guidance, support, or technology from police administrators for dealing with problems. But the routine application of problem-solving techniques is new. It is premised on two facts: that problem solving can be applied by officers throughout the agency as part of their daily work and that routine problem-solving efforts can be effective in reducing or resolving problems.

TABLE 6-1

Traditional versus Community Policing: Questions and Answers

Question	Traditional Policing	Community Policing
Who are the police?	A government agency principally responsible for law enforcement.	The police are the public, and the public are the police: The police officers are those who are paid to give full-time attention to the duties of every citizen.
What is the relationship of the police force to other public-service departments?	Priorities often conflict.	The police are one department among many responsible for improving the quality of life.
What is the role of the police?	To focus on solving crimes.	To take a broader problem-solving approach.
How is police efficiency measured?	By detection and arrest rates.	By the absence of crime and disorder.
What are the highest priorities?	Crimes that are high value (e.g., bank robberies) and those involving violence.	Whatever problems disturb the community most.
What, specifically, do police deal with?	Incidents.	Citizens' problems and concerns.
What determines the effectiveness of police?	Response times.	Public cooperation.
What view do police take of service calls?	Deal with them only if there is no real police work to do.	View them as a vital function and a great opportunity.
What is police professionalism?	Responding swiftly and effectively to serious crime.	Keeping close to the community.
What kind of intelligence is most important?	Crime intelligence (study of particular crimes or series of crimes).	Criminal intelligence (information about the activities of individuals or groups).
What is the essential nature of police accountability?	Highly centralized; governed by rules, regulations, and policy directives; accountable to the law.	Emphasis on local accountability to community needs.
What is the role of headquarters?	To provide the necessary rules and policy directives.	To preach organizational values.
What is the role of the press liaison department?	To keep the "heat" off operational officers so they can get on with the job.	To coordinate an essential channel of communication with the community.
How do the police regard prosecutions?	As an important goal.	As one tool among many.

Source: Malcolm K. Sparrow, Department of Justice, National Institute of Justice, "Implementing Community Policing" (Washington, DC: U.S. Government Printing Office, November 1988), pp. 8–9.

Problem-oriented policing was grounded on different principles than COP, but they are complementary. POP is a strategy that puts the COP philosophy into practice. It advocates that police examine the underlying causes of recurring incidents of crime and disorder. The problem-solving process helps officers identify problems, analyze them completely, develop response strategies, and assess the results.

Herman Goldstein is considered by many to be the principal architect of POP. Goldstein coined the term "problem-oriented policing" in 1979 out of frustration with the dominant model for improving police operations: "More attention [was] being focused on how quickly officers responded to a call than on what they did when they got to their destination."[4]

Goldstein argued for a radical change in the direction of efforts to improve policing. The first step in POP is to move beyond just handling incidents and to recognize that incidents are often overt symptoms of problems. It requires that officers take a more in-depth interest in incidents by acquainting themselves with some of the conditions and factors that cause them. The expanded role of police officers under problem-oriented policing is discussed later.

The Problem-Solving Process: SARA

POP has at its nucleus a four-stage problem-solving process known as **SARA**, for scanning, analysis, response, and assessment.[5]

Scanning: Problem Identification. Scanning involves problem identification. As a first step, officers should identify problems on their beats and look for a pattern, or persistent repeat incidents. At this juncture, the question might well be asked, "What is a problem?" *Problem* has been defined as "a group of two or more incidents that are similar in one or more respects, causing harm and, therefore, being of concern to the police and the public." Incidents may be similar in various ways, including

- *Behaviors:* This is the most frequent indicator and includes activities such as drug sales, robberies, thefts, and graffiti.
- *Location:* Problems may occur in area hot spots, such as downtown, and in housing complexes plagued by burglaries and in parks in which gangs commit crimes.
- *People:* This can include repeat offenders or victims; both account for a high proportion of crime.
- *Time:* Incidents may be similar in terms of the season, the day of the week, or the hour of day; examples include rush hours, bar closing times, and tourist seasons.
- *Events:* Crimes may peak during events such as university spring break, rallies, and gatherings.

Once disorder begins to descend on a location, crime soon follows—and the police will become involved.

(Courtesy Reno, Nevada, Police Department)

There does not appear to be any inherent limit on the types of problems patrol officers can face, because all types of problems are candidates for problem solving.

Numerous resources are available to the police to help them identify problems, including calls for service (CFS) data, especially repeat calls from the same location or a series of similar incidents. Other ways include citizen complaints, census data, data from other government agencies, newspaper and media coverage of community issues, officer observations, and community surveys.

The primary purpose of scanning is to conduct a preliminary inquiry to determine whether a problem really exists and whether further analysis is needed. During this stage, priorities should be established if multiple problems exist, and a specific officer or team of officers should be assigned to handle the problem. Scanning initiates the problem-solving process.

Analysis: The Heart of Problem Solving. The second stage, analysis, is the heart of the problem-solving process. Crime analysis has been defined as "a set of systematic, analytical processes providing timely and pertinent information to assist operational and administrative personnel."[6]

Effective, tailor-made responses cannot be developed unless people know what is causing the problem. Thus the purpose of analysis is to learn as much as possible about a problem in order to identify its causes. Complete analysis includes identifying the seriousness of the problem, identifying all the individuals or groups involved and affected, identifying all of the causes of the problem, and assessing current responses and their effectiveness.

Over time, several methods have been developed for analyzing crime and disorder. We examine some of them now, including the problem-analysis triangle; analyses of crime maps, offense reports, and calls for service; and the use of surveys.

Problem-Analysis Triangle. One tool that may be used for analyzing problems is the **problem-analysis triangle**, which helps officers visualize the problem and understand the relationship between the three elements of the triangle (see Figure 6-1). Additionally, it suggests where more information is needed and helps with crime control and prevention. Generally, three elements must be present before a crime or harmful behavior—problem—can occur: an offender (someone who is motivated to commit harmful behavior), a victim (a desirable and vulnerable target), and a location (although the victim and offender are not always in the same place at the same time; we discuss locations later) If these three elements show up over and over again in patterns and recurring problems, removing one of these elements can stop the pattern and prevent future harm.[7]

Mapping and Offense Reports. Computerized crime mapping (discussed in greater detail in Chapter 14) also assists with crime analysis. Mapping combines geographic information from global positioning satellites with crime statistics gathered by the department's computer-aided dispatching (CAD) system and demographic data provided by private companies or the U.S. Census Bureau.

Police offense reports can also be useful, analyzed for suspect characteristics, modi operandi (MOs), victim characteristics, and many other factors. Offense reports are also a potential source of information about high-crime areas and addresses, since they capture exact descriptions of locations. In a typical department, however, patrol officers may write official reports on only about 25 to 30 percent of all calls to which they respond. Another limitation is that there may be a considerable lag between when the officer files a report and when the analysis is complete.[8]

Computer software now exists for COPPS, to assist with beat profiling and demographics, finding patterns of problems, helping plan daily officer activities, balancing beat and officer workloads, and identifying current levels of performance. Such software can scan through hundreds of millions

FIGURE 6-1 Problem-analysis triangle.

Source: Department of Justice, Bureau of Justice Assistance, Comprehensive Gang Initiative: Operations Manual for Implementing Local Gang Prevention and Control Programs *(Draft, October 1993), p. 3.*

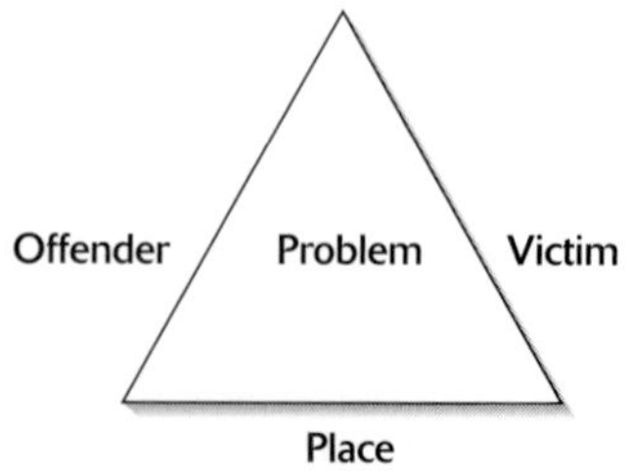

of pieces of data for patterns, trends, or clusters in beats and neighborhoods while ranking and reranking problems. In the field, the officer simply highlights the neighborhood, beat, or grid under consideration, then selects the problem or problems to be worked from a menu on the computer.

Call for Service Analysis. With the advent of CAD systems, a more reliable source of data on CFS has become available. CAD systems, containing information on all types of calls for service, add to information provided by offense reports, yielding a more extensive account of what the public reports to the police.[9] The data captured by CAD systems can be sorted to reveal hot spots of crime and disturbances—specific locations from which an unusual number of calls to the police are made.

A study in Minneapolis on hot spots analyzed nearly 324,000 calls for service for a one-year period over all 115,000 addresses and intersections. The results showed relatively few hot spots accounting for the majority of calls to the police:

- Fifty percent of all calls came from 3 percent of the locations.
- All robbery calls came from 2.2 percent of the locations.
- All rape calls came from 1.2 percent of the locations.
- All auto thefts came from 2.7 percent of the locations.[10]

Many police agencies have the capability to use CAD data for repeat call analysis (which is related to repeat victimization, discussed later). The repeat call locations identified in this way can become targets of directed patrol efforts, including problem solving. For example, a precinct may receive printouts of the top twenty-five calls-for-service areas to review for problem-solving assignments. In Houston, the police and Hispanic citizens were concerned about violence at cantinas (bars). Through repeat call analysis, police learned that only 3 percent of the cantinas in the city were responsible for 40 percent of the violence. The data narrowed the scope of the problem and enabled a special liquor-control unit to better target its efforts.[11]

Repeat alarm calls are another example of how CAD data can be used to support patrol officer problem solving. In fact, when an experiment began in Baltimore County, Maryland, some commanders preferred that officers start with alarm projects. Data documenting repeat alarm calls by address were readily available, and commanders anticipated that solving alarm problems would be relatively simple and would bring considerable benefits compared to the investment of time.[12]

Surveys. Not to be overlooked in crime analysis is the use of community surveys to analyze problems. For example, an officer may canvass all the business proprietors in shopping centers on his or her beat. In Baltimore, an officer telephoned business owners to update the police department's after-hours business contact files. Although the officer did not conduct a formal survey, he used this task to inquire about problems the owners might want to bring to police attention.

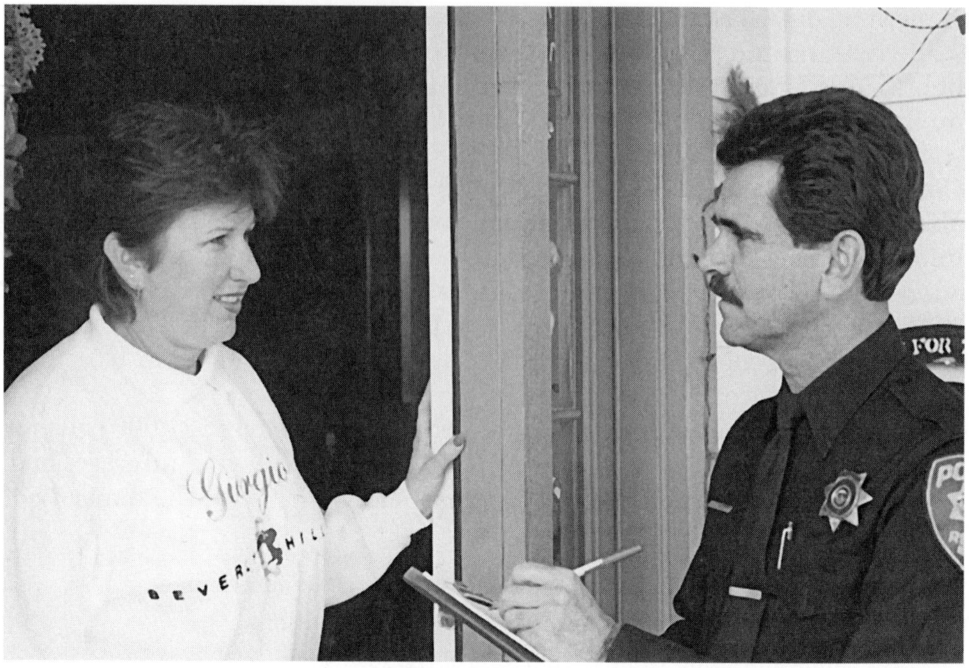

Citizen surveys provide the police with valuable information about citizen concerns and police performance.

(Courtesy Reno, Nevada, Police Department)

On a larger scale, a team of officers may survey residents of a housing complex or neighborhood known to have particular crime problems. The survey could assist in determining residents' priority concerns, acquiring information about hot spots, and learning more about residents' expectations of police.[13] Residents are also more likely to keep the police abreast of future problems when patrol officers leave their cards and encourage residents to contact them directly.

Many police agencies now provide citizens with crime analysis information via the Internet. As an example, Exhibit 6-1 shows the home page of the Tempe, Arizona, Police Department's Crime Analysis Unit.

Response: Formulating Tailor-Made Strategies. After a problem has been clearly defined and analyzed, the officer confronts the ultimate challenge in problem-oriented policing: the search for the most effective way of dealing with it. The response may be quite simple (such as reprogramming a public telephone at a convenience store where drug dealers conduct their "business" so that it only makes outgoing calls) or quite involved (for example, screening and evicting some tenants from a housing complex; cleaning up a neighborhood that is overcome with graffiti, debris, and junk cars; taking legal action to create a curfew; or condemning and razing a drug house). A number of examples of responses are provided in the two COPPS case studies discussed later.

This stage of the SARA process focuses on developing and implementing responses to the problem. Before entering this stage, the police agency must overcome the temptation to implement a response prematurely and must be certain that it has thoroughly analyzed the problem; attempts to fix problems quickly are rarely effective in the long term.

Assessment: Evaluating Overall Effectiveness. Finally, in the assessment stage, officers evaluate the effectiveness of their responses. A number of measures have traditionally been used by police agencies and community members to assess effectiveness. These include numbers of arrests; levels of reported crime; response times; clearance rates; citizen complaints; and various workload indicators, such as CFS and the number of field interviews conducted.[15] Several of these measures may be helpful in assessing the impact of a problem-solving effort.

A number of nontraditional measures will also shed light on whether a problem has been reduced or eliminated:

- Reduced instances of repeat victimization
- Decreases in related crimes or incidents
- Neighborhood indicators, which can include increased profits for businesses in the target area, increased usage of the area, increased property values, less loitering and truancy, and fewer abandoned cars
- Increased citizen satisfaction regarding the handling of the problem, determined through surveys, interviews, focus groups, electronic bulletin boards, and so on
- Reduced citizen fear related to the problem[16]

Assessment is obviously key in the SARA process; knowing that we must assess the effectiveness of our efforts emphasizes the importance of documentation and baseline measurement. Supervisors can help officers assess the effectiveness of their efforts.

A Collaborative Approach: Basic Principles of COPPS

The two concepts of community-oriented policing and problem-oriented policing are separate but complementary notions that can work together. Both COP and POP share some important characteristics: (1) decentralization (to encourage officer initiative and the effective use of local knowledge); (2) geographically defined rather than functionally defined subordinate units (to encourage the development of local knowledge); and (3) close interactions with local communities (to facilitate responsiveness to, and cooperation with, the community).[17] The following definition accurately captures the essence of this concept:

> Community Oriented Policing and Problem Solving (COPPS) is a proactive philosophy that promotes solving problems that are criminal, affect our quality of life, or increase our fear of crime, as well as other community issues. COPPS involves identifying, analyzing, and addressing community problems at their source.[18]

For COPPS to succeed, the following measures are required:

- Conducting accurate community needs assessments
- Mobilizing all appropriate players to collect data and brainstorm strategies

EXHIBIT 6-1

The Home Page of the Tempe, Arizona, Police Department's Crime Analysis Unit

ABOUT CRIME ANALYSIS

Historically, the causes and origins of crime have been the subject of investigation by varied disciplines. Some factors known to affect the volume and type of crime occurring from place to place are

- Population density and degree of urbanization with size locality and its surrounding area
- Variations in composition of the population, particularly youth concentration
- Stability of population with respect to residents' mobility, commuting patterns, and transience
- Modes of transportation and highway system
- Economic conditions, including median income, poverty level, and job availability
- Cultural factors and educational, recreational, and religious characteristics
- Family conditions with respect to divorce and family cohesiveness
- Climate
- Effective strength of law enforcement agencies
- Administrative and investigative emphases of law enforcement
- Policies of other components of the criminal justice system (*e.g.,* prosecutorial, judicial, correctional, and probational)
- Citizens' attitudes toward crime
- Crime-reporting practices of the citizenry

Crime Analysis Is Defined as . . .

"A set of systematic, analytical processes directed at providing timely and pertinent information relative to crime patterns and trend correlations to assist the operational and administrative personnel in planning the deployment of resource for the prevention and suppression of criminal activities, aiding the investigative process, and increasing apprehensions and the clearance of cases. Within this context, Crime Analysis supports a number of department functions including patrol deployment, special operations, and tactical units, investigations, planning and research, crime prevention, and administrative services (budgeting and program planning)." [Steven Gottlieb et al., 1994, "Crime Analysis: From First Report to Final Arrest"]

Types of Crime Analysis

Tactical crime analysis: An analytical process that provides information used to assist operations personnel (patrol and investigative officers) in identifying specific and immediate crime trends, patterns,

- Determining appropriate resource allocations and creating new resources where necessary
- Developing and implementing innovative, collaborative, comprehensive programs to address underlying causes and causal factors
- Evaluating programs and modifying approaches as needed[19]

series, sprees, and hot spots; providing investigative leads; and clearing cases. Analysis includes associating criminal activity by method of the crime, time, date, location, suspect, vehicle, and other types of information.

Strategic: Concerned with long-range problems and projections of long-term increases or decreases in crime (crime trends). Strategic analysis also includes the preparation of crime statistical summaries, resource acquisition, and allocation studies.

Administrative: Focuses on provision of economic, geographic, or social information to administration.

Crime Analysis Personnel

The Tempe Police Department's Crime Analysis Unit consists of three full-time crime analysts and a full-time crime analysis clerk. The Tempe Police Department's Crime Analysis Unit performs all three types of crime analysis: tactical, strategic, and administrative.

Interesting Statistics

The following reflect 2000 figures unless otherwise noted:

- The population of Tempe is 163,000.
- There were a total of 122,830 citizen-generated calls for service in 2000, up 3 percent from 1999.
- The citizen-generated calls for service rate per person is 754 per 1,000 persons. It was 734 per 1,000 persons in 1999.
- The most common type of citizen-generated call for service is the burglary alarm call. These calls are 11.6 percent of the total calls for service. Approximately 84.5 percent of alarm calls are false, 1.7 percent result in a report, and the remaining 15.6 percent of alarm calls are unknown in outcome (no evidence of a false alarm or of a crime committed). Officers spend an average of 18 minutes on an alarm call.
- The average amount of time it took an officer to respond to an emergency call for service is 6 minutes and 28 seconds.
- Approximately one report is generated for every five calls for service (not necessarily a criminal report).
- Tempe's crime rate is 9,353 Part I crimes per 100,000 persons.

To develop tailored responses, problem solvers should review their findings about the three sides of the crime triangle—victims, offenders, and location—and develop creative solutions that will address at least two sides of the triangle.[14] It is also important to remember that the key to developing tailored responses is making sure that the responses are very focused and directly linked to the findings from the analysis phase of the project.

Responses may be wideranging and often require arrests, referral to social service agencies, or changes in ordinances. Note that apprehension is not always the most effective solution.

Implementing COPPS

Since COPPS came into being, most police executives have implemented the strategy throughout the entire agency; some executives, however, have attempted to introduce the concept in a small unit or an experimental district,[20] often in a specific geographic area of the jurisdiction.

It is strongly argued that a departmentwide implementation of COPPS be used. When COPPS is established as a distinct unit within patrol rather than departmentwide, the introduction of this "special unit" seems to exacerbate the conflict between community policing's reform agenda and the more traditional outlook and hierarchical structure of the agency. A perception of elitism is created—a perception that is ironic because COPPS is meant to close the gap between patrol and special units and to empower and value the rank-and-file patrol officer as the most important functionary of police work.

The key lesson from research in **implementation**, however, is that there is no golden rule or any universal method to ensure the successful adoption of COPPS. Two general propositions are important, however, for implementing the concept: the role of the rank-and-file officer and the role of the environment (or "social ecology") where COPPS is to be implemented.[21] The social ecology of COPPS includes both the internal/organizational and external/societal environments. These factors are discussed next.

Principal Components of Successful Implementation

Moving an agency from the reactive, incident-driven mode to COPPS is a complex endeavor, often requiring a complete change in the culture of the police organization. Four principal components of implementation profoundly affect the way agencies do business: leadership and administration, human resources, field operations, and external relations.[22]

Leadership and Administration. It is essential that the chief executive communicate the idea that COPPS is departmentwide in scope. To get the whole agency involved, the chief executive must adopt four practices as part of the implementation plan:

1. Communicate to all department members the vital role of COPPS in serving the public. They must understand why handling problems is more effective than just handling incidents.
2. Provide incentives to all department members to engage in COPPS. This includes a new and different personnel evaluation and reward system as well as positive encouragement.
3. Reduce the barriers to COPPS that can occur. Procedures, time allocation, and policies all need to be closely examined.
4. Show officers how to address problems. Training is a key element of COPPS implementation. The executive must also set guidelines for innovation. Officers must know they have the latitude to innovate.[23]

Middle managers (captains and lieutenants) and first-line supervisors (sergeants) also play a crucial role in planning and implementing COPPS and in encouraging their officers to be innovative, take risks, and be creative.[24] First-line supervisors and senior patrol officers seem to generate the greatest resistance to community policing, largely because of longstanding working styles cultivated from years of traditional police work and because these officers can feel disenfranchised by a management system that takes the best and brightest out of patrol and that (they often believe) has left them behind.

Furthermore, the mechanisms that motivate, challenge, reward, and correct employees' behaviors must be compatible with the principles of COPPS. These include recruiting, selection, training, performance evaluation, promotion, honors and awards, and discipline, all of which should be reviewed to ensure that they promote and support the tenets of COPPS. First, recruiting literature should reflect the principles of COPPS. A job-task analysis identifying the new knowledge, skills, and abilities should be conducted and become a part of the testing process for entry-level employees. COPPS should also be integrated into academy training, field-training programs, and in-service training. Performance evaluations and reward systems should reflect new job descriptions and officers' application of their COPPS training. Finally, promotion systems should be expanded from their usual focus on tactical decision making, should include knowledge of the research on community policing, and should test an officer's ability to apply problem solving to various crime and neighborhood problems.

External Relations. Collaborative responses to neighborhood crime and disorder are essential to the success of COPPS. This requires new relationships and the sharing of information and resources between the police and the community, local government agencies, service providers, and businesses. The media provide an excellent means for police to educate the community about COPPS and crime and disorder.

Political support is another essential consideration when implementing COPPS. The political environment varies considerably, say, with the strong-mayor and council-manager forms of government. These and other rapidly changing political environments make the implementation of COPPS more difficult—especially when we add to the mix the at-will employment of most police executives.

A Broader Role for the Street Officer

A major departure of problem-oriented policing from the conventional style lies with POP's view of the line officer, who is given much more discretion and decision-making ability and is trusted with a much broader array of responsibilities.

Problem-oriented policing values "thinking" officers, urging that they take the initiative in trying to deal more effectively with problems in the areas they serve. This concept effectively uses the potential of college-educated officers, "who have been smothered in the atmosphere of traditional policing."[25] It also gives officers a new sense of identity and self-respect; they are more challenged and have opportunities to follow through on individual cases—to analyze and solve problems, which will give them greater job satisfaction. Using patrol officers in this manner allows the agency to provide sufficient challenge for both better-educated officers and those who remain a patrol officer throughout their entire career.[26]

Under problem-oriented policing, officers continue to handle calls, but they also do much more. They combine the information gathered in their responses to incidents with information obtained from other sources to get a clearer picture of the problem. They then address the underlying conditions. If they are successful in ameliorating these conditions, fewer incidents may occur; those that do occur may be less serious. The incidents may even cease. At the very least, information about the problem can help police design more effective ways of responding to each incident. Police administrators ought to be recruiting people as police officers who can "serve as mediators, as dispensers of information, and as community organizers."[27]

Did It Succeed? Evaluating COPPS

Rigorous **evaluation** is an essential component of the COPPS initiative. Until rigorous evaluations are completed, there will be no clear verdict about whether the COPPS approach made a difference in controlling crime and disorder. An evaluation will also help to determine whether a crime-prevention initiative has achieved such goals as reducing crime and the fear of crime, has raised the community's quality of life, and is worthy of continued funding.

Evaluating the outcomes of problem-solving projects is not the same as the assessment stage of the SARA problem-solving process. Evaluation is the more overarching concept, and it involves large projects—surveys, performance evaluations, and so on. Broken down into simplified steps, evaluation asks some or all of the following questions:

- What is the problem? (Define it by such measures as community indicators, police data, and public surveys.)
- How does the project intend to address the problem? (Look at the project's goal statements.)
- What does the project do to resolve the problem? (Look at the project's objectives.)
- How does the project carry out its objectives? (Look, for example, at collaborative efforts among the police, other governmental agencies, and private businesses.)
- What impact (over time) does the prevention project have on the problem? (For example, over a specified time period, reported crimes increased or decreased by what percentage?)[28]

The evaluative criteria employed in the professional policing model, such as crime rates, clearance rates, and response times, have been problematic when applied to the professional model itself and are even less appropriate for the COPPS model. These measures do not gauge the effect of crime-prevention efforts. A decrease in the reliance on these quantitative measures of police success is also important because communities differ in the services they desire, depending on their particular characteristics.[29]

Several criteria can assist in assessing the success of a COPPS effort. An effective COPPS strategy has a positive impact on reducing neighborhood crime, allays citizen fear of crime, and enhances the quality of life in the community.[30] Assessing the effectiveness of COPPS efforts includes determining whether problems have indeed been solved and how well the managers and patrol officers have used community partnerships.

COPPS evaluations can include outcome measures and impact measures. Outcome measures might include the following:

- Control of crime—compare, for example, the present rates of serious and violent crime with those of an earlier time period. Included in this category are behavioral changes, such as increased use of a once drug-infested park or a greater number of students attending drug-education programs.
- Citizen satisfaction with police services and fear of crime, which are measured with basic survey techniques (discussed later). Content analysis of media portrayals of police work, analysis of letters from citizens, and analysis of citizen complaints can also be used to evaluate citizen satisfaction with police services.[31]

Outcome measures can also reflect environmental changes (such as number of street lights installed, traffic patterns altered, graffiti removed).

Impact measures describe and monitor changes in community indicators (such as community efforts to prevent or deal with crime and violence, community perception of quality of life, level of business, and other activity in the area).[32]

Crime Prevention

An important corollary of COPPS—a critical and rapidly developing concept that all police officers should understand—is crime prevention. It stands to reason that it is preferable as well as much less expensive (in terms of both financial and human resources) to prevent a crime from occurring in the first place rather than having to try to solve the offense and arrest, prosecute, and possibly incarcerate the offender. A focus on crime prevention shifts a police organization's purpose. Once the question becomes "How can we prevent the next crisis?" all kinds of approaches become possible.[33]

Crime prevention once consisted primarily of exhorting people to "lock it or lose it" and giving advice to citizens about door locks and window bars for their homes and businesses. It typically was (and often still is) an add-on program for the police agency, which normally included a few officers who were trained to go to citizens' homes and perform security surveys or to speak publicly on the subject of target hardening. Times are rapidly changing in this regard.

Crime prevention and COPPS are close companions, attempting to define the problem, identify the contributing causes, seek out the proper people or agencies to assist in identifying potential solutions, and work as a group to implement the solution. The problem drives the solution.[34] At its heart, COPPS is about preventing crime.

Next we briefly discuss two important aspects of crime prevention: crime prevention through environmental design and repeat victimization.

Crime Prevention through Environmental Design

Crime prevention through environmental design (CPTED) is defined as the "proper design and effective use of the environment that can lead to a reduction in the fear and incidence of crime, and an improvement in the quality of life."[35] At its core are three principles that support problem-solving approaches to crime:

- *Natural access control:* Employing elements such as doors, shrubs, fences, and gates to deny access to a crime target and to create a perception among offenders that there is a risk in selecting the target.
- *Natural surveillance:* Placing windows, lighting, and landscaping properly to increase the ability to observe intruders as well as regular users, allowing observers to challenge inappropriate behavior or to report it to the police or to the property owner.
- *Territorial reinforcement:* Using elements such as sidewalks, landscaping, and porches to distinguish between public and private areas and to help users exhibit signs of ownership that send hands-off messages to would-be offenders.[36]

Five types of information are needed for CPTED planning:

- Crime analysis information, including crime mapping, police crime data, incident reports, and victim and offender statistics
- Demographics, including statistics about residents, such as age, race, gender, income, and income sources
- Land use information, including zoning information (such as residential, commercial, industrial, school, and park zones) as well as occupancy data for each zone
- Observations, including observations of parking procedures, maintenance, and residents' reactions to crime
- Resident information, including resident crime surveys and interviews with police and security officers[37]

Studying Prey: Repeat Victimization

Our society—including the police—gives far greater attention to criminal offenders than to crime victims. Just as at the zoo, where there always seem to be more spectators around the lions and tigers than around wildebeests and antelope, more attention is focused on the predators than on their prey. However, an evolving body of research in Great Britain suggests that crime victims should be placed on the national agenda. In the United States—where POP has spread across the country—patterns of **repeat victimization (RV)** have not been examined or assimilated into problem solving. Police officers in the United States would benefit from this developing body of knowledge, which can play a major role in crime prevention and analysis.

The premise underlying RV is that if the police want to know where a crime will occur next, they should look at where it happened last. RV is not new; police officers have always been aware that the same people and places are victimized again and again. What is new, however, are attempts abroad to incorporate repeat victimization knowledge into formal crime-prevention efforts.

One in three burglaries reported in the United States is a repeated burglary of a household. Furthermore, a 48 percent RV was found for sexual incidents (including grabbing, touching, and assault), 43 percent for assaults and threats, and 23 percent for vehicle vandalism.[38] A study of white-collar crime indicated that the same people are victims of fraud and embezzlement time and time again[39] and that banks that have been robbed also have high rates of repeat victimization.[40] These data show that providing crime-prevention assistance to potential victims is not only morally justifiable in most instances, it is also an efficient and practical way of allocating limited police resources.

Why would, say, a burglar return to burgle the same household again? One could argue that, for several reasons, the burglar would be stupid not to return: Temporary repairs to a burgled home will make a subsequent burglary easier, the burglar is familiar with the physical layout and surroundings of the property, the burglar knows what items of value were left behind at the prior burglary, and the burglar also knows that items that were taken at an earlier burglary are likely to have been replaced through insurance policies.

Repeat victimization is arguably the best single predictor routinely available to the police in the absence of specific intelligence information. A small number of victims accounts for a disproportionate number of victimizations.[41]

Drug Abuse Resistance and Education

A related attempt to prevent crime should be discussed briefly: the well-known Drug Abuse Resistance and Education (DARE) program. The program, launched in 1983 and now administered by the police in 80 percent of schools, has not fared well among researchers. Over the past decade, studies have repeatedly shown that the $226 million program has little effect on keeping kids from abusing drugs. Indeed, the mayor of Salt Lake City recently halted the city's budget for DARE, declaring it "a complete waste of money, a fraud on the American people."[42] One of its key flaws, researchers allege, has been that students are taught that all drugs are equally dangerous; when students find that this is not true, the DARE message is undercut.[43]

Now DARE officials are admitting that the program needs a new direction. Officials are revamping the program, reducing the lecturing role of local officers, and involving kids in a more active way. A new curriculum is being developed for use in some schools that will show brain scans after drug use to demonstrate the harm, shift officers into more of a coaching role, and have kids engage in role-playing about peer pressure.[44]

COPPS Case Studies

Following are two excellent case studies of COPPS efforts using the SARA model, the first in Charlotte-Mecklenburg, North Carolina,[45] and the second in Tulsa, Oklahoma.[46] In each case, instead of merely showing up at a crime scene, taking offense reports, and leaving the scene, the police employed a variety of responses to combat crime and disorder.

Addressing Domestic Violence in Charlotte-Mecklenburg

Scanning. For several years, the Charlotte-Mecklenburg, North Carolina, Police Department (CMPD) had made domestic assaults a priority and had worked to analyze those cases, intervene, and reduce the occurrence of domestic violence in the community. Then an officer working a particularly serious domestic case became concerned about the overall number of domestic assaults in his patrol district in a year's time: 305 domestic assaults, or 30 percent of the total assaults. Many of these assaults involved the same individuals but at different locations in the county; rather than a repeat call location being the "hot spot" for crime, he surmised that tracking the *participants* might be a better indicator of future violence.

Analysis. A much more thorough analysis of domestic assault reports showed that the average victim had filed nine previous police reports, most involving the same suspect but sometimes crossing police district boundaries. Many of the prior reports were for other indicator crimes, such as trespassing, threatening, and stalking. Most repeat call locations were domestic situations. It became clear that it was best to regard the victim and suspect as the hot spots instead of a fixed geographic location.

Response. Officers developed a tailored response plan for each repeat offense case, including zero tolerance of criminal behavior by the suspect and assistance from other criminal justice and social service agencies. A Police Watch Program was implemented in which systematic zone checks of both the victim's residence and workplace were made when appropriate. A Domestic Violence Hotline voice-mail system was also initiated, which victims could use to report miscellaneous incidents involving the suspect. Officers developed detailed case files and created a separate database with victim and offender background data. The database tracks victims and offenders as moving hot spots from one address to another and across patrol district boundaries.

Assessment. Repeat calls for service were reduced by 98.9 percent at seven target locations. Domestic assaults decreased 7 percent in this targeted patrol district, while increasing 29 percent in the rest of the city. Only 14.8 percent of domestic violence victims in the project reported repeat victimization, as opposed to a benchmark figure of 35 percent. No internal affairs complaints were generated by officer contacts with suspects.

Ameliorating Juvenile Problems in Tulsa

Scanning. North Tulsa experienced consistently higher crime rates than the rest of the city. Nearly half of the violent crimes that were reported occurred in this section of the city—a depressed, low-income area lacking in adequate services. The Tulsa Housing Authority was established to support the city's low-income public housing. In an attempt to determine the nature of the crime problem in North Tulsa, a special management team of Tulsa police officials conducted a study and decided to concentrate on five public-housing complexes where high crime rates and blatant street dealing existed.

Analysis. A residential survey conducted by patrol officers revealed that 86 percent of the occupants lived in households headed by single females. Officers in the target area noticed large groups of school-age youth in the housing complexes who appeared to be selling drugs during school hours. A comparison of the dropout and suspension rates in North Tulsa schools with those in other areas of the city determined that the city's northernmost high school, serving most of the high school–age youth in the five complexes, had the highest suspension (4.4 percent) and dropout (10 percent) rates of any school in the city. It also reported the highest number of pregnant teenagers in the school system. Few of the juveniles observed in the complexes had legitimate jobs, and most of them appeared to be attracted to drug dealing by the easy money.

Supervisors at Uniform Division North placed volunteers into two-officer foot teams, assigned to the complexes on eight-hour tours. The teams established a rapport with residents and assured them that police were present to ensure their safety. Within a month, officers verified juvenile involvement in drug trafficking. A strategy was needed to provide programs to deter youth from selling or using drugs.

Response. Officers S. and N., assigned to foot patrol at one of the complexes, believed that the youth needed programs that would improve their self-esteem, teach them values, and impart decision-making skills. Eighty-six percent of the boys came from homes without fathers. To provide positive role models for young men, the officers started a Boy Scout troop in the complex for boys between 11 and 17 years of age. Officer N., a qualified Boy Scout leader, and Officer S. began meeting with the boys on Saturdays in a vacant apartment.

Officers J. and E. also organized a Boy Scout troop. In addition, they started a group that worked to raise money for needy residents and police-sponsored youth activities. Officer J. spoke at civic group meetings and local churches throughout the city to solicit donations and increase awareness of the needs of young people on the city's north side. Volunteers came from the churches and the civic groups where Officer J. spoke.

Officers B. and F., foot patrol officers at another complex, developed plans for unemployed young people. Officer B. organized a group called the Young Ladies Awareness Group, which hosted guest speakers who taught different job-related skills each week. Programs instructed young women how to dress for job interviews and employment; role-playing officers demonstrated proper conduct during interviews. The women were also instructed in résumé writing and makeup, hair care, and personal hygiene. Officer F. worked with a government program that sponsored sessions on goal setting and self-esteem building to prepare young people to enter job-training programs. Officer F. also helped area youth apply for birth certificates and arranged for volunteers from the Oklahoma Highway Patrol and a local school to help teach driver's education. Officers even provided funds for young people who were unable to pay the fees to obtain birth certificates or driver's licenses. Officers F. and B. also tried to explain the value of an education and persuade youth in their complex to return to school. Unfortunately, parents too often appeared unconcerned when their children missed classes.

The foot patrol officers became involved in a day camp project conducted at "the Ranch," a 20-acre north-side property that the police had confiscated from a convicted drug dealer. The project used the property for a day camp for disadvantaged youth recruited from the target projects. Tulsa's mayor and chief of police came to the Ranch to meet with the youth, as did psychologists, teachers, ministers, and celebrities. Guests tried to convey the value of productive and drug-free lives, among other ethical values.

To combat dropout and suspension problems, a program called Adopt a School had police officers patrol the schools during classes, not to make arrests but rather to establish rapport with the students. The program was intended to reduce the likelihood of student involvement in illegal activities.

Assessment. The police noted a decline in street sales of illegal drugs in the five target complexes. Youth reacted positively to the officers' efforts to help them, and the programs seemed to deter them from drug involvement. The police department continued to address the problems of poor youth in North Tulsa. Foot patrol officers met with the Task Force for Drug Free Public Housing to inform the different city, county, and statewide officials of the needs of youth in public housing. Other social service agencies began working with the police department, establishing satellite offices on the north side of the city, scheduling programs, and requesting police support in their efforts.

SUMMARY

This chapter set out the basic principles and strategies of the community-policing and problem-oriented policing concepts. It also described a combined approach, which is popular today and which represents the best strategy for the future: community-oriented policing and problem solving, or COPPS. Blending these two concepts results in a better, more comprehensive approach to providing quality police service, combining the emphasis on forming a police-community partnership to fight crime with the use of the SARA problem-solving process. It was shown that two very important components of this philosophy are the expanded role of the street officer and the focus on crime analysis.

REVIEW QUESTIONS

1. Define *community policing*, and describe the major ways this concept differs from traditional policing.
2. List and explain the four parts of the SARA problem-solving process for police.
3. Briefly describe the importance of implementation and evaluation of COPPS.
4. Explain what is meant by crime prevention, and describe how it relates to community policing and problem solving.
5. Summarize the case studies of COPPS at work with domestic violence and juvenile problems.

INDEPENDENT STUDENT ACTIVITIES

1. Determine whether the community-oriented policing and problem-solving strategy has been adopted by agencies in your local area; if so, how does it differ in terms of agency philosophy and methods from the traditional, professional model of policing?
2. Using information provided in this chapter concerning the SARA problem-solving process, perform a problem-solving exercise with a particularly crime-ridden neighborhood, beat, or area of your jurisdiction.

RELATED WEB SITES

Community Policing Consortium
http://www.communitypolicing.org/

National Crime Prevention Council
http://www.ncpc.org

Office of Community Oriented Policing Services (COPS)
http://www.usdoj.gov/cops

NOTES

1. W. L. MELVILLE LEE, *A History of Police in England* (London: Methuen, 1901), ch. 12.
2. ROBERT TROJANOWICZ and BONNIE BUCQUEROUX, *Community Policing: A Contemporary Perspective* (Cincinnati: Anderson, 1990), p. 154.
3. MARK H. MOORE and ROBERT C. TROJANOWICZ, Department of Justice, National Institute of Justice, *Corporate Strategies for Policing* (Washington, DC: U.S. Government Printing Office, 1988), pp. 8–9.
4. HERMAN GOLDSTEIN, "Problem-Oriented Policing" (paper presented at the Conference on Policing: State of the Art III, National Institute of Justice, Phoenix, June 12, 1987).
5. Ibid., pp. 43–52.
6. NOAH FRITZ, "Crime Analysis" (Tempe, AZ: Tempe Police Department, no date), p. 9.
7. JOHN ECK, "A Dissertation Prospectus for the Study of Characteristics of Drug Dealing Places" (College Park: University of Maryland, November 1992).
8. BARBARA WEBSTER and EDWARD F. CONNORS, "Community Policing: Identifying Problems" (Alexandria, VA: Institute for Law and Justice, March 1991), p. 9.

9. See LAWRENCE W. SHERMAN, PATRICK R. GARTIN, and MICHAEL E. BUERGER, "Hot Spots of Predatory Crime: Routine Activities and the Criminology of Place," *Criminology* 27 (1989): 27.
10. Ibid., p. 36.
11. WILLIAM SPELMAN, *Beyond Bean Counting: New Approaches for Managing Crime Data* (Washington, DC: Police Executive Research Forum, January 1988).
12. WEBSTER and CONNORS, "Community Policing," p. 11.
13. For an example of this type of survey process, see WILLIAM H. LINDSEY and BRUCE QUINT, *The Oasis Technique* (Fort Lauderdale: Florida Atlantic University/Florida International University Joint Center for Environmental and Urban Problems, 1986).
14. RANA SAMPSON, "Problem Solving," in *Neighborhood-Oriented Policing in Rural Communities: A Program Planning Guide* (Washington, DC: Department of Justice, Office of Justice Programs, Bureau of Justice Assistance, 1994), p. 4.
15. DARREL STEPHENS, "Community Problem-Oriented Policing: Measuring Impacts," in *Quantifying Quality in Policing*, ed. LARRY T. HOOVER (Washington, DC: Police Executive Research Forum, 1995).
16. DEPARTMENT OF JUSTICE, Office of Community Oriented Policing Services, *Problem-Solving Tips: A Guide to Reducing Crime and Disorder through Problem-Solving Partnerships* (Washington, DC: Author, 2002), p. 20.
17. MOORE and TROJANOWICZ, *Corporate Strategies for Policing*, p. 11.
18. KENNETH J. PEAK and RONALD W. GLENSOR, *Community Policing and Problem Solving: Strategies and Practices*, 4th ed. (Upper Saddle River, NJ: Prentice Hall, 2004), p. 159.
19. Ibid.
20. HERMAN GOLDSTEIN, *Problem-Oriented Policing* (New York: McGraw-Hill, 1990), p. 172.
21. GREGORY SAVILLE and D. KIM ROSSMO, "Striking a Balance: Lessons from Community-Oriented Policing in British Columbia, Canada" (unpublished manuscript, June 1993), pp. 29–30.
22. RONALD W. GLENSOR and KENNETH J. PEAK, "Implementing Change: Community-Oriented Policing and Problem Solving," *FBI Law Enforcement Bulletin* 7 (July 1996): 14–20.
23. JOHN E. ECK and WILLIAM SPELMAN, *Problem-Solving: Problem-Oriented Policing in Newport News* (Washington, DC: Police Executive Research Forum, 1987), pp. 100–101.
24. Ibid., p. 9.
25. HERMAN GOLDSTEIN, "Toward Community-Oriented Policing," *Crime and Delinquency* 33 (1987): 6–30.
26. Ibid., p. 21.
27. Ibid.
28. JOHN E. ECK, *Assessing Responses to Problems: An Introductory Guide for Police Problem-Solvers* (Washington, DC: Department of Justice, Office of Community Oriented Policing Services, 2002), p. 6.
29. COMMUNITY POLICING ADVISORY COMMITTEE, *Community Policing Advisory Committee Report* (Victoria, British Columbia: Author, 1993), p. 61.

30. DEPARTMENT OF JUSTICE, Bureau of Justice Assistance, Community Policing Consortium, *Understanding Community Policing: A Framework for Action* (Washington, DC: Author, 1993), p. 86.

31. CALIFORNIA DEPARTMENT OF JUSTICE, Attorney General's Office, Crime Prevention Center, *COPPS: Community Oriented Policing and Problem Solving* (Sacramento: Author, November 1992), pp. 90–91.

32. Ibid., pp. 4–5.

33. JIM JORDAN, "Shifting the Mission: Seeing Prevention as the Strategic Goal, Not a Set of Programs," *Subject to Debate* (Washington, DC: Police Executive Research Forum, December 1999), pp. 1–2.

34. Ibid., p. 8.

35. C. R. JEFFREY, *Crime Prevention through Environmental Design* (Beverly Hills, CA: Sage, 1971).

36. NATIONAL CRIME PREVENTION COUNCIL, *Designing Safer Communities: A Crime Prevention through Environmental Design Handbook* (Washington, DC: Author, 1997), pp. 7–8.

37. Ibid., p. 3.

38. G. FARRELL and W. SOUSA, "Repeat Victimization in the United States and Ten Other Industrialized Countries" (paper presented at the National Conference on Preventing Crime, Washington, DC, October 13, 1997).

39. Ibid.

40. Ibid.

41. G. FARRELL, "Preventing Repeat Victimization," in *Building a Safer Society*, ed. M. TONRY and D. P. FARRINGTON (Chicago: University of Chicago Press, 1995), pp. 469–534.

42. ROCKY ANDERSON, quoted in CLAUDIA KALB, "DARE Checks into Rehab," *Newsweek*, February 26, 2001, p. 56.

43. Ibid.

44. Ibid.

45. Adapted from POLICE EXECUTIVE RESEARCH FORUM, *Excellence in Problem-Oriented Policing: The 2002 Herman Goldstein Award Winners* (Washington, DC: Author, November 2002), pp. 19–26.

46. DEPARTMENT OF JUSTICE, Bureau of Justice Assistance, *Problem-Oriented Drug Enforcement: A Community-Based Approach for Effective Policing* (Washington, DC: Police Executive Research Forum, October 1993), pp. 27–28.

CHAPTER 7

Criminal Investigation: The Science of Detection

Murder though it hath no tongue will speak.

—*Shakespeare, Hamlet, Act II, Scene 2*

And the Lord said unto Cain, Where is thy brother Abel? [The first recorded instance of a criminal interrogation] And he said, I know not; am I my brother's keeper? [The first recorded instance of perjury] And He said, what hast thou done? The voice of thy brother's blood crieth unto me from the ground. [The first recorded instance of criminal evidence]

—*Genesis 4:9–10*

The truth is rarely pure and never simple.

—*Oscar Wilde*

Key Terms

Bertillon system
cold case
corpus delicti
criminalistics
criminal profiling
cybercrook
dactylography
forensic science
interrogation
investigative stages
mitochondrial DNA
modus operandi
polygraph examination
stalking

To these chapter-opening quotes, one more, by Ludwig Wittgenstein, could have been added: "How hard I find it to see what is right in front of my eyes!"[1] Investigating crimes has indeed become a complicated art as well as a science, as will be seen in this chapter.

The art of sleuthing has long fascinated the American public. Certainly the O. J. Simpson trial of 1995, which received more media attention than any other case before or after, heightened America's interest in detective work and forensic science. For decades, Americans have feasted on the exploits of dozens of well-known television- and novel-based detectives. Some fictional masterminds, like Sherlock Holmes and Agatha Christie's Hercule Poirot, epitomized the intellectual detective, using a minimum of clues and a lot of psychology and logic to solve crimes. Others, like Clint Eastwood's Dirty Harry character, relied more on weaponry and machismo, capturing bad guys—often using very violent means—while paying little attention to the rule of law (covered in Chapter 9).

In reality, investigative work is largely misunderstood, often boring, and generally overrated; it results in arrests only a fraction of the time; and it relies strongly on the assistance of witnesses and even some luck. Nonetheless, the related fields of forensic science and criminalistics are the most rapidly developing areas of policing—and probably in all of criminal justice. This is an exciting time to be in the investigative or forensic disciplines.

This chapter begins by defining forensic science and criminalistics and by looking at their origins. Then we discuss the evolution of criminal investigation, emphasizing the identification of people and firearms. Next we analyze the application of forensic science within the larger context of the criminal justice system, followed by a review of the qualities detectives should have.

Next we consider undercover police work, the use of polygraph testing, and DNA analysis. We examine behavioral science applications in investigations, including criminal profiling, psychics, and hypnosis. Then we examine some recent investigative developments and problems in the field, including the interrogation of terrorists, forensic entomology, investigating stalkers and "cybercrooks," and working cold cases. A chapter summary, review questions, independent student activities, and related Web sites conclude the chapter.

The Scope of Forensic Science and Criminalistics

The terms *forensic science* and *criminalistics* are often used interchangeably. Forensic science is the broader term; it is that part of science used to answer legal questions. It is the examination, evaluation, and explanation of physical evidence in law. Forensic science encompasses pathology, toxicology, physical anthropology, odontology (development of dental structure and dental diseases), psychiatry, questioned documents, ballistics, tool work comparison, and serology (the reactions and properties of serums), among other fields.[2] Criminalistics is one branch of forensic science; it deals with the study of physical evidence related to crime. From such a study, a crime may be reconstructed.

Technology is rapidly advancing in forensic laboratories. The lab technicians shown here are performing DNA, ballistics, shoeprint, hair and fiber, fingerprint, and drug analysis.
(Markus Matzel / Das Foto, Peter Arnold, Inc. [top left]; © Spencer Grant / Photo [top right]; Mikael Karlsson, Arresting Images [middle left]; Dr. Jurgen Scriba, Photo Researchers [middle right]; Mikael Karlsson, Arresting Images [bottom left]; and Getly Images, Inc. [bottom right])

EXHIBIT 7-1

Making His Bones: Famed Sculptor Is a Secret Weapon in Missing-Person Cases

He's a sculptor of international renown, but to those in law enforcement, Philadelphia artist Frank Bender is a secret weapon capable of recreating from just the bones a face so uncannily like that of its owner that he is credited with helping investigators around the country solve their most stubborn missing-persons cases....

Bender has done 28 sculptures for police. Each takes approximately one month, and he charges $1,700—the amount he says agencies are willing to pay. In his most recent case, he was asked to help identify a man whose decapitated and dismembered body was found in two burn barrels last summer in the Pocono Mountains of Pennsylvania....

Bender, 61, is also a founding member of the Vidocq Society, an organization of 82 individuals who, upon request, will put their considerable forensic expertise to work on tough investigations....

When constructing his sculptures, Bender works with a chart that gives tissue thickness for 21 points of the face, depending on a victim's age, race and ethnicity. But it is the skull that is the "road map of the face," abetted by a healthy dose of Bender's own intuition....

Among his most famous recreations was that of John List, an accountant who murdered his mother, wife and three children in their New Jersey home in 1971, then disappeared. Working with a profiler, Bender was able to come up with a clay bust that was shown on "America's Most Wanted." List was captured a few days after the program aired in 1989.

Another was Anna Mary Duval, a 62-year-old Phoenix woman who had been shot three times in the head. Years later, mobster John Martini was convicted of her murder.

Bender also does age reconstructions, some of which have led to the capture of drug traffickers and gangsters....

And it was Bender's pastel-and-charcoal renderings, along with busts, of Robert Nauss, a convicted killer and former head of the Warlocks motorcycle gang, and Hans Vorhauer, a methamphetamine manufacturer with a genius IQ, that helped investigators find the pair after they broke out of a Maryland prison in the mid-1980s....

Source: "Making His Bones: Famed Sculptor Is a Secret Weapon in Missing-Person Cases," *Law Enforcement News*, April 15, 2003, p. 4. John Jay College of Criminal Justice, CUNY, 555 W 57th St., New York, NY 10019.

Criminalistics is interdisciplinary, drawing on mathematics, physics, chemistry, biology, anthropology, and many other scientific fields.[3] Dr. Paul Kirk, a leader in the criminalistics movement in this country, once remarked that "criminalistics is an occupation that has all of the responsibilities of medicine, the intricacy of the law, and the universality of science."[4] Criminalistics has occasionally reached plateaus, but on the whole it is a dynamic and progressive discipline.

Basically, the analysis of physical evidence is concerned with identifying traces of evidence, reconstructing criminal acts, and establishing a common origin of samples of evidence. Peter DeForest and colleagues described the types of information that physical evidence can provide:[5]

- Information on the ***corpus delicti*** (or "body of the crime"): physical evidence showing that a crime was committed, such as tool marks, a broken door or window, a ransacked home, and missing valuables in a burglary or a victim's blood, a weapon, and torn clothing in an assault.
- Information on the ***modus operandi*** (or method of operation): physical evidence showing means used by the criminal to gain entry, tools that were used, types of items taken, and other signs, such as urine left at the scene, an accelerant used at an arson scene, the way crimes are committed, and so forth. Many well-known criminals have left their "calling card" at their crimes, either in terms of what they did to their victims or the physical condition of the crime scene.
- Linking a suspect with a victim: one of the most important linkages, particularly with violent crimes. It includes hair, blood, clothing fibers, and cosmetics that may be transferred from victim to perpetrator. Items found in a suspect's possession, such as bullets or a bloody knife, can also be linked to a victim.
- Linking a person to a crime scene: also a common and significant linkage. It includes fingerprints, glove prints, blood, semen, hairs, fibers, soil, bullets, cartridge cases, tool marks, footprints or shoeprints, tire tracks, and objects that belonged to the criminal. Stolen property is the most obvious example.
- Disproving or supporting a witness's testimony: Evidence can indicate whether or not a person's version of events is true. An example is a driver whose car matches the description of a hit-and-run vehicle. If blood is found on the underside of the car and the driver claims that he hit a dog, tests on the blood can determine whether the blood is from an animal or from a human.
- Identification of a suspect: One of the best forms of evidence for identifying a suspect is fingerprints, which prove "individualization." Without a doubt, that person was at the crime scene.

Origins of Criminalistics

The study of **criminalistics** began in Europe. The first major book describing the application of scientific disciplines to criminal investigations was written in 1893 by Hans Gross, a public prosecutor and later a judge from Graz, Austria.[6] Translated into English in 1906, the book remains a highly respected work in the field. Two prominent aspects of criminalistics, personal identification and firearms analysis, are discussed next.

Personal Identification: Anthropometry and Dactylography

Historically there have been two major systems for personal identification of criminals: anthropometry and **dactylography**. The former did not survive long; the latter, better known as fingerprint identification, is widely used throughout the world today.

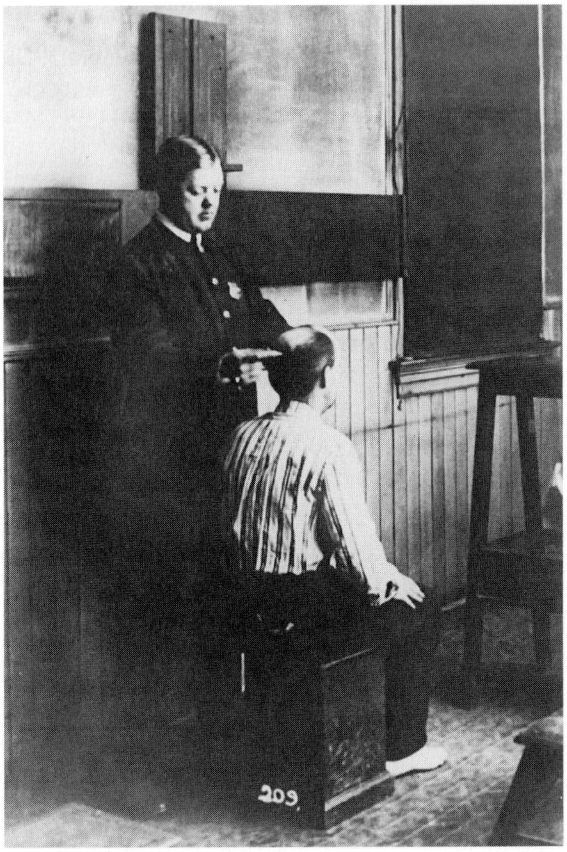

A police officer taking Bertillon measurements.

(Courtesy St. Louis, Missouri, Police Department)

Anthropometry was developed by Alphonse Bertillon (1853–1914) in 1882. This method, the first attempt at criminal identification that was thought to be reliable and accurate, was based on the facts that every human being differs from everyone else in the exact measurements of their bodies and that the sum of these measurements yields a characteristic formula for each individual.[7] Bertillon, largely a failure at everything he tried, performed menial tasks in 1879 for the Paris Police Department, filing cards that described criminals so vaguely as to have little meaning—"stature: average... face: ordinary."[8]

Bertillon became increasingly frustrated with the senselessness of his work. He began comparing photographs of criminals and taking measurements of those who had been arrested. He eventually concluded that if eleven physical measurements of a person were taken, the chances of finding another person with the same eleven measurements were 4,191,304 to 1.[9]

Bertillon's report to his superiors outlining his criminal identification system was not met with enthusiasm. His chief said, "Bertillon? If I am not mistaken, you are a clerk of the twentieth grade and have been with us for only eight months, right? And already you are getting ideas? Your report sounds like a joke."[10] In 1883, however, Bertillon's "joke" was given worldwide attention when it was implemented on an experimental basis and Bertillon correctly made his first criminal identification.[11]

Around the turn of the century, many countries abandoned anthropometry, or the **Bertillon system**, adopting the simpler and more reliable system of fingerprint identification. Bertillon recognized the potential of fingerprinting in 1902, when he discovered a defendant's prints on a glass cupboard and solved a murder case. Yet he persisted in his view that anthropometry was superior to dactylography. He explored other ideas as well, developing the prototype of the "mug shot" (to which he reluctantly added fingerprints) and pioneering police photography. But fingerprinting was eventually found superior to the Bertillon system. After Bertillon's death in 1914, France became the last major country to replace anthropometry with dactylography as its system of criminal identification.[12] Bertillon's pioneering work in personal identification has earned him a place in history; today Bertillon is considered the "father of criminal investigation."[13]

Fingerprints Prevail over Bertillonage. Dactylography was first used in 1900 in England as a system of criminal identification; however, fingerprints have a long legal and scientific history. In the first century, a Roman lawyer named Quintilianus introduced a bloody fingerprint at trial, successfully defending a child accused of murdering his father.[14] Fingerprints were also used on contracts during the Chinese T'ang Dynasty in the eighth century. In 1684, in England, Dr. Nehemiah Grew first called attention to the system of pores and ridges in the hands and feet. And in 1823, John Perkinje, a professor at the University of Breslau, named nine standard types of fingerprint patterns and outlined a broad method of classification.[15] In spite of these developments, fingerprinting would not emerge as a prominent means of criminal identification for another seventy-five years.

Beginning in 1858, William Herschel, a British official in India, requested the palm prints and fingerprints of those with whom he did business in an attempt to get people to keep their agreements. Over a twenty-year period, Herschel noticed that the patterns of the lines on the fingerprints for an individual never changed, despite growth and other physical changes. Excited by the prospect of using fingerprints to identify criminals, he wrote in 1877 to the Inspector General of the Prisons of Bengal. The reply implied in kind terms that Herschel's idea was insane. Discouraged by this, Herschel never pursued his discovery.[16] Meanwhile, Henry Faulds, a Scottish physician teaching in Tokyo, had been interested in fingerprints for several years. After clearing a theft suspect by comparing his fingerprints with those found in a home, Faulds reported his findings in the journal *Nature* in 1880. Herschel read Faulds's article and published a reply, claiming credit for the discovery more than twenty years earlier. A controversy arose that was never resolved, and still no official interest was shown in using fingerprints for criminal identification.

In 1888, Sir Francis Galton (1822–1911), a cousin of Charles Darwin, became interested in criminal investigation and contacted Herschel, who unselfishly turned over all of his files in the hope that Galton could apply fingerprinting to practical police uses.[17] In 1892, Galton published the first definitive book on dactylography, *Finger Prints*, in which he presented statistical proof of the uniqueness of fingerprints and of their applications.[18] In Argentina two years later, Juan Vucetich outlined his method of fingerprint classification. A disciple of Vucetich's, Inspector Alvarez, obtained the first American criminal conviction based on fingerprints in 1892. They helped convict a woman who beat her two sons to death.[19]

The major breakthrough for fingerprints was made by Edward Henry (1850–1931), who went to India at the age of twenty-three and became inspector general of police in Nepal in 1891. Henry developed an interest in fingerprints. He instituted Bertillon's system, but he added fingerprints to the cards. In 1893, Henry began working on a simple, reliable method of classification, and in 1897 he recommended that anthropometry be dropped in favor of his own fingerprint-classification system. Six months later, his recommendations were followed throughout British India. In 1901, Henry published his *Classification and Use of Finger Prints* and was appointed assistant police commissioner of London, rising to the post of commissioner two years later.[20]

The Jones and West Cases. In 1904, Detective Sergeant Joseph Faurot of New York City was sent to England to study fingerprints, becoming the first foreigner trained in the Henry classification system. Upon his return to New York, where he reported his findings, Faurot was told by his superiors to forget such scientific nonsense, and he was transferred to a walking beat. In 1906, Faurot arrested a man dressed in formal evening wear but no shoes who was creeping out of a suite at the Waldorf-Astoria Hotel; the man claimed to be a respected citizen named James Jones. Faurot sent the man's fingerprints to Scotland Yard and learned that "James Jones" was actually Daniel Nolan, who had twelve prior convictions for hotel thefts and was wanted for burglary in England. Nolan, confronted with this information, confessed to several thefts in the Waldorf-Astoria and was sent to prison for seven years. Publicity surrounding this case greatly advanced the credibility of fingerprinting in America.[21]

An even more important and amazing incident furthered the use of fingerprints in America. In 1903, Will West arrived at the federal penitentiary in Leavenworth, Kansas. While West was being processed into the institution, a staff member said that a photograph was already on file for him, along with Bertillon measurements. West denied ever having been in Leavenworth. A comparison of fingerprints showed that despite nearly identical physical appearance and Bertillon measurements, the identification card on file belonged to a William West who had been in Leavenworth since 1901. The incident served to establish the superiority of fingerprints over anthropometry as a system of personal identification.

Firearms Identification

Firearms are perennially the leading instrument of death for Americans, causing about 70 percent of the nation's 22,000 homicide deaths each year.[22]

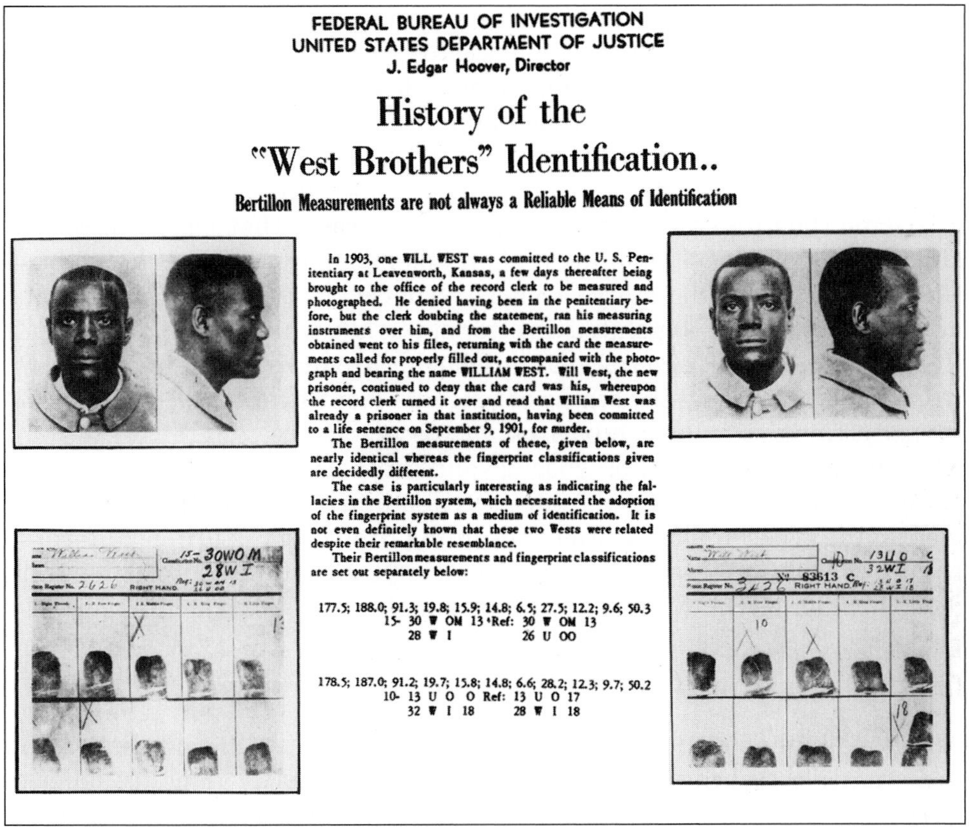
FEDERAL BUREAU OF INVESTIGATION
UNITED STATES DEPARTMENT OF JUSTICE
J. Edgar Hoover, Director

History of the "West Brothers" Identification..

Bertillon Measurements are not always a Reliable Means of Identification

In 1903, one WILL WEST was committed to the U. S. Penitentiary at Leavenworth, Kansas, a few days thereafter being brought to the office of the record clerk to be measured and photographed. He denied having been in the penitentiary before, but the clerk doubting the statement, ran his measuring instruments over him, and from the Bertillon measurements obtained went to his files, returning with the card the measurements called for properly filled out, accompanied with the photograph and bearing the name WILLIAM WEST. Will West, the new prisoner, continued to deny that the card was his, whereupon the record clerk turned it over and read that William West was already a prisoner in that institution, having been committed to a life sentence on September 9, 1901, for murder.

The Bertillon measurements of these, given below, are nearly identical whereas the fingerprint classifications given are decidedly different.

The case is particularly interesting as indicating the fallacies in the Bertillon system, which necessitated the adoption of the fingerprint system as a medium of identification. It is not even definitely known that these two Wests were related despite their remarkable resemblance.

Their Bertillon measurements and fingerprint classifications are set out separately below:

177.5; 188.0; 91.3; 19.8; 15.9; 14.8; 6.5; 27.5; 12.2; 9.6; 50.3
15- 30 W OM 13 Ref: 30 W OM 13
28 W I 26 U OO

178.5; 187.0; 91.2; 19.7; 15.8; 14.8; 6.6; 28.2; 12.3; 9.7; 50.2
10- 13 U O O Ref: 13 U O 17
32 W I 18 28 W I 18

The West Brothers Case.

(Courtesy Federal Bureau of Investigation)

Furthermore, the Centers for Disease Control recently found in an eight-year study that 93 percent of all firearms-related deaths involve the intentional use of guns.[23] It is plain that the frequency of shootings in this country has made firearms identification very important.

In 1835, Henry Goddard, one of the last of the Bow Street Runners, made the first successful attempt to identify a murderer from a bullet recovered from the body of a victim. Goddard noticed that the bullet had a distinctive slight gouge on it and seized a bullet mold with a corresponding gouge at the home of a suspect; the defendant confessed.[24] In 1889, Professor Lacassagne removed a bullet from a corpse in France; upon examining it, he found seven grooves made as the bullet passed through the barrel of a gun. Shown the guns of a number of suspects, Lacassagne identified the one that could have left seven grooves. With this evidence, a man was convicted of the murder.[25]

In 1898, a German chemist named Paul Jeserich was given a bullet taken from the body of a man murdered near Berlin. After firing a test bullet from the defendant's revolver, Jeserich took microphotographs of the fatal and test bullets, later testifying that the defendant's revolver fired the fatal bullet. Although he was at the threshold of eminence, Jeserich did not pursue his technique further.[26] Attention gradually shifted to other aspects of firearms. In 1913, Professor Balthazard published a major article on firearms identification, noting that the firing pin, breechblock, extractor, and ejector all leave marks on cartridges and that these markings vary among different types of weapons. With World War I approaching, Balthazard's article did not receive wide attention.

Chicago witnessed the St. Valentine's Day Massacre in 1929. A special grand jury inquiring into the matter noted that there were no facilities for analyzing the numerous bullets and cartridge cases that had been strewn about. As a result, several influential jury members raised funds to establish a permanent crime laboratory. Colonel Calvin Goddard (1858–1946), a retired army physician, was appointed director of the lab, which was established at the Northwestern University Law School.[27] Goddard is the person most responsible for raising the status of firearms identification to a science and for perfecting the bullet comparison microscope.[28]

Firearms identification goes beyond comparing a bullet found in the victim and a test bullet fired from the defendant's weapon. It also includes identifying types of ammunition, designing firearms, restoring obliterated serial numbers on weapons, and estimating the distance between a gun's muzzle and a victim when the weapon was fired.[29]

Contributions of August Vollmer and Others

August Vollmer's contributions to the development of criminalistics and investigative techniques were considerable. In 1907, as police chief of Berkeley, California, he enlisted the services of a University of California chemistry professor named Loeb to identify a suspected poison during a murder investigation. Vollmer instituted a formal training program to ensure that his officers properly collected and preserved criminal evidence. Vollmer called on scientists on campus on several other occasions. His support helped John Larson produce the first workable polygraph in 1921.

Vollmer also established the first full forensic laboratory in Los Angeles in 1923; the concept soon spread to other cities, including Sacramento (a state laboratory), San Francisco, and San Diego. Although they were small, the influence of these laboratories is still seen today. Furthermore, Vollmer's efforts in establishing a relationship between his police department and the university led other scientists to get involved in forensic science. For example, Paul Kirk became so interested in criminalistics that he soon began offering courses in it as part of the biochemistry curriculum at the University of California at Berkeley.[30] Many of the graduates of that program went on to become criminalists and crime laboratory directors.

Other contributors included Albert Osborn, who in 1910 wrote *Questioned Documents*, a definitive work; Edmond Locard, who maintained a central interest in locating microscopic evidence; and Leone Lattes, who in 1915 developed a blood-typing procedure from dried blood—a key event in serology.[31]

THE EVOLUTION OF CRIMINAL INVESTIGATION

Investigative Beginnings: The English Contribution

To fully understand the development of criminal investigation in America, it is important to first understand the social, economic, political, and legal contexts in which it evolved. To do so, we will briefly discuss the impact of (1) the agricultural and industrial revolutions, (2) the Fielding brothers and their Bow Street Runners, and (3) London's Metropolitan Police.

It is probably difficult to see any relationship between agriculture and fingerprinting or surveillance, but as Charles Swanson and his colleagues observed,

> During the eighteenth century two events, an agricultural and industrial revolution, began a process of change that profoundly affected how police services were delivered and investigations conducted. Improved agricultural methods gave England increased agricultural productivity in the first half of the eighteenth century. Improvements in agriculture [led to] the Industrial Revolution, in the second half of the eighteenth century, because they freed people from farm work for city jobs. As the population of England's cities grew, slums also grew, crime increased and disorders became more frequent. Consequently, public demands for government to control crime grew louder.[32]

In 1748, Henry Fielding became chief magistrate of London's Bow Street, and in 1750 he established a small band of volunteer "thief takers," known as the Bow Street Runners. These homeowners hurried to the scenes of reported crimes and began investigations. In 1752, Fielding began publishing the *Covent Garden Journal*, which included descriptions of wanted persons. When Henry Fielding died in 1754, his blind brother, John, carried on his work for the next twenty-five years (although less successfully; the effectiveness of the amateur force declined during John's tenure). By 1785, the government was so impressed by the work of the Runners that each of them was paid a salary, and an attempt was made to expand the detective concept to other areas of London.

Following the creation of London's Metropolitan Police in 1829, the British public became suspicious and even hostile toward its new force. The French, they knew, had experienced oppression under their centralized police force. Thus high standards were set for the London bobbies (discussed in Chapter 1); there were five thousand dismissals and six thousand forced resignations during the first three years of operation. High standards of conduct were expected and maintained. Despite the eventual reputation for fairness and professionalism that the London force earned, the fear remained that the use of police "spies"—detectives in plain clothes—would reduce civil liberties.[33] Occasionally, bobbies were temporarily removed from patrol duties to investigate crimes on their beats, but the public was uneasy. As an example, in 1833, a sergeant was dismissed from duty after Parliament learned that he had infiltrated a radical group, acquired a leadership position, and argued for the use of violence.

Until 1842, Metropolitan constables competed with Bow Street Runners to investigate crimes; in that year, a regular detective branch was opened at Scotland Yard, superseding the Runners.[34] The detective force was to have no more than sixteen investigators, and its operations were restricted because of concern about "clandestine methods."[35] In 1878, following a scandal in which three of four chief inspectors of detectives were convicted of taking bribes, a separate, centralized Criminal Investigation Division (CID) was established at Scotland Yard. It was headed by an attorney; uniformed constables who had shown an aptitude for investigation were recruited to become CID detectives.[36]

Investigative Techniques Come to America

Meanwhile, the success of the Metropolitan Police in London was not going unnoticed in America. Beginning with a paid, twenty-four-hour professional police force in New York City in 1844, by 1880 virtually all major cities had a police force that used Peel's principles. Ironically, while the bobbies were striving for public acceptance that would allow them to work out of uniform, American police administrators were having difficulty getting their officers to accept uniforms (see Chapter 1). Only after the Civil War did the wearing of a uniform—which was invariably blue—become widely accepted by American police officers.[37]

Following the advent of private police in America in the mid-1840s (most notably Pinkerton's National Detective Agency), the concept of plainclothes officers spread in America. As early as 1845, New York City had eight hundred such officers; however, not until 1857 was the department authorized to appoint twenty patrol officers as "detectives."[38] In November 1857, the New York Police Department established a rogues' gallery—photographs of known offenders arranged by criminal specialty and offender height. By June 1858, it had over seven hundred photographs for detectives to study for future recognition.[39] Photographs in the rogues' gallery showed some offenders grimacing, puffing their cheeks, rolling their eyes, and otherwise trying to distort their appearance to thwart detectives and lessen the chance of later recognition.[40]

To assist its detectives, in 1884 Chicago established the nation's first municipal Criminal Investigation Bureau.[41] The Atlanta Police Department's Detective Bureau was organized in 1885 with a staff of one captain, one sergeant, and eight detectives.[42] In 1886, Thomas Byrnes, chief detective of New York City, published *Professional Criminals in America*, which included pictures, descriptions, and methods of all criminals known to him.[43] To supplement the rogues' gallery, Byrnes instituted the Mulberry Street Morning Parade. At 9:00 every morning, all criminals arrested in the past twenty-four hours were marched before his detectives, who were expected to take notes and to recognize the criminals later.[44] Byrnes had personal shortcomings, however; in 1894, he was forced to leave the department when he admitted that he had grown wealthy by tolerating gambling dens and brothels.[45]

State and Federal Developments

From its earliest days, the federal government employed investigators to detect revenue violations, but their responsibilities were narrow and their numbers few.[46] In 1865, Congress created the U.S. Secret Service to combat counterfeiting. In 1903—two years after the assassination of President McKinley—the guarding of the president was made a permanent Secret Service responsibility.[47]

In 1905, the California Bureau of Criminal Identification was established to share information about criminal activity; that same year, the state of Pennsylvania created a state police force. Serving as a prototype for modern state police organizations, one of the functions of the Pennsylvania State Police was to provide local police with assistance in investigations; that tradition continues among today's state police agencies.[48]

The forerunner of what was to become the Federal Bureau of Investigation (FBI) (discussed in Chapter 2) was created in 1908. In 1924, J. Edgar Hoover assumed leadership of the Bureau of Investigation; eleven years later, Congress enacted legislation giving the FBI its present designation. Under Hoover, who understood the importance and uses of information, records, and publicity, the FBI became known for investigative efficiency. In 1932, the FBI established a crime laboratory and made its services free—they remain free of charge today to state and local police. In 1935, it opened its National Academy, providing training courses for state and local police as well as federal officers. And in 1967, the National Crime Information Center (NCIC) was made operational by the FBI, providing data on wanted persons and property stolen in all fifty states. These developments gave the FBI considerable influence over policing in America; Hoover and the FBI vastly improved policing practices in this country, keeping crime statistics and assisting investigations.[49]

Forensic Science and the Criminal Justice System

Investigative Stages and Activities

The police, more specifically investigators and criminalists, operate on the age-old theory that there is no such thing as a perfect crime; criminals either leave a bit of themselves (such as a hair or clothing fiber) at the crime scene or they take a piece of the crime scene away with them. Thus it is the job of the police and the crime lab to unify their efforts and to find that incriminating piece of evidence, which they can use in conjunction with other pieces of evidence to determine "whodunit" and to bring the guilty party to justice.

Homicide investigation is the most important and challenging work performed by detectives.

(Courtesy City of New York Police Department Photo Unit)

In the apprehension process, when a crime is reported or discovered, police officers respond, conduct a search for the offender (it may be a "hot" crime-scene search, where the offender is likely present, a "warm" search in the general vicinity, or a "cold" investigative search), and check out suspects. If the search is successful, evidence for charging the suspect is assembled, and the suspect is apprehended.[50] Cases not solved in the initial phase of the apprehension process are assigned either to an investigative specialist or, in smaller police agencies, to an experienced uniformed officer who functions as a part-time investigator. According to Paul Weston and Kenneth Wells, what follows are the basic **investigative stages**:[51]

The preliminary investigation: The work of the preliminary investigation is crucial, involving the first police officer at the scene. Duties to be completed include establishing whether a crime has been committed; securing from any witnesses a description of the perpetrator and his or her vehicle; locating and interviewing the victim and all witnesses; protecting the crime scene (and searching for and collecting all items of possible physical evidence); determining how the crime was committed and what the resulting injuries were, as well as the nature of property taken; recording in field notes and sketches all data about the crime; and arranging for photographs of the crime scene.

The continuing investigation: This stage, which begins when preliminary work is done, includes follow-up interviews; developing a theory of the crime; analyzing the significance of information and evidence; continuing the search for witnesses; beginning to contact crime lab technicians and assessing their analyses of the evidence; conducting surveillances, interrogations, and polygraph tests, as appropriate; and preparing the case for the prosecutor.

Reconstructing the crime: The investigator seeks a rational theory of the crime. Most often, inductive reasoning is used: The collected information and evidence are carefully analyzed to develop a theory. Often, a rational theory of a crime is developed with some assistance from the careless criminal. *Verbrecherpech*, or "criminal's bad luck," is an unconscious act of self-betrayal. One of the major traits of criminals is vanity; their belief in their own cleverness, not chance, is the key factor in their leaving a vital clue. Investigators look for mistakes.

Focusing the investigation: When this stage is reached, all investigative efforts are directed toward proving that one suspect (perhaps with accomplices) is guilty of the crime. This decision is based on the investigator's analysis of the relationship between the crime, the investigation, and the habits and attitudes of the suspect.

Arrest and Case Preparation

A lawful arrest brings the investigation into even greater focus and provides the police with several investigative opportunities. The person arrested can be searched and booked at the police station and fingerprinted for positive identification and future use. Evidence may be found at these stages. The prisoner may wish to talk to the police. Here, the officer must obviously know and understand the laws of arrest and search and seizure as well as the laws of evidence (especially the "chain of custody"). Any evidence found during the arrest must be collected, marked, transported, and preserved as carefully as that found at a crime scene.

"Case preparation is organization."[52] For an investigation to succeed at trial, all reports, documents, and exhibits must be arrayed in an orderly manner. This package must then be forwarded to the prosecutor. At this point, the investigator never injects personal opinions or conclusions into the case. The identification of the accused leads to an array of witnesses and physical evidence. The corpus delicti of the crime has been established, and the combination of "what happened" and "who did it" has occurred, at least in the mind of the investigator. The investigator must also prepare for the almost inevitable negative evidence that must be countered at trial, where the accused may contend that he or she did not commit the crime. (He or she may try to attack the investigative work, use an alibi, or get the evidence suppressed.) The defendant may offer an affirmative defense, admitting that he or she committed the acts charged but claiming that he or she was coerced, acted in self-defense, was legally insane, and so forth. Or the defendant may attack the corpus delicti, contending that no crime was committed or that there was no intent present.[53]

In the prosecutor's office, the case is reviewed, assigned for further investigation, and, if warranted, prepared for trial. Conferences with the investigator and witnesses are usually held. The prosecutor may waive prosecution if the case appears to be too weak to result in a conviction; if the accused will inform on other (usually more serious) offenders; if a plea bargain is more attractive than a trial; or if there are mitigating circumstances in the case (such as emotional disturbance).

An investigation is successful when the crime being investigated is solved and the case closed. Often a case is considered cleared even if no arrest has been made, as when the offender dies, the case is found to be a murder-suicide, the victim refuses to cooperate with the police or prosecutor, or the offender has left the jurisdiction and the cost of extradition is not justified.[54]

Detectives: Qualities, Myths, and Attributes

The **detective** function is now well established within the police community. A survey by the RAND Corporation revealed that every city with a population of more than 250,000, along with 90 percent of the smaller cities, has officers specifically assigned to investigative duties.[55]

Several myths surround police detectives, who are often portrayed in movies as rugged, confident (sometimes overbearing), independent, streetwise individualists who bask in glory, are rewarded with big arrests, and adorned by beautiful women. Detective work carries a strong appeal for many patrol officers, young and veteran alike. In reality, detective work is seldom glamorous or exciting. Investigators, like their bureaucratic cousins, often wade in paperwork and spend many hours on the telephone. Furthermore, studies have not been kind to detectives, showing that their vaunted productivity is overrated. Not all cases have a good or even a 50-50 chance of being cleared by an arrest. Indeed, in a study of over 150 large police departments, a RAND research team learned that only about 20 percent of their crimes could have been solved by detective work.[56] Another study, involving the Kansas City, Missouri, Police Department, found that fewer than 50 percent of all reported crimes received more than a minimal half hour's investigation by detectives. In many of these cases, detectives merely reported the facts discovered by the patrol officers during the preliminary investigations.[57]

Yet the importance and role of detectives should not be understated. Detectives know that a criminal is more than a criminal. As Weston and Wells said,

> John, Jane and Richard are not just burglar, prostitute and killer. John is a hostile burglar and is willing to enter a premises that might be occupied. Jane is a prostitute who wants a little more than pay for services rendered and is suspected of working with a robbery gang and enticing her customers to secluded areas. Richard is an accidental, a person who, in a fit of rage, killed the girl who rejected him.[58]

To be successful, the investigator must possess four personal attributes to enhance the detection of crime: an unusual capability for observation and recall; extensive knowledge of the law, rules of evidence, scientific aids, and laboratory services; power of imagination; and a working knowledge of social psychology.[59] Successful detectives (and even patrol officers) also appear to empathize with the suspect; if a detective can appear to understand why a criminal did what he did ("You robbed that store because your kids were hungry, right?"), a rapport is often established that results in the suspect's telling the officer his or her life history—including how and why he or she committed the crime in question. Perhaps first and foremost, however, detectives need logical skills, the ability to exercise deductive reasoning, to assist in their investigative work. (An interesting example of the logical skills needed for police work was provided by Al Seedman, former chief of detectives for the New York Police Department, in Chapter 3.)

Officers Who "Disappear": Working Undercover

Undercover work is a highly sought-after and valued type of investigative police work. Undercover work can be defined as the assignment of police officers to investigative roles in which they adopt fictitious civilian identities for a sustained period of time in order to uncover criminal activities that are not usually reported to police.[60] (For more about undercover work, see the Practitioner's Perspective by former FBI special agent George Togliatti in Chapter 8.)

Undercover police operations have increased greatly since the 1970s, owing largely to expanded drug investigations. The selection process typically is intense and very competitive. Since only a few officers are actually selected for undercover assignments, these officers enjoy a professional mystique, in large measure because of wide discretionary and procedural latitude in their roles, minimal departmental supervision, the ability to exercise greater personal initiative, and a higher degree of professional autonomy than regular patrol officers.[61]

Problems with the Role

However, the conditions of undercover work may lessen officer accountability and lower adherence to procedural due process and confidence in the rule of law.[62]

One of the most important requirements is the ability to cultivate informants for information on illegal activities and for contacts with active criminals. Deals and bargains must be struck and honored. Therefore close association with criminals—both the informants and the targeted offenders—heightens the challenges of the undercover role considerably. Undercover officers must sustain a deceptive front over extended periods of time, thereby facing increased risk of stress-induced illness, physical harm, and corruption. One study determined that the greater the number of undercover assignments undertaken, the more drug, alcohol, and disciplinary problems federal officers had during their careers.[63]

Undercover agents can experience profound changes in their value systems, often resulting in overidentification with criminals and a questioning of certain criminal statutes they are sworn to enforce.[64] These isolated assignments may also involve a separation of self, disrupting or interfering with officers' family relationships and activities and perhaps even leading to a loss of identity and the adoption of a criminal persona as they distance themselves from a conventional lifestyle.[65]

> A good example of this is the case of a Northern California police officer who participated in a "deep cover" operation for eighteen months, riding with the Hell's Angels. He was responsible for a very large number of arrests, including previously almost untouchable higher-level drug dealers. But this was at the cost of heavy drug use, alcoholism, brawling, the break-up of his family, an inability to fit back into routine police work, resignation from the force, several bank robberies, and a prison term.[66]

The stressful nature of undercover work is discussed further in Chapter 12.

Returning to Patrol Duties

Ending an undercover assignment and returning to patrol duty is an awkward experience for many officers, who experience difficulty in adjusting to the everyday routine of traditional police work. These officers may suffer from such emotional problems as anxiety, loneliness, and suspiciousness, and they may experience marital problems. Officers will quickly have less autonomy and diminished initiative in job performance; they are no longer working with a tight-knit unit with expanded freedom and control. They no longer feel as though they are behind enemy lines in the battle against crime, where their work experiences are intense and inherently dangerous. The return to routine patrol may be analogous to coming down from an emotional high, and officers in this position may feel depressed and lethargic.[67]

Uses of the Polygraph

The polygraph has been used by the police in the investigation of serious crimes since at least the early 1900s. The modern polygraph is a briefcase-sized device or computerized model that records changes in skin resistance (perspiration), blood pressure, pulse rate, and breathing activity. Activity in each of these physiological measurements is monitored and recorded on a paper chart.[68]

The polygraph, commonly referred to as a lie detector, cannot actually detect when a lie is told; therefore, the **polygraph examination** is an inferential process in which "lying" is inferred from comparisons of the aforementioned physiological responses to questions that are asked during polygraph testing. In police work, the two major uses of polygraph testing are specific issue testing and preemployment screening. In specific issue testing, the polygraph is used to investigate whether a particular person is responsible for or involved in the commission of a specific offense. The use of the polygraph for preemployment screening is very controversial and is, in fact, illegal in some jurisdictions. When used, however, polygraph testing can help to verify information collected during traditional background investigations and to uncover information not otherwise available. Studies show that polygraph procedures may yield an accuracy of about 90 percent.[69]

The commonly held belief that polygraph examination results are not admitted into court is untrue. Some courts admit polygraph evidence even over the objection of counsel. In other jurisdictions, polygraph results are admitted by stipulation. At the federal level, there is no single standard governing admissibility. It is also common for prosecutors to use polygraph results to decide which charges to file, if any, and defense attorneys rely on polygraph testing to plan their defense and to negotiate pleas. Some judges also use polygraph results in sentencing decisions.[70]

DNA Analysis

Methods

O. J. Simpson's criminal trial in 1995 brought DNA testing to the attention of most Americans and heightened their interest in and possibly their concern about its use. More recent cases involving the exoneration of innocent death-row inmates across the country, however, have caused DNA to be cast in a more positive light.

"DNA fingerprinting" has been used in legal cases in the United States since 1987; it is viewed as the greatest advance since fingerprinting and has been called the "magic bullet" of criminal investigations.[71] Proponents hope that DNA fingerprinting will end the search for the perfect means of personal identification.

DNA (deoxyribonucleic acid) is the chemical dispatcher of genetic information found in almost all human cells. Except for identical twins, no two people share the same DNA sequences. Developed in England in 1984 by Alec Jeffreys, DNA fingerprinting uses purified DNA obtained from whole blood, sperm, hair roots, skin, or other tissues; blood and semen are the richest sources.[72] Actually, two DNA testing methods are used for creating the DNA profile. The most widely used method, known as restriction fragment length polymorphism (RFLP) uses highly dangerous radioactive material to produce a DNA image on an X-ray film. The second method, polymerase chain reaction (PCR), employs no radioactive material. PCR is the principal method for forensic science DNA testing.[73] (See Figure 7-1.)

DNA profiling has rapidly spread across the country. The FBI began DNA analysis in December 1988, and in 1990 it began developing a national DNA identification index.[74] DNA testing by the FBI is performed free of charge for all police agencies, which do not incur any travel expenses for DNA examiners who must testify in court. In addition, more than fifty police laboratories now perform DNA analysis.

The chances that two people (except for identical twins) could have the same DNA profile range anywhere from 1 in 50,000 to 1 in 5 million, according to scientists' most conservative estimates.[75] For some people, the

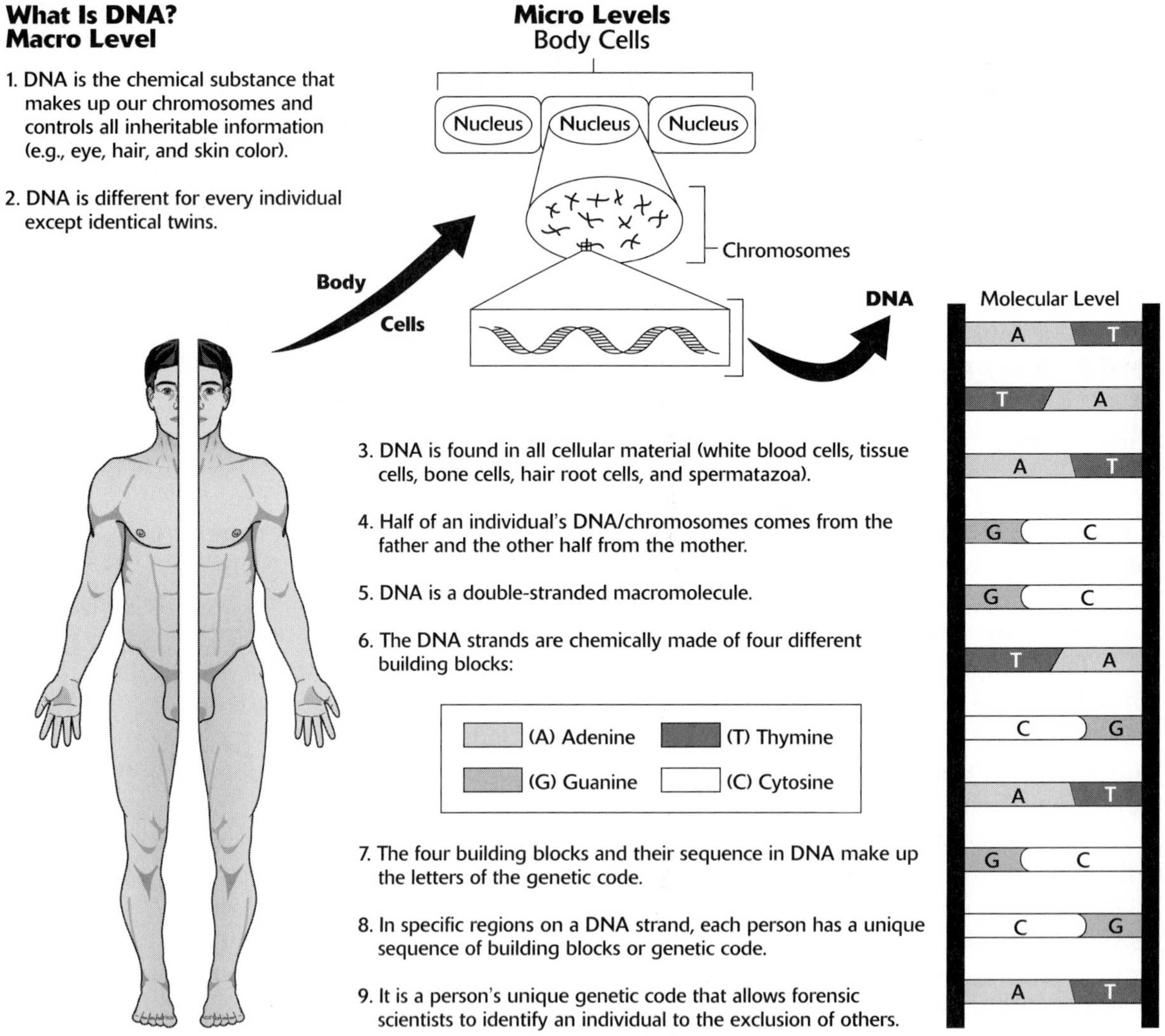

What Is DNA?
Macro Level
1. DNA is the chemical substance that makes up our chromosomes and controls all inheritable information (e.g., eye, hair, and skin color).
2. DNA is different for every individual except identical twins.
Micro Levels
Body Cells
Nucleus
Nucleus
Nucleus
Chromosomes
Body
Cells
DNA
Molecular Level
A T
T A
A T
G C
G C
T A
C G
A T
G C
C G
A T
3. DNA is found in all cellular material (white blood cells, tissue cells, bone cells, hair root cells, and spermatazoa).
4. Half of an individual's DNA/chromosomes comes from the father and the other half from the mother.
5. DNA is a double-stranded macromolecule.
6. The DNA strands are chemically made of four different building blocks:
(A) Adenine
(T) Thymine
(G) Guanine
(C) Cytosine
7. The four building blocks and their sequence in DNA make up the letters of the genetic code.
8. In specific regions on a DNA strand, each person has a unique sequence of building blocks or genetic code.
9. It is a person's unique genetic code that allows forensic scientists to identify an individual to the exclusion of others.

FIGURE 7-1 What Is DNA?

Source: Federal Bureau of Investigation, Laboratory Division

lesser odds and other factors (discussed later) combine to make the test vulnerable to legal attack; for others, the higher odds make any question about the value of DNA testing a nonissue.

Methods and Standards for Testing

Although offenders have been convicted and even executed largely on DNA evidence (the first such execution occurred in Virginia in April 1994),[76] DNA profiling has been under judicial scrutiny since 1988.[77] Questions about population statistics, matching, contamination, and interpretation are commonly raised. Defense attorneys argue that the statistics are inaccurate or overstated and that they do not weigh enough variations between races and ethnicities.

Even with the reluctance of some juries to accept DNA evidence, courts have recognized that genetic profiles developed from DNA are reliable and objective.[78] At issue is the ability of crime laboratories to match similar DNA profiles reliably and to assess the frequency with which the matched profile is expected to occur in the U.S. population.

Traditionally, the *Frye* standard, established in 1923, was the primary test of admissibility of scientific evidence; under this standard, a court would admit scientific evidence only after it had gained general acceptance in the relevant scientific community.[79] In 1993, the U.S. Supreme Court set a new standard, significantly easing the rules for the admissibility of scientific evidence in *Daubert* v. *Merrell Dow Pharmaceuticals, Inc.*[80] *Daubert*, which superseded the much stricter *Frye* standard, allows the following factors to determine whether any form of scientific evidence is reliable: whether it has been subjected to testing and peer review, whether there are known or potential rates of error, and whether there are standards controlling application of the techniques involved. Using this standard, the Court held that DNA testing at the FBI's crime laboratory easily met the necessary criteria for scientific acceptability.

A majority of courts have admitted DNA profiling results from the three major laboratories involved in DNA analysis: the FBI, Cellmark, and Lifecodes. Courts in at least forty-nine states have admitted DNA evidence; more than thirty appellate courts, including eleven state supreme courts, have reported favorable decisions after reviewing DNA profiling.[81] When defense challenges have arisen against DNA evidence or when the courts have balked at admitting it, such reluctance is usually on the grounds of how common or rare the reported DNA profile is in the U.S. population. In other words, the prosecution must demonstrate the significance of the DNA match based on population genetics. The FBI estimates that the likelihood of two DNA samples matching each other is as low as one in a trillion. And in *United States* v. *Jakobetz* (1990),[82] population statistics produced by the FBI indicated that the DNA profile of the defendant was extremely rare—it was expected to occur only once in every 300 million people.[83] DNA critics, however, charge that the FBI has incorrectly applied the theories

EXHIBIT 7-2

DNA and the Green River Killer

For nearly two decades, evidence from crimes committed by Washington State's Green River Killer—three tiny swabs of semen recovered from the decomposing bodies of prostitutes—sat in a sheriff's office evidence locker in Seattle. Until recently, technicians could not identify suspects using such small DNA samples. In 2001, however, the specimens, along with saliva and blood taken from three possible suspects, were sent to the state crime lab for advanced DNA testing. In November 2003, Gary Ridgway, a 54-year-old truck painter, confessed to forty-eight strangulation murders, ending a nearly twenty-year investigation and making him the serial killer convicted of the most murders in U.S. history. Mitochondrial DNA, which attempts to match DNA found outside the nucleus of cells, was used to match bones in this case.

Source: Adapted from Andrew Murr, "Reeling in a Monster," *Newsweek*, November 17, 2003, p. 44; and Tracy Johnson, "Listed as Green River Victim, Family Learns Truth: Girl Is Dead," *Seattle Post-Intelligencer*, http://seattlepi.nwsource.com/local/gree03/shtml (accessed January 8, 2004).

of population biology underlying such calculations and that, as a result, the chances of a mismatch are artificially minimized in the courtroom.

In August 1993, the Washington Supreme Court became the first state high court to endorse forced genetic testing of everyone convicted of a sexual offense or violent crime. Such testing is done to generate a DNA database to identify and prosecute future sex offenders or violent criminals. Washington is one of more than thirty states that have enacted such statutes. Although opponents of forced testing believe it is a waste of money and an unnecessary invasion of privacy with the sole purpose of investigating future crimes, the Washington Supreme Court found a "rational connection between the DNA testing statute and law enforcement."[84]

Recent Developments: Mitochondrial DNA and National Databases

The latest development in the use of DNA is **mitochondrial DNA** evidence, which has been deemed "shaky" by some defense attorneys and is inadmissible in many courts. It is, however, rapidly becoming a mainstream investigative tool. Mitochondrial DNA—a tiny ring-shaped molecule that's much smaller than the more familiar nuclear DNA that reveals genetic makeup—can be extracted from hair and bones when little else remains of a body. This technique was involved in solving the Green River Killer case in Washington State (see Exhibit 7-2) and recently came under scrutiny in the high-profile case involving Scott

Peterson, who was convicted in November 2004 of drowning his pregnant wife, Lacy, in Modesto, California. In the latter case, prosecutors tried to link to the victim a hair that was wrapped around pliers found in Peterson's boat. Defense attorneys attempted to discredit this genetic identification method on the grounds that it is unreliable and unproven. Nonetheless, it is increasingly seen as a legitimate type of science, and the more it is used, the more difficult it is going to be to attack it.[85]

Another relatively recent development in this field is the creation of a national DNA database. Since 1994, states have been entering DNA profiles into an index known as the Combined DNA Index System (CODIS), which enables crime labs to exchange and compare DNA profiles electronically. In 1998, the FBI launched a national version of the index, known as the National DNA Index System (NDIS). Today, more than a hundred labs upload DNA profiles into the system, and the DNA profiles of more than 1.2 million convicted felons are in the NDIS database.[86] Problems exist, however, with backlogs of DNA samples that need to be examined and the findings that must be written up; there currently is not enough time or staffing to keep up with the workload. Figure 7-2 shows that the number of cases analyzed, the samples collected from convicted offenders, and the cases awaiting analysis have at least doubled since 1997, while laboratory staffing has not kept pace.

Status of Workloads in DNA Crime Laboratories, by Type of Case, 1997–2000

Case Status and Type of Work	1997	2000	Percent Change
Work Received			
Casework*	20,793	31,394	51
Convicted offender	115,681	177,184	53
Work Analyzed			
Casework*	14,289	24,790	73
Convicted offender	44,810	148,347	231
Backlog of Work			
Casework*	6,800	15,981	135
Convicted offender	286,819	265,329	−7
Full-time Employees	672	893	33

Note: Workloads and backlogs do not include all DNA crime laboratories because of nonresponses of some laboratories.

*Casework includes known and unknown subject cases.

FIGURE 7-2 Status and workloads in DNA crime laboratories, by type of case, 1997–2000.

Source: Greg W. Steadman, Survey of DNA Crime Laboratories, 2001 *(Washington, DC: Department of Justice, Bureau of Justice Statistics, January 2002), p. 2.*

Behavioral Science in Criminal Investigation

Criminal Profiling

The **criminal profiling** of serial killers has captured the public's fancy more than any other investigative technique used by the police. The success of profiling depends on the profiler's ability to draw on investigative experience, training in forensic and behavioral science, and empirically developed information about the characteristics of known offenders. It is more art than science. The focus of the analysis is the behavior of the perpetrator within the crime scene.[87]

There are various types of investigative profiles. Drug courier profiles have been developed from collections of observable characteristics that experienced investigators believe indicate a person who is carrying drugs. Other types of profiles include loss-control specialists' profiles of shoplifters and threat assessments, such as the Secret Service's profiles of potential presidential assassins. Criminal profiling of violent offenders, however, is the area for which the most descriptive information has been collected and analyzed and the most extensive training programs developed.[88] Unfortunately, most people associate criminal profiling with the psychic profiler on television's *The Profiler* or with Agent Starling in the film *The Silence of the Lambs*—both of which are inaccurate portrayals.[89]

Profiling is not a new discovery; indeed, Sir Arthur Conan Doyle's fictional character Sherlock Holmes often engaged in profiling. For example, in "A Study in Scarlet," published in 1887, Holmes congratulated himself on the accuracy of his psychological profile: "It is seldom that any man, unless he is very full-blooded, breaks out in this way through emotion, so I hazarded the opinion that the criminal was probably a robust and ruddy-faced man. Events proved that I had judged correctly."[90] Profiling was used by a psychiatrist to study Adolph Hitler during World War II and to predict how he might react to defeat.[91]

Psychological profiling, while not an exact science, is obviously of assistance to investigators; however, it does not replace sound investigative procedures. Profiling works in harmony with the search for physical evidence. Victims play an important role in the development of a profile, as they can provide the investigator with the offender's exact conversation. Other items needed for a complete profile include photographs of the crime scene and any victims, autopsy information, and complete reports of the incident, including the weapon used. From this body of information the profiler looks for motive.[92]

Serial murderers—killers who are driven by a compulsion to murder again and again—are also profiled. Many psychologists believe that serial murderers fulfill violent sexual fantasies they have had since childhood. They satisfy their sexual needs by thinking about their killings, but when the satisfaction wears off, they kill again. Most serial murderers, the FBI has learned, are solitary males; an alarming number are doctors, dentists, or other health-care professionals. Almost one-third are ex-convicts and former mental patients. Many, like Kenneth Bianchi, the Los Angeles Hillside Strangler, are attracted to policing. (Bianchi, who was working as a security guard when he was finally caught in Washington State, often wore a police uniform during his crimes.) Serial killers seem normal, and they principally attack lone women, children, older people, homeless people, hitchhikers, and prostitutes.[93]

Another psychology-related investigative tool is psycholinguistics, which provides an understanding of those who use criminal coercion and provides strategies for dealing with threats. The 1932 kidnapping case of Charles Lindbergh's infant son (perpetrated by a German-born illegal alien, whose notes revealed his background and ethnicity) marked the beginning of this investigative method. Concentrating on evidence obtained from a message, spoken or written, the psycholinguistic technique microscopically analyzes the threats or messages for clues to the origins, background, and psychology of the maker. Every sentence, syllable, phrase, word, and comma is computer-scanned. A "threat dictionary" containing more than 350 categories and 15 million words is consulted; these "signature" words and phrases are then used to identify possible suspects.[94]

Clearly, profiling can be useful in criminal inquiries in several ways: focusing the investigation on more likely types of offenders, suggesting proactive strategies, suggesting trial strategies, and preventing violent crimes. From 1984 to 1991, the FBI trained thirty-three state and local police investigators in the profiling process. The program required twelve months of intensive training and hands-on profiling experience and consisted of an academic phase and an application phase.[95]

Psychics and Hypnosis

Psychics are also brought in from time to time, usually as a last resort when an investigation has stalled and no solution is imminent. Psychics are believed to possess extrasensory perception (ESP) or paranormal powers. National interest was focused on parapsychology—the discipline dealing with ESP, clairvoyance, and so forth—with the publicity accompanying the solving of three sex murders of youths in South Gate, California, in 1978. After two fruitless years of investigation, police resorted to the services of a local psychic, who helped an artist sketch a drawing of a face that had appeared to the psychic in a vision. With this information, police apprehended a suspect. However, Martin Reiser, a prominent LAPD psychologist, has studied the use of psychics and has found no support for the "contention that psychics can provide significant information leading to the solution of major crimes."[96]

In the early 1970s, policing turned to hypnosis as an investigative tool. A number of police practitioners were trained in how to place witnesses, victims, arresting officers, and even investigators in a hypnotic state.[97] Hypnosis has been used to help people recall license plate numbers, names, places, or details of an incident. Although a trend toward acceptance of hypnosis by appellate courts began to develop in the early and mid-1970s, a 1976 California ruling reflected current skepticism with the technique. Hypnosis was used in a murder case to secure details of the suspect's identity and to obtain his conviction.[98] Following this case, the courts, increasingly concerned with the suggestibility of potential witnesses while under hypnosis, began rendering adverse rulings against such testimony. It then became clear to police and prosecutors that witnesses whose recall had been enhanced through hypnosis could not be put on the witness stand. Today, hypnosis is used sparingly, generally for people who would otherwise be useless as material witnesses.

Today, only two states—Nevada and Texas—expressly allow such evidence. Officials in those states believe that forensic hypnotists can help otherwise frustrated investigators solve crimes and that investigators with information obtained through hypnotism are free to either confirm, corroborate, or refute that information through the use of other evidence.[99]

Recent Developments in Forensic Science and Investigation

Technological opportunities—as well as new scientific and investigative problems—are rapidly developing for federal, state, and local police practitioners. In this section, we discuss several of them.

Interrogations of a Different Sort: Terrorism Suspects

Any good criminal investigation textbook or police manual that deals with **interrogation** and interviewing will convey a number of time-tested techniques for use with most criminal suspects. Since the terrorist attacks of September 11, 2001, information has become the most vital weapon against terrorism, and another form of interrogation has taken center stage among federal law enforcement agencies and counterterrorism organizations: the interrogation of terrorism suspects. Although the techniques used with such individuals are classified information and largely unknown to the American public, following is some general information about what is known.

First, torture is repulsive, and deliberate cruelty is thought to be the classic shortcut for lazy and incompetent interrogators; furthermore, the Geneva Convention bans any mistreatment of prisoners. But fear works; it is more effective than any tactic, drug, or torture device. It is an article of faith that an unfrightened prisoner makes an unlikely informer.[100]

People change when in custody; they may be heroes on the outside, but inside, where conditions are different, they change. They will look out for number one, and the isolation, fear, and deprivation of normal comforts cause people to retreat, to reorient themselves, and to reorder their priorities. When pushed hard enough, they will act to preserve themselves—at the expense of anyone or anything else (thus, the high degree of success police have always had in, say, getting lower-level drug suspects to "snitch" on their suppliers). An old Arab saying is, "Let one hundred mothers cry, but not my mother—but better my mother than me."[101]

Preparing terrorist suspects for interrogation—perhaps someone like Sheikh Mohammed, operations chief for Osama bin Laden and the biggest catch in America's war on terror—means softening them up first. They may be kept awake for long periods, isolated, ill-fed, and unsure of where they are or what time it is. Ideally, the interrogator knows the prisoner's language and has a large amount of information about him; nothing rattles a captive more than to be confronted with an interrogator who seems to know everything or to suspect that a trusted comrade has betrayed him. Once a prisoner begins to talk, rapid follow-up is needed to separate fact from fiction, to determine whether the subject is being truthful or deceptive.[102]

Religious extremists pose the greatest challenge; they are usually well educated, financially and emotionally stable, and disrespectful of nonbelievers. Their cause allows them to commit any offense without remorse. But they can be persuaded to talk if the proper techniques are employed.[103]

Forensic Entomology: Using "Insect Detectives"

An example of how the field of **forensic science** is quickly developing is the use of new "investigators": insects. Anyone involved in death investigations is aware of the connection between dead bodies and insects, especially maggots. As one forensic entomologist stated, "Insects are major players in nature's recycling effort, and in nature a corpse is simply organic matter to be recycled. Left to its own devices, nature quickly populates a corpse with a diverse community of organisms, all dedicated to reducing the body to its basic components."[104]

Until recently, most death investigators regarded insects as merely a sign of decay to be washed away rather than as potentially significant evidence. Yet the application of insect evidence to criminal investigations is not a new idea. In 1255, a Chinese "death investigator" named Sung Ts'u wrote a book entitled *The Washing Away of Wrongs*. Sung tells of a murder in a Chinese village in which the victim was repeatedly slashed. The local magistrate thought the wounds might have been inflicted by a sickle and ordered all the village men to assemble, each with his own sickle. In the hot summer sun, flies were attracted to one sickle because of the residue of blood and small tissue fragments still clinging to the blade and handle. The owner of the sickle confessed.[105]

Not until several centuries later, in 1668, was the link between fly eggs and maggots discovered in the West. Before then, people did not realize that maggots hatched from the eggs flies laid on exposed meat or decomposing bodies. Unfortunately, it was not until much later, in 1855, that this discovery would be used in a forensic investigation. During a remodeling of a house outside Paris, the mummified body of an infant was discovered behind a mantelpiece. An autopsy determined that a flesh fly had exploited the body during the first year and that mites had laid their eggs on the dried corpse the following year. The logical suspects were people who were the occupants of the house in 1848—a young couple—who were subsequently arrested and convicted.[106]

In the mid-1930s, entomological evidence came to the fore in a brutal murder case. A woman saw a severed human arm while looking over a bridge spanning a small stream in Scotland. Ultimately, more than seventy pieces of two badly decomposed corpses—the wife of a local physician and her personal maid—were recovered from the area. Some maggots were discovered feeding on the decomposing body parts and were sent to the laboratory; they were identified as belonging to a type of blow fly and were thought to be between twelve and fourteen days old. For a number of reasons, suspicion fell on the physician: the entomological estimate of the time of death, the skillful manner of the dismemberment, and the fact that the doctor had been seen with a cut finger. He was convicted of both murders.[107]

Today, forensic entomology can be of tremendous assistance to investigators. When a person dies, hundreds of species of insects descend on the corpse and the crime scene. Attracted by what scientists think may be a "universal death scent," common green flies, ground beetles, and other insects that thrive on flesh migrate to a corpse to lay eggs or to feast. The death of a human triggers very predictable patterns of insect activity that can be traced backward through time. There are several waves of insects, and their presence is informative. The life cycles of these creatures are so fixed and precise that they act as a natural clock to the trained eye.[108]

There is also the phenomenon of succession: As each organism feeds on a body, it changes the body. This change in turn makes the body attractive to another group of organisms, which changes the body for the next group, and so on until the body has been reduced to a skeleton. This is a predictable process.[109] This process is now being studied scientifically at the so-called Body Farm at the University of Tennessee in Knoxville—the only place in the world where corpses rot in the open air to advance human knowledge (see also Exhibit 7-3). William Bass III, the Body Farm's founder, trains anthropologists and FBI agents in human decomposition. More than twenty corpses are decomposing there as maggots do their work; over the years, more than three hundred bodies have decayed at this location, some in car trunks, others under water or under the earth or hung from scaffolds. The overarching goal of the study is to produce an atlas for the police that will provide a "gold standard" for decomposition—a page-by-page, color-by-color, insect-by-insect depiction of the process of human decay on a time and temperature line. The study also includes burying multiple bodies under four pads of concrete to assist the FBI's tests of its latest ground-penetrating radar.[110]

EXHIBIT 7-3

A New Crime Scene Academy

A number of assessments have found that the quality of evidence collection and identification could be improved, particularly at the local level. Now help is on the way. The Knoxville, Tennessee, Police Department is spearheading a project to create a National Forensic Academy for in-service criminalists. The 400-hour curriculum includes 180 hours of class work and 220 hours of field practicum. The academy session ends with 10 hours of testing. It covers arson, autopsy, trace evidence (including DNA and serology), mass fatalities, death investigations, cold case studies, emerging trends, fingerprinting, blood splatter, child fatality investigations, and computer forensics, among other topics. Applicants for the fourteen available slots must be first-line responders, computer literate, willing to participate in group activities, and prepared to work with human cadavers. The first academy class was held in September 2001.

Source: Adapted from "Is Your Crime-Scene Work a Crime? Help Will Soon Be on the Way," *Law Enforcement News*, March 15, 2001, p. 1. Used with permission from *Law Enforcement News*, John Jay College of Criminal Justice, CUNY, 555 West 57th St., New York, NY 10019.

Often the strongest circumstantial evidence in a criminal prosecution is the fact that the victim and a suspect were seen together. For example, the body of a nine-year-old girl who had been missing for three weeks was found in Kenosha, Wisconsin; insect evidence put her death at midnight twenty-one days before—the exact day she had gone to a carnival with the suspect, who was convicted.[111]

There are other uses of insects as well. A man claiming to have found his girlfriend dead was convicted of her murder when none of the usual creatures were present on the body (it was shown that the man opened the windows before the police arrived, therefore the absence of insects). A Florida murderer who dropped his victim in a swamp was convicted when mayflies, only active in a swamp region a few days of the year, were found in his car radiator. In a rape case, the offender was convicted when his ski mask was found to contain larvae from caterpillars that emerged only in late summer and were known to dwell in the woods next to the rape scene. Furthermore, insects feeding on infected tissues where children's diapers have not been changed or under bandages and bedsheets of the elderly have often been the only evidence that neglect has occurred.[112]

Stalking Investigations

Stalking was recently described as "the crime of the 1990s."[113] California enacted the first antistalking law in 1990, following the stalking and subsequent death of Rebecca Shaeffer, the costar of the television series *My Sister Sam*. Today, all but two states have their own antistalking laws. (Arizona and Maine use their harassment and terrorizing statutes to combat stalking.)[114]

There are four types of stalking situations:

Erotomanic: The stalker has a delusional disorder in which the victim, usually a person of higher status and opposite gender (often a celebrity or a public figure), is believed to be in love with the stalker. In fact, the victim does not know the stalker, and the stalking is usually short-lived, lasting one to four months.

Love obsessional: Similar to the erotomanic, here the stalker does not know the victim except through the media and has a psychiatric diagnosis; stalkers usually write letters and make telephone calls in a campaign to make their existence known to the victim. This behavior lasts much longer, often exceeding ten years.

Simple obsessional: In this type of incident, the stalker had a prior relationship with the victim, as a former spouse or employer, for example, and the stalking began after the relationship soured. The stalking usually lasts about five months.

The false victimization syndrome: This is the rarest form, in which a person claims that someone is stalking him or her in order to gain attention as a victim. There is no stalker, and this phenomenon is similar to Munchausen syndrome by proxy, in which people intentionally produce physical symptoms of illness in their children in order to gain attention and sympathy.[115]

Evidence collection for crimes of stalking begins with the victims. Victims should record each time they see the stalker or when any contact is made. Further, victims should document specific details, such as time, place, location, and any witnesses. Messages on answering machines, faxes, letters, and computer e-mail messages provide useful evidence for building a case against the offender. Police agencies should also consider providing the victim with a small tape recorder to facilitate the collection of this information and should encourage victims to report in a journal how the stalking has affected them and their lifestyle, to later help convince a jury of the victim's fear and trauma. Another investigative strategy is surveilling suspects at times when they are likely to stalk the victim. Executing a search warrant for the suspect's personal and work computers, residence, and vehicle can prove useful in many circumstances. Officers should look for spying equipment (such as binoculars and cameras), photos, and any property belonging to the victim.[116]

Investigating "Cybercrooks"

Today an estimated 605 million people around the world are plugged into cyberspace, and thousands more enter the online world each day.[117] The Internet has revolutionized the way people communicate, shop, entertain themselves, learn, and conduct business. But as the saying goes, "The fleas come with the dog"; this high-tech revolution in our homes and offices has opened a whole new world for the criminal element, creating a new type of criminal: the "**cybercrook**." Indeed, the problem of cybercrime has become so prevalent that a new Computer Crime and Intellectual Property Section has been created in the Criminal Division of the U.S. Department of Justice; it can be accessed at www.cybercrime.gov. CyberAngels, an organization founded by a twenty-one-year-old man that assists victims of Internet crimes, receives 650 online stalking complaints every day. The Federal Trade Commission receives more than eighteen thousand Internet-related complaints each year. At least three hundred Web sites offer counterfeit drivers' licenses, law enforcement credentials, passports, Social Security cards, and military identification cards.[118]

Pornographers and pedophiles (discussed below) are also on the Web, as well as other, newer types of criminals: better educated, upscale, older, and increasingly female. Computer crimes include identity theft; cyberterrorism; software piracy; industrial espionage; credit card, consumer, and stock market fraud; baby adoption scams; and embezzlement. These crimes compel the development of new investigative techniques, specialized and ongoing training for police investigators, and the employment of individuals with strong technical backgrounds. Obviously, the police must become better educated, better equipped, and more adaptable.[119]

The technical staff of many, if not most, police agencies are civilians, who are generally kept away from the operational side of the organization. They understand what computers do but not necessarily how that capability supports the operational needs of the police officer on the street. Thus the sworn officer or detective is generally unprepared for the types of criminal schemes described above. This situation must change.

We discuss liability issues concerning the handling of computer evidence in Chapter 10.

Protecting the Innocents: Investigating Crimes against Juveniles and Missing Youths

Although the number of crimes against children has been declining in America, children still have very high rates of victimization. Pedophiles and pornographers are now increasingly engaging in Internet sex crimes against minors. Some writers have estimated that about 89,000 such cases occur each year,[120] but that figure has almost certainly grown. The possession of child pornography is an element in two-thirds of all Internet sex crimes against minors.[121] Furthermore, juveniles age twelve through seventeen constitute 23 percent of all violent crime victims, and one victim survey found that 1.38 million Americans were victims of violent crimes from birth through age seventeen; 555,000 of them were victimized violently from birth through age eleven.[122]

In addition, according to a study by the U.S. Department of Justice's Office of Juvenile Justice and Delinquency Prevention, about 1,315,000 children are missing from their caretakers each year; about 800,000 of them are reported to the authorities for the purpose of locating them. Nearly all (99.8 percent) of the children reported missing by a caretaker were located or returned home alive.[123]

EXHIBIT 7-4

Looking at "Cold" Cases

At the new Institute for Cold Case Evaluation at West Virginia University, a nonprofit consulting center, law-enforcement agencies will have at their disposal a diverse array of scientists in fields ranging from anthropology to entomology, according to the institute's creator, Max Houck, a forensic anthropologist who previously worked at the FBI crime laboratory.

Each year, the number of cold cases in the nation grows by about another 6,000, on top of the 200,000 unsolved murder cases that have accumulated since 1960.

"At other agencies, they just take the last retiree, hire him back as a contractor and give him a desk and a phone because that's all they have," Houck told The AssociatedPress. "Then they put a stack of files in front of him... with no resources."

Houck, who teaches at the university, said the ICCE will provide departments with free or discounted services from at least two dozen scientists. It will launch a Web site as well, with a free electronic newsletter and a secure chat room for investigators. The public can browse the site, searching through cases and making donations what will help fund the center.

Source: "Case Studies," *Law Enforcement News*, November 15/30, 2003, p. 7. John Jay College of Criminal Justice, CUNY, 555 West 57th St., New York, NY 10019.

Fortunately, the police have valuable resources for investigating such cases. The National Center for Missing and Exploited Children (NCMEC), for example, provides police training and other services nationwide for investigating instances where children are abducted, endangered, and sexually exploited. The NCMEC also

- Age-enhances photographs of children missing for two years or more
- Reconstructs facial images from morgue photographs of unidentified juveniles so that posters can be made
- Distributes photographs and descriptions of missing children worldwide
- Maintains a free and secure lost child Web site for the police[124]

The NCMEC was established in 1984 and is a private, not-for-profit organization located in Alexandria, Virginia.

No Stone Unturned: Handling Cold Cases

Many jurisdictions plagued by a significant number of unsolved murders, or **cold cases**, have created a cold case squad. These squads can be especially useful in locating and working with past and potential witnesses and in reviewing physical evidence to identify suspects. (See Exhibit 7-2, concerning the case of the Green River Killer.)

The most important component of cold case squads is personnel; the squads must have the right mix of investigative and supervisory talent.

Squads may also use, as needed, the services of federal law enforcement agencies, medical or coroners' offices, retired personnel, criminalists or other specialists, or college or student interns. Cold cases selected for investigation are usually at least a year old and cannot be addressed by the original investigative personnel because of workload, time constraints, or the lack of viable leads. Cases are prioritized on the basis of the likelihood of an eventual solution. The highest priority cases are those in which there is an identified homicide victim; suspects were previously named or identified through forensic methods; an arrest warrant was previously issued; significant physical evidence can be reprocessed; newly documented leads have arisen; and critical witnesses are available and willing to cooperate.[125]

SUMMARY

The evolution of forensic evidence, criminalistics, and criminal investigation is the product of a successful symbiosis of science and policing. This chapter has shown the truly interdisciplinary nature of police work; we discussed not only the influence of the so-called hard sciences—computer science, chemistry, biology, and physics—but also the assistance of psychology.

There is little doubt that the future holds greater advances in the realm of forensic science. This discipline has traveled a great distance, especially since the advent of the computer. The potential of the computer to assist in solving crimes is limited only by our funds and imagination. Thus policing should continue to reap the benefits of continually progressing scientific aids for years to come.

REVIEW QUESTIONS

1. Distinguish between the terms *forensic science* and *criminalistics*.
2. Explain the origins of criminalistics, and compare anthropometry and dactylography.
3. How did August Vollmer and other pioneers in law enforcement contribute to the development of criminal investigation techniques?
4. What qualities do detectives need and use?
5. Review the basic functions of the polygraph, and discuss its legal status in the courts.
6. Explain how DNA analysis operates. What is its future outlook, both legally and scientifically?
7. Describe the contributions of behavioral science to criminal investigation, providing actual case studies.

8. Explain the fundamental advantages of forensic entomology for criminal investigators.
9. Review the four types of stalking situations and describe how detectives must go about addressing them.
10. How has the Internet provided new opportunities for criminals? Give examples.
11. What is the purpose of a cold case squad? How does it operate?

INDEPENDENT STUDENT ACTIVITIES

1. Tour a modern forensics laboratory (or interview a forensic examiner) to learn about the laboratory's existing capabilities, areas of service, and other related information. Also learn about how the chain of evidence is protected and how evidence is stored until trial. Ask the technicians what they see as the most rapidly developing areas of forensics.
2. Interview several detectives about the methods and technologies they use for processing a crime scene, their training and education, the primary obstacles in bringing a case to trial, the greatest challenges in their work, the methods they use for interviewing suspects, recent changes in the investigative field, and so on.
3. Determine the method that is predominantly used to extract and examine DNA in your jurisdiction, and learn about some of the local cases in which DNA evidence has been employed.
4. Interview someone in the investigative field to learn his or her views toward such controversial methods as hypnosis and the use of psychics.

RELATED WEB SITES

American Academy of Forensic Sciences
http://www.aafs.org

Crime Mapping Research Center (CMRC)
http://www.ojp.usdoj.gov/cmrc

Forensic Science Information
http://ash.lab.rl.fws.gov

National Center for Missing and Exploited Children
http://www.missingkids.com

National Domestic Violence Hotline
http://www.inetport.com/ndvh

National Fraud Information Hotline
http://www.fraud.org

National White Collar Crime Center
http://www.iir.com/nwccc/nwccc.htm

NOTES

1. Quoted in LEONARD ROY FRANK, ed., *Random House Webster's Quotationary* (New York: Random House, 1999), p. 761.
2. MARC H. CAPLAN and JOE HOLT ANDERSON, *Forensic: When Science Bears Witness* (Washington, DC: U.S. Government Printing Office, 1984), p. 2.
3. CHARLES R. SWANSON Jr., NEIL C. CHAMELIN, and LEONARD TERRITO, *Criminal Investigation*, 4th ed. (New York: Random House, 1988), pp. 223–24.
4. PAUL L. KIRK, "The Ontogeny of Criminalistics," *Journal of Criminology and Police Science* 54 (1963): 238.
5. PETER R. DEFOREST, R. E. GAENSSLEN, and HENRY C. LEE, *Forensic Science: An Introduction to Criminalistics* (New York: McGraw-Hill, 1983), p. 29.
6. RICHARD SAFERSTEIN, *Criminalistics* (Englewood Cliffs, NJ: Prentice Hall, 1977), p. 5.
7. JURGEN THORWALD, *Crime and Science* (New York: Harcourt, Brace and World, 1967), p. 4.
8. JURGEN THORWALD, *The Century of the Detective* (New York: Harcourt, Brace and World, 1965), p. 7.
9. Ibid., pp. 9–10.
10. Ibid., p. 12.
11. SWANSON, CHAMELIN, and TERRITO, *Criminal Investigation*, p. 13.
12. Ibid., pp. 14–15.
13. Ibid., p. 15.
14. ANTHONY L. CALIFANA and JEROME S. LEVKOV, *Criminalistics for the Law Enforcement Officer* (New York: McGraw-Hill, 1978), p. 20.
15. FREDERICK R. CHERRILL, *The Finger Print System of Scotland Yard* (London: Her Majesty's Stationery Office, 1954), p. 3.
16. THORWALD, *The Century of the Detective*, p. 18.
17. Ibid., p. 33.
18. SAFERSTEIN, *Criminalistics*, p. 4.
19. JURGEN THORWALD, *The Marks of Cain* (London: Thames and Hudson, 1965), p. 81.
20. THORWALD, *The Century of the Detective*, p. 62.
21. THORWALD, *The Marks of Cain*, pp. 78–79.
22. DEPARTMENT OF JUSTICE, Federal Bureau of Investigation, *Crime in the United States, 2000* (Washington, DC: U.S. Government Printing Office, 2001), p. 17.
23. Reported in *Newsweek*, September 30, 1991, p. 10.
24. THORWALD, *The Marks of Cain*, pp. 87–88.

25. THORWALD, *The Century of the Detective*, pp. 418–19.
26. THORWALD, *The Marks of Cain*, p. 164.
27. DEFOREST, GAENSSLEN, and LEE, *Forensic Science*, p. 14.
28. SWANSON, CHAMELIN, and TERRITO, *Criminal Investigation*, p. 19.
29. SAFERSTEIN, *Criminalistics*, p. 30.
30. DEFOREST et al., *Forensic Science*, pp. 13–14.
31. Ibid., p. 19.
32. SWANSON, CHAMELIN, and TERRITO, *Criminal Investigation*, p. 1.
33. Ibid., p. 3.
34. THOMAS A. REPPETTO, *The Blue Parade* (New York: Free Press, 1978), pp. 26–28.
35. Ibid., p. 29.
36. JOHN COATMAN, *Police* (New York: Oxford, 1959), pp. 98–99.
37. SWANSON, CHAMELIN, and TERRITO, *Criminal Investigation*, p. 4.
38. AUGUSTINE E. COSTELLO, *Our Police Protectors* (1885; reprint, Montclair, NJ: A. Patterson Smith, 1972), p. 402.
39. JAMES F. RICHARDSON, *The New York Police* (New York: Oxford, 1970), p. 37.
40. SWANSON, CHAMELIN, and TERRITO, *Criminal Investigation*, p. 8.
41. WILLIAM J. BOPP and DONALD SHULTZ, *Principles of American Law Enforcement and Criminal Justice* (Springfield, IL: Charles C. Thomas, 1972), pp. 70–71.
42. WILLIAM J. MATHIAS and STUART ANDERSON, *Horse to Helicopter* (Atlanta: Community Life Publications, Georgia State University, 1973), p. 22.
43. THORWALD, *The Marks of Cain*, p. 136.
44. Ibid.
45. Ibid., p. 137.
46. REPPETTO, *The Blue Parade*, p. 26.
47. Ibid., p. 267.
48. SWANSON, CHAMELIN, and TERRITO, *Criminal Investigation*, p. 10.
49. Ibid., p. 11.
50. PRESIDENT'S COMMISSION ON LAW ENFORCEMENT AND THE ADMINISTRATION OF JUSTICE, *Task Force Report: Science and Technology* (Washington, DC: U.S. Government Printing Office, 1967), pp. 7–18.
51. PAUL B. WESTON and KENNETH M. WELLS, *Criminal Investigation: Basic Perspectives*, 4th ed. (Englewood Cliffs, NJ: Prentice Hall, 1986), pp. 5–10.
52. Ibid., p. 207.
53. Ibid., pp. 207–209.
54. Ibid., p. 214.
55. PETER W. GREENWOOD and JOAN PETERSILIA, *The Criminal Investigation Process*, vol. 1, *Summary and Policy Implications* (Santa Monica, CA: RAND , 1975). The entire report is found in PETER W. GREENWOOD, JAN M. CHAIKEN, and JOAN PETERSILIA, *The Criminal Investigation Process* (Lexington, MA: D. C. Heath, 1977).
56. Ibid.
57. Ibid., p. 19.

58. WESTON and WELLS, *Criminal Investigation*, p. 5.
59. DEFOREST et al., *Forensic Science*, p. 11.
60. MARK R. POGREBIN and ERIC D. POOLE, "Vice Isn't Nice: A Look at the Effects of Working Undercover," *Journal of Criminal Justice* 21 (1993): 383–94.
61. Ibid., pp. 383–84.
62. PETER K. MANNING, *The Narc's Game: Organizational and Informational Limits on Drug Enforcement* (Cambridge, MA: MIT Press, 1980).
63. M. GIRODO, "Drug Corruption in Undercover Agents: Measuring the Risk," *Behavioral Sciences and the Law* 3 (1991): 299–308; also see DAVID L. CARTER, "An Overview of Drug-Related Conduct of Police Officers: Drug Abuse and Narcotics Corruption," in *Drugs, Crime, and the Criminal Justice System*, ed. RALPH WEISHEIT (Cincinnati: Anderson, 1990).
64. DEPARTMENT OF JUSTICE, Federal Bureau of Investigation, *The Special Agent in Undercover Investigations* (Washington, DC: Author, 1978).
65. A. L. STRAUSS, "Turning Points in Identity," in *Social Interaction*, ed. C. CLARK and H. ROBBOY (New York: St. Martin's, 1988).
66. GARY T. MARX, "Who Really Gets Stung? Some Issues Raised by the New Police Undercover Work," in *Moral Issues in Police Work*, ed. F. ELLISON and M. FELDBERG (Totowa, NJ: Bowman and Allanheld, 1988), pp. 99–128.
67. G. FARKAS, "Stress in Undercover Policing," in *Psychological Services for Law Enforcement*, ed. J. T. REESE and H. A. GOLDSTEIN (Washington, DC: U.S. Government Printing Office, 1986).
68. FRANK HORVATH, "Polygraph," in *The Encyclopedia of Police Science*, 2nd ed., ed. WILLIAM G. BAILEY (New York: Garland, 1995), pp. 640–42.
69. Ibid., p. 643.
70. Ibid., p. 642.
71. SHARON BEGLEY, GINNY CARROLL, and KAREN SPRINGEN, "Blood, Hair, and Heredity," *Newsweek*, July 11, 1994, p. 24.
72. JAY V. MILLER, "The FBI's Forensic DNA Analysis Program," *FBI Law Enforcement Bulletin* 60 (July 1991): 11–15.
73. RICHARD M. RAU, "Forensic Science and Criminal Justice Technology: High-Tech Tools for the 90's," *National Institute of Justice Reports* (Washington, DC: U.S. Government Printing Office, 1991), pp. 6–10.
74. JOHN R. BROWN, "DNA Analysis: A Significant Tool for Law Enforcement," *Police Chief*, March 1994, p. 51.
75. LYNNELL HANCOCK and MARK MILLER, "Testing the Gene Fit," *Newsweek*, January 9, 1995, p. 64.
76. BEGLEY, CARROLL, and SPRINGEN, "Blood, Hair, and Heredity," p. 24.
77. See *PEOPLE* v. *WESLEY*, 533 N.Y.S.2d 643 (Sup. Ct., 1988) (the first reported decision passing on the admissibility of forensic DNA profiling).
78. For a complete listing of court decisions, see JOHN T. SYLVESTER and JOHN H. STAFFORD, "Judicial Acceptance of DNA Profiling," *FBI Law Enforcement Bulletin* 60 (July 1991): 26–31.
79. *FRYE* v. *UNITED STATES*, 293 F. 1013, 1014 (D.C. Cir. 1923).
80. *DAUBERT* v. *MERRELL DOW PHARMACEUTICALS, INC.,* 113 S.Ct. 2786, decided June 28, 1993.

81. William J. Cook, "Courtroom Genetics," *U.S. News and World Report*, January 27, 1992, pp. 60–61.
82. *United States* v. *Jakobetz*, 747 F. Supp. 250, 254–255 (D.Vt. 1990).
83. Sylvester and Stafford, "Judicial Acceptance of DNA Profiling," pp. 28–29.
84. Victoria Slind-Flor, "Court OKs Forced DNA Test," *National Law Journal*, September 6, 1993, p. 10.
85. Jim Wasserman, Associated Press, "Justice System's Use of Mitochondrial DNA Grows," *Reno Gazette Journal*, November 3, 2003, p. 4B.
86. Tod Newcombe, "The Truth Machine," *Government Technology: Crime and the Tech Effect*, April 2003, pp. 37–39.
87. Patrick E. Cook and Dayle L. Hinman, "Criminal Profiling: Science and Art," *Journal of Contemporary Criminal Justice* 15 (August 1999): 230.
88. Ibid., p. 232.
89. Steven A. Egger, "Psychological Profiling," *Journal of Contemporary Criminal Justice* 15 (August 1999): 243.
90. Ibid., p. 242.
91. Walter C. Langer, *The Mind of Adolph Hitler* (New York: World, 1978).
92. Swanson, Chamelin, and Territo, *Criminal Investigation*, pp. 601–2.
93. Brad Darrach and Joel Norris, "An American Tragedy," *Life*, August 1984, p. 58.
94. Swanson, Chamelin, and Territo, *Criminal Investigation*, pp. 606–7.
95. Cook and Hinman, "Criminal Profiling," p. 234.
96. Martin Reiser, Louise Ludwig, Susan Saxe, and Clare Wagner, "An Evaluation of the Use of Psychics in the Investigation of Major Crimes," *Journal of Police Science and Administration* 7 (1979): 18–25.
97. Joseph Deladurantey and Daniel Sullivan, *Criminal Investigation Standards* (New York: Harper and Row, 1980), p. 72.
98. *People* v. *Quaglino*, Cal. Ct. App., 2d Dist., 1977; cert. denied, 439 U.S. 875, 99 S. Ct. 212 (1978).
99. Bill O'Driscoll, "Hypnotist Keeping Busy Since Law Let His Evidence into State Courts," *Reno Gazette Journal*, June 21, 1999, p. 1c.
100. Mark Bowden, "The Dark Art of Interrogation," *Atlantic Monthly* 292, no. 3 (October 2003): 53, 60.
101. Ibid., p. 62.
102. Ibid.
103. Ibid., pp. 62–64.
104. M. Lee Goff, *A Fly for the Prosecution: How Insect Evidence Helps Solve Crimes* (Cambridge, MA: Harvard University Press, 2000), p. 9. An excellent source of information concerning forensic entomology, this book contains not only the effects of insects but also the consequences of predators, air, fire, and water and provides a number of related case studies.
105. Ibid., p. 10.
106. Ibid., p. 11.
107. Ibid., pp. 12–13.

108. JOANNIE M. SCHROF, "Murder, They Chirped," *U.S. News and World Report*, October 14, 1991, pp. 67–68.
109. GOFF, *A Fly for the Prosecution*, p. 14.
110. DANIEL PEDERSEN, "Down on the Body Farm," *Newsweek*, October 23, 2000, pp. 50–52.
111. Ibid., p. 67.
112. Ibid., p. 68.
113. HARVEY WALLACE, *Victimology: Legal, Psychological, and Social Perspectives* (Boston: Allyn and Bacon, 1998), p. 333.
114. Ibid.
115. Ibid., pp. 333–34.
116. GEORGE E. WATTENDORF, "Stalking: Investigation Strategies," *FBI Law Enforcement Bulletin* (March 2000):10–15.
117. NUA Archives, "How Many Online?" http://www.nua.ie/surveys/how_many_online/ (accessed January 20, 2005).
118. Ibid., p. 45.
119. D. PETTINARI, "Are We There Yet? The Future of Policing/Sheriffing in Pueblo—Or in Anywhere, America," http://www.policefuturists.org/files/yet.html (accessed February 13, 2001).
120. JANIS WOLAK, KIMBERLY MITCHELL, and DAVID FINKELHOR, *Internet Sex Crimes against Minors: The Response of Law Enforcement* (Alexandria, VA: National Center for Missing and Exploited Children, November 2003), p. 17.
121. Ibid.
122. CRIMES AGAINST CHILDREN RESEARCH CENTER, "Fact Sheet: Overall Crime Victimization of Juveniles," http://www.unh.edu.ccrc/factsheet/overallcrime.htm (accessed August 17, 2004).
123. ANDREA J. SEDLAK, DAVID FINKELHOR, HEATHER HAMMER, and DANA J. SCHULTZ, *National Estimates of Missing Children: An Overview* (Washington, DC: Office of Juvenile Justice and Delinquency Prevention, National Incidence Studies of Missing, Abducted, Runaway, and Throwaway Children [NISMART], October 2002), p. 6.
124. NATIONAL CENTER FOR MISSING AND EXPLOITED CHILDREN, http://www.missingkids.com (accessed February 4, 2004), p. 1.
125. RYAN TURNER and RACHEL KOSA, *Cold Case Squads: Leaving No Stone Unturned* (Washington, DC: Department of Justice, Bureau of Justice Assistance, July 2003), pp. 2–4.

CHAPTER 8

Extraordinary Problems and Methods

Never before have good and evil been so completely massed against one another.

—Dwight D. Eisenhower

In utrumque paratus / Seu versare dolos seu certae occumbere morti. [Prepared for either event / to set his traps or to meet with certain death.]

—Virgil, 70–19 B.C.

Key Terms

bioterrorism
coyote
gang
graffiti
hate crime
homeland security
Mafia
Racketeer Influenced and Corrupt Organizations Act (RICO)
terrorism
USA PATRIOT Act

Certain types of people in the United States, through their actions or status, pose unique challenges for the police. A common thread running through the types of offenders that are discussed in this chapter—terrorists, hate crime offenders, mafiosi, gang members, and illegal immigrants—is that the police are often compelled to engage in clandestine operations in order to arrest them. Another common thread is that the police must constantly attempt to develop new methods and practices for dealing with them. As contemporary American society becomes more complex and rife with problems and violence, the police will increasingly be compelled to approach such groups differently. This chapter examines each of these unique challenges to police and their methods, and then concludes with a chapter summary, review questions, independent student activities, and related Web sites.

TERRORISM AND HOMELAND SECURITY

As shown in Chapter 2, nothing has changed the structure and function of U.S. law enforcement—particularly federal law enforcement—more than the events of September 11, 2001, and their aftermath. While compelled to become much more knowledgeable about terrorists' methods and how to respond in the event of an attack, at the same time our law enforcement agencies were given a mandate to become much more strategic in their approach to their work, adopting a long-term view of **homeland security**.

A Nation Changed and Challenged

Unquestionably, historians of the future will maintain that the terrorist attacks of the early twenty-first century changed forever the nature of policing and security efforts in the United States. Words are almost inadequate to describe how the events of September 11 forever altered and heightened the fears and concerns of all Americans with regard to domestic security and the methods and technologies necessary for safeguarding the general public.

The ongoing conflict between Israel and the Palestinians, the antigovernment narcoterrorists in several South American countries, the spread of radical Islamic fundamentalism, and our own homegrown terrorist groups strongly suggest that North Americans will face the threat of **terrorism** for some time to come.[1] Our local police departments are our first line of defense. Within the fifty states, there are three thousand counties and eighteen thousand cities that must be protected. The job of getting law enforcement, emergency services, public-health agencies, and private enterprises coordinated and working together at local, state, and federal levels is a daunting task.[2]

Definitions and Types

The Federal Bureau of Investigation (FBI) defines *terrorism* as "the unlawful use of force against persons or property to intimidate or coerce a government, the civilian population, or any segment thereof, in furtherance of political or social objectives."[3] Terrorism can take many forms, however, and does not always involve bombs and guns. For example, the Earth Liberation Front (ELF) and a sister organization, the Animal

Liberation Front, have been responsible for the majority of terrorist acts committed in the United States for several years. These ecoterrorists have burned greenhouses, tree farms, logging sites, ski resorts, and new housing developments.[4] The FBI considers ELF to be one of the nation's most prolific domestic terrorist organizations, responsible for such acts as a $12 million fire at a ski resort in Vail, Colorado, and the arsons of mink farms and auto dealerships that sell sports utility vehicles in Pennsylvania.[5]

The FBI divides the current international terrorist threat into three categories:

> *Foreign sponsors of international terrorism:* Seven countries—Iran, Iraq, Syria, Sudan, Libya, Cuba, and North Korea—are designated as sponsors and view terrorism as a tool of foreign policy. They fund, organize, network, and provide other support to formal terrorist groups and extremists.
>
> *Formalized terrorist groups:* Autonomous terrorist organizations have their own infrastructures, personnel, finances, and training facilities. Examples of this type are Osama bin Laden's al Qaeda terrorists, who attacked the World Trade Center towers and the Pentagon in 2001. Other formalized terrorist groups include Afghanistan's Taliban, Iranian-backed Hezbollah, Egyptian Al-Gama'a Al-Islamiyya, and Palestinian Hamas.
>
> *Loosely affiliated international radical extremists:* Loosely affiliated extremists like those who bombed the World Trade Center in 1993 do not represent a particular nation. They may pose the most urgent threat to the United States because they remain relatively unknown to law enforcement agencies.[6]

Police officers confronting terrorists in the United States find themselves vulnerable in six types of situations:[7]

> *Traffic stops:* During a traffic stop, the law enforcement officer lacks prior knowledge of the individual being stopped; the officer may be isolated and the extremist in a heightened state of suspicion or anger as a result of the stop.
>
> *Residence visits:* During a residence visit, the officer is on the extremist's home turf, putting the officer at a disadvantage; the visit may be routine, but the extremist may not view it as such, and the home may be fortified and its occupants armed.
>
> *Rallies and marches:* The risk to police at rallies and marches usually comes not from the group holding the event but from counterprotestors—often anarchists who hate the police and who believe the best way to confront the demonstrators is through physical violence.
>
> *Confrontations and standoffs:* A confrontation or standoff can arise from any of the three preceding situations.
>
> *Revenge and retaliation:* A terrorist may be motivated by the desire for revenge. An example is a person who attempts to blow up an Internal Revenue Service office because he was audited.

The horrifying destruction of the World Trade Center in New York City in 2001 (right) and the Murrah Building in Oklahoma City in 1993 (left) demonstrated for all Americans that terrorism is a very real threat to our security at home.
(Corbis / Sygma)

Incident responses: Incident responses can take many forms, ranging from activities of terrorists to acts of nature.

Terrorist attacks in the United States are caused by both foreign and domestic terrorists. Examples of the former are the terrorist attacks in September 2001 on the World Trade Center in New York and the Pentagon in Virginia, which resulted in the deaths of more than three thousand people. Another example is the bombing of the World Trade Center in February 1993, which killed six and injured one thousand people. An example of domestic terrorism is the April 1995 bombing of the Murrah Building in Oklahoma City by Timothy McVeigh; 168 people were killed, and more than five hundred were injured.[8] (McVeigh was executed in June 2001.)

Greater Law Enforcement Powers: The USA PATRIOT Act

Police have several possible means to address domestic terrorism. The first, and perhaps the most fruitful, is military support of domestic law enforcement. The Posse Comitatus Act of 1878 prohibits using the military to execute the laws generally; the military may be called on, however, to provide personnel and equipment for certain special support activities, such as domestic terrorist events involving weapons of mass destruction.[9]

On a broad level, there are four primary means available to law enforcement agencies for dealing with terrorist organizations:

- Gather raw intelligence on the organization's structure, its members, and its plans (or potential for the use of violence).
- Determine what measures can be taken to counter, or thwart, terrorist activities.
- Assess how the damage caused by terrorists can be minimized through rapid response and containment of the damage.
- Apprehend and convict individual terrorists and dismantle their organizations.[10]

Toward those ends, a number of new investigative measures have been provided federal law enforcement agencies through the enactment of the **USA PATRIOT Act** shortly after the September 11 attacks. The act dramatically expands the federal government's ability to investigate Americans for "intelligence purposes" without establishing probable cause and to conduct searches if there are "reasonable grounds" to believe the suspects pose a threat to national security. Federal agencies like the FBI are given access to financial, mental health, medical, library, and other records.[11]

Broad new authority for the use of wiretaps against suspected terrorists has also been granted federal agencies. Included are "roving wiretaps"—taps not on a particular phone but on any (mobile or land) phone that a terrorism suspect uses or might use.[12] The USA PATRIOT Act has not been without its critics, however. Because of the act's broad language and what it permits federal agents to do, many fear that these new governmental powers will be abused or that the act will become a "permanent fixture" in our legal system.[13] Indeed, a federal district court blocked the expanded wiretapping law, but the law was upheld by a special panel of federal appeals court judges in late 2002.[14] Critics also bemoan the fact that federal agents are using the act in cases that "have nothing to do with terrorism." An example cited is the act's money-laundering language, which allows the government to search every financial institution in the country for the records of suspected terrorists, resulting in about sixty-four hundred such searches in 2003 alone.[15]

Furthermore, the treatment of Arab-Americans since September 11 has been termed a form of "persecution," as many of those under scrutiny have been fingerprinted, photographed, detained, and deported under the act's mandatory registration program. Tensions have also been raised among Arab-Americans and Muslims because hate crimes against them have increased dramatically—1,700 percent in the eighteen months following September 11.[16]

Still, many Americans seem willing to sacrifice civil liberties in the interest of homeland security and to allow the government to use "every legal means" at its disposal to prevent further terrorist activity.[17]

Spiking Resources

Chasing terrorists is very expensive. The U.S. Congress appropriated more than $60 billion from September 2001 to January 2002 to combat terrorism at home and abroad, including $1.5 billion for the new Homeland Security Department.[18] Law enforcement resources available for the task have also greatly increased. From 1993 to 2001, the counterterrorism budget of the FBI (which created a new Counterterrorism Division in April 2000) increased 388 percent, from $77 million to $376 million.[19] The costs of trying to secure the nation's people and places are projected to skyrocket even more in the future ($150 billion more by 2010).[20] In a related vein, in February 2002, President Bush announced a plan to strengthen our homeland security and proposed allocating $38 billion for border security (including $3.5 billion for the nation's first responders (police, firefighters, and medical teams), $700 million to improve intelligence gathering and sharing abilities, and $230 million to create a citizens' initiative to help communities become better prepared for an attack.[21]

In addition to terrorism and other critical incidents of human origin, the police must be prepared for major tragedies like airplane crashes and natural disasters like floods, hurricanes, and tornadoes.

(Courtesy City of New York Police Department Photo Unit)

An Intelligence Overhaul

In July 2004, Congress released the final report of the National Commission on Terrorist Attacks upon the United States, also known as the 9/11 Commission. This report's thirteen chapters and 567 pages outlined forty-one recommendations for change in the nation's federal intelligence community and its preparations against future terrorist attacks. Included was the commission's major recommendation for the appointment of a national intelligence director above the director of the Central Intelligence Agency (CIA) to oversee more than a dozen intelligence agencies. The commission would also create a national counterterrorism center to direct the war on terror.[22] Much of the report detailed intelligence shortcomings and what was not known prior to the September 11 attacks.

As a result, in December 2004, Congress passed, and President Bush signed into law the *Intelligence Reform and Terrorism Prevention Act of 2004*, Public Law 108–458, which creates a new Director of National Intelligence position to be the principal adviser to the president and coordinate the nation's spy agencies. The position will be above the CIA director. It also established a National Counterterrorism Center for planning intelligence missions and coordinating information on terror threats and responses, as well as a Privacy and Civil Liberties Board of private citizens to oversee privacy protections.

The intelligence community now comprises a sprawling network of fifteen federal agencies and a budget of $40 billion, with personnel ranging from the three hundred staffers in a State Department office to the thirty-eight thousand people at the National Security Agency. The CIA chief also serves as director of Central Intelligence and is tasked with leading the community, but he wields little actual influence outside the CIA. Eight of the agencies and most of the total intelligence budget are controlled by the Department of Defense. Other agencies, like the FBI and Homeland Security, run their own operations.[23]

Clearly, the time had come for the U.S. intelligence community to be examined and redesigned. The problems found by the 9/11 Commission are so many and so extensive that it is hard to even know where to begin. The budgetary and personnel systems are archaic; individual spy agencies resemble not so much modern corporations as feudal fiefdoms. There is only the most tenuous central authority, widespread duplication of effort, and secrecy bordering on paranoia.[24] Intelligence reform is now on the national agenda. The intelligence community had to be streamlined quickly if terrorism is to be prevented.

A Companion Threat: Bioterrorism

The use of anthrax in the United States in late 2001 left no doubt about our vulnerability to biological weapons—or about the intention of some people to develop and use them for the purpose of **bioterrorism**. Smallpox, botulism, and plague also constitute major threats, and many experts feel that it is only a matter of time before biological weapons get into the wrong hands and are used like explosives have been used in the past.[25]

EXHIBIT 8-1

With Biochem Terror No Longer "Unthinkable," NYPD Gets Ready

Forced to think the unthinkable, as New York City Police Commissioner Raymond W. Kelly put it, the N.Y.P.D. has put together over the past year a response, which experts contend is unrivaled in the nation, to a potential catastrophic attack using chemical, biological or nuclear weapons.

"We're thinking about the unthinkable—what a few years ago was the unthinkable," said Kelly. . . .

Among the drills and training exercises being conducted by the New York City Police Department are those that will prepare officers for their role in a sweeping citywide plan to get emergency antibiotics to every resident after an attack with biological weapons.

The plan, which was formulated prior to the Sept. 11, 2001, terrorist attacks, would involve tens of thousands of city workers and volunteers, and at least a dozen agencies. More than 200 points of distribution, or PODs, would be set up in the five boroughs in specially selected city buildings, including public schools. New York's more than 8 million inhabitants would report to those locations for medication or vaccinations. . . .

During a daylong exercise called Operation TriPod conducted in May 2002, one POD was able to process more than 1,400 people in an hour—a far greater number than the 400-an-hour rate that would be necessary for all 200 locations to vaccinate 8 million people in five days, officials said. . . .

Source: "With Biochem Terror No Longer 'Unthinkable,' NYPD Gets Ready," *Law Enforcement News*, Spring 2004, pp. 1, 13. John Jay College of Criminal Justice, CUNY, 555 W. 57th St., New York, NY 10019.

All of this brings to mind *The Andromeda Strain*. In that movie, a toxic agent was genetically engineered in large quantities and sprayed into the population; it then reproduced itself and killed many people. The person who controls such a toxin could sell it to terrorists. One has to wonder why international terrorists have not already developed and used a biological weapon. This form of terrorism can wipe out an entire civilization. All that is required is a toxin that can be cultured and, in spray form, disseminated into the population. Fortunately, biological agents are extremely difficult for all but specially trained individuals to make in large quantities and in the correct dosage; they are tricky to transport because live organisms are delicate; and they must be dispersed in a proper molecule size to infect the lungs of the target. Like chemical weapons, they are also dependent on the wind and the weather and are difficult to control.[26]

The Practitioner's Perspective by Dr. Kenneth Hunter very expertly lays out the nature of bioterrorism and the role that local police would need to assume if an act of bioterrorism were to occur. Some cities, including New York, have developed a planned response to such a catastrophic attack, with drills and training exercises that attempt to prepare officers for their roles in getting emergency antibiotics to every resident, enforcing a quarantine, and using personal radiation detectors to check vehicles.[27]

PRACTITIONER'S PERSPECTIVE

Bioterrorism: The Challenges for Local Law Enforcement

KENNETH W. HUNTER JR., Sc.D.

Kenneth W. Hunter Jr., Sc.D., is professor of microbiology and immunology at the University of Nevada School of Medicine. Dr. Hunter served for eleven years as vice president for research and dean of the graduate school at the University of Nevada, Reno. He received the doctor of science degree in immunology from the Johns Hopkins University in 1978, and for more than twenty years, he has done research and published scientific articles on the diagnosis and treatment of exposure to toxic chemicals, biological toxins, and infectious microorganisms. His experience includes research and consultation in chemical and biological warfare for the U.S. Army Medical Research Institute for Chemical Defense (Edgewood Arsenal, Maryland) and for the U.S. Army Medical Research Institute for Infectious Disease (Fort Detrick, Maryland).

The use of biological agents in warfare and terrorism is not new. In 1346, after a protracted siege of Kaffa in the Crimea, the Tartars catapulted bodies of plague victims into the city with the intent of killing their adversaries.[1] During the French and Indian Wars (1754–1763), several American Indian tribes were decimated by smallpox when British troops gave them blankets from smallpox victims.[2] Ironically, these events occurred long before microorganisms were identified as the cause of plague and smallpox. In the 1930s, fleas carrying plague were released into Chinese cities by the Japanese, not to attain a strategic military advantage, but to create widespread public panic.[3]

Though history is replete with examples of the use of biological agents as weapons, it has taken letters filled with anthrax spores delivered to the offices of a U.S. senator to make bioterrorism a modern reality.[4] Notwithstanding the fact that most of us are now aware of the threat of bioterrorism,[5] few of us, including most law enforcement personnel, understand its complexity. For instance, as bad as the release of anthrax spores upwind of a large city would be, there are bioterrorism scenarios that are even more horrifying.

A wide variety of contagious microorganisms (that is, microorganisms that spread by person-to-person contact) have the potential to be used by terrorists, but those listed in Table 8-1 have been suggested as the most probable.[6] However, sophisticated terrorists may have access to modern molecular biology laboratories, and bioagents could be genetically engineered to have characteristics even more devastating than naturally occurring microorganisms (Table 8-2). In bioterrorism with contagious agents, there would be no gunshots, no explosions, and no mass casualties in the streets. Instead, the first evidence of an attack would be increasing numbers of sick and dying individuals transported to local clinics and hospitals with a similar constellation of symptoms. With many of these biological agents, the initial symptoms would look like common febrile illnesses (for example, influenza), causing a delay in the recognition of the terrorist microorganism. Once it was

TABLE 8-1

Contagious Microorganisms That Could Be Used as Bioterrorist Agents
Varicella major (smallpox)
Yersinia pestis (plague)
Franciscella tularensis (tularemia)
Hemorrhagic fever viruses (e.g., Ebola, Marburg, Lassa)

recognized that an infectious agent was being transmitted in the local population, public health officials would be notified, and attempts would immediately be made to identify and characterize it, usually with the help of federal laboratories like the Centers for Disease Control and Prevention.

At that time, local law enforcement agencies would be alerted that a possible bioterrorist attack had occurred. The time frame from initial recognition of the disease to its identification could be several days given present technology. Moreover, if the offending organism had been genetically manipulated, identification could be even more protracted. Eventually, local public health officials working in concert with federal specialists would decide whether it was a natural epidemic or bioterrorism. The critical task for public health officials would be to quickly identify prophylactic and therapeutic modalities to address the problem, and assistance from local police agencies in the distribution of drugs and vaccines would be needed.

As strange as it may seem, the easier forms of bioterrorism to deal with involve the release of toxins or spores from noncontagious organisms (for example, anthrax spores); the spread would be limited by environmental parameters and would be local in distribution. Such terrorist attacks could have grave consequences, however. A 1993 congressional study modeled the release of 100 kg of anthrax spores upwind of a major city of five million people and suggested that between 130,000 and three million people would die.[7] This would have an effect approaching the magnitude of a nuclear weapon.

TABLE 8-2

How Bioterrorists Could Use Genetic Engineering to Produce Highly Contagious and Lethal Microorganisms

Microorganisms could be engineered to

- Contain one or more antibiotic resistance plasmids (e.g., multi-drug-resistant bacteria)
- Lack characteristic molecules that respond to antibodies induced by present vaccines (e.g., vaccine-resistant microorganisms)
- Express lethal virulence factors like toxins (e.g., common cold viruses engineered to produce lethal botulinum toxin)
- Make them more contagious
- Produce disease only after a protracted incubation period, thus assuring widespread dissemination before the first clinical cases are recognized
- More easily disperse by aerosol or water and be much more stable in the environment

(continued)

Clearly, in a mass casualty situation, law enforcement agencies would have to respond to extraordinary public panic. However, as terrible as the release of anthrax spores would be, because anthrax is not transmitted from person to person, the devastation would be limited to the region inundated with the spores; perhaps tens of kilometers.[8] The principal tasks for law enforcement in the anthrax scenario would be to manage public panic and to prevent uninfected people from coming in contact with residual anthrax spores until the spores were decontaminated or had dissipated naturally to noninfectious levels.

On the other hand, if the terrorist attack employed highly contagious microorganisms, the primary task of law enforcement would instead be containment of the disease. While it might seem that some police resources should be devoted to catching the perpetrators, terrorists wielding biological agents could disperse them in a clandestine fashion, and these attackers could be on the other side of the world before the first signs of illness appeared in the public.

Contagious disease containment by voluntary or forced sequestration of infected individuals is called "quarantine."[9] The concept of quarantine goes back many centuries, even before the discovery that microbes cause disease. Indeed, the word *quarantine* derives from the Latin term *quadraginta*, which was used to describe the forty-day isolation of merchant ships arriving at Mediterranean ports in the thirteenth century to prevent spread of the "black death" (the plague). Quarantine was used in the late nineteenth century to control relatively small outbreaks of contagious microorganisms, but quarantine has not been used in the United States for nearly a century[10]—and never with a large population. As previously mentioned, inhalation of anthrax is a deadly situation, but because it is not a contagious organism, drastic quarantine measures are probably unnecessary.[11] Even some microorganisms that spread from person to person may be of insufficient risk to warrant full-scale quarantine.

The process whereby medical and public health officials determine whether quarantine is feasible and justifiable to contain the spread of a contagious microorganism is complex.[12] However, if it is determined that the microorganism responsible for the initial cases is a potentially lethal terrorist weapon and is highly contagious, a decision to implement quarantine to prevent spread of the disease may be appropriate.

A bioterrorist attack with a highly contagious microorganism may initially be a local epidemic, but it has the potential of expanding into a worldwide pandemic if infected individuals disperse to other locations. Though quarantine will clearly involve state and federal resources, early quarantine will perforce be implemented at the local level, and therefore local law enforcement agencies need to be aware of the array of potentially negative attributes of quarantine that may come into play.

Because there have been no actual bioterrorist attacks for American cities to deal with, there is no direct experience for law enforcement agencies to draw on. Most police departments are only marginally prepared to deal with a highly contagious agent spreading in the community. Terrorist attacks using conventional explosives would probably engage an incident command system with the fire department in charge initially, followed by a command switch to local police, and, finally, federal authorities (that is, the FBI). However, the critical need to provide rapid containment of a contagious agent by limiting dispersal of infected people would require the initial incident command structure to shift to a lead by local police, working closely with public-health officials and supported rapidly by National Guard and federal military resources.

The first inclination of citizens in a community subjected to the release of a bioterrorist agent would be to flee, particularly if they realize that sequestration of all residents, including those who have not been infected, would markedly increase the chance of disease transmission to the uninfected. Unfortunately, there would be no way for them to know whether they were harboring the microorganism in the preclinical stage, and thus fleeing individuals must be prevented from leaving the quarantine area and infecting others.

It has been recognized since the late nineteenth century that extraordinary police powers would be needed to implement a quarantine for the sake of public health.[13] In 1893, civil disobedience and violence against local officials resulted from an attempt to implement quarantine to quell a smallpox outbreak in the small community of Muncie, Indiana.[14] Imagine how much more problematic it would be for local officials to implement an effective quarantine of a large metropolitan area. If feasible at all, it probably would require the rapid mobilization of federal resources. J. Barbara and colleagues proposed a list of alternatives to full-scale quarantine that might be implemented with fewer negative consequences; they include the widespread use of disposable masks, short-term voluntary home curfew, restrictions on the assembly of groups, and the closure of mass transportation. Whether implementing full-scale quarantine or one or more of these alternatives, local law enforcement agencies would need to work closely with the media, public health organizations, and other local and state government agencies.

During the first few days after a bioterrorist attack with a highly contagious agent, local law enforcement personnel would play a critical role in maintaining order and enforcing quarantine or other measures. Since police officers would be just as susceptible to the effects of the biological agent as the public, and many would already have been exposed by the time the problem had been identified, they would justifiably be concerned about their own health. Even if police officers had protective clothing and respirators (a completely inadequate situation at present for most police departments), they would know that their relatives and friends were unprotected, thus causing extraordinary stress on performance.

Finally, and most importantly, would police officers be able to use the force necessary to maintain quarantine, knowing that infected individuals leaving the local area could transmit the disease and potentially cause the deaths of millions?

1. V. J. Derbes, "De Mussis and the Great Plague of 1348: A Forgotten Episode of Bacteriological Warfare," *Journal of the American Medical Association* 196 (1966): 59–62.
2. E. A. Fenn, "Biological Warfare in Eighteenth-Century North America: Beyond Jeffrey Amherst,"*Journal of American History* 86 (2000): 1552–80.
3. S. Harris, "Japanese Biological Warfare Research on Humans: A Case Study of Microbiology and Ethics," *Annals of the New York Academy of Science* 666 (1990): 21–52.
4. A. C. Revkin, "The Odyssey of an Anthrax-Tainted Envelope and a Trail of Death," *New York Times*, October 31, 2001, p. B8.
5. A. Carter, J. Deutsch, and P. Zelicow, "Catastrophic Terrorism," *Foreign Affairs* 77 (1998): 80–95.
6. D. A. Henderson, T. V. Inglesby, and T. O'Toole, eds., *Bioterrorism: Guidelines for Medical and Public Health Management* (Chicago: American Medical Association Press, 2002).
7. Office of Technology Assessment, U.S. Congress, *Proliferation of Weapons of Mass Destruction*, publication OTA-ISC-559 (Washington, DC: U.S. Government Printing Office, 1993).
8. J. Simon, "Biological Terrorism: Preparing to Meet the Threat," *Journal of the American Medical Association* 278 (1997): 428–30.
9. P. S. Sehdev, "The Origin of Quarantine," *Clinical Infectious Diseases* 35 (2002): 1071–72.
10. H. Cumming, "The United States Quarantine System during the Past Fifty Years," in *A Half Century of Public Health*, ed. M.Ravenel (New York: American Public Health Association, 1921), pp. 118–32.
11. T. V. Ingelsby, D. A. Henderson, J. G. Bartlett et al., "Anthrax as a Biological Weapon," *Journal of the American Medical Association* 281 (1999): 1735–45.
12. J. Barbara, A. Macintyre, L. Gostin et al., "Large-Scale Quarantine Following Biological Terrorism in the United States," in Henderson, Inglesby, and O'Toole, eds., *Bioterrorism*, pp. 187–220.
13. E. Freund, *The Police Power: Public Policy and Constitutional Rights* (New York: Arno Press, 1904), pp. 124–30.
14. W. Eidson, "Confusion, Controversy, and Quarantine: The Muncie Smallpox Epidemic of 1893," *Indiana Magazine of History* 86 (1990): 374–98.

Policing Hate

In the past, the police often tended to dismiss the context in which crimes occurred; an assault, for example, was simply an assault. In 1990, however, Congress passed the Hate Crimes Statistics Act, which forced the police to collect statistics on **hate crimes**; 41 states have enacted statutes that place higher penalties on crimes that have a "hate motive." Hate crimes and hate incidents—those that are motivated by an offender's bias against an individual's or group's race, religion, ethnic or national origin, gender, age, disability, or sexual orientation[28]—are major issues for the police because of their unique impact on victims and the community.[29]

There are numerous hate groups in the United States. They include the American Nazi Party, the Arizona Patriots, the Aryan Brotherhood and the Aryan Nations, the Christian Defense League, the Identity Church Movement, the Ku Klux Klan, Posse Comitatus, and the Skinheads, to name a few. In addition, there are more than two hundred militias operating in thirty-nine states.[30]

The rationale for police involvement in hate crimes is that one of their primary roles is the enforcement or reinforcement of community values.[31] Even though a particular hate crime may be relatively minor and unorganized (for example, graffiti, simple assault, or disorderly conduct), it may attack the very fiber of a community and result in special or unusual effects on the victim or the community as a whole.

But preventing and responding to hate crimes can be a daunting task; about seventy-five hundred hate crimes are reported each year in the United States, about half (51.4 percent) of which are motivated by racial bias; about 18 percent are motivated by religious bias, 17 percent by sexual orientation bias, and 14 percent by ethnic or national origin bias. Of the incidents that were motivated by religious bias, 69 percent were directed against Jews and Jewish institutions.[32] Furthermore, hate crimes committed against Arab-Americans and Muslims increased 1,700 percent in the eighteen months following September 11. Table 8-3 shows the distribution of hate crimes by victim group.

At present, forty-one states and the District of Columbia have crime statutes that address hate violence and enhance the penalties for hate crimes. At the federal level, hate crimes are investigated by the Bias Crimes Unit of the FBI and the church arson and explosives experts of the Bureau of Alcohol, Tobacco, Firearms, and Explosives.[33]

There is much a law enforcement organization can do with respect to hate crimes. They can provide victims with a point of contact in the department to whom they can report hate crimes and express concerns. They can inform victims on case progress, participate in hate-crime training and educate the public about these crimes, establish a "zero tolerance" of prejudice within the department, track the criminal activities of hate groups,

TABLE 8-3

Incidents, Offenses, Victims, and Known Offenders by Bias Motivation, 2003

Bias Motivation	Incidents	Offenses	Victims[a]	Known Offenders[b]
Total	**7,489**	**8,715**	**9,100**	**6,934**
Single-Bias Incidents	7,485	8,706	9,091	6,927
Race	**3,844**	**4,574**	**4,754**	**3,886**
Anti-White	830	969	1,006	1,019
Anti-Black	2,548	3,032	3,150	2,456
Anti-American Indian/Alaskan Native	76	83	85	80
Anti-Asian/Pacific Islander	231	277	289	196
Anti-Multiracial Group	159	213	224	135
Religion	**1,343**	**1,426**	**1,489**	**574**
Anti-Jewish	927	987	1,025	332
Anti-Catholic	76	78	80	32
Anti-Protestant	49	50	54	20
Anti-Islamic	149	155	171	94
Anti-Other Religious Group	109	118	120	69
Anti-Multireligious Group	24	25	26	17
Anti-Atheism/Agnosticism/etc.	9	13	13	10
Sexual Orientation	**1,239**	**1,430**	**1,479**	**1,313**
Anti-Male Homosexual	783	881	910	863
Anti-Female Homosexual	187	220	230	167
Anti-Homosexual	247	305	314	257
Anti-Heterosexual	14	15	15	10
Anti-Bisexual	8	9	10	16
Ethnicity/National Origin	**1,026**	**1,236**	**1,326**	**1,119**
Anti-Hispanic	426	529	595	577
Anti-Other Ethnicity/National Origin	600	707	731	542
Disability	**33**	**40**	**43**	**35**
Anti-Physical	24	30	32	24
Anti-Mental	9	10	11	11
Multiple-Bias Incidents[c]	4	9	9	7

[a]The term *victim* may refer to a person, business, institution, or society as a whole.
[b]The term *known offender* does not imply that the identity of the suspect is known, but only that the race of the suspect is identified, which distinguishes him or her from an unknown offender.
[c]A multiple-bias incident is a hate crime in which two or more offense types were committed as a result of two or more bias motivations.

Source: Department of Justice, Federal Bureau of Investigation, "Hate Crime Statistics/2003," http://www.fbi.gov/ucr/03hc.pdf, November 2004 (accessed January 23, 2005).

and sponsor and participate in community events that promote tolerance and diversity.[34]

The Madison, Connecticut, Police Department has been educating its officers about hate crimes. At a departmental roll call, every officer received a laminated hate-crimes response card with important information for responding to hate crimes, working with victims, and pursuing perpetrators. The card includes the definition of a hate crime, questions responding officers should ask, and tips for recognizing signs of organized hate groups. In October 2002, the Anti-Defamation League took the effort further, distributing these cards to more than seventy-five hundred police officers throughout Connecticut.[35]

A unique problem that exists with hate crimes is that they are difficult to prosecute. Hate-crime charges are the only ones in which proving motive is as important as proving method. Juries often find it too difficult to conclude with any certainty what was going on in the defendant's mind during the crime. Defending a hate crime can also be a daunting task. Defense attorneys argue that a defendant might, for example, dress and talk like a Skinhead but not identify with the group, while juries can be prejudiced toward guilt by the mere allegation of such a cruel crime. Furthermore, defending against hate-crime allegations can take on the appearance of defending a hate group, and jurors may force a defendant to pay for the sins of the group.[36]

Policing the Mafia

Origin and Organization

Imagine devoting your entire police career to the collection and analysis of intelligence information and making only a few or even no arrests. Visualize yourself investigating crime by watching newspaper obituaries and appearing at funerals to log license plates and take photographs of the mourners from a safe distance, then tracing names to the fifth cousins. Consider spending years investigating a single case, combing through records and files that go back twenty years. Picture yourself going undercover for several years to investigate a crime organization, never knowing whether your cover will be blown and you will be targeted for death. (See the Practitioner's Perspective on George Togliatti.)

Enter the world of organized crime. These are only some of the unusual methods and schemes employed by police agents who are assigned to the underworld. *Organized crime* is defined by the FBI as "any group having some manner of formalized structure and whose primary objective is to obtain money through illegal activities." Under this definition, several organized-crime syndicates or organizations exist in America, such as street youth gangs, prison gangs, Asian gangs (like the Chinese Triads, some Vietnamese and Tong immigrants, and the Japanese Boryokudan), bikers, and Gypsies. Probably the oldest, most profitable, and dangerous crime organization in America is the **Mafia**, also known as La Cosa Nostra, or "this thing of ours."

Mafia origins can be traced to thirteenth-century Sicily. The history of the Mafia is a confusing hodgepodge of lore and legend, but the story with the most appeal (probably due to its romantic nature) involves the French occupation of Sicily and Italy in 1282. The local people used a form of guerrilla warfare to fight the French military, engaging in hit-and-run tactics and using their knowledge of the rugged terrain to fight the superior French army. A legend holds that a young French soldier and an Italian maiden fell in love during this military occupation; when their tryst was discovered, they were both assassinated by the French army. Following the deaths of these two young people, a vindictive cry arose among the people: "Morte alle Francia Italia anela," meaning "Death to the French is Italy's cry." The acronym of this cry is MAFIA.

Many Sicilian and Italian mafiosi immigrated to the United States in the late 1800s and early 1900s, maintaining their criminal lifestyle of intimidation and force. It has been argued that organized crime existed even in the Wild West, focusing on the crimes of gambling, prostitution, robbery, and cattle rustling.[37]

Mafia families have a formally organized nature (see Figure 8-1) consisting of El Capo (or "godfather"), Sotto Capo ("underboss"), the consigliere ("counselor"), caporegimas ("lieutenants" or enforcers), and the soldatos (or "soldiers"). The major obstacle to investigating and apprehending these criminals is that they shun the public spotlight. In fact, their primary, centuries-old code of honor is that of *omerta* (silence).

For the most part, mafiosi loathe unwelcomed attention; it has been said that it is almost as if the mafiosi are products of "parthenogenesis"— as if they just arose out of the dust, like the mythical "phoenix" bird. When confronted by a police officer and asked questions about himself (the Mafia is an all-male organization), the mafioso seems to have no roots, no parentage, or any other background that the police can maintain as intelligence information.

Successful Police Offensives

For forty years, FBI Director J. Edgar Hoover denied that the Mafia even existed. Until very recently, the "Mob" had a veritable choke hold on America, being involved in killing for hire, extortion, loan-sharking, money laundering, narcotics, prostitution, smuggling, bookmaking, bribery, business infiltration, embezzlement, hijacking, horse-race fixing, racketeering, pornography, bank fraud, and fencing. By the 1960s, the Mafia's influence extended from America's largest labor unions into trucking, construction, longshoring, waste disposal, gambling, and garment making; it had grown into a multibillion-dollar syndicate of criminal enterprises run by twenty-six "families" nationwide.[38]

PRACTITIONER'S PERSPECTIVE

Going Undercover: An FBI Agent's Two-Year Experience

GEORGE TOGLIATTI

George Togliatti joined the FBI in 1973 and was subsequently assigned to offices in Boise, Detroit, and Las Vegas. In Las Vegas, he supervised the White Collar Crime, the Property Crime, and the Organized Crime Investigations and Drug Programs. He holds a bachelor's degree in economics from Iona College and a master's in criminal justice administration from the University of Detroit. He retired from the FBI in 1996. The following is a case study of his role as a supervisory special agent.

Togliatti is soft spoken, part Italian and part Irish. He flew search-and-rescue helicopter missions for five years in North Vietnam. He then worked in the computer industry and took graduate accounting courses. Not happy with his career path, he joined the FBI at age twenty-eight. After short assignments in Butte, Montana, and Boise, Idaho, he acquired his first undercover experience in Detroit. But none of that could have prepared Togliatti for his undercover role as "George Dario"—the undercover mafioso who loved partying and the criminal lifestyle in the Las Vegas underworld.

Information was obtained that mobsters from Detroit and New York were attempting to gain a major foothold in Las Vegas. Wiretaps also revealed serious attempts to skim casino profits before they were counted for tax purposes, some mafiosi were killing one another, and ties between organized labor and the mob were deepening. The FBI conceived Operation Desert Fox, in which Togliatti would operate on the fringe of mob

Beginning in the mid-1980s, however, the FBI spearheaded an unprecedented assault on the Mafia, putting away two generations of godfathers on racketeering charges. That initiative continues today, and the bureau has had tremendous success in dealing with this very elusive group.

How has this success been obtained? Through tenacity, hard work, and some luck. The FBI has been successful for three practical reasons:

The expanded use of electronic eavesdropping ("wiretapping"): With federal agents listening in on more conversations each year, mobsters are forced to operate in a climate of constant suspicion. Cooperation between federal and state law enforcement authorities also speeds up convictions. Furthermore, the Internal Revenue Service can legally share information, enabling it to assist in almost two-thirds of all organized crime prosecutions.

The use of informants: A significant tool in the toppling of mob kingpins has been the use of former gangsters who have proved willing to violate the code activities and gather information for later prosecutions. Although it was originally intended to be a two-week assignment, Togliatti would be undercover for two years.

"George Dario" sported a Rolex watch, drove a Cadillac Seville, and had access to a $500,000 home in a country club addition. He had little trouble assuming his new identity, and he was readily accepted by the mob. He quickly made new friends, his glib, streetwise New York background serving him well. He assumed a phony background as a sales manager for a legitimate New York music company. Cruising casinos, bars, and restaurants, he noted criminal activities, such as extortion cases and drug deals. He was once approached by a man with an offer of $10,000 to beat up a girlfriend's ex-husband.

To fit into the underworld, where crime, sex, and drugs were easily available, Dario's values were often compromised, as when he would have to fake snorting cocaine. But he realized that one improper move would blow his cover and possibly cost him his life. He avoided committing several illegal and unsafe acts by turning ugly, telling associates he preferred alcohol to drugs and saying he wanted a clear head during his crimes. He saw rampant drug addiction among his associates, though, and today many of Dario's former associates who cheated on their wives wonder if that information is still tucked away in some FBI file.

Two close friends—fellow FBI agents—kept Dario informed of developments with the information he had uncovered. The trio often met in hideaway restaurants to discuss goings-on in the bureau office and the outside world in general. The friends also performed support work, such as checking license plate numbers or hotel registrations to identify people.

After two years had passed, Dario realized that it was time to become Togliatti again; the mob had learned he was a fake, and the telephone lines were abuzz. Operation Desert Fox was a huge success. Would Togliatti do it again? Today he says no; he can never recover the two years lost from his family and feels it was too high a price to pay. Yet he says it made him a better special agent; indeed, several promotions came his way in the next five years. He plays down the danger surrounding what he did, saying a lot of people in the FBI could have done the job. And, he says, "Vietnam was tougher, hands down."

Source: Portions excerpted from, and used with permission of, the *Reno Gazette Journal*, November 1, 1987, pp. 1A, 14A.

of secrecy, turning state's evidence against their old cronies. More youthful gangsters do not possess the level of loyalty to the family that their ancestors did, and government prosecutors have managed to exploit this new, less-than-loyal breed of mafioso. The willingness of some hoodlums to defy the Mafia is also partly due to the existence of the federal Witness Protection Program, within the U.S. Marshals Service, which helps people move to different locations and acquire new identities and jobs.

The ***Racketeer Influenced and Corrupt Organizations Act (RICO)****:* The single most important piece of legislation ever enacted against organized crime, RICO defines racketeering in a very broad manner, includes many offenses that do not otherwise violate federal statutes, and attempts to prove a pattern of crimes conducted through an organization. Under RICO, it is a separate crime to *belong* to an enterprise that is involved in a "pattern of racketeering."

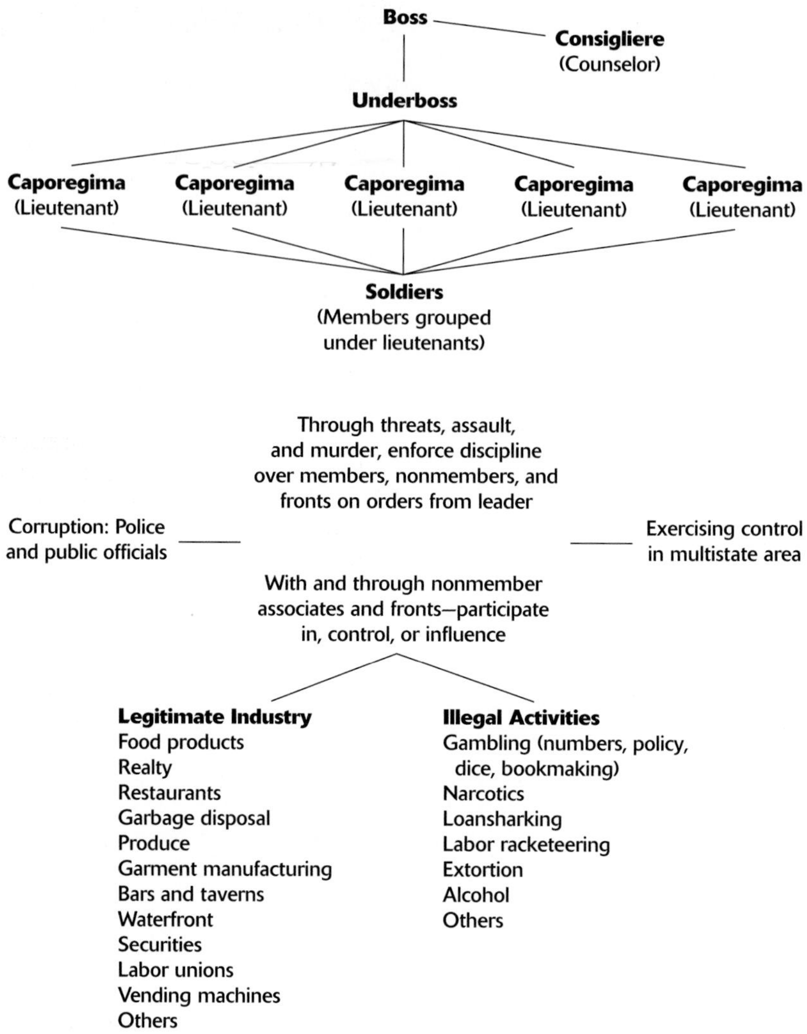

FIGURE 8-1 An organized crime family.

Source: The President's Commission on Law Enforcement and Administration of Justice, Task Force Report: Organized Crime *(Washington, DC: Author, 1967), p. 9.*

The number of Mafia families has fallen to just nine today. And while the estimated number of full-fledged (sworn, or "made") members has remained at about eleven hundred for more than three decades, half of those are now in jail or inactive. Experts believe that the Mafia's Commission—a ruling body of godfathers who mediate disputes—has not met since 1996. Once thriving Mafia families in Cleveland, Detroit, Kansas City, and Milwaukee are "down to two or three guys doing low-level scams."[39]

The FBI can take well-earned credit for the Mafia's change in fortune. During the tenure of Director Louis Freeh (1993–2001), the agency compiled 274 convictions of Mafia figures, including twenty top bosses. During the year 2000 alone, the FBI and New York City police arrested more than seventy people in the New Jersey crime family, decimating its leadership.[40]

But the Mob has proved to be remarkably resilient, and the FBI needs linguists and ethnic agents who can penetrate the new wave of mobsters.[41]

Policing Street Gangs

Definition and Extent of the Problem

A street **gang** is an association of individuals who have a gang name and recognizable symbols, a geographic territory, a regular meeting pattern, and an organized, continuous course of criminality.[42] Street gang activity was first recognized in the early twentieth century in southern California. Indeed, a major study of gangs in 1927 found that most gangs were small (six to twenty members) and formed spontaneously in poor and socially disorganized neighborhoods. Several factors were found to play a role in the popularity of street gangs: disintegration of family life, inefficiency of schools, formalism and externality of religion, corruption and indifference in local politics, low wages and monotony in occupational activities, unemployment, and lack of opportunity for wholesome recreation.[43] This explanation of the causes of gang affiliation still applies in large measure today.

According to U.S. Justice Department estimates,[44] there are more than sixteen thousand gangs and over a half million gang members in the United States.[45] Nearly half of all gang members (47.8 percent) are African-American youth, while Hispanic youngsters account for 42.7 percent and Asians make up 5.2 percent. (Specific types of ethnic and racial gangs are discussed later in this section.)

Gangs are a substantial problem in America today, and their members are becoming younger. Most research on youth gangs in the United States has concluded that the typical gang member is between fourteen and twenty-four years old; researchers are aware of gang members as young as ten, however, and in some areas (such as southern California, where some Latino gangs originated more than a hundred years ago), one can find several generations of gang members in the same family, with active members in their thirties. Youngsters generally begin hanging out with gangs at twelve or thirteen years of age, join the gang at thirteen or fourteen, and are first arrested at fourteen.[46]

Organization and Revenues

Studies of individual gangs have found a leadership class (typically a leader and three officers), a "foot soldier" class (ranging from twenty-five to one hundred members aged sixteen to twenty-five years), and "rank and file" members (usually two hundred children younger than high school age). More than 70 percent of a gang's total annual revenue of approximately $280,000 is generated from the sale of crack cocaine. Dues provide some additional gang revenue (about 25 percent), and extortion directed at local businesses and entrepreneurs represents about 5 percent. The gang generally operates in a neighborhood of roughly four city blocks.[47]

When a gang member is killed, the gang pays funeral expenses (about $5,000 per funeral) and typically provides compensation to the slain member's family. Leaders in the studies were found to retain about $4,200 per month from the gang's revenues, for an annual wage of about $50,000. The longer a member has been in a leadership position, however, the more his "salary," which could go as high as $130,000. Officers (runners, enforcers, and treasurers) earn about $1,000 per month, and foot soldiers are paid about $200 per month for working about twenty hours per week (but foot soldiers are also allowed to sell drugs outside the gang structure).[48]

Ethnic and Racial Gangs

Gangs are composed of three types of members: hardcore (those who commit violent acts and defend the reputation of the gang); associates (members who frequently affiliate with known gang members for status and recognition but who move in and out on the basis of interest in gang functions); and peripherals, who are not gang members but identify with a gang—usually the dominant gang in their neighborhood—for protection. Most females fall into this latter category.

There are several levels of gun-toting "gangbangers" who want to earn their stripes. The "wannabe" begins by having target practice and handling the guns; he may shoot but doesn't actually aim. The next level is the gang-involved youth who wants a tough-guy reputation; he will eventually kill somebody, but he's not seen as a hard-core crazy person. When a teenager reaches that level—the crazed killer—he doesn't care about himself or his victims; his violence is random and cold-blooded.

The most prominent African-American gangs are the Crips and the Bloods. The Crips began in Los Angeles in 1969, reportedly on the campus of Washington High School, supposedly as Community Resources for an Independent People; one of the school's colors was blue, which is now the color of gang identification. Another popular belief is that their name derived from "crypt," from the then-popular *Tales from the Crypt* horror movie. Crips address each other with the nickname "Cuzz." Crip graffiti can be identified by the symbol *B/K*, which stands for "Blood Killers." The Bloods are reported to have formed near Compton, California, as a means of protection against the Crips. Bloods use the color red and address each other as "Blood." Gang graffiti frequently uses the terms BS for "Bloodstone" or *C/K* for "Crip Killers." Both Crips and Bloods refer to fellow gang members as "homeboys" or "homeys."[49]

Hispanic gangs invariably name themselves after a geographic area, or "turf," that they feel is worth defending. Hispanic gang activity often becomes a family affair, with the young boys (ten to thirteen years old) as the "pee wees," the fourteen- to twenty-two-year-olds as the hardcore, and those living beyond age twenty-two as the "vetranos," or veterans. Standard trappings for Hispanic gangs includes headgear (knit cap or monikered bandanna), shirts (Pendleton or T-shirt), pants (highly starched khakis or blue jeans), tattoos (of gang identification), and vehicles (preferably older model Chevrolets, lowered and with extra chrome and fur).

White gangs are also expanding their membership, as growing numbers of young neo-Nazi Skinheads are linking up with old-line hate groups in the United States. This unity has bolstered the morale and criminal activity of the Ku Klux Klan and other white supremacist organizations.

Graffiti and Hand Signals

Nonverbal forms of communication not only allow gang members to communicate with one another and with rival gangs, but also bring recognition that the members need and seek out. The style and quality of **graffiti** can create and enhance the gang's image; thus, those who draw them are given additional status. Graffiti also serve to mark the gang's turf; if a gang's graffiti is untouched or unchallenged for a period of time, the gang's control in that area is reaffirmed. To stem the spread of graffiti, five states (Arizona, California, Massachusetts, Rhode Island, and Texas) currently have laws that ban spray paint sales to minors. and Chicago bans spray paint sales to the public altogether.[50]

Chicano gangs use a nonverbal communication system that has existed for over fifty years. This method, called a "placa," allows the Chicano gang member to express himself, support his gang, and direct challenges to others. A full placa expresses the gang's opinion of itself, its control of the area, and a warning that other gangs are helpless to do anything about it. An example of a full placa is given in Figure 8-2, with the translation given at the right (the actual graffiti would be written in unique gang style). Figure 8-3 provides a guide to reading gang graffiti.

Hand signals, or "throwing signs," are made by forming letters or numbers with the hands and fingers, depicting the gang symbol or initials. This allows the gang member to show which gang he belongs to and issue challenges to other gangs in the vicinity. Figure 8-4 shows some examples of hand signals that are commonly used in the western United States.

Police agencies in jurisdictions experiencing gang problems must develop expertise in gang movements and activities and in all forms of nonverbal communication. Police have also developed intelligence files on known or suspected gang members.

Obviously, something more is needed than police work alone to break the cycle of gang delinquency. In too many communities, gang violence is tolerated as long as gang members victimize each other and do not bother the rest of society.[51] Without community support, the contemporary cycle of youth gang activities will continue; even gang members who are imprisoned join branches of their gang behind bars while replacements are found to take their place on the street.[52]

FIGURE 8-2 A full placa (Chicano gang graffiti).

-EZ	He or She (El or La)
WINO	Moniker (Wino)
DE	From (De)
ZOS CHICOS	The gang name (Los Chicos)
-R-	I'm the best
C/S	There is nothing you can do about it (C/S)
ZOS NEIGHBORHOOD	Gang (Los Neighborhood)
TOTAZ	United (Total)
CONTROZZA	Controls (Controlla)
-R	We're the best

Across the country, many cities have responded to their gang problems by forming some type of special unit—often suppression oriented—as an initial response to major episodes of gang violence.[53] Today, about two-thirds of all large cities in the United States with more than 200,000 residents have a specialized gang unit, while about half of all other cities have such a unit.[54] These gang intelligence units (GIUs) identify the core members of the gangs and target them for enforcement. Intelligence is collected by questioning suspected gang members who are arrested and talking with rival gang members and with residents in gang neighborhoods. At the same time, officers collect information on gang activities, monitor graffiti, collect information on assaults and homicides of gang members by rival gangs, and observe disputes involving drug sales. They have also enhanced collaboration with agencies external to the police agency (schools, local code enforcement agencies, probation agencies, community groups, and so on).[55]

Over time, however, many police agencies have shifted from an emphasis on suppression to an emphasis on education. A well-known police response to gangs is the Gang Resistance Education and Training (GREAT) program, which originated in 1991 in Phoenix, Arizona. GREAT emphasizes the acquisition of information and skills that students need to resist peer pressure and gang influences; Formal training programs now include a thirteen-week curriculum for middle-school students, six

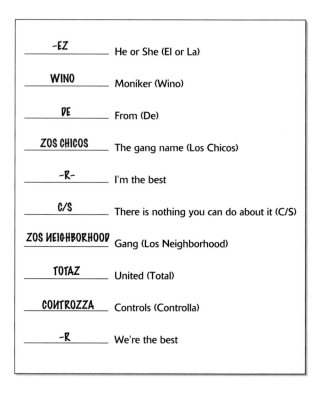

Guide to Reading Gang Graffiti

1. Step One Barrio or Varrio Meaning Neighborhood or Group/Clique	B H G R PQS -13- L's
2. Step Two The "HG" Meaning Hawaiian Gardens City and Gang/Clique	B H G R PQS -13- L's
3. Step Three The Letter "R" Meant to Be "RIFA" Meaning Rule, Reign, or Control	B H G R PQS -13- L's
4. Step Four The actual gang group abbreviation of "PQS" "PEQUENOS" from Hawaiian Gardens. (Normally younger groups, e.g., Chicos, Midgets, or Tiny's.)	B H G R PQS -13- L's
5. Step Five The Number "13"* stands for "SUR" meaning Southern California	B H G R PQS -13- L's
6. Step Six The letter "L" or "L's" is used to mean the Vato Locos or the Crazy Ones/ Brave Ones. Not normally a separate gang or clique.	B H G R PQS -13- L's

* The number 13 is sometimes used by younger gang members to mean marijuana.

FIGURE 8-3 Guide to reading gang graffiti.

30–45 minute lessons for elementary school pupils, and summer and family programs.[56]

A fundamental question to ask is this: How do we as a society replace the gang's social importance and financial benefits (with children "earning" literally hundreds of dollars a day in drug-related activities) with education or work programs that pay minimum wage? This is a complex issue, with no simple answers.

New Threats

Two areas of the United States are currently witnessing exploding numbers of gang members and related crimes of violence. In Los Angeles, California, long known for its gang violence, the growing numbers of hardcore prison parolees—being released at a rate of five hundred per month—combined

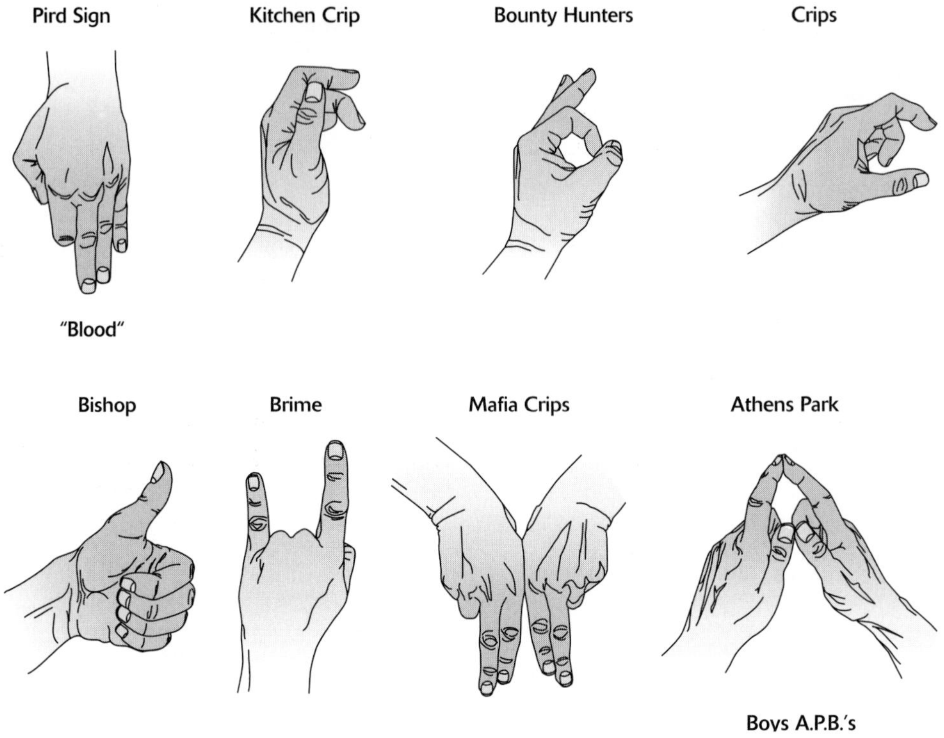

FIGURE 8-4 Gang hand signals.

with young recruits are fueling a sharp increase in gang-related crimes. Gang violence contributed to an 80 percent increase in the city's homicide rates in a recent two-year period.[57]

The southern United States, particularly areas in North Carolina, Virginia, and Georgia, have witnessed similar trends due to an immigration wave of Latinos (nearly 400 percent growth) in the 1990s. A malignant gang, Mara Salvatrucha 13, or MS-13, has developed in just a few years, forcing police to become knowledgeable about the Latino culture, form a database of gang members, and develop a multiagency task force.[58]

Gangs and Terrorism

While the relationship between gangs and terrorism is rarely studied and little understood, there are links between the two that demand further investigation. First, some gangs share with terrorists the inclination toward the use of violence to achieve political and economic ends. Some have even suggested that "urban terrorism," in which aggressive gangs dominate the social lives of some American neighborhoods, is a more tangible and daily threat to societal safety than the activities of foreign terrorists. In this sense, then, gang activity could be regarded as a subset of terrorist threats that should be addressed. Furthermore, there might be actual links between street gangs and foreign terrorists. For example, there is evidence that Sri Lankan ethnic gangs in Toronto might be funneling funds to terrorist operations.[59]

There is also evidence of an intersection among drug and terror operations, such as in Latin America and the Middle East. Traffickers might benefit from a terror organization's security assurances, while the terrorists can funnel drug money for operations.[60]

Third, gang members and terrorists might be drawn from similar ranks of disaffected youths who are either subconsciously or ideologically convinced that the existing social order has betrayed or exploited them and who see participation in deviant groups as a means to lash out against the social order.

Still, it is too early to assume a definitive link between gangs and terrorist groups. The most sophisticated terror networks, such as al Qaeda, might not yet find marginalized Westerners to be promising recruits. At this point, it seems best to evaluate and address the gang-terrorism connection with caution.[61]

Policing America's Borders

In Chapter 2, we discussed the new federal directorate within the Department of Homeland Security, Customs and Border Protection (CBP), which was formed in March 2003 and has a workforce of over forty thousand employees. CBP combined some employees of the Department of Agriculture, the former U.S. Customs Service, the U.S. Border Patrol, and the Immigration and Naturalization Service.

The task of protecting our nation's borders is now more important and poses a greater challenge than ever before. Next we discuss law enforcement attempts to thwart illegal entries by terrorists at all U.S. borders and by Mexicans at the southwestern border.

A New Terrorist Watch Program

In early 2004, a new program began entitled U.S. Visitor and Immigrant Status Indicator Technology (US-VISIT), under which twenty-four million foreigners are expected to be checked annually at the nation's airports. The program allows Customs agents to check passengers instantly against terrorist watch lists and a national database; the database is only available to law enforcement authorities on a need-to-know basis. Foreigners arriving at U.S. airports also have their fingerprints checked with an inkless scanner, and then they have their photograph taken as they make their way through customs. The only exceptions are visitors from twenty-seven mostly European countries as well as Canadians and Mexicans coming into the country for a short time and not venturing far from the border.[62]

Illegal aliens watch Border Patrol vehicles, waiting for an opportunity to cross the border.

(Courtesy U.S. Border Patrol)

The Southwestern Border

Each night, a drama is played out in many American cities as a hide-and-seek game unfolds at the nation's southwestern border, as thousands of people gather to make a run for American soil and grab their fortune and a new way of life. About three million of the 8.5 million Mexican-born people living in the United States are believed to be living here illegally.[63]

Many people do not consider these undocumented immigrants to be a crime problem. In fact, because of their clandestine lifestyle, they are likely to avoid contacting the police even when they are victimized. One crime that has been disproportionately associated with undocumented migrants in the Southwest is drug trafficking. This, police officials say, is a false impression. While a few illegal aliens do carry drugs across the border, the typical alien comes from a rural area and wants only to work. Most aliens do not trust banks and carry large sums of money in their pockets, which makes them a prime target for criminals.[64]

As the United States has fortified the southwestern border, the price and the profits have shot up for the smugglers, or **coyotes**, who transport migrants to Phoenix for a fee of $1,000. Although the coyotes are reviled by U.S. authorities, they are hailed as heroes by tens of thousands of migrants. The coyotes use several types of employees: A *vendepollo*, or "chicken seller," works the streets in Mexico looking for new clients, and a *brincador*, or "fence jumper," guides migrants across the border.[65] For the $1,000 fee, the smugglers take migrants to Nogales, Mexico, and arrange for a taxi to take them to the border, where smugglers lift them over the fourteen-foot-high fence. On the U.S. side of the border, other smugglers drive them to Phoenix.[66]

Violence has become rampant at the fortified Arizona border as rival smuggling groups and ripoff gangs, known as *bajadores*, battle over migrants in that sector. Because of the violence associated with smuggling in Arizona, in late 2003 federal officials launched Operation Ice Storm, arresting more than five hundred undocumented immigrants in the Phoenix area, prosecuting eighty people on related charges, and seizing $300,000 in smuggling proceeds as well as a large number of weapons.[67]

This border's immigration problem has been termed an "alien invasion" by two civilian patrol groups that have sprung up recently: the Civil Homeland Defense, whose members patrol the Arizona border on foot, and the American Border Patrol (its motto: "The Eyes of America"), which uses surveillance technology. These groups, calling Arizona the "last stand" against the migration invasion, believe they can do the job as well as and more cheaply than the CBP's agents. The CBP, meanwhile, strongly discourages private parties from taking matters into their own hands.[68]

New Technologies: Border Drones

A pilot program that uses two unmanned aerial vehicles (UAVs, discussed in more detail in Chapter 15) to monitor illegal activity along the Arizona-Mexico border was begun in July 2004. The UAVs, or drones, use thermal and night-vision equipment to spot illegal immigrants. They can detect movement from fifteen miles of altitude, read a license plate, and even detect weapons. In thirty-nine days of surveillance at the border, the UAVs led to the apprehension of 248 illegal immigrants and the seizure of 518 pounds of marijuana. The vehicles are waist high, weigh about a thousand pounds, and have a thirty-five-foot wingspan. They fly faster than 100 miles per hour and can stay aloft for twenty hours at a time.[69]

SUMMARY

Although police work generally tends to be very much the same from region to region and from jurisdiction to jurisdiction, this chapter has demonstrated several functions—some of them unusually dangerous in nature—that require special methods. The police, to borrow a phrase, must put on different faces for different people.

As society and its problems become more diverse, the police will continue to face new challenges. It is important that police officers receive training and education that allow them to be prepared for impending exigencies and to ensure that they maintain a professional approach to any such emergencies.

REVIEW QUESTIONS

1. Define the three types of terrorism, and describe how terrorism has changed policing. What kinds of new legal authority and resources have the police been given to combat terrorism?
2. Describe how hate crimes differ from other crimes. Why must the police be vigilant in enforcing laws against such offenses? Describe some potential responses to the problem of hate crime.
3. How did the Mafia originate? Describe some of the more successful methods the police have developed to investigate and prosecute mafiosi.
4. Describe the nature, causes, and extent of our nation's gang problem. Name some tactics that the police have used to deal with gang members.
5. Discuss some of the new methods that are available to the police for controlling illegal border crossings. Why are immigrant smugglers reviled by some people and respected by others?

INDEPENDENT STUDENT ACTIVITIES

1. This chapter is replete with interesting areas of inquiry for inquisitive students. Contact federal, state, or local police practitioners to determine the methods they are employing to control the kinds of problems that are addressed in this chapter.
2. How attractive is your local area with respect to terrorist attack, organized crime, gang activity, and illegal immigration? What unique challenges do these extraordinary problems present, and what are the police doing to combat them? What kinds of training and education must the police undergo to be able to work these assignments? What is the community's apparent attitude toward these problems?

RELATED WEB SITES

Department of Homeland Security
http://www.whitehouse.gov/homeland/

Nathanson Centre for the Study of Organized Crime and Corruption
http://www.yorku.ca/nathanson/default.htm

National Youth Gang Center
http://www.emergency.com/doj-gang.htm

U.S. Customs and Border Patrol
http://www.customs.gov/

NOTES

1. E. J. Tully and E. L. Willoughby, "Terrorism: The Role of Local and State Police Agencies," http://www.neiassociates.org/state-local.htm (accessed July 31, 2002).
2. J. Meisler, "The New Frontier of Homeland Security," *Government Technology's Tech Trends 2002: Combined Effort* (August 2002): 26–30.
3. Quoted in M. K. Rehm and W. R. Rehm, "Terrorism Preparedness Calls for Proactive Approach," *Police Chief* (December 2000): 38–43.
4. D. Westneat, "Terrorists Go Green," *U.S. News and World Report*, June 4, 2001, p. 28.
5. Associated Press, "SUVs Torched in Pennsylvania," *Reno Gazette Journal*, January 5, 2003, p. 4A.
6. J. F. Lewis Jr., "Fighting Terrorism in the Twenty-first Century," *FBI Law Enforcement Bulletin* (March 1999): 3.
7. K. Garrett, "Terrorism on the Homefront," *Law Enforcement Technology* (July 2002): 22–26.
8. Lewis, "Fighting Terrorism in the Twenty-first Century," p. 3.
9. D. G. Bolgiano, "Military Support of Domestic Law Enforcement Operations: Working within Posse Comitatus," *FBI Law Enforcement Bulletin* (December 2001): 16–24.
10. Tully and Willoughby, "Terrorism."
11. Gary Peck and Laura Mijanovich, "Give Us Security While Retaining Freedoms," *Reno Gazette Journal*, August 28, 2003, p. 9A.
12. Sharon Begley, "What Price Security?" Newsweek, October 1, 2001, pp. 58–62.
13. Peck and Mijanovich, "Give Us Security While Retaining Freedoms."
14. Dan Eggen, "Feds Win Wiretap Appeal," *Washington Post*, November 19, 2002, p. 1A.
15. Michael Isikoff, "Show Me the Money," *Newsweek*, December 1, 2003, p. 36.
16. Lorraine Ali, "'We Love This Country,'" *Newsweek*, April 7, 2003, p. 50.
17. John Ashcroft, quoted in Begley, "What Price Security?" p. 58.
18. A. Fram, Associated Press, "Terror's $60 Billion Price Tag," January 7, 2002.
19. C. Ragavan, "FBI, Inc.: How the World's Premier Police Corporation Totally Hit the Skids," *U.S. News and World Report*, June 18, 2001, p. 14.
20. Fram, "Terror's $60 Billion Price Tag."
21. CNN.com/inside politics, "Bush presents a $2.1 trillion wartime budget" (http://archives.cnn.com/2002/ALLPOLITICS/02/04/bush.budget/ (accessed January 23, 2005).
22. David E. Kaplan, "Mission Impossible," *U.S. News and World Report*, August 2, 2004, p. 35. The full report can be found at http://www.gpoaccess.gov/911/.
23. Ibid., p. 38.

24. Ibid., pp. 37–38.
25. K. Strandberg, "Bioterrorism: A Real or Imagined Threat?" *Law Enforcement Technology* (June 2001): 88–97.
26. D. Rogers, "A Nation Tested: What Is the Terrorist Threat We Face and How Can We Train for It?" *Law Enforcement Technology* (November 2001): 16–21.
27. "With Biochem Terror No Longer 'Unthinkable,' NYPD Gets Ready," *Law Enforcement News* (Spring 2004): 1, 13.
28. International Association of Chiefs of Police, *Responding to Hate Crimes: A Police Officer's Guide to Investigation and Prevention* (Arlington, VA: Author, 2000), p. 27.
29. Michael Lieberman, "Responding to Hate Crimes," *Community Policing Exchange* (Washington, DC: Community Policing Consortium, January/February 2000): 3.
30. Southern Poverty Law Center, "Over 200 Militias and Support Groups Operate Nationwide," *Klan Watch Intelligence Report* 78 (June 1995).
31. J. Garofalo and S. Martin, "The Law Enforcement Response to Bias-Motivated Crimes," in *Bias Crime: American Law Enforcement and Legal Responses* (2d ed.), ed. R. Kelly (Chicago: Office of International Criminal Justice, University of Illinois at Chicago, 1993), pp. 12–23.
32. U.S. Department of Justice, Federal Bureau of Investigation, "Hate Crime Statistics/2003," http://www.fbi.gov/ucr/03hc.pdf, November 2004 (accessed January 23, 2005).
33. Ibid.
34. International Association of Chiefs of Police, "Responding to Hate Crimes: A Police Officer's Guide to Investigation and Prevention," http://www.theiacp.org/documents (accessed April 28, 2003).
35. Madison, Connecticut Police Department, "Special Programs: ADL and Police Launch Statewide Effort to Fight Hate Crimes," http://www.madisonct.org/pdspcprog.htm (accessed April 28, 2003).
36. Sean Webby and Knight Ridder, "Hate-Crime Prosecutions Have Proved to Be Difficult," *Reno Gazette Journal*, October 25, 2002, p. 8C.
37. James N. Gilbert, "Organized Crime on the Western Frontier," paper presented at the annual conference of the Western Social Science Association, April 27, 1995, Oakland, California, p. 1.
38. David E. Kaplan, "Getting It Right: The FBI and the Mob," *U.S. News and World Report*, June 18, 2001, p. 20.
39. Ibid.
40. Ibid.
41. Ibid.
42. Carolyn R. Block and Richard Block, *Street Gang Crime in Chicago* (Washington, DC: National Institute of Justice Research in Brief, 1993), p. 2.
43. Frederic M. Thrasher, *The Gang* (Chicago: University of Chicago Press, 1927), pp. 33, 339, 346.

44. See G. David Curry, Richard A. Ball, and Scott H. Decker, *Estimating the National Scope of Gang Crime from Law Enforcement Data* (Washington, DC: National Institute of Justice Research in Brief, 1996).
45. Scott H. Decker and G. David Curry, "Responding to Gangs: Comparing Gang Member, Police, and Task Force Perspectives," *Journal of Criminal Justice* 28 (2000): 129–37.
46. Ronald C. Huff, *Comparing the Criminal Behavior of Youth Gangs and At-Risk Youths* (Washington, DC: National Institute of Justice Research in Brief, 1998).
47. S. Ventakesh, "The Financial Activity of a Modern American Street Gang," in *Looking at Crime from the Street Level: Plenary Papers of the 1999 Conference on Criminal Justice Research and Evaluation—Enhancing Policing and Practice through Research*, vol. 1 (Washington, DC: Department of Justice, Office of Justice Programs, National Institute of Justice, 1999).
48. Ibid.
49. Gregory Vistica, "'Gangstas' in the Ranks," *Newsweek*, July 24, 1995, p. 48.
50. Bob Hills, "Officials Looking for Regional Solution to Problem," *Reno Gazette Journal*, December 1, 2003, p. 5A.
51. Ruth Horowitz, "Community Tolerance of Gang Violence," *Social Problems* 34 (December 1987): 437–50.
52. James B. Jacobs, *New Perspectives on Prisons and Imprisonment* (Ithaca, NY: Cornell University Press, 1983).
53. D. L. Weisel and E. Painter, *The Police Response to Gangs: Case Studies of Five Cities* (Washington, DC: Police Executive Research Forum, 1997).
54. Ibid.
55. Ibid.
56. http://www.great-online.org (accessed January 23, 2005).
57. Associated Press, "Parolees, Recruits Fuel Increase in Gang Crimes," *Reno Gazette Journal*, April 10, 2003, p. 2B.
58. Arian Campo-Flores, "Gangland's New Face," *Newsweek*, December 8, 2003, p. 41.
59. High Commission of Sri Lanka, "Street Gangs in Toronto Fund Terrorism in Sri Lanka," press release, http://203.115.21.154/news/press/27th_march_2000.html (accessed November 27, 2002).
60. Neil A. Pollard, *Terrorism and Transnational Organized Crime: Implications of Convergence* (No place: Terrorism Research Center, 1996).
61. Kenneth J. Peak and Timothy Griffin, "Gangs: Origin, Status, Community Responses, and Policy Implications," in *Visions for Change: Crime and Justice in the Twenty-first Century*, ed. Roslyn A. Muraskin and Albert R. Roberts, 4th ed. (Upper Saddle River, NJ: Prentice Hall, 2005), p. 49.
62. Associated Press, "U.S. Airports Boost Security," *Reno Gazette Journal*, January 6, 2004, p. 2A.
63. Reed Karaim, "South of the Border: Illegal Crossings Dip," *U.S. News and World Report*, February 26, 2001, p. 28.

64. Ibid., p. 8.
65. Alan Zarembo, "People Smugglers Inc.," *Newsweek*, September 13, 1999, p. 36.
66. Daniel Gonzalez and Sergio Bustos, "U.S. Reviles Border Smugglers; Migrants Hail 'Coyote' Heroes," *Reno Gazette Journal*, November 29, 2003, p. 9C.
67. Ibid.
68. Bay Fang, "Between Two Lands," *U.S. News and World Report*, August 4, 2003, pp. 18–23.
69. Amanda Lee Myers, Associated Press, "Officials Say Border Drones Producing Positive Results," *Reno Gazette Journal*, August 34, 2004, p. 4C.

CHAPTER 9

The Rule of Law

Justice lives through those who practice it, by those who deliver it and in those who believe in it.

—*National Judicial College, Reno, Nevada*

We must never forget that it is a constitution we are expounding.

—*John Marshall, in* McCulloch *v.* Maryland

Key Terms

affidavit
crime-control model
due process model
entrapment
exclusionary rule
exigent circumstance
Fifth Amendment
Fourth Amendment
in loco parentis
interrogation
lineup
parens patriae
probable cause
search and seizure
Sixth Amendment

The Bill of Rights—the first ten amendments to the U.S. Constitution—was passed largely to protect all citizens from excessive governmental power. The police are expected to control crime within the framework of these rights; they must conduct themselves in a manner that conforms to the law as set forth in the U.S. Constitution, state constitutions, statutes passed by state legislatures, and the precedent of prior interpretations by the courts.

In other words, under the rule of law of the United States, the means are more important than the ends. A nation's democratic form of government would be of little value if the police could arrest, search, and seize its citizens and their property at will. If one considers the policing systems of some nondemocratic countries (such as those discussed in

Chapter 13), it is readily apparent that from the citizen's standpoint, legal curbs on those who enforce the law are absolutely necessary.

This chapter examines three constitutional amendments that regulate the police and prevent abuses of power: the Fourth Amendment (probable cause, the exclusionary rule, arrest, search and seizure, electronic surveillance, and lineups), the Fifth Amendment (confessions, interrogation, and entrapment), and the Sixth Amendment (right to counsel and interrogation). To avoid overwhelming the reader with case titles, only better-known court cases—such as *Miranda* v. *Arizona*—are included in the body of the chapter; others are cited in the Notes section. Finally, we discuss a related, yet in some ways very different, area of law and procedure: the law pertaining to juvenile offenders. A chapter summary, review questions, independent student activities, and related Web sites conclude the chapter.

Because of space limitations, many Supreme Court decisions affecting police powers in this country have necessarily been omitted from this discussion. Many publications cover those decisions, however. Among them are monthly police periodicals like the *FBI Law Enforcement Bulletin* and *The Police Chief* magazine; other sources include the *Criminal Law Reporter*, *U.S. Law Week*, and the *Supreme Court Bulletin*.

THE RULE OF LAW

The Fourth Amendment

> The right of the people to be secure in their persons, papers, and effects, against unreasonable **searches and seizures**, shall not be violated, and no Warrants shall issue, but upon probable cause, supported by Oath or affirmation, and particularly describing the place to be searched, and the persons or things to be seized.

The **Fourth Amendment** is intended to limit overzealous behavior by the police. Its primary protection is the requirement that a neutral, detached magistrate, rather than a police officer, issue warrants for arrest and search and seizure. Crime, though a major concern to society, is balanced by the concern that officers might thrust themselves unnecessarily into our homes. The Fourth Amendment requires that the necessity for a person's right of privacy to yield to society's right to search is best decided by a neutral judicial officer, not by an agent of the police.[1]

Probable Cause. The standard for a legal arrest is **probable cause**. This important concept is elusive at best; it is often quite difficult for professors to explain and even more difficult for students to understand. One way to define *probable cause* is to say that for an officer to make an arrest, he or she must have more than a mere hunch yet less than actual knowledge that the arrestee committed the crime. I often use the following example to better explain the concept.

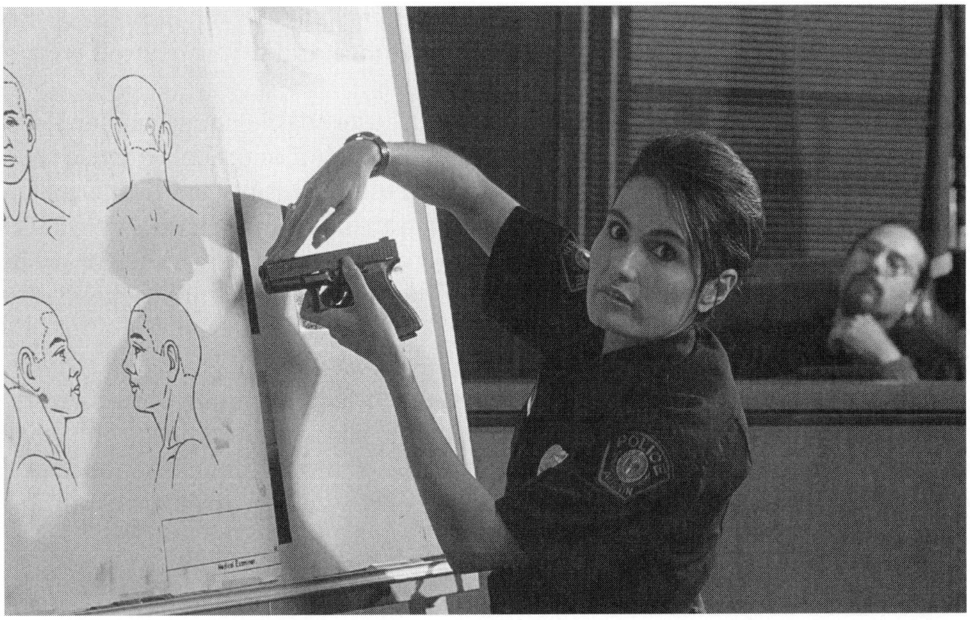

Officers have a responsibility to testify in court.

(Bob Daemmrich, The Image works)

At midnight, a fifty-five-year-old woman, having spent several hours at a city bar, wished to leave the bar and go to a nightclub in a rural part of the county. A man offered her a ride, but rather than driving directly to the nightclub, he drove to a remote place and parked the car. There he raped the woman and forced her to sodomize him. She fought him and later told the police she thought she had broken the temples (side pieces) of his black glasses. After the act, he drove her back to town; when she got out of the car, she saw the license plate number and thought that the hood of the car was colored red. Her account of the crime and her physical description of the rapist immediately prompted a photograph lineup; a known rape/sodomy suspect's picture was shown to her, along with those of several other men with a similar description. She tentatively identified the suspect in the mug shot but could not be certain; the suspect's mug shot had been taken several years earlier.

With this preliminary information, two police officers (one of whom was the author) hurried to the suspect's home to question him. They did not have a warrant. Upon entering the suspect's driveway, the officers observed a beige car — but with a red hood; probable cause was beginning to build. Next the officers noted that the vehicle's license number matched the one given by the victim; probable cause was now growing by leaps and bounds. Then the suspect exited the house and walked toward his car; the officers observed that his eyeglasses frame was black but the temples were gold, indicating that the black temples had probably been broken and replaced by spare gold temples. The officers now had, by any standard, adequate probable cause to lead a "reasonable and prudent" person to believe that this suspect was the culprit; the failure to arrest him would have been a gross miscarriage of justice. The suspect was thus arrested and placed in an actual lineup, where the victim identified him. This was one of those rare cases where the evidence was so compelling that the defendant pleaded guilty at his initial appearance and threw himself on the judge's mercy.

Of course, the facts of each case and the probable cause present are different; the court will examine the type and amount of probable cause that the officer had at the time of the arrest. It is important to note that a police officer cannot add to the probable cause used to make the arrest after effecting the arrest; the court will determine whether there existed sufficient probable cause to arrest the individual based on the officer's knowledge of the facts at the time of the arrest.

The Supreme Court has upheld convictions when probable cause was provided by a reliable informant,[2] when it came in an anonymous letter,[3] and when a suspect fit a Drug Enforcement Administration profile of a drug courier.[4] The Court has also held that police officers who "reasonably but mistakenly conclude that probable cause is present" are granted qualified immunity from civil action.[5]

The Exclusionary Rule. The Fourth Amendment recognizes the right to privacy, but its application raises some perplexing questions. First of all, not all searches are prohibited—only those that are unreasonable. Another issue has to do with how to handle evidence that is illegally obtained. Should murderers be released, Justice Benjamin Cardozo asked, simply because "the constable blundered"?[6] The Fourth Amendment says nothing about how it is to be enforced; this is a problem that has stirred a good amount of debate for a number of years. Most of this debate has focused on the wisdom of, and the constitutional necessity for, the so-called **exclusionary rule**, which requires that all evidence obtained in violation of the Fourth Amendment be excluded from government's use in a criminal trial.

The exclusionary rule has an interesting history. It first appeared in the federal criminal justice system in 1914, when the Supreme Court ruled in *Weeks* v. *United States* that all illegally obtained evidence was barred from use in federal prosecutions.[7] The practice has not existed in the state systems for nearly as long, however. Relatively few states employed the rule until 1950. Indeed, as of 1949, only seventeen states followed the *Weeks* doctrine. There was considerable objection both within and outside the Supreme Court about the states being able to do what was forbidden to the federal government. The ludicrous nature of this situation becomes evident in that until 1960, any evidence illegally seized by state or local police officers could be turned over to and used by federal officers in federal courts; this was known as the "silver platter doctrine."[8]

In 1926, a police officer arrested a man in a hallway for stealing an overcoat—a misdemeanor. The officer then entered the defendant's room and searched it, discovering a bag containing a blackjack. Appealing his conviction for possessing the weapon, the defendant made a motion to suppress the blackjack as evidence, as it had been obtained through a warrantless search. Justice Cardozo delivered a classic objection to the rule and considered its far-reaching effects:

> A room is searched against the law, and the body of a murdered man is found. The privacy of the home has been infringed, and the murderer goes free. On the one side is the social need that crime shall be repressed. On the other hand, the social need that the law shall not be flouted by the insolence of office. There are dangers in any choice.[9]

Justice Oliver Wendell Holmes took an opposite view of the rule in his dissenting opinion in a wiretapping case.[10] Holmes said that we must consider two desirable objects—that criminals should be detected and all available evidence used and that the government should not itself commit other crimes while gathering evidence. Holmes was repulsed by the manner in which government "dirtied" itself by engaging in snooping and wiretapping activities. In *Olmstead* v. *United States* (1928), Holmes made his classic statement, "For my part, I think it is a less evil that some criminals should escape than that the government should play an ignoble part."

The 1961 Supreme Court decision in *Mapp* v. *Ohio*[11] put an end to confusion over the admissibility of illegally seized evidence in the state courts. (See the Court Closeup box on page 262.) But the Court's decision in *Mapp* did not end the controversy surrounding the exclusionary rule. Opponents of the rule are left with the suspicion that the rule is invoked only by someone—usually a guilty person—who does not want evidence of his or her crimes to be used at trial; furthermore, they believe that the suspect's behavior has been much more reprehensible than that of the police.[12]

The Supreme Court has objected to police behavior when it "shocks the conscience," excluding evidence, for example, that was obtained by forcible extraction (by stomach pump) from a man who had swallowed two morphine capsules in police presence.[13]

Modifications of the Exclusionary Rule. Three major decisions during the 1983–1984 term of the Supreme Court served to modify the exclusionary rule. Justice William Rehnquist established a "public safety exception" to the doctrine. In that case, the defendant was charged with criminal possession of a firearm after a rape victim described him to the police. The officers located him in a supermarket and, upon questioning him about the weapon's whereabouts (without giving him the *Miranda* warning), they found it located behind some cartons. Rehnquist said that the case presented a situation in which concern for public safety outweighed a literal adherence to the rules. The police were justified in questioning the defendant on the ground of "immediate necessity."[14]

Another 1984 decision announced the "inevitability of discovery exception." A ten-year-old girl was murdered and her body hidden. While transporting the suspect, detectives—who had promised the suspect's attorney that they would not question him while in transit—appealed to his sensitivities by saying it would be proper to find the body so that the girl's parents

COURT CLOSEUP

Mapp v. *Ohio,* 367 U.S. 643 (1961)

In May 1957, three Cleveland police officers went to the home of Dolree Mapp to follow up on an informant's tip that a suspect in a recent bombing was hiding there. They also had information that a large amount of materials for operating a numbers game would be found. Upon arrival at the house, officers knocked on the door and demanded entrance, but Mapp, after telephoning her lawyer, refused them entry without a search warrant.

Three hours later, the officers again attempted to enter Mapp's home, and again she refused them entry. They then forcibly entered the home. Mapp confronted the officers, demanding to see a search warrant; an officer waved a piece of paper at her, which she grabbed and placed in her bosom. The officers struggled with Mapp to retrieve the piece of paper, at which time Mapp's attorney arrived at the scene. The attorney was not allowed to enter the house or to see his client. Mapp was forcibly taken upstairs to her bedroom, where her belongings were searched. One officer found a brown paper bag containing books that he deemed to be obscene.

Mapp was charged with possession of obscene, lewd, or lascivious materials. At the trial, the prosecution attempted to prove that the materials belonged to Mapp; the defense contended that the books were the property of a former boarder who had left his belongings behind. The jury convicted Mapp, and she was sentenced to an indefinite term in prison.

In May 1959, Mapp appealed to the Ohio Supreme Court, claiming that the obscene materials were not in her possession and that the evidence was seized illegally. The court disagreed, ruling the evidence admissible. In June 1961, the U.S. Supreme Court overturned the conviction, holding that the Fourth Amendment's prohibition against unreasonable search and seizure had been violated and that as

> *the right to be secure against rude invasions of privacy by state officers is . . . constitutional in origin, we can no longer permit that right to remain an empty promise. We can no longer permit it to be revocable at the whim of any police officer who, in the name of law enforcement itself, chooses to suspend its enjoyment.*

could give her a Christian burial. (This became known as the "Christian Burial Speech.") The suspect directed them to the body. In 1977, the Supreme Court ruled that the detectives had violated the defendant's rights by inducing him to incriminate himself without the presence of counsel. But the Court left open the possibility that the state could introduce evidence that the body would have been found even without the suspect's help. Using this "inevitability of discovery" opening, the Iowa courts found the defendant guilty, and in 1984 the Supreme Court upheld his conviction.[15]

Also in 1984, the Court ruled that evidence can be used even if obtained under a search warrant that is later found to be invalid. The Court held that evidence obtained by police officers acting in good faith on a reasonable reliance on a search warrant issued by a neutral magistrate could be used at trial even if the warrant was later found to be lacking in probable cause. This decision prompted a strong dissenting opinion by three justices, including William Brennan Jr., who said, "It now appears that the Court's victory over the Fourth Amendment is complete."[16]

Another ruling favorable to the police was handed down in 1988. Federal agents, observing suspicious behavior in and around a warehouse, illegally entered the building (with force and without a warrant) and observed marijuana in plain view. They left and obtained a search warrant for the building, then returned and arrested the defendant for conspiracy to deliver illegal drugs. The Court allowed the evidence to be admitted at trial, saying that it ought not to have been excluded simply because of unrelated illegal conduct by the police. If probable cause could be established apart from their illegal activity, the Court said, evidence obtained from the search should be admitted.[17]

Views on the Exclusionary Rule. Today there are basically two schools of thought, or models, regarding the use of illegally seized evidence. The **crime-control model** holds that the police are going to make mistakes occasionally. The victim is entitled to sue and have his or her complaint considered by a jury. Most important, this model holds, there is no reason why the evidence should not be used against the suspect at trial, even if obtained illegally. Proponents of the **due process model**, on the other hand, believe that the only way to deal with illegally obtained evidence is to suppress it before trial. When such evidence is allowed at trial, convictions based wholly or in part on it should be reversed. The victim of an illegal seizure usually is in no financial position to sue, and departmental discipline of officers is totally ineffective as a deterrent. Thus the only way to control the illegal collection of evidence is to take the profit out of it.[18]

The current trend is clearly toward the crime-control model, which weakens the impact of the exclusionary rule. Not only do many court watchers expect the Supreme Court to continue this trend, but a large number of law-and-order citizens also favor the rule's decline. Indeed, Chief Justice Rehnquist has openly called for its removal. Acknowledging that the primary reason for the rule is to control police misconduct, Rehnquist notes that since *Mapp* was decided, redress is more easily obtainable by a defendant whose constitutional rights have been violated, including the *Bivens* decision and the long-dormant Section 1983 actions. (See Chapter 11.) Further, Rehnquist believes that modern juries can be trusted to return fair awards to injured parties, saying that "I feel morally certain that the United States is the only nation in the world in which the most relevant, most competent evidence as to the guilt or innocence of the accused is mechanically excluded because of the manner in which it may have been obtained."[19]

In summary, since the Warren Court expanded the rights of criminal defendants in the 1960s, a surge of cases to the Supreme Court has raised further questions concerning the exclusionary rule. Many observers expected the Court to overturn *Mapp*. Yet the Court has not done so, apparently believing that without *Mapp*, the flagrant abuses that occurred before it could resurface.

Arrests with and without a Warrant. A restriction on the right of the police to arrest is the hallmark of a free society. A basic condition of freedom is that one cannot be legally seized in an arbitrary and capricious manner at the discretion or whim of any government official. It is customary to refer to the writ of habeas corpus—the "Great Writ"—as the primary guarantee of personal freedom in a democracy. *Habeas corpus* is defined simply as a writ requiring an incarcerated person to be brought before a judge for an investigation of the restraint of that person's liberty. It should be noted that habeas corpus is the means of remedying wrongful arrest or other detention that has already occurred and that may have been illegal. The constitutional or statutory provisions for making an arrest are of crucial importance because they prevent police action that could be very harmful to the individual.[20]

It is always best for a police officer to effect an arrest with a warrant. In fact, in 1980, the Supreme Court required police officers to obtain warrants when making felony arrests, should there be time to do so—that is, when there are no **exigent circumstances**.[21] To obtain an arrest warrant, the officer or a citizen swears in an **affidavit** (as an "affiant") that he or she possesses certain knowledge that a particular person has committed an offense. This could be, for example, a private citizen who tells police or the district attorney that he or she attended a party at a residence where drugs or stolen articles were present. Or, as is often the case, a detective gathers physical evidence or interviews witnesses or victims and determines that probable cause exists to believe that a particular person committed a specific crime. In any case, a neutral magistrate, if he or she agrees that probable cause exists, will issue the arrest warrant. Officers will execute the warrant, taking the suspect into custody to answer the charges.

An arrest without a warrant requires exigent circumstances and that the officer possess probable cause (as explained earlier in the sodomy case). Street officers rarely have the time or opportunity to effect an arrest with warrant in hand. Although the following real-life case involves a search preceding an arrest, it will make the point: One afternoon a police officer was sent to the residence of several college students. They reported that four men left their party and soon thereafter another guest discovered that a stereo had been taken from a car parked in the yard. A description of the men and their vehicle was given to the officer, who soon observed a vehicle and four men matching the description. The men were stopped in their vehicle, and the officer called for backup.

The law does not require that the officer ask the subjects to stay put while he speeds off to the courthouse to attempt to secure a search warrant. The doctrine of probable cause allows the officer to search the vehicle and arrest the occupants if stolen or contraband items are found (as in this case, where the stolen stereo was found under the driver's seat). Police officers encounter these kinds of situations thousands of times each day. Such searches and arrests without benefit of a warrant are legally permissible, provided the officer had probable cause (which can later be explained to a judge) for his or her actions.

In 1979, the Supreme Court rendered two decisions relating to arrests. Police, the Court said, must have probable cause to take a person into custody and on to the police station for **interrogation**.[22] Police may not randomly stop a single vehicle to check the driver's license and registration; there must be probable cause for stopping drivers.[23] However, in 1990, the Court ruled that the stopping of all vehicles passing through sobriety checkpoints—a form of seizure—did not violate the Constitution, although singling out individual vehicles for random stops without probable cause is not authorized.[24] Several days later, it ruled that police were not required to give drunk-driving suspects a *Miranda* warning and could videotape their responses.[25]

In related decisions in the 2003–2004 term, the Supreme Court held that police may arrest *everyone* in a vehicle in which drugs are found. A Baltimore officer, stopping a speeding car and finding cocaine in an armrest in the backseat, was told by the driver and the two passengers that none of them owned the contraband; he arrested all three. Chief Justice Rehnquist wrote that, in a small space like a car, officers can reasonably infer "a common enterprise" among a driver and passengers and would have probable cause to suspect that the drugs might belong to any or all of them.[26] A few months later, the Court ruled that police may set up roadblocks to collect information from motorists about crime. Short stops, "a very few minutes at most," are not too intrusive considering the value in crime solving; police may also hand out fliers or ask drivers to volunteer information, the Court noted.[27]

Finally, since 1975, police practice has been to ensure that a person arrested without a warrant receives a "prompt" initial appearance for a probable cause determination to see if the police were justified in arresting and holding the detainee. In its 1990–1991 term, the Supreme Court said that "prompt" does not mean "immediate," and that within forty-eight hours is generally soon enough.[28]

Search and Seizure in General. Because of the serious nature of police invasion of private property, the Supreme Court has had to examine several issues, particularly as they relate to searches of suspects' homes. In late 2003, the Court clarified how long police must wait before breaking into a home to serve a warrant, ruling unanimously that it was constitutional for police to wait fifteen to twenty seconds before knocking down the door of a drug suspect, because to wait any longer would give the suspect time to flush evidence down the toilet. (The justices refused, however, to state exactly how long is reasonable in serving warrants.)[29] However, in 1995, the Court affirmed without decision an opinion of the Pennsylvania Supreme Court that the police violated the Fourth Amendment when they broke down the door of a residence only one or two seconds after they knocked, announced their presence, and said that they had a warrant. There were no exigent circumstances present.[30] Furthermore, in *Wilson* v. *Arkansas* (1995),[31] the Court found a search invalid when police in Arkansas, armed with a search warrant after receiving an informant's tip that drugs were being sold at the defendant's home, identified themselves *as they entered* the residence, where they subsequently found drugs and paraphernalia.

However, the Court upheld a search (with a warrant) of a third party's property when police had probable cause to believe it contained fruits or instrumentalities of a crime (for example, a newspaper office containing photographs of a disturbance),[32] a search of a wrong apartment conducted with a warrant but with a mistaken belief that the address was correct,[33] and a warrantless search and seizure of garbage in bags outside the defendant's home.[34]

The Court has also attempted to define when a person is considered "seized," an important issue because seizure involves Fourth Amendment protections. Is a person "seized" while police are pursuing him or her? Basically, there is no rule that determines the point of seizure in all situations. The standard is whether a suspect believes his or her liberty is restrained. This is ultimately a question for a judge or jury to decide.[35] In a recent roadblock case, the Court did provide some guidance, however. Where a police roadblock resulted in the death of a speeder, the Court said roadblocks involve a "governmental termination of freedom of movement," that the victim was therefore seized under the Fourth Amendment, and so the police were liable for damages.[36]

Two decisions in the 1990–1991 Supreme Court term expanded police practices. The Court looked at a police drug-fighting technique known as "working the buses." Police board a bus at a regular stopping place, approach seated passengers, and ask permission to search their luggage for drugs. Justice O'Connor, writing for the majority, said that such a situation should be evaluated in terms of whether a person in the passenger's position would have felt free to decline the officer's request or to otherwise terminate the encounter; it was held that such police conduct does not constitute a search.[37] In a companion decision in 2002, the justices held that the police—focusing on possible terrorists as well as drug couriers—may question passengers on buses and trains and may search for evidence without informing passengers that they can refuse. Police in Florida were on a Greyhound bus, asking questions of each passenger, when two men wearing heavy clothing on a warm day consented to a search of their luggage and bodies; police found bricks of cocaine strapped to their legs. The Court said the men were not coerced into consenting and that nothing about the fact that they were seated on a bus forced them to give their consent.[38]

The Court also decided that no "seizure" occurs when a police officer seeks to apprehend a person through a show of authority but applies no physical force (such as in a foot pursuit). In this case, a juvenile being chased by an officer threw down an object, later determined to be crack cocaine. The Supreme Court found no seizure or actual restraint in this situation.[39] Also, it should be noted that the Court held that no individualized suspicion of misconduct was required in either of these cases.

Supreme Court decisions have authorized a warrantless seizure of blood from a defendant to obtain evidence. (This was a case of driving under the influence, the drawing of blood was done by medical personnel in a hospital, and there were exigent circumstances—the evidence would have been lost by dissipation in the body.)[40] However, when police compelled a robbery suspect to submit to surgery to remove a bullet, the Court held that such an intrusion to seize evidence was unreasonable; this case said there are limits to what police can do to solve a crime.[41]

Searches and Seizures with and without a Warrant. As is the case with making an arrest, the best means by which the police can search a person or premises is with a search warrant issued by a neutral magistrate. Such a magistrate has determined, after receiving information from a sworn affiant, that probable cause exists to believe that a person possesses the fruits or instrumentalities of a crime or that they are present at a particular location. Again, as with arrest, the "luxury" of searching and seizing with a warrant is usually confined to investigative personnel, who can interview victims and witnesses and gather other available evidence, then request the warrant. Street officers rarely have the opportunity to perform such a search, as the flow of events normally requires quick action to prevent escape and to prevent the evidence from being destroyed or hidden.

Five types of searches may be conducted without a warrant: (1) searches incidental to lawful arrest, (2) searches during field interrogation (stop-and-frisk searches), (3) searches of automobiles under special conditions, (4) seizures of evidence that is in "plain view," and (5) searches when consent is given.

Searches Incidental to Lawful Arrest. In *United States* v. *Robinson* (1973), the defendant was arrested and taken to the police station for driving without a permit—an offense for which a full-scale arrest could be made. Robinson was taken to jail and searched, and heroin was found. He tried to suppress the evidence on the ground that the full-scale arrest and custodial search were unreasonable for a driver's-license infraction. The Supreme Court disagreed, saying that the arrest was legal and that when police assumed custody of him, they needed total control and therefore could perform a detailed inventory of his possessions: "It is the fact of the lawful arrest that establishes the authority to search and we hold that in the case of lawful custodial arrest a full search of the person is not only an exception to the warrant requirement of the Fourth Amendment, but is also a 'reasonable' search under that Amendment."[42]

The rationale for this decision was in part the possibility that the suspect might destroy evidence unless swift action was taken. But in *Chimel* v. *California* (1969), when officers without a warrant arrested an individual in one room of his house and then proceeded to search the entire three-bedroom house, including the garage, attic, and workshop, the Supreme Court said that searches incidental to lawful arrest are limited to the area within the arrestee's immediate control or that area from which he or she might obtain a weapon. Thus if the police are holding a person in one room of the house, they are not authorized to search and seize property in another part of the house, away from the arrestee's immediate physical presence.[43]

The Court approved the warrantless seizure of a lawfully arrested suspect's clothes even after a substantial time period had elapsed between the arrest and the search.[44] Another advantage given the police was the Court's allowing a warrantless, in-home "protective sweep" of the area in which a suspect is arrested to reveal the presence of anyone else who might pose a danger. Such a search, if justified by the circumstances, is not a full search of the premises and may only include a cursory inspection of those spaces where a person could be hiding.[45]

Stop and Frisk: Lesser Intrusions during Field Interrogation. In 1968, the U.S. Supreme Court heard a case challenging the constitutionality of on-the-spot searches and questioning by the police. The case, *Terry* v. *Ohio*, involved a suspect who was stopped and searched while apparently "casing" a store for robbery.

COURT CLOSEUP

Terry v. *Ohio,* 319 U.S. 1 (1968)

Cleveland Detective McFadden, a veteran of nineteen years of police service, first noticed Terry and another man at about 2:30 P.M. on the afternoon of the arrest in October 1963. McFadden testified that it appeared the men were "casing" a retail store. He observed the suspects making several trips down the street, stopping at a store window, walking about a half block, turning around and walking back again, pausing to look inside the same store window. At one point they were joined by a third party, who spoke with them and then moved on. McFadden claimed that he followed them because he believed it was his duty as a police officer to investigate the matter further.

Soon the two rejoined the third man; at that point McFadden decided the situation demanded direct action. The officer approached the subjects and identified himself, then requested that the men identify themselves as well. When Terry said something inaudible, McFadden "spun him around so that they were facing the other two, with Terry between McFadden and the others, and patted down the outside of his clothing." In a breast pocket of Terry's overcoat, the officer felt a pistol. McFadden found another pistol on one of the other men. The two men were arrested and ultimately convicted for concealing deadly weapons. Terry appealed on the ground that the search was illegal and that the evidence should have been suppressed at trial.

The U.S. Supreme Court disagreed with Terry, holding that the police have the authority to detain a person briefly for questioning even without probable cause if they believe that the person has committed a crime or is about to commit a crime. Such detention does not constitute an arrest. The officer may also frisk a person if the officer reasonably suspects that he or she is in danger.

The Court's dilemma in this case was whether to rule that in some circumstances the police do not need probable cause to stop and search people and thus appear to invalidate *Mapp* v. *Ohio*, or to insist on such a high standard for action by the police that they could not function on the streets.[46] The Court held that a brief on-the-spot stop for questioning, accompanied by a superficial search (a pat-down search) of external clothing for weapons, was something less than a full-scale search and therefore could be performed with less than the traditional amount of probable cause. This case instantly became, and remains, a major tool for the police.

While *Terry* said the stop and frisk is legal under the Fourth Amendment in cases involving direct police observation, other cases have said that such a stop is legal when based on information provided by an informant[47] and when an individual is the subject of a "wanted" flier from another jurisdiction.[48] In summary, police officers are justified, both for their own safety and in order to detect past or future crimes, in stopping and questioning people. A person may be frisked for a weapon if an officer fears for his or her life, and the officer may go through the individual's clothing if the frisk indicates the presence of a weapon. Regardless of the rationale for the stop and frisk, there will always be some argument about whether this search is being used frivolously or to harass individuals. However, in balancing the public's need for safety against individual rights, the Court was willing to tip the scales in favor of community protection, especially when the safety of the officer was concerned.[49]

An important expansion of the *Terry* doctrine was handed down in 1993 in *Minnesota* v. *Dickerson*,[50] in which a police officer observed a man leave a notorious crack house and then try to evade the officer. The man was eventually stopped and patted down, during which time the officer felt a small lump in the man's front pocket that was suspected to be drugs. After manipulating and squeezing the lump, the officer removed it from the man's pocket; the object was crack cocaine wrapped in a cellophane container. Although the defendant's arrest and conviction were later thrown out (the Supreme Court reasoned that the search was illegal because it went beyond the limited frisk for weapons, as permitted by *Terry*), the Court also allowed such seizures in the future when officers' probable cause is established by the sense of touch.

Another case extending *Terry*, *Illinois* v. *Wardlow*,[51] was decided in January 2000. The Court held that a citizen's running away from the police—under certain conditions—supports reasonable suspicion to justify a search. Two Illinois police officers investigating drug transactions in an area of heavy drug activity observed Wardlow holding a bag. Upon seeing the two officers, Wardlow fled, but he was soon stopped. The officers conducted a protective pat down and then squeezed the bag; they felt a gun and arrested Wardlow. The Court reasoned that, taken together, several factors (e.g., the stop occurred in a high-crime area; the suspect acted in a nervous, evasive manner; and the suspect engaged in unprovoked flight upon noticing the police)[52] were sufficient to establish reasonable suspicion.

Another important Supreme Court decision in February 1997 took officer safety into account. In *Maryland* v. *Wilson*,[53] the Court held that police may order passengers out of vehicles they stop, regardless of any suspicion of wrongdoing or threat to the officer's safety. Chief Justice Rehnquist cited statistics showing officer assaults and murders during traffic stops and noted that the "weighty interest" in officer safety is present whether a vehicle occupant is a driver or a passenger. (Here, a Maryland state trooper initiated a traffic stop and ordered an apparently nervous passenger, Wilson, to exit the vehicle. While doing so, Wilson dropped a quantity of crack cocaine, for which he was arrested and convicted.)

Searches and Pursuits of Automobiles. The third general circumstance allowing a warrantless search is when an officer has probable cause to believe that an automobile contains criminal evidence. The Supreme Court has traditionally distinguished searches of automobiles from searches of homes on the ground that a car involved in a crime can be rapidly moved and its evidence irretrievably lost. The Court first established this doctrine in *Carroll* v. *United States* (1925). In this case, officers searched the vehicle of a known bootlegger without a warrant but with probable cause, finding sixty-eight bottles of illegal booze. On appeal, the Court ruled that the seizure was justified. However, *Carroll* established two rules: First, to invoke the *Carroll* doctrine, the police must have enough probable cause that if there had been enough time, a search warrant would have been issued; second, urgent circumstances must exist that require immediate action.[54]

A police officer engages in a vehicle search.

(Courtesy Reno, Nevada, Police Department)

Extending the creation of the *Carroll* doctrine, however, two new questions confronted the justices: whether impounded vehicles were subject to warrantless search and whether searches could be made of vehicles stopped in routine traffic inspections. In *Preston* v. *United States* (1964), the Court ruled that once the police had made a lawful arrest and then towed the suspect's car to a different location, they could not conduct an incidental search of the vehicle. The Court reasoned that because such a search was remote in time and place from the point of arrest, it was not incidental and therefore was unreasonable.[55]

Harris v. *United States* (1968) upheld the right of police to enter an impounded vehicle following a lawful arrest in order to inventory its contents.[56] Building on this decision, the Court later upheld a warrantless search of a vehicle in custody, saying that because the police had probable cause to believe it contained evidence of a crime and could be easily moved, it made little difference whether a warrant was sought or an immediate search conducted.[57]

In 1974, the expectation of citizens to privacy in their vehicles was further diminished; the Court said an automobile has "little capacity for escaping public scrutiny [as] it travels public thoroughfares where both its occupants and its contents are in plain view."[58] This position was reinforced in 1976, when the Court said that a validly impounded car may be searched without probable cause or warrant as it is reasonable for an inventory of its contents to be made as a protection against theft or charges of theft while the car is in police custody.[59]

An automobile may be searched following the lawful search of its driver or another occupant. Following the rationale of *Chimel*, the Court ruled that the entire interior of the car, including containers, may be examined even if the items are not within the driver's reach.[60] The Court went on to say that a warrantless search of an automobile incidental to a lawful arrest, including its trunk and any packages or luggage, is permissible if there is probable cause to believe that it contains evidence of a crime.[61] The Court also authorized a protective pat-down of vehicle passenger compartments for weapons (similar to that of persons in *Terry* v. *Ohio*) after a valid stop and when officers have a reasonable belief that they may be in danger.[62] Finally, it was decided in 1987 that evidence seized by opening a closed container during a warrantless inventory search of a vehicle incidental to lawful arrest is admissible.[63]

During its 1990–1991 term, the Supreme Court extended the long arm of the law with respect to automobiles. In a May 1991 decision, the Court declared that a person's general consent to a search of the interior of an automobile justifies a search of any closed container found inside the car that might reasonably hold the object of the search; thus, an officer, after obtaining a general consent, does not need to ask permission to look inside each closed container.[64] One week later, the Court ruled that probable cause to believe that a container within a car holds contraband or evidence allows a warrantless search of that item under the automobile exception, even in the absence of probable cause extending to the entire vehicle.[65] This decision clarified the *Carroll* doctrine.

During its 1998–1999 term, the Court held that when an officer has probable cause to search a vehicle, the officer may search objects belonging to a passenger in the vehicle, provided the item the officer is looking for could reasonably be in the passenger's belongings.[66] (Here the officer was searching an automobile for contraband and searched a passenger's purse, finding drug paraphernalia there.)

Then, in January 2005, the Supreme Court decided by a 6-2 vote that a motorist has no legitimate expectation of privacy during a traffic stop for contraband hidden in a vehicle and detected by a drug-sniffing dog. In *Illinois* v. *Caballes*,[67] the defendant had been stopped for speeding; while the state trooper was issuing a citation, another trooper walked a drug-sniffing dog around the car. The dog alerted at the trunk, and after a search the troopers found marijuana, for which Caballes was arrested and convicted. The Court noted that Caballes was stopped lawfully and that the entire episode lasted less than ten minutes; also, drug-sniffing dogs only detect illegal activity (as opposed to, say, thermal-imaging devices that police once used to seek out marijuana growing in a home; the Court said in 2001 that such devices were illegal because they can also detect, for example, lawful activities such as a person's taking a daily sauna or a bath).

Plain-View and Open-Field Searches. The police do not have to search for items that are seen in plain view. If such items are believed to be fruits or instrumentalities of a crime and the police are lawfully on the premises, they may seize them. For example, if an officer has been admitted into a home with an arrest or search warrant and sees drugs and paraphernalia on a living-room table, he or she may arrest the occupants on drug charges as well as the earlier ones. If an officer performs a traffic stop for an offense and observes drugs in the backseat of the car, he may arrest for that as well. Provided that the officer was lawfully in a particular place and that the plain-view discovery was inadvertent, the law does not require the officer to ignore contraband or other evidence of a crime that is in plain view.

The Supreme Court has said that officers are not required to immediately recognize an object in plain view as contraband before it may be seized. (For instance, an officer may see a balloon in a glove box with a white powdery substance on its tip and later determine the powder to be heroin.)[68] Furthermore, fences and the posting of "No Trespassing" signs afford no expectation of privacy and do not prevent officers from viewing open fields without a search warrant.[69] Nor are police prevented from making a naked-eye aerial observation of a suspect's backyard or other curtilage (the grounds around a house or building).[70]

Two decisions in the late 1980s have further defined the plain-view doctrine. In one case, an officer found a gun under a car seat while looking for the vehicle identification number; the Court upheld the search and the resulting arrest as being a plain-view discovery.[71] However, in another similar situation, the Court disallowed an arrest when an officer, during a legal

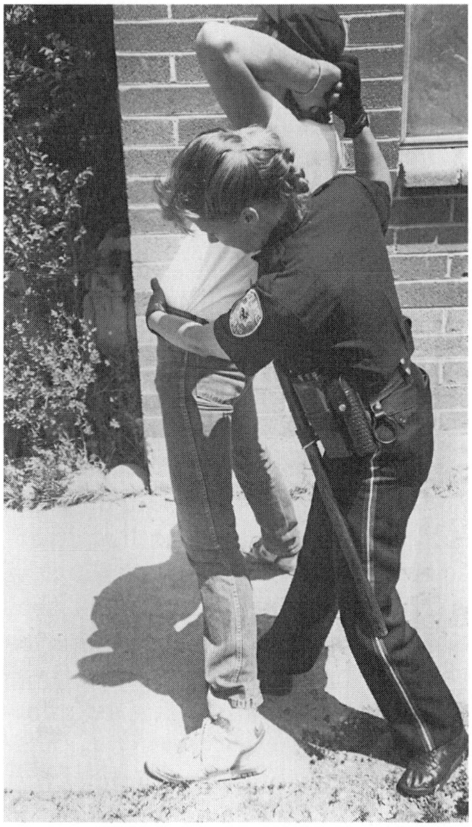

Police officers must often engage in warrantless searches of persons.

(Courtesy Reno, Nevada, Police Department)

search for weapons, moved a stereo system to locate its serial number, saying that this constituted an unreasonable search and seizure.[72]

Consent to Search. Another permissible warrantless search involves citizens' waiving their Fourth Amendment rights and consenting to a search of their persons or effects. It must be established at trial, however, that the defendant's consent was given voluntarily. In some circumstances, as with metal detectors at airports, an agent's right to search is implied.

In the leading case on consent searches, *Schneckloth* v. *Bustamonte* (1973), a police officer stopped a car for a burned-out headlight. Two other backup officers joined him. When asked if his car could be searched, the driver consented. The officers found several stolen checks in the trunk. The driver and passenger were arrested and convicted. On appeal, the defendants argued that the evidence should have been suppressed, as they did not know they had the right to refuse the officers' request to search the car. The Supreme Court upheld their convictions, reasoning that the individuals, although poor, uneducated, and alone with three officers, could reasonably be considered capable of knowing and exercising their right to deny officers permission to search their car.[73]

However, police cannot deceive people into believing they have a search warrant when they in fact do not. For example, the police, looking for a rape suspect, announced falsely to the suspect's grandmother that they had a search warrant for her home; the evidence they found was ruled to be inadmissible.[74] Nor can a hotel clerk give a valid consent to a warrantless search of the room of one of the occupants; hotel guests have a reasonable expectation of privacy, and that right cannot be waived by hotel management.[75]

Electronic Surveillance. It was the original view of the Supreme Court, in *Olmstead* v. *United States* (1928), that wiretaps were not searches and seizures and did not violate the Fourth Amendment; this represented the old rule on wiretaps.[76] However, that decision was overruled in 1967 in *Katz* v. *United States*, which held that any form of electronic surveillance, including wiretapping, is a search and violates a reasonable expectation of privacy.[77] The case involved a public telephone booth, deemed by the Court to be a constitutionally protected area where the user has a reasonable expectation of privacy. This decision expressed the view that the Constitution protects people, not places. Thus the Court has required that warrants for electronic surveillance be based on probable cause, describe the conversations that are to be overheard, be for a limited period of time, name subjects to be overheard, and be terminated when the desired information is obtained.[78]

However, the Supreme Court has held that while electronic eavesdropping (that is, an informant wearing a "bug," or hidden microphone) did not violate the Fourth Amendment (a person assumes the risk that whatever he or she says may be transmitted to the police),[79] the warrantless monitoring of an electronic beeper in a private residence violated the suspect's right to privacy. A federal drug agent had placed a beeper inside a can of ether, which was being used to extract cocaine from clothing imported into the United States, and had monitored its movements.[80]

Lineups and Other Pretrial Identification Procedures. A police **lineup** or other face-to-face confrontation after the accused has been arrested is considered a critical stage of criminal proceedings; therefore, the accused has a right to have an attorney present. If counsel is not present, the evidence obtained is inadmissible.[81] However, the suspect is not entitled to the presence and advice of a lawyer before being formally charged.[82]

Lineups that are so suggestive as to make the result inevitable violate the suspect's right to due process. (In one case, the suspect was much taller than the other two people in the lineup, and he was the only person wearing a leather jacket similar to that worn by the robber. In a second lineup, the suspect was the only person who had participated in the first lineup.[83]) In short, lineups must be fair to suspects; a fair lineup guarantees no bias against the suspect.

The Supreme Court has held that a suspect may be compelled to appear before a grand jury and give voice exemplars for comparison with an actual voice recording. Appearance before a grand jury is not a search, and the giving of a voice sample is not a seizure that is protected by the Fourth Amendment.[84]

The Fifth Amendment

> No person shall be held to answer for a capital, or otherwise infamous crime, unless on a presentment or indictment of a Grand Jury, except in cases arising in the land or naval forces, or in the Militia, when in actual service in time of war or public danger; nor shall any person be subject for the same offense to be twice put in jeopardy of life or limb; nor shall be compelled in any criminal case to be a witness against himself, nor be deprived of life, liberty, or property, without due process of law; nor shall private property be taken for public use, without just compensation.

A major tool used in religious persecutions in England during the sixteenth century was the oath. Ministers were called before the Court of Star Chamber (which, during much of the sixteenth and seventeenth centuries, enforced unpopular political policies and meted out severe punishments, including whipping, branding, and mutilation, without a jury trial) and questioned about their beliefs. Being men of God, they were compelled to tell the truth and admitted to their nonconformist views; for this, they were often severely punished or even executed.[85] In the 1630s, the Star Chamber and similar bodies of cruelty were disbanded by Parliament. People had become repulsed by compulsory self-incrimination; the privilege against self-incrimination was recognized in all courts when claimed by defendants or witnesses. Today, the **Fifth Amendment** clause applies not only to criminal defendants but also to any witness in a civil or criminal case and anyone testifying before an administrative body, a grand jury, or a congressional committee. However, the privilege does not extend to blood samples, handwriting exemplars, and other such items not considered to be testimony.[86]

The right against self-incrimination is one of the most significant provisions in the Bill of Rights. Basically it states that no criminal defendant shall be compelled to take the witness stand and give evidence against himself or herself. No one can be compelled to answer any question if his or her answer can later be used to implicate or convict him or her. Some people view the defendant's "taking the Fifth" as an indication of guilt; others view this as a basic right in a democracy, wherein defendants do not have to contribute to their own conviction. In either case, the impact of this amendment is felt daily by the criminal justice system.

Voluntary Confessions and Decisions Supporting *Miranda*. Traditionally, the U.S. Supreme Court has excluded physically coerced confessions on the ground that such confessions might very well be untrustworthy or unreliable in view of the duress surrounding them.

As the quality of police work has improved, police use of physical means to obtain confessions has diminished. Some cases that have come before the Supreme Court involved psychological rather than physical pressure on the defendant to confess. One such case involved an accused who was questioned for eight hours by six police officers in relays and was told falsely that the job and welfare of a friend who was a rookie cop depended on his confession. He was also refused contact with his lawyer. The Court reversed his conviction, not so much on the ground that the confession was unreliable, but on the ground that it was obtained unfairly.[87]

In the 1960s, the Supreme Court ruled in *Escobedo* v. *Illinois* (1964),[88] discussed later, and in *Miranda* v. *Arizona* (1966)[89] that confessions made by suspects who have not been notified of their constitutional rights cannot be admitted into evidence. In these cases, the Court emphasized the importance of a defendant's having the "guiding hand of counsel" present during the interrogation process.

Once a suspect has been placed under arrest, the *Miranda* warning must be given before interrogation for any offense, be it a felony or a misdemeanor.

COURT CLOSEUP

Miranda v. *Arizona,* 384 U.S. 436 (1966)

While walking to a Phoenix, Arizona, bus stop on the night of March 2, 1963, eighteen-year-old Barbara Ann Johnson was accosted by a man who shoved her into his car, tied her hands and ankles, and drove her to the edge of the city, where he raped her. He then drove Johnson to a street near her home, letting her out of the car and asking that she pray for him.

The Phoenix police subsequently picked up Ernesto Miranda for investigation of Johnson's rape and included him in a lineup at the police station. Miranda was identified by several women; one identified him as the man who had robbed her at knifepoint a few months earlier, and Johnson thought he was the rapist.

Miranda was a twenty-three-year-old eighth-grade dropout with a police record dating back to age fourteen and he had also served time in prison for driving a stolen car across a state line. During questioning, the police told Miranda that he had been identified by the women; Miranda then made a statement in writing that described the rape incident. He also noted that he was making the confession voluntarily and with full knowledge of his legal rights. He was soon charged with rape, kidnapping, and robbery.

At trial, Miranda's court-appointed attorney got the officers to admit that during the interrogation the defendant was not informed of his right to have counsel present and that no counsel was present. Nonetheless, Miranda's confession was admitted into evidence. He was convicted and sentenced to serve twenty to thirty years for kidnapping and rape.

On appeal, the U.S. Supreme Court held that

> *the current practice of incommunicado interrogation is at odds with one of our Nation's most cherished principles—that the individual may not be compelled to incriminate himself. Unless adequate protective devices are employed to dispel the compulsion inherent in custodial surroundings, no statement obtained from the defendant can truly be the product of free choice.*

An exception is the brief, routine traffic stop; however, a custodial interrogation of a DUI (driving under the influence) suspect requires the *Miranda* warning.[90] Moreover, after an accused has invoked the right to counsel, the police may not interrogate the same suspect about a different crime.[91] Once a "Mirandized" suspect invokes his or her right to silence, interrogation must cease. The police may not readminister *Miranda* and interrogate the suspect later unless the suspect's attorney is present. If, however, the suspect initiates further conversation, any confession he or she provides is admissible.[92]

Decisions Eroding *Miranda*. *Miranda*, *Escobedo*, and *Mapp* combined to represent the centerpiece of the Warren Court's "due process revolution" of the 1960s. However, several decisions, including many by the Burger Court, have dealt severe blows to *Miranda*.

It has been held that a second interrogation session held after the suspect had initially refused to make a statement did not violate *Miranda*.[93] If a suspect waives his or her *Miranda* rights and makes voluntary statements while irrational (allegedly "following the advice of God"), those statements too are admissible.[94] The Court also decided that when a suspect waived his or her *Miranda* rights, believing the interrogation would focus on minor crimes, but the police shifted their questioning to a more serious crime, the confession was valid—there was no police deception or misrepresentation.[95] And when a suspect invoked his or her right to assistance of counsel and refused to make written statements, then voluntarily gave oral statements to police, the statements were admissible (defendants have "the right to choose between speech and silence").[96] Finally, a suspect need not be given the *Miranda* warning in the exact form as it was outlined in *Miranda* v. *Arizona*. In one case, the waiver form said the suspect would have an attorney appointed "if and when you go to court." The Court held that as long as the warnings on the form reasonably convey the suspect's rights, they need not be given verbatim.[97]

In 1994, the Supreme Court ruled that after police officers obtain a valid *Miranda* waiver from a suspect, they may continue questioning him or her when he or she makes an ambiguous or equivocal request for counsel during questioning. In this case,[98] the defendant stated during an interview and after waiving his rights, "Maybe I should talk to a lawyer." The officers inquired about this statement, determined that he did not want a lawyer, and continued their questioning. When a suspect unequivocally requests counsel, all questioning must cease. However, here the Court held that when the suspect mentions an attorney, the officers need not interrupt the flow of the questioning to clarify the reference but may continue questioning until there is a clear assertion of the right to counsel, such as "I want a lawyer."

Entrapment. The due process clause of the Fifth Amendment requires "fundamental fairness"; government agents may not act in a way that is "shocking to the universal sense of justice." Thus the police may not induce or encourage a person to commit a crime that he or she would otherwise not have attempted; that is **entrapment**.[99] This is the current test used by many courts to evaluate police behavior. Some states take a broader view than others as to what constitutes entrapment. For example, a police department in a western state had police officers impersonate homeless people. The decoys pretended to be asleep or passed out from intoxication on a public bench, and paper money visibly protruded from their pockets. Several passersby helped themselves to the money and were arrested on the spot. On appeal, the prosecution argued that a thief is a thief, the people had the intent to commit theft, and the decoy operation simply provided an opportunity for dishonest people to get caught. The state supreme court disagreed, calling the operation entrapment, adding that the situation could cause even honest people to be overcome by temptation.

However, the Supreme Court approved an undercover drug agent's provision of an essential chemical for the manufacture of illegal drugs. (The defendant, the majority said, was an "unwary criminal" who was already "predisposed" to commit the offense).[100] Nor is it entrapment when a drug agent sells drugs to a suspect, who then sells it to government agents. Government conduct in this case is shocking to civil libertarians, but the focus here is the conduct of the defendant, not the government. As long as government's conduct is not outrageous and the defendant was predisposed to crime, the arrest is valid.[101]

The Supreme Court has held that police officers "may not originate a criminal design, implant in an innocent person's mind the disposition to commit a criminal act, and then induce commission of the crime."[102]

The Sixth Amendment

> In all criminal prosecutions the accused shall enjoy the right to a speedy and public trial, by an impartial jury of the State and district wherein the crime shall have been committed, which district shall have been previously ascertained by law, and to be informed of the nature and cause of the accusation; to be confronted with the witnesses against him; to have compulsory process for obtaining witnesses in his favor, and to have the assistance of counsel for his defense.

Right to Counsel. Many people believe that the **Sixth Amendment** right of the accused to have the assistance of counsel before and at trial is the greatest right we enjoy in a democracy. Indeed, a close reading of the cases mentioned here would reveal the negative outcomes that are possible when a person, rich or poor, illiterate or educated, has no legal representation.

Over a seventy years ago, in *Powell* v. *Alabama* (1932), it was established that in a capital case, when the accused is poor and illiterate, he or she enjoys the right to assistance of counsel for his or her defense and due process.[103] In *Gideon* v. *Wainwright* (1963), the Supreme Court mandated that all indigent people charged with felonies in state courts be provided counsel.[104]

Note that *Gideon* applied only to felony defendants. In 1973, *Argersinger* v. *Hamlin* extended the right to counsel to indigent people charged with misdemeanor crimes if they face the possibility of incarceration (however short the incarceration may be).[105]

Another landmark decision concerning the right to counsel is *Escobedo* v. *Illinois* (1964).[106] Danny Escobedo's brother-in-law was fatally shot in 1960; Escobedo was arrested without a warrant and questioned, but he made no statement to the police. He was released after fourteen hours of interrogation. Following police questioning of another suspect, Escobedo was again arrested and questioned at police headquarters. Escobedo's request to confer with his lawyer was denied, even after the lawyer arrived and asked to see his client. The questioning of Escobedo lasted several hours, during which time he was handcuffed and forced to remain standing. Eventually, he admitted being an accomplice to murder. Under Illinois law, an accomplice was as guilty as the person firing the fatal bullet. At no point was Escobedo advised of his rights to remain silent or to confer with his attorney.

Escobedo's conviction was ultimately reversed by the Supreme Court, based on a violation of Escobedo's Sixth Amendment right to counsel. However, the real thrust of the decision was his Fifth Amendment right not to incriminate himself; when a defendant is scared, flustered, ignorant, alone, and bewildered, he or she is often unable to effectively make use of protections granted under the Fifth Amendment without the advice of an attorney.[107] The *Miranda* decision set down two years later simply established the guidelines for the police to inform suspects of all of these rights.

What Constitutes an Interrogation? The Supreme Court has stated that an interrogation takes place not only when police officers ask direct questions of a defendant, but also when the police make remarks designed to appeal to a defendant's sympathy, religious interest, and so forth. This has been deemed soliciting information through trickery and deceit. The "Christian Burial Speech" case (see page 262) and *Escobedo* demonstrated that even before and certainly after a suspect has been formally charged, a suspect in police custody should not be interrogated without an attorney present unless he or she has waived the right to counsel.

However, the Supreme Court upheld a conviction when two police officers, in a suspect's presence, discussed the possible whereabouts of the shotgun used in a robbery and expressed concern that nearby schoolchildren might be endangered by it. Hearing this conversation, the suspect led officers to the shotgun, thereby implicating himself. On appeal, the Court said that interrogation includes words and actions intended to elicit an incriminating response from the defendant and that no such interrogation occurred here; this was a mere conversation between officers, and the evidence was admissible.[108]

In another case, the Court ruled that if the police were present at and recorded a conversation between a husband and wife (this tape was later used against the husband at trial, where he claimed insanity in the killing of his son), an interrogation did not occur. The Court believed that the police merely arranged a situation in which it was likely the suspect would make incriminating statements, so anything recorded could be used against him in court.[109]

Two cases on police interrogations were heard during the 1990–1991 Supreme Court term. First, the Court held that a defendant who is in custody and has been given the *Miranda* warning may be questioned later on a separate, as-yet-uncharged offense. In this case, the defendant appeared with an attorney at a bail hearing on robbery charges. Later, while he was still in custody, the police, after reading him his rights, questioned him about a murder; the defendant agreed to discuss the murder without counsel and made incriminating statements that were used to convict him.[110] Second, in the one victory for the defense, the Court held that once a criminal suspect has asked for and consults with a lawyer, interrogators may not later question him without his lawyer being present.[111]

Juvenile Rights

The criminal justice system's philosophy toward juveniles is very different from its philosophy toward adults. Consequently, police officers, who are constantly dealing with juvenile offenders, must know and apply a different standard of treatment in these situations. The approach toward juvenile offenders is generally that society, through poor parenting, poverty, and so forth, is primarily responsible for their criminal behavior.

The prevailing doctrine that guides our treatment of juveniles is ***parens patriae***, meaning that the "state is the ultimate parent" of the child. In effect, this means that as long as we adequately care for and provide at least the basic amenities for our children as required under the law, they are ours to keep. But when children are physically or emotionally neglected or abused by their parents or guardians, the juvenile court and police may intervene and remove the children from that environment. Then the doctrine of ***in loco parentis*** takes hold, meaning that the state will act in place of the parent. The author can state from experience that there is probably no more overwhelming or awe-inspiring duty for a police officer than having to testify in juvenile court that a woman is an unfit mother and that parental ties should be legally severed. However, when a person chooses to be a negligent or abusive parent, it is clearly in everyone's best interest for the state to assume care and custody of the child.

The juvenile justice system, working through and with the police, seeks to protect the child. It seeks to rehabilitate, not punish; its procedure is generally amiable, not adversarial. That is why the term *In Re*, meaning "concerning" or "in the matter of," is commonly used in many juvenile case titles—for example, a case would be called *In Re Smith* rather than the adversarial and more formal *State* v. *Smith*. Juvenile court proceedings are generally shrouded in privacy, heard before a judge only. However, when a juvenile commits an act that is so heinous that the protective and helpful juvenile court philosophy will not work, the child may be remanded to the custody of the adult court to be tried as an adult.

Juvenile delinquency (an ambiguous term that has no widespread agreed-upon meaning but has a multitude of definitions under state statutes[112]) became recognized as a national problem in the 1950s. As a result, several important decisions by the Supreme Court between 1960 and 1970 addressed the rights of juveniles. *Kent* v. *United States* (1966)[113] involved a sixteen-year-old male who was arrested in the District of Columbia for robbery, rape, and burglary. The juvenile court, without holding a formal hearing, waived the matter to a criminal court, and Kent was tried and convicted as an adult. Kent appealed, arguing that the waiver without a hearing violated his right to due process. The Supreme Court agreed.

Another landmark case extending due process to juveniles was *In Re Gault* (1967).[114] Gerald Gault was a fifteen-year-old who resided in Arizona and allegedly made obscene telephone calls. When a neighbor complained to police, Gault was arrested and eventually sent to a youth home (a previous crime, stealing a wallet, was also taken into account), to remain there until he either turned twenty-one or was paroled. Before his hearing, Gault did not receive a timely notice of charges; at his hearing, Gault had no attorney present, nor was his accuser present; no transcript was made of the proceedings; and Gault was not read his rights or told he could remain silent. Gault appealed on the grounds that all of these due process rights should have been provided. The Supreme Court reversed his conviction, declaring that these Fourteenth Amendment protections applied to juveniles as well as adults. This case remains the most significant juvenile-rights decision ever rendered.

In 1970, the Supreme Court decided *In Re Winship*, involving a twelve-year-old boy convicted in New York of larceny.[115] At trial, the court relied on the "preponderance of the evidence" standard of proof against him rather than the more demanding "beyond a reasonable doubt" standard used in adult courts. At that time, juvenile courts could apply any of three standards of proof (the third was "clear and convincing evidence"). The Court reversed Winship's conviction on the ground that the "beyond a reasonable doubt" standard had not been used.

Other precedent-setting juvenile cases followed. In *McKeiver* v. *Pennsylvania* (1971), the Supreme Court said juveniles do not have an absolute right to trial by jury; whether or not a juvenile receives a trial by jury is left to the discretion of state and local authorities.[116] Finally, in *Breed* v. *Jones* (1975), the Court concluded that the Fifth Amendment protected juveniles from double jeopardy, or being tried twice for the same offense. (Breed had been tried both in California Juvenile Court and later in Superior Court for the same offenses.)[117]

SUMMARY

Our society places great importance on individual freedom, and the power of government has traditionally been feared; therefore, our Constitution, courts, and legislatures have seen fit to rein in the power of government agents through what is commonly referred to as the "rule of law." This necessary aspect associated with having police in a democracy carries with it a responsibility for police practitioners to understand the law and—more important, perhaps—to keep abreast of the legal changes our society is constantly undergoing.

The law is dynamic; that is, it is constantly changed by the Supreme Court and other federal courts and by state courts and legislatures. It is imperative that police agencies have a formal mechanism for imparting these legal changes to their officers.

The number of successful criminal and civil lawsuits against police officers today demonstrates that the police have not always done their homework and simply do not apply the law in the manner in which the federal courts intended. Officers must understand and enforce the law properly. In this grave business of adult cops and robbers, the means are in many respects more important than the ends. The courts and the criminal justice system should expect and allow nothing less.

REVIEW QUESTIONS

1. Outline the protections afforded citizens by the Fourth, Fifth, and Sixth Amendments.
2. Define and give an example of probable cause.
3. Discuss, from both the police and community perspectives, the ramifications of having an exclusionary rule. What would be the ramifications for the police and the public if the rule were discontinued?
4. Distinguish between arrests and searches and seizures with and without a warrant. Which form is best? Why? Cite examples of each.
5. In what significant ways has the *Miranda* decision been eroded? What is its long-term outlook, given the shifting composition of judges on the Supreme Court?
6. Delineate the major rights of juveniles. What are the major differences in philosophy and treatment between juvenile and adult offenders? How are these differences manifested toward the offender in court?

INDEPENDENT STUDENT ACTIVITIES

1. Read a primer on legal research methods, and then go to a law library and locate the following landmark U.S. Supreme Court decisions: *Miranda* v. *Arizona*, *Terry* v. *Ohio*, and *Mapp* v. *Ohio* (their case citations are given below, in the Notes section).
2. Have an attorney or a police officer explain the elusive concept of probable cause. Ask him or her to provide some real-life examples of this concept as it has been applied on the street.
3. Interview officers or court personnel concerning their views on the advantages and disadvantages of the exclusionary rule. Try to imagine the ramifications of a justice system in which the exclusionary rule did not exist. What kinds of safeguards or penalties for the police would need to be put in place to operate in its absence?
4. Imagine scenarios involving different types of criminal activities in which an officer might need to search a person or a vehicle without a warrant. (For example, assume that an officer stops a vehicle matching the description of one used in a convenience store robbery where a bank bag containing cash and various food items were taken. What kinds of items might the officer view in the back seat of the vehicle that would constitute probable cause and justify a warrantless search?)

RELATED WEB SITES

Administrative Office of the Courts
http://www.uscourts.gov

American Bar Association
http://www.abanet.org

Justice Information Center
http://www.ncjrs.org

U.S. Supreme Court
http://www.supremecourtus.gov

NOTES

1. David Neubauer, *America's Courts and the Criminal Justice System*, 7th ed. (Belmont, CA: Wadsworth, 2002), pp. 294–300.
2. *Draper* v. *United States*, 358 U.S. 307 (1959).
3. *Illinois* v. *Gates*, 462 U.S. 213 (1983).
4. *United States* v. *Sokolow*, 109 S.Ct. 1581 (1989).

5. *HUNTER* v. *BRYANT*, 112 S.Ct. 534 (1991).
6. *PEOPLE* v. *DEFORE*, 242 N.Y. 214, 150 N.E. 585 (1926).
7. *WEEKS* v. *UNITED STATES*, 232 U.S. 383 (1914).
8. This doctrine was overruled by the Supreme Court in *ELKINS* v. *UNITED STATES*, 364 U.S. 206 (1960).
9. *PEOPLE* v. *DEFORE*, 242 N.Y. 214, 150 N.E. 585 (1926).
10. *OLMSTEAD* v. *UNITED STATES*, 277 U.S. 438, 48 S.Ct. 564 (1928).
11. *MAPP* v. *OHIO*, 367 U.S. 643 (1961).
12. JOHN KAPLAN, JEROME H. SKOLNICK, and MALCOLM M. FEELEY, *Criminal Justice: Introductory Cases and Materials*, 5th ed. (Westbury, NY: Foundation Press, 1991), pp. 258–59, 269.
13. *ROCHIN* v. *CALIFORNIA*, 342 U.S. 165 (1952).
14. In *NEW YORK* v. *QUARLES*, 467 U.S. 649 (1984).
15. *NIX* v. *WILLIAMS*, 52 LW 4732 (1984). This case began as *BREWER* v. *WILLIAMS*, 430 U.S. 387 (1977).
16. *UNITED STATES* v. *LEON*, 82 L.Ed.2d 677 (1984).
17. *MURRAY* v. *UNITED STATES*, 487 U.S. 533 (1988).
18. KAPLAN, SKOLNICK, and FEELEY, *Criminal Justice*, p. 269.
19. *CALIFORNIA* v. *MINJARES*, 443 U.S. 916 (1979).
20. ALEXANDER B. SMITH and HARRIET POLLACK, *Criminal Justice: An Overview* (New York: Holt, Rinehart and Winston, 1980), pp. 154–55.
21. *PAYTON* v. *NEW YORK*, 445 U.S. 573 (1980).
22. *DUNAWAY* v. *NEW YORK*, 442 U.S. 200 (1979).
23. *DELAWARE* v. *PROUSE*, 440 U.S. 648 (1979).
24. *MICHIGAN DEPARTMENT OF STATE POLICE* v. *SITZ*, 110 S.Ct. 2481, 110 L.Ed.2d 412 (1990).
25. *PENNSYLVANIA* v. *MUNIZ*, 110 S.Ct. 2638, 110 L.Ed.2d 528 (1990).
26. *MARYLAND* v. *PRINGLE*, 124 S.Ct. 795 (2004).
27. *ILLINOIS* v. *LIDSTER*, 124 S.Ct. 885 (2004).
28. *RIVERSIDE COUNTY, CALIF.* v. *MCLAUGHLIN*, 59 LW 4413 (May 13, 1991).
29. *U.S.* v. *BANKS*, 124 S.Ct. 521 (2003).
30. *PENNSYLVANIA* v. *BULL*, 63 LW 3695 (1995).
31. *WILSON* v. *ARKANSAS,* 115 S.Ct. 1914 (1995).
32. *ZURCHER* v. *STANFORD* DAILY, 436 U.S. 547 (1978).
33. *MARYLAND* v. *GARRISON*, 480 U.S. 79 (1987).
34. *CALIFORNIA* v. *GREENWOOD*, 486 U.S. 35 (1988).
35. ROLANDO V. DEL CARMEN and JEFFREY T. WALKER, *Briefs of One Hundred Leading Cases in Law Enforcement* (Cincinnati: Anderson, 1991), p. 49.
36. *BROWER* v. *COUNTY OF INYO*, 109 U.S. 1378 (1989).
37. *FLORIDA* v. *BOSTICK*, 59 LW 4708 (June 20, 1991).
38. *U.S.* v. *DRAYTON*, 536 U.S. 194, 231 F. 3d 787 (2002).
39. *CALIFORNIA* v. *HODARI D.*, 59 LW 4335 (April 23, 1991).
40. *SCHMERBER* v. *CALIFORNIA*, 384 U.S. 757 (1966).
41. *WINSTON* v. *LEE*, 470 U.S. 753 (1985).

42. *UNITED STATES* v. *ROBINSON,* 414 U.S. 218 (1973).
43. *CHIMEL* v. *CALIFORNIA*, 395 U.S. 752 (1969).
44. *UNITED STATES* v. *EDWARDS*, 415 U.S. 800 (1974).
45. *MARYLAND* v. *BUIE*, 58 LW 4281 (1990).
46. SMITH and POLLACK, *Criminal Justice*, p. 161.
47. *ADAMS* v. *WILLIAMS*, 407 U.S. 143 (1972).
48. *UNITED STATES* v. *HENSLEY*, 469 U.S. 221 (1985).
49. SMITH and POLLACK, *Criminal Justice*, p. 162.
50. *MINNESOTA* v. *DICKERSON*, 113 S.Ct. 2130 (1993).
51. *ILLINOIS* v. *WARDLOW,* 120 S.Ct. 673 (2000).
52. Ibid., at 673.
53. *MARYLAND* v. *WILSON*, 117 S.Ct. 882 (1997).
54. *CARROLL* v. *UNITED STATES*, 267 U.S. 132 (1925).
55. *PRESTON* v. *UNITED STATES*, 376 U.S. 364 (1964).
56. *HARRIS* v. *UNITED STATES*, 390 U.S. 234 (1968).
57. *CHAMBERS* v. *MARONEY*, 399 U.S. 42 (1970).
58. *CARDWELL* v. *LEWIS*, 417 U.S. 583 (1974).
59. *SOUTH DAKOTA* v. *OPPERMAN*, 428 U.S. 364 (1976).
60. *NEW YORK* v. *BELTON*, 453 U.S. 454 (1981).
61. *UNITED STATES* v. *ROSS*, 456 U.S. 798 (1982).
62. *MICHIGAN* v. *LONG*, 463 U.S. 1032 (1983).
63. *COLORADO* v. *BERTINE*, 479 U.S. 367 (1987).
64. *FLORIDA* v. *JIMENO*, 59 LW 4471 (May 23, 1991).
65. *CALIFORNIA* v. *ACEVEDO*, 59 LW 4559 (May 30, 1991).
66. *WYOMING* v. *HOUGHTON*, 119 S.Ct. 1297 (1999).
67. *ILLINOIS* v. *CABALLES*, 543 U.S. ___ (2005).
68. *TEXAS* v. *BROWN*, 460 U.S. 730 (1983).
69. *OLIVER* v. *UNITED STATES*, 466 U.S. 170 (1984).
70. *CALIFORNIA* v. *CIRAOLO*, 476 U.S. 207 (1986).
71. *NEW YORK* v. *CLASS*, 54 LW 4178 (1986).
72. *ARIZONA* v. *HICKS*, 55 LW 4258 (1987).
73. *SCHNECKLOTH* v. *BUSTAMONTE*, 412 U.S. 218 (1973).
74. *BUMPER* v. *NORTH CAROLINA*, 391 U.S. 543 (1968).
75. *STONER* v. *CALIFORNIA*, 376 U.S. 483 (1964).
76. *OLMSTEAD* v. *UNITED STATES*, 277 U.S. 438 (1928).
77. *KATZ* v. *UNITED STATES,* 389 U.S. 347 (1967).
78. *BERGER* v. *NEW YORK*, 388 U.S. 41 (1967).
79. *LEE* v. *UNITED STATES*, 343 U.S. 747 (1952).
80. *UNITED STATES* v. *KARO*, 468 U.S. 705 (1984).
81. *UNITED STATES* v. *WADE*, 388 U.S. 218 (1967).
82. *KIRBY* v. *ILLINOIS*, 406 U.S. 682 (1972).
83. *FOSTER* v. *CALIFORNIA*, 394 U.S. 440 (1969).
84. *UNITED STATES* v. *DIONISIO*, 410 U.S. 1 (1973).

85. KAPLAN, SKOLNICK, and FEELEY, *Criminal Justice*, pp. 219–20.
86. Ibid., pp. 220–21.
87. *SPANO* v. *NEW YORK*, 360 U.S. 315 (1959).
88. *ESCOBEDO* v. *ILLINOIS*, 378 U.S. 478 (1964).
89. *MIRANDA* v. *ARIZONA*, 384 U.S. 436 (1966).
90. *BERKEMER* v. *MCCARTY*, 468 U.S. 420 (1984).
91. *ARIZONA* v. *ROBERSON*, 486 U.S. 675 (1988).
92. *EDWARDS* v. *ARIZONA*, 451 U.S. 477 (1981).
93. *MICHIGAN* v. *MOSLEY*, 423 U.S. 93 (1975).
94. *COLORADO* v. *CONNELLY*, 479 U.S. 157 (1986).
95. *COLORADO* v. *SPRING*, 479 U.S. 564 (1987).
96. *CONNECTICUT* v. *BARRETT*, 479 U.S. 523 (1987).
97. *DUCKWORTH* v. *EAGAN*, 109 S.Ct. 2875 (1989).
98. *DAVIS* v. *UNITED STATES*, 114 S.Ct. 2350 (1994).
99. *SHERMAN* v. *UNITED STATES*, 356 U.S. 369 (1958).
100. *UNITED STATES* v. *RUSSELL*, 411 U.S. 423 (1973).
101. *HAMPTON* v. *UNITED STATES*, 425 U.S. 484 (1976).
102. Ibid., at 1540.
103. *POWELL* v. *ALABAMA*, 287 U.S. 45 (1932).
104. *GIDEON* v. *WAINWRIGHT*, 372 U.S. 335 (1963).
105. *ARGERSINGER* v. *HAMLIN*, 407 U.S. 25 (1973).
106. *ESCOBEDO* v. *ILLINOIS*, 378 U.S. 478 (1964).
107. SMITH and POLLACK, *Criminal Justice*, p. 177.
108. *RHODE ISLAND* v. *INNIS*, 446 U.S. 291 (1980).
109. *ARIZONA* v. *MAURO*, 481 U.S. 520 (1987).
110. *MCNEIL* v. *WISCONSIN*, 59 LW 4636 (June 13, 1991).
111. *MINNICK* v. *MISSISSIPPI*, 59 LW 4037 (1990).
112. ARNOLD BINDER, GILBERT GEIS, and DICKSON BRUCE, *Juvenile Delinquency: Historical, Cultural, Legal Perspectives* (New York: Macmillan, 1988), pp. 6–9.
113. *KENT* v. *UNITED STATES*, 383 U.S. 541 (1966).
114. IN RE GAULT, 387 U.S. 9 (1967).
115. IN RE WINSHIP, 397 U.S. 358 (1970).
116. *MCKEIVER* v. *PENNSYLVANIA*, 403 U.S. 528 (1971).
117. *BREED* v. *JONES,* 421 U.S. 519 (1975).

CHAPTER 10

Accountability: Ethics, Force and Corruption, and Discipline

I don't care if a rookie thinks the Duke of Wellington is a man, a horse, or a smoking tobacco. What counts is a man's character.

—Bruce Smith

This is your duty, to act well the part that is given to you.

—Epictetus

Key Terms

bias-based policing
code of silence
complaint
ethics
Garrity v. *New Jersey*
Lautenberg Amendment
limitations on officers' constitutional rights
police brutality
police corruption
police firearms regulations
police use of force
slippery slope perspective

The new millennium certainly came in like a lion with respect to controversial police practices and public outcry; we can hope in this regard that its first decade will go out more like a lamb. Citizens in some communities took their anger against police to the streets, engaging in violent civil unrest (see, for example, the description of recent actions in Cincinnati, discussed later). Perhaps no aspect of policing carries more controversy, problems, and questions than how to maintain police accountability; this topic includes ethical conduct, police use of force and corruption, and officer discipline. This chapter addresses that triad.

First is an examination of the complicated concept of police ethics, including types of corruption and potential problems under community policing. Next we review the use of violence and force against the public, including police brutality in general and the use and control of lethal force; also discussed is the contemporary hot-button issue of bias-based policing and other field tactics. Then we consider police corruption: types and causes, problems posed by the police code of silence, and how to deal with it. Next is an overview of areas in which the federal courts have placed limitations on police behaviors by virtue of their unique role: freedom of speech, search and seizure, self-incrimination, freedom of religion, sexual misconduct, residency requirements, moonlighting, misuse of firearms, and alcohol and drug abuse. Finally, the chapter examines disciplinary policies and practices, including handling citizens' complaints and doling out sanctions. A chapter summary, review questions, independent student activities, and related Web sites conclude the chapter.

This chapter necessarily lays bare several sordid aspects of police behavior, especially the use of force. We must keep in mind the positive findings of a recent federal study, however: Of nearly 44 million contacts the police had with the public in a year's time, less than 1 percent resulted in force being used or threatened. And in more than half of the cases in which force was used by the police, citizens acknowledged having argued with, disobeyed, or resisted police during the interaction or were drunk or high on drugs at the time.[1]

In the Beginning: Problems Greet the New Millennium

Troubles in Cities Large and Small

There was no dearth of high-profile investigations of, and outcomes involving, metropolitan police problems during the early part of the new millennium:

- Seventy officers of the Los Angeles Police Department's (LAPD's) Rampart Division came under scrutiny in early 2000 after a disgraced former officer (who was eventually sentenced to five years in prison for stealing cocaine) told investigators that he and other antigang-unit officers framed suspects

and falsified evidence. Nearly one hundred people were framed by "rogue" officers over a three-year period, and a few unarmed citizens were shot. Dozens of cases brought by the unit were thrown out, and dozens of officers were convicted, fired, suspended, or quit.[2] In early 2000, the Los Angeles police chief, Bernard C. Parks, issued a stinging indictment of his own department, saying that lax oversight and poor adherence to departmental policies allowed corruption to flourish in the LAPD. Parks said he needed at least $9 million and hundreds of new positions (primarily in the internal affairs division) to fix the problems.[3]
- Also in early 2000, the verdict was rendered in the New York police killing of an unarmed West African, Amadou Diallo. In February 1999, officers, mistaking Diallo's wallet for a handgun, fired forty-one shots at Diallo, striking him nineteen times. The four police officers who were involved in the shooting were acquitted.

While police problems have plagued the cities of Los Angeles and New York for forty years, big-city policing abuses have also been seeping into smaller towns and suburbs:

- Following a confrontation, a police detective in Prince George's County, Maryland, killed a black twenty-five-year-old university student in September 2000, shooting him in the back five times; he was one of twelve people shot in the county in thirteen months, five fatally.
- In Riverside, California, in 1998, an unconscious nineteen-year-old woman in a parked car died after being shot twelve times by local police.
- And in mid-2000, the Department of Justice began probing racial profiling in Eastpointe, Michigan, and Orange County, Florida.[4]

Possible explanations for such problems in small-town and suburban police agencies abound, with a *Washington Post* columnist offering that "it is the police culture, more than race, that is at the crux of the problem...a mentality of brutality."[5] (See Exhibit 10-1, which discusses methods of measuring a police department's "culture of integrity.")

A New Tool: Federal Investigations

The federal government—specifically, the Department of Justice—has a new legal means to investigate allegations of racial bias in police departments. The law authorizing such investigations, passed in 1994 after the Rodney King beating in Los Angeles, has gotten results while generating a lot of controversy. It compels police agencies to initiate safeguards against excessive force and racial bias—for instance, computer systems to track complaints and disciplinary actions. The Fraternal Order of Police filed a lawsuit against the law in 2001, arguing that the Justice Department's use of the law was unconstitutional.

The law was applied in April 2001 in the fatal Cincinnati police shooting of Timothy Thomas, an unarmed nineteen-year-old black man. Thomas's killing—he was the fifteenth young black man killed by Cincinnati police

The police have always been criticized for a variety of reasons, as shown in this 1874 caricature of police as pigs.

(Courtesy The Granger Collection, New York)

in six years—ignited a storm of violence and looting. As a result, the city's mayor asked U.S. Attorney General John Ashcroft to review the "practices, procedures, and training" of the police department. At the same time, the Justice Department was investigating twelve other local police departments (in Buffalo, New York; Charleston, West Virginia; Cleveland; Detroit; Eastpointe, Michigan; New Orleans; New York City; Orange County, Florida; Prince George's County, Maryland; Riverside, California; Tulsa, Oklahoma; and Washington, D.C.) to determine whether they engaged in "a pattern and practice" of racial discrimination or brutality.[6]

Police Ethics

A Scenario

Assume that the police have strong suspicions that Jones is a serial rapist, but they have not secured enough probable cause to obtain a search warrant for Jones's car and home, where evidence might be found.

EXHIBIT 10-1

Measuring a Police Department's "Culture of Integrity"

Researchers believe they have found a quantitative method that allows police executives to assess their agency's level of resistance to corruption. A national survey of 3,235 officers in thirty police departments asked them to examine eleven common scenarios of police misconduct. The study was based on the premise that organizational and occupational culture can create an atmosphere in which corruption is not tolerated. Survey questions were designed to indicate whether officers knew the rules governing misconduct and how strongly they supported those guidelines, whether they knew the disciplinary penalties for breaking those rules and believed them to be fair, and whether they were willing to report misconduct. Respondents found some types of transgressions to be significantly less serious than others. The more serious the transgression was perceived to be, the more willing officers were to report a colleague and to believe that severe discipline was appropriate. Four scenarios that were not considered major transgressions by officers included operating a private security business while off duty, receiving free meals, accepting free holiday gifts, and covering up a police drunk-driving accident. Indeed, a majority of respondents said they would not report a fellow officer for accepting free gifts, meals, or discounts or for having a minor traffic accident while under the influence of alcohol.

The intermediate levels of misconduct included using excessive force on a car thief following a foot pursuit, a supervisor's offering time off during holidays in exchange for a tune-up on his personal vehicle, and accepting free drinks in return for ignoring a late bar closing. Very serious forms of misconduct, as perceived by the respondents, included accepting a cash bribe, stealing money from a found wallet, and stealing a watch from a crime scene.

Source: Adapted from "How Do You Rate? The Secret to Measuring a Department's 'Culture of Integrity.'" Reprinted with permission from *Law Enforcement News*, October 15, 2000, pp. 1, 6. John Jay College of Criminal Justice, CUNY, 555 W. 57th St., New York, NY 10019.

Officer Brown feels frustrated and, early one morning, uses a razor blade to remove the current registration decal from the license plate on Jones's car. The next day he stops Jones for operating his vehicle with an expired registration; he impounds and inventories the vehicle and finds evidence of several sexual assaults, which ultimately leads to Jones's conviction on ten counts of forcible rape and possession of burglary tools and stolen property. Brown receives accolades for the apprehension. Was Officer Brown's removal of the registration decal legal? Should Brown's actions, even if improper or illegal, be condoned for "serving the greater public good"? Did Brown use the law properly?

This hypothetical sequence of events and the accompanying questions should be kept in mind as we consider the problem of police **ethics**.

EXHIBIT 10-2

Law Enforcement Code of Ethics

All law enforcement officers must be fully aware of the ethical responsibilities of their position and must strive constantly to live up to the highest possible standards of professional policing.

The International Association of Chiefs of Police believes it is important that police officers have clear advice and counsel available to assist them in performing their duties in accordance with these standards. The association has adopted the following ethical mandates as guidelines to meet these ends.

PRIMARY RESPONSIBILITIES OF A POLICE OFFICER

A police officer acts as an official representative of government who is required and trusted to work within the law. The officer's powers and duties are conferred by statute. The fundamental duties of a police officer include serving the community; safeguarding lives and property; protecting the innocent; keeping the peace; and ensuring the rights of all to liberty, equality and justice.

PERFORMANCE OF THE DUTIES OF A POLICE OFFICER

A police officer shall perform all duties impartially, without favor or affection or ill will and without regard to status, sex, race, religion, political belief or aspiration. All citizens will be treated equally with courtesy, consideration and dignity.

Officers will never allow personal feelings, animosities or friendships to influence official conduct. Laws will be enforced appropriately and courteously and, in carrying out their responsibilities, officers will strive to obtain maximum cooperation from the public. They will conduct themselves in appearance and deportment in such a manner as to inspire confidence and respect for the position of public trust they hold.

DISCRETION

A police officer will use responsibly the discretion vested in the position and exercise it within the law. The principle of reasonableness will guide the officer's determinations, and the officer will consider all surrounding circumstances in determining whether any legal action shall be taken.

Consistent and wise use of discretion, based on professional policing competence, will do much to preserve good relationships and retain the confidence of the public. There can be difficulty in choosing between conflicting courses of action. It is important to remember that a timely word of advice rather than arrest—which may be correct in appropriate circumstances—can be a more effective means of achieving a desired end.

USE OF FORCE

A police officer will never employ unnecessary force or violence and will use only such force in the discharge of duty as is reasonable in all circumstances.

Force should be used only with the greatest restraint and only after discussion, negotiation and persuasion have been found to be inappropriate or ineffective. While the use of force is occasionally unavoidable, every police officer will refrain from applying the unnecessary infliction of pain or suffering and will never engage in cruel, degrading or inhuman treatment of any person.

CONFIDENTIALITY

Whatever a police officer sees, hears or learns which is of a confidential nature will be kept secret unless the performance of duty or legal provision requires otherwise.

Members of the public have a right to security and privacy, and information obtained about them must not be improperly divulged.

INTEGRITY

A police officer will not engage in acts of corruption or bribery, nor will an officer condone such acts by other police officers.

The public demands that the integrity of police officers be above reproach. Police officers must, therefore, avoid any conduct that might compromise integrity and thus undercut the public confidence in a law enforcement agency. Officers will refuse to accept any gifts, presents, subscriptions, favors, gratuities or promises that could be interpreted as seeking to cause the officer to refrain from performing official responsibilities honestly and within the law. Police officers must not receive private or special advantage from their official status. Respect from the public cannot be bought; it can only be earned and cultivated.

COOPERATION WITH OTHER OFFICERS AND AGENCIES

Police officers will cooperate with all legally authorized agencies and their representatives in the pursuit of justice.

An officer or agency may be one among many organizations that may provide law enforcement services to a jurisdiction. It is imperative that a police officer assist colleagues fully and completely with respect and consideration at all times.

PERSONAL/PROFESSIONAL CAPABILITIES

Police officers will be responsible for their own standard of professional performance and will take every reasonable opportunity to enhance and improve their level of knowledge and competence.

Through study and experience, a police officer can acquire the high level of knowledge and competence that is essential for the efficient and effective performance of duty. The acquisition of knowledge is a never-ending process of personal and professional development that should be pursued constantly.

PRIVATE LIFE

Police officers will behave in a manner that does not bring discredit to their agencies or themselves.

A police officer's character and conduct while off duty must always be exemplary, thus maintaining a position of respect in the community in which he or she lives and serves. The officer's personal behavior must be beyond reproach.

Source: Adopted by the Executive Committee of the International Association of Chiefs of Police on October 17, 1989. Used with permission.

Definition and Types

Proper ethical behavior has always been the cornerstone of policing (see the Law Enforcement Code of Ethics, Exhibit 10-2) and is what the public expects of its public servants. Ethics usually involves standards of moral conduct and what we call "conscience," the ability to recognize right from wrong, and acting in ways that are good and proper. One definition for *ethics* is "the discipline dealing with what is good and bad and with moral duty and obligation."[7]

There are both absolute and relative ethics. Absolute ethics is a concept wherein an issue only has two sides: Something is either good or bad, black or white. The original interest in police ethics focused on such unethical behaviors as bribery, extortion, excessive force, and perjury. Few communities can tolerate the absolute unethical behavior of rogue officers; for instance, anyone would have a hard time trying to rationally defend a police officer's stealing.

Relative ethics is more complicated and can have a multitude of sides and varying shades of gray. What is considered ethical behavior by one person may be deemed highly unethical by someone else. However, not all police ethical issues are clear-cut. For example, communities seem willing at times to tolerate extralegal behavior by the police if there is a greater public good, especially in dealing with such problems as gangs and the homeless—and with offenders like the serial rapist in our scenario. As one police captain put it, "When you're shoveling society's garbage, you gotta be indulged a little bit."[8]

Another type of ethical dilemma faced by police officers involves situational ethics, which is related to relativism. For instance, consider a situation in which a police officer stops her father for driving while intoxicated. The officer must decide whether to do her duty—make an arrest—or allow the offender to go free.

Ethics and Community Policing

With the shift to community-oriented policing and problem solving (COPPS, discussed in Chapter 6), some concerns have been raised about the increased number of ethical dilemmas that COPPS officers confront because they have greater discretion and more public interaction than other officers.

Gratuities—free gifts that are supposedly given to the police without obligation—are an example of an ethical problem that can arise with more frequency under COPPS. Whether the police should receive such minor gratuities as free coffee and meals is a longstanding and controversial issue, one for which there will probably never be widespread consensus of opinion. Proponents argue that police deserve such perks and that minor gratuities are the building blocks of positive social relationships. Harmless gratuities, it is maintained, may create good feelings in the community toward police officers, and vice versa. Opponents believe, however, that the receipt of gratuities can lead to future deviance. This is the **slippery slope perspective**, which holds that the acceptance of minor gratuities begins a process wherein the recipient's integrity is gradually subverted, which eventually leads to more serious unethical conduct.[9] Given that judges, educators, and other professionals neither expect nor receive such gifts, some people (and police agencies) conclude that gratuities are unethical. As an example, after firing an officer for stealing cigars, sandwiches, magazines, and other goods from merchants, the Bradenton, Florida, Police Department established a policy prohibiting sworn personnel from accepting discounted meals from restaurant owners.[10]

The following scenario involves COPPS and gratuities:

> The sheriff's department has a long-standing policy concerning the solicitation and acceptance of gifts. (The policy is similar to the one in Figure 10-1.) A deputy has been working a problem-solving project in a strip mall area that has experienced juvenile loitering, drug use, prostitution, and vandalism after hours in the parking lot. The mall manager, Mr. Chang, believes it is his moral duty to show his appreciation to the deputy and has made arrangements for the deputy and his family to receive a 15 percent discount at every store in the mall. Knowing that the department policy requires that such offers be declined, the deputy is also aware that Chang will feel very hurt if the proffered gift is refused.[11]

A particularly strong consideration in this scenario is that the mall manager is Asian-American and might be extremely hurt if his gift were rejected. Some policy issues are also presented in this scenario. For example, in developing a rapport with a mall restaurant manager, is an officer who was formerly prohibited from accepting a free meal now free to do so? Assume that other deputies learn of Chang's new discount arrangement and go to the mall expecting to be treated similarly, resulting in complaints to the sheriff by several business owners. Certainly some people would hold this action to be unethical, given their motivation (personal gain) and their exploitation of the situation.

In sum, the subject of police ethics is not simplistic in nature. We all know that officers should do right, not wrong, but the existence and use of relative ethics makes this a complicated issue at best. What can be said is that police officers must be recruited and trained with ethics in mind because they will be given much freedom to become more involved in their community and given wider discretion to make important decisions when addressing neighborhood disorder.

Use of Violence and Force

A Tradition of Problems

Throughout our history, police agencies have faced allegations of brutality and corruption. In the late nineteenth century, New York police sergeant Alexander "Clubber" Williams epitomized police brutality; he spoke openly of using his nightstick to knock a man unconscious, batter him to pieces, or even kill him. Williams supposedly coined the term *tenderloin* when he commented, “I've had nothing but chuck steaks for a long time, and now I'm going to have me a little tenderloin.”[12] Williams was referring to opportunities for graft in an area in downtown New York that was the heart of vice and nightlife, often termed Satan's Circus. This was Williams's beat, where his reputation for brutality and corruption became legendary.[13]

Although police brutality and corruption are no longer openly tolerated, a number of events have demonstrated that the problem still exists and requires the attention of police officials. Several of these events, such as the so-called police riot in 1968 during the Democratic National Convention, were discussed in Chapter 1.

The Prerogative to Use Force

Our society recognizes three legitimate and responsive forms of force: the right of self-defense, including the valid taking of another person's life in order to protect oneself from harm; the power to control those for whom one is responsible (such as a prisoner or a patient in a mental hospital); and the relatively unrestricted authority of police to use force as required. Police work is dangerous; a routine arrest may result in a violent confrontation, sometimes triggered by drugs, alcohol, or mental

“Clubber” Williams.

(Courtesy The Granger Collection, New York)

illness. To cope, police officers are given the unique right to use force, even deadly force, against others. There are, of course, limitations on when an officer may exercise deadly force; they are discussed later in this chapter.

Egon Bittner defined **police use of force** as the "distribution of non-negotiably coercive remedies."[14] He asserted that the duty of police intervention in matters of societal disorder "means above all making use of the authority to overpower resistance. This feature of police work is uppermost in the minds of people who solicit police aid. Every conceivable police intervention projects the message that force may... have to be used to achieve a desired objective."[15] The exercise of force by police can take several forms—for example, a simple verbal command, a light touch on the arm to encourage someone to move along or comply with an order, the use of a baton or Mace to control an individual, the use of the carotid restraint (the so-called sleeper hold), and the use of lethal force.

Police Brutality

Many people contend that there are actually three means by which the police can be "brutal." There is the literal sense of the term, which involves the physical abuse of others. There is the verbal abuse of citizens, exemplified by slurs or epithets. Finally, for many who feel downtrodden, the police symbolize brutality because the officers represent the establishment's law, which serves to keep the minority groups in their place. It is perhaps the latter form of **police brutality** that is of the greatest concern for anyone who is interested in improving community relations. Because it is a philosophy or frame of mind, it is probably the most difficult to overcome.

Citizen use of the term *police brutality* encompasses a wide range of practices, from the use of profane and abusive language to the actual use of physical force or violence.[16] Some would claim that there is little, if any, police brutality in today's enlightened police agencies. Others acknowledge that police brutality exists today but add that "*brutality is the prerogative of the police state. To tolerate any of it is to differ from the police state only in degree*" (emphasis in original).[17]

While no one can deny that some police officers use brutal practices, it is impossible to know with any degree of accuracy how often and to what extent these incidents occur. They are low-visibility acts, and many victims decline to report them. Although it is widely believed that brutality is a racial matter primarily involving white police and black victims, Albert Reiss found that lower-class white men were as likely to be brutalized by the police as lower-class black men.[18] What is most disturbing is that 37 percent of the instances of excessive force occurred in settings controlled by the police—station houses and patrol cars. In half

EXHIBIT 10-3

Good News, Better News on Use of Force

First, the good news: Of more than 43 million contacts law enforcement had with the public during 1999, less than 1 percent resulted in force being used or threatened. Now the better news: In more than half of those cases, the subjects acknowledged having argued with, disobeyed or resisted police during the interaction, or had been drunk or high on drugs at the time.

The Bureau of Justice Statistics reported this month that an estimated 43.8 million people age 16 or older had face-to-face contact with police in 1999, with about half of those involving a vehicle stop. Of the nation's 18.1 million black licensed drivers, 12.3 percent were pulled over at least once, compared with 10.4 percent of the 143 million licensed white drivers.

The study, "Contacts Between Police and the Public—Findings from the 1999 National Survey," was based on data from BJS's Police-Public Contact Survey, which was conducted during the last six months of that year. Some 80,000 participants were used to develop the representative sample.

In addition to a larger percentage of blacks being subject to traffic stops, researchers also found that both blacks and Hispanics proportionately accounted for more searches, as well. Some 1.3 million drivers or vehicles were searched in 1999, said the study. Eleven percent of African Americans and 11.3 percent of Hispanics were searched by police, compared with 5.4 percent of whites. In nearly 90 percent of the searches conducted without the express consent of drivers, no drugs, alcohol, illegal weapons or evidence of criminal wrongdoing was found.

"What I think is important is when we asked drivers whether they felt it was a legitimate stop, about 84 percent of white drivers said yes, and about 74 percent of black drivers said yes," said Lawrence Greenfeld, a BJS statistician and co-author of the study. "There is some disparity there, but for the vast majority of black and white drivers who said yes, there was a legitimate reason."

The study also found that the race of the officer involved in the stop played little or no role in whether the motorists felt it was justified, Greenfeld told *Law Enforcement News*. "It suggests that the perception of whether the stop was valid or not has nothing to do with the officer's race," he said....

Of those who had contact with police during 1999, the report found that 422,000 contacts resulted in force or the threat of force. An estimated 20 percent of those incidents involved only the threat of force. Among blacks and Hispanics, 2 percent said they experienced the threat or use of force by police, compared to 1 percent of whites....

An estimated 49 percent of those involved in a force situation had charges filed against them, ranging from a traffic offense to assaulting an officer, said the study. Whites were as likely as blacks in such incidents to describe the force used against them as excessive, and the vast majority, 92 percent, said police had acted improperly.

Some 90 percent of respondents overall, however, said police had acted properly during the encounter. An estimated 51 percent of drivers said they had been speeding, 24 percent cited reckless driving, an illegal turn or some other traffic violation.

Source: Reprinted with permission from *Law Enforcement News*, March 15, 2001, p. 1. John Jay College of Criminal Justice, CUNY, 555 W. 57th St., New York, NY 10019.

the situations, a police officer did not participate but did not restrain his or her colleague, indicating that the informal police culture did not disapprove of the behavior.[19]

EXHIBIT 10-4

Study Links Use of Force to Suspect's Back Talk

Mouthing off to a police officer is not illegal, but it can be hazardous to your health, according to a new study sponsored by the National Institute of Justice, which found that when force is used during an arrest, it was more likely to have been prompted by a suspect's uncivil demeanor or resistance than by such characteristics as race, gender or age....

The study's authors—Joel H. Garner of the Joint Centers for Justice Studies, and Christopher D. Maxwell and Cedric Heraux, both of Michigan State University—measured force that they defined as involving the use of any weapon or weaponless tactic, such as hitting, kicking, grabbing, and any severe restraint, such as leg cuffs. When force was used, they found, it typically involved grabbing—in 7.8 percent of arrests. In only 2.1 percent of arrests was a firearm, baton, chemical agent, flashlight or other weapon used. A chemical agent was used most frequently, in 1.1 percent of the cases....

The characteristics most associated with police use of force [were] resistance by the suspect, demeanor, and "to a lesser extent," race. This was consistent across the diverse samples, jurisdictions, measures and analyses the study drew upon.

According to Garner and his colleagues, the odds that police would use force increased by a factor of 19 when suspects resisted physically. Demeanor was the second most consistent characteristic, with the likelihood of an officer using physical force increasing by a factor of 2.5 when a suspect was antagonistic but not physical. When suspects were uncivil to police, the odds of force being used in their arrest increased by 163 percent, the study found....

In addition to suspect resistance, the authors found other characteristics that increased the likelihood of force being used. They included a suspect's alcohol impairment; gang involvement; a reputation for carrying weapons or being combative; a prior arrest for a violent offense; the presence of bystanders; an increased police presence; male officers; male suspects; and the use of "contact and cover" arrest tactics.

The age of the suspect was found to play virtually no role in the use of force. On the other hand, Garner noted, the age of the officer is significant. Younger officers, male officers and Hispanic officers tended to use more force than older or female officers. Force is most often used in these cases against male suspects....

Bystanders also played a role in use of force, said the study. "We also found that police used less force when there were no bystanders," said the authors. "The presence of bystanders increases the amount of force used by the police; if the bystanders are strangers to the suspect, the severity of the force increases."

Source: "Study Links Use of Force to Suspect's Back talk," *Law Enforcement News*, January 15–31, 2003, p. 5. John Jay College of Criminal Justice, CUNY, 555 West 57th St., New York, NY 10019.

It is impossible to realistically expect that police brutality will at some point disappear forever. There are always going to be, in the words of A. C. Germann, Frank Day, and Robert Gallati, "Neanderthals" who enjoy their absolute control over others and become tyrannical in their

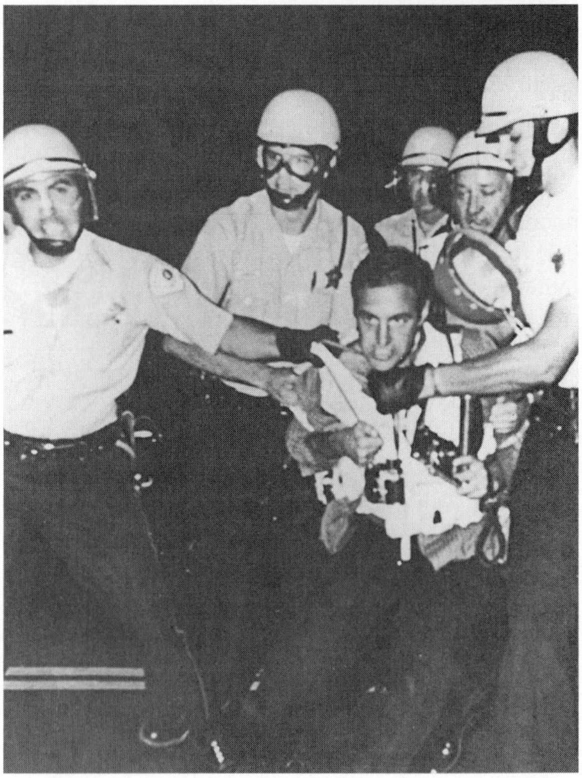

Scenes from the *Walker Report* of the 1968 Chicago Democratic National Convention.

arbitrary application of power.[20] The need is obvious for a formal citizen complaint review procedure within police agencies for investigating allegations of brutality and excessive use of force.

Use and Control of Lethal Force

The lethal use of force by a police officer is one of the most tragic and unfortunate circumstances that can occur in our society. It is tragic for the victim, the victim's family, the officer, and often the officer's family. Estimates of the number of citizens killed annually by the police range from three hundred to six hundred; about fifteen hundred more are wounded each year.[21] These numbers appear to be declining from the high level set in the 1970s.[22] However, it remains a notable fact that the typical victim of deadly force is a young African-American male.[23] For this reason, deadly force has become one of the major sources of tension between the police and minority communities.

When the colonists came to this country from England, they brought with them a common law principle that authorized the use of deadly force to apprehend any and all fleeing felony suspects. In such circumstances, it was reasoned, deadly force was appropriate and not disproportionate to the punishments arrestees received. As our laws and society evolved, however, it became possible for police to use deadly force against people who were at great distances from them, including people suspected of nonviolent property crimes. The justification and necessity for the fleeing-felon rule came into question.[24] Many states modified their criminal laws, narrowing the range of fleeing suspects that police were authorized to shoot.

Then the Supreme Court's 1985 decision in *Tennessee* v. *Garner*[25] greatly curtailed the use of deadly force. The Court held that the use of deadly force to prevent the escape of all felony suspects was constitutionally unreasonable. It is not better, the Court reasoned, that all felony suspects die than that they escape. Where the suspect poses no immediate threat to the officer or to others, the harm resulting from failing to apprehend him or her does not justify the use of deadly force to do so. In short, the Fourth Amendment prohibits the seizure of an unarmed, nondangerous suspect by means of deadly force.

Only recently has any meaningful attempt been made to examine or control the use of deadly force by police officers. Before the 1970s, police officers had tremendous discretion regarding their use of firearms, and police departments often had poorly defined or nonexistent policies on this issue. Investigations of police shootings were sometimes conducted halfheartedly, and police agencies did not always keep records of all firearm discharges by officers.[26] This situation has changed dramatically. First, many states modified the old fleeing-felon doctrine that had allowed police to use deadly force to prevent a suspected felon from escaping. Second, the U.S. Supreme Court ruled that shootings of any unarmed, nonviolent fleeing felony suspects violated the Fourth Amendment to the Constitution. Third, almost all major urban police departments enacted restrictive policies regarding deadly force. And finally, the Supreme Court made it easier for a private citizen to successfully sue and collect damages after a questionable police shooting.[27]

The misuse of firearms, generally, is discussed more fully later in this chapter.

Further Sources of Tension: Bias-Based Policing and Other Field Tactics

Bias-based policing—also known as "driving while black or brown" (DWBB)—involves unequal treatment of any person on the basis of race, ethnicity, religion, gender, sexual orientation, or socioeconomic status. This issue has driven a deep wedge between the police and minorities, many of whom claim to be victims of this practice. Indeed, the New Jersey governor fired the state police superintendent in March 1999 for statements concerning biased policing that were perceived as racially insensitive.

In today's climate, there is considerable pressure on the police to be watchful of certain minorities who live in our nation and might do us harm. Indeed, since September 11, 2001, law enforcement's targeting of Arabs and Muslims, in their search for suspected terrorists, is viewed by two-thirds of Americans as "understandable."[28]

Incidents of bias-based policing can take various forms, as demonstrated by the following accounts by people who were stopped by police on questionable grounds and subjected to disrespectful behavior or intrusive questioning:

- A young African-American woman traded her new sports car for an older model because police repeatedly stopped her on suspicion of possessing a stolen vehicle.
- An elderly African-American couple returning from a social event in formal dress were stopped and questioned at length, allegedly because their car resembled one identified in a robbery.
- A prominent African-American lawyer driving a luxury car was frequently stopped on various pretexts.
- A Hispanic deputy police chief was stopped various times in neighboring jurisdictions on "suspicion."
- An African-American judge far from her hometown was stopped, handcuffed, and laid facedown on the pavement while police searched her car. (They issued no citations.)[29]

Some police executives defend officers' selective stopping of citizens as effective crime fighting, based not on prejudice but on probabilities—or the statistical reality that certain people are disproportionately likely to commit crimes. As explained by Bernard Parks, former African-American police chief of Los Angeles,

> We have an issue of violent crime against jewelry salespeople. The predominant suspects are Colombians. We don't find Mexican-Americans, or blacks, or other immigrants. It's a collection of several hundred Colombians who commit this crime. If you see six in a car in front of the Jewelry Mart, and they're waiting and watching people with briefcases, should we play the percentages and follow them? It's common sense.[30]

Still, bias-based policing has become a despised police practice in the new millennium. Profiling on the basis of race is given no public

EXHIBIT 10-5

Sacramento Searches for Biased Policing

In the late 1990s, the Sacramento, California, Police Department (SPD) began a study on racially biased policing. The goal was to determine the degree of intrusiveness of traffic stops and whether or not such stops were indicative of racially biased policing. Even though there were no reported complaints of such policing, the SPD recognized the importance of responding to national concern about the problem. The researchers began by collecting reports, editorials, and anecdotal information for insight into approaches taken by other agencies. Meetings were held with the community, civil rights organizations, the police union, and agency staff. Officers were invited to provide input on how to conduct the study. The SPD also invited the American Civil Liberties Union, the Mexican American Legal Defense and Education Fund, and neighborhood associations to participate.

Once the study began, officers filled out data-collection forms for each traffic stop, which included the officer's badge number, age, race, and unit assignment. The study examined data on traffic patterns and type of crimes throughout the city.

In the end, the SPD came to the conclusion that rarely could an officer identify the race of the driver or occupants of cars before they were actually stopped. The study did find that traffic stops involving African-Americans occurred at a disproportionately higher rate than their overall population, so the study was extended for two years in order to examine whether systems existed that encouraged bias-based policing. Now, as part of its community policing program, "Police as Problem Solvers/Peacemakers Initiative," the SPD is providing technical assistance to other local police agencies interested in collecting data on biased policing.

Source: Adapted from Tammy Jones, "Sacramento Searches for Bias Policing," in *Community Links* (Washington, DC: Community Policing Consortium, February 2003), pp. 1–2.

support. The best defense for the police may be summarized in two words: *collect data*. Collecting traffic stop data helps chiefs and commanders to determine whether officers are stopping or searching a disproportionate number of minorities and enables them to act on this information right away. Technology—including mobile data computers and wireless handheld devices—can be used for this purpose.

Exhibit 10-5 shows what the Sacramento, California, Police Department has done to study and address biased policing, although no such complaints had been reported in the city.

Other police field practices, such as the following, can be sources of tension between minorities and police as well:

> *Delay in responding to calls for service:* Studies of police work have found that patrol officers sometimes delay responding to calls for service, especially in cases of family disturbances.[31] Although this delay may be justified on grounds of officer safety (that is, an officer must await backup) and while these studies did not demonstrate any pattern of racial bias, delays do not improve public perceptions of the police.

Verbal abuse, epithets, and other forms of disrespect: Offensive labels for people are a regular aspect of the working language of some police officers. One study found that 75 percent of all officers used some racially offensive words, most of which were not uttered in the presence of citizens; however, police openly ridicule and belittle citizens in 5 percent of all encounters.[32] In some situations, the police use the terms as a control technique, in an attempt to establish their authority.[33] Nonetheless, verbal abuse should be avoided at all times.

Excessive questioning and frisking of minority citizens: Allegations of harassment by police are often raised by racial minorities who believe they have been unnecessarily subjected to field interrogations. Many officers, because they are trained to be suspicious and must often confront individuals in questionable circumstances, regard such activities as legitimate and effective crime-fighting tactics.

Discriminatory patterns of arrest and traffic citations: African-Americans are arrested more often than whites relative to their numbers in the population.[34] African-American complainants request arrests more often than whites. Since most incidents are intraracial, this can result in more arrests of African-Americans.[35] Police have been found more likely to arrest both white and African-American suspects in low-income areas. Insofar as African-Americans are disproportionately represented among the poor, however, this factor is likely to result in a disproportionately high arrest rate for African-Americans.[36]

Excessive use of physical force: Police have been found to use force in about 5 percent of all encounters involving offenders. In about two-thirds of the incidents involving force, its application was judged to be reasonable. White and African-American officers used excessive force at nearly the same rate. It is known that "a sizable minority of citizens experience police misconduct at one time or another."[37] The result, of course, is that many racial minorities perceive that their race is being unduly brutalized. And, to them, perception is reality.

A Related Issue: Domestic Violence

A 1996 federal law, entitled the Domestic Violence Offender Gun Ban (popularly known as the **Lautenberg Amendment**), bars anyone—including police and military personnel—from carrying firearms if they have a conviction for domestic violence. Although no figures are available regarding loss of jobs, that has been the case for hundreds of police officers across the nation. In many cases, officers found to have past misdemeanor convictions have lost their jobs.[38]

No one denies that a police officer who beats a spouse or child should be fired. The ban's supporters maintain that the police must also be held accountable when they commit any type of domestic violence and that their easy access to firearms can cause a domestic argument to escalate to homicide.[39] However, critics of the law, including many politicians, police associations, and unions, argue that the law is too broad.

Assume, for example, that a police officer tells her fifteen-year-old son that he cannot leave the house and hang out with some kids she knows to be using drugs. He attempts to leave and calls her some names, so she grabs him by the arm and sits him down. Except for a bruise on his arm, he is not injured, but he calls the police, a report is filed, and she is convicted of misdemeanor assault in a trial by judge with no right to trial by jury. Because of the domestic-violence law, she loses her right to carry a gun, and thus her career is ended.[40] Because police agencies typically have no unarmed positions, the law in effect ends the careers of officers who are affected by it.

The issue is not whether abusive police officers should be fired, but whether the law as it is written is effective and legal. Several state lawsuits have challenged the constitutionality of the law, including lawsuits by the National Association of Police Officers (which argues that officers are being "sacrificed on the altar of political correctness"[41]). In August 1998, the U.S. Court of Appeals for the District of Columbia Circuit exempted police and federal law enforcement agents within its jurisdiction from the law.

POLICE CORRUPTION

A Long-Standing "Plague" on Policing

"For as long as there have been police, there has been **police corruption**."[42] Thus observed Lawrence Sherman about the oldest and most persistent problem in American policing. To make the point, corruption has long plagued the New York City Police Department, as determined by the Knapp Commission, which investigated police corruption there in the early 1970s.[43] Knapp's 1973 report stated that there are two primary types of corrupt police officers: the "meat-eaters" and the "grass-eaters." Meat-eaters, who probably constitute a small percentage of police officers, spend a good deal of their working hours aggressively seeking out situations that they can exploit for financial gain, including gambling, narcotics, and other lucrative enterprises. No change in attitude is likely to affect meat-eaters; their income is so large that the only way to deal with them is to get them off the force and prosecute them. Grass-eaters constitute the overwhelming majority of those officers who accept payoffs. They are not aggressive but will accept gratuities from contractors, tow-truck operators, gamblers, and the like.

The Knapp Commission also identified several factors that influence how much graft police officers receive, the most important of these being the character of the individual officer. The branch of the department and the type of assignment also affect opportunities for corruption. Typically, plainclothes officers have more varied opportunities than uniformed patrol officers, and uniformed officers located in beats with, say, several vice dens will have more opportunities for payoffs. Another factor is rank; the amount of the payoff received generally ascends proportionally with rank.

Police corruption can be defined broadly, from major forms of police wrongdoing to the pettiest forms of improper behavior. Another definition is "the misuse of authority by a police officer in a manner designed to produce personal gain for the officer or for others."[44] Police corruption is not limited to monetary gain, however. Gains may be made through the acceptance of services received, status, influence, prestige, or future support for the officer or someone else.[45]

Events like those described in Los Angeles and other cities have focused attention on the broader issue of rogue cops in police departments across the country, especially in minority neighborhoods.[46] The brazenness and viciousness of today's corrupt police officers trouble even their staunchest defenders.

Types and Causes

Several factors contribute to police corruption, among them the rapid hiring of personnel, civil service and union protections that make it difficult to fire officers,[47] and temptations from money and sex.

Two theories—the "rotten apple" theory and the "environmental" theory—have been suggested to explain police corruption. The rotten apple theory holds that corruption is the result of having a few bad apples in the barrel who probably had character defects prior to employment. The environmental theory suggests that corruption is more the result of a widespread politically corrupt environment; politically corrupt cities create an environment in which police misconduct flourishes.[48]

Police corruption takes two basic forms: external and internal. The external form includes those activities (such as gratuities and payoffs) that occur from and through police contacts with the public. Internal corruption involves the relationships among police officers within the workings of the police department; this includes payments to join the police force, for better shifts or assignments, for promotions, and the like.[49]

Ellwyn Stoddard, who coined the term "blue-coat crime," described several different forms of deviant practices among both police and citizens. In the following list, those coming first would probably elicit the least fear of prosecution, and those at the end would probably invoke major legal ramifications:

Mooching: Receiving free coffee, meals, liquor, groceries, laundry services, and so forth.

Chiseling: Demanding free admission to entertainment or price discounts on goods and services.

Favoritism: Using license tabs, window stickers, or courtesy cards to gain immunity from traffic arrest.

Prejudice: Behaving less than impartially toward minority group members or others who are less likely to have influence in city hall.

Bribery: Receiving payments of cash or gifts for past or future assistance in avoiding prosecution; also includes political payoffs for favoritism in promotions. Police officers who accept payoffs or protection money are said to be "on the pad."

Shakedown: Stealing expensive items for personal use and attributing the loss to criminal activity when investigating a burglary or unlocked door.

Perjury: Following the "code" that demands that officers lie to provide an alibi for fellow officers apprehended in unlawful activity.

Premeditated theft: Planned burglaries that involve the use of tools or keys to gain entry; any prearranged act of unlawful acquisition of property that cannot be explained as a "spur of the moment" theft.[50]

The most common and extensive form of corruption involves the receipt by police officers of small gratuities or tips. Officers may regard discounts and free services as relatively unimportant, while the payment of cash—bribery—is a very different matter.[51] Former New York Police Commissioner Patrick V. Murphy was one of those who "drew the short line," telling his officers that "except for your paycheck, there is no such thing as a clean buck."[52] Such police officials would argue that even the smallest gratuities can create an expectation of some patronage or favor in return. Retail establishments do not offer gratuities to other persons in professional positions (e.g., doctors, lawyers, educators) for performing their duties, and the argument can certainly be made that the police should be similarly viewed and treated.

Another serious form of police corruption is related to drugs. Until the 1960s, most police corruption was associated with the protection of gambling operations, illegal liquor establishments, prostitution, and similar "victimless" activities. More recently, however, drug-related police corruption has probably surpassed those earlier forms of deviance. A typology of drug-related corruption has been developed by David Carter, who believes that the numbers of such cases "have notably increased":[53]

Type I drug corruption occurs when an officer seeks to use his or her position simply for personal gain. This type of drug corruption includes the following: giving information to drug dealers about investigations, names of informants, planned raids, and so forth; accepting bribes from drug dealers in exchange for nonarrest, evidence tampering, or perjury; theft of drugs from the police property room for personal consumption; "seizure" of drugs for personal use without arresting the person possessing the drugs; taking the profits of drug dealers' sales or their drugs for resale; extorting drug traffickers for money or property in exchange for nonarrest or nonseizure of drugs.

Type II drug corruption involves the officer's search for legitimate goals and may not even be universally perceived as being corrupt. "Gain" may involve organizational benefit—perhaps a form of "winning" or "revenge." Included are such actions as giving false statements to obtain arrest or search warrants against suspected or known drug dealers; perjury during hearings and trials of drug dealers; "planting," or creating evidence against known drug dealers; entrapment; and falsely spreading rumors that a dealer is a police informant in order to endanger that person.

The Code of Silence

Patrick V. Murphy wrote that "the most difficult element to overcome in the fight against corruption in the department was the code of silence."[54] This **code of silence**—keeping quiet in the face of misconduct by other officers—has been well documented. Evidence of the fraternal bond that exists in policing was found by William Westley as early as 1970, when more than 75 percent of the officers surveyed said that they would not report another officer for taking money from a prisoner, nor would they testify against an officer accused by a prisoner.[55] (In a related vein, see Exhibit 10-1.)

Officer Jack Smith finds himself in a moral dilemma. He knows of another officer's misconduct; he witnessed the officer putting expensive ink pens in his pocket while securing an unlocked office supply store on the graveyard shift. If reported, the misconduct will ruin the officer, but if not reported, the behavior could eventually cause enormous harm. To outsiders, this is not a dilemma at all; the only proper path is for Smith to report the misconduct. To philosophers, the doctrines of utilitarianism (the ethic of good consequences) and deontology (the ethic of rights and duties) require that Officer Smith work to eliminate corruption. But the outsiders and the philosophers are not members of the close fraternity of police, nor do they have to depend on other officers for their own safety.

There are several arguments for and against Officer Smith's informing on his partner. Reasons for informing include the fact that the harm caused by a scandal would be outweighed by the public's knowing that the police department is free of corruption; also, individual episodes of corruption would be brought to a halt. The officer, moreover, has a sworn duty to uphold the law. Any employee has a right to be allowed to do his or her duty, including blowing the whistle on employers or colleagues. Reasons against Officer Smith's informing include the fact that a skilled police officer is a valuable asset whose social value far outweighs the damage done by moderate corruption. Also, discretion and secrecy are obligations assumed by joining and remaining within the police fraternity; dissenters should resign rather than inform. Furthermore, it would be unjust to inflict punishment of dismissal and disgrace on an otherwise decent officer.[56]

How does one reconcile these two varying points of view? Probably the first thing to do is to realize that each view is morally defensible. A person who is in charge of investigating police corruption would no doubt be warmer toward the punitive view, while at the other extreme would be the person who would overlook such behaviors at all times. The ideal position might be in the middle—to maintain a commitment to professionalism and ethics without overreacting (for example, without insisting that officers report on their fellows every time they accept a cup of coffee).

The good news is that a recent survey by the National Institute of Justice found that about 83 percent of all officers in the United States do not accept the code of silence as an essential part of the mutual trust necessary to good policing.[57]

Investigation and Prosecution

Federal powers and jurisdiction for investigating and prosecuting police corruption were significantly expanded through the Hobbs Act in 1970. (See 18 U.S.C., Section 1955.) Two important elements of this federal statute that allow the investigation of police corruption are extortion and commerce. Whenever a police officer solicits a payoff from a legitimate business owner to overlook law violations (for example, a tavern owner who was selling alcohol to minors), extortion (involving fear) occurs, and that extortion affects legitimate commerce. The Hobbs Act may be employed by the prosecutor when these two elements are present. The meaning of extortion has been expanded so that it now covers most payoff arrangements that involve public officials.[58] The only areas of police corruption that may be beyond the reach of the Hobbs Act are internal corruption and the acceptance of isolated gratuities.

The federal perjury statute (18 U.S.C. 1621) and the federal false sworn declaration statute (18 U.S.C. 1623), both enacted in 1970, have also become powerful weapons for prosecutors in investigating public corruption. Both statutes deal with false testimony under oath, and in an investigation of corruption they are pertinent at the grand jury stage.[59]

Possible Solutions

There are several other possible measures for overcoming the pernicious effects of police corruption. In addition to the obvious need for an honest and effective police administration, it is also necessary to train recruits on the need for a corruption-free department. The creation and maintenance of an internal affairs unit and the vigorous prosecution of law-breaking police officers are also critical to maintaining the integrity of officers. Finally, there should be some mechanism for rewarding the honest police officers, which should minimally include protection from retaliation when they inform on crooked cops. All police officers should be given formal written guidelines on the departmental policy on soliciting and accepting gifts and gratuities. This apprises officers of the administration's view of such behavior and assists the chief executive in maintaining integrity and disciplining wayward officers. Figure 10-1 is an example of a good policy concerning gratuities.

Finally, computers can also assist with investigations of police corruption. Indeed, information that was uncovered about corruption within the Chicago Police Department was obtained through an $850 software program known as "Brainmaker," an early-warning program intended to

FIGURE 10-1 The gratuity policy of the Washoe County, Nevada, Sheriff's Office.

Courtesy Washoe County Sheriff's Office

1. Without the express permission of the Sheriff, members shall not solicit or accept any gift, gratuity, loan, present, or fee where there is any direct or indirect connection between this solicitation or acceptance of such gift and their employment by this office.
2. Members shall not accept, either directly or indirectly, any gift, gratuity, loan, fee, or thing of value, the acceptance of which might tend to improperly influence their actions, or that of any other member, in any matter of police business, or which might tend to cast an adverse reflection on the Sheriff's Office.
3. Any unauthorized gift, gratuity, loan, fee, reward, or other thing falling into any of these categories coming into the possession of any member shall be forwarded to the member's commander, together with a written report explaining the circumstances connected therewith. The commander will decide the disposition of the gift.

flag at-risk officers before they commit acts that could get them arrested or fired. With this type of approach, at-risk officers can be provided with counseling before serious problems occur.[60]

Limitations on Officers' Constitutional Rights

Police officers are generally afforded the same rights, privileges, and immunities outlined in the U.S. Constitution for all citizens. However, by virtue of their position, they may be compelled to give up certain rights in connection with an investigation of on-duty misbehavior or illegal acts. These rights are the basis for legislation such as the Peace Officers' Bill of Rights (discussed in Chapter 12), labor agreements, and civil service and departmental rules and regulations that guide an agency's disciplinary process.

Following is a brief overview of some areas in which the federal courts have placed **limitations on officers' constitutional rights** and have held sworn officers more accountable by virtue of the higher standard required by their occupation.

Free Speech

Although the right of freedom of speech is one of the most fundamental and cherished of all American rights, the Supreme Court has indicated that "the State has interests as an employer in regulating the speech of its employees that differ significantly from those it possesses in connection with regulation of the speech of the citizenry in general."[61] Thus the state may impose restrictions on its police employees that it would not be able to impose on civilians. However, these restrictions must be reasonable. For example, a department may not prohibit "any activity, conversation, deliberation, or discussion which is derogatory to the Department," as such a rule obviously prohibits all criticism of the agency by its officers, even in private conversation.[62]

Some police agencies maintain an internal affairs division for investigating citizen complaints against officers.

(Reno, Nevada, Police Department)

Another First Amendment–related area is that of personal appearance. The Supreme Court has upheld several grooming standards for officers (regarding the length of hair, sideburns, and mustaches) to make officers readily recognizable to the public and to maintain the esprit de corps within the department.[63]

Searches and Seizures

The Fourth Amendment to the U.S. Constitution protects "the right of the people to be secure in their persons, houses, papers, and effects, against unreasonable searches and seizures." The Fourth Amendment usually applies to police officers when they are at home or off duty in the same manner as it applies to all citizens. However, because of the nature of their work, police officers can be compelled to cooperate with investigations of their behavior when ordinary citizens would not. For example, regarding equipment and lockers provided by the department to the officers, the officers have no expectation of privacy that affords or merits protection.[64]

However, lower courts have established limitations on searches of employees themselves. The question of whether prison authorities have the right to search their employees arose in a 1985 Iowa case in which employees were forced to sign a consent form as a condition of hire. The court disagreed with such a broad policy, ruling that the consent form did not constitute a blanket waiver of all Fourth Amendment rights.[65]

Police officers may also be forced to appear in a lineup, a clear "seizure" of their person.

Self-Incrimination

The Supreme Court has addressed questions concerning the Fifth Amendment as it applies to police officers who are under investigation. In ***Garrity* v. *New Jersey***,[66] a police officer was ordered by the attorney general to answer questions or be discharged. The officer testified that information obtained as a result of his answers was later used to convict him of criminal charges. The Supreme Court held that the information obtained from the officer could not be used against him at his criminal trial because the Fifth Amendment forbids the use of coerced confessions.

However, it is proper to fire a police officer who refuses to answer questions that are related directly to the performance of his or her duties, provided that the officer has been informed that any answers may not be used later in a criminal proceeding.[67]

Religious Practices

Police work requires that personnel be available and on duty twenty-four hours a day, seven days a week. Although it is not always convenient or pleasant, shift configurations require that many officers work weekends, nights, and holidays. It is generally assumed that an officer who takes such a position agrees to work such hours and abide by other such conditions; it is usually the personnel with the least seniority on the job who must work the most undesirable shifts. However, there are occasions when the requirements of the job interfere with an officer's ability to attend religious services or observe religious holidays. The carrying of firearms may even conflict with an officer's beliefs. In these situations, the employee may be forced to choose between his or her job and religion.

Title VII of the Civil Rights Act of 1964 prohibits religious discrimination in employment. It requires reasonable accommodation of religious beliefs but not to the extent that the employee has complete freedom of religious expression.[68]

Sexual Misconduct

To be blunt, there is ample opportunity for police officers to become engaged in adulterous or extramarital affairs. Few other occupations or professions offer the opportunities for sexual misconduct that police work does. Police officers frequently work alone, usually without direct supervision, in activities that involve frequent contact with citizens, usually in relative isolation. The problem seems to be pervasive in police departments of all sizes. Unfortunately, it is also an area of police behavior that is not easily quantified or understood.[69]

Allen Sapp suggested several possible categories of sexually motivated behaviors by police officers (again, the extent to which each occurs is unknown):[70]

Sexually motivated nonsexual contacts: Officers initiate contacts with female citizens, without probable cause or any legal basis, for the purpose of obtaining names and addresses for possible later contact.

Voyeuristic contacts: Officers seek opportunities to view unsuspecting women partially clad or nude, such as in parked cars on "lovers' lanes."

Contacts with crime victims: A wide variety of behavior can occur, including unnecessary callbacks to homes of female victims, bodily contact with accident victims, and sexual harassment by officers.

Contacts with offenders: Officers may also harass female offenders by conducting body searches and pat-downs or frisks.

Sexual shakedowns: Officers may demand sexual services from prostitutes or other citizens.

Citizen-initiated sexual contacts: "Police groupies"—often young women who are sexually attracted to the uniform, weapons, or power of the police officer—may seek to participate in sexual activities with officers. This category may also include offers of sexual favors in return for preferential treatment or calls to officers from lonely or mentally disturbed women seeking officers' attention.

Sex crimes by officers: Officers may sexually assault jail inmates and citizens.

In a related vein, several federal courts have recently considered whether police agencies have a legitimate interest in the sexual activities of their officers when such activities affect job performance. In one such case, the court held that the dismissal of a married police officer for living with another man's wife was a violation of the officer's privacy and associational rights.[71]

Other courts, however, have found that off-duty sexual activity can affect job performance. When a married city police officer was found to be having consensual sexual relations with unmarried women other than his wife, the department contended that the officer's conduct—which became public—severely damaged public confidence in the department. A Utah court held that adultery was not a fundamental right and refused to strike down a statute criminalizing adultery.[72] And in a Texas case, when a male officer's extramarital affair led to his being passed over for promotion, the city civil service commission, the Texas Supreme Court, and the U.S. Supreme Court upheld the denial. They concurred with the city police chief's argument that such a promotion would adversely affect the efficiency and morale of the department and would be disruptive.[73]

Residency Requirements

Many government agencies specify that all or certain members in their employ must live within the geographic limits of their jurisdiction. In other words, employees must reside within the county or city of employment. Such residency requirements have been justified on the grounds that officers should become familiar with and be visible in the jurisdiction of employment or that they should reside where they are paid by the taxpayers to work. Perhaps the strongest rationale given by employing agencies is that criminal justice employees must live near their work so they can respond quickly in the event of an emergency.

Moonlighting

To *moonlight* means to hold a second job in addition to one's normal full-time occupation. The courts have traditionally supported the limitations police agencies have placed on the amount and kinds of outside work their employees can perform.[74] For example, police restrictions on moonlighting range from a complete ban on outside employment to permission to engage in certain forms of work, such as investigations, private security, and police science education. The rationale for agency limitations is that "outside employment seriously interferes with keeping the [police and fire] departments fit and ready for action at all times."[75]

Misuse of Firearms

Police agencies typically attempt to restrain the use of firearms through written policies and frequent training of a "shoot/don't shoot" nature. Still, a broad range of potential and actual problems remains with respect to the use and possible misuse of firearms. Police agencies generally have policies regulating the use of handguns and other firearms by their officers, both on and off duty. The courts have held that such regulations need only be reasonable and that the burden rests with the disciplined police officer to show that the regulation was arbitrary and unreasonable.[76]

Police firearms regulations may address several basic topics: shooting in defense of life, shooting to stop fleeing felons, identifying juveniles, shooting at or from vehicles, firing warning shots, shooting animals, carrying secondary weapons, carrying weapons off duty, and registering weapons.[77] Next we briefly discuss each of these topics.

Following the 1985 *Tennessee* v. *Garner* decision, discussed earlier, firearms policies are likely to be written from the "defense-of-life" perspective, which permits shooting only to defeat an imminent threat to an officer's life or to another person's life (as opposed to previous policies which included and allowed for the killing of fleeing felons).[78] Regarding juveniles, agencies generally do not instruct their officers to make a distinction between adults and juveniles when using deadly force. This is based on the pragmatic view that an armed juvenile can kill as well as an adult and that it is often impossible to tell if an offender is a juvenile or an adult.[79]

Shooting at or from moving vehicles has been severely limited in recent years. Some of the reasons include difficulty in hitting the target, ricochets striking innocent bystanders, difficulty in penetrating the automobile body and tires, and injuries and damages that might result should the vehicle go out of control.[80] A general consensus among police administrators is that warning shots should be prohibited, as they might strike an innocent person.[81] From a safety standpoint, "what goes up, must come down," and even firing a warning shot into the ground or into a tree, if allowed at all, is restricted to only a few kinds of situations.

Police agencies generally allow their officers to kill animals in self-defense or to prevent substantial harm to others, or when the animal is injured so badly that humanity requires its relief from suffering.[82] Secondary, or "backup," weapons are generally permitted in case officers are disarmed during a confrontation and so they can less conspicuously be prepared to protect themselves during routine citizen stops. A concern is that backup weapons may be used as "throwaways" in the event that an officer shoots an unarmed suspect, but the practice is generally accepted as long as the weapons are registered.[83] Similarly, carrying weapons off duty has also been controversial; however, given that while in their jurisdictions they are viewed as being on duty twenty-four hours a day, officers are generally allowed to carry such weapons, provided the weapons are registered and officers qualify on the pistol range regularly with them.[84]

Finally, most agencies require their officers to use only department-approved weapons on and off duty and may require that the weapons be inspected, fired, and certified by the department's armorer. In addition, some agencies require that the firearms be registered by make, model, serial number, and even ballistics sample.[85]

Courts and juries are increasingly becoming more harsh in dealing with police officers who misuse their firearms. The current tendency is to investigate police shootings to determine whether the officer acted negligently or whether the employing agency was negligent in training and supervising the officer.

Alcohol and Drug Abuse

Alcoholism and drug abuse problems are much more acute when they involve police employees. It is obvious, given the law of most jurisdictions and the nature of their work, that police officers must not be walking time bombs; they must be able to perform their work with a clear head that is unbefuddled by alcohol or drugs.[86] Police departments typically specify in their policy manual that no alcoholic beverages may be consumed within a specified period prior to reporting for duty. Such regulations have uniformly been upheld as rational because of the hazards of police work.

Enforcing such regulations occasionally means that police employees are ordered to submit to drug or alcohol tests. In 1989, the U.S. Supreme Court issued a major decision on drug testing: *National Treasury Employees Union* v. *Von Raab*,[87] which dealt with drug-testing plans for U.S.

customs workers. This decision addressed all three of the most controversial drug-testing issues: whether testing should be permitted when there is no indication of a drug problem in the workplace, whether the testing methods are reliable, and whether a positive test proves there was on-the-job impairment.[88]

The Supreme Court held that although only a few customs employees tested positive, drug use is such a serious problem that the program was warranted. Second, the Court found nothing wrong with the testing protocol. And, finally, while tests may punish and stigmatize a person for extracurricular drug usage that may have no effect on the worker's on-the-job performance, the Court indicated that this dilemma is still no impediment to testing.

Disciplinary Policies and Practices

Maintaining the Public Trust

Clearly, the public's trust and respect are precious commodities, quickly lost through improper behavior by police employees and the improper handling of an allegation of misconduct. Serving communities professionally and with integrity should be the goal of every police agency and its employees in order to ensure that trust and respect are maintained. The public expects that police agencies will make every effort to identify and correct problems and respond to citizens' complaints in a judicious, consistent, fair, and equitable manner.

Employee misconduct and violations of departmental policy are the two principal areas in which discipline is involved.[89] Employee misconduct includes acts that harm the public, such as corruption, harassment, brutality, and violations of civil rights. Violations of policy may involve a broad range of issues, from substance abuse and insubordination to minor violations of dress or tardiness.

Due Process Requirements

There are well-established minimum due process requirements for discharging public employees. Employees must

- Be afforded a public hearing
- Be present during the presentation of evidence against them and have an opportunity to cross-examine their superiors
- Have an opportunity to present their own witnesses and other evidence concerning their side of the controversy
- Be represented by counsel if they want
- Have an impartial referee or hearing officer presiding
- Have an eventual decision based on the weight of the evidence introduced during the hearing

Such protections apply to any disciplinary action that can significantly affect a police employee's reputation or future chances for special assignment or promotion.[90]

At times, police administrators determine that an employee must be disciplined or terminated. Grounds for discipline or discharge can vary widely from agency to agency. The agency's formal policies and procedures should specify what constitutes proper and improper behavior.

Dealing with Complaints

Origin of Complaint. A personnel **complaint** is an allegation of misconduct or illegal behavior against an employee by anyone inside or outside the organization. Internal complaints—those made from within the organization—may involve supervisors who observe officer misconduct, officers who complain about supervisors, civilian personnel who complain about officers, and so on. External complaints originate from outside the organization and usually involve the public.

Every complaint, regardless of the source, must be accepted and investigated in accordance with established policies and procedures. Anonymous complaints are the most difficult to investigate because there is no opportunity to obtain further information or to question the complainant about the allegation. Such complaints can have a negative impact on employee morale, as officers may view them as unjust and frivolous.

Types and Causes. Complaints may be handled informally or formally, depending on the seriousness of the allegation and the preference of the complainant. A formal complaint occurs when a written and signed or tape-recorded statement of the allegation is made and the complainant asks to be informed of the investigation's disposition. Figure 10-2 provides an example of a complaint form used to initiate a personnel investigation.

An informal complaint is an allegation of minor misconduct, made for informational purposes, that can usually be resolved without the need for more formal processes. The supervisor may simply discuss the incident with the employee and resolve it through informal counseling as long as more serious problems are not discovered and there is no history of similar complaints.

The majority of complaints against officers fall under the general categories of verbal abuse, discourtesy, harassment, improper attitude, and ethnic slurs.[91] It is clear that the verbal behavior of officers generates a significant number of complaints. Finally, minority citizens and those with less power and fewer resources are more likely to file complaints of misconduct and to allege more serious forms of misconduct than citizens with greater power and more resources.

FIGURE 10-2 Formal complaint form.

****

Control Number ___________

Date & Time Reported ________________ Location of Interview ________________ Interview _______Verbal ______ Written _______Taped

Type of complaint: _____Force _____Procedural _____Conduct _____Other (Specify)

Source of complaint: _____In Person _____ Mail _____Telephone _____Other (Specify)

Complaint originally Received by: _____Supervisor _____On Duty Watch Commander _____Chief _____IAU _____Other (Specify)

Notifications made: Received by: _______Division Commander _______Chief of Police _______On-Call Command Personnel _______Watch Commander _______Other (Sepcify)

Copy of formal personnel complaint given to complainant? _____Yes _____ No

****

Complainant's name: ________________ Address: ________________ Zip ________

Residence Phone: ________________ Business Phone: ________________

DOB: ________ Race: ________ Sex: ________ Occupation: ________

****

Location of Occurence: ________________ Date & Time of Occurrence: ________________

Member(s) Involved:
(1)________________
(3)________________

Member(s) Involved:
(2) ________________
(4) ________________

Witness(es) Involved:
(1)________________
(3)________________

Witness(es) Involved:
(2) ________________
(4) ________________

****

(1) ____ Complainant wishes to make a formal statement and has requested an investigation into the matter with a report back to him/her on the findings and actions.

(2) ____ Complainant wishes to adivise the Police Department of a problem, understands that some type of action will be taken, but does not request a report back to him/her on the findings and actions.

****

CITIZEN ADVISEMENTS

(1) If you have not yet provided the department with a signed written statement or a tape-recorded statement, one may be required in order to pursue the investigation of this matter.

(2) The complainant(s) and/or witness(es) may be required to take a polygraph examination in order to determine the credibility concerning the allegations made.

(3) Should the allegations prove to be false, the complainant(s) and/or witness(es) may be liable for criminal and/or civil prosecution.

________________ Signature of Complainant ________________ Date & Time

________________ Signature of Member Receiving Complaint

Receipt and Referral. Administrators must have a process for receiving complaints that is clearly delineated by departmental policy and procedures. Generally, a complaint is made at a police facility and is referred to a senior officer in charge to determine its seriousness and whether immediate intervention is needed.

In most cases, the senior officer will determine the nature of the complaint and will identify the employee involved; he or she then refers the matter to the employee's supervisor to conduct an initial investigation. The supervisor completes the investigation, recommends any discipline, and sends the matter to the internal affairs unit (IAU) and the agency head to finalize the disciplinary process. This method of review ensures that consistent and fair standards of discipline are applied.

The Investigative Process. Generally, the employee's supervisor will conduct a preliminary inquiry of the complaint, commonly known as "fact-finding." If it is determined that further investigation is necessary, the supervisor may question employees and witnesses, obtain written statements from those who were involved in the incident, and gather any necessary evidence, including photographs. Care must be exercised that the accused employee's rights are not violated. The initial investigation is sent to an appropriate division commander and forwarded to the IAU for review.

Making a Determination and Disposition. Once an investigation has been completed, the supervisor or IAU officer must make a determination about the culpability of the accused employee and report that determination to the administrator. The following categories of dispositions are commonly used:

Unfounded: The alleged act did not occur.

Exonerated: The act occurred, but it was lawful, proper, justified, or in accordance with departmental policies, procedures, rules, and regulations.

Not sustained: There is insufficient evidence to prove or disprove the allegation made.

Misconduct not based on the complaint: Sustainable misconduct was determined but is not a part of the original complaint. For example, a supervisor investigating an allegation of excessive force may find that the force used was within departmental policy but that the officer made an unlawful arrest.

Closed: An investigation may be halted if the complainant fails to cooperate or if it is determined that the action does not fall within the administrative jurisdiction of the police agency.

Sustained: The act did occur, and it was a violation of departmental rules and procedures. Sustained allegations include misconduct that falls within the broad outlines of the original allegation.

Once a determination of culpability has been made, the complainant should be notified of the department's findings. Details of the investigation or recommended punishment should not be included in the correspondence. As shown in Figure 10-3, the complainant will normally receive only information concerning the outcome of the complaint.

FIGURE 10-3 Citizen's notification-of-discipline letter.

POLICE DEPARTMENT
3300 Main Street
Downtown Plaza
Anywhere, U.S.A. 99999

June 20, 2002

Mr. John Doe
2200 Main Avenue
Anywhere, U.S.A.

Re: Internal Affairs #000666-98
Case Closure

Dear Mr. Doe,

Our investigation into your allegations against Officer Smith has been completed. It has been determined that your complaint is SUSTAINED, and the appropriate disciplinary action has been taken.

Our department appreciates your bringing this matter to our attention. It is our position that when a problem is identified, it should be corrected as soon as possible. It is our goal to be responsive to the concerns expressed by citizens so as to provide more efficient and effective services.

Your information regarding this incident was helpful and of value in our efforts to attain that goal. Should you have any further questions about this matter, please contact Sergeant Jane Alexander, Internal Affairs, at 555-9999.

Sincerely,

I.M. Boss
Lieutenant
Internal Affairs Unit

Appealing Disciplinary Measures. If an officer disagrees with a supervisor's recommendation for discipline, the first step of an appeal may involve a hearing before the division commander, who usually holds the rank of captain or deputy chief. The accused employee may be allowed labor representation or an attorney to assist in asking questions of the investigating supervisor, clarifying issues, and presenting new or mitigating evidence. If the employee is still not satisfied, an appeal hearing before the chief executive is granted. This is usually the final step in appeals within the agency. The chief or sheriff communicates a decision to the employee in writing. Depending on labor agreements and civil service rules and regulations, some agencies extend their appeals of discipline beyond the department. For example, employees may bring their issue before the civil service commission or city or county manager for a final review. Employees may also have the right to an independent arbiter's review.

Determining the Level and Nature of Sanctions

When an investigation against an employee is sustained, the sanctions and level of discipline must be decided. Management must be very careful when recommending and imposing discipline because of its impact on the overall morale of the agency's employees. If employees view the recommended discipline as too lenient, it may send the wrong message that the misconduct was insignificant. On the other hand, discipline that is viewed as too harsh may have a demoralizing effect on the officer involved and on other agency employees and may result in allegations that the leadership is unfair.

Listed here, in order of severity, are disciplinary actions that police agencies commonly use:

Counseling: This is usually a conversation between the supervisor and the employee about a specific aspect of the employee's performance or conduct. It is warranted when an employee has committed a relatively minor infraction or when the nature of the offense is such that oral counseling is all that is required. No documentation or report is placed in the employee's personnel file.

Documented oral counseling: This is usually the first step in a progressive disciplinary process and is intended to address relatively minor infractions. It takes place when the employee has had no previous reprimands or more severe disciplinary action of the same or similar nature.

Letters of reprimand: These are formal written notices regarding significant misconduct, more serious performance violations, or repeated offenses. It is usually the second step in the disciplinary process and is intended to provide the employee and the agency with a written record of the violation of behavior. It identifies what specific corrective action must be taken to avoid subsequent and more serious disciplinary action.

Suspension: This is a severe disciplinary action that results in an employee being relieved of duty, often without pay. It is usually administered when an employee commits a serious violation of established rules or after written reprimands have been given and no change in behavior or performance has resulted.

Demotion: In this situation, an employee is placed in a position of lower responsibility and pay. It is normally used when an otherwise good employee is unable to meet the standards required for the higher position or when the employee has committed a serious act requiring that he or she be removed from a position of management or supervision.

Termination: This is the most severe disciplinary action that can be taken. It usually occurs when previous serious discipline has been imposed and there has been inadequate or no improvement in behavior or performance. It may also occur when an employee commits an offense so serious that continued employment would be inappropriate.

Transfer: Many agencies use the disciplinary transfer to deal with problem officers; officers can be transferred to a different location or assignment, and this action is often seen as an effective disciplinary tool.[92]

SUMMARY

This chapter has examined the serious nature of police misbehavior and society's attempts to hold officers accountable. Police behavior is being closely scrutinized today. The police are held to a much higher standard of behavior than ordinary citizens, especially since incidents of misprision of office often harm innocent or undeserving people and receive national attention.

REVIEW QUESTIONS

1. Define ethics, and delineate some of the unique ethical problems that community policing can pose.
2. What are the types of police brutality? Can it ever be totally eliminated?
3. What are some factors that contribute to police violence? What is the U.S. Supreme Court precedent regarding police use of lethal force?
4. Define bias-based policing, and explain why it is a tinderbox in relations between minorities and police.
5. Review how and why police corruption began and what factors within both the community and policing seem to foster and maintain it.
6. Delineate the constitutional limitations that federal courts have placed on officers' rights and behavior.
7. Describe the general process that police agencies use to deal with citizen complaints.
8. Review some of the factors used to determine the level and nature of sanctions for officers who are to be disciplined.

INDEPENDENT STUDENT ACTIVITIES

1. Interview local police administrators or internal affairs investigators to determine their policy and philosophy concerning police gratuities. In general, how are their officers held accountable for their performance? What precautionary measures are taken to prevent graft and corruption? What policies are in place? What are the penalties for violation of these policies?
2. What process exists within the police department for investigating citizen complaints? Is there a citizen review board in your community? If so, what is its role and function? If not, would such a board be beneficial?
3. Using newspaper editorials or interviews, ascertain the level of citizen satisfaction with the police. What seems to be the greatest area of discontent toward the police? Do citizens feel that their police are a part of the community?

RELATED WEB SITES

Amnesty International USA
http://www.amnestyusa.org/countries/usa/document.do? id = 133746465C2D34CA8025690000692D98

Human Rights Watch
http://www.hrw.org

Institute for Criminal Justice Ethics
http://www.lib.jjay.cuny.edu/cje/html/policeethics.html

NOTES

1. "Good News, Better News on Use of Force," *Law Enforcement News*, March 15, 2001, p. 7.
2. "L.A. Police Corruption Case Continues to Grow," *Washington Post*, February 13, 2000, p. 1A.
3. SCOTT GLOVER and MATT LAIT, "LA Police Chief Issues Critical Review of Department," *Los Angeles Times*, February 5, 2000, p. 1A.
4. ANGIE CANNON, "Cop-Shop Woes in the Burbs," *U.S. News and World Report*, September 25, 2000, p. 26.
5. COURTLAND MILLOY, quoted in ibid.
6. KIT R. ROANE, "Policing the Police Is a Dicey Business: But the Feds Have a Plan to Root Out Racial Bias," *U.S. News and World Report*, April 30, 2001, p. 28.
7. *Webster's New World Dictionary* (New York: World, 1981), p. 389.
8. DEPARTMENT OF JUSTICE, National Institute of Justice, Office of Community Oriented Policing Services, *Police Integrity: Public Service with Honor* (Washington, DC: U.S. Government Printing Office, 1997), p. 62.
9. BRIAN WITHROW and JEFFREY D. DAILEY, "When Strings Are Attached: Understanding the Role of Gratuities in Police Corruptibility," in *Contemporary Policing Controversies, Challenges, and Solutions: An Anthology*, eds. QUINT THURMAN and JIHONG ZHAO (Los Angeles: Roxbury, 2004), pp. 319–326.
10. "No Free (or Discounted) Lunch for Bradenton Cops," *Law Enforcement News*, October 15, 2000, p. 6.
11. KENNETH J. PEAK, B. GRANT STITT, and RONALD W. GLENSOR, "Ethics in Community Policing and Problem Solving," *Police Quarterly* 1 (1998): 30–31.
12. L. MORRIS, *Incredible New York* (New York: Bonanza, 1951).
13. JAMES A. INCIARDI, *Criminal Justice*, 5th ed. (Orlando, FL: Harcourt Brace, 1996).
14. EGON BITTNER, "The Functions of the Police in Modern Society," in *Policing: A View from the Street*, ed. PETER K. MANNING and JOHN VAN MAANEN (Santa Monica, CA: Goodyear, 1978), pp. 32–50.

15. Ibid., p 36.
16. George F. Cole and Christopher E. Smith, *The American System of Criminal Justice*, 8th ed. (Belmont, CA: West/Wadsworth, 1998), p. 228.
17. A. C. Germann, Frank D. Day, and Robert R. J. Gallati, *Introduction to Law Enforcement and Criminal Justice* (Springfield, IL: Charles C. Thomas, 1976), p. 225.
18. Albert J. Reiss Jr., "Police Brutality: Answers to Key Questions," *Transaction* (July–August 1968): 10–19.
19. Ibid.
20. Germann, Day, and Gallati, *Introduction to Law Enforcement and Criminal Justice*, p. 225.
21. Ibid.; also see William Geller, "Deadly Force: What We Know," *Journal of Police Science and Administration* 10 (1982): 151–77.
22. Lawrence Sherman and Ellen G. Cohn, "Citizens Killed by Big City Police: 1970–84" (unpublished manuscript, Crime Control Institute, Washington, DC, October 1986).
23. James J. Fyfe, "Reducing the Use of Deadly Force: The New York Experience," in Department of Justice, *Police Use of Deadly Force* (Washington, DC: U.S. Government Printing Office, 1978), p. 28.
24. James J. Fyfe, Jack R. Greene, William F. Walsh, et al., *Police Administration*, 5th ed. (New York: McGraw-Hill, 1997), pp. 197–198.
25. Tennessee v. Garner, 471 U.S. 1, 105 S.Ct. 1694, 85 L.Ed.2d 1 (1985).
26. Mark Blumberg, "Controlling Police Use of Deadly Force: Assessing Two Decades of Progress," in *Critical Issues in Policing: Contemporary Readings*, eds. Roger G. Dunham and Geoffrey P. Alpert (Prospect Heights, IL: Waveland Press, 1989), pp. 442–64.
27. Monell v. Department of Social Services, 436 U.S. 658, 98 S.Ct. 2018 (1978).
28. "Since Sept. 11: Racial Profiling of Arabs and Muslims," http://www.publicagenda.org/specials/terrorism/terror_pubopinion6.htm (accessed April 28, 2003).
29. Lorie Fridell, Robert Lunney, Drew Diamond, et al., *Racially Based Policing: A Principled Response* (Washington, DC: Police Executive Research Forum, 2001), pp. 4–5.
30. Randall Kennedy, "Suspect Policy," *New Republic*, September 13, 1999, pp. 30–35.
31. Donald Black, *Manners and Customs of the Police* (New York: Academic Press, 1980), p. 117; and Richard J. Lundman, "Domestic Police-Citizen Encounters," *Journal of Police Science and Administration* 2 (March 1974): 25.
32. Jerome Skolnick, *The Police and the Urban Ghetto* (Chicago: American Bar Foundation, 1968).
33. Samuel Walker, *The Police in America: An Introduction* (New York: McGraw-Hill, 1983), p. 234.
34. Ibid., p. 235.
35. Robert Friedrich, "Racial Prejudice and Police Treatment of Blacks," in *Evaluating Alternative Law Enforcement Policies*, ed. Ralph Baker and Fred A. Meyers (Lexington, MA: Lexington Books, 1979), pp. 160–61.

36. Douglas A. Smith and Christy A. Visher, "Street-Level Justice: Situational Determinants of Police Arrest Decisions," *Social Problems* 29 (December 1981): 167–87.
37. Albert J. Reiss, *The Police and the Public* (New Haven: Yale University Press, 1971), p. 151.
38. "Beat Your Spouse, Lose Your Job," *Law Enforcement News*, December 31, 1997, p. 9.
39. Ibid.
40. Adapted from Jerry Hoover, "Brady Bill Unfair in Broad Approach to Police Officers," *Reno Gazette Journal*, September 25, 1998, p. 11A.
41. "Denver Cop's Case Galvanizes Opponents of Lautenberg Gun Ban," *Law Enforcement News*, February 14, 1999, p. 1.
42. Lawrence W. Sherman, ed., *Police Corruption: A Sociological Perspective* (Garden City, NY: Anchor, 1974), p. 1.
43. See Peter Maas, *Serpico* (New York: Viking, 1973).
44. Herman Goldstein, *Policing a Free Society* (Cambridge, Mass.: Ballinger, 1977), p. 188.
45. Ibid.
46. Gordon Witkin, "When the Bad Guys Are Cops," *Newsweek*, September 11, 1995, p. 20.
47. Ibid., p. 22.
48. Lawrence W. Sherman, "Becoming Bent," in *Moral Issues in Police Work*, ed. F. A. Elliston and M. Feldberg (Totowa, NJ: Rowan and Allanheld, 1985), pp. 253–65.
49. Christian P. Potholm and Richard E. Morgan, eds., *Focus on Police: Police in American Society* (New York: Schenkman, 1976), p. 140.
50. Ellwyn R. Stoddard, "Blue Coat Crime," in *Thinking about Police: Contemporary Readings*, ed. Carl B. Klockars (New York: McGraw-Hill, 1983), pp. 338–50.
51. Walker, *The Police in America*, p. 175.
52. "Police Aides Told to Rid Commands of All Dishonesty," *New York Times*, October 29, 1970.
53. David L. Carter, "Drug Use and Drug-Related Corruption of Police Officers," in *Policing Perspectives: An Anthology*, ed. Larry K. Gaines and Gary W. Cordner (Los Angeles: Roxbury, 1999), pp. 311–23.
54. Patrick V. Murphy and Thomas Plate, *Commissioner: A View from the Top of American Law Enforcement* (New York: Simon and Schuster, 1977), p. 226.
55. William A. Westley, *Violence and the Police* (Cambridge, MA: MIT Press, 1970), pp. 113–14.
56. Thomas E. Wren, "Whistle-Blowing and Loyalty to One's Friends," in *Police Ethics: Hard Choices in Law Enforcement*, ed. William C. Heffernan (New York: John Jay Press, 1985), pp. 25–43.
57. David Weisburd and Rosanne Greenspan, *Police Attitudes toward Abuse of Authority: Findings from a National Study* (Washington, DC: Department of Justice, National Institute of Justice Research in Brief, May 2000), p. 5.

58. See, for example, *UNITED STATES* v. *HYDE*, 448 F.2d 815 (5th Cir. 1971), cert. den., 404 U.S. 1058 (1972); *UNITED STATES* v. *ADDONIZIA*, 451 F.2d 49 (3d Cir.), cert. den., 405 U.S. 936 (1972); and *UNITED STATES* v. *KENNEY*, 462 F.2d 1205 (3d Cir.) as amended, 462 F.2d 1230 (3d Cir.), cert. den., 409 U.S. 914 (1972).
59. HERBERT BEIGEL, "The Investigation and Prosecution of Police Corruption," in POTHOLM and MORGAN, eds., *Focus on Police*, pp. 139–66.
60. "Artificial Intelligence Tackles a Very Real Problem—Police Misconduct Control," *Law Enforcement News*, September 30, 1994, p. 1.
61. PICKERING v. BOARD OF EDUCATION, 391 U.S. 563 (1968), p. 568.
62. MULLER v. CONLISK, 429 F.2d 901 (7th Cir. 1970).
63. KELLEY v. JOHNSTON, 425 U.S. 238 (1976).
64. See PEOPLE v. TIDWELL, 266 N.E.2d 787 (Ill. 1971).
65. MCDONELL v. HUNTER, 611 F. Supp. 1122 (SD Iowa, 1985), affd. as mod., 809 F.2d 1302 (8th Cir. 1987).
66. GARRITY v. NEW JERSEY, 385 U.S. 483 (1967).
67. See GABRILOWITZ v. NEWMAN, 582 F.2d 100 (1st Cir. 1978).
68. UNITED STATES v. CITY OF ALBUQUERQUE, 12 EPD 11, 244 (10th Cir.); also see *TRANS WORLD AIRLINES* v. *HARDISON*, 97 S.Ct. 2264 (1977).
69. ALLEN D. SAPP, "Police Officer Sexual Misconduct: A Field Research Study," in *Crime and Justice in America: Present Realities and Future Prospects*, ed. PAUL F. CROMWELL and ROGER G. DUNHAM (Upper Saddle River, NJ: Prentice Hall, 1997), pp. 139–51.
70. Ibid.
71. See BRIGGS v. NORTH MUSKEGON POLICE DEPARTMENT, 563 F. Supp 585 (W.D. Mich. 1983), aff'd. 746 F.2d 1475 (6th Cir. 1984).
72. OLIVERSON v. WEST VALLEY CITY, 875 F. Supp.1465 (D. Utah 1995).
73. HENERY v. CITY OF SHERMAN, 928 S.W.2d 464 (Sup. Ct. Texas), cert. denied, 17 S.Ct. 1098 (1997).
74. See, for example, COX v. MCNAMARA, 493 P.2d 54 (Ore. 1972); BRENCKLE v. TOWNSHIP OF SHALER, 281 A.2d 920 (Pa. 1972); FLOOD v. KENNEDY, 239 N.Y.S.2d 665 (1963); and HOPWOOD v. CITY OF PADUCAH, 424 S.W.2d 134 (Ky. 1968).
75. RICHARD N. WILLIAMS, *Legal Aspects of Discipline by Police Administrators*, Traffic Institute Publication 2705 (Evanston, IL: Northwestern University, 1975), p. 4.
76. See LALLY v. DEPARTMENT OF POLICE, 306 So.2d 65 (La. 1974).
77. CHARLES R. SWANSON, LEONARD TERRITO, and ROBERT W. TAYLOR, *Police Administration*, 5th ed. (Upper Saddle River, NJ: Prentice Hall, 2005), p. 586.
78. Ibid.
79. Ibid.
80. KENNETH JAMES MATULIA, *A Balance of Forces: Model Deadly Force and Policy Procedure* (Alexandria, VA: International Association of Chiefs of Police, 1985), pp. 23–24.
81. CATHERIN H. MILTON, JEANNE WAHL HALLECK, JAMES LARNDEW, et al., *Police Use of Deadly Force* (Washington, DC: Police Foundation, 1977), p. 52.
82. MATULIA, *A Balance of Forces*, p. 52.

83. Ibid., p. 177.
84. Ibid.
85. Ibid., p. 78.
86. See KROLICK v. LOWERY, 302 N.Y.S.2d 109 (1969), p. 115; and HESTER v. MILLEDGEVILLE, 598 F.Supp. 1456, 1457 (M.D.Ga. 1984).
87. NATIONAL TREASURY EMPLOYEES UNION v. VON RAAB, 489 U.S. 656 (1989).
88. ROBERT J. AALBERTS and HARVEY W. RUBIN, "Court's Rulings on Testing Crack Down on Drug Abuse," *Risk Management* 38 (March 1991): 36–41.
89. V. MCLAUGHLIN and R. BING, "Law Enforcement Personnel Selection," *Journal of Police Science and Administration* 15 (1987): 271–76.
90. Ibid.
91. ALLEN E. WAGNER and SCOTT H. DECKER, "Evaluating Citizen Complaints against the Police," in ROGER G. DUNHAM and GEOFFREY P. ALPERT, eds., *Critical Issues in Policing: Contemporary Readings,* 3d ed. (Prospect Heights, IL: Waveland, 1989), pp. 302–318.
92. KENNETH J. PEAK, LARRY K. GAINES, and RONALD W. GLENSOR, *Police Supervision and Management: In an Era of Community Policing*, 2d ed. (Upper Saddle River, NJ: Prentice Hall, 2004), pp. 271–72.

CHAPTER

11

Civil Liability: Failing the Public Trust

All men are liable to error; and most men are . . . under temptation to it.

—John Locke

Where laws end, tyranny begins.

—William Pitt

Key Terms

Bivens tort
negligence
qualified immunity
respondeat superior
Section 242
Section 1983
sovereign immunity
stare decisis
tort liability
vicarious liability
wrongful death

Policing is a challenging occupation. The police must enforce the laws, perform welfare tasks, protect the innocent, and attempt to prevent crime. They see people at their worst and participate in searches and seizures, major incidents (such as hostage situations), and high-speed pursuits. They make split-second decisions. And they are custodians of offenders in local jails.

Legal actions can arise against the police in the course of these and many other kinds of actions. Perhaps no other occupation, with the exception of medicine, is as vulnerable to legal attack for the actions of its practitioners. Some observers believe that community-oriented policing and problem solving (COPPS, discussed in Chapter 6) could lead to an increase in civil liability filings because of the greater degree of involvement of police in the lives of citizens.[1]

This chapter discusses the current and developing laws that serve to make criminal justice practitioners legally accountable, both civilly and criminally, for acts of misconduct and negligence. For many years, this has been a rapidly growing area of litigation and body of legal precedent; lawyers are becoming very knowledgeable about the relevant statutes and court decisions, are more experienced, and are more willing to seek redress in the federal court system as they protect the rights of their clients.

It cannot be overstated how important it is for students of criminal justice and police personnel to know and understand the area of liability. It is far better to learn which police actions are blameworthy—and potentially costly—through education and training than to learn it as a defendant in a lawsuit. Today's police executives must be proactive and follow appropriate laws and guidelines in order to avoid legal difficulty; their failure to do so will place them and their jurisdiction at serious financial risk.

This chapter analyzes the legal history of federal civil liability suits, the kinds of police actions that promote liability suits, the liability of supervisors who fail to control their personnel, and some cases in which police officers have been criminally punished for misconduct. After a discussion of three expanding areas of potential liability—vehicle pursuits, handling computer evidence, and disseminating public information—the chapter concludes with a chapter summary, review questions, independent student activities, and related Web sites.

A Legal Foundation

Laws are enacted in three ways: by legislation, by regulation, and by court decision. Statutes and ordinances are laws passed by legislative bodies, such as the U.S. Congress, state legislatures, county commissions, and city councils. These bodies sometimes create a general outline of the laws they enact, leaving to a particular governmental agency the authority to fill in the details of the law through rules and regulations; during the past two decades, administrative rules and regulations constituted one of the fastest growing bodies of new law.

When the solution to a legal dispute cannot be found in the existing body of law—statutes, rules, or regulations—judges must rely on prior decisions that their own or other courts have made on similar issues. These judicial decisions are known as ***stare decisis;*** meaning "let the decision stand," and the judges who follow them are said to be relying on precedent.

Of course, prior court decisions can be overruled or modified by a higher court or by the passage of new legislation. Furthermore, judges sometimes create their own tests to fairly resolve an issue. Statutes, judicial decisions, and tests may differ greatly from state to state; therefore, it is important for lawyers or criminal justice practitioners to read and understand the laws as they apply in their own jurisdictions.

It is also important to have a basic understanding of **tort liability**. A tort is an injury inflicted upon one person by another. Three categories of torts generally cover most of the lawsuits filed against criminal justice practitioners: negligence, intentional torts, and constitutional torts.

Negligence arises when a police officer's conduct creates a danger to others. In other words, the officer did not conduct his or her affairs in a manner so as to avoid subjecting others to a risk of harm. The officer will be held liable for the injuries caused to others through his or her negligent acts. The law recognizes various levels or degrees of negligence: simple, gross, and willful or criminal negligence. Simple negligence involves a reasonable act performed by a reasonable officer in the scope of employment but performed without due care; the result is usually a charge of mental pain and anguish, for which an employer or an insurance company will pay damages. Gross negligence involves an unreasonable act for which damages for mental pain and anguish will be paid by either the employer (if the officer's acts were within the scope of employment) or the officer. Willful or criminal negligence involves an intentional act rather than negligence; the plaintiff will receive actual damages, plus mental pain and anguish damages, plus punitive damages. The damages will be paid by the individual officer only; neither the employer nor the insurance company will be compelled to pay.[2]

Intentional torts occur when an officer engages in a voluntary act that had a substantial likelihood of resulting in injury to another; examples are assault and battery, false arrest and imprisonment, malicious prosecution, and abuse of process. Constitutional torts involve police officers' duty to recognize and uphold the constitutional rights, privileges, and immunities of others; violations of these guarantees may subject the officer to civil suit, most frequently brought in federal court under 42 U.S.C. Section 1983, which is discussed later.[3]

Assault, battery, false imprisonment, false arrest, invasion of privacy, negligence, defamation, and malicious prosecution are examples of torts that are commonly brought against police officers.[4] False arrest is the arrest of a person without probable cause—an arrest that is made even though an ordinarily prudent person would not have concluded that a crime had been committed or that the person arrested had committed it. False imprisonment is the intentional illegal detention of a person, not only jailing but any confinement to a specified area. Most false arrest suits result in a false imprisonment charge as well, but a false imprisonment charge sometimes can follow a valid arrest. For example, the police might fail to release an arrested person after a proper bail or bond has been posted, they might delay the arraignment of an arrested person unreasonably, or they might fail to release a prisoner after they no longer have authority to hold him or her. "Brutality" is not a legal tort action per se; rather, it must be brought as a civil assault and/or battery.[5]

A single act may also be a crime as well as a tort. For example, if Officer Smith, in an unprovoked attack, injures Citizen Jones, the state will attempt to punish Smith in a criminal action by sending him to prison or fining him or both. The state would have the burden of proof at criminal trial, having to prove Smith guilty "beyond a reasonable doubt." Furthermore, Jones may sue Smith for money damages in a civil action for the personal injury he suffered. Jones would argue that Smith failed to carry out his duty to act reasonably and prudently and that this failure resulted in Jones's injury. This legal wrong, of course, is a tort; Jones would have the burden of proving Smith's acts were tortious by a "preponderance of the evidence"—a lower standard and thus easier to satisfy in civil court.

Our system of government has both federal and state courts. Federal courts are intended to have somewhat limited jurisdiction, and they tend not to hear cases involving private (as opposed to public) controversies unless federal law is involved or both parties agree to have their dispute settled there. Thus most tort suits are filed in state courts. There are two means by which a federal court may acquire jurisdiction of police misconduct suits. The first means is the predominant source of our later discussions, referred to as a "1983 suit." This name is derived from the fact that the suits are brought under the provisions of Title 42, Section 1983, of the U.S. Code. The significant part of this statute and its legislative history follow.

The second means by which a federal court may assume jurisdiction over a police misconduct suit is to allege what some legal commentators call a ***Bivens*** tort. This name derives from a 1971 case, *Bivens* v. *Six Unknown Named Agents of the Federal Bureau of Narcotics*.[6] The U.S. Supreme Court held that a civil suit based directly on the Fourth Amendment could be filed. In *Bivens*, federal narcotics agents conducted an illegal search, arrest, and interrogation, but a suit by the plaintiffs could not be filed under Section 1983 because that section covers only police agents acting under state law. Civil suits to recover damages for violations of constitutional rights by federal officers have thus become known as *Bivens* suits.

A preliminary question is "Who can sue whom?" Under common law, police officers were held personally liable for damage they caused to someone while exceeding the boundaries of permissible behavior. This law applied even when the officer was ignorant of the law. Today, this rule is the basis for one of the major risks of policing.[7]

A suit may also be filed against an employer under the doctrine of ***respondeat superior***, an old legal maxim meaning "let the master answer." This doctrine is also termed **vicarious liability**. In sum, an employer is liable in certain instances for the wrongful acts of the employee. It is generally inapplicable if a jury determines that the employee's negligent or malicious acts were outside the legitimate scope of the employer's authority. Although U.S. courts have expanded the extent to which employers can be sued for the torts of their employees, they are still reluctant to extend this doctrine to police supervisors (sergeants and lieutenants) and administrators. The courts realize that, first of all, police supervisors have little discretion in hiring decisions. Second, the duties of police officers are largely established by the governmental authority that hired them rather than by their supervisors. However, if a supervisor has abused his or her authority, was present when the misconduct occurred and did nothing to stop it, or otherwise participated in the misconduct, he or she can be held liable for the tortious behavior of his or her officers.[8] This issue is discussed at greater length later in this chapter.

Another issue that involves the question of who may be sued involves immunity and whether police department and the employing governmental unit can be sued for damages caused by police misconduct. Under common law, the government could not be sued, because the king could do no wrong; This doctrine, known as **sovereign immunity**, was also adopted in 1795 in the Eleventh Amendment to the U.S. Constitution, which says: "The judicial power of the United States shall not be construed to extend to any suit in law or equity, commenced or prosecuted against one of the United States by citizens of another state, or by citizens or subjects of any foreign state." This amendment therefore bars suits against states, state agencies, and instrumentalities in federal courts; the Supreme Court has also said it bars suits by citizens of the same state.[9]

Municipal governments, however, do not enjoy the same protection, as they are creations of state laws and, as such, are not truly "sovereigns." Thus, they do not enjoy blanket immunity and are only cloaked with immunity to the extent that the state sees fit to do so.[10]

History and Growth of Section 1983 Litigation

In the years following the Civil War, Congress, in reaction to the states' inability to control the Ku Klux Klan's lawlessness, enacted the Ku Klux Klan Act of 1871. This was later codified as Title 42, **Section 1983**, of the U.S. Code. Its statutory language is as follows:

> Every person who, under color of any statute, ordinance, regulation, custom, or usage of any State or Territory, subjects, or causes to be subjected, any citizen of the United States or any other person within the jurisdiction thereof to the deprivation of any rights, privileges, or immunities secured by the Constitution and laws, shall be liable to the party injured in an action at law, suit in equity, or other proper proceeding for redress.

This legislation was intended to provide civil rights protection to all "persons" protected under the act, when a defendant acted "under color of law" (misused power of office). It was also meant to provide an avenue to the federal courts for relief of alleged civil rights violations.

The original intent of the law did not include police misconduct litigation. In fact, the law was virtually ignored for ninety years, until the U.S. Supreme Court's decision in *Monroe* v. *Pape* in 1961.[11] In that case, thirteen members of the Chicago Police Department broke into a home without a warrant, forced the family out of bed at gunpoint, made them stand naked while the officers ransacked the house, and subjected the family to verbal and physical abuse. Monroe was then taken to the police station, where he was held incommunicado and questioned for ten hours before being released without charges. The plaintiffs (Monroe and his family) claimed that the officers acted "under color of law" as set forth in Section 1983, thus violating their constitutional rights. The U.S. Supreme Court agreed, holding the officers liable; however, the Court also held the city of Chicago immune from liability under the statute.

In the five-year period following *Monroe*, only a few police misconduct suits were filed in the federal courts under Section 1983. As an example, the New York City Police Department led the country in lawsuits during the five-year period from 1967 to 1972, but only 5 percent of those cases were brought to the federal forum.[12] There was a virtual boom of Section 1983 suits from 1967 through 1976, however. Studies conducted by a national group, Americans for Effective Law Enforcement, found that police misconduct suits in state courts rose from 1,556 in 1967 to 8,007 in 1976 (an increase of 415 percent). During the same period, however, federal civil rights actions alleging police misconduct rose from 167 to 2,226 (or an increase of 1,233 percent). Combining state and federal jurisdictions, misconduct suits grew from 5.5 per 1,000 officers to 19.6 per 1,000 in this ten-year period. And from 1972 through 1976, 32 percent of all legal actions were arrest related, and 32 percent alleged excessive nondeadly force.[13]

Several factors contributed to this surge in Section 1983 actions. First, some lawyers believe that clients receive more competent judges and juries in the federal forum than in state courts. Federal judges, who are appointed for life, may be less concerned about the political ramifications of their decisions than locally elected judges often are. Federal prosecutors may be more aggressive in arguing to jurors from a multicounty area; local prosecutors must argue to jurors who elected them and may know the defendant-officer. Furthermore, federal rules of pleading and evidence are uniform, federal procedures of discovery are more liberal, and lawyers have easier access to published case law in assisting them to prepare a federal suit.[14]

Just as important, Congress passed Section 1988 of the Civil Rights Act in 1976, which allows attorney's fees to the prevailing party over and above the award for compensatory and punitive damages. This provision in the law did as much to spur the use of Section 1983 as any other factor. Attorneys usually accept personal injury cases on a contingency basis. If they win, they receive one-third of the amount awarded. Thus a plaintiff's verdict in a police shooting case can be quite profitable; a lawsuit that may not have been worth the time and effort is now, thanks to Sections 1983 and 1988, potentially quite lucrative.

Initially, the Supreme Court concluded that Congress did not intend Section 1983 to apply to municipalities; the cities believed they had absolute immunity. However, in 1978, upon examining this question in *Monell* v. *Department of Social Services*,[15] the Court modified its earlier thinking. This decision has been another major factor in the increased use of Section 1983. In *Monell*, a class of female employees filed a Section 1983 suit alleging that their employers had, as a matter of official policy, forced female employees to take unpaid leaves of absence before such leaves were required for medical reasons. The Supreme Court overruled its previous decisions in *Monroe* and other cases, stating that Congress, in the Civil Rights Act of 1871, did intend that municipalities and other local governments be included as "persons" to whom Section 1983 applies. Local governing bodies and corporate "persons," therefore, can be sued for damages under Section 1983. *Monell* made it clear that an individual had legal recourse when he or she had been deprived of a right or privilege guaranteed under the Constitution and laws if such deprivation was the direct result of an official policy or custom of a local unit of government.

Defenses and immunities against Section 1983 suits exist, however. The states themselves, for example, are granted absolute immunity from Section 1983 suits,[16] as are judges, prosecutors, legislators, and federal officials. Federal officials usually act under color of federal law, as opposed to state law, as specified in the act. Police officers are granted **qualified immunity**, meaning that as long as they acted in "good faith" and their conduct was reasonable, they have a defense. Over the years, the courts have struggled to develop a test for "good faith." In 1975, the Supreme Court developed a test that considered both the officer's state of mind at the time of the act in question (the subjective element) and whether or not the officer's act violated clearly established legal rights (the objective element).[17] Overzealous conduct that is not undertaken in good faith and that occurs without regard for the rights of citizens can and will result in a finding of liability.

Police Actions Leading to Section 1983 Liability

As indicated in the introduction, probably no group of workers in the private or public sectors (with the exception of medical professionals) is more susceptible to work-related litigation and liability than police officers. The police are frequently cast into confrontational situations and, given the complex nature of their work, will from time to time act in a manner that provokes public scrutiny and complaint. Compounding this problem is the fact that some officers are overzealous in the pursuit of their work; intentionally or not, some officers do violate the rights of the citizens they are sworn to protect. We now look at some police behaviors that have resulted in officer or supervisor liability in the areas of brutality, off-duty activity, wrongful death, false arrest, illegal search and seizure, and negligence.

Section 1983 is an appropriate legal tool for citizens who believe they have been victims of police brutality. Such cases abound. Following are a few that illustrate the police behaviors that have resulted in officer liability. In *Jennings* v. *City of Detroit*,[18] a twenty-two-year-old single African-American man was permanently paralyzed following a beating at a police station. Jury award: $8 million (settled for $3.5 million). In *Gilliam* v. *Falbo*,[19] the U.S. District Court for Ohio awarded $72,000 to a young man beaten by two officers. And in *Haygood* v. *City of Detroit*,[20] a thirty-five-year-old plaintiff was awarded $2.5 million punitive damages and $500,000 compensatory damages after being subjected to racial slurs, beaten, and chained to a bed for twelve hours; charges were never filed.

Even off-duty activities may get police officers into serious difficulty for acting "under color of law." Part-time work as security guards often opens the door to legal problems. In *Carmelo* v. *Miller*,[21] two off-duty officers were working security at a baseball game. They received information that someone was displaying a gun and stopped a man who fit the description. The officers searched, arrested, beat, and kicked the suspect and his companion. No gun was found in the area, and one of the beaten men required medical treatment. The officers were found liable. In *Stengel* v. *Belcher*,[22] an off-duty officer entered a bar carrying a .32-caliber handgun (which he was required to carry off duty at all times) and a can of Mace. An altercation broke out and, without identifying himself, the officer got involved, killing two men and seriously wounding another. The plaintiffs recovered $800,000 in compensatory damages.

Clearly, the use of off-duty weapons and policies requiring that they be carried pose a risk of liability. In *Bonsignore* v. *City of New York*, a mentally unstable twenty-three-year veteran police officer shot his wife five times and then killed himself, using a .32-caliber pistol that departmental policy required him to carry when off duty. Evidence produced at trial demonstrated that Officer Bonsignore's unsuitability for police duties was well known by the department—it had even provided him a limited-duty assignment as station house janitor—yet the police code of silence protected him. The jury awarded Mrs. Bonsignore nearly a half million dollars.

Wrongful death suits are also becoming more frequent. The following cases illustrate how the law applies in this regard. In *Prior* v. *Woods*,[23] a twenty-four-year-old man was killed outside his home by police officers who mistook him for a burglar. The jury awarded his estate $5.75 million. In *Burkholder* v. *City of Los Angeles*,[24] a Los Angeles police officer killed a man in his early twenties who, while naked and under the influence of drugs, was climbing a light pole. The man had seized the officer's club but had not struck the officer. The jury awarded $450,000 in damages and $150,000 in attorney's fees. In *Webster* v. *City of Houston*,[25] an officer killed an unarmed seventeen-year-old boy, who was stopped in a stolen vehicle, and then attempted to cover up the killing by using a "throwaway" weapon. The jury awarded the boy's estate nearly $1.5 million in punitive and compensatory damages.

Generally, police officers are not liable for damages under Section 1983 for merely arresting someone. However, that protective shroud vanishes if the plaintiff proves the officer was negligent or violated an established law or right (as in cases of false arrest). As an illustration, in *Murray* v. *City of Chicago*,[26] the plaintiff's purse and checkbook were stolen; she reported the theft to the police. Later, some of the stolen checks were cashed and the plaintiff was arrested; she appeared in court and cleared up the matter, all charges being dropped. Several months later, she was arrested again at her home by Chicago officers who used an invalid arrest warrant that was related to the earlier mix-up. Murray was taken to the police station, was strip searched by male officers, and was detained for six hours before being released. The federal court ruled that the officers acted in good faith, but if the policy or custom of the city was shown to have encouraged such unwarranted arrests, the city could be held liable. In similar cases (see, for example, *Powe* v. *City of Chicago*, 664 F.2d 639, 1981), when a person's name was not properly removed from the police warrants list, resulting in arrest, the plaintiff has been successful in Section 1983 suits for false arrest.

Search and seizure, an especially complicated area of criminal procedure, is ripe for Section 1983 suits, primarily because of the ambiguous nature of the probable cause doctrine. In *Duncan* v. *Barnes*,[27] police officers obtained a warrant to search a suspect's home for heroin. The officers executed the warrant in early morning hours, using a sledgehammer to break down the rear door of the apartment. With guns drawn, officers entered two bedrooms, forcing the two females and one male inside to stand nude, spread-eagled against a wall, while their rooms were searched. Soon the officers realized that they had entered the wrong apartment, and they left. They left the apartment in total disarray—several doors, a television, and a tape recorder were broken. The occupants, students at a court-reporting school, were so upset that they missed classes for two weeks; as a result, their certification and employment as court reporters were delayed. The court had little difficulty finding that the officers had acted in an unreasonable manner.

Negligence by police officers is another cause of action under Section 1983. Negligence can be found in the supervision and training of personnel, among other things. In *Sager* v. *City of Woodlawn Park*,[28] an officer accidentally killed a person when the shotgun he was pointing at the head of the prisoner discharged; the officer was attempting to handcuff the prisoner with his other hand. At trial, the officer stated that he had seen the technique in a police training film. The training officer, however, testified that the film was intended to show how not to handcuff a prisoner; unfortunately, none of the trainers had made that important distinction to the class. The court ruled that improper training resulted in the prisoner's death. In *Popow* v. *City of Margate*,[29] an innocent bystander was killed on his front porch at night by a police officer engaged in foot pursuit. The court held the city negligent because the officer had had no training on night firing, shooting at moving targets, or using firearms in a residential area. And in *Beverly* v. *Morris*,[30] a police chief was held liable for improper training and supervision of his officers following the blackjack beating of a citizen by a subordinate officer.

In June 1998, the Supreme Court rendered a significant decision concerning police liability in high-speed pursuits. Each year, police pursuits result in accidental deaths of hundreds of citizens.[31] In the past, courts have disagreed about when the police are liable for those deaths. This decision involved police in Sacramento, California, who chased a motorcyclist. When the motorcyclist braked abruptly in front of the officers, a passenger fell from the bike and was struck and killed by the pursuing police car. A lower court held that the police could be sued for "reckless indifference to life," but the Supreme Court reversed that decision, noting the need for split-second decisions by officers. The Court asserted that officers could be held liable only for activities that "shock the conscience."[32]

Criminal Prosecutions for Police Misconduct

Whereas Section 1983 is a civil statute, Title 18, **Section 242**, of the U.S. Code makes it a *criminal* offense for any person acting willfully "under color of law," statute, regulation, or custom to deprive any person of the rights and privileges guaranteed under the Constitution and laws of the United States. This law, like Section 1983, dates from the post–Civil War era and applies to all people regardless of race, color, or national origin. Section 242 not only applies to police officers, but also to other public officials; prosecutions of judges, bail-bond agents, public defenders, and even prosecutors are possible under the statute.

An example of the use of Section 242 is the murder of a drug courier by two U.S. customs agents while the agents were assigned to the San Juan International Airport. The courier flew to Puerto Rico to deposit approximately $700,000 in cash and checks into his employer's account. He was last seen being interviewed by the two customs agents in the airport; ten days later, his body was discovered in a Puerto Rican rain forest. An investigation revealed that the agents had lured the victim away from the airport and had murdered him for his money, later disposing of the body. They were convicted under Section 242 and related federal statutes, and each agent was sentenced to a prison term of 120 years.[33]

The two major federal entities involved in investigating civil rights cases are the Civil Rights Division of the Department of Justice and the Civil Rights Unit of the Federal Bureau of Investigation (FBI). The FBI investigates these cases and presents them to the Department of Justice to review and determine whether prosecution is warranted.

A great amount of weight is attached to the willfulness of the misconduct. The Supreme Court has ruled that in Section 242 prosecutions, the federal government must prove the defendant's specific intent to engage in misconduct. When the misconduct is deliberate and willful (for example, when a suspect is beaten to obtain a confession or an arrestee is beaten in retaliation for resisting arrest), the Justice Department will not hesitate to prosecute.[34]

A frequent complaint by police officers in the past was the lack of prosecutions against people who falsely accused the police of misconduct. In 1984, however, the Supreme Court held that Title 18, Section 1001, of the U.S. Code does cover false statements made to FBI agents, thus allowing prosecution. One such case occurred in Louisiana, where a jail inmate falsely reported to the FBI that he had been assaulted and kicked by a deputy sheriff; in reality, the inmate had received his injuries during a fight with another inmate. He was convicted under Section 1001 and sentenced to three additional years of imprisonment for his false statements.[35]

Liability of Police Supervisors

As already shown, Section 1983 allows for a finding of personal liability on the part of police supervisory personnel if improper training is proved or if it is proved that they knew, or should have known, of the misconduct of their officers yet failed to take corrective action and prevent future harm.

McClelland v. *Facteau*,[36] a Section 1983 suit against a state police agency chief as well as a local police chief, was such a case. McClelland was stopped by Officer Facteau (a state employee) for speeding. He was taken to the city jail; there he was not allowed to make any phone calls, he was questioned but not advised of his rights, and he was beaten and injured by Facteau in the presence of two city police officers. McClelland sued, claiming that the two police chiefs were directly responsible for his treatment and injuries due to their failure to properly train and supervise their subordinates. Evidence was produced of prior misbehavior by Facteau. The court ruled that the chiefs could be held liable if they knew of prior misbehavior yet did nothing about it.

Another related case was that of *Brandon* v. *Allen*.[37] In this case, two teenagers who were parked in a "lovers' lane" were approached by an off-duty police officer, Allen, who showed his police identification and demanded that the boy exit the car. Allen struck the boy with his fist and stabbed him with a knife, then attempted to break into the car where the girl was seated. The boy was able to reenter the car and manage an escape. As the two teenagers sped off, Allen fired a shot at them with his revolver; the shattered windshield glass severely injured the youths to the point that they required plastic surgery. Allen was convicted of criminal charges, and the police chief was also sued under Section 1983. The plaintiffs charged that the chief and others knew of Allen's reputation for being mentally unstable; none of the other police officers wanted to ride in a patrol car with him. At least two formal charges of misconduct had been filed previously, yet the chief failed to take any remedial action or even to review the disciplinary records of officers. The court called this behavior "unjustified inaction," held the police department liable, and allowed the plaintiffs' damages. The U.S. Supreme Court upheld this judgment.[38]

Police supervisors have also been found liable for injuries arising out of an official policy or custom of their department. Injuries resulting from a chief's verbal or written support of heavy-handed behavior resulting in excessive force by officers have resulted in such liability.[39]

Today's police supervisors are definitely in a "need-to-know" position where the law is concerned. They are caught in the middle; not only can they be sued for improper hiring, training, and supervision of their officers, but there are other civil rights laws that can be used by officers who believe they were improperly disciplined or terminated. Indeed, Section 1983 can also be used by unsuccessful job applicants if they can show that the administrator's tests were not job related, included inherent bias, or were not properly administered or graded. The same holds true if it can be shown that proper testing methods were not used in promotions or in the discipline or firing of personnel. Police supervisors have lost in suits in which they disciplined male and female officers who were having a private relationship,[40] in which they disciplined African-American officers who removed the U.S. flag from their uniforms to protest perceived discriminatory acts by the city,[41] and in which they disciplined officers for "improper" political party membership.[42]

New Areas of Potential Liability

Recently, three areas of potential liability were established by the courts: police vehicle pursuits, the handling of computer evidence, and the dissemination of information to the public.

Police Vehicle Pursuit: A High-Stakes Operation

Few operational patrol issues are of greater concern to police leadership than police pursuits because of the tremendous potential for injury, property damage, and liability that accompanies them. As one police procedure manual describes it, "The decision by a police officer to pursue a citizen in a motor vehicle is among the most critical that can be made."[43] Civil litigation arising out of collisions involving police pursuits reveals such pursuits to be high-stakes undertakings with serious and sometimes tragic results.[44] Indeed, several hundred people are killed each year during police pursuits,[45] many of whom are innocent third parties.

Pursuits place the police in a delicate balancing act. On one hand is the need for police to show criminals that flight from the law is no way to freedom. If a police agency completely bans high-speed pursuits, its credibility with both law-abiding citizens and law violators may suffer; public knowledge that the agency has a no-pursuit policy may encourage people to flee, decreasing the probability of apprehension.[46] Still, according to one observer, because of safety and liability concerns, "a growing number of agencies have the position that if the bad guy puts the pedal to the metal, its a 'freebie.' They will not pursue him."[47]

PRACTITIONER'S PERSPECTIVE

Police and Civil Liability

SAMUEL G. CHAPMAN

Samuel G. Chapman, a police consultant, teaches police officers at home and abroad. He was a Berkeley, California, police officer and a student at the University of California, Berkeley, where he took degrees in criminology and studied under August Vollmer. He later taught at Michigan State University, served as chief of the Multnomah County Sheriff's Office (Portland, Oregon), and was assistant director of the President's Commission on Law Enforcement and the Administration of Justice in Washington. In 1967, he began a twenty-four-year career as professor of political science at the University of Oklahoma, where he authored a number of books and monographs on various aspects of policing and the use of police dogs.

"Sue? Me? For what? Why? What do I do now? Will I lose everything?" Such thoughts preoccupy police officers when they learn that they have been named as defendants in a civil rights lawsuit. Officers need help and direction at this juncture, including assurance that this isn't the end of the world. But they need to know that being sued is not a parlor game, either.

Police departments and their personnel must take civil rights litigation seriously, for such actions have been on the increase over the past three decades. Actually, civil rights lawsuits are seen by many as an occupational hazard in policing. Just when this virtual flood tide of litigation will ebb, if it ever will, is not clear.

When a lawsuit has been filed, the allegations should be evaluated by the government's defense attorneys. Fact-finding may disclose that the allegations appear to have little merit. It could be that the plaintiff's counsel has seemingly filed a case of dubious substance, really seeking what is called a "convenience settlement," which occurs when a defendant pays the plaintiff a dollar amount less than what the defendant's costs would be to prepare for trial. But if after fact-finding it appears that the department and its officers are culpable, the defense team should start settlement negotiations early. The defense should make a meaningful offer, keeping it in the range of settlements in cases of a similar sort elsewhere.

At the same time, the defense must get under way with discovery within the context of a game plan aimed at minimizing loss should the case eventually go to trial. Settlements that occur just before trial are invariably costly. The defense team should also evaluate the courtroom record of the plaintiff's law firm, since

On the other hand, there is indeed the high-speed threat to everyone within range of the pursuit, including suspects, their passengers, other drivers, and bystanders. One police trainer asks a simple question to help officers determine whether to continue a pursuit: "Is this person a threat to the public safety other than the fact the police are chasing him?" If the officers cannot objectively answer yes, the pursuit should be terminated.[48]

The Supreme Court's View. In May 1990, two Sacramento County, California, deputies responded to a call about a fight. At the scene, they observed a motorcycle with two riders approaching their vehicle at high some firms are more competent than others. Moreover, knowledge about the track record of the opposing attorneys may bear on whether to settle and the amount of an offer.

In many instances, fact-finding will reveal that a case is realistically defensible. When this is so, the defense team may decide to reject a convenience settlement and prepare for trial. Such a stance will cause the plaintiff's law firm to evaluate whether to expend resources and time in pursuing a case that they are not likely win. Clearly, when the defense feels it can be successful and decides to stand up and fight, it establishes the jurisdiction as a "hard target" and sends a message that lawsuits with little merit are going to be stridently defended.

Of course, it is urgent that whomever is named to defend officers and police agencies be skilled in handling civil rights cases. It is a grave mistake for the government to take a bargain-basement approach to defending civil rights lawsuits by assigning staff attorneys who have little or no experience working these highly technical types of litigation.

A popular misconception is that only officers in the nation's largest police forces are sued. The truth is that although personnel in major forces are frequent targets of litigation, officers in very small forces are named as defendants too, far more often than one might imagine. In fact, members of very small forces may be more vulnerable to litigation because they may not be as well trained and supervised as their counterparts on large forces, and their rules, regulations, and procedures manuals may not be as thorough and up-to-date.

With the upsurge in litigation against police, officers may become demoralized, dispirited, and defensive. They are easy prey for cynical locker-room jockeys who proclaim that the best way to avoid trouble is to slow down, cool it, and do no more police work than one has to. Such advice, which is of the worst sort, poses a special urgent challenge for police supervisors, who must ensure that officers execute their duties faithfully and in accord with departmental guidelines.

Yes, the police can fight back by suing those who sue them. But this means hiring counsel, which is expensive. And even if the lawsuit is successful and brings a dollar judgment against the defendant, such defendants are usually poor and hence unable to meet any financial judgment levied against them. In short, suing back is not a realistic course of action.

Government's best defense against an adverse judgment in a civil rights lawsuit is to thoroughly train and regularly retrain its police personnel and to supervise them well. In addition, the police department's rules and regulations, as well as its procedures manuals, must be kept current and as complete and practical as possible. The content of these important documents must be understood by all officers. If all these things are in place and if officers perform as trained and execute their roles in accord with departmental guidelines and policies, a persuasive defense can be mounted against any allegations of misconduct.

speed. Turning on their red lights, the deputies ordered the driver to stop. The motorcycle operator began to elude the officers, who initiated a pursuit that reached speeds of more than 100 miles per hour over about 1.3 miles. The pursuit ended when the motorcycle crashed; the deputies' vehicle could not stop in time and struck the bike's passenger, killing him. His family brought suit, claiming that the pursuit violated the crash victim's due process rights under the Fourteenth Amendment.

In *County of Sacramento* v. *Lewis*,[49] decided in May 1998, the U.S. Supreme Court held that the proper standard to be employed in these cases is whether the officer's conduct during the pursuit "shocks the conscience" (that is, was the conduct offensive to a reasonable person's sense of moral goodness?). The Court further determined that high-speed chases with no intent to harm suspects do not give rise to liability under the Fourteenth Amendment. The Court closed the door on the liability for officers involved in pursuits that do not "shock the conscience." But the Court left unanswered many important questions, such as whether it will allow an innocent third party to file a claim against the police for damages and whether a municipality can be held liable for its failure to train officers in pursuit issues.

In sum, a pursuit is justified only when the necessity of apprehension outweighs the degree of danger created by the pursuit. Agencies generally require field supervisors (sergeants) to discontinue the pursuit when it is unjustified or becomes too dangerous.[50]

Computer Evidence

It is almost impossible to investigate a fraud, embezzlement, or child pornography case today without dealing with some sort of computer evidence. Even evidence in a homicide or narcotics case may be buried deep within a computer's hard disk drive. As a result, many police agencies have recruited self-taught "experts" to fill the role of computer evidence specialists. These specialists are usually highly motivated and have some knowledge of the rules of evidence and some experience in testifying in court. Other police agencies have enlisted the support of personnel at local universities or computer repair shops to help them with computer evidence.[51]

The increased exposure to computer evidence by people both inside and outside policing brings an increase in potential legal liabilities. For example, if a police agency seizes the computerized records of an ongoing business, there may be negative financial consequences for the business. If it can be shown that the police accidentally destroyed business records through negligence, a criminal investigation might well become the civil suit of the decade. Furthermore, if a seized computer contains a newsletter, a draft of a book, or any computer bulletin board system, there may be liability under the Privacy Protection Act.[52]

The risk of liability in these kinds of cases may be reduced substantially if police investigators follow generally accepted forensic computer evidence procedures. Guidelines approved by the Department of Justice's Computer Crime and Intellectual Property Section dictate how the police are to search, seize, and analyze computers. It is crucial that the police be trained in the proper procedures for handling computers as well as in the rules of evidence. The federal government has made computer evidence training a priority for federal, state, and local law enforcement officers.[53]

Disseminating Public Information

In 1997, the Louisiana Supreme Court held that police department public information officers (PIOs) can be held liable for unfounded statements they make in news releases. The case involved a defamation suit against the state police, in which the PIO told a reporter that the defendant was running a large-scale illegal gambling operation and was bilking customers. The court found that the PIO had no reasonable basis for saying that the defendant had cheated customers and thus made injurious statements that he had no reason to believe were true. Although the ruling applies only to PIOs in Louisiana, it could grow to have national implications in the future.[54]

SUMMARY

This chapter examined the high legal cost of misconduct and negligence in policing. Included were discussions of police actions leading to liability, a number of police civil liability cases decided by federal courts, and new areas of potential police liability: hot pursuits, computer evidence, and the dissemination of information to the public.

Implicit in this chapter are the dire consequences of failing to properly hire, train, and supervise police personnel. Furthermore, students and criminal justice practitioners must remember that the law is fluid and constantly changing; officers and students must therefore keep abreast of the laws concerning liability and must conduct themselves accordingly.

REVIEW QUESTIONS

1. Explain the basic means by which laws are enacted, and differentiate between civil and criminal law.
2. Define negligence, and discuss Title 42, Section 1983, of the U.S. Code.
3. Give reasons for the recent increase in Section 1983 lawsuits.
4. Delineate some types of police actions that are vulnerable to Section 1983 actions.
5. Explain how police officers might be held criminally liable for their misconduct.
6. How might police supervisors be held liable under Section 1983?
7. Describe some of the liability issues related to computer evidence.

INDEPENDENT STUDENT ACTIVITIES

1. Interview police executives to learn of the challenges they face in trying to provide police services in a litigious society. What are they doing in terms of training and policies to minimize the chances of successful lawsuits against their officers? In which areas are the police the most vulnerable to charges of negligence?

2. In a related vein, determine from discussions with police practitioners the technical areas of their work in which they must constantly be retrained and certified to avoid harming citizens and to avoid litigation.
3. Determine how police officers try to protect themselves against lawsuits, such as purchasing false-arrest insurance, keeping abreast of court decisions involving police negligence, and subscribing to related literature.

RELATED WEB SITES

Association of Trial Lawyers
http://www.atlanet.org

International Perspectives on Justice
http://pap01.adt.jjay.cuny.edu

Labor Relations Information System
http://www.lris.com/index.cfm

National District Attorney Association
http://www.ndaa-apri.org

NOTES

1. See, for example, JOHN L. WORRALL and OTWIN MARENIN, "Emerging Liability Issues in the Implementation and Adoption of Community Oriented Policing," *Policing: An International Journal of Police Strategies and Management* 22 (1998): 121–36.
2. H. E. BARRINEAU III, *Civil Liability in Criminal Justice* (Cincinnati: Pilgrimage, 1987), p. 58.
3. Ibid., p. 5.
4. CHARLES R. SWANSON, LEONARD TERRITO, and ROBERT W. TAYLOR, *Police Administration: Structures, Processes, and Behavior*, 5th ed. (Upper Saddle River, NJ: Prentice Hall, 2001), p. 438.
5. Ibid., pp. 357–58.
6. *BIVENS* v. *SIX UNKNOWN NAMED AGENTS OF THE FEDERAL BUREAU OF NARCOTICS*, 403 U.S. 388, 29 L.Ed.2d 619, 91 S.Ct. 1999 (1971).
7. SWANSON, TERRITO, and TAYLOR, *Police Administration*, p. 438.
8. Ibid., pp. 438–39.
9. *HANS* v. *LOUISIANA*, 134 U.S. 1 (1890); also see "Sovereign Immunity," 17 *Alaska Bar Rag* No. 3 (Sep/Oct 1993), http://touchngo.com/lglcntr/usdc/bnkrptcy/briefs/bnk21.htm (accessed January 28, 2005), p. 2.
10. Ibid.
11. *MONROE* v. *PAPE*, 365 U.S. 167, 81 S.Ct. 473 (1961).

12. WAYNE W. SCHMIDT, "Section 1983 and the Changing Face of Police Management," in *Police Leadership in America*, ed. WILLIAM A. GELLER (Chicago: American Bar Foundation, 1985), pp. 226–36.
13. Ibid., p. 228.
14. Ibid., p. 227.
15. *MONELL* v. *DEPARTMENT OF SOCIAL SERVICES*, 436 U.S. 658 7 (1978).
16. *ALABAMA* v. *PUGH*, 438 U.S. 781 (1978).
17. SWANSON, TERRITO, and TAYLOR, *Police Administration*, p. 449.
18. *JENNINGS* v. *CITY OF DETROIT*, Wayne County Circuit Court, Michigan (August 1979).
19. *GILLIAM* v. *FALBO*, U.S. District Court, Southern District of Ohio (April 1982).
20. *HAYGOOD* v. *CITY OF DETROIT*, Wayne County Circuit Court, Michigan, No.77–728013 (December 29, 1980).
21. *CARMELO* v. *MILLER*, 569 S.W. 365 (1978).
22. *STENGEL* v. *BELCHER*, 522 F.2d 438 (6th Cir., 1975).
23. PRIOR v. WOODS, U.S. Dist. Ct., E.D. Mich. (October 1981).
24. *BURKHOLDER* v. *CITY OF LOS ANGELES*, L.A. Cty. Sup. Ct., California (October 1982).
25. *WEBSTER* v. *CITY OF HOUSTON*, 735 F.2d 838 (5th Cir., 1994).
26. *MURRAY* v. *CITY OF CHICAGO*, 634 F.2d 365 (1980).
27. *DUNCAN* v. *BARNES*, 592 F.2d 1336 (1979).
28. *SAGER* v. *CITY OF WOODLAWN PARK*, 543 F.Supp. 282 (D.Colo., 1982).
29. *POPOW* v. *CITY OF MARGATE*, 476 F. Supp. 1237 (1979).
30. *BEVERLY* v. *MORRIS*, 470 F.2d 1356 (5th Cir., 1972).
31. GORDON WITKIN, "Police Chases Get a Green Light," *U.S. News and World Report*, June 8, 1998, p. 25.
32. SACRAMENTO COUNTY, *CALIF.* v. *LEWIS*, 66 LW 4407 (May 26, 1998).
33. On appeal, the Section 242 convictions were vacated, as the victim was not an inhabitant of Puerto Rico; therefore, he enjoyed no protection under the U.S. Constitution. On resentencing, in January 1991, the agents each received fifty years in prison for convictions of several other federal crimes under Title 18.
34. JOHN EPKE and LINDA DAVIS, "Civil Rights Cases and Police Misconduct," *FBI Law Enforcement Bulletin* 60 (August 1991): 14–18.
35. Ibid., p. 17.
36. *MCCLELLAND* v. *FACTEAU*, 610 F.2d 693 (10th Cir., 1979).
37. *BRANDON* v. *ALLEN*, 516 F.Supp. 1355 (W.D. Tenn., 1981).
38. *BRANDON* v. *HOLT*, 469 U.S. 464, 105 S.Ct. 873 (1985).
39. See, for example, *BLACK* v. *STEPHENS*, 662 F.2d 181 (1991).
40. *SWOPE* v. *BRATTON*, 541 F.Supp. 99 (W.D. Ark., 1982).
41. *LEONARD* v. *CITY OF COLUMBUS*, 705 F.2d 1299 (11th Cir., 1983).
42. *ELROD* v. *BURNS*, 427 U.S. 347 (1975).
43. Tulsa, Oklahoma, Police Department, procedure manual, RONALD PALMER, chief of police, June 10, 1998, p. 1.

44. JOHN HILL, "High-Speed Police Pursuits: Dangers, Dynamics, and Risk Reduction," *FBI Law Enforcement Bulletin* (July 2002): 14–18.
45. NATIONAL HIGHWAY TRAFFIC SAFETY ADMINISTRATION, *National Highway Traffic Safety Administration Statistics* (Washington, DC: Author, 1995).
46. C. B. EISENBERG, "Pursuit Management," *Law and Order* (March 1999): 73–77.
47. A. BELOTTO, "Supervisors Govern Pursuits," *Law and Order* (January 1999): 86.
48. G. T. WILLIAMS, "When Do We Keep Pursuing? Justifying High-Speed Pursuits," *Police Chief* (March 1997): 24–27.
49. *COUNTY OF SACRAMENTO* v. *LEWIS* 118 S.Ct. 1708 (1998).
50. Oklahoma County Sheriff John Whetsel, quoted in NICOLE MARSHALL, "Hot Pursuit," *Tulsa World*, June 15, 1998, p. A11.
51. MICHAEL R. ANDERSON, "Reducing Computer Evidence Liability," *Government Technology* (February 10, 1997): 24, 36.
52. Ibid.
53. Ibid.
54. "Be Careful What You Say," *Law Enforcement News*, December 15, 1997, p. 1.

CHAPTER 12

Issues and Trends

Debate on public issues should be uninhibited, robust, and wide open.

—Justice William Brennan

History has many cunning passages, contrived corridors, and issues.

—T. S. Eliot

Key Terms

accreditation
collective bargaining
Commission on Accreditation for Law Enforcement Agencies (CALEA)
double marginality
Fair Labor Standards Act (FLSA)
female police officer
grievance
impasse
job action
labor relations
minority police officer
Peace Officer Bill of Rights
private police
stress
unionization

This chapter addresses a number of important policing matters that could have been included in earlier chapters. But because of their common nature—all represent a relatively recent and substantial degree of change, controversy, and/or influence within the operations of their agencies—they are consolidated here for discussion.

The chapter is divided into two major sections: contemporary policing trends and contemporary policing issues. In the first section, we examine the rights of police officers, labor relations (including unionization and collective bargaining), women and minorities in policing, the private police, and the accreditation of police agencies.

The issues section includes two primary subjects: higher education for the police and police stress—not as an issue per se but because of its myriad causes, physical and emotional effects, and possible solutions. In this section, we also briefly discuss what officers can do to maintain an edge. A chapter summary, review questions, independent student activities, and related Web sites conclude the chapter.

Contemporary Policing Trends

Labor Relations: Officers' Rights, Unionization, and Collective Bargaining

In an earlier time, police supervisors, middle managers, and chief executives were largely unrestricted and unchallenged in their treatment of rank-and-file officers. Disciplinary action was subjective, and the prevailing theme was often "Do as I say, not as I do." Today, the labor-management relationship has changed significantly. **Labor relations**—a broad term that includes officers' employment rights and the related concepts of **unionization** and **collective bargaining**—has become an important issue in policing. This section explores these topics.

Rights of Police Officers. Chapter 10 delineated several restrictions on police officers' rights (such as place of residence, religious practice, freedom of speech, and search and seizure). Because of the nature of their position, police officers may encounter treatment by employers—and federal courts—that is quite different from that received by regular citizens. Officers do give up certain constitutional privileges when they put on a police uniform. In this section, we look at some measures the police have taken to maintain their rights on the job to the extent possible.

In the 1980s and 1990s, police officers began to insist on greater procedural safeguards to protect themselves against what they perceived as arbitrary infringement on their rights. These demands have been reflected in a statute enacted in many states, generally known as the **Peace Officer Bill of Rights**. This legislation confers upon police employees a property interest in their position and mandates due process rights for peace officers who are the subject of internal investigations, that could lead to disciplinary action. The legislation identifies the type of information that must be provided to the accused officer, the officer's responsibility to cooperate during the investigation, the officer's rights to representation during the process, and the rules and procedures concerning the collection of certain types of evidence. Following are some common provisions of state Peace Officer Bill of Rights legislation:

> *Written notice:* The department must provide the officer with written notice of the nature of the investigation, a summary of the alleged misconduct, and the name of the investigating officer.

Right to representation: The officer may have an attorney or a representative of his or her choosing present during any phase of questioning or any hearing.

Polygraph examination: The officer may refuse to take a polygraph examination unless the complainant submits to an examination and is determined to be telling the truth. In this case, the officer may be ordered to take a polygraph examination or may be subject to disciplinary action.

Officers expect to be treated fairly, honestly, and respectfully during the course of an internal investigation. In turn, the public expects that the agency will develop sound disciplinary policies and will conduct thorough inquiries into allegations of misconduct.

It is imperative that supervisors be thoroughly familiar with statutes, contract provisions, and existing rules between employer and employee to ensure that procedural due process requirements are met, particularly in disciplinary cases in which an employee's property interest is affected.

Police officers today are also more likely to file a **grievance** when they believe their rights have been violated. Grievances may cover a broad range of issues, including salaries, overtime, leave, hours of work, allowances, retirement, opportunity for advancement, performance evaluations, workplace conditions, tenure, disciplinary actions, supervisory methods, and administrative practices. The preferred method for settling officers' grievances is through informal discussion during which the employee explains his or her grievance to the immediate supervisor; most complaints can be handled this way. Complaints that cannot be dealt with informally are usually handled through a more formal grievance process, which may involve several different levels of action.

Unionization. Probably as a result of their often difficult working conditions and traditionally low salary and poor benefits packages, police have often elected to band together to fight for improvement. Another major force in the development and spread of unionization was the authoritarian, unilateral, and "do as I say, not as I do" management style that characterized many police administrators of the past.

The first campaign to organize the police started shortly after World War I, when the American Federation of Labor (AFL) reversed a long-standing policy and issued charters to police unions in Boston, Washington, D.C., and about thirty other cities. Many police officers were suffering from the rapid inflation following the outbreak of the war and believed that if their chiefs could not get them long-overdue pay raises, then perhaps unions could. Capitalizing on their sentiments, the fledgling unions signed about 60 percent of all officers in Washington, 75 percent in Boston, and a similar proportion in other cities.[1]

The unions' success was short-lived, however. The Boston police commissioner refused to recognize the union, forbade officers to join it, and filed charges against several union officials. Shortly thereafter, on September 9, 1919, the Boston police initiated a famous strike of three days' duration, causing major riots and a furor against the police all across the nation; nine rioters were killed, and twenty-three were seriously injured. During the strike, Massachusetts governor Calvin Coolidge uttered his now-famous statement: "There is no right to strike against the public safety by anybody, anywhere, anytime."

During World War II, the unionization effort was reignited. Unions issued charters to a few dozen locals all over the country and sent in organizers to help enlist the rank and file. Most police chiefs continued speaking out against unionization, but their subordinates were moved by the thousands to join, sensing the advantage in having unions press for higher wages and better benefits.[2] But in a series of rulings, the courts upheld the right of police authorities to ban police unions.

The unions were survived in the early 1950s by many benevolent and fraternal organizations of police. Some were patrolmen's benevolent associations (PBAs), like those formed in New York, Chicago, and Washington; others were fraternal orders of police (FOPs). During the late 1950s and early 1960s, a new group of rank-and-file association leaders came into power. They were more vocal in articulating their demands. Soon a majority of the rank and file vocally supported higher salaries and pensions, free legal aid, low-cost insurance, and other benefits. For the first time, rank-and-file organizations were legally able to insist that police administrators sit down at the bargaining table.[3]

Since the 1970s, the unionization of the police has continued to flourish. Today, the majority of U.S. police officers belong to unions.[4] The International Brotherhood of Police Officers touts itself as the largest police union, but it is rivaled by the American Federation of State, County, and Municipal Employees union, which represents about 1.4 million workers and one hundred affiliated associations.[5] This dramatic rise in union membership was fomented by several factors: job dissatisfaction, the belief that the public is hostile to police needs, and an influx of younger officers who hold less traditional views on relations between officers and the department hierarchy.[6]

Collective Bargaining: Types, Relationships, Negotiation, and Job Actions.

Three Models. Each state is free to decide which public-sector employees, if any, will have collective bargaining rights and under what terms; therefore there is considerable variety in collective bargaining arrangements across the nation. In states with comprehensive public-sector bargaining laws, the administration of the statute is the responsibility of a state agency, such as a public employee relations board (PERB) or a public employee relations commission (PERC). Three basic models are used in the states: (1) binding arbitration, (2) meet and confer, and (3) bargaining not required.[7]

The binding-arbitration model is used in twenty-five states. Under this model, public employees are given the right to bargain with their employers. If the bargaining reaches an **impasse**, the matter is submitted to a neutral arbiter, who decides what the terms and conditions of the new collective bargaining agreement will be.[8]

Only three states use the meet-and-confer model, which grants very few rights to public employees. As with the binding-arbitration model, police employees in meet-and-confer states have the right to organize and to select their own bargaining representatives.[9] However, when an impasse is reached, employees are at a distinct disadvantage. Their only legal choices are to accept the employer's best offer, try to influence the offer through political tactics (such as appeals for public support), or take some permissible **job action**.[10]

The twenty-two states that follow the bargaining-not-required model have statutes that either do not require or do not allow collective bargaining by public employees.[11] In the majority of these states, laws permitting public employees to engage in collective bargaining have not been passed.

The Bargaining Relationship. In those states and agencies seeking to organize for collective bargaining, the process is as follows. First, a union will begin an organizing drive seeking to get a majority of the classes of employees it seeks to represent to sign authorization cards. At this point, agency administrators may attempt to convince employees that they are better off without the union. Questions may also arise, such as whether certain employees (for example, police lieutenants) are part of management and therefore ineligible for union representation.

Once a majority of the eligible employees have signed cards, the union notifies the criminal justice agency. If management believes that the union has obtained a majority legitimately, it will recognize the union as the bargaining agent of the employees it seeks to represent. Once recognized by the employer, the union will petition the PERB, or other body responsible for administering the legislation, for certification.

Negotiations. Figure 12-1 depicts a typical configuration of the union and management bargaining teams. Positions shown in dashed boxes typically serve in a support role and may or may not actually partake in the bargaining. The management's labor relations manager (lead negotiator) is often an attorney assigned to the human resources department who reports to the city manager or assistant city manager and represents the city in grievances and arbitration matters. The union's chief negotiator will normally not be a member of the bargaining unit; rather, he or she will be a specialist brought in to represent the union's position and to provide greater experience, expertise, objectivity, and autonomy. The union's chief negotiator may be accompanied by individuals who have conducted surveys on wages and benefits, trends in the consumer price index, and so on.[12]

Management's chief negotiator may be the director of labor relations or the human resource director for the unit of government involved or a professional labor relations specialist. The agency's chief executive

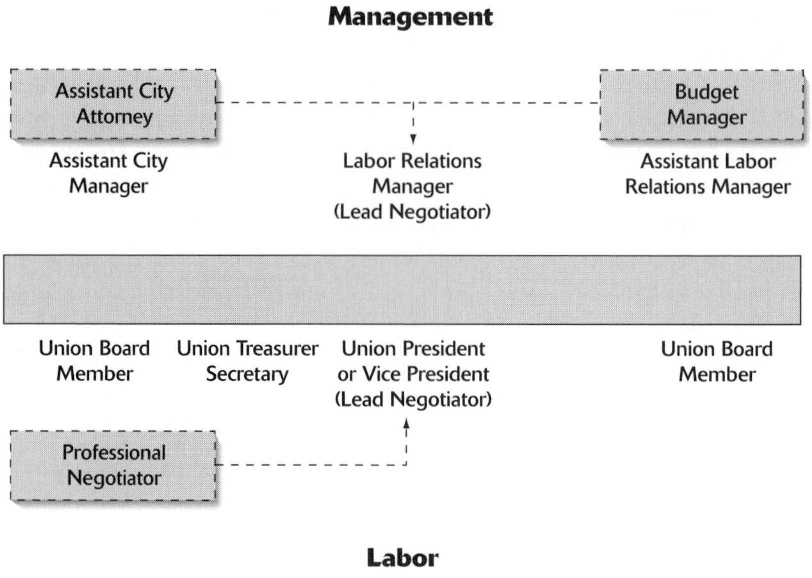

FIGURE 12-1 Union and management collective bargaining teams.

Source: *Jerry Hoover, Chief of Police, Reno, Nevada*

should not appear at the table personally; it is extremely delicate for the chief to represent management one day and then return to work among the employees the next. Rather, management is represented by a key member of the command staff who has the executive's confidence.

In the Event of an Impasse. The purpose of bargaining is to produce a bilateral written agreement to which both parties will bind themselves during the lifetime of the agreement. Even parties bargaining in good faith may not be able to resolve their differences by themselves, and an impasse may result. In such cases, a neutral third party may be appointed to facilitate, suggest, or compel an agreement. Three major forms of impasse resolution are mediation, fact-finding, and arbitration.

> *Mediation:* Mediation occurs when a third party, called the "mediator," comes in to help the adversaries with the negotiations.[13] This person may be a professional mediator or someone in whom both parties have confidence. In most states, mediation may be requested by either labor or management. The mediator's task is to build agreement about the issues involved by reopening communication between the two sides. The mediator has no way to compel an agreement, so an advantage of the process is that it preserves the nature of collective bargaining by maintaining the decision-making power in the hands of the parties involved.[14]
>
> *Fact-finding:* Fact-finding primarily involves the interpretation of facts and the determination of what weight to attach to them. Appointed in the same way as mediators, fact-finders also do not have a way to impose a settlement of the dispute. Fact-finders may sit alone or as part of a panel, which normally consists of three people. The fact-finding hearing is quasi-judicial, although less strict rules of evidence are applied. Both labor and management may be

represented by legal counsel, and verbatim transcripts are commonly made. In most cases, the fact-finder's recommendations are made public at some point.[15]

Arbitration: Arbitration parallels fact-finding, but it differs in that the "end product of arbitration is a final and binding decision that sets the terms of the settlement and with which the parties are legally required to comply."[16] Arbitration may be compulsory or voluntary. It is compulsory when mandated by state law, and it is binding upon the parties even if one of them is unwilling to comply. It is voluntary when the parties undertake of their own volition to use the procedure. Even when entered into voluntarily, arbitration is binding upon the parties who have agreed to it.

Grievances. The establishment of a working agreement between labor and management does not mean that the possibility for conflict no longer exists; the day-to-day administration of the agreement may also be the basis for strife. Questions can arise about the interpretation and application of the document and its various clauses. Grievances—complaints or expressions of dissatisfaction by an employee concerning some aspect of employment—may arise. The grievance procedure is a formal process that involves the seeking of redress of the complaints through progressively higher channels within the organization. The sequence of grievance steps will be spelled out in the collective bargaining agreement and will typically include the following five steps: (1) the employee presents the grievance to the immediate supervisor, and if he or she does not receive satisfaction, (2) a written grievance is presented to the division commander, then (3) to the chief executive officer, then (4) to the city or county manager, and finally (5) to an arbiter, who is selected according to the rules of the American Arbitration Association.[17]

The burden of proof is on the grieving party except in disciplinary cases, in which it is always on the employer. The parties may be represented by counsel at the hearing, and the format will include opening statements by each side, examination and cross-examination of any witnesses, and closing arguments in the reverse order in which opening arguments were made.[18]

Job Actions. A job action is an activity in which employees engage to express their dissatisfaction with a particular person, event, or condition or to attempt to influence the outcome of some matter pending before decision makers.[19] Job actions are of four types: the vote of confidence, work slowdowns, work speedups, and work stoppages.

Vote of confidence: The vote of confidence is used sparingly; a vote of no confidence signals employees' collective displeasure with the chief administrator of the agency. Although such votes have no legal standing, they may have high impact due to the resulting publicity.

Work slowdowns: In work slowdowns, employees continue to work, but they do so at a leisurely pace, causing productivity to fall. As productivity declines, the government is pressured to resume normal work production—for example, a police department may urge officers to issue more citations so revenues are not lost.[20]

Work speedups: Work speedups involve accelerated activity in the levels of services. For example, a police department may conduct a "ticket blizzard" to protest a low pay increase or to pressure government leaders to make more concessions at the bargaining table or to abandon some policy change that affects their working conditions.

Work stoppages: Work stoppages constitute the most severe job action. The ultimate work stoppage is the strike, or the withholding of all employee services. This tactic is most often used by labor to force management back to the bargaining table when negotiations have reached an impasse. However, criminal justice employee strikes are now rare. Briefer work stoppages, which do not involve all employees and are known in policing as "blue flu," last only a few days.

Fair Labor Standards Act. An area of policing that is at the heart of management-labor relations is the **Fair Labor Standards Act (FLSA)**. For some police administrators, the Fair Labor Standards Act has become a budgetary and operational nightmare. Indeed, one observer referred to the FLSA as the criminal justice administrator's "worst nightmare come true."[21] The act provides minimum pay and overtime provisions covering both public- and private-sector employees and contains special provisions for firefighters and police officers. Although there is currently some discussion in Congress concerning the repeal or modification of the act, at the present time it is still a legislative force that administrators, mid-level managers, and supervisors must reckon with.

The act was passed in 1938 to protect the rights and working conditions of employees in the private sector. During that time, long hours, poor wages, and substandard work conditions plagued most businesses. The FLSA placed a number of restrictions on employers to improve these conditions. In 1985, the U.S. Supreme Court brought local police employees under the coverage of the FLSA. In this major (and very costly) decision, *Garcia* v. *San Antonio Transit Authority*,[22] the Court held, 5 to 4, that Congress imposed the requirements of the FLSA on state and local governments.

Police operations, which take place twenty-four hours a day, seven days a week, often require overtime and participation in off-duty activities such as court appearances and training sessions. The FLSA comes into play when overtime salaries must be paid. It provides that an employer must generally pay employees time and a half for all hours worked over forty per week. Overtime must also be paid to personnel for all work in excess of forty-three hours in a seven-day cycle or 171 hours in a twenty-eight-day period. Public-safety employees may accrue a maximum of 480 hours of "comp" (compensation) time, which, if not utilized as leave, must be paid off upon separation from employment at the employee's final rate of pay or at the average pay over the last three years, whichever is greater.[23] Furthermore, employers usually cannot require employees to take compensatory time in lieu of cash. The primary issue with FLSA is the rigidity of application of what is compensable work. The act prohibits an agency from taking "volunteered time" from employees.

Today, an officer who works the night shift must receive pay for attending training or testifying in court during the day. Furthermore, officers who are ordered to remain at home in anticipation of emergency actions must be compensated. Notably, however, the FLSA's overtime provisions do not apply to those who are employed in a bona fide executive, administrative, or professional capacity. In criminal justice, the act has generally been held to apply to detectives and sergeants but not to those of the rank of lieutenant and above.

Garcia prompted an onslaught of litigation by police and fire employees of state and local government entities. The issues are broad but may include paying overtime compensation to K-9 and equestrian officers who care for department animals while "off duty," overtime pay for officers who access their work computer and conduct business from home, pay for academy recruits who are given mandatory homework assignments, and standby and on-call pay for supervisors and officers who are assigned to units that require their unscheduled return to work. These are just a few of the many FLSA issues that are being litigated in courts across the nation.

Women Who Wear the Badge

Over the past thirty years, the proportion of **female police officers** has grown steadily. During the 1970s, some formal barriers to hiring women were eliminated, such as height requirements, and subjective physical agility tests and oral interviews were modified.[24] Some job discrimination suits further expanded women's opportunities. A 1980 lawsuit by Los Angeles police officer Fanchon Blake opened up the ranks above sergeant to women; the case of New York City detective Kathleen Burke, who in May 1991 won a settlement and a promotion to detective first grade, broadened their possibilities even more.[25]

Agency and Chief Executive Representation. Women represent 14.5 percent of sworn personnel in municipal agencies, 13.5 percent of sworn personnel in county agencies, and 8.2 percent in small agencies. State agencies as a whole have a much lower percentage of female officers than either local or federal law enforcement agencies: 6.8 percent.[26] Women account for 14.8 percent of all federal officers, which is a bit higher than in local agencies.[27]

Although the representation of female officers is low compared to their overall population, underrepresentation is even more evident in the leadership ranks, where women constitute only 1 percent of the police chiefs in the United States.[28] The number of women serving as chiefs has expanded considerably, however, since Penny Harrington took over as chief in Portland, Oregon (becoming the first woman chief in a large agency), in 1985 and Elizabeth (Betsy) Watson assumed the helm in Houston (becoming the first in a city of more than one million population) in 1990. As examples, in early 2004 newly appointed women were serving as chiefs of police in

TABLE 12-1

Gender and Race or Ethnicity of Federal Officers with Arrest and Firearm Authority, Agencies Employing 500 or More Full-Time Officers, June 1998

		Percentage of Full-Time Federal Officers with Arrest and Firearm Authority							
			Gender		Race/Ethnicity				
	Number of Officers[a]	Total	Male	Female	White	Native American	Black or African-American	Asian or Pacific Islander	Hispanic or Latino of Any Race
Immigration and Naturalization	16,888	100%	88.3%	11.7%	59.2%	0.5%	5.3%	2.3%	32.0%
Federal Bureau of Prisons	12,751	100	87.9	12.1	62.6	1.4	23.4	0.9	11.7
Federal Bureau of Investigation	11,451	100	84.1	15.9	83.9	0.5	6.3	2.5	6.9
U.S. Customs Service	10,863	100	81.4	18.6	66.3	0.7	7.2	3.5	22.3
U.S. Secret Service	3,594	100	91.4	8.6	79.7	0.8	12.9	1.3	5.3
U.S. Postal Inspection Service	3,537	100	85.5	14.5	67.1	0.4	22.5	3.0	7.0
Internal Revenue Service	3,370	100	74.8	25.0	80.2	0.9	9.4	3.3	6.1
Drug Enforcement Administration[b]	3,396	100	92.1	7.9	80.5	0.6	8.2	2.0	8.8
U.S. Marshals Service	2,755	100	88.6	11.4	83.8	0.7	7.1	1.9	6.5
National Park Service	2,207	100	86.8	13.2	86.4	1.3	6.5	2.4	3.4
Ranger Activities Division	1,534	100	85.0	15.0	90.0	1.9	3.1	2.2	2.8
U.S. Park Police	673	100	90.8	9.2	78.2	0.0	14.3	3.0	4.6
Bureau of Alcohol, Tobacco, and Firearms	1,732	100	87.8	12.2	78.6	1.3	10.8	1.7	7.6
U.S. Capitol Police	1,055	100	82.1	17.9	67.4	0.4	29.8	0.8	1.7
GSA—Federal Protective Service	904	100	91.2	8.8	57.7	0.2	30.4	2.1	9.5
U.S. Fish and Wildlife Service	836	100	90.0	10.0	91.7	1.9	1.4	0.6	4.3
U.S. Forest Service	604	100	83.9	16.1	82.5	7.3	3.1	1.0	6.1

[a]Includes employees in U.S. territories.

[b]Gender and race/ethnicity data for the Drug Enforcement Administration are estimates based on Department of Justice data. Data on gender and race/ethnicity of officers were not provided by the Administrative Office of the U.S. Courts. Detail may not add to total because of rounding.

Source: Brian A. Reaves and Timothy C. Hart, *Federal Law Enforcement Officers, 1998* (Washington, DC: Department of Justice, Bureau of Justice Statistics Bulletin, 2000), p. 6.

San Francisco, Boston, Detroit, and Milwaukee, providing further evidence that today's "mayors are looking for sophisticated CEOs who can oversee large budgets, negotiate thorny management problems, and set sound departmentwide policy."[29]

A recent survey identified 157 women serving as chiefs of police and twenty-five who were sheriffs; ninety-six of these chiefs participated in a survey intended to establish a demographic profile of the women.[30] Forty-eight (49 percent) of these chief executives were in charge of municipal police departments, while forty (42 percent) led college and university police departments. Only six of the respondents led agencies with at least one hundred sworn officers (five being municipal, one a campus police agency, and one a tribal agency). Conversely, twenty-three (25.8 percent) were in agencies with ten or fewer officers. These female CEOs reflect the increasing levels of education achieved by today's chiefs, with three-fourths having either a bachelor's or a master's degree. About a third had a partner who was also in policing.[31]

Certainly, a large enough proportion of women have now been employed in policing long enough to be considered for promotion. A number of researchers question the commitment of police agencies and their male administrators in promoting women and have made recommendations for changing the evaluation and promotion process.[32]

Key Issues. Peter Horne identified several key issues that have been problematic in the past and must be addressed in the future:[33]

Recruitment. This is the first critical step in getting qualified women to enter policing. Unfocused, random recruiting is unlikely to attract diversity. Recruiting literature, such as flyers, posters, and brochures, should feature female officers working in all areas of policing. The variety of assignments (for example, victim/witness assistance, domestic violence, community policing) is often cited by prospective policewomen as attractive, and recruitment should stress this quality. Furthermore, agencies should recruit from a variety of places and resources (local colleges, women's groups, female community leaders, gyms, martial arts schools) and use all types of media to attract qualified applicants.

Preemployment Physical Testing. Historically, women have been screened out disproportionately in the preemployment physical testing used by many agencies. Tests that include such components as scaling a six-foot wall, bench pressing one's own weight, and throwing medicine balls are likely to have an adverse impact on female applicants, so agencies should examine their physical tests to determine why women are screened out more than men. Also, agencies should permit all candidates to practice for the preemployment physical exam.

PRACTITIONER'S PERSPECTIVE

Women in Policing: Past, Present, and Future

CHIEF PENNY HARRINGTON

Chief Penny Harrington, author of *Triumph of Spirit*, her autobiography, is the director of the National Center for Women and Policing, a division of the Feminist Majority Foundation. She spent twenty-three years in the Portland, Oregon, Police Bureau, where she started in 1964 as a policewoman in the Women's Protective Division. Based on her record in the bureau and her support from the community, Harrington was named chief of police in 1985, making her the first woman to become chief of a major U.S. city. After leaving the Portland Police Bureau, she became the assistant director of investigations for the State Bar of California. As director of the National Center for Women and Policing, she is working nationally to bring more women into policing and to help women reach the higher levels of command within their agencies. For more information on the National Center for Women and Policing, see www.feminist.org/police.

When Lola Baldwin joined the Portland, Oregon, Police Bureau in 1905, she was the first woman in the field of law enforcement. In 1985, the Portland Police Bureau again made history by promoting me to be the first female police chief of a major U.S. city. In those eighty years, a lot of progress was obviously made. Yet women remain underrepresented in policing, and the current rate of progress is such that we will not achieve equality with men for about another seventy-seven years. Here, I'll briefly outline the past and present status of women in policing. I'll also chart a course for the future that includes increasing women's representation and transforming the police force toward a more community-oriented style of policing.

A Brief History

Pioneers like Lola Baldwin led the way for women in policing, but even when I began my career in the 1960s I was hired as a policewoman. The position wasn't equal in pay or stature to that of patrolman, which was explicitly described as being available only to men. In 1968, the Indianapolis Police Department was the first to assign women to patrol on an equal basis with the men. Other agencies followed, including the Federal Bureau of Investigation, which hired its first female agent in 1972.

Throughout this period of change, women entered the field of law enforcement in larger numbers, but their service was nonetheless seen as an experiment. In fact, several research studies were conducted in the early 1970s to see whether women could actually perform the job successfully. The answer was a unanimous yes. Not only were female officers just as competent as their male peers, but—as the research began to illuminate—women brought some unique advantages to the field. For example, female officers were often better at communicating with citizens, and they used these skills to deescalate situations that might otherwise have turned violent. This is something that I have certainly found to be true, and female officers from around the country all say the same thing—they prefer to talk through a situation rather than resort to physical force because it is a smarter way to do business.

As women made gains in the field of policing, we were helped by groundbreaking legislation. Perhaps the most important was the 1964 Civil Rights Act, which Congress passed to extend legal protection to both women and minorities in the workplace. This was followed in 1972 by the guidelines published by the Equal Employment Opportunity Commission for law enforcement agencies about the employment of minorities and women.

However, much of the progress has been the result of brave female officers who used the court system to challenge the discrimination and harassment they experienced. Over the years, lawsuits filed around the country have improved the practices involved in hiring, assignment, and promotion. In Portland, we filed many civil rights complaints and negotiated agreements in each of these areas. It is perhaps unfortunate that women have so often had to file a lawsuit to improve their situation, but by doing so they have reduced discrimination and opened the field to other women who followed them.

Current Status

Despite the many important gains women have made in policing, research consistently reveals that we are still vastly underrepresented. As director of the National Center for Women and Policing, I oversee our annual research into the current status of women in policing. Each year, we identify a random sample of police agencies with a hundred or more sworn officers, and we ask them to provide detailed information regarding the women within their agency. In 2000, we found that women represented only 13 percent of sworn personnel in these large agencies.[1] This is a paltry four percentage points higher than 1990, when women represented 9 percent of sworn law enforcement. Considering that women accounted for 46.5 percent of the adult labor market in 2000,[2] it is clear that we have a long way to go before we will be equally represented. Worse, the pace of increase is so slow that women gain only half a percentage point every year. This means that it will be decades before women will achieve equality with men in policing.

The reasons for women's underrepresentation in policing are many. Research indicates that discrimination continues to exist in hiring and promotion practices and that many women experience a wide range of harassing behaviors once on the job. Only a small number of women who experience harassment report the misconduct, however, out of fear of retaliation. Unfortunately, this fear is well founded. Women who report discrimination or harassment do often experience retaliation, and it is sometimes so severe that they leave the field as a result.

There are signs, however, that this is beginning to change. In recent years, many agencies have had a difficult time recruiting qualified personnel, and police executives are beginning to realize that they cannot overlook half of the pool of potential applicants. There is also a growing body of research documenting the many advantages of female officers. As I've previously described, research conducted both in the 1970s and more recently demonstrates that women often use a style of policing that relies more on communication and less on physical force. Women also tend to ascribe more to the ideals of community policing and are much less likely to use excessive force than their male colleagues. Finally, female officers respond more effectively to crimes of violence against women, and our very presence often brings about positive change in the culture of policing.[3] For all of these reasons, police executives across the country are redesigning their agencies to better recruit and retain women.

(*continued*)

PRACTITIONER'S PERSPECTIVE (*continued*)

Looking to the Future

There is still a long way to go. We all read the headlines and know that police agencies around the country are struggling with problems of excessive force, corruption, and public mistrust. Much of the problem is due to the structure of the agencies themselves, which often provide too little supervision and reinforce all the wrong behaviors. However, another significant part of the problem is the type of person that police agencies have historically sought. With the "he-man" stereotype of policing as a profession for only those with the thickest necks, police agencies have placed too much emphasis on factors like upper-body strength and military experience.

As agencies shift toward a more community-oriented style of policing, we must rethink these stereotypes and look for people who possess the kinds of skills this new kind of officer will need. Recruitment must begin to focus on interpersonal skills, including communication and an appreciation for diversity. Agencies must seek out individuals who can creatively solve neighborhood problems and work with citizens to build trust and partnerships. In many cases, these individuals will be women.

I have a lot of hope for the future of policing. I believe that agencies will (perhaps slowly) improve their recruitment and retention of women. At the National Center for Women and Policing, we do everything we can to promote that change and to transform the face of policing. Our communities deserve the best police services, and women and men must work together to see that this happens.

[1] *Equality Denied: The Status of Women in Policing 2000* (National Center for Women and Policing, 2000), available at www.feminist.org/police.
[2] Bureau of Labor Statistics, 2000. Available at www.bls.gov.
[3] *Hiring and Retaining More Women: The Advantages to Law Enforcement Agencies* (National Center for Women and Policing, 2000), available at www.feminist.org/police.

Academy Training. Recruits must be trained in sexually integrated academy classes to ensure full integration between female and male officers. Female instructors are especially important during academy training because they are positive role models and help female rookies develop skills and confidence. These instructors should teach more than the stereotypical "feminine" parts of the curriculum (such as child abuse or juvenile delinquency). Involving female instructors in firearms and physical/self-defense training will send a message that trained female officers can effectively handle the physical aspects of policing.

Field Training. Field training officers (FTOs, discussed in Chapter 3) play a crucial role in transforming the academy graduate into a competent field officer. FTOs should be both supportive of female rookies and effective evaluators of their competence. Female officers should serve as FTOs.

Assignments. A rookie's assignments have long-term effects on his or her policing career; agencies should routinely review the daily assignments of all probationary officers to ensure that they have equal opportunity to become effective patrol officers. If women are removed from patrol early in their careers (for any reason), they will miss vital field patrol experience. The majority of supervisory positions exist in the patrol division, and departments generally believe that field supervisors must have adequate field experience in order to be effective and respected by subordinates. Special assignments are often quite attractive, with better working shifts and days off, greater independence, and increased salaries and benefits. These positions are highly sought after, and male officers may resent women who receive coveted assignments merely because of their gender. Furthermore, agencies should conduct audits of such assignments to ensure that women are not assigned to stereotypical jobs, as was the case in the past.

Promotions. For a number of reasons, women are not getting promoted in proportion to their numbers. The so-called glass ceiling continues to restrict women's progress through the ranks. Performance evaluations and the overall promotional system utilized by agencies should be scrutinized for gender bias. For example, studies show that the more subjective the promotion process, the less likely women are to pass it. To provide more objectivity (in terms of ability to measure aptitude), the process should include more hands-on (practical, applied) tasks and the selection of board members who represent both sexes.

Harassment and Discrimination. Police agencies across the nation have paid millions of dollars in compensation for acts of harassment and discrimination against female officers. Aside from the obvious financial toll, sexual discrimination and harassment exact a human cost from the women involved—including a negative impact on their performance and careers (and, probably, a negative impact on the recruitment of other women into policing). A Police Foundation study found that "most women officers have experienced both sex discrimination and harassment on the job."[34] Departments need to have policies in place concerning sexual harassment and gender discrimination—and they need to enforce them. Furthermore, all supervisory candidates should be screened for their own treatment of women and attitudes about women in policing.

Mentoring. Retention issues are also significant in policing. Female officers have a higher turnover rate (about 6 percent) than men (about 4 percent). The employee's experience as he or she transitions into the organization can be a deciding factor in whether the employee remains with the organization. Formal mentoring programs—which can begin even before the rookie enters the academy—have helped some agencies raise their retention rates for women; such programs might include having a veteran employee provide new hires with information concerning what to expect at the academy and during field training and the probationary period. Mentors can also act as confidants and can provide access to informal organizational networks.

Today, women in law enforcement have a variety of assignments, including investigations, SWAT, and motorcycle patrol.

(Monica Geddry [top] and Vivian Lord [bottom])

Career and Family. Police work can create a considerable amount of conflict between one's work life and one's family life. The fact that women have a slightly higher turnover rate and use somewhat more sick leave than their male counterparts are related to their family lives and responsibilities as wives and mothers. The treatment of pregnant officers has been one of the more complex (and heavily litigated) personnel issues in recent years. To reduce this conflict, police agencies should have a leave policy covering pregnancy and maternity leave. Light- or limited-duty assignments (for example, desk, communications, records) can be made available to female officers when reassignment is necessary. Other issues include the availability of quality child care, shift rotation (which can more heavily burden single parents), and uniforms, body armor, and firearms that fit women.

As the community-oriented policing and problem solving (COPPS) concept continues to expand, female officers can likewise play an increasingly vital role. (COPPS is examined in Chapter 6.)

Experts maintain that the verbal skills many women possess often have a calming effect that defuses potentially explosive situations. Such a style is especially effective in handling rape and domestic violence calls.[35] As former Madison, Wisconsin, police chief David Couper put it, female officers have helped usher in a "kinder, gentler organization."[36]

Still, this clearly remains an area in which policing has been slow to change. For women to serve effectively as police officers, police managers must see the value of employing women and vigorously recruiting, hiring, and retaining them. As shown earlier, a basic task for the chief executive is to consider how departmental policies affect female officers with respect to selection, training, promotion, sexual harassment, and family leave. Most important, executives must set a tone of welcoming women into the department.

Minorities as Police Officers

In the last decade of the 1990s, **minority police officers** made dramatic gains in their representation in local police agencies. From 1987 to 2000, minorities accounted for 22.7 percent of municipal police officers (up from 14.5 percent in 1987) and 17.1 percent of sworn personnel in sheriff's offices (compared to 13.4 percent in 1987).[37] And, as with women, federal law enforcement agencies are major employers of members of racial or ethnic minorities—32.4 percent overall.[38]

Several developments of the early 1970s spurred the growth of African-Americans in policing, including federal reports (such as that from the U.S. Commission on Civil Rights[39]), the Supreme Court's decision in *Griggs* v. *Duke Power Company* (1971) banning the use of intelligence tests and other artificial barriers that were not job-related,[40] and federal legislation like the Equal Employment Opportunities Act of 1972. The mid-1970s witnessed the advent of the National Black Police Association and the National Organization of Black Law Enforcement Executives (NOBLE), which advocated increased hiring of minority officers and improvement of community relations. In the 1980s, several lawsuits successfully challenged such requirements as height, age, weight, sex, and a clean arrest record.[41]

Recruitment of minority officers remains a difficult task. Probably the single most difficult barrier has to do with the image that minority communities have of police officers. Unfortunately, police officers have been

Police departments must strive to enhance diversification in their ranks.

(Michael Newman, Photo Edit)

seen as symbols of oppression and have been charged with using excessive brutality; they are often seen as an army of occupation. Many minorities view African-American police officers as people who have "sold out." For many of those African-Americans in uniforms, a so-called **double marginality** has existed, whereby the African-American officers feel accepted neither by their own minority group nor by the white officers. However, many African-Americans view police work as an opportunity to leave the ghetto and enter the middle class. As one officer put it, "There were two ways to get out of my neighborhood and not end up dead or in prison. You either became a minister or a cop. I always fell asleep in church so I decided to become a cop."[42]

African-American police officers face problems similar to those of women who attempt to enter and prosper in police work. Until more African-American officers are promoted and can affect police policy and serve as role models, they are likely to be treated unequally and have difficulty being promoted—a classic catch-22 situation. African-Americans considering a police career may be encouraged by a survey of African-American officers, which found that most thought their jobs were satisfying and offered opportunities for advancement.[43]

Interestingly, a study of African-American high school students found that although negative experiences with the police increased negative attitudes toward the police, these attitudes did not in themselves reduce interest in police work. The findings suggested that police recruiters need not expend a lot of effort trying to neutralize perceptions that African-American people are treated unfairly by the police. A greater concern among the students was the danger of the job itself. Therefore, it may be more important for police departments to educate the parents of potential African-American recruits about the benefits and objectives of police work rather than focus excessively on dealing with negative attitudes.[44]

On Guard: The Private Police

A burgeoning industry in this country is one that is both a "trend" and an "issue," as we will see; this industry is that of the **private police**, which provide protective services for profit.

Historical Overview. Since prehistoric times, people have sought security from enemies and from beasts of prey by developing weapons, building and fortifying caves, and using fire, stone, hemp, and water to punish and control their fellow humans. We have sought to protect ourselves from a hostile environment.[45]

In the early nineteenth century in England, private police were hired as watchmen by shipping docks, industrial firms, and railroad companies. In the mid-nineteenth century, America's western frontier was awash with train robbers, pickpockets, bootleggers, and common outlaws; as a result, railroad companies were allowed to establish their own in-house, proprietary security forces. This was also the beginning of the contract (fee-for-service) security system for private concerns.[46]

In 1851, a pioneer in the private security industry, Allan Pinkerton, initiated the Pinkerton National Detective Agency, which specialized in railroad security. Pinkerton established the first private security contract operation in the United States. His motto was "We Never Sleep," and his logo, an open eye, was probably the genesis of the term *private eye*. Pinkerton also established a code of ethics for his agents. Other pioneers in the security industry were Henry Wells and William Fargo, who in 1853 formed a contract security company, Wells Fargo, that provided private detectives and shotgun riders on stagecoaches west of the Missouri River.

Later, in 1909, William J. Burns, a former head of the forerunner agency of the Federal Bureau of Investigation (FBI), founded a detective agency. (Pinkerton and Burns had the only national investigative agencies until the formation of the FBI in 1924.) In 1917, the Brinks armored car was unveiled. In 1954, George R. Wackenhut and three other former FBI agents formed the Wackenhut Corporation, another large contract guard and investigative firm in the United States.[47]

In "a Nation of Thieves." Saul Astor said, "We are a nation of thieves."[48] And, it might be added, a nation of rapists, robbers, and other dangerous offenders. About 23 million offenses are committed in America each year,

William A. Pinkerton, principal of the western branch of Pinkerton's National Detective Agency.

(International Association of Chiefs of Police)

5.3 million of which are violent.[49] As a result, this nation has become security minded concerning its computers, lotteries, celebrities, college campuses, casinos, nuclear plants, airports, shopping centers, mass transit systems, hospitals, and railroads.

Given this crime picture and level of concern and the limited capabilities of the nation's full-time sworn federal, state, and local agents, officers, and deputies, it is not surprising that Americans have increasingly turned to the "other police"—those of the private sector—for protection.

There are now more than ten thousand private security companies in the United States, employing over seven hundred thousand uniformed officers as well as about one hundred thousand managers and store detectives.[50] Thus the private policing field is larger in both personnel and resources than the federal, state, and local forces combined.[51]

In-house security services, directly hired and controlled by the company or organization, are called "proprietary services"; contract services are outside firms or individuals who provide security services for a fee. The most common security services provided include contract guards, alarm services, private investigators, locksmith services, armored-car services, and security consultants.[52]

Although some of the duties of the security officer are similar to those of the public police officer, their overall powers are entirely different. First, because security officers are not police officers, court decisions have stated that the security officer is not bound by the

Miranda decision concerning suspects' rights. Furthermore, security officers generally possess only the same authority to effect an arrest as does the common citizen (the exact extent of citizen's arrest power varies, however, depending on the type of crime, jurisdiction, and the status of the citizen). In most states, warrantless arrests by private citizens are allowed when a felony has been committed and reasonable grounds exist for believing that the person arrested committed it. Most states also allow citizen's arrests for misdemeanors committed in the arrester's presence.[53]

The tasks of the private police are very similar to those of their public counterparts: protecting executives and employees, tracking and forecasting security threats, monitoring alarms, preventing and detecting fraud, conducting investigations, providing crisis management and prevention, and responding to substance abuse.[54] Still, the security industry and security officers are not always portrayed in a positive manner in popular culture; movies often cast them as poorly trained, incompetent individuals. Indeed, one study found that security officers and their work are viewed significantly *less* positively by males, whites, those who have had an encounter with a security officer, and the middle class.[55]

Recruitment and Training. With the boom of the industry, in terms of both numbers of employees and dollars spent, there have also been problems and concerns. As one author noted, "Of those individuals involved in private security, some are uniformed, some are not; some carry guns, some are unarmed; some guard nuclear energy installations, some guard golf courses; some are trained, some are not; some have college degrees, some are virtually uneducated."[56]

Studies have shown that security officer recruits generally have minimal education and training; because the pay is usually quite low, the work attracts only people who cannot find other jobs or who seek only temporary work. Thus most of the work is done by the young and the retired.[57] The recruitment and training of lower-level private security personnel presents a major concern to both law enforcement officials and civil liberties groups.[58] All too often, the new security officer is taught only the security "primer": the chain of command, how to use a radio, and uniform dress standards. Some organizations "train" their employees by merely having them accompany other security officers around the company's facility.[59] For these reasons, security training has been an issue in court cases involving claims of negligent security.

Carrying Weapons. A long-running debate is whether the private police should even be armed at all. When an employer decides to arm security personnel, the type and level of firearms training that is provided is justifiably called into closer scrutiny. Much ado has been made about security officers who have received little or no prior training or have undergone no checks on their criminal history records but are carrying a weapon. This debate will probably not be settled in the foreseeable future. However, both sides agree that there are some roles in which security officers must be armed, such as protecting high-risk or high-value assets, such as nuclear power plants or money transported in armored cars. Twenty-three hours of firearms instruction is recommended for all security personnel, as well as another twenty-four hours on general matters and proper legal training.[60]

The Problem of Liability. Civil liability has become an increasing concern in the private security industry. Civil actions may be brought against any private security officer who commits an unlawful action against another person. Often, the officer's employer is sued as well.[61] The typical scenario develops when a person is attacked on property that either is patrolled by a private security company, has a security officer stationed on the premises, or has no security present. Then, when the assailant is not caught or has no assets to compensate the injured victim, the victim sues the landowner and security company for damages. Thus reasonable precautions must be taken to try to prevent innocent people from being victimized.

Accreditation

In 1979, the **accreditation** of police agencies began slowly with the creation of the **Commission on Accreditation for Law Enforcement Agencies (CALEA)**, located in Fairfax, Virginia. CALEA is a nonprofit organization that has developed and administers 439 voluntary standards for law enforcement agencies to meet. These standards cover the role and responsibilities of the agency; its organization and administration; law enforcement, traffic, and operational support; prisoner- and court-related services; and auxiliary and technical services. Accreditation, a voluntary process, is quite expensive, both in actual dollars and in human resources; it often takes a year to eighteen months for an agency to prepare for the assessment.[62] Today, there are nearly 700 agencies accredited or recognized in one of the Commission's various programs, with several hundred others working toward their first award.[63]

Once an agency believes it is ready to be accredited, an application is filed and the agency receives a self-evaluation questionnaire to determine its current status. If the self-evaluation indicates that the agency is ready to attempt accreditation, an on-site team appointed by CALEA conducts an assessment and writes a report on its findings. After becoming accredited, the agency must apply for reaccreditation after five years.[64]

Several unanticipated consequences of the accreditation process have emerged. A number of states have formed coalitions to assist police agencies in the process of accreditation. Also, some departments also report decreased insurance costs as a result of accreditation. Finally, the national transition to community-oriented policing and problem solving (COPPS, discussed in Chapter 6) has not been lost on CALEA. Today, the accreditation self-assessment process provides many opportunities to institutionalize community policing. Not only do the accreditation standards help weave community policing into an agency's internal fabric, they also provide a way to integrate such objectives into external service delivery, such as:

- enhancing the role and authority of patrol officers;
- improving analysis and information management; and
- managing calls for service.[65]

In comparing accredited and nonaccredited police agencies, Kimberly McCabe and Robin Fajardo found that accredited police agencies (1) provided more training for their officers and required higher minimum educational requirements for new officers; (2) were nearly twice as likely to require drug testing for sworn applicants; and (3) were more likely to operate special units for the enforcement of drug laws and laws against child abuse.[66] However, the study "did not always reveal positive support for accreditation."[67] Notwithstanding the rigorous standards that must be met in order for agencies to become accredited, McCabe and Fajardo found that there were no differences in accredited versus nonaccredited agencies in terms of their starting salaries or annual budgets, officer demographics (for example, race and sex of the officers), or the officers' wearing of body armor. (Because many researchers view accreditation as a means of reducing liability insurance, it was expected that officers in accredited agencies would be required to wear protective body armor.)[68]

Contemporary Policing Issues

Higher Education for Police

An Enduring Controversy. One of the most enduring and controversial issues in policing is whether police officers benefit from, and should pursue, higher education.

Efforts to involve college-educated personnel in police work were first made by August Vollmer in 1917, when he recruited University of California students as part-time police officers in Berkeley.[69] However, few departments elsewhere in the country took any immediate steps to follow Vollmer's example. Rank-and-file officers strongly resisted the concept of college-level studies for police, and officers with a college education remained very much an exception; they were often referred to disparagingly as "college cops."[70]

However, the movement toward higher education for police continued to spread; by 1975, there were 729 community college programs and 376 four-year programs.[71] The Law Enforcement Education Program (LEEP) provided tuition assistance for in-service police officers and preservice students. In 1973, ninety-five thousand college and university students were receiving LEEP assistance; these were unquestionably the "glory days" of higher education in criminal justice.[72] Many patrol officers who otherwise could not have afforded to do so received quality higher education.

Rationales for and against Higher Education for Police. In 1973, the National Advisory Commission on Criminal Justice Standards and Goals, recognizing the need for college-educated police officers, recommended that all police officers have a four-year college education by 1982.[73] That goal obviously went unmet. Nevertheless, from 1967 to 1986, every national commission that studied crime, violence, and policing in America came to the conclusion that a college education could help the police do their jobs better.[74] Advocates of higher education for the police maintain that it will improve the quality of policing by making officers more tolerant of people who are different from themselves; in this view, college-educated officers are more professional, communicate better with citizens, are better decision makers, and have better written and verbal skills than less-educated officers.

A ringing endorsement for higher education for the police came in 1985, when a lawsuit challenged the Dallas, Texas, Police Department's requirement that all applicants for police officer positions possess 45 credit hours and at least a C average at an accredited college or university. The Fifth Circuit Court of Appeals, and eventually the U.S. Supreme Court, upheld the educational requirement. The circuit court said,

> Even a rookie police officer must have the ability to handle tough situations. A significant part of a police officer's function involves his ability to function effectively as a crisis intervenor, in family fights, teen-age rumbles, bar brawls, street corner altercations, racial disturbances, riots and similar situations. Few professionals are so peculiarly charged with individual responsibilities as police officers. Mistakes of judgment could cause irreparable harm to citizens or even to the community. The educational requirement bears a manifest relationship to the position of police officer. We conclude that the district court's findings... are not erroneous.[75]

Conversely, critics believe that educated officers are more likely to become frustrated with their work and that their limited opportunities for advancement will cause them to leave the force early. Furthermore, they argue that police tasks that require mostly common sense or street sense are not performed better by officers with higher education.[76]

EXHIBIT 12-1

For Florida Police, Higher Education Means Lower Risk of Disciplinary Action

Police officers with just a high school diploma made up just over half of all sworn law enforcement personnel in Florida between the years 1997 and 2002, yet they accounted for nearly three quarters of all disciplinary actions issued by the state, according to a preliminary study commissioned by the International Association of Chiefs of Police.

The findings in "Discipline and Educational Levels of Law Enforcement Officers: An Exploratory Report" are based on statistics gathered by the Florida Criminal Justice Standards and Training Commission. As of August 2002, Florida had 42,910 sworn officers. Of those, 24,800 had high school diplomas; 6,777 had associate's degrees, and 10,364 had bachelor's degrees. Another 867 officers held master's degrees and 102 had earned doctorates, said the report.

Officers with no degree above high school accounted for a startling 74.8 percent of the 727 disciplinary actions issued by the CJSTC during the five-year period. Those with bachelor's degrees made up 11.9 percent of the total, and those with two-year degrees represented 12.2 percent. Only six of the 867 officers with master's degrees were disciplined by the agency, and one of the 102 who hold doctorates.

"Education and law enforcement has been debated for decades," said Deputy Chief Scott A. Cunningham of the Tampa Police Department, the study's author and chairman of the IACP's police administrative committee. . . .

"We needed to finally put it to rest, and say that all the rest of society values higher-educated people," said Cunningham, who holds a Ph.D. degree in adult education from the University of South Florida. "Law enforcement, just on the bare face, shouldn't be any different there."

The committee is ready to go forward on a "massive study on education," he said.

Cunningham noted that the discipline imposed on the officers in the cases studied was severe. The study looked at the harshest penalties—revocation and voluntary relinquishment of certification—and found that those with the lowest levels of education were disproportionately represented, accounting for 76 percent of certification losses. Officers holding bachelor's degree and above accounted for only 11.6 percent of decertifications, the study said.

Officers with high school diplomas accounted for 80.4 percent of the 332 revocations between 1997 and 2002, and 70.9 percent of the voluntary relinquishments.

"From this base review of state-administered discipline, it is apparent that higher educated officers have significantly less discipline than less educated counterparts," said the report.

Source: "For Florida Police, Higher Education Means Lower Risk of Disciplinary Action, *Law Enforcement News*, October 31, 2002, pp. 1, 10. John Jay College of Criminal Justice, CUNY, 555 W. 57th St., New York, NY 10019.

Police administrators fear that having a formal educational requirement will prompt discrimination suits from minorities who do not possess such an education, that the police officers' union would seek higher pay and benefits for such a requirement, and that academy classes would go unfilled; many administrators also lack the conviction that higher education is beneficial for officers.

However, abundant empirical evidence indicates that college-educated police officers are better officers. Compared to less-educated officers, they have significantly fewer founded citizen complaints;[77] have better peer relationships;[78] are likelier to take a leadership role in the organization;[79] tend to be more flexible;[80] are less dogmatic and less authoritarian;[81] take fewer leave days, receive fewer injuries, have less injury time, have lower rates of absenteeism, use fewer sick days, and are involved in fewer traffic accidents;[82] have greater ability to analyze situations and make judicious decisions; and have a more desirable system of personal values.[83] Furthermore, college graduates are significantly less likely to violate their department's internal regulations regarding insubordination, negligent use of a firearm, and absenteeism than officers who lack a college degree.[84]

Some studies, however, have found negative effects of higher education. These studies found that it had no positive effect on officers' public service orientation (those with a degree displayed less orientation toward public service than those without a degree)[85] and that college-educated officers attach less value on obedience to supervisors than officers without a college education.[86]

Because a number of views and arguments for both sides of the issue remain, it is unlikely that this question will be resolved soon. Perhaps the entry of federal courts into the foray will help to expedite a resolution. Change is also indicated by such developments as the Tulsa, Oklahoma, Police Department requirement as of January 1998 that all new hires possess a bachelor's degree. The Tulsa police chief, Ron Palmer, has observed "a world of difference between a high school graduate and a college graduate in regard to the skill levels and the handling of people."[87] Palmer also found that the requirement has not hampered the department's efforts to attract more minority recruits. Another indicator of change is the existence of the American Police Association, based in Alexandria, Virginia, which is composed of college-educated officers.

It seems paradoxical—given the research, the increase in educational level of society in general, and the need for police agencies to recruit the best people—that in this new millennium, our society still does not require higher educational standards for police officers. No true profession requires less than a college degree. Police, in their quest for greater professionalism, should take notice.[88]

A Related Program: The Police Corps

The era of police higher education may be returning through the Violent Crime Control and Law Enforcement Act of 1994 (the so-called Crime Act), which provided $200 million for a Police Corps program and an in-service scholarship program. The Police Corps program is discussed more thoroughly in Appendix II.

Stress: Sources, Effects, and Management

There is a side of policing that many people would prefer to ignore: job-related **stress**. Indeed, Sir W. S. Gilbert observed that "when constabulary duty's to be done, the policeman's lot is not a happy one."[89]

Stress can be defined as "a force that is external in nature that causes strain upon the body, both physical and emotional, from its normal process." The late Hans Selye, who is known as the "father of stress research," defined *stress* as a nonspecific response of a body to demands placed upon it.

William Westley observed more than thirty years ago that "the policeman's world is spawned of degradation, corruption and insecurity. He walks alone, a pedestrian in Hell."[90] Being a cop today has been described as a "stop-and-go nightmare."[91] As noted in Chapter 5, the job of policing has never been easy, but the danger, frustration, and family disruption of the past have been made worse by the drug war and by violent criminals who are heavily armed and hold more contempt for the police than ever before.

Sources of Stress. There are several potential sources of stress for police officers:

I. Stressors Originating within the Organization
   A. Intra-Agency Practices and Characteristics
      1. *Poor supervision:* Stress can be fostered by supervisors who go by the book and issue a constant flurry of memos, won't back up their subordinates, or fail to attend to their basic needs. These behaviors can contribute substantially to the stress levels of subordinates.
      2. *Absence of career development opportunities:* The vast majority of police officers start and end their careers as patrol officers. Promotional oppor-

Dr. Hans Selye, the "father of stress research."

(Courtesy Edward Donovan)

tunities are limited, and the promotion process can lack fairness and generate frustration.

3. *Inadequate reward system:* Recognition and compensation are limited for work that is well done. A lot of negative reinforcement exists in police work. Punishment—demotion, reprimand, suspension, termination, reassignment—is commonly meted out when things go wrong.
4. *Offensive policy:* Police organizations possess numerous policies and guidelines that officers find offensive, such as locking and unlocking municipal parking lots, emptying parking meters, and running all kinds of errands.
5. *Offensive paperwork:* The volume of paperwork that police officers must complete is incredible. Computerization has generally created more paperwork for police officers because management now wants additional kinds of information.
6. *Poor equipment:* In policing, inadequate vehicles, communication equipment, and safety equipment (flares, for example) can become sources of frustration.

II. Stressors External to the Organization

Stressors that come from outside of the organization can cause a great deal of tension; with few exceptions, the individual officer or agency normally has little or no control over them.

A. Interorganizational Practices and Characteristics

1. *Absence of career development opportunities:* Few chances for mobility exist in police work; rank and seniority are seldom transferable to another agency, so opportunities for lateral moves are limited. Thus the officer must remain with the same agency unless he or she retires or is willing to start anew.
2. *Jurisdictional isolationism:* Police agencies are not always the tight, congenial fraternity that the public often imagines. Jurisdictional boundaries can be guarded zealously. Some police agencies are notorious for withholding information or for grabbing credit for good arrests.

B. Criminal Justice System Practices and Characteristics

1. *Seemingly ineffective corrections system:* The police often see corrections agencies (for example, probation and parole agencies and prisons) as a revolving door for criminals; attempts to rehabilitate offenders at these agencies often fail.
2. *The courts:* Unfavorable court decisions and misunderstood judicial procedure (for example, plea bargaining) lead to considerable frustration for the police.

C. Distorted Press Accounts of Police Incidents

Reporters sometimes distort the news because they gather the facts hastily to meet deadlines, do not understand the facts, or simply do not care enough to report them accurately. Overzealous reporters can interfere with investigations.

D. Unfavorable Civilian Attitudes

Minorities often accuse police of over- or underpolicing their neighborhoods or being brutal and racist. Similarly, the majority often complain about police response time and argue that the police should be out trying to catch bank robbers instead of issuing traffic citations.

E. Derogatory Remarks by Neighbors and Others

In a sense, police officers are never completely off duty; they are always cops, accosted at home and while attending social functions by people who want to complain about the police or who want legal advice.

F. Adverse Government Actions

Units of government often make decisions without consulting police officers or managers, including decisions about budgeting, recruitment, hiring, firing, and downsizing. Public officials may monitor and chase police calls, make and enforce policy, check on officers, and seek to "fix" arrests of friends or family members.

III. Stressors Connected with the Performance of Police Duties

A. Police Work Itself

1. *Role conflict:* Police must determine when to maintain a crime fighter image and when to portray an order-maintenance role. The public expects officers to be all things to all people—social worker, minister, physician, babysitter, psychologist, and so forth.
2. *Adverse work scheduling:* Shift work, especially the graveyard shift and a rotating shift schedule, can adversely affect an officer's health as well as family and social life,[92] causing constant adjustment to new sleeping and eating patterns.
3. *Fear and danger:* As noted in Chapter 5, fear and danger are constant companions of police officers, so officers need to keep their survival instincts honed. An annual FBI publication, *Law Enforcement Officers Killed and Assaulted*, regularly reveals an unsettling fact: Police officers often are overpowered, outmuscled, disarmed, and murdered by offenders whom they try to arrest. Different types of assignments can bring greater stress; for example, working undercover[93] and homicide investigation[94] have been identified as particularly stressful. Also, many times officers are simply in poorer physical condition than the criminals they chase. Today more than ever, officers need to maintain a good physical state. In addition, they must also properly maintain their equipment; use deescalation techniques (sometimes termed "verbal judo"); employ physical defense, approach, and positioning tactics; properly use backup personnel; deploy proper weapon and driving skills; use safe techniques when searching buildings; and handle prisoners with care.[95]
4. *Sense of uselessness and inefficiency of referral agencies:* Many officers entered the police service to help people. However, in many jurisdictions few agencies are available to which the police can refer people with problems. Police see firsthand the outcomes of the absence of such social services—suicides, murders, spousal or child abuse, and so on.

5. *Absence of closure:* Police can seldom close their cases through disposition; furthermore, plea bargaining affects much of what they did in the first place (what is believed to be a "righteous" arrest is often reduced down by the prosecutor).
6. *People pain:* The police see firsthand the gamut of violence humans employ against one another, and they witness both crime victims and offenders at their worst. Police deal constantly with people in pain and are expected to remain calm and collected during the entire affair.

IV. Stressors Particular to the Individual Officer

A. The Police Officer Himself/Herself

1. *The fear-ridden:* Some, although not many, police officers are overcome by the fear and danger of the job; they are in constant fear for their physical well-being. These officers generally leave the force well before retirement.
2. *The nonconformist:* Police work demands a certain amount of conformity and adherence to a chain of command, allowing little room for individualism or freedom of expression. Court decisions have allowed police administrators to have residency requirements, a dress code, and so on. Pressures to conform can be severe, and some nonconforming officers cannot endure such pressure.
3. *The minority officer:* Both African-American and female police officers suffer discrimination by virtue of entering a predominantly white, male occupation.

An Orlando, Florida, police officer cries after telling a mother that her child died in a house fire.

(Courtesy Bobby Coker / Orlando Sentinel)

A New York Police Department scuba diver is overwhelmed by what he has just seen at the bottom of a body of water.

(Courtesy City of New York Police Department Photo Unit)

V. Effects of Critical Incidents

Several stressful repercussions can follow a police shooting. The officer is generally suspended from work pending a full investigation. He or she is secluded from work and peers, and the officer's gun, badge, and other trappings of the job are taken away.[96] Relationships with family may become strained, and the officer may experience time distortion, emotional numbing, a feeling of isolation, denial, flashbacks, sleep disturbances, legal problems, and guilt.[97] A high percentage of police officers who kill another person leave the force within five years.[98]

Effects and Management of Stress. It has been estimated that at any one time, 15 percent of a department's officers will be in a burnout phase. These officers account for 70 to 80 percent of all the complaints against their department, including physical abuse, verbal abuse, and misuse of firearms.[99] If they do not relieve the pressure, they may eventually suffer heart attacks, nervous breakdowns, back problems, headaches, psychosomatic illnesses, and alcoholism.[100] They may also manifest excessive weight gain or loss; combativeness or irritability; excessive perspiration; excessive use of sick leave; excessive use of alcohol, tobacco, or drugs; marital or family disorders; inability to complete an assignment; loss of interest in work, hobbies, and people in general; more than the usual number of "accidents," including vehicular and other types; and more shooting incidents.[101] An extreme reaction to stress is suicide. Police are at a higher risk for committing suicide because of their access to firearms, continuous exposure to human misery, shift work, social strain and marital difficulties, physical illness, and alcohol problems. Police are eight times more likely to commit suicide than to be killed in a homicide, three times more likely to kill themselves than to die in a job-related accident.[102]

EXHIBIT 12-2

The Blue Plague of American Policing

Cops kill themselves three times more often than other Americans. They suffer more depression, divorce more, and drink more—as many as one in four police officers have alcohol abuse problems. Cops are unhappy. They feel estranged from their departments and from a public eager to find a scapegoat for their own social, economic and political woes. This problem should give pause to everyone, to supporters and critics of the police department alike. Society needs police officers, and we need them to be happy and healthy.

The numbers are staggering. . . . Researchers at the University of Buffalo have found that police officers are eight times more likely to commit suicide than to be killed in a homicide. The most recent U.S. Census estimates that police officers divorce twice as often as the national average. The respected researchers J. J. Hurrell and W. H. Kroes say that as many as 25 percent of police officers have alcohol abuse problems. This evidence cannot be ignored. Police officers are suffering from anomie; they believe that society is turning its back on them. . . .

So what's going wrong? Why do cops feel unappreciated even as their performance improves? . . . The truth . . . is that the most common and debilitating source of stress in law enforcement comes from within the agency itself. Cops don't complain about the added complexity of their jobs nearly as much as they do about the agency for which they work. . . . Ask cops what they don't like about their jobs and they cite internal politics, favoritism and impersonal treatment as their most common criticisms of their work environment. Internal surveys reveal that cops rate personal stress management as their most pressing need. Working in a paramilitary structure depersonalizes and marginalizes people from top to bottom. Decision-making structures that deprive them of input embitter officers and breed cynicism. They resent supervisors who treat them as numbers, who have no consideration for their personal or family lives, who play favorites in terms of choice assignments, shifts, and recognition. They doubt whether or not they will be backed up by their superiors in times of trouble. . . .

Police officers have an incredible capacity to deal with incidental stress. What police cannot deal with is the chronic stress of a system that marginalizes them. . . .

So what do we do?

We need to create a non-toxic work environment for the men and women that protect us. The training and education a police officer receives . . . offers little or nothing to prepare the future police officer to successfully adjust to the new and very different working environment of law enforcement. . . . Along with body armor, every man and woman entering this profession deserves a "stress vest" that provides them with the knowledge, skills and on-going services to combat the deadly consequences of stress.

Like any problem, the solution begins with awareness and education. . . . Beginning with the police academy experience, future police officers (cadets) need to learn about working in a complex bureaucracy. They need to learn how to deal with human tragedy and separate it from the way they interact with their own families and loved ones. Police officers need on-going services in stress management to maintain their identities as human beings first and understand that law enforcement is a job and career, not who they are. . . .

Source: Robert A. Fox, "The Blue Plague of American Policing," *Law Enforcement News*, May 15/31, 2003, p. 9. John Jay College of Criminal Justice, CUNY, 555 W. 57th St., New York, NY 10019.

No human being can exist in a continuous state of alarm. The body, striving to maintain its normal state, or homeostasis, and adapt to the alarm can actually develop a disease in the process. Often, however, the problem of stress is exacerbated by the reluctance of police to admit they have problems. They often avoid seeking professional psychological help; officers fear being placed on limited duty or being labeled "psychos" by their peers.[103] As they start to acknowledge the problem, many police departments are attempting to improve their recruit screening and provide better counseling programs.

It is imperative that officers learn to manage their stress before it causes deep physical or emotional harm. One means is to view the mind as a "mental bucket" and strive to keep it full through hobbies or activities that provide relaxation. Exercise, proper nutrition, and positive lifestyle choices (such as not smoking or abusing alcohol) are also essential for good health.

The federal government has taken official notice of the problem of police stress. In 1997, the National Institute of Justice awarded grants to eight police agencies and organizations for devising effective stress-reduction programs.[104]

SUMMARY

This chapter has examined contemporary trends and issues in policing. Despite its 150-year history, policing still has not resolved several longstanding problems and areas of controversy. For example, women and minorities have yet to be accepted in this occupation, even though studies have shown their tremendous value. Furthermore, higher education remains a questionable element of policing for many people, irrespective of the fact that major national commissions have been advocating this requirement for nearly three decades.

REVIEW QUESTIONS

1. Review the employment rights of today's police officers, including the common provisions of state Peace Officer Bill of Rights legislation.
2. Explain the major reasons for the development and expansion of police unions, and describe their impact today.
3. Describe the three models of collective bargaining. What happens under each model when there is an impasse?
4. Describe the four kinds of job actions.
5. Describe the Fair Labor Standards Act, and explain how it operates in policing.
6. Discuss the difficulty of recruiting and retaining women and minorities. What are the primary issues that concern women who are already working in policing?
7. What advantages does private policing offer? What problems are associated with private policing?
8. What are the benefits of accreditation for police agencies?

9. What are the benefits of hiring officers with a college degree?
10. List the major causes of stress, and explain how officers can manage it.

INDEPENDENT STUDENT ACTIVITIES

1. Interview local police practitioners about the kinds of calls for service that create the most stress for them. What lifestyle changes, if any, have they adopted to manage their stress? You might also probe into other possible contributors of stress, such as working the night shift, seeing crime victims at their worst, and so on.
2. Observe private security officers at work, noting the kinds of tasks they perform that are similar to and different from those of the public police.
3. Interview a police officer who is currently attending a college or university. What prompted the decision to attend school? What does the officer see as the benefits of higher education?
4. Interview a female or minority officer to determine the challenges or difficulties he or she confronted when entering law enforcement.
5. Determine whether the local police engage in formal collective bargaining. If so, what are the kinds of protections and provisions afforded officers under the contract or agreement?

RELATED WEB SITES

American Society for Industrial Security
http://www.securitymanagement.com

Commission on Accreditation for Law Enforcement Agencies
http://www.calea.org

National Labor Relations Board
http://www.nlrb.gov/nlrb/home/default.asp

Police-Stress.Com
http://police-stress.com

NOTES

1. W. Clinton Terry III, *Policing Society: An Occupational View* (New York: Wiley, 1985), p. 168.
2. Ibid.
3. Ibid., pp. 170–71.

4. Samuel Walker, *The Police in America: An Introduction*, 3d ed. (Boston: McGraw-Hill, 1999), p. 368.
5. American Federation of State, County and Municipal Employees, "About AFSME," http://www.afscme.org/about/officers.htm (accessed January 30, 2005).
6. Ibid., p. 318.
7. Will Aitchison, *The Rights of Police Officers*, 3d ed. (Portland, OR: Labor Relations Information System, 1996), p. 7.
8. Ibid.
9. Ibid.
10. Ibid., p. 8.
11. Ibid., p. 9.
12. Charles R. Swanson, Leonard Territo, and Robert W. Taylor, *Police Administration: Structures, Processes, and Behavior*, 6th ed. (Upper Saddle River, NJ: Prentice Hall, 2005), p. 517.
13. Arnold Zack, *Understanding Fact-Finding and Arbitration in the Public Sector* (Washington, DC: U.S. Government Printing Office, 1974), p. 1.
14. Thomas P. Gilroy and Anthony V. Sinicropi, "Impasse Resolution in Public Employment," *Industrial and Labor Relations Review* 25 (July 1971): 499.
15. Robert G. Howlett, "Fact Finding: Its Values and Limitations—Comment," *Arbitration and the Expanded Role of Neutrals*, proceedings of the twenty-third annual meeting of the National Academy of Arbitrators (Washington, DC: Bureau of National Affairs, 1970), p. 156.
16. Zack, *Understanding Fact-Finding and Arbitration in the Public Sector*, p. 1.
17. Charles W. Maddox, *Collective Bargaining in Law Enforcement* (Springfield, IL: Charles C. Thomas, 1975), p. 54.
18. Swanson, Territo, and Taylor, *Police Administration*, p. 530.
19. Ibid., p. 423.
20. Ibid.
21. L. Lund, "The 'Ten Commandments' of Risk Management for Jail Administrators," *Detention Reporter* 4 (June 1991): 4.
22. Garcia v. San Antonio Transit Authority, 469 U.S. 528 (1985).
23. Swanson, Territo, and Taylor, *Police Administration*, p. 392.
24. Barbara Raffel Price, "Sexual Integration in American Law Enforcement," in *Police Ethics: Hard Choices in Law Enforcement*, ed. William C. Heffernan and Timothy Stroup (New York: John Jay Press, 1985), pp. 205–14.
25. Jeanne McDowell, "Are Women Better Cops?" *Time*, February 17, 1992, p. 71.
26. National Center for Women and Policing, *Equality Denied: The Status of Women in Policing* (Washington, DC: Feminist Majority Foundation, 2001), p. 5.
27. Department of Justice, Bureau of Justice Statistics, "Federal Law Enforcement Officers, 2002," http//www.ojp.usdoj.go/bjs/abstract/fleo02.htm (accessed January 21, 2004).
28. Dorothy Moses Schulz, "Women Police Chiefs: A Statistical Profile," *Police Quarterly* 6, no. 3 (September 2003): 330–45.

29. PEG TYRE, "Ms. Top Cop," *Newsweek*, April 12, 2004, p. 49.
30. SCHULZ, "Women Police Chiefs," p. 333.
31. Ibid.
32. Ibid.
33. PETER HORNE, "Policewomen: 2000 A.D. Redux," *Law and Order* (November 1999): 53
34. Quoted in HORNE, "Policewomen," p. 59.
35. MCDOWELL, "Are Women Better Cops?" p. 71.
36. Quoted in ibid., p. 72.
37. DEPARTMENT OF JUSTICE, Bureau of Justice Statistics, "State and Local Law Enforcement Statistics," http://www.ojp.usdoj.gov/bjs/sandlle.htm (accessed January 21, 2004).
38. DEPARTMENT OF JUSTICE, Bureau of Justice Statistics, "Federal Law Enforcement Officers, 2002."
39. RICHARD MARGOLIS, *Who Will Wear the Badge? A Study of Minority Recruitment Efforts in Protective Services: A Report of the United States Commission on Civil Rights* (Washington, DC: U.S. Government Printing Office, n.d.).
40. GRIGGS v. DUKE POWER COMPANY, 401 U.S. 424 (1971).
41. ROBERT PURSLEY, *Introduction to Criminal Justice* (Encino, CA: Glencoe Press, 1977).
42. Quoted in PEGGY S. SULLIVAN, "Minority Officers: Current Issues," in *Critical Issues in Policing: Contemporary Readings*, ed. ROGER G. DUNHAM and GEOFFREY P. ALPERT (Prospect Heights, IL: Waveland Press, 1989), p. 338.
43. LENA WILLIAMS, "Police Officers Tell of Strains of Living as a 'Black in Blue,'" *New York Times*, February 14, 1988, pp. 1, 26.
44. ROBERT J. KAMINSKI, "Police Minority Recruitment: Predicting Who Will Say Yes to an Offer for a Job as a Cop," *Journal of Criminal Justice* 21 (1993): 395–409.
45. KEN PEAK, "The Quest for Alternatives to Lethal Force: A Heuristic View," *Journal of Contemporary Criminal Justice* 6 (1990): 8–22.
46. Ibid.
47. Ibid.
48. SAUL D. ASTOR, "A Nation of Thieves," *Security World* 15 (September 1978).
49. DEPARTMENT OF JUSTICE, Bureau of Justice Statistics, National Crime Victimization Survey, *Criminal Victimization, 2002* (Washington, DC: Author, August 2003), p. 1.
50. MAHESH K. NALLA and CEDRICK G. HERAUX, "Assessing Goals and Functions of Private Police," *Journal of Criminal Justice* 31 (2003): 237.
51. Ibid.
52. K. PEAK and K. BRAUNSTEIN, "On Guard: The Private Security Industry in America," in *Introduction to Criminal Justice: Theory and Practice*, ed. DAE CHANG and MICHAEL PALMIOTTO (Wichita, KS: MidContinent Academic Press, 1997), pp. 281–300.
53. Ibid.
54. NALLA and HERAUX, "Assessing Goals and Functions of Private Police," p. 238.

55. Ibid., pp. 243–44.
56. LAWRENCE J. FENNELLY, ed., *Handbook of Loss Prevention and Crime Prevention*, 2d ed. (Boston: Butterworths, 1989), in foreword.
57. GEORGE F. COLE and CHRISTOPHER E. SMITH, *The American System of Criminal Justice*, 10th ed. (Belmont, CA: Wadsworth, 2004), p. 266.
58. Ibid.
59. THOMAS T. CHUDA, "Taking Training Beyond the Basics," *Security Management* 39 (February 1995): 57–59.
60. NATIONAL ADVISORY COMMISSION ON CRIMINAL JUSTICE STANDARDS AND GOALS, *Private Security* (Washington, DC: U.S. Government Printing Office, 1976), p. 99.
61. KAREN M. HESS and HENRY M. WROBLESKI, *Introduction to Private Security*, 3d ed. (St. Paul, MN: West, 1992).
62. STEVEN M. COX, *Police: Practices, Perspectives, Problems* (Boston: Allyn and Bacon, 1996), p. 90.
63. FULTON COUNTY, GEORGIA, SHERIFF's OFFICE, "CALEA Law Enforcement Accreditation," http:/www.fultonsheriff.org/misc/accreditation.asp (accessed January 30, 2005); also see the CALEA Web site, http://www.calea.org/newweb/AboutUs/Aboutus.htm.
64. COX, *Police*, p. 90.
65. FULTON COUNTY, GEORGIA, SHERIFF's OFFICE, "CALEA Law Enforcement Accreditation," p. 2.
66. KIMBERLY A. MCCABE and ROBIN G. FAJARDO, "Law Enforcement Accreditation: A National Comparison of Accredited versus Nonaccredited Agencies," *Journal of Criminal Justice* 29 (2001): 127–31.
67. Ibid., 130.
68. Ibid., pp. 129–30.
69. ALBERT DEUTSCH, *The Trouble with Cops* (New York: Crown, 1955), p. 122.
70. HERMAN GOLDSTEIN, *Policing a Free Society* (Cambridge, MA: Ballinger, 1977), pp. 283–84.
71. DEUTSCH, *The Trouble with Cops*, p. 213; *Law Enforcement and Criminal Justice Education: Directory, 1975–76* (Gaithersburg, MD: International Association of Chiefs of Police, 1975), p. 3.
72. LAW ENFORCEMENT ASSISTANCE ADMINISTRATION, *Fifth Annual Report, Fiscal Year 1973* (Washington, DC: U.S. Government Printing Office, 1973), p. 119.
73. NATIONAL ADVISORY COMMISSION ON CRIMINAL JUSTICE STANDARDS AND GOALS, *Police* (Washington, DC: U.S. Government Printing Office, 1973), p. 369.
74. GERALD W. LYNCH, "Why Officers Need a College Education," *Higher Education and National Affairs* (September 20, 1986): 11.
75. DAVIS v. CITY OF DALLAS, 777 F.2d 205 (5th Cir. 1985).
76. ROBERT E. WORDEN, "A Badge and a Baccalaureate: Policies, Hypotheses, and Further Evidence," *Justice Quarterly* 7 (September 1990): 565–92.
77. VICTOR E. KAPPELER, ALLEN D. SAPP, and DAVID L. CARTER, "Police Officer Higher Education, Citizen Complaints and Departmental Rule Violations," *American Journal of Police* 11 (1992): 37–54.

78. CHARLES L. WEIRMAN, "Variances of Ability Measurement Scores Obtained by College and Non-College Educated Troopers," *Police Chief* 45 (August 1978): 34–36.

79. Ibid.

80. ROBERT TROJANOWICZ and T. NICHOLSON, "A Comparison of Behavioral Styles of College Graduate Police Officers versus Non-College Going Police Officers," *Police Chief* 43 (August 1976): 56–59.

81. A. F. DALLEY, "University and Non-University Graduated Policemen: A Study of Police Attitudes," *Journal of Police Science and Administration* 3 (1975): 458–68.

82. WAYNE F. CASCIO, "Formal Education and Police Officer Performance," *Journal of Police Science and Administration* 5 (1977): 89–96; BERNARD COHEN and JAN M. CHAIKEN, *Police Background Characteristics and Performance* (New York: RAND, 1972); B. E. SANDERSON, "Police Officers: The Relationship of College Education to Job Performance," *Police Chief* (August 1977): 62–63.

83. JAMES W. STERLING, "The College Level Entry Requirement: A Real or Imagined Cure-All?" *Police Chief* 41 (April 1974): 28–31.

84. GERALD W. LYNCH, "Cops and College," *America* (April 4, 1987): 274–75.

85. JON MILLER and LINCOLN FRY, "Reexamining Assumptions about Education and Professionalism in Law Enforcement," *Journal of Police Science and Administration* 4 (1976): 187–98.

86. JOHN K. HUDZIK, "College Education for Police: Problems in Measuring Component and Extraneous Variables," *Journal of Criminal Justice* 6 (1978): 69–81.

87. Quoted in "Men and Women of Letters," *Law Enforcement News*, November 30, 1997, p. 1.

88. NATIONAL ADVISORY COMMISSION ON CRIMINAL JUSTICE STANDARDS AND GOALS, *Police*, p. 367.

89. JOHN BARTLETT, ed., *Familiar Quotations*, 16th ed. (Boston: Little, Brown, 1992), p. 529.

90. WILLIAM A. WESTLEY, *Violence and the Police* (Cambridge, MA: MIT Press, 1970), p. 3.

91. GORDON WITKIN, TED GEST, and DORIAN FRIEDMAN, "Cops Under Fire," *U.S. News and World Report*, December 3, 1990, pp. 32–44.

92. MICHELLE INGRASSIA and KAREN SPRINGEN, "Living on Dracula Time," *Newsweek*, July 12, 1993, pp. 68–69.

93. See, for example, STEPHEN R. BAND and DONALD C. SHEEHAN, "Managing Undercover Stress: The Supervisor's Role," *FBI Law Enforcement Bulletin*, February 1999, pp. 1–6.

94. See, for example, J. SEWELL, "The Stress of Homicide Investigations," *Death Studies* 18 (1994): 565–82.

95. Adapted from GERALD W. GARNER, "Prepare to Survive," *Police*, January 1994, pp. 18–19, 90.

96. ANNE COHEN, "I've Killed That Man Ten Thousand Times," in *Annual Editions: Criminal Justice, 88/89*, ed. JOHN J. SULLIVAN and JOSEPH L. VICTOR (Guilford, CT: Dushkin, 1988), pp. 86–90.

97. JOHN G. STRATTON, *Police Passages* (Manhattan Beach, CA: Glennon, 1984), pp. 235–36.

98. JAMES M. HORN and ROGER M. SOLOMON, "Peer Support: A Key Element for Coping with Trauma," *Police Stress* 9 (winter 1989): 25–27.
99. BEN DAVISS, "Burnout," *Police Magazine*, May 1982, p. 10.
100. Ibid., p. 50.
101. GERALD L. FISHKIN, *Police Burnout: Signs, Symptoms and Solutions* (Gardena, CA: Harcourt Brace Jovanovich, 1988), pp. 233–39.
102. "What's Killing America's Cops?" *Law Enforcement News*, November 15, 1996, p. 1.
103. Ibid.
104. "Stressed Out? Help May Be on the Way," *Law Enforcement News*, January 31, 1997, p. 5.

CHAPTER 13

Comparative Perspectives: Policing in Foreign Countries

Courts and camps are the only places to learn the world in.

—*Earl of Chesterfield*

Key Terms

Diyya crime
Holy Koran
Hudud crime
International Criminal Police Organization (Interpol)
Irish Republican Army (IRA)
law of Islam (the Sharia)
paramilitary group
Police Service of Northern Ireland
Quesas crime
Tazir crime
Ulster
writ of *amparo*

Crime is an international problem. Life in general and crime in particular have become globalized. Crime easily transcends national borders, and the fruits of crime are also dispatched with ease across geographic boundaries, to be laundered and used in other criminal enterprises. In an era of rapidly advancing technology and mobility, the world order has become interdependent, and crime and justice issues are clearly transcontinental.[1]

It has therefore become increasingly important to understand the structure and function of international criminal justice systems. It has been said that the comparative approach provides the opportunity to search for order.[2] A comparative view of foreign policing systems provides the opportunity to better assess the methods, role, and functions of our democratic American policing system. We can also look for the common properties of all systems and determine where each political system and, consequently, each policing system stands in its regard for human rights and its respect for the private lives of its citizens.[3]

We will look at policing in five countries: Iraq, Saudi Arabia, China, Northern Ireland, and Mexico. One might ask, "Why were those countries chosen? What do they have to do with policing in the United States?" The answer is that they actually have little in common with the American system of policing, and that is precisely why they were chosen. These countries all employ police systems that are uniquely different from ours, making them ideal for comparison; also, it is hoped that an understanding of these systems will give the reader a deeper appreciation for policing methods in our democracy.

Then we analyze the International Criminal Police Organization, or Interpol, the most effective international effort at crime fighting in the world. Included are the history, organization, and methods of this unique organization. A chapter summary, review questions, independent student activities, and related Web sites conclude the chapter.

Iraq

A History of Dictators and Disorder

Iraq is located in the Middle East, between Iran and Kuwait. Its capital is Baghdad, and its population of about 25.3 million is 97 percent Muslim (about two-thirds Shiite and one-third Sunni). An interim government was appointed in June 2004, and on January 30, 2005, Iraqis voted for a 275-member Transitional National Assembly to make its laws, elect a president, choose a prime minister, and establish the new government.[4] This was the country's first free national election in more than fifty years. Defying death threats, mortars, and suicide bombers, Iraqis turned out in great numbers to vote; forty-four deaths were attributed to ten suicide bombers and mortar shells directed toward voting polls and the nation's government center.[5]

Formerly part of the Ottoman Empire, Iraq was occupied by Britain during World War I; Iraq attained its independence as a kingdom in 1932, and a "republic" was proclaimed in 1958, but in actuality a series of military strongmen ruled the country; the latest was Saddam Hussein. Territorial disputes with Iran led to a costly eight-year war (1980–1988). In August 1990 Iraq seized Kuwait but was expelled by U.S.-led coalition forces in February 1991. Following this incursion, the United Nations Security Council required Iraq to scrap all weapons of mass destruction and long-range missiles, but 12 years of noncompliance with UN resolutions resulted in the U.S.-led invasion of Iraq in March 2003 and the ouster of Saddam. Coalition forces remain in Iraq, hoping to restore its infrastructure facilitate a democratic government through Iraq's first national election held in January 2005.[6]

Policing the World's Most Perilous Place

Until recently, it could be stated with a high degree of certainty that, on the whole, Northern Ireland was the most dangerous country in which to be a police officer. (See the discussion later in this chapter.) It is clear, however, that today that dubious distinction belongs to Iraq.

On the one side is the U.S. military, the most advanced fighting force in history; on the other side, a group of insurgents and terrorists, who—particularly after former dictator Saddam Hussein's capture in December 2003—quickly went on the offensive. The U.S. military is trained to obliterate its enemy with overwhelming firepower, but it is not a police force; it is not trained to track down dangerous groups or individuals in heavily populated areas. In Iraq, that job has fallen to the local police.

The insurgents, retaliating against U.S. occupation after Saddam's capture, turned Iraq's voting places and many local police stations and officers into targets; following are some examples:

- In January 2005, fierce clashes leading up to the national elections left at least eleven Iraqi police officers and a senior judge dead in eastern Baghdad.[7]
- In September 2004, a suicide attacker detonated a car bomb outside the Iraqi police station in Kirkuk as hundreds of trainees and civilians were leaving, killing twenty and wounding thirty-six.[8]
- On February 15, 2004, insurgents using rocket-propelled grenades, machine guns, and mortars staged a brazen daylight attack on a Fallujah police station, freeing dozens of prisoners in a battle that killed twenty-three people and wounded thirty-seven.[9]
- A truck bomb exploded on February 10, 2004, at a police station south of Baghdad as dozens of would-be police recruits lined up to apply for jobs, killing at least fifty-four people and wounding sixty others.[10]
- On December 15, 2003, a suicide bomber killed eight and injured ten Iraqi police officers in an attack on the northern outskirts of Baghdad.[11]
- Many Iraqi officers stopped wearing their blue uniform shirts because they made them an easy target for insurgents.

Since Saddam's Fall: A Poorly Trained and Equipped Force

Without U.S. military backing, the poorly trained and badly equipped Iraqi police would have been hard-pressed to keep basic order, much less battle well-armed insurgents who have attacked relentlessly after the fall of Saddam Hussein. A former instrument of the Saddam government, the

Iraqi police initially seemed to be clueless as to how to deal with either revenge or reconciliation following Saddam's brutal dictatorship. But the U.S. military had little choice but to try to build the Iraqi officers into an effective force; thus the task of stopping the revenge killings and other types of crimes fell to thirty-five thousand Iraqi officers. They quickly became targets of convenience for those opposed to the U.S. occupation of the country because the Iraqi people viewed them as collaborators with American soldiers (who did in fact train these officers) and knew their faces and where they lived.[12]

The Iraqi officers' duties have been varied. At times, they clashed almost daily with demonstrators in Baghdad and Basra; 420 men were assigned, sometimes armed only with a "rusting pair of binoculars, an AK-47, and a half magazine of bullets," to guard the country's vast borders.[13] They were also expected to control the widespread vice—prostitution, pornographic adult cinemas, and drug abuse—that pervaded Baghdad and other cities after Saddam's fall.[14] This dismal situation was compounded by police corruption, civilian looting, and chaotic traffic problems. The police battled these problems with little in the way of key equipment—such as radios, vehicles, uniforms, or computers—and for a notoriously low pay of $20 per month.[15]

The Future

Clearly, policing in Iraq carries tremendous challenges and dangers for years to come. Following the national elections of 2005, prospects for the country's future stability still depend on creation of well-trained police force—which could take months, possibly years—and success is far from certain.[16] Increasing the number of Iraqi police officers, soldiers, and guardsmen is paramount, as is the weeding out of about one-fourth (as many as 30,000) of its officers who served under Saddam's corrupt, hated, and feared Interior Ministry.[17]

The following discussion is of another Middle Eastern country, Saudi Arabia, whose Muslim-based criminal code—and punishments—are grounded on the Koran.

Saudi Arabia

An Exodus over Terrorism

The struggle against terrorism and the war in Iraq have had a major effect on U.S.-Saudi relations. In early 2004, the U.S. State Department began authorizing all nonessential diplomats and families of U.S. officials to leave Saudi Arabia because of ongoing security concerns.[18] The terrorist group al Qaeda, which originated in Saudi Arabia, conducted suicide attacks against Riyadh housing compounds in May and November of 2003, killing

EXHIBIT 13-1

Changing Bad Cops to Good

Faculty at John Jay College of Criminal Justice in New York City have developed a course meant to reverse the effects of years of bad police practices in countries with authoritarian rule. Since 1994, more than three thousand police officers in fifty troubled countries have taken the course, "Human Dignity and Policing," which is funded by the U.S. Department of Justice. Realizing that straight lectures cannot change behavior, the course emphasizes group therapy and role-playing to help foreign officers examine their practices and confront their past. Bosnian officers noted that their superiors strip-searched them at the end of each shift to take whatever bribes they had collected. In Latin America, officers were regularly forced to do menial work for their bosses, such as building houses. An El Salvadoran officer admitted that his superiors told him to kill a prisoner that he was escorting, which he did, receiving a hero's medal for murder. These officers need to return to their homelands wanting to do good for others; as a college dean says, "All cops want to have their jobs mean something."

Source: Adapted from "Teaching Cops Right from Wrong," *Time*, March 19, 2001, p. 59.

40 people and wounding 122 others, most of them Muslims.[19] U.S. officials were assuming that further attacks were imminent.

Americans at home were also urged to avoid all nonessential travel to the kingdom because of intelligence concerning terrorist threats to western airlines; Saudi Arabia, meanwhile, began spending large sums of money on public-relations advertising and lobbying in an effort to convince Americans that it is committed to fighting terrorism—despite the fact that fifteen of the nineteen hijackers who participated in the September 11, 2001, attacks were Saudi citizens.[20]

Social Behavior in a Patriarchal Land

The kingdom of Saudi Arabia is the largest country in the Middle East and occupies four-fifths of the Arabian Peninsula—873,000 square miles. At about one-fourth of America's size, it covers an area roughly the size of the United States east of the Mississippi.

The government is patriarchal with attributes of democracy. At a given hour of the day, the king makes himself accessible to his subjects. Sitting as a supreme court of appeal, he hears the complaints brought before him by even the humblest members of society. The king's decisions cannot be appealed.

Arabic is the language of the country, but many of the younger educated businessmen were schooled in English-speaking countries; thus English is widely spoken in business and the military. The population in most of the cities of Saudi Arabia is a cosmopolitan mixture of Arabs from all over the

Muslim world. The family structure is undergoing marked changes. Monogamy is becoming the norm, even though Saudi Arabian men still have the right to take four wives and divorce is comparatively simple. The social life is also very much male oriented—women still wear the veil and must be covered from ankles to wrists in public to avoid calling attention to themselves. Women are not allowed to drive or work, and it is still considered a primary function for women to bear a son.[21]

Westerners will find some matters of Arabian social etiquette to be curious, particularly those forms of etiquette relating to Arab courtesy and hospitality. For example, to admire an Arab's possession is to put him under obligation to present the item to you as a gift; to refuse the offer would be to offend the host. A famous Arab hospitality is the serving of coffee, black and sweetened, in tiny cups and poured from a brass pot; it is customary to accept two cups. Handshaking is more frequent than in the West, and before discussing business, Arabs will normally indulge in sincere small talk about each other's health, work, and interests; undue haste in a business transaction is considered bad form.

There are innumerable anecdotes about Arabs who gave their last morsel to feed a guest. One popular story involves a poor bedouin who had endured the loss of his livestock until only one horse was left. A man who had long coveted the horse and had offered to buy it visited one day and was invited by the bedouin to dine. After eating, the man offered again to buy the horse from the poor man, who listened attentively and then replied, "I thank you for your generosity, but we have just consumed my horse!"[22]

Westerners are considered a temporary commercial colony in Saudi Arabia today and are generally concentrated in Jidda, Riyadh, Taif, and Khamis Mushayt. Many Americans work in oil-related and other business and commercial enterprises, and they need schools and other amenities for their families.

Religious Underpinnings

To describe Saudis is to speak of their religion, culture, and customs, all of which are bound closely together. The national flag of Saudi Arabia, bearing the Islamic creed and unsheathed sword, symbolizes strength rooted in faith. Saudi Arabia is the center of the Islamic faith and contains its two holiest cities, Mecca (Muhammad's birthplace) and Medina (his burial place). Mecca is the focal point of religious devotion; five times daily, Muslims throughout the world turn toward the holy city to pray.

Few acts are performed that do not have their basis in the **Holy Koran**. *Islam* means complete submission to the will of God. Five primary duties, known as the Five Pillars of Faith, are required of every Muslim: the profession of faith (a statement of loyalty to God and Muhammad); prayer; almsgiving (helping poor Muslims); fasting (during Ramadan, the ninth month of the Muslim year); and pilgrimage (for those who are able to make the trip to Mecca or Medina).[23]

Laws and Prohibitions

To provide a well-ordered society, the interpretation of Islamic law is stricter in Saudi Arabia than in any other Islamic country. Saudi Arabian law, like other facets of Saudi life, is governed by the Koran. If an American or any other foreigner breaks the law in Saudi Arabia, there is little anyone can do to assist; he or she must expect to receive the full penalty for the offense. In fact, in March 1993, the U.S. Supreme Court held that a U.S. worker could not sue the Saudi government in an American court for torture and other abuses received at the hands of Saudi authorities.[24] The appellant, Scott Nelson, charged that he had been detained and tortured by Saudi police for thirty-nine days for issuing complaints about safety in the Saudi-run hospital in which he worked. Writing for the majority, Justice David Souter observed that the police power of a nation was "particularly sovereign in nature" and was sheltered from lawsuits in U.S. federal courts according to the Foreign Sovereign Immunities Act, a 1976 law governing suits against foreign states.

A mannequin wearing the Saudi Arabian police uniform, displayed at the International Police Museum, Central Police University, Taoyuan, Taiwan.

Alcohol is forbidden in Saudi Arabia; those who brew, sell, smuggle, or drink alcohol are punished. Any case involving alcohol will result in a police investigation to determine the source of the alcohol. There are three kinds of narcotics offenses: possession, trafficking, and smuggling. Possession includes small amounts of hashish or marijuana, for which the maximum punishment is two years' imprisonment. An individual arrested for trafficking faces a maximum sentence of five years in prison. Possession of large amounts of narcotics carries a possible death sentence by public beheading. Many drug offenders are deported.[25]

The **law of Islam (the Sharia)** is recognized as the fundamental code in Saudi Arabia. Islamic criminal legislation is divided into three categories: (1) *Hudud* crimes—those against the divine or God's rights, (2) *Quesas* and *Diyya* crimes—those against the individual, and (3) *Tazir* crimes—those that are left undetermined by religious law. ***Hudud* crimes** harm the property or security interests of society. The seven types of *Hudud* crimes are theft, slander (falsely accusing someone of adultery or defaming a married woman), adultery, highway robbery, consuming alcohol, transgression (revolting against a legitimate religious leader, known as an "imam"), and apostasy (renouncing Islam).

For the crime of theft, even for the first offense, the penalty may be amputation of the left hand at the wrist. The penalty for slander is flogging, usually with eighty lashes, and the same penalty may be applied for consuming alcohol. The penalty for adultery is flogging one hundred times. A woman who engages in adultery may be flogged or buried to the waist in a pit; stoning may follow. Highway robbery is punishable by execution or crucifixion, the amputation of opposite hands and feet, or exile from the land. Transgressors are those who attack the government; they will be confronted by the Saudi armed forces until they are defeated, and apostasy carries the death penalty.[26]

Public executions are commonplace in Saudi Arabia. The country's public executioner has carried out more than six hundred executions since 1989. Hundreds of worshippers, including children and women, often gather to observe these and other punishments. The crowd usually applauds after the execution, and some bystanders spit on the blood of the deceased and curse them.[27]

***Quesas* and *Diyya* crimes** involve compensation (*Diyya*) from the offender to the victim and normally involve acts of intentional or unintentional bodily injury or maiming. Even murder may be punished by compensation, with the consent of the victim's family.[28] ***Tazir* crimes**—a broad category meant to include those crimes that are harmful to the public order—carry penalties that are left to the discretion of the judge or other public authority.

Guardians of Religious Purity

Due in large measure to the harsh criminal code and its penalties, there is comparatively little for the Saudi police to do in terms of crime prevention or investigation; nor are they actively engaged in random patrolling or traffic enforcement. Thus there is ample time for other endeavors. The religious police—Mutawin—wear short, coarse, white cotton robes and sandals; as one writer observed, they look like "desert nomads who have stumbled unexpectedly into the 20th century."[29] These police patrol in jeeps and stroll through the streets and malls looking for people who are improperly dressed or women who have a loose strand of hair falling across their face or who need to adjust their *tarhas* (head coverings).

For the religious police—officially known as the Committee for the Promotion of Virtue and the Prevention of Vice—such encounters are all part of a day's work. While these minions of the law view their corrective actions as a small victory for Islam, many citizens view the police actions as nothing more than harassment. The police are currently at the heart of a fierce debate about the country's future, one that pits a mostly Western-oriented elite against those who want a stricter Islamic rule. In an effort to draw the Muslim fundamentalist opposition into the system and bolster its own religious credentials, the government has steadily expanded the scope and power of the police.[30] This expansion of powers does not bode well for those who want to see liberal democratic reforms.

Around-the-clock patrols ensure that shops are closed in time for daily prayers and that only married couples are sitting in the family section of restaurants. The squads often follow people suspected of being involved in what is deemed immoral behavior, such as drug use, homosexuality, gambling, and begging. Teams of religious police destroy home satellite dishes, which bring uncensored western television broadcasts into Saudi homes. For young men and women, social life often becomes a cat-and-mouse game with the roving bands of religious police. The religious officers, who are often accompanied by uniformed police officers, are viewed with open hostility by many Saudi youth, who see the police as the enemy. University students in Jidda hang out at a shopping mall next to campus, a place that is frequently raided by special squads. But as evidence of their effectiveness, the police point to their ordered society, where violent crime and theft are rare.[31]

The religious police have a broad scope of authority in a country dominated by Wahhabism, a puritanical sect of Islam embraced by the ruling Saud family and most of the population. Under this sect's influence, theaters and many western publications are banned, in addition to alcohol. Women and men are segregated in workplaces, restaurants, and schools. Wahhabism views daily life as a war against vice, including an "infusion" of imported pornographic videos. Police officials acknowledge that their officers have committed some abuses—such as beating guest workers from foreign countries—but they deny any widespread mistreatment.[32]

The police also assist with the so-called chop-chops, which are conducted in many cities, including on the Justice Square in Riyadh, on Fridays.

Believing that these public amputations are a deterrent to other would-be offenders, the police encourage anyone who is in the vicinity of the Square—including American visitors—to witness these affairs of state; thus Riyadh's streets are largely empty on Fridays. When a thief's right hand is cut off in public, a string is tied to the middle finger and the hand is hung from a hook high on a streetlight pole on Justice Square for all to see; this announces the thief's transgression and casts shame on the family.[33]

Notwithstanding the harsh criminal code, forms of punishment, and police presence, many people residing in Saudi Arabia report feeling safer than they do living in the United States, largely owing to the absence in Saudi Arabia of gangs, drive-by shootings, purse snatchings, and drugs, alcohol, and weapons on the streets. Many Americans report that their biggest fear while living in Saudi Arabia is being caught by the police for improper dress. The police busily patrol the streets in Chevrolets, BMWs, and Volvos, looking for such infractions. The police also check vehicles for bombs near the U.S. Embassy building. Furthermore, a concern with terrorism keeps the police alert.[34]

CHINA

Policing a Vast Land

China is a vast country, encompassing 3.7 million square miles and sharing borders with fourteen other nations, and has about 1.2 billion people—the world's largest population.[35] The Chinese police bear the responsibility for maintaining law and order in the world's most populous nation.

Although there is no official estimate of the numbers of police officers or of the police-to-population ratio in China, unofficial estimates put the ratio between 1:745 and 1:1,400. By whatever estimate, the ratio is much lower than those in almost all Western nations. Even so, since the founding of the People's Republic in 1949, the Chinese police have maintained one of the lowest crime rates in the world.[36]

Reform under Police Law 1995

Since the early 1980s, China has implemented a series of police reforms. But the most significant is the passage of Police Law 1995, which contains specific provisions regarding police organization, recruitment and training, powers and functions, accountability, and styles and strategies. Next we briefly discuss each of these provisions.

Organization. According to Police Law 1995, the Chinese police consist of five components: public security police, state security police, prison police, judicial police in people's courts, and judicial police in people's procuratorates

Chinese police officers.

(Courtesy Office of International Criminal Justice)

(prosecutors' offices). Public security police, the largest and oldest police force, perform a wide range of ordinary police duties as well as administering the household registration system. When people talk about police in China, they usually think of the public security police.[37] At the helm of this police force is the Ministry of Public Security, which represents the central government and directs police operation throughout the country. Figure 13-1 shows the organization of public security police in China.

State security police are responsible solely for protecting state security—that is, preventing foreign espionage, sabotage, and conspiracies. Prison police supervise convicted offenders, make general regulations with regard to prison management, and make policies concerning supervision and rehabilitation of inmates. Judicial police are officers who work in both people's courts and people's procuratorates; they provide physical security, serve subpoenas, conduct searches, and execute court orders (including death sentences).

Recruitment and Training. Because of the relatively low police-to-population ratio and China's increasing problems with law and order, police agencies in China face an urgent need with respect to recruitment and training. Recently, the quality of new recruits has been deemed less than satisfactory, resulting in incidences of police corruption, abuse of powers, and other misconduct.[38] Police Law 1995 set out basic qualifications for police officers: Recruits must be over eighteen years old, support the Constitution, have good character, be in excellent physical condition, and have at least a high school degree. Qualified applicants must take a competitive entrance examination and must complete a one-year probationary period, during which time they receive training in an academy. The Police Law sets out additional qualifications for those who seek to hold leadership

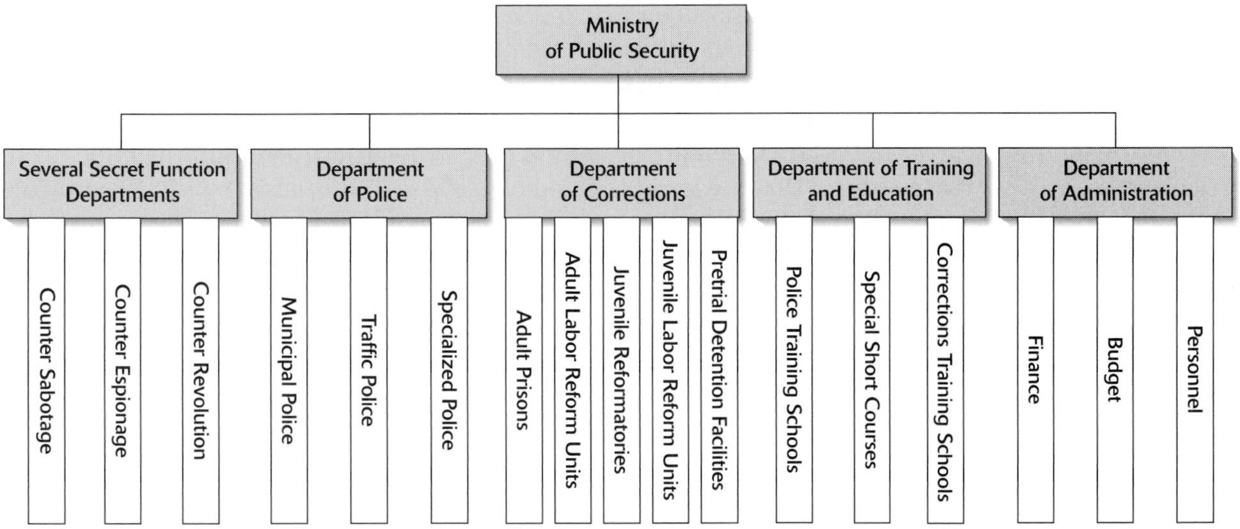

FIGURE 13-1 Organizational structure of the Chinese police.

Source: Richard A. Myren, "The Developing Legal System of China," CJ International 2 *(March–April 1986): 13. Reproduced with permission.*

positions: These candidates must have a college degree, legal knowledge, practical police experience, administrative talent, management skills, and requisite in-service training.[39]

Powers and Functions. The powers and functions of the Chinese police are much broader than those of their counterparts in many other nations; indeed, the list of functions of China's police appears to represent a combination of the kinds of work found in an array of federal and state law enforcement agencies in the United States. In addition to routine police duties of investigation and traffic control, the Chinese police also engage in fire prevention; controlling firearms, ammunition, knives, and explosive and radioactive materials; supervising the operation of certain types of professions and industries; guarding high-ranking government officials, dignitaries, buildings, and facilities; administering the household registration system and handling entry into or exit from the country; maintaining borders; supervising offenders on parole; supervising the security and protection of computer information; and guiding and supervising the security of government offices and social organizations.[40]

The Chinese police's wide powers have been a subject of controversy and criticism, stemming from the fact that they are given wide detention power, which can result in an individual's loss of freedom for months or even years. Although the Criminal Procedural Law (CPL) regulates the power of police to arrest and detain without judicial or prosecutorial approval, these regulations are nevertheless compromised by the wide detention power of the police. Administrative detention can be used by the police for up to fifteen days for investigation or interrogation; this is a very powerful weapon in the police arsenal. The use of physical torture to force confessions is widely reported. But the most disturbing problem is extended detention, which in many cases runs for more than three months. After taking suspects into custody, police often do not engage in a diligent investigation. The police may also send offenders to farms or camps for reeducation through labor for up to three years; this measure is the most severe administrative sanction police may take against an offender without court approval.[41]

Police Law 1995 also granted the police a new power: If police have reasonable suspicion to believe that a person has committed a crime, they may stop and question that person after identifying themselves. If their suspicions are not allayed, they may then take the individual to a police station for further questioning for up to twenty-four hours—and up to forty-eight hours under "exceptional circumstances."

Accountability. Police accountability is obviously a matter of concern in China. The Chinese police in general enjoy a positive image in the eyes of the public; one national survey showed that 70 percent of the public expressed confidence that if they reported personal victimizations to the police, their complaints would be addressed.[42] The Chinese police, however, are not immune from misconduct; there have been increasing numbers of reported cases of police corruption, abuse of power, and infringement of citizens' rights. Public Law 1995 also established an internal police supervisory system, however, requiring that higher-level police agencies oversee and inspect the legality of law enforcement activities of lower-level police agencies. The law also established an internal supervisory system within each police bureau; a committee has the authority to receive and investigate complaints against officers and to impose disciplinary sanctions against them as necessary.

Styles and Strategies. The policing styles and strategies in China have also been transformed in order to deal with the country's changing social and economic environment. The key to success remains the police's ability to keep a tight control over the population through the household registration system and extensive surveillance. Every citizen must register his or her residence with the police, and neighborhood committees are established in all neighborhoods. This system has the advantage of enabling officers to keep close contacts with community residents and to keep a tight surveillance on every neighborhood. No strangers can enter a neighborhood without being noticed immediately and reported promptly to the police.[43] Although this might seem quite intrusive to Americans, the system does allow the police to monitor large city populations and criminals, especially gangs. Community policing (examined in Chapter 6) has also worked well in China; to combat the current rise in crime, the government advocates an overall strategy known as "comprehensive management"—the mobilization of all possible social forces to strengthen public security and to prevent crime.[44]

NORTHERN IRELAND

Recent Developments and Violence in a Long Civil War

About thirty-two hundred people have been killed in Northern Ireland since 1970; fathers have been shot in front of their children, and children have been blown up while playing in their own backyards.[45] More than forty thousand people were injured and at least fifteen thousand families driven from their homes in Belfast in the 1970s alone. In addition to bombs, terrorists have employed other forms of savagery: stapling a person's tongue to a table; shooting an informer's kneecaps (so common was this form of punishment that a Limerick factory once produced plastic kneecaps);[46] and tarring and feathering.[47] As a result of the violence, two groups of people—speaking the same language, having the same skin color, and sharing a Christian heritage—regard themselves as separate races.[48]

On April 10, 1998—Good Friday—voters in Ireland approved referendums that, it was hoped, would end the civil conflicts, creating a new regional legislature, a cross-border council, and an eventual repeal of articles in the Irish constitution that committed the Dublin government to seek a united Ireland.[49] For a while, the agreement seemed to be working, but in mid-2003 it was revealed that the **Irish Republican Army (IRA)** was operating a spy ring within the Northern Ireland government, and the IRA refused to fully "decommission" its arms. In response, British prime minister Tony Blair suspended the Northern Ireland government and postponed further elections indefinitely. In the end, elaborate negotiations and attempts at goodwill do not seem to be working. In the words of William Butler Yeats, "Things fall apart; the center cannot hold."[50]

Both sides have extremists, and dissidents vowed to continue their violence.[51] Indeed, the carnage continued: In July 1998, ten Roman Catholic churches were burned by pro-British loyalists, Protestant mobs injured forty-two police officers of the Royal Ulster Constabulary (RUC), and 314 vehicles were set on fire or damaged.[52] The next month, the single deadliest blast in Northern Ireland's decades of conflict occurred when a car bomb exploded in the center of a bustling market town, Omagh, killing more than thirty people and injuring more than two hundred.[53]

In July 2000, the peace process seemed to tumble further into chaos. In a week of rioting, thousands of hard-line Protestants lit towering bonfires and fired volleys of shots in connection with marches and parades across Northern Ireland. The police arrested 146 people and seized a thousand gasoline bombs. Nearly one hundred vehicles were hijacked and burned, and fifty-seven officers were wounded.[54]

Violence flared again in January 2002, when thirty officers were injured as Protestant and Catholic rioters attacked police in northern Belfast. About

350 people hurled gasoline bombs, acid bombs, and stones at officers. At least two homemade grenades exploded near police, who fired plastic bullets in response. In another series of attacks a few days earlier, forty-eight officers were injured in disturbances when Protestant rioters vandalized seventeen cars parked at a Catholic school. (The children at the school were in hysterics and had to be hurried home.)[55]

A Divided Land

Since 1921, Ireland has been divided into two political units: Northern Ireland, with about 1.7 million people and 5,241 square miles, and the Republic of Ireland, with 2 million people and 21,895 square miles.[56] Northern Ireland is composed of the six northeastern counties of Ireland; this area, often referred to as **Ulster**, enjoys a measure of self-government within the United Kingdom of Great Britain and Northern Ireland. As with the other countries discussed in this chapter, one must first understand some of the political history of Ireland before attempting to grasp the policing system that has evolved.

In 1801, England and Ireland became the United Kingdom of Great Britain and Ireland. This entire period was in fact characterized by several centuries of anti-British agitation and demands for Irish home rule. The Government of Ireland Act of 1920 attempted to give self-government to Ireland and prohibit control of Ulster by the Roman Catholic majority of southern Ireland. This plan was accepted in Northern Ireland but was rejected by the south. Nevertheless, the act continued to serve as the basis of a constitution for Northern Ireland. The essential feature of the constitution is that Northern Ireland is a province of the United Kingdom. The IRA has argued since 1920 that its right to kill people comes from this partition of Ireland into two illegitimate states.[57]

Political Factions

The Irish Free State (Eire) was established by King George V in June 1921. From that point on, there was civil war in Ireland that included acts of bombing, shooting, and incendiarism. In 1922, 232 people were killed and one thousand were injured. In 1949, the Republic of Ireland withdrew from the British Commonwealth. This gave Northern Ireland greater status within the United Kingdom but further soured its relationship with the Irish Republic.

During and prior to this time, most Irish Protestants regarded themselves as British and valued their membership in the United Kingdom. They were and are opposed to a united Ireland. Thus inhabitants of Northern Ireland, who are mostly Protestant, of British ancestry, and in the majority, have historically maintained the strongest opposition to the return of home rule and Irish self-government. Most Catholics regard

The Police Service of Northern Ireland (PSNI).

(Courtesy Office of International Criminal Justice)

themselves as Irish and cherish the prospect of a united Ireland. Roman Catholics in all of Ireland still hold a fervent desire to become an independent nation.

Terrorist groups seek to bring Northern Ireland into the Republic through violent methods. Many Protestant loyalists (who are pro-British) consider the police to be traitors to their cause and have employed terrorist attacks against them. Some of the predominant terrorist groups in this camp are the Ulster Defense Association, the Ulster Freedom Fighters, and the Ulster Volunteer Force. The majority of the terrorist murders and other acts of violence have been carried out by the IRA, a secret terrorist group comprised mainly of Catholics. Other groups in this camp include Sinn Fein, the political mouthpiece of the IRA, and the Irish National Liberation Army.

Policing the Terrorist War

Since 1922, it has been the task of the Northern Ireland police force—the **Police Service of Northern Ireland (PSNI)**, formerly the Royal Ulster Constabulary—to combat acts of terrorism and other forms of criminal activity. Over time, these acts of terrorism brought a bunker attitude to PSNI officers, who view themselves as fighting a terrorist war. They have had to guard against acts of terrorism directed against themselves as well. Officers have refused to allow their children to answer the door at their homes, and they routinely check their police vehicles for bombs.[58] The PSNI is in a precarious position, locked between two groups of paramilitary extremists. As one PSNI officer stated, they are truly "the piggies in the middle."[59]

Many officers have been attacked by the pro-British Protestant loyalists, and some officers have had their cars bombed or their homes burned. If a plainclothes officer happens to be in the "wrong" neighborhood (Catholic areas known as "hard green" neighborhoods that are hotbeds of terrorist activity) and is recognized, his or her life could be in danger.[60]

Both the Protestant paramilitary groups (discussed below), who are battling to keep Northern Ireland British, and the Irish nationalists, who are seeking unification with the Irish Republic, have used terrorist attacks for discipline and control. The PSNI's banning and rerouting of traditional parades have also sparked numerous attacks on officers and their homes.[61]

A vital tool for combating terrorism in the United Kingdom is the Terrorism Act of 2000. Put into force in February 2001, the law outlaws certain terrorist groups and makes it illegal for them to operate in the United Kingdom. It also gives the police enhanced powers to investigate terrorism, including wider stop-and-search powers, and the power to detain suspects after arrest for up to seven days. The law also created new criminal offenses, including inciting terrorist acts.[62]

Notwithstanding its uniquely dangerous situation, the PSNI is recognized by police experts and terrorists alike as one of the world's most experienced and best police forces. With about eight thousand personnel

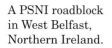

A PSNI roadblock in West Belfast, Northern Ireland.

(Courtesy Ron Glensor)

	Establishment	Actual
Chief Constable	1	1
D/CC Constable	1	1
ACC	6	6
C. Supt	29	29
Supt	70	74
C/Inspector	140	131.5
Inspector	410	388
Sergeant	1154	1101.25*
Constable	5689	5342
Total regular officers	7500	7330.75
FTR*	1682	1652.75
PTR*	2500	870

*FTR = Full-Time Reserve

*PTR = Part-Time Reserve

FIGURE 13-2 Strength of police service, Police Service of Northern Ireland

Source: Police Service of Northern Ireland

(seventy-three hundred of whom are full-time; see Figure 13-2), the department adheres to high standards of professionalism and behavior.

The current recruitment practice is for 50 percent of the officers who are hired to be Catholic and 50 percent non-Catholic; minimum qualifications include being a British subject, a Commonwealth or Republic of Ireland citizen; eighteen to fifty-two years of age; in good physical and mental health; in possession of certain skills or competencies to carry out the duties of a police officer; and without specified criminal convictions.[63]

The PSNI is very supportive of the community policing philosophy (discussed in Chapter 6). Indeed, recently the PSNI won several prestigious Tilley Awards—the United Kingdom's top policing awards for community policing achievement.

The organizational structure of the PSNI is shown in Figure 13-3.

A New Source of Terror: Paramilitary Groups

Northern Ireland is described as having an "imperfect peace" in which "acceptable levels of violence" persist. The government is said to have adopted a "see no evil, hear no evil" philosophy, by conceding that **paramilitary groups** "police" the informal criminal justice system in their areas with political and even legal impunity.[64]

Paramilitary groups are very active in working-class communities and employ a range of punitive measures against individuals who "violate some community norm, as defined by the paramilitary group."[65] The alternative system features a graduated scale of sanctions escalating from threats or warnings, through curfew, public humiliation, exile, and punishment beating to kneecapping or even execution.[66]

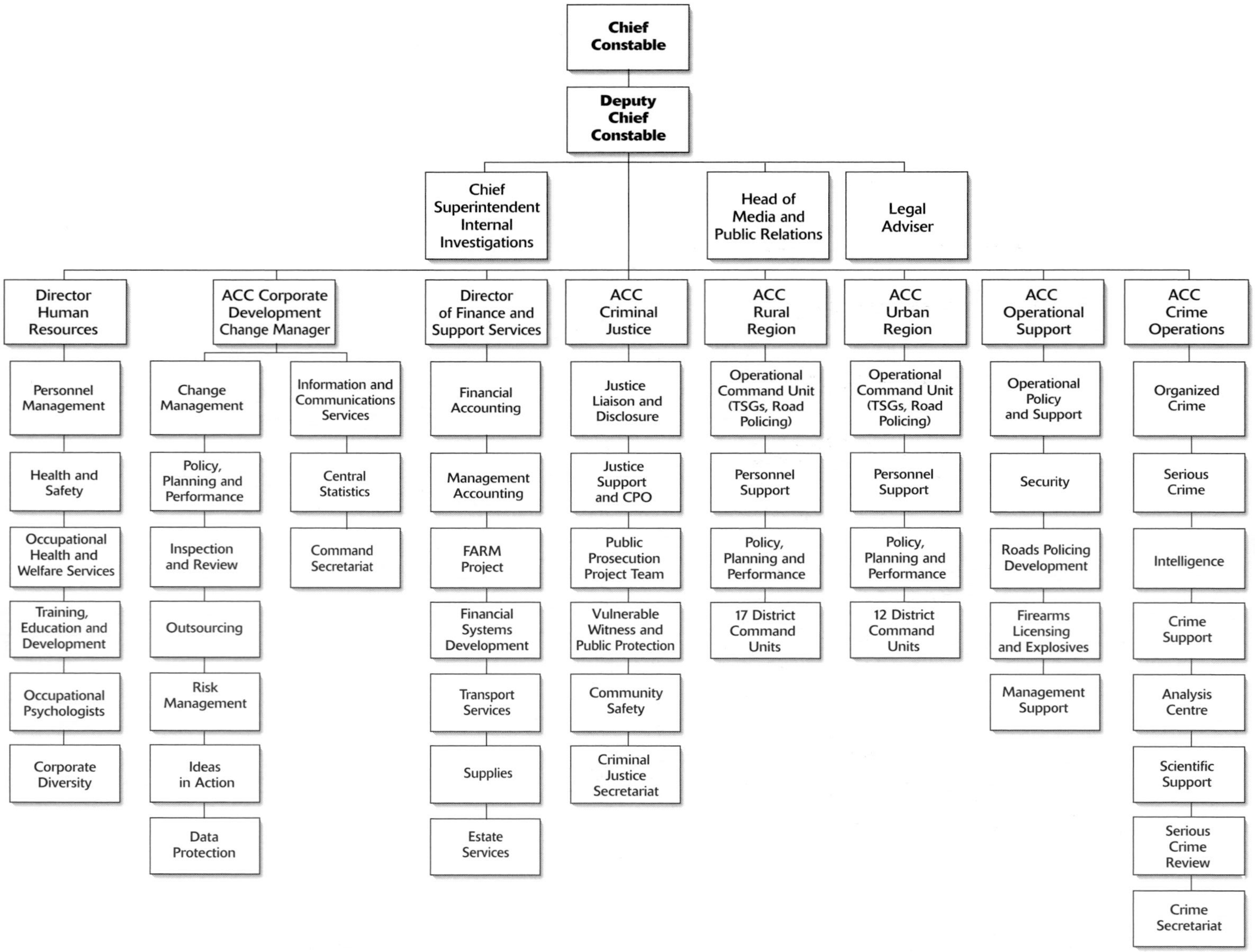

FIGURE 13-3 Organizational structure of the Police Service of Northern Ireland.

Source: Police Service of Northern Ireland

A fortified police station in West Belfast, Northern Ireland.

(Courtesy Ron Glensor)

The paramilitary groups are portrayed as community protectors, but that ignores the grotesque and brutal nature of their criminal acts; beatings are carried out using weapons like baseball bats, golf clubs, pickax handles, drills, iron bars, hammers, and sticks spiked with nails. According to PSNI statistics, from 1973 to 2000 there were 2,303 paramilitary shootings, about one-half committed by loyalists (mostly in North and East Belfast) and one-half by republicans (mostly in West Belfast). In the absence of what is seen as a legitimate police force, communities often turn to paramilitaries for protection. Communities are discouraged from going to the PSNI, as their experience has been that charges will be dropped against the perpetrators in exchange for providing information useful to the PSNI. The PSNI, on the other hand, contends that its hands are tied if victims won't file a police report. In sum, the PSNI is limited in its response, the communities want protection from paramilitaries, and the victims are fearful of paramilitary reprisal if they go to the police—a catch-22 situation. Therefore, the PSNI acquiesces to the status quo by minimizing the extent of the problem.[67]

MEXICO

Mexico, or the United Mexican States, covers an area of 756,000 square miles and has a population of almost 100 million people. The country consists of 31 states and a federal district; a limited democratic form of government exists. The country's capital is Mexico City.

A New President and Unfulfilled Promises

If Americans were to choose one word to describe Mexico's government and criminal justice system of the past, it would probably be *corruption*. Mexico's President Vicente Fox, who was elected in 2000, hoped to reverse that image—and reality—by creating a new government commission to investigate past scandals, to overhaul the nation's police forces from top to bottom, and to bring about much greater effort in combating drug trafficking.[68]

The election of President Fox—a charismatic Harvard MBA—defeated former Mexican president Ernesto Zedillo and ended the seventy-one-year reign of the Institutional Revolutionary Party, the world's longest-running political dynasty. Fox promised major social and economic reform in a country where more than 40 million people live in poverty, 39 percent are malnourished, and 10 percent are illiterate.[69] In addition, Fox promised to closely examine one of Mexico's unassailable institutions, the military, to root out corruption, examine its human rights record, and review its struggle against the nation's drug lords.

Fox's promises generally did not materialize, however, and in 2003 and 2004 thousands of people protested out of frustration with a poor economy and what they perceived to be political paralysis.[70] Another indication of national discontentment is that national elections have weakened Fox's National Action Party; indeed, lawmakers have chastised him for spending too much time catering to other countries and have even blocked him from traveling to the United States. Mexico's lack of support for the war in Iraq disappointed President Bush, and U.S.-Mexico relations cooled. Furthermore, Fox's detractors view him as a do-nothing president who simply travels about the country giving daily speeches touting his administration.[71]

Still, Fox has had some successes. He has worked to clean up corruption and crack down on Mexico's drug trade (the police made several arrests of high-profile drug lords and tightened border security), but there is still much to accomplish, and atrocities are still reported. For example, in February 2004, thirteen Ciudad Juarez state police officers were reportedly held and questioned about drug trafficking and the murders of at least a dozen people, feeding fears that officers there were taking part in the crime they were supposed to be fighting. In addition, the state police acknowledged that about three hundred Ciudad Juarez officers were fired between 2002 and 2004, and that hundreds of murders had gone unsolved—including dozens of young women who were strangled and dumped in the desert outside of the city.[72]

Police Organization

Mexican police forces exist at the federal, state, and municipal levels through many overlapping levels of authority. The primary federal police, the General Directorate of Police and Traffic, are part of the Ministry of Government. The General Directorate is divided into four divisions: preventive, riot, auxiliary, and traffic and investigation (formerly called the Secret Service). The total strength of the General Directorate is about thirty thousand, including about one thousand female officers. The Federal Judicial Police are also on the federal level, under the command of the Public Ministry, which performs criminal investigations and represents Interpol in Mexico.[73] The Federal Highway Police, who number about two thousand, patrol the federally designated highways and investigate auto accidents. Small police forces are also maintained in the health, railway, and petroleum industries.[74]

The federal police are organized along military lines and comprise thirty-three battalions, thirty-one of which are numbered and include the preventive police, auxiliary police, auxiliary private police, administrative police, and women's police. The unnumbered battalions are the Grenadiers (a riot-control force that includes a motorized brigade) and the Transport Battalion.

The federal district, and each of the states, has its own police force. The state police enforce state laws within their jurisdiction and assist the federal police in enforcing federal laws. Large cities have special units, such as the Park Police and the Foreign Language Police. Large urban areas have many precincts, called "police delegations." A typical delegation has between 200 and 250 police assigned to it, under the command of a *comandante*, who is usually an officer with the rank of first captain. Lesser officers, usually lieutenants, are in charge of each eight-hour shift. They are assisted by first sergeants, second sergeants, and corporals. Most of the officers operate out of a command headquarters called a *comandancia*, but two-officer kiosks are scattered about as well. Auxiliary police also patrol on the night shift.[75]

Recruitment and Training

Generally, the Mexican police are underfunded and understaffed at all levels and jurisdictions. As a result, the recruitment and training of police officers are severely affected. Corruption among Mexican police is a long-standing problem, and the media on both sides of the border report regularly on police corruption, immorality, and incompetence. Bribes are commonplace and even required for the performance of some tasks. A close relationship exists between the police and the criminal elements of Mexico; indeed, a former police chief of Mexico City is in prison for organized graft on a massive scale.[76]

The General Directorate of Police and Traffic operates a police academy, where four- to six-month-long courses are taught. A few states have academies for state police; the best are in the states of Nuevo Leon, Jalisco, and Mexico. Courses at these academies usually last for four months. In cities where no formal academies exist, police officers are appointed by political bosses.

Criminal Codes and the Legal System

Mexico has separate federal and state codes of criminal procedure. Crimes are broadly categorized as those against persons, property, the state, public morals, and public health. Capital punishment was prohibited by the Federal Penal Code of 1931; although the Constitution provides for the death penalty for parricide, abduction, and highway robbery, it does not require that the penalty be imposed. The next severest punishment is thirty years in prison, which may be imposed for kidnapping.[77]

The most distinctive feature of the Mexican legal system is the **writ of *amparo***, which is similar to both the American writ of *habeas corpus,* used to challenge a prisoner's confinement, and to Section 1983, the instrument used against police officers (see Chapter 11). Considered to be Mexico's contribution to jurisprudence, the *amparo* has been adopted in part by several Latin American countries. An *amparo* may be sought by any citizen for the redress of an infringement of his or her civil rights or against the act of any official, tribunal, police officer, legislature, or bureaucrat; it is issued only by a federal judge. No class action suits are permitted in Mexico, so each person aggrieved by a law, a body, or an individual must file a separate *amparo* for redress.[78]

Another distinctive feature of the Mexican criminal process is the Public Ministry, which dates back to the nineteenth century and exists at the federal, state, and municipal levels. Agents of the Public Ministry, called *fiscales*, are charged with suppressing crime and initiating proceedings in criminal cases. They are usually assigned to police stations to determine the facts of a given case. They turn over their findings to a central office, which determines whether to initiate prosecution in a criminal case. Public prosecutors are independent of the courts and may not be censured by the judiciary. Since the Public Ministry represents the public, the office may not be sued by defendants if they are found innocent. The Public Ministry also commands the Federal Judicial Police.[79]

Except when an offender has been apprehended in the act of committing a crime (in flagrante delicto), arrest and detention must be preceded by a warrant issued by a competent judicial authority. The accused is entitled to counsel from the moment of arrest, and detention cannot exceed three days without a formal order of commitment. Bail is permitted except in cases of offenses that carry a prison term of more than five years as a penalty.

Jail Atrocities

Human rights activists have long implored the Mexican government to clamp down on the country's brutal police and crooked judges. The Mexican-U.S. "war on drugs" initiative that began in the early 1990s has resulted in the capture and imprisonment of an increasing number of U.S. citizens.[80] Thousands of cases have been logged in which the police have allegedly taken innocent citizens off the streets and held them incommunicado in jail without allowing them to see a judge. Many have also reported paying exorbitant "legal fees" while seeking their release from Mexican jails; only after signing a confession are they allowed to contact the U.S. embassy. Vigorous protests by the U.S. embassy against these practices appear to have had little effect.[81] It has also been alleged that the Mexican police use torture to obtain confessions, including beating, electrical shocks, and the *tehuacanazo*—blasts of chili powder and seltzer water up the nose. Amnesty International reports that another technique is to put a suspect's head inside a plastic bag filled with ammonia fumes.[82]

Many U.S. citizens have spent at least twenty months in prison before conviction, adding to rights violations and prison overcrowding. The prisoner exchange treaty between the United States and Mexico applies only to U.S. citizens who have been convicted.[83] Thus it may be several years before U.S. offenders can transfer to the United States to serve their sentences.

Toward Democratizing the Police Abroad: Lessons Learned

What must be done in order to democratize a police organization? What has history taught, and what lessons have we learned about police reform in the aid of democracy? In a federal report, noted police author David Bayley provided some practical advice for foreign police forces in countries that wish to become more democratic. Bayley noted that although the police cannot bring about political democracy through their own unaided efforts, they can contribute to democratic political development by acting in accord with the following four norms:[84]

Police must give top operational priority to servicing the needs of individual citizens and private groups: In the United States, any citizen with access to a telephone can summon a uniformed representative of the state who is imbued with the authority of law and is equipped with instruments of force to attend to his or her particular need. This is a major orientation of police that is still very rare among the world's police forces; it enhances the legitimacy of government by demonstrating that the authority of the state will be used in the interests of the people.

Police must be accountable to the law rather than to the government: In a democracy, the actions of government are constrained by law. Police actions in a democracy must therefore be governed by the rule of law rather than by directions given arbitrarily by particular regimes and their members.

Police must protect human rights, especially those that are required for the sort of unfettered political activity that is the hallmark of democracy: Democracy requires that the police make a special effort to safeguard activities that are essential to the exercise of democracy: freedom of speech, association, and movement; freedom from arbitrary arrest, detention, and exile; and impartiality in the administration of justice.

Police should be transparent in their activities: Police activity must be open to observation and regularly reported to outsiders. This requirement applies to information about the behavior of individual officers as well as to the operations of the institution as a whole.

INTERPOL

Tracking International Criminals

Donald Martin (alias Arman Esterhazy, alias Rene Tronter, alias Estaban Villarejo) left Kennedy Airport six months ago, posing as a businessman. He went from New York to London to Paris to Wiesbaden to Tel Aviv to Beirut in a crime spree that netted him $1 million by conning dozens of importers into ordering commodities ranging from crude rubber to machine tools. Fleeced merchants began contacting police, who eventually contacted the **International Criminal Police Organization (Interpol)**. This organization checked its master file and concluded that Martin, Tronter, and Villarejo were all the same man. His photograph, his fingerprints, and a national alert were distributed to member countries. An airport stakeout spotted Martin in Bombay, where he was Mr. Tronter on the passenger list. Extradition proceedings commenced immediately.[85]

This account is fictional, but the general scenario is not. Many crimes are conducted on an international scale, such as drug trafficking, bank fraud, money laundering, and counterfeiting. The crooks may escape detection for years while they enjoy their profits. Interpol is the oldest, best-known, and probably only truly international crime-fighting organization charged with the responsibility of capturing the "Martins" of the globe who seek to keep one country or continent ahead of the long arm of the law. To most people, the term *Interpol* probably conjures up a *Man from U.N.C.L.E.* image of worldwide secret agents; indeed, a *Man from Interpol* television show popularized the organization. In reality, however, Interpol agents do not patrol the globe; nor do they make arrests or engage in shoot-outs. They are basically intelligence gatherers who, since 1923, have helped many nations work together in attacking international crime.

Today, Lyon, France, serves as the headquarters for Interpol's crime-fighting tasks. One cardinal rule is observed: Interpol deals only with common criminals; it does not become involved with political, racial, or religious matters. Today, 176 countries belong to Interpol. U.S. participation in Interpol began in 1938, when Congress, under 22 U.S.C. 263a, authorized the attorney general to accept membership in the organization on behalf of the federal government. With the onset of World War II, however, the United States delayed membership until 1947, under the jurisdiction of the Federal Bureau of Investigation. In 1958, the Treasury Department was designated the official representative to Interpol, and in 1969 Treasury created the Interpol–U.S. National Central Bureau (USNCB). In 1977, dual authority was established between Treasury and Justice Department officials in administering the USNCB, and in 1981, the USNCB was again placed under the purview of the Justice Department.[86]

Police departments frequently request assistance from Interpol in locating a fugitive or obtaining information about a criminal. Interpol headquarters may issue an international circulation of information, known as a "diffusion"—an electronic dissemination of information about a wanted person—to agencies in a particular country or area; the information is immediately broadcast to the police officers in that country. Interpol may also issue a "notice," which is similar to a diffusion and communicates various types of information that are color-coded into ten categories (see Figure 13-4). Using the color code, officers receiving the notice immediately know the nature of the alert. For example, Interpol issues a red notice to alert officers at all locations, especially border and immigration checkpoints, that their subject has outstanding arrest warrants.[87]

Terrorism, drug and arms trafficking, and money laundering are unquestionably the most pressing international crime problems at present. Interpol has those crimes at the top of its list of concerns. The issue of

Red	Seeks arrest of subjects for whom arrest warrants have been issued and where extradition will be requested (e.g., fugitives)
Blue	Seeks information (e.g., identity, criminal records) for subjects who have committed criminal offenses and is used to trace and locate a subject where extradition may be sought (e.g., unidentified offenders, witnesses)
Green	Provides information on career criminals who have committed, or are likely to commit, offenses in several countries (e.g., habitual offenders, child molesters, pornographers)
Yellow	Seeks missing or lost persons (includes missing and abducted children)
Black	Provides details of unidentified dead bodies or deceased people who may have used false identities
White	Circulates details and descriptions of all types of stolen or seized property, including art and cultural objects
Purple	Provides details of unusual *modus operandi,* including new methods of concealment
Gray	Provides information on various organized crime groups and their activities
Orange	Provides information on criminal activity with international ramifications but not involving a specific person or group
FOPAC	Provides money-laundering information for use in countering international money laundering

FIGURE 13-4 Types of Interpol notices.

Source: John J. Imhoff and Stephen P. Cutler, "Interpol: Extending Law Enforcement's Reach around the World," FBI Law Enforcement Bulletin, *December 1998, p. 13.*

terrorism raised some problems in Interpol because of its constitutional provisions against becoming involved in political matters. The member countries decided it was imperative nonetheless to strengthen cooperation in the area of terrorism. Lately, Interpol has been fighting international crime "on a shoestring," as one author stated.[88] Its level of technology has been wanting throughout most of its history, especially in comparison to the resources employed by criminals.[89]

A Formula for Success

Interpol has a basic three-step formula for improving multinational police cooperation. Interpol requires member countries to pass laws specifying the offense is a crime; to prosecute offenders and cooperate in other countries' prosecutions; and to exchange information with Interpol about crime and its perpetrators. This formula could reverse the worldwide trend that is currently forecast: an increasing capability by criminals for violence and destruction.

The rule of thumb governing extradition treaties seems to be that the offenses specified must involve double criminality. They must be recognized as crimes by both parties: the country in which the offender was caught and the country in which the crime was committed. The following crimes are covered by almost all U.S. treaties of extradition: murder, rape, bigamy, arson, robbery, burglary, forgery, counterfeiting, embezzlement, larceny, fraud, perjury, and kidnapping.

(Courtesy of Interpol)

EXHIBIT 13-2

Needs of Police Training and Education Transcend International Boundaries

Law enforcement trainers and educators from around the world will have a chance to exchange ideas and information under the auspices of a new international organization dedicated to serving the needs of those in the field.

"As nations begin to cooperate with each other, it becomes clear that the international aspects of delivering education and training to society's protectors are more important as terrorism reaches virtually every nation," said Ed Nowicki, executive director of the International Law Enforcement Educators and Trainers Association, which will be headquartered in Twin Lakes, Wis.

Nowicki, who has served as a law enforcement trainer for more than two decades, said the widely varied backgrounds of the professional trainers on the group's advisory board will benefit members....

Moreover, the executive director's position will be permanent, providing continuity to the association, said Nowicki....

Membership in ILEETA will be open to any active law enforcement educator or trainer, supervisor or manager of criminal justice education. Among other perquisites, membership will entitle one to a quarterly periodical, *The ILEETA Digest,* and free or discounted subscriptions to a number of other professional journals and publications.

ILEETA also plans to hold a conference and expo in the Chicago area each spring.

Source: "Needs of Police Training and Education Transcend International Boundaries," *Law Enforcement News,* March 15/31, 2003, p. 11. John Jay College of Criminal Justice, CUNY, 555 W. 57th St., New York, NY 10019.

SUMMARY

The national police systems discussed in this chapter are similar in some ways. With the exception of the PSNI of Northern Ireland, each force is in effect a pawn of its national government. And each, again except for the PSNI, offers its officers low wages and benefits and is held in low esteem by the citizens. Some of the police organizations described here train their officers well for the heavy-handed duties they must perform. Most are granted considerable powers of arrest for investigation and interrogation and are known to be brutal and unrelenting to their prisoners; thus their citizens fear them.

Although some of these elements may seem to exist in relationships of U.S. citizens with their police officers, there are many differences between U.S. police methods and those in the countries discussed here. While U.S. police are well trained on the whole (and probably also consider themselves to be underpaid and accorded low esteem by the public), U.S. citizens do not have to fear an omnipotent national police force as citizens of other countries obviously must.

As we have seen in previous chapters, police officers in the United States perform defined, limited functions under a constitutionally grounded rule of law that governs arrests, searches, and seizures and that prohibits excessive methods of interrogation and detention by the police. This comparative perspective has provided the opportunity to compare and contrast various police systems. It has demonstrated that although U.S. police have their own problems, a democratic system appears to be unequivocally better than those systems discussed in this chapter.

Finally, the discussion of Interpol shows that even with political problems and the isolation of countries around the globe, foreign countries must, can, and do succeed in tracking and prosecuting international offenders.

REVIEW QUESTIONS

1. Why it is helpful and important to examine criminal justice systems in other countries?
2. Analyze the police systems discussed in this chapter. What are the main characteristics of each with regard to the following?
   a. Political and legal foundation
   b. Organization and jurisdiction
   c. Methods of operation
   d. Respect for human rights
3. How do the police agencies of each of these countries differ from the U.S. system of policing in terms of the items listed in question 2?
4. What organization exists to combat international crime and to catch transient fugitives? How does this organization accomplish its mission?

INDEPENDENT STUDENT ACTIVITIES

1. Select one of the countries described in this chapter. Imagine that you are traveling in that country and are arrested on suspicion of being a drug courier. (You are innocent.) How would you likely be treated by that country's police and its justice system in general? Then, based on your knowledge of American policing, compare how you would likely be treated by the local police if you were arrested for the same offense in the United States.
2. From a human rights perspective, which of the countries discussed in this chapter do you think would be the worst country in which to live?
3. Try to imagine a national police force being proposed in the United States, in the image of the police in China or Mexico. How would U.S. citizens receive such a proposal?
4. Do the foreign police systems discussed in this chapter have any attributes that might be adopted in America for the betterment of our police system?

RELATED WEB SITES

Office of International Criminal Justice
http://www.oicj.org

United Nations Crime and Justice Information Network
http://www.ifs.univie.ac.at/uncjin/uncjin.html

United Nations Online Crime and Justice Clearinghouse
http://www.unojust.org

NOTES

1. KEN PEAK, "The Comparative Systems Course in Criminal Justice: Findings from a National Survey," *Journal of Criminal Justice Education* 2 (1992): 267–72.
2. MARK KESSELMAN, "Order or Movement? The Literature of Political Development as Ideology," *World Politics* 26 (1973): 139–54.
3. GABRIEL S. ALMOND and JOHN S. COLEMAN, *The Politics of the Developing Areas* (Princeton, NJ: Princeton University Press, 1960), p. 2.
4. "Q & A: Iraqi Election," BBC News, UK Edition, http://news.bbc.co.uk/1/hi/world/middle_east/3971635.stm (accessed January 31, 2005).
5. "Iraq Vote a 'Historic Victory'," The Kansas City Star, KansasCity.com, http://www.kansascity.com/mld/kansascity/news/world/10775453.htm?1c (accessed January 31, 2005).
6. CIA—The World Factbook, "Iraq," http://www.cia/gov/cia/publications/factbook/geos/iz.html (accessed January 31, 2005).
7. "Judge, 11 police killed in Baghdad attacks," MSNBC News, http://www.msnbc.msn.com/id/68472225/ (accessed January 25, 2005).
8. YEHIA BARZANJI, "Bomb at Iraqi Police Station Kills Twenty; U.S. Troops Battle Insurgents," *Army Times,* September 4, 2004, http://www.armytimes.com/story.php (accessed September 7, 2004).
9. ANTHONY SHADID, "Insurgents Storm Iraq Police Station, Twenty-three Die in Fighting," *Washington Post*, February 15, 2004, p. 1A.
10. "Fifty-Four Iraqis Killed in Car Bombing during Job Fair," *New York Times*, February 11, 2004, p. A2.
11. "Explosion Kills Eight Iraqi Police," Associated Press, *Reno Gazette Journal*, December 15, 2003, p. 2A.
12. JOEL BRINKLEY, "The Struggle for Iraq: Violence, Revenge Drives String of Killings in Basra," *New York Times*, November 1, 2003, p. A6.
13. DAN MURPHY, "Iraqi Police in the Cross Hairs of Anti-U.S. Forces," *Christian Science Monitor*, October 10, 2003, p. 7.
14. JOSHUA HAMMER, "Holding the Line," *Newsweek*, February 16, 2004, p. 32.
15. CHRISTINE CARYL, "Iraqi Vice," *Newsweek*, December 22, 2003, p. 38.

16. "U.S. sees training as the key to success," The Baltimore Sun, http://www.baltimoresun.com/news/nationworld/bal-te.baghdad30Jan30,1,2276781.story?c (accessed January 31, 2005).
17. BETH POTTER, "Iraqi police to get the boot," United Press International, http://www.wpherald.com/storyview.pho?StoryID520050112–024620–6336r (accessed January 31, 2005).
18. "U.S. Diplomats Urged to Leave Saudi Arabia," CNN.com, http://www.cnn.com/2033/US/12/17/saudi, warning/ (accessed January 7, 2004).
19. "U.S. Citizens Advised to Avoid Saudi Arabia," Guardian Unlimited, http://www.guardian.co.uk.saudi.story/0,11599,1072596.html (accessed January 7, 2004).
20. Ibid.
21. SAUDI ARABIAN INTERNATIONAL SCHOOLS, *An Introduction to the Kingdom of Saudi Arabia* (Spring 1992), p. 11.
22. Ibid., p. 12.
23. Ibid., p. 4.
24. SAUDI ARABIA v. NELSON, 113 S.Ct. 1471, 123 L.Ed.2d 47 (1993).
25. SAUDI ARABIAN INTERNATIONAL SCHOOLS, *An Introduction to the Kingdom of Saudi Arabia,* p. 17.
26. ADEL MOHAMMED EL FIKEY, "Crimes and Penalties in Islamic Criminal Legislation," *CJ International 2* (July–August 1986), p. 13.
27. Gulf News, May 19, 1989, p. 1.
28. EL FIKEY, "Crimes and Penalties in Islamic Criminal Legislation," p. 14.
29. CHRIS HEDGES, "Everywhere in Saudi Arabia, Islam Is Watching," *New York Times,* January 6, 1993, p. A4(N), col. 3.
30. Ibid.
31. Ibid.
32. Ibid.
33. Confidential personal communication, July 27, 1994.
34. Ibid.
35. RICHARD J. TERRILL, *World Criminal Justice Systems,* 5th ed. (Cincinnati: Anderson, 2003), pp. 513–14.
36. YUE MA, "The Police Law 1995: Organization, Functions, Powers and Accountability of the Chinese Police," *Policing: An International Journal of Police Strategy and Management* 20 (1997): 113–35.
37. Ibid., p. 115.
38. Z. MA and M. TIAN, *The People's Police Law of the People's Republic of China: Explanations and Seminars* (Beijing: China University Press, 1995).
39. YUE MA, "The Police Law 1995," p. 119.
40. Ibid., pp. 120–21.
41. Ibid., pp. 123–25.
42. X. WANG, "Preliminary Analysis of Current Situation of Chinese Young People's Feeling of Safety," *Public Security Studies* 4 (1991).
43. YUE MA, "The Police Law 1995," pp. 130–31.
44. Ibid., p. 132.

45. Fintan O'Toole, "A Novel Question for Ireland," *U.S. News and World Report*, May 25, 1998, p. 22.
46. Richard Ward, "Gangs Deal in Fear and Savagery," *Criminal Justice International* 4 (November–December 1988): 3.
47. Royal Ulster Constabulary, *RUC: The Grim Statistics* (July 1989), p. 27.
48. Ibid., p. 22.
49. Stryker McGuire, "The Easter Peace," *Newsweek,* April 20, 1998, p. 34.
50. Michael Barone, "An Irish Parable, Unfinished," *U.S. News and World Report*, August 4, 2003, p. 31.
51. McGuire, "The Easter Peace," p. 34.
52. "Britain Bolsters Troops: Northern Ireland's Mayhem Unchecked," Associated Press, July 8, 1998.
53. "Phone Call Causes Dozens of Deaths in Terrorist Bomb Blast in Ireland," Associated Press, August 16, 1998.
54. Shawn Pogatchnik, "Bonfires in Belfast," Associated Press, July 12, 2000; also see Thomas K. Grose, "It's Back to the Streets," *U.S. News and World Reports*, July 17, 2000, p. 34.
55. "Violence Continues in Belfast; Thirty Hurt," Associated Press, January 11, 2002.
56. Yahoo! Education, "Ireland Population," http://education.yahoo.com/reference/factbook/ei/popula.html (accessed February 26, 2004).
57. O'Toole, "A Novel Question for Ireland," p. 23.
58. Personal communication, Tim Lewis, May 10, 1990.
59. Paul K. Clare, "The Royal Ulster Constabulary: Northern Ireland's Beleaguered Police Force," *Criminal Justice International* 3 (May–June 1987): 3–6.
60. Ibid., pp. 4–5.
61. *RUC: The Grim Statistics*, p. 30.
62. United Kingdom Home Office, "Terrorism Act, 2000," http: //www.homeoffice.gov.uk/terrorism/govprotect/legislation/ (accessed August 26, 2004).
63. United Kingdom, Statutory Rules of Northern Ireland, "Police Recruitment Regulations, 2001," http://www.hmso.gov.uk/sr/sr2001/20010140.htm (accessed August 26, 2004).
64. Colin Knox, "See No Evil, Hear No Evil," *British Journal of Criminology* 22, no. 42 (2002): 164; see also Rachel Monaghan, "The Return of 'Captain Moonlight': Informal Justice in Northern Ireland," *Studies in Conflict and Terrorism* 24, no. 41 (2002): 41–56.
65. L. Kennedy, "Nightmares within Nightmares: Paramilitary Repression within Working-Class Communities," in *Crime and Punishment in West Belfast*, ed. L. Kennedy (West Belfast: Summer School, 2000), pp. 62–112.
66. W. Thompson and B. Mulholland, "Paramilitary Punishments and Young People in West Belfast: Psychological Effects and the Implications for Education," in Kennedy, ed., *Crime and Punishment in West Belfast*, pp. 114–141.
67. Knox, "See No Evil, Hear No Evil," pp. 174–75.
68. Elliot Blair Smith, "Fox Ready for 'Revolution of Hope,' " *USA Today*, December 1, 2000, p. 1.
69. Ibid.

70. "Thousands Demonstrate against Mexican Leader," Associated Press, November 28, 2003.
71. Traci Carl, "Three Years Later, Mexico Disenchanted with Vicente Fox," Associated Press, July 13, 2003.
72. "Thirteen Officers Held after Bodies Found in Mexico," Associated Press, January 30, 2004.
73. George Thomas Kurian, *World Encyclopedia of Police Forces and Penal Systems* (New York: Facts on File, 1989), p. 258.
74. Ibid., pp. 258–59.
75. Ibid., p. 258.
76. Ibid., p. 259.
77. Ibid., p. 259.
78. Ibid., pp. 259–60.
79. Ibid., p. 260.
80. America's Watch, *Human Rights in Mexico: A Policy of Impunity* (Los Angeles: Author, 1990).
81. J. Michael Olivero, "The 'War on Drugs' and Mexican Prisons," *Criminal Justice and the Americas* 4 (April–May 1991): 3–4.
82. Tim Padgett, "Tijuana's Midnight Express," *Newsweek,* November 23, 1992, p. 41.
83. U.S. Congress, House Committee on the Judiciary, *Providing Implementation of Treaties for Transfer of Offenders to or from Foreign Countries: Report of the Judiciary on S1682, October 19, 1977* (Washington, DC: U.S. Government Printing Office, 1977).
84. David H. Bayley, *Democratizing the Police Abroad: What to Do and How to Do It*. (Washington, DC: Department of Justice, National Institute of Justice, June 2001), pp. 13–15.
85. Michael Fooner, *Interpol* (Chicago: Henry Regnery, 1973), pp. 2–3.
86. Interpol, *An Overview of Interpol and the U.S. National Central Bureau* (October 1994), pp. 6–7.
87. John J. Imhoff and Stephen P. Cutler, "Interpol: Extending Law Enforcement's Reach around the World," *FBI Law Enforcement Bulletin,* December 1998, pp. 10–17.
88. Richard Ward, "Interpol: Fighting Crime on a Shoestring," *Criminal Justice International* (winter 1985): 1.
89. Michael Fooner, *Interpol: Issues in World Crime and International Criminal Justice* (New York: Plenum Press, 1989), p. 179.

CHAPTER 14

Technology Review

Knowledge is power.

—Francis Bacon

Intelligence . . . is the faculty of making artificial objects, especially tools to make tools.

—Henri Bergson

Give us the tools, and we will finish the job.

—Winston Churchill

Key Terms

automated fingerprint identification system (AFIS)
computer-aided dispatching (CAD)
crime mapping
geographic profiling
homicide investigation and tracking system (HITS)
less-lethal
mobile data system

Several photographs and some discussions in Chapter 7 demonstrated the kinds of technologies now available for forensic analyses. This chapter reviews more broadly the kinds of technologies that are either currently available to the police or on the horizon.

The new millennium brings exciting, ongoing opportunities for policing with regard to technology; since the advent of computers, we are limited only by our collective imagination and willingness to provide the funding necessary for technology to evolve. While our crime laboratories have arguably provided the greatest technological advances in recent years, tremendous opportunities exist in other areas as well. It is not surprising that most technological innovations in criminal justice were developed for and involve the police, given the nature of their work, tools, and problems.

We begin by considering some fundamental problems that exist in the area of policing and technology, particularly the need for better trained personnel who understand computer hardware and software. Next we discuss technologies that are being developed to combat terrorism; then we look at the development and status of less-lethal police weapons, followed by a look at wireless technology for use in databases, in crime mapping, and in dealing with serial offenders and gunshots. Then we examine how electronic capabilities are being applied to several traffic functions. Following is a brief look at technological advances with DNA, and then we review developments with fingerprints and mug shots. New uses of technologies in the area of crime-scene investigations are presented, and we then consider how computers are assisting with regard to firearms, particularly in training officers and in solving cases involving guns. Following a short commentary on intelligence systems of gangs, we conclude with a chapter summary, review questions, independent student activities, and related Web sites.

Several of the technologies discussed in this chapter may be—and are being—applied to community-oriented policing and problem solving (COPPS, examined in Chapter 6). Some crime-analysis methods and tools (such as computer mapping) that were briefly mentioned in Chapter 6 are examined in more detail in this chapter. Furthermore, Chapter 15 will discuss future technologies in more detail as they relate to policing. Three technologies in particular are still "out there" in terms of research and development: nanotechnology, augmented reality, and unmanned aerial vehicles.

Police and Technology of the Future: Problems and Prospects

First, the good news. It is anticipated that police officers of the future will function in very different ways and on very different terms than officers of the past. There will be few time and space constraints because all officers will be equipped with a pager, a cellular phone, and a laptop computer with software that includes encryption programs and sophisticated databases and search engines. Officers will have software that allows them to have real-time chats with officers from other agencies, in other states, or even in other countries. Before going on the streets, every rookie will be an expert at using computers and will be able to use crime-analysis software.[1] Exhibit 14-1 describes how one form of handheld technology—the handheld minicomputer—already allows officers to be removed from their patrol car laptops.[2]

As the saying goes, however, "The fleas come with the dog." Aspects of the alliance between police and technology presage problems for the foreseeable future. From 1995 to 1998 (the last year of the program), the federal Office of Community Oriented Policing Services poured hundreds of millions of dollars into police agencies for new equipment.[3] But this federal largesse brought problems. First, many departments lacked the in-house computer expertise to install or run the software and equipment. Even today, many police executives believe that they hire people to be police officers—not to be

EXHIBIT 14-1

The Power of Information, in a Palm-Sized Package

What the newest hand-held minicomputers lack in heft, they more than make up for in the wealth of information they can supply to police in those crucial moments before they approach a suspect. The devices, which tip the scales at a mere four ounces or so, are finding their way onto the equipment belts of law enforcement officers in a steadily growing number of jurisdictions, including New York City, Charleston, S.C., and Franklin County, Ohio....

New York is the first city in the nation to have officers use the devices during routine street patrols. Worn on the officers' gun belts, they come with small keyboards that can be used to enter license numbers, names and other data. What sets them apart from existing NYPD computers that can provide the same information, however, is their speed and stealth.

Said Ari Wax, the NYPD's deputy commissioner for technology and development: "It can be just like the cop on the street is checking his e-mail."

In April, two housing officers demonstrated how effective the hand-helds could be when police are faced with quality-of-life crimes. Confronting a man drinking beer on a Harlem stoop, the officers entered his name into a device they were testing. It turned out that the subject, Adrian Bowman, was wanted for a triple homicide in St. Louis....

Det. Chris Floyd noted that in the past, when suspects are detained, deputies might use a walkie-talkie to call the dispatcher for arrest information. Those results, transmitted over the radio, could then be heard by the suspect. "Now this guy knows I know who he is," said Floyd. "It's giving this guy a warning to run or fight."

While it is the portability of hand-held computers that has garnered the greatest appreciation thus far from police, they also cost much less than laptops, noted Sgt. Robert Flynn, director of computer services for the Charleston Police Department. The agency handed out 25 minicomputers last month to its traffic officers as part of a 60-day trial. It is the only department in the state to try out the devices so far, according to the *Charleston Post and Courier*....

"It's tremendous in that respect," he said, "but the cost can't be ignored." To install a laptop in a vehicle costs approximately $7,100; the hand-held computers, with software and network data time through a provider, cost approximately $1,900. "It's substantial. We can do everything a laptop was doing for us in the palm of the officer's hand for less money."

Source: Reprinted with permission from *Law Enforcement News*, May 31, 2001, p. 11. John Jay College of Criminal Justice, CUNY, 555 W. 57th St., New York, NY 10019.

computer programmers or database experts. But the nature of the policing business is changing; officers with such skills are not only desirable and valuable, but also increasingly and rapidly becoming a necessity as a problem-solving aid.

In many police agencies, information technology staff are often civilians and are generally kept away from the operational side of the organization. They understand what computers do but not necessarily how that capability supports the operational needs of the police officer on the street.

These problems are in addition to other technology-related shortcomings. For example, the police are also playing catch-up to counter a host of evasive criminal schemes, such as digital compression, remote storage, audit disabling, anonymous remailers, digital cash, computer penetration and looping, and cloning of cellular phones and phone cards.[4]

In this chapter, we examine the kinds of advances that are rapidly being made in the field. It should be emphasized that several of the systems described here are extremely expensive and too costly for most agencies. Furthermore, these systems are not a panacea and cannot replace the traditional forms of police work; rather, they are simply a way of managing information and focusing an investigation or search in a small area.

Technology versus Terrorists

The terrorist attacks on September 11, 2001, not only changed the way federal, state, and local law enforcement agencies approach their mission (in essence, they now also protect citizens against attack from the outside, rather than only from within), but also set in motion research and development of new technologies for protecting against terrorist acts. And Americans seem accepting of more surveillance and screening technologies even if it means giving up some of their privacy: Polls conducted immediately after the September 11 attacks revealed that an overwhelming majority of Americans—about 75 percent—thought it necessary to give up some personal freedoms for the sake of security.[5] Following are some technologies that are being or have been developed to supplement luggage scanners and metal detectors to assist in detecting and foiling terrorists.

A low-dose X-ray imager can see through garments to detect stashed weapons, drugs, or other contraband. (The September 11 terrorists slipped through checkpoints with box cutters.) Surveillance cameras can scan faces and feed the images to a computer that scours a database of digital mug shots for a match. These devices were used during the 2001 Super Bowl in Tampa, Florida, and identified several petty criminals in the crowd. Soon after that, however, many Floridians and the state's civil liberties union protested against their use.[6] Better bomb-detecting technology is also being developed, including machines that perform a cross-sectional X-ray scan of checked baggage. Ion-detecting swabs can find bomb residue on hand luggage. Also being considered for limited use are "smart cards"—IDs equipped with memory chips that store personal data and can track movements and transactions.[7]

The Development of Less-Lethal Weapons

A Historical Overview

Since the dawn of time, people have sought to control the behavior of their fellows. Our recorded history is full of accounts of the need to protect ourselves from a hostile environment.[8] Certainly, international police forces have attempted to employ many means to protect themselves and the public at large.

Although the term *nonlethal weapon* is often used, this term is inappropriate because any tool or weapon can be lethal if it is used in an improper or unintended manner. For this reason, the term **less-lethal** is more properly used to designate a weapon designed to produce only a temporary effect and minimal medical consequences for healthy people.[9]

The Unveiling: 1829. When London's new bobbies began patrolling the streets in September 1829, they were armed with a baton, or truncheon, that still is a standard-issue weapon. Traditionally, it was made of hardwood and was two to four centimeters in diameter and thirty to sixty-five centimeters in length.[10]

Social turmoil in America between 1840 and 1870 brought increased use of force by the police, who themselves were frequent victims of assault. The New York City police and other departments were armed with thirty-three-inch clubs, which officers were not reluctant to use. Charges of police brutality were common in the mid-nineteenth century, when officers allegedly clubbed "respectable" citizens with frequency.[11]

Until the end of the nineteenth century, the baton remained a staple tool among American police. As late as 1900, when the Chicago Police Department numbered 3,225 officers, the only tools given the new patrolmen were "a brief speech from a high-ranking officer, a hickory stick, whistle, and a key to the call box."[12] Charges of police brutality continued.

Chemical Weapons: 1860s–1950s. From 1860 to 1959, there was only one major addition to the small array of less-lethal police tools: chemical weapons. CN gas was synthesized by German chemists in 1869 and was the first tear gas; it produced a burning sensation in the throat, eyes, and nose. It became available for use in aerosol cans in 1965. Chemical Mace was the most well-known brand. By 1912, chemical weapons were increasingly used in riots and when subduing criminals.[13]

CS gas was first synthesized in 1928 as a white powder that stored well. It was adopted by many police forces as it had a greater effect than CN, causing a very strong burning sensation in the eyes that often caused them to close involuntarily. Severe pain in the nose, throat, and chest; vomiting; and nausea are also associated with its use.[14]

A Technological Explosion: The 1960s. The 1960s witnessed major technological advances in less-lethal weaponry. This was the age of rioting, on both domestic and foreign soil. Aerosol chemical agents, developed to provide alternatives to police batons and firearms, became the most popular less-lethal weapons for police use. Mace seemed like "manna from heaven."[15]

CR gas appeared in 1962; six times more potent than CS and twenty times more potent than CN, it caused extreme eye pressure and occasionally hysteria. CS gas cartridges, which were fired by shotguns at a range of 125 meters, were used in the United States and Britain as early as 1968.

In 1967, alternatives to lethal lead bullets were first used in Hong Kong. Wooden rounds, fired from a signal pistol with a range of twenty to thirty meters, were designed to be ricocheted off the ground, striking the victim in the legs. The wooden rounds proved to be fatal, however, and direct fire broke legs at forty-six meters. Rubber bullets were developed and issued to British troops and police officers in 1967, only a few months after the wooden rounds appeared. Intended to deliver a force equivalent to a hard punch at twenty-five meters, the rubber bullets caused severe bruising and shock. Also intended to be ricocheted off the ground, the rubber bullet was designed so that riot police could outrange stone throwers.[16] Rubber bullets were employed by Seattle police officers in December 1999 during protests against the World Trade Organization meeting.[17]

During the 1960s, British riot police also began employing water cannons, which were designed to fire large jets of water at demonstrators. Resembling armored fire engines, water cannons were also used in Germany, France, Belgium and the United States. Nontoxic blue dye was added to the water for marking the offenders. For a time, the firing of a CR solution was contemplated.[18]

In 1968, another unique riot-oriented weapon was unveiled in America: the Sound Curdler, which consisted of amplified speakers that produced loud shrieking noises at irregular intervals. Attached to vehicles or helicopters, the device was first used at campus disturbances.

The 1970s: Beanbag Guns, Strobe Lights, and "New Age" Batons. Another unique tool was introduced in 1970: a gun that shot beanbags rather than bullets. The apparatus fired a pellet-loaded bag that unfurled into a spinning pancake and was capable of knocking down a two-hundred-pound person at a range of three hundred feet. Although its manufacturer warned that it had potentially lethal capabilities, it quickly became popular in several countries, including South Africa and Saudi Arabia.[19]

Several other inventions were added to the less-lethal arsenal in the 1970s. The Photic Driver, first used by police in South Africa, produced a strobe effect; its light caused giddiness, fainting, and nausea. A British firm developed a strobe gun that operated at five flickers per second. Some of these devices also had a high-pitched screamer device attached. Another apparatus, known as the Squawk Box, had two high-energy ultrasound generators operating at slightly different frequencies that produced sounds that also caused nausea and giddiness.[20]

Other inventions of the early 1970s included an electrified water jet; a baton that carried a six-thousand-volt shock; shotgun shells filled with plastic pellets; plastic bubbles that immobilized rioters; a chemical that created slippery street surfaces for combating rioters; and an instant "cocoon," an adhesive substance that, when sprayed over crowds, made people stick together.[21]

Two new types of projectiles were developed in 1974: the plastic bullet and the Taser. The "softer" plastic bullets could be fired from a variety of riot

EXHIBIT 14-2

Reducing the Death Toll from Nonlethal Weapons

With 12 people dead and dozens injured around the country in recent years by beanbag rounds, the Santa Ana, Calif., Police Department has decided to switch to a less dangerous less-than-lethal weapon.

The FN 303 Launcher, sold by FNH USA Inc. of McLean, Va., weighs five pounds and uses compressed air to shoot only those projectiles it was designed to fire. It has a red-dot sight and propels a round at 290 feet per second, roughly twice as fast as a beanbag shotgun. the device also has an optimum range of nearly 55 yards. Eight of the $1,500 weapons have been deployed to patrol officers, who began training on them earlier this year.

"Beanbags, depending on the type you use, [had] problems with accuracy," Sgt. Baltazar De La Riva of the department's media relations unit told *Law Enforcement News*. "Depending on the distance between the round and the suspect, they were causing some serious injuries. "That was one of the aspects that was considered in the purchase and use of these launchers."

Although it looks somewhat like a shotgun, the launcher has a round barrel—like a Tommy gun—and can hold 15 rounds, giving it greater capabilities than shotguns converted to fire less-than-lethal munitions, said De La Riva. The pellets it uses, which can be filled with water, paint or pepper spray, will explode on impact and disintegrate. Another safety measure is the launcher's orange strap, which will help officers distinguish the weapon from an actual shotgun, he said.

Last October [2002], a Redondo Beach, Calif., officer killed an unarmed man suspected of being a car thief when he was inadvertently handed a shotgun instead of a beanbag stun gun. The 40-year-old victim was killed instantly when he was hit in the chest. And in 1995, a Contra Costa County, Calif., deputy killed a 42-year-old man when he fired a shotgun instead of a beanbag round....

Source: "Reducing the Death Toll from Non-lethal Weapons," *Law Enforcement News*, March 15/31, 2003, p. 8. John Jay College of Criminal Justice, CUNY, 555 W. 57th St., New York, NY 10019.

weapons at a speed of 160 miles per hour and a range of thirty to seventy meters, making them attractive to riot police. Like wooden bullets, however, these new plastic bullets could be fatal. Seven people in Northern Ireland died during the early 1980s after being struck in the head by these bullets.[22]

The Taser resembled a flashlight and shot two tiny darts into its victim. Attached to the darts were fine wires through which a transformer delivered a fifty-thousand-volt electrical shock, which would knock down a person at a distance of fifteen feet. Police officers in every state except Alaska had tried the device by 1985, but its use was not widespread because of limitations of range and because it was not always effective on people under the influence of drugs. Heavy clothing could also render it ineffective.[23] The current status of the Taser is discussed later.

The stun gun, also introduced in the mid-1970s, initially competed with the Taser as the police tool of choice. Slightly larger than an electric razor, it also delivered a fifty-thousand-volt shock when its two electrodes were pressed directly against the body. Like the Taser, its amperage was so small that it did not provide a lethal electrical jolt. Its target, who was rendered rubbery-legged and fell to the ground, was unable to control physical movement for several minutes.[24]

The Quest Continues

The quest continues today for effective alternatives to lethal force. It is a paradox in this high-technology age that reliable substitutes for lethal police weapons have not yet been developed. As the discussion shows, the innovations of the past were sometimes deadly or ineffective. So the search for the "perfect" less-lethal weapon continues.

The Taser underwent considerable revision in the late 1990s, evolving into a much better tool, one that is now widely adopted by police agencies. The newer models are shaped like a handgun, use twenty-six watts to deliver fifty thousand volts (as opposed to the older five- or six-watt versions) for five seconds, and can penetrate up to three inches of clothing. Their range is up to twenty-one feet. Even if only one probe sticks to the person, the newer versions will still work most of the time.[25]

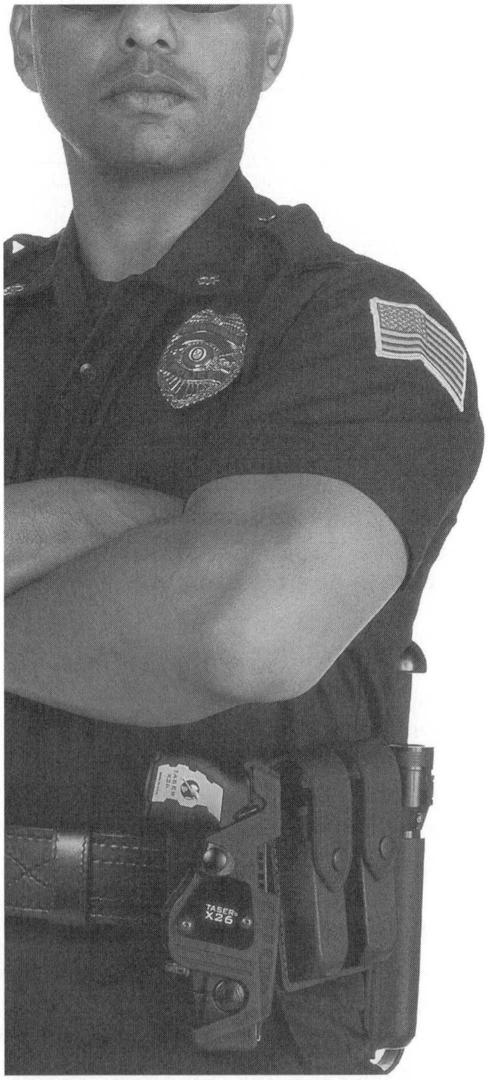

By late 2004, more than one hundred thousand police officers in fifty-five hundred police agencies were carrying a Taser.

(Courtesy of TASER International, Inc.)

Also recently introduced are two types of foam that may hold promise. One is supersticky; offenders are drenched in a substance that, when exposed to the air, turns into taffy-like glue. The other creates an avalanche of very dense soap bubbles that leave offenders unable to see or move but still able to breathe. Other chemical compounds, known as "stick 'ems" and "slick 'ems," make pavements either too sticky or too slippery for vehicles to move on.[26]

Police departments nationwide—many of them beleaguered by protests after fatal shootings—continue to look to new weapons that offer a less-lethal alternative, an "intermediate" weapon between the voice and the gun. Many of these alternatives are relatively inexpensive for agencies to adopt and can significantly reduce a department's liability.[27]

Interest has been renewed in beanbag rounds (sometimes called kinetic batons) and capture nets. Beanbag rounds have become extremely popular; they have been adopted by police agencies across the country and have been used successfully to help end a number of standoffs.[28] A Spiderman-style net gun known as the WebShot is designed to wrap and immobilize a suspect. The WebShot gun has been on the market since 1999 and is being tried in Los Angeles and San Diego. WebShot is ideally used against an unarmed person who is being combative.[29]

The Less Than Lethal program for the National Institute of Justice coordinates research on such weapons, ensuring that they are both technically feasible and practical for police officers. In addition to the WebShot gun, the program recently provided funding for research into the following technologies:

- The Laser Dazzler, a flashlight device designed to disorient or distract suspects with a green laser light
- The Sticky Shocker, a wireless projectile fired from a gas gun that sticks to the subject with glue or barbs and delivers an electric shock
- The Ring Airfoil Projectile, a doughnut-shaped, hard rubber weapon that is being redesigned to disperse a cloud of pepper powder on impact[30]

Pepper spray, or oleoresin capsicum, is now used by an estimated 90 percent of police agencies, according to the National Institute of Justice.[31] This spray inflames the mucous membranes of the eyes, nose, and mouth, causing a severe burning sensation for twenty minutes or less.[32] The spray is highly effective in subduing suspects without causing undue harm or long-term aftereffects.[33]

Another promising new innovation is the Option, which offers lethal and less-lethal capabilities in a single unit; the weapon has a cylinder of pepper spray that is mounted to the barrel of a pistol or shoulder weapon.[34] It was invented by a member of the Oxnard, California, Police Department's SWAT team.

This compressed-air gun fires small pellets filled with OC ("pepper spray") or other gases.

(Courtesy Sparks, Nevada, Police Department)

The Use of Wireless Technology

Instant Access to Information

Mobile data systems have been available since the 1970s. But the first-generation systems were based on large, proprietary computers that were very costly and were often beyond the reach of many small and medium-sized police agencies. The first digital data were not transmitted from police headquarters to a cruiser until the mid-1980s. Today, armed with a notebook computer and a radio modem, police officers can have almost instant access to information in numerous federal, state, and local databases. Even small agencies can now afford a network and mobile data terminals (MDTs).[35]

A growing number of American police departments, including small agencies, are using laptop computers with wireless connections to crime and motor vehicle databases. These systems are believed to pay for themselves in increased fines and officer safety. Officers can access court documents, in-house police department records, and a **computer-aided dispatching (CAD)** system, as well as enter license numbers into their laptop computers. And, through a national network of motor vehicle and criminal history databases, they can locate drivers with outstanding warrants, expired or suspended licenses, and so on. Furthermore, rather than using open radio communications, police officers use their computers to communicate with one another via e-mail.[36]

Integrated Databases

In 1999, a "railroad killer" was engaged in a rampage across the southwest. Texas Border Patrol agents unknowingly picked up the killer near the

An officer uses a relatively new handheld pocket computer.

(Courtesy Aether Systems, Inc.)

Mexican border and dutifully checked the agency's database for any outstanding warrants. Finding none, they released him, and within a few days he struck again, killing two women. Several federal and local law enforcement agencies wanted the suspect for questioning, but the Border Patrol had no way of searching those agencies' databases; had it done so, the killing spree might have ended sooner.[37]

Agencies will be able to cross-search databases when the U.S. Department of Justice builds its proposed Global Justice Information Network to link crime networks—including police, courts, and corrections agencies—at the local, state, national, and international levels. This is being termed a new course for the criminal justice community, which is at a historic turning point with these integration efforts. Such systems will improve the quality of information and decisions made by criminal justice officials.[38]

We will discuss integrating DNA databases later.

Crime Mapping

Conclusive evidence from clay tablets found in Iraq proves that maps have been around for several thousand years—perhaps tens of millennia.[39]

A relatively recent development in policing is computerized **crime mapping**, which has become increasingly popular among law enforcement agencies.[40] In fact, a federal study found that departments with one hundred or more officers used computer crime mapping 35 percent of the time.[41] Computerized crime mapping combines geographic information from global positioning satellites with crime statistics gathered by the department's computer-aided dispatching (CAD) system and demographic data provided by private companies or the U.S. Census Bureau. (Some agencies acquire information from the Census Bureau's Internet site.) The result is a picture that combines disparate sets of data for a whole new perspective on crime. For example, maps of crimes can be overlaid with maps or layers of causative data: unemployment rates in the areas of high crime, locations of abandoned houses, population density, reports of drug activity, or geographic features (such as alleys, canals, or open fields) that might be contributing factors.[42] Furthermore, the hardware and software are now available to nearly all police agencies, costing a few thousand dollars.

The importance of crime mapping is evidenced by the fact that in 1997, the National Institute of Justice established the Crime Mapping Research Center (CMRC) to promote research, evaluation, development, and dissemination of geographic information systems technology for criminal justice research and practice. The CMRC holds annual conferences on crime mapping to give researchers and practitioners an opportunity to gain both practical and state-of-the-art information on the use and utility of computerized crime mapping.[43]

Exhibit 14-3 discusses the use of interactive crime mapping on the Internet; and Figure 14-1 is the initial screen that appears when the user chooses "vehicle and traffic incidents" from the San Diego County Web site. The screen provides information about auto thefts and burglaries as well as traffic accidents.

An excellent example of mapping success is the New York Police Department's Compstat program, which provides up-to-the-minute statistics, maps patterns, and establishes causal relationships among crime categories. Compstat also puts supervisors in constant communication with the department's administration, provides updates to headquarters every week, and makes supervisors responsible for responding to crime in their assigned areas.[44]

Locating Serial Offenders

Most offenders operate close to home. Offenders tend to operate in target-rich environments to "hunt" for their prey. **Geographic profiling**—a relatively new development in the field of environmental criminology—analyzes the geography of such locations and the sites of the victim encounter, the attack, the murder, and the body dump and maps the most probable location of the suspect's home.[45]

Geographic profiling is most effective when used in conjunction with linkage analysis. For example, the Washington State Attorney General's office uses a **homicide investigation and tracking system (HITS)** that includes crime-related databases and links to vice and gang files, sex offender registries, corrections and parole records, and department of motor vehicle databases. HITS can scan these databases simultaneously. When an agency in the state has a major crime in its jurisdiction, the case is loaded into a central system, which scans every database and linking file for connections by comparing eyewitness descriptions of a suspect and vehicle. It then builds a dataset containing profiles of the

EXHIBIT 14-3

Interactive Crime Mapping on the Internet

Recently, San Diego County's Automated Regional Justice Information System (ARJIS) developed the first multiagency, interactive crime mapping Web site in the nation, making interactive crime maps available to the public on the Internet. These systems not only enable citizens to obtain much more information than was previously available, but also preclude their having to make formal requests for information while freeing crime analysts to devote more time to analyzing crime instead of providing reports to the public. Now, anyone in the world can query and view certain crime, arrest, call, and traffic data for the county. Searches can be geographic (by street, neighborhood, police beat, or city, as well as by time of day or day of week. People access ARJIS for a variety of purposes, including to learn about crime in their area, for a grant proposal, to support a debate on an issue, for citizen patrol, and even for real estate information.

Source: Adapted from *Crime Mapping News*, a Police Foundation newsletter, 3 (Summer 2001): 1–6.

offender, the victims, and the incidents. The dataset then goes into a geographic information system (GIS), where the program selects and maps the names and addresses of those suspects whose method of operation fits the crimes being investigated.[46]

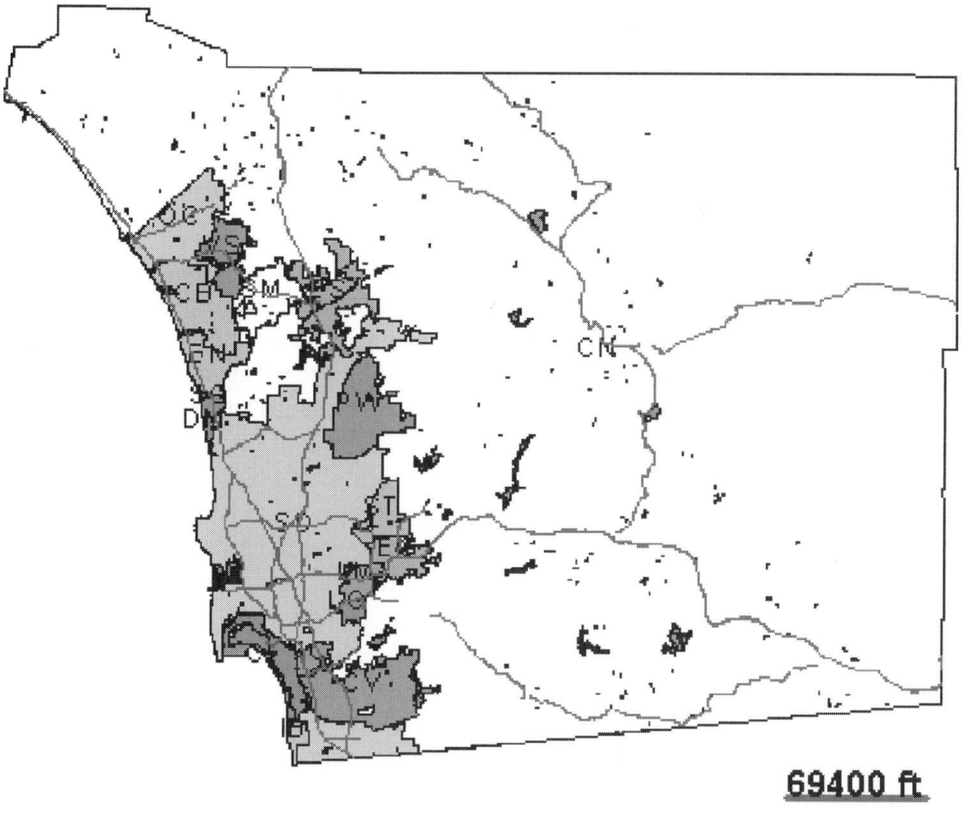

FIGURE 14-1 San Diego County's "Automated Regional Justice Information System" (ARJIS) vehicle and traffic map.

Source: City of El Cajon Police Department

EXHIBIT 14-4

Twenty-First-Century Police Department

Naperville, Illinois

Over the last decade, companies in the manufacturing, entertainment, and defense industries have used a tool called "process mapping" to help them describe, analyze, and ultimately improve how their organizations operate. Members of the City of Naperville, Illinois, Police Department and twenty-three other police agencies were invited to attend training in process mapping, which involves the development of three different flowcharts that visually depict the series of activities involved in carrying out one of the organization's major functions:

- The *as-is map* describes the organization as it currently exists. This map is based on interviews and observations of people and is used to diagnose waste, duplication of effort, coordination of problems, or breakdowns in the flow of information.
- The *should-be map* makes short-term changes to reduce waste, remove duplication, and improve coordination and flow of information. This map is based on management analysis of the as-is map and suggestions gathered from field personnel during interviews.
- The *could-be map* describes the ideal process for the future. This map is based on the organization's vision and highlights the long-term changes that are needed to get there.

For example, Naperville is focusing on "crime solving" as the major function to be mapped and is focusing on one crime type: burglary. Process mapping allows the agency to increase the clearance rate for crimes by identifying areas where new work methods or organizational changes might improve police ability to investigate crimes and arrest offenders; and it makes more widespread and effective use of automation and technology by identifying areas where work processes can be improved, such as automated case reporting.

Source: Adapted from City of Naperville, Illinois, Web page, "Twenty-First Century Police Department," 1997, pp. 1–2.

Gunshot Locator System

A primary difficulty for the police is determining the location of gunshots. Technology is now being tested that is similar to that used to determine the strength and epicenter of earthquakes. Known as a "gunshot locator system," it uses microphone-like sensors placed on rooftops and telephone poles to record and transmit the sound of gunshots by radio waves or telephone lines. Software is then used to alert a dispatcher and to pinpoint the origin of gunshots via a flashing icon on a computerized map. Ideally, the system, which triangulates based on how long it takes the sound to reach the sensors, would greatly reduce police response time to crime scenes, meaning quicker aid for victims and a greater likelihood of arrests.[47]

Initial results of available technologies for gunshot detection have not been promising, however. An examination of about 750 gunshots in three areas of Dallas, Texas, found the following: Not a single offender was apprehended in response to reports of random gunfire; officers were dispatched to a scene where youths were setting off fireworks; there was a 16 percent reduction in the amount of time required to dispatch officers to a random gunfire call and a one-minute decrease in the time it took police to respond to the scene. In fact, call takers, dispatchers, and patrol officers ended up spending less time processing citizen calls about random gunfire and more time processing such calls using the technology, suggesting that the technology tends to lengthen rather than reduce the time spent on random gunfire calls.[48]

Dogs and Searches for Lost Persons

Another related use of geographic technology—used extensively with military tanks during Operation Desert Storm and in the private sector (such as in taxicab firms and car rental express delivery companies)—is the Global Positioning System (GPS), which plots locations of vehicles and even people with remarkable accuracy. The police, for example, have adapted GPS to the problem of knowing exactly where search-and-rescue dogs are and how effective they have been in their search efforts. A small, specially designed backpack containing software is attached to the dog; after a search for lost persons, data from the backpack are downloaded to show where the dog has searched as well as areas that may need to be searched further.[49]

Dogs provide many vital functions for the police, including searching for lost persons.

(Courtesy Washoe County, Nevada, Sheriff's Department)

Electronics in Traffic Functions

Accident Investigation

A multicar accident can turn a street or highway into a parking lot for many hours, sometimes days. The police must collect evidence relating to the accident, including measurements and sketches of the scene, vehicle and body positions, skid marks, street or highway elevations, intersections, and curves. These tasks typically involve a measuring wheel, steel tape, pad, and pencil. The cost of traffic delays—especially for commercial truck operators—is substantial.

Some police agencies have begun using a Global Positioning System to determine such details as vehicle location and damage, elevation, grade, radii of curves, and critical speed. A transmitter takes a series of "shots" to find the exact location and measurements of accident details like skid marks, area of impact, and debris. That information is then downloaded into the system, and the coordinates are plotted out onto an aerial shot of the intersection or roadway. Using computer technology, the details are then superimposed onto the aerial shot, thus recreating the accident scene to scale. Finally, digital photos of the accident are incorporated into the final product, resulting in a highly accurate depiction of the accident. Furthermore, with a fatal or major injury accident, what once required several officers up to eighteen hours' time is reduced to mere minutes.[50]

Similarly, other agencies use a version of a surveyor's "total station," electronically measuring and recording distances, angles, elevations, and the names and features of objects. Data from the system can be downloaded into a computer for display or printed out on a plotter. The system consists of four components: a base station, a data collector, a tripod, and

Some agencies use a Global Positioning System to accurately draw accident scenes. Here, police and technical personnel employ the system at the scene of a fatal accident.

(Source: City of Sparks, Nevada, City Works Department)

a prism, which reflects an infrared laser beam back to the tripod-mounted base station. With this device, officers can get measurements in an hour or so at major traffic accidents, push a button, and have lines drawn for them to scale; this process enables officers to get 40 percent more measurements in about 40 percent of the time, allowing the traffic flow to resume much more quickly. This system is also being used at major crime scenes, such as murders.[51]

Arresting Impaired Drivers

During a vehicle stop for driving under the influence (DUI), officers might spend a long time questioning the driver and conducting a barrage of screening tests. Then, if an arrest is made, the officer necessarily devotes a lot of time transporting and processing the arrestee at the jail before beginning formal testing of urine or blood. This delay in formal testing can skew test results because the alcohol has had time to metabolize.

New instruments now help automate the DUI arrest process. One tool used routinely during a drunk-driving stop is a breath-screening device—a small, portable machine that resembles a video game cartridge. The DUI suspect blows into the device, and the officer gets a reading of the amount of alcohol in the suspect's system. It is hoped that this device can be adapted in such a way that the test can be used in court. Fewer hours would then be spent transporting DUI suspects and testing them, only to find that they were below the legal limit and thus cannot be prosecuted for DUI.

The revamped instrument would be attached to a notebook or a laptop computer that officers would use to help speed them through the process; an officer would simply run a magnetic-stripe driver's license through a reader on the computer to bring up all of the driver's information. The computer would then prompt the officer to start the test and would supply a readout of the results on the screen. The officer would then transmit the test results over telecommunications lines to a central location for recording.[52]

Preventing High-Speed Pursuits

Chapter 11 discussed the current controversy over the tremendous potential for injury, property damage, and liability that accompanies high-speed pursuits by police; indeed, this is such a concern that some agency policies completely prohibit such pursuits by officers. Such techniques as bumping, crowding, the three-cruiser rolling roadblock, and tire spikes can all result in significant damage to vehicles and personal injury.

Tire spikes can be deployed when a fleeing vehicle is approaching and then retracted so that other vehicles and police cars can pass safely. However, tire spikes often do not work effectively, or they result in the suspect's losing control of the vehicle (although some spike devices are designed to prevent loss of control by breaking off in the tires and thus deflating them slowly).[53] Furthermore, use of the spikes is limited to times and places where other traffic can be diverted.

One new device stops the suspect's vehicle with a short pulse of electric current that disrupts the vehicle's ignition system. Once pulsed, the vehicle rolls to a controlled stop, similar to running out of fuel, and will not restart until the affected parts are replaced. Since this device requires near-direct contact with the suspect vehicle, other nearby vehicles and people are not affected. This device, which is still being refined and miniaturized, is now being demonstrated for federal, state, and local law enforcement agencies across the country, as well as for transportation officials.[54]

DNA

New success stories involving the use of DNA in criminal justice are reported nearly each day. Here's an example:

> A case file in the rape of a twelve-year-old Englewood, Colorado, girl was starting to yellow. A sketch of the suspect had not produced anything concrete. Then the Colorado Bureau of Investigation linked a DNA "fingerprint" from the evidence file to a man recently imprisoned for another sexual assault.[55]

Today, some of the nation's most effective crime fighters wear white lab coats instead of blue uniforms and study DNA fingerprinting. Unfortunately, successes such as the Colorado case are severely limited by the scarcity of DNA fingerprints on file.

Integrated databases were discussed earlier; it was shown that today's police are exchanging information quickly and with good results. There have certainly been successful outcomes in the area of DNA databases as well. For example, in the late 1980s, states began passing laws mandating that DNA samples be collected from people convicted of sexual assault or other violent crimes. This data could then be used to solve existing cases and to identify the felons if they committed further crimes after they were released. All fifty states now have such laws, and by the end of 1999 they had gathered nearly 750,000 DNA samples and made the data accessible to police agencies. The downside, however, is that this figure represents less than 5 percent of the total number of DNA samples that need to be analyzed for thirteen genetic markers.[56]

The U.S. Department of Justice has stepped in to help the states process their backlog of more than 700,000 DNA samples. The government has funded a private firm to develop and use a process called "laser desorption mass spectrometry" in conjunction with robotics; this process enables a sample to be analyzed in a matter of seconds. Once this process becomes available, states will be able to clear their backlogs in a matter of months, enabling DNA to be used much more broadly in identifying, apprehending, and prosecuting criminals.[57]

FINGERPRINTS AND MUG SHOTS

Though perhaps not as exotic as DNA identification, fingerprints are still a reliable means of positively identifying someone. Throughout the country, filing cabinets are filled with ink-smeared cards that hold the keys to countless unsolved crimes if only the data could be located. **Automated fingerprint identification systems (AFISs)** allow this legacy of data to be rapidly shared throughout the nation. One such system is the Western Identification Network (www.winid.org), established by nine states as a way to share their 17 million fingerprint records. These states were later joined by local agencies and the FBI, the Internal Revenue Service, the Secret Service, and the Drug Enforcement Administration. The system can generally provide a match within a few hours and has helped solve more than five thousand crimes. A digital photo exchange facility known as WINPHO is now being added to supplement fingerprint data.[58]

The Boston Police Department, like most others in the country, was devoting tremendous resources to identifying prisoners with mug shots and fingerprints. Then the department replaced all of its mug shots and inked fingerprints with a citywide, integrated electronic imaging identification

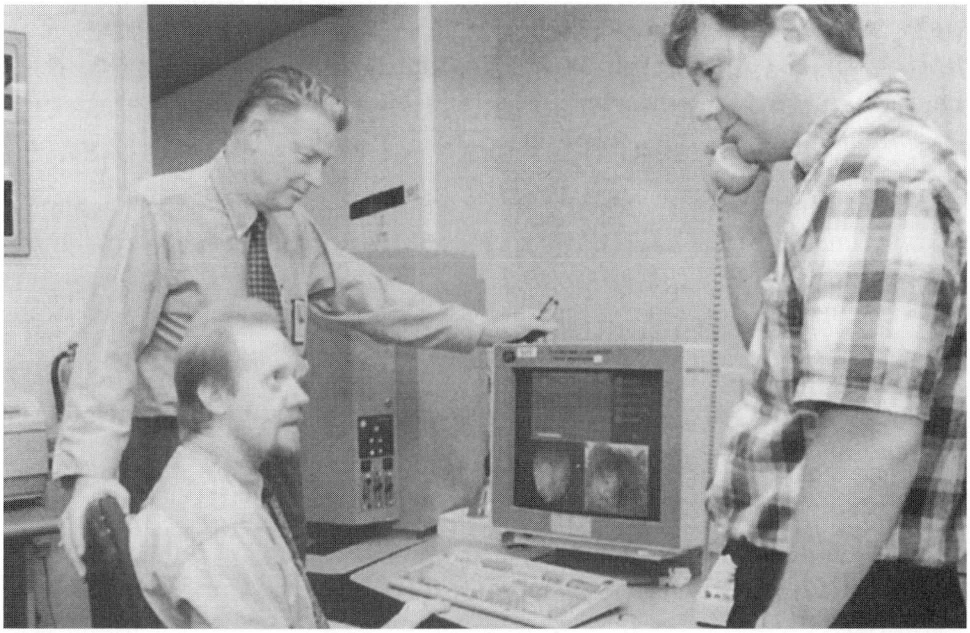

Major advances are being made toward a national automated fingerprint identification system, which would connect thousands of police agencies in the United States and abroad.

(City of New York Police Department Photo Unit)

system—the first system of its kind in North America. The Boston Police Department is also the first city to receive the FBI's certification for electronic fingerprint submission.

Instead of transporting prisoners to a central booking facility in downtown Boston—a task that took forty thousand hours of officers' time per year—officers at the eleven district police stations can electronically scan a prisoner's fingerprints, take digital photographs, and then route the images to a central server for easy storage and access. This network gives investigators timely access to information and mug shot lineups and is saving the police department $1 million per year in labor and transportation costs while freeing officers from prisoner transportation duties.[59]

Technology involving mug shots and imaging systems can be useful in a variety of situations. For example, as a police officer responds to a domestic violence call, the CAD system searches the address and finds a restraining order against the ex-husband or boyfriend; moments later, a street map and digital mug shot of the suspect appear on the officer's laptop computer monitor. The officer is thus aided with an image of the suspect and his criminal history before arriving at the scene.[60]

Crime Scenes: Computers to Explore and Draft Evidence

Several technologies exist or are being developed that are relevant to crime-scene investigations. Three-dimensional computer-aided drafting (3-D CAD) software is now available and can be purchased for a few hundred dollars. Working in 3-D, CAD users create scenes that can be viewed from any angle. Suddenly, nontechnical people can visualize very technical evidence. Juries can "view" crime scenes and see the location of evidence; they can view just what the witness says he or she saw. Police give the CAD system the exact dimensions and get a scaled drawing. A five-day, forty-hour course teaches 3-D CAD to police investigators, traffic accident reconstructionists, and evidence technicians.[61]

Often, crime-scene evidence is too sketchy to yield an obvious explanation of what happened. New software called Maya has been developed for the field of forensic animation; this software helps experts determine what probably occurred. Maya is so packed with scientific calculations that it can create a virtual house from old police photos and can replicate the effects of several types of forces, including gravity: how a fall could or could not have produced massive injuries; how flames would spread in a house fire; and how smoke might have cut a pilot's visibility in a plane crash.[62]

The federal Department of Energy is testing a prototype laptop computer equipped with digital video and still cameras, laser range finders, and a Global Positioning System. A detective using it can "beam" information from a crime scene back to a laboratory to get input from experts. Researchers are also working on a so-called lab-on-a-chip that would give police the ability to process more evidence—including DNA samples—at the crime scene, eliminating the risk of contamination en route to the lab.[63]

Developments Relevant to Firearms

Handguns are, and nearly always have been, the weapon of choice for violent criminals, especially murderers. Handguns are also used with greatest frequency—in about seven of every ten incidents—when police officers are murdered.[64] It is therefore important that everything that is technologically possible be done to train the police to use lethal force against citizens, to identify those who would use lethal force against others, and to keep out of harm's way.

Computer-Assisted Training

A device known as FATS, for firearms training system, is said to be "as close to real life as you can get."[65] Recruits and in-service officers alike use the system. The students are given a high-tech lesson in firearms and can be shown a wide variety of computer-generated scenarios on a movie screen. An instructor at a console can control the scene. Using laser-firing replicas of their actual weapons, they learn not only sharpshooting but also judgment—when to shoot and when not to shoot. The system—consisting of a container about the size of a large baby buggy, with a computer, a laser disk player, a projector, and a hit-detect camera—can be transported to sites throughout the state. Some sites combine FATS with a driving simulator and have recruits drive to the scene of a bank robbery and then bail out of their car into a FATS scenario.[66]

Recent developments have made firearms simulators even more realistic than the basic FATS system just described. One new version has a synchronized "shootback cannon." If an individual on a projection screen pulls a gun and fires toward the trainee, a cannon, which hangs above the screen, pelts the trainee with painful .68-caliber nylon balls. The newest generation of firearms training systems—which are getting more realistic and better at breaking down how the trainee reacted under stress—now cost between $25,000 for a small system to $200,000 for a trailer that police departments can haul from station to station.[67]

Using Gun "Fingerprints" to Solve Cases

Every gun leaves a unique pattern of minute markings on ammunition. If gun makers test-fire their weapons before the guns leave their factories, the police can use spent ammunition recovered from crime scenes to trace guns, even when the gun itself is not recovered. This technology could even be taken to the next level: creating an automated database of the fingerprints of new guns. A $45 million multiyear contract was recently awarded to a Montreal, Canada, firm by the U.S. Bureau of Alcohol, Tobacco and Firearms to help fund the development of such technology.[68]

Several problems need to be resolved, however: (1) Criminals can easily use a nail file to scratch a new gun's firing pin; (2) even if the system worked and turned up a serial number, the number could be used to trace the gun to its initial owner and not necessarily to the criminal; (3) the database would not include the estimated 200 million weapons already in circulation; and (4) gun lobbies would undoubtedly oppose the system as being "suspiciously like a national gun registry."[69]

GANG INTELLIGENCE SYSTEMS

Often a witness to gang violence has only a brief view of the incident—a glimpse of the offenders and their distinguishing characteristics and their vehicles and license plate numbers. Police are now armed with laptop computers and cellular phones to assist in solving gang-related crimes. Recently, for example, the California Department of Justice began installing CALGANG (known as GangNet outside California), an intranet-linked software package linked to nine other sites throughout the state. It is essentially a clearinghouse for information about individual gang members, the places they frequent or live, and the cars they drive. Within a few minutes, a police officer in the field can be linked to CALGANG through a laptop and cellular phone, type in information, and wait for matches. Other officers can be moving to make the arrest even before the crime laboratory technicians have dusted the scene for fingerprints.[70]

SUMMARY

This chapter examined the exciting high-technology developments in policing, including those in the areas of less-lethal weapons, wireless technology, electronics, imaging systems, firearms, and communications. This is an exciting time for the police: More new technologies than ever are being made available to aid them in their efforts to analyze and address crimes. This chapter has shown the breadth of research and development that is under way.

The rapid expansion in computer technology, while certainly a strong advantage for society overall, bodes ill as well. The first problem lies in adapting the computer technologies to the needs of policing. While this nation's air force can drop a smart bomb down a smokestack and our army is rapidly moving toward the electronic battlefield, modern-day crooks and hackers engage in a variety of cybercrimes, and (even though the technology exists) the police are still unable to halt a high-speed chase that threatens the lives of officers and citizens.[71]

Obviously, many challenges remain. For example, we must continue to seek a weapon with less-lethal stopping power that can effectively and safely be employed. We must also strive to enhance police effectiveness and efficiency through electronic means. As has been noted, "It is not enough to shovel faster. Criminal justice must enter the Information Age by incorporating technology as a tool to make the system run efficiently and effectively."[72]

REVIEW QUESTIONS

1. Briefly describe some of the major discoveries in less-lethal weapons for use by the police.
2. How has the development of wireless technology benefited the police?
3. How can mapping and profiling systems aid the police, and what do these systems specifically provide?
4. How does technology assist the police traffic function? How has it affected gang intelligence?
5. Describe recent developments in the area of firearms training and investigation.
6. How are the police training and communications functions enhanced by technology?

INDEPENDENT STUDENT ACTIVITIES

1. Using the Internet or interviews, identify a few major corporations that sell technological products for police use to learn of their current efforts in terms of product research and development.
2. Interview local police administrators to determine what kinds of technologies are planned for the future, especially for addressing computer-related, identity-theft, financial, and other complicated types of crimes. Also, what type of less-lethal weapon do they feel is most promising? If money were no object, what kinds of technologies would they find most helpful?
3. For comparative purposes, consult some old issues of police trade magazines (for example, *Police Chief* or *Law and Order*) and examine the product advertisements. What tools were available to the police in the "olden days?"

RELATED WEB SITES

Crime Mapping Research Center (CMRC)
http://www.ojp.usdoj.gov/cmrc

Government Technology
http://www.govtech.net

Justice Technology Information Network (JUSTNET)
http://www.nlectc.org

NOTES

1. Dave Pettinari, "Are We There Yet? The Future of Policing/Sheriffing in Pueblo—Or in Anywhere, America," http://www.policefuturists.org/files/yet.html(accessed February 13, 2001).
2. Ibid.
3. Jennifer Nislow, "Big Benefits, Huge Headaches," *Law Enforcement News*, May 15/31, 2000, p. 1.
4. "Cybergame for the Millennium: Cops 'n' Robbers Playin' Hide 'n' Seek on the Net," *Police Futurist* 8, no. 1 (Spring 2000): 4.
5. "Polls: Trade Some Freedom for Security," *Law Enforcement News*, September 15, 2001, p. 1.
6. "Surveillance Cameras Stir up Static," *Law Enforcement News*, July–August 2001, p. 13.
7. Dana Hawkins and David LaGesse, "Tech versus Terrorists," *U.S. News and World Report*, October 8, 2001, pp. 16–17.
8. Kenneth J. Peak, "The Quest for Alternatives to Lethal Force: A Heuristic View," *Journal of Contemporary Criminal Justice* 6, no. 1 (1990): 8–22.
9. S. Sweetman, *Report on the Attorney General's Conference on Less Than Lethal Weapons* (Washington, DC: Department of Justice, National Institute of Justice, 1987).
10. Peak, "The Quest for Alternatives to Lethal Force," p. 10.
11. Ibid.
12. Ibid.
13. T. S. Crockett, "Riot Control Agents," *Police Chief* (November 1968): 8–18.
14. M. H. Haller, "Historical Roots of Police Behavior: Chicago, 1890–1925," *Law and Society Review* 13, no. 2 (1976): 303–23.
15. T. F. Coon, "A Maze of Confusion over Amazing Mace," *Police* (November-December1968): 46.
16. Sarah Manwaring-White, *The Policing Revolution: Police Technology, Democracy, and Liberty in Britain* (Brighton, Sussex: Harvester Press, 1983).
17. Luis Cabrera, Associated Press, "Police Explore 'Less-Than-Lethal' Weapons," June 19, 2000.
18. Manwaring-White, *The Policing Revolution*, pp. 141–42.
19. Peak, "The Quest for Alternatives to Lethal Force," pp. 15–16.
20. Ibid., p. 16.
21. Manwaring-White, *The Policing Revolution*, pp. 145–46.
22. Ibid., pp. 142–43.
23. Sweetman, *Report on the Attorney General's Conference on Less Than Lethal Weapons*, pp. 4–5.
24. M. S. Serrill, "ZAP! Stun Guns: Hot But Getting Heat," *Time*, May 1985, p. 59.
25. Darren Laur, "More Powerful, but Still Less Lethal," *Law Enforcement Technology* (October 1999): 10.
26. John Barry and Tom Morganthau, "Soon, 'Phasers on Stun,' " *Newsweek*, February 7, 1994, pp. 24–25.

27. "Rethinking Stopping Power," *Law Enforcement News*, November 15, 1999, pp. 1, 9.
28. Ibid.
29. Cabrera, "Police Explore 'Less-Than-Lethal' Weapons."
30. Ibid.
31. "Rethinking Stopping Power," pp. 1, 9.
32. "Effectiveness Times Three," *Law Enforcement News*, May 15, 1993, p. 1.
33. Ibid., p. 6.
34. "Rethinking Stopping Power," pp. 1, 9.
35. Blake Harris, "Goin' Mobile," *Government Technology* 10 (August 1997): 1.
36. Kaveh Ghaemian, "Small-Town Cops Wield Big-City Data," *Government Technology* 9 (September 1996): 38.
37. Tod Newcombe, "Combined Forces," *Crime and the Tech Effect* (Folsom, CA: Government Technology, April 2001), p. 15.
38. Ibid.
39. Department of Justice, National Institute of Justice, *Crime Mapping and Analysis by Community Organizations in Hartford, Connecticut* (Washington, DC: Author, March 2001): 1.
40. Donna Rogers, "Getting Crime Analysis on the Map," *Law Enforcement Technology* (November 1999): 76–79.
41. Department of Justice, National Institute of Justice, *Crime Mapping Research Center* (Washington, DC: Author, 2000), pp. 1–3.
42. Lois Pilant, "Computerized Crime Mapping," *Police Chief* (December 1997): 58.
43. Department of Justice, *Crime Mapping Research Center*, pp. 1–3; the CMRC Web site address is http://www.ojp.usdoj.gov/cmrc.
44. Pilant, "Computerized Crime Mapping," pp. 64–65.
45. Bill McGarigle, "Crime Profilers Gain New Weapons," *Government Technology* 10 (December 1997): 28–29.
46. Ibid.
47. Justine Kavanaugh, "Locator System Targets Shooters," *Government Technology* 9 (June 1996): 14–15.
48. Lorraine Green Mazerolle, Cory Watkins, Dennis Rogan, et al., "Using Gunshot Detection Systems in Police Departments: The Impact on Police Response Times and Officer Workloads," *Police Quarterly* 1 (1998): 21–50.
49. "GPS-Loaded Dogs to the Rescue," *Government Technology* 10 (April 1997): 24.
50. Alison Bath, "Accident Scene Investigation Is High Tech," *Reno Gazette Journal* (Sparks Today section), November 18, 2003, p. 4.
51. Bill McGarigle, "Electronic Mapping Speeds Crime and Traffic Investigations," *Government Technology* 9 (February 1996): 20–21.
52. Justine Kavanaugh, "Drunk Drivers Get a Shot of Technology," *Government Technology* 9 (March 1996): 26.
53. Ibid.
54. Jaycor, Inc., "Freshnews.com: Less-than-Lethal Technologies," http://www.jaycor.com/jaycor_main/web-content/eme_ltlt.html (accessed February 1, 2005).

55. RUTT BRIDGES, "Catching More Criminals in the DNA Web," *Law Enforcement News*, September 15, 2000, p. 9.
56. DREW ROBB, "The Long New Arm of the Law," in *Crime and the Tech Effect* (Folsom, CA: Government Technology, April 2001), pp. 44–46.
57. Ibid.
58. Ibid., p. 46.
59. TOD NEWCOMBE, "Imaged Prints Go Online, Cops Return to Streets," *Government Technology* 9 (April 1996): 1, 31.
60. COREY GRICE, "Technologies, Agencies Converge," *Government Technology* 11 (April 1998): 24, 61.
61. TOD NEWCOMBE, "Adding a New Dimension to Crime Reconstruction," *Government Technology* 9 (August 1996): 32.
62. JOHN MCCORMICK, "Scene of the Crime," *Newsweek*, February 28, 2000, p. 60.
63. JOAN RAYMOND, "Forget the Pipe, Sherlock: Gear for Tomorrow's Detectives," *Newsweek*, June 22, 1998, p. 12.
64. SAMUEL G. CHAPMAN, *Murdered on Duty: The Killing of Police Officers in America*, 2d ed. (Springfield, IL: Thomas, 1998), p. 33.
65. PATRICK JOYCE, "Firearms Training: As Close to Real as It Gets," *Government Technology* 8 (July 1995): 14–15.
66. Ibid.
67. JOHN MCCORMICK, "On a High-Tech Firing Line," *Newsweek*, December 6, 1999, p. 64.
68. VANESSA O'CONNELL, "The Next Big Idea: Using 'Fingerprints' of Guns to Solve Cases," *Wall Street Journal*, February 10, 2000, p. A1.
69. Ibid.
70. RAY DUSSAULT, "GangNet: A New Tool in the War on Gangs," *Government Technology* (January 1998): 34–35.
71. PETTINARI, "Are We There Yet?" p. 2.
72. GEORGE NICHOLSON and JEFFREY HOGGE, "Retooling Criminal Justice: Interbranch Cooperation Needed," *Government Technology* 9 (February 1996): 32.

CHAPTER 15

Focus on the Future

My interest is in the future because I am going to spend the rest of my life there.

—Charles F. Kettering

Where there is no vision, the people perish.

—Proverbs 29:18

Key Terms

accelerators
augmented reality (AR)
Futures Working Group
nanotechnology
Society of Police Futurists International (SPFI)
unmanned aerial vehicle (UAV)

It has been said that the only thing that is permanent is change. Perhaps more than anything else, the foregoing chapters have demonstrated that even in the relatively tradition-bound domain of policing, we certainly live in a dynamic world in which society and its problems and challenges are constantly changing. As a result, our lives will be drastically altered as the world continues to change.

Given that, the question at the forefront of our minds is, What will the future bring? That troublesome question becomes even more important and ominous when we consider the world's present state of affairs. As we will see here, there are indicators of future problems and turmoil. Our choice is either to ignore the future until it is upon us or to try to anticipate what the future holds and gear our resources to cope with it.

Peering into the future is not easy. Many variables—such as war, technology, and economic upheaval—can greatly affect otherwise sound predictions and trends. Indeed, much of our planning and predictive efforts revolve around the unstable future of finance. As someone once said, "There's a lot of crime prevention in a T-bone steak." While all predictions are grounded in past trends and future likelihood, unforeseen variables and major events can and do change the course of the future in ways that no one could have anticipated. In other words, the best we can possibly do in this chapter is to render an educated guess.[1]

The chapter begins with an overview of how the Federal Bureau of Investigation (FBI) and other state and local police futurists have taken steps to better plan for the future by banding together and creating formal futures groups. Then we shift to what the future might hold for the police, especially in the areas of technology (including augmented reality, unmanned aerial vehicles, and nanotechnology), community-oriented policing and problem solving (COPPS), and the role of the beat officer. Then we consider the influence of drugs and guns on crime and violence. A chapter summary, review questions, independent student activities, and related Web sites conclude the chapter.

Taking Futures Seriously: A Working Group and a Futurists' Society

To build a stronger partnership between all facets of law enforcement and the FBI, the **Futures Working Group** was formed in April 2002. It represents a partnership between the FBI and the **Society of Police Futurists International(PFI)** which was founded in 1991 and is now located at Sam Houston State University, Huntsville, Texas. (See Exhibit 15-1.) The goals of the partnership include the development of forecasts and strategies to maximize the effectiveness of all law enforcement entities as they strive to maintain peace and security. Breakthrough technologies, such as nanotechnology, artificial intelligence, and genetic engineering; changing demographic and cultural conditions; and the threat of international crime and terrorism will provide tremendous challenges for the members of these groups, who represent some of the best and brightest in policing.[2]

What the Future Might Hold for the Police

Defining solutions to the problems that police will face in the future is difficult at best. Factors such as locale, political environment, and economics determine how an agency and its employees will view and react to future events. For some police leaders, the future is next Friday, and their goal is to survive without a crisis until their next day off. As Sheldon Greenberg has noted, for some police leaders the future is the next fiscal year; they subscribe to the notion expressed by Albert Einstein, who said "I never think of the future. It comes soon enough."[3] For others, however, the future is a three- to five-year span of time toward which they have set into motion a strategic planning process. Any discussion of the future must include the short term as well as the long term and must give attention to operational issues, administrative issues, the community, and the basic philosophy of policing.[4]

EXHIBIT 15-1

Police Futurists International

The Society of Police Futurists International (PFI) is an organization of law enforcement practitioners, educators, researchers, private security specialists, technology experts and other professionals dedicated to improving criminal and social justice through the professionalization of policing. Futures Research (long-range planning and forecasting) is the pivotal discipline that constitutes the philosophical underpinnings of PFI. The tools and techniques of this field are applied in order to more accurately anticipate and prepare for the evolution of law enforcement ten, twenty, and even fifty years into the future. Futures Research offers both philosophical and methodological tools to analyze, forecast, and plan in ways rarely seen in policing in the past.

Source: Adapted from Society of Police Futurists International Web site.

Futures Research

Because change is inevitable, law enforcement professionals must understand the importance of futures research—to have the capacity not only to manage change but also to thrive on it. Futures research leads to the examination of the probable, possible, and preferable outcomes of the future and provides a basis for decision making today that will lead to a preferable future. This research provides the tools to analyze, forecast, and plan in ways rarely seen in policing in the past.

High Technology: Coming Attractions

In Chapter 14, we discussed a number of contemporary technologies that are, or soon will be, available to the police. In this chapter, we discuss several technologies that are still far removed from day-to-day use but that promise to greatly alter police methods and training.

One of the most powerful technologies that is emerging, **augmented reality (AR)**, uses wearable components to overlay virtual (computer-generated) information onto one's real-world view in a way that improves and enhances one's ability to accomplish a variety of missions and tasks. Still in the early stages of research and development, AR combines the real and the virtual, displaying information in real time.[5] AR is already here: If you watch televised sports, you may have noticed the yellow first-down lines superimposed on a football field and the driver and speed information tagged to race cars speeding around a track. At a more advanced level, today's military fighter pilots can observe critical information superimposed on the cockpit canopy.[6]

Fundamentally, an AR system consists of a wearable computer, a head-mounted display, and tracking and sensing devices along with advanced software and virtual three-dimensional applications. It is a mobile technology designed to improve situational awareness and to speed human decision making. Among the many possible uses in the future of policing are these:

- Real-time language translation, along with data on cultural customs and traditions
- Real-time intelligence about crimes and criminals in the patrol area
- Facial, voiceprint, and other biometric recognition data of known criminals
- Integration of chemical, biological, and explosive sensors that denote local contamination
- Accessibility of scalable, three-dimensional maps (with building floor plans, utilities systems, and so forth)[7]

Similarly, special weapons and tactics officers could be provided with advanced optics that provide zoom, thermal, and infrared imaging for locating fleeing criminals, as well as a friend-or-foe indicator that could reduce or eliminate friendly-fire casualties. Investigative personnel could use speaker-recognition technology for accurately matching voices against known criminals and for lip-reading from a distance; thermal imaging might improve interrogations by indicating the truthfulness of suspects' statements. Supervisors could use video feed from their personnel on the street to determine what their officers are seeing in real time and to monitor their physical status during critical incidents.[8] Certainly, a number of issues would accompany the planned adoption of AR; acceptance by officers themselves may prove problematic, given the bulk and mobility issues associated with additional equipment. The public—including the courts—may be uncomfortable with the constitutional issues and legal ramifications that AR abilities might raise.

Would AR bring us dangerously close to a real-life "Robo-Cop" scenario? The answer to that question is in the eye of the beholder. It cannot be questioned, however, that AR technology and the uses described above will soon be available and could provide the police with a new degree of efficiency and effectiveness never seen before. The question is whether or not the public—and the police—will be willing to accept this "virtual intrusion" in their daily lives.

In a similar vein, technology will also be available soon to allow realistic simulated humans to be used as a tool for training decision making. Law enforcement personnel need experience making decisions in which other people—whether suspects, bystanders, or team members—are involved. A three-dimensional computer graphic would represent a variety of settings; the trainee would have the ability to move about, look around, and direct actions toward a variety of computer graphic representations of human figures that move naturally, display appropriate gestures and expressions, and exhibit realistic patterns of speech. Such simulation technology, which should be available and affordable within the next five to ten years, will have a very positive impact on police training.[9]

Another technology that warrants close attention is that of **unmanned aerial vehicles (UAVs)** (discussed briefly in Chapter 8 in relation to border security). UAVs are powered aerial vehicles that do not carry human operators. They are designed to carry nonlethal payloads for missions such as reconnaissance, command and control, and deception. UAVs, which are directed by a ground or airborne controller, come in a variety of designs, from those that fit into a backpack to one with a longer wingspan than a Boeing 747. More than two dozen companies in the United States are currently involved in production of prototype UAV products.[10]

While UAV research and development are almost totally focused on military applications at present, their potential uses for law enforcement should not be ignored. For example, a low-flying UAV could patrol a given stretch of road, on vigil for speeders; images could be piped to a monitor in a patrol car along with rate of speed, direction of travel, and Global Positioning System coordinates, which can be overlaid on a map for the officer on the ground.[11] UAVs could also provide real-time reconnaissance, surveillance, and target spotting in a variety of situations.[12]

Sandy Boyd and colleagues[13] argue that, overall, government and law enforcement seem to lag behind the private sector in both the use of new technologies and the development of expertise in such applications. A common theme among members of the Society of Police Futurists International is the fear that the law enforcement profession will never "catch up" with the necessary computer-based investigative skills to keep pace with criminals who use computer technology. But technology involves much more than using computers to hack into systems or to commit identity theft. Whether through nanotechnology, AR, or biometrics, criminals will always attempt to steal, misuse, or exploit others. If law enforcement does not anticipate such illicit uses, the victims of these crimes will eventually rely on private sources for relief.

Nanotechnology

The term **nanotechnology** is based on the root *nanos*, meaning "one billionth." It is the engineering of components that have at least one physical dimension the size of 100 nanometers or less. (For perspective, a human hair is gigantic in the realm of nanotechnology.) This technology allows for "getting small," which means making objects smarter, more powerful, and more economical (for example, the computers of the 1940s were the size of a room, compared to those of today). Nanotechnology allows for revolutionary new products using new materials and substances that are not accessible with other technologies. Such products will be stronger, lighter, and even interactive, ranging from knives that never need sharpening to better space ships and computers—and possibly the end of disease as we know it.[14]

Community-Oriented Policing and Problem Solving

As noted in Chapter 6, the conventional style of reactive, incident-driven policing employed during the professional era had several drawbacks. That type of police department was hierarchical, impersonal, and rule based, and most important, policy decisions were made at the top; line officers made few decisions on their own. In this section, we analyze where the current policing era—that of community-oriented policing and problem solving (COPPS)—fits into the challenges of the future.

Many fundamental questions remain concerning COPPS. For example, how many police agencies have made a commitment to community policing? How many agencies have demonstrated the link between community policing and the quality of the communities they serve? How many have embraced community policing just to gain a share of available federal dollars? Will community policing endure without federal funding?[15]

From 1994 to 2001, the federal Office of Community Oriented Policing Services (COPS), created by the Violent Crime Control and Law Enforcement Act of 1994, spent about $9 billion to help police agencies implement COPPS, adding officers to the beat and providing technical assistance, technology, equipment, and training. By mid-2000, the COPS office had provided funding to 82 percent of America's police departments by awarding more than thirty thousand grants to more than twelve thousand departments. This included funding more than 105,000 community policing officers and training more than ninety thousand officers and citizens.[16] However, the future remains uncertain for the office.[17] Any police agency that is currently hanging its COPPS efforts on federal funds may find itself in desperate straits in the years ahead.

Another central issue with respect to COPPS concerns community partnerships. Much of society—including the police—has come to realize that the police cannot function independently to address crime and disorder. The challenge to leaders, now and in the future, is to develop meaningful and lasting partnerships rather than the superficial relationships that exist in many communities. For many police officers, the concept of partnership means simply attending occasional neighborhood association meetings or periodically visiting neighborhood leaders who live on their beat. Partnerships for the sake of partnership do not endure; they will work only when the mutual benefits to the parties involved are well defined, well understood, and attainable.

Several other issues for the future must be addressed if COPPS is to survive and thrive, including whether police chief executives will change the culture of their agencies, implement the concept, decentralize their department (pushing decision making downward), invest in the necessary technology to locate "hot spots," and develop the necessary mechanisms to support COPPS. These challenges also include recruitment, selection, training, performance appraisals, and reward and promotions systems. Police unions must work with administrators to effect the kinds of changes that are needed for COPPS. The answers to these issues could be critical, not only to the future of COPPS but also to policing and society.

Some futurists believe that policing in general will undergo a metamorphosis in the near future. They predict the following changes:

- Ethics will be woven into everything the police do: the hiring process, the field training officer (FTO) program, the decision-making processes. There will be increased emphasis on accountability and integrity within police agencies as policing is elevated to a higher standing and reaches more toward being a true profession. Concomitantly, the majority of officers will be required to possess a college degree.
- Formal awards ceremonies will recognize officers who have improved citizens' quality of life as well as those who have made felony arrests or engaged in other high-risk activities.
- Communications will be greatly improved through internal intranets that contain local and agency operational data, phone books, maps, calendars, calls for service, crime data sheets, speeches, newsletters, news releases, and so on.[18]
- Major cities will no longer require that the chief police executive have prior policing experience; instead, they may begin to recruit from private industry. The future heads of police agencies will essentially be recognized as CEOs with good business sense as a trend toward the privatization of certain services expands. Knowledge will continue to increase at lightning speed, forcing the CEO to be involved in trend analysis and forecasting in order to keep ahead of the curve.
- The rigid paramilitary style of police organization currently in effect will become obsolete, replaced by work teams consisting of line officers, community members, and business and corporation people.
- The current squad structure will give way to more productive, creative teams of officers who, empowered with more autonomy, will become efficient problem solvers, thus strengthening ties between the police and the citizenry.
- Neighborhoods will more actively participate in the identification, location, and capture of criminals.

On a more negative note, however, some authors point to what they believe are several unfavorable social forces that militate against the future of COPPS: Local governments are being pushed toward a more legalistic crime-control model of policing; the public is less willing to pay more taxes to address fundamental social problems; and public policy does not allow the police to focus on the root causes of crime but only on their symptoms—such as criminal conduct—through aggressive strategies rather than through COPPS.[19] Indeed, the landscape of policing is littered with the skeletons of strategies and approaches that died after the departure of a dedicated COPPS chief or sheriff. Although one would hope that such a fate would not befall COPPS, history has shown it to be a possibility that cannot be ignored.

In sum, several questions for the future remain concerning COPPS:

- Will police organizations come to believe that they cannot control crime alone and truly enlist the aid of the community in this endeavor?
- Will police chief executives acquire the innovative drive necessary to change the culture of their departments, implement COPPS, flatten the organizational structure of their departments, and see that officers' work is properly evaluated?
- Will police executives have the necessary job security to accommodate COPPS? Or will the at-will employment of chiefs place COPPS at risk?
- Will police departments work with their communities, other city agencies, businesses, elected officials, and the media to sustain COPPS?
- Will police unions work with administrators to effect the changes needed for COPPS?
- Will police employees who have not yet done so, from top to bottom, sworn and civilian, realize that the traditional reactive mode of policing has obviously not been successful and cannot work in the future?
- Can those police organizations, from top to bottom, become more customer and value oriented?
- Will police executives and supervisors come to develop the necessary policies and mechanisms to support COPPS, including recruitment, selection, training, performance appraisals, and reward and promotions systems?
- Will police executives and supervisors begin viewing the patrol officer as a problem-solving specialist? Will they give street officers enough free time and latitude to engage in proactive policing?
- Will police organizations come to view COPPS as a departmentwide and citywide strategy? Will they invest in technology to support problem-oriented policing?
- Will those agencies attempt to bring diversity into their ranks to reflect the changing demographics and cultural customs of our society?

The Role of the Beat Officer

The changing role of rank-and-file officers also looms large in future police service. The good news is that future generations of police officers will have been raised to be at ease and fluent with information technologies. This bodes well for recruiting, hiring, and developing officers who possess the skills needed in the future and are familiar with the kinds of technologies that both police and offenders will use, such as those described earlier.

Another area of interest for the future of policing concerns the attitude and cognitive abilities of the recruits as they relate to the management styles they will confront. In the past—particularly under the professional model of policing—while undergoing the academy phase of their training, recruits adopted a new identity and a system of discipline in which they learned to take orders and to not question authority. Recruits learned that loyalty to fellow officers, a professional demeanor and bearing, and respect for authority are highly valued qualities. That theme—and the police executive's set of expectations for recruits—must change. Only those candidates who can think critically, plan, and evaluate will be hired. At the same time, chiefs, sheriffs, commanders, and even sergeants will wield less power and control and will filter less information; instead, they will move into enhanced roles as coaches, supporters, and resource developers.[20]

People entering police service in the future will probably not have military experience and its inherent obedience to authority, but they will have higher levels of education and will tend to be more independent and less responsive to traditional authoritarian leadership styles. These recruits will have been exposed to more participative, supportive, and humanistic approaches and will want more opportunities to provide input into their work and to address the challenges posed by problem solving. The autocratic leader of the past will not work in the future. The watchwords of the new leadership paradigm are *coach, inspire, gain commitment, empower, affirm, flexibility, responsibility, self-management, shared power, autonomous teams,* and *entrepreneurial units.* Therefore, a major need for police leadership will be the surrendering of power to lower organizational employees, creating a flattened hierarchy.

The tools and functions of police in the future, as seen by futurists, were discussed in Chapter 14.

Other Personnel Issues

Some traditional police personnel problems are not likely to go away. Such matters as the need for more women and minorities in policing, unionization and job actions, contract and consolidated policing, civilianization, accreditation, higher education, and stress recognition and management will not be resolved in the near future. Furthermore, changing societal values, court decisions about the rights of employees, and the Peace Officers' Bill of Rights will make police leadership increasingly challenging. Nor will opportunities decline for officers to engage in graft and corruption, so administrators must develop personnel policies that will protect the integrity of the profession.

Crime, Violence, and the Influence of Drugs and Guns

There are about 23 million violent and property crime victimizations each year in this nation.[21] A number of factors contribute to the high number of victimizations: immediate access to firearms, alcohol and substance abuse, drug trafficking, poverty, racial discrimination, and cultural acceptance of violent behavior.[22] While that figure is certainly massive, the good news is that the crime rate fell from 1992 through 2003, to its lowest point in a generation. Certainly, the robust economy that preceded the September 11, 2001, terrorist attacks and the overall aging of the population contributed in large fashion to those declines. More and more, however, experts are also crediting community-oriented policing and problem solving for the drop in crime.

Why did this decline in crime occur? First, state legislators have imposed tougher sentences on violent criminals, and second, local officials are implementing aggressive and intelligent methods of community policing. The effectiveness of good police work and the extended incarceration of hardened criminals is beyond dispute.[23] Notwithstanding this recent decline in offenses, serious challenges remain. New criminal types will dot the national landscape in the future: better educated, upscale, older, and increasingly female.

Still, there are serious problems with respect to violence in the United States. In both the immediate and distant future, police will continue to deal with the "new violence" that has emerged over the past ten to fifteen years. In the past, violence was a means to an end. Revenge, robbery, and jealousy were among the many reasons that people resorted to violence. Today, an entire culture has emerged that sees the use of violence as an end unto itself. The people who make up this culture—gangs, pseudo-gangs, well-armed young people, and others—are not going to change their way of thinking or relax their hostility and aggression. For these people, the wanton use of violence—aggression for the sake of aggression—is not abhorrent behavior. Taken in combination, these factors present challenges for police leaders. Police will need training and education far beyond what they are given today to understand such violent behavior.[24]

Furthermore, the reduction in crime has had a minimal effect on reducing the public's fear of crime. Reducing fear, not simply crime statistics, will be a major challenge facing police leaders in the future. Few police leaders and officers know anything about fear. What is it? How does it work? What is the cycle of fear? How can the police intervene to break the cycle? Why is fear contagious? Do problem solving, partnering, and the implementation of crime-control strategies and tactics reduce fear? Officers should be trained to assess causes and levels of individual, neighborhood, and community fear.[25]

Drugs are also a major factor in crime and violence; 277,000 offenders are in prison for drug-law violations—that's 21 percent of state prisoners and more than 60 percent of federal prisoners. More than 80 percent of state prisoners and 70 percent of federal prisoners have engaged in some form of illicit drug use. One-third of state prisoners and 22 percent of federal prisoners report that they were under the influence of drugs when they committed the crime for which they are in prison.[26]

Most police agencies remain reactive to the drug trade. They sweep street corners, arrest users and low-level dealers, rely on specialists (narcotics units) to assume primary responsibility for drug-law enforcement, and participate in regional task forces (generally when funded by the federal government). Police leaders will have to "think outside the box" in the future in response to a changing drug market. All agencies will need a well-planned, strategic approach to the drug trade and problem solving related to drugs. More agencies must become involved in teaching employees about market analysis and forecasting in the drug trade.

In addition to drugs, two more likely crime **accelerators**—guns and alcohol—might still increase the risk of victimization and a general fear of crime. This is a well-armed nation: An estimated 250 million guns are legally owned in the United States. With roughly 83 to 96 guns per 100 people, we are approaching a statistical level of one gun per person.[27] Consequently, gun violence in the United States has become both a criminal justice and a public-health problem; firearms are still the weapons most frequently used for murder; they are the weapons of choice in nearly two-thirds of all murders. Strategies and programs to reduce gun violence include interrupting sources of illegal guns, deterring illegal possession and carrying of guns, and responding to illegal gun use.[28]

Alcohol also remains a major factor in crime and violence. Almost four in ten violent crimes involve alcohol.[29] Nearly two million offenders (about 36 percent of the total) reported that they were using alcohol at the time of their offense.[30]

SUMMARY

The cup is half full. The cup is half empty. Should we be optimistic or pessimistic about the nation's future? One thing is for certain: Our society is changing.

This is a very exciting and challenging time in the history of police service. No matter what issues lie ahead, the public will continue to expect a high degree of service from its police. Today's leaders and those who follow will determine whether police agencies embrace their communities or return to being distant and aloof. They will deal with unforeseen problems caused by new drugs, small but hostile groups of extremists, young people who were raised in an environment of violence, and more. They have the opportunity to deal with these issues supported by advanced technology, highly evolved information resources, better-trained officers and deputies, and a heightened commitment to interjurisdictional cooperation.

The police will benefit greatly by anticipating what the future holds so that appropriate resources and methods may be brought to bear on the problems ahead. And there is no indication that a significant abatement of today's social problems is looming on the horizon. The police will be affected in many ways by the social and economic changes to come; they can no longer be resistant to change or unmindful of the future.

It is hoped that at some point in the future, Americans can reflect back on the challenges of today and say with total certainty and sincerity, "The police profession today is the intellectual leadership of the criminal justice profession in the United States. The police are in the lead. They're showing the world how things might better be done."[31]

REVIEW QUESTIONS

1. Why it is important for law enforcement administrators to study futures? Identify two prominent groups that have recently been formed for this purpose.
2. What are augmented reality, unmanned aerial vehicles, and nanotechnology? How might these technologies benefit law enforcement?
3. Delineate how community policing and problem solving will fit into the future crime picture.
4. Describe how the role of beat police officers might change in the future.
5. What are some problematic police personnel issues that loom on the horizon?
6. Explain the specific changes in crime that are predicted for the future.

INDEPENDENT STUDENT ACTIVITIES

1. Assume that you have unlimited financial resources and a favorable political climate. Design a futuristic police organization for 2050 that would completely prevent crime while upholding the constitutional rights of all citizens. What kinds of people would be recruited for your agency, and how would they be educated, trained, uniformed, and equipped? What would be their primary mission and day-to-day tasks? What kinds of equipment would officers need? What role would women and minorities fill in your futuristic police force? What classes of criminals must you guard against?
2. Interview local law enforcement administrators to learn about their current strategic-planning activities to prepare for the future. How are they making projections?

RELATED WEB SITES

Futures Working Group
http://www.fbi.gov/hq/td/fwg/workhome.htm

Police Futurists International
http://www.policefuturists.org

NOTES

1. To keep abreast of trends and changes, join the World Future Society; its publication, *The Futurist*, is excellent.
2. "Focus on the Future: A Look Forward," *FBI Law Enforcement Bulletin* (January 2004): 1.

3. Quoted in Sandy Boyd, Alberto Melis, and Richard Myers, "Preparing for the Challenges Ahead: Practical Applications of Futures Research," *FBI Law Enforcement Bulletin* (January 2004): 2.
4. Sheldon Greenberg, "Future Issues in Policing: Challenges for Leaders," in *Policing Communities: Understanding Crime and Solving Problems*, ed. Ronald W. Glensor, Mark E. Correia, and Kenneth J. Peak (Los Angeles: Roxbury, 2000), p. 315.
5. Thomas Cowper, "Improving the View of the World: Law Enforcement and Augmented Reality Technology," *FBI Law Enforcement Bulletin* (January 2004): 13.
6. Ibid.
7. Ibid., p. 15.
8. Ibid., p. 16.
9. Chris Forsythe, "The Future of Simulation Technology for Law Enforcement: Diverse Experience with Realistic Simulated Humans," *FBI Law Enforcement Bulletin* (January 2004): 19–21.
10. Brian P. Tice, "Unmanned Aerial Vehicles: The Force Multiplier of the 1990s," http://www.airpower.maxwell.af.mil/airchronicles/apj/4spr91.html (accessed January 17, 2004).
11. SPI Corp., "UAV ONE – The Unmanned Aerial Vehicle Source," http://www.uav1.com (accessed February 2, 2005).
12. Tice, "Unmanned Aerial Vehicles."
13. Boyd, Melis, and Myers, "Preparing for the Challenges Ahead," p. 5.
14. Nanoink, Inc., "What Is Nanotechnology"?. http://www.nanoink.net/4100_whatis.html (accessed February 2, 2005).
15. Greenberg, "Future Issues in Policing," pp. 318–19.
16. Thomas C. Frazier, "Community Policing Efforts Offer Hope for the Future," *Police Chief*, August 2000, p. 11.
17. Ibid.
18. Dave Pettinari, "Are We There Yet? The Future of Policing/Sheriffing in Pueblo—Or Anywhere, in America," http://www.policefuturists.org/files/yet.html (accessed February 2, 2005).
19. Roy Roberg, John Crank, and Jack Kuykendall, *Police and Society*, 2d ed. (Los Angeles: Roxbury, 2000), pp. 522–23.
20. Pettinari, "Are We There Yet?" p. 2.
21. Department of Justice, Bureau of Justice Statistics, Criminal Victimizations, 2002, http://www.ojp.usdoj.gov/bjs/cvictgen.htm (accessed January 18, 2004).
22. Lee P. Brown, "Violent Crime and Community Involvement," *FBI Law Enforcement Bulletin* (May 1992): 2–5.
23. Ibid., p. 3.
24. Greenberg, "Future Issues in Policing," pp. 315–21.
25. Ibid.
26. Department of Justice, Bureau of Justice Statistics, press release, "More Than Three-Quarters of Prisoners Had Abused Drugs in the Past," January 5, 1999.

27. EDITH M. LEDERER, "Americans Have Far More Guns Than Any Other Population," Associated Press, July 8, 2003.
28. DAVID SHEPPARD, "Strategies to Reduce Gun Violence" (Department of Justice, Office of Juvenile Justice and Delinquency Prevention fact sheet no. 93, February 1999), p. 1.
29. DEPARTMENT OF JUSTICE, Bureau of Justice Statistics, *Alcohol and Crime* (Washington, DC: Author, 1998), p. 20.
30. Ibid.
31. JAMES Q. WILSON, "Six Things Police Leaders Can Do about Juvenile Crime," in *Subject to Debate* (newsletter of the Police Executive Research Forum), September/October 1997, p. 1.

Appendix A

Career Information

This book has examined policing from many perspectives. For those who have decided to try to enter into a policing career or are interested in learning about the processes involved, this appendix discusses some methods for preparing for career opportunities at the federal, state, and local levels. It also provides some general advice about obtaining a police position.

Preparing for Job Hunting

Police recruiters often ask what the applicant has done to prepare for a police career. In fact, you can take several steps to prepare for a career in policing. For example, it is to your benefit if you can point to criminal justice studies, participation in a police ride-along program or auxiliary police service, a clean criminal record, good physical shape, and so on.

Also, you may wish to read about the federal, state, and local law enforcement agencies that are described in Chapter 2; you'll find information about police recruitment and the hiring process in Chapter 3. Both chapters will serve as a good resource in your job search. Then you can more objectively determine your areas of interest and possible suitability for such employment. The primary limitations to the ability to secure employment are often characteristics that you can address: mobility, appearance, character, physical ability, academic performance, experience, the quality of your résumé, your performance during an interview, and so forth. Above all, be patient and heed the old adage that "Rome wasn't built in a day."

At some point, you will want to determine whether you have the background, personality, interest, and physical abilities to pass the entry-level examinations and to handle the challenges of police work. Can you work well under pressure? Write well? Take action when necessary? Accept the cultural differences of others? You might want to enroll in an internship program through your college or university. Look to your college or university placement office for job announcements and for assistance in preparing your résumé, interviewing, and so on. There are also private, for-profit organizations that assist with résumé preparation and developing interviewing skills. Do not underestimate the value of a good résumé.

You must also determine which agencies have job vacancies., Govtjobs.com, for example, provides job listings on the Internet (see: http://www.govtjobs.com/crim). *Knight Line USA,* published semimonthly in Tallahassee, Florida, provides general information about career planning and also offers a job search service. Another excellent resource are books such as *Seeking Employment in Criminal Justice and Related Fields,* by J. Scott Harr and Karen M. Hess.[1]

Careers in Federal Law Enforcement

You can use several methods to learn of openings in federal law enforcement agencies. First, many federal law enforcement agencies have agents who are assigned specifically as recruitment coordinators; you can contact them in their respective agencies for general information about the application process and the hiring outlook. Some people have been successful in finding federal law enforcement positions through the Internet (for example, see the FBI's job link at FBIjobs.com, at the following Web site: http://www.fbi.gov/employment/employ.htm). You can also look for announcements of state level openings at your state employment office.

Before considering a career in any federal law enforcement agency, you must first complete and submit an application form—the SF-171 form—for federal employment. The federal Office of Personnel Management (OPM) coordinates the testing for most federal law enforcement agencies, although requirements for federal positions are determined by the individual agencies. (The Federal Bureau of Investigation and some other agencies do not use the OPM.) Once you have passed the exam for a particular agency (you'll need a minimum score of 70), you will receive an employment rating for that agency. The recruiting agency will interview the best candidates and initiate a background investigation.

The minimum salary, or Government Service (GS) grade, at hiring depends on the applicant's education, experience, and training, although some agencies do not hire above a specific level (generally GS-5, 7, or 9).

Careers with the State Police

As discussed in Chapter 2, most states have a state police or highway patrol agency; many have an investigative agency as well. A number of other specialized investigative units also exist at the state level, such as a separate office of alcoholic beverage control, a fire marshal, a state revenue office, and an office of wildlife or natural resources.

Nearly all of the state police, highway patrol, and investigative agencies require a high school degree or its equivalent as a minimal requirement for trooper, investigator, or agent positions.

If you are interested in state employment, watch for hiring notices on television, in the newspapers, on the radio, or at your state employment office, or contact your state personnel office and ask for information concerning a particular state agency.

Careers in Local Policing

Most of this book has examined the roles and functions of local police departments and sheriff's offices. The seventeen thousand municipal police agencies constitute the largest segment of police personnel in the nation. They also offer a broad spectrum of specialized assignments. At the county level, policing is primarily in the hands of an elected sheriff; investigators may be assigned to the county prosecutor's office, or the office may hire its own separate investigative unit. Counties may have other specialized police personnel, such as county park police or part-time deputies.

If you are interested in local police employment, contact the human resources department for the city or county agency in which you are interested, or contact the agency directly. (Many smaller agencies do not have a human resources department or do not advertise position vacancies.) Also watch for hiring notices on television, in the newspapers, or on the radio.

1. J. Scott Harr and Karen M. Hess, *Seeking Employment in Criminal Justice and Related Fields*, 3d ed. (Belmont, CA: Wadsworth, 2000).

Appendix B

The Police Corps

The Police Corps is a federally funded program administered by the U.S. Department of Justice, Office of the Police Corps and Law Enforcement Education (OPCLEE). It operates in about half of the states and is designed to motivate highly qualified individuals to serve as peace officers in state and local agencies. The program is designed to address violent crime by increasing the number of police officers and sheriff's deputies with advanced education and training. The program has three components:

- It provides scholarships on a competitive basis to students who agree to earn their bachelor's degrees, complete approved Police Corps training, and then serve for four years on patrol, as assigned, with law enforcement agencies in great need.
- It provides funds to states to develop and provide sixteen to twenty-four weeks of rigorous Police Corps training. Undergraduates must attend college full time and may receive up to $7,500 per academic year to cover the expenses of study toward a bachelor's or master's degree. (Recent college graduates or undergraduate juniors or seniors may qualify for reimbursement for their degree or for funds to assist with completing graduate studies.)
- It provides state and local agencies that hire Police Corps officers with $10,000 for each of an officer's first four years of service.

Individuals apply to the state where they are willing to serve. Allowable educational expenses for full-time students include reasonable room and board. A student may receive up to $30,000 under the program, including a monthly stipend of $1,600 during the academy phase, regardless of family income or resources. To be eligible, a student must attend a public or nonprofit four-year college or university. Participants may choose to study criminal justice or may pursue degrees in other fields. They must also possess the necessary mental and physical capabilities and moral characteristics to be an effective police officer, must be of good character, must meet the standards of the police agency with which they will serve, and must demonstrate sincere motivation and dedication to law enforcement and public service.

Police Corps participants have all the rights and responsibilities of other members of the police department in which they serve, and they are subject to all rules and regulations that apply to other officers. If a Police

Corps participant does not satisfactorily complete his or her education, training, and service obligations, he or she must repay all scholarships and reimbursements received through the program, plus interest.

Because not all states participate in the Police Corps program and because some of the conditions vary from state to state, individuals and police agencies interested in learning about the Police Corps may contact the Office of the Police Corps and Law Enforcement Education at 810 Seventh St., NW, Washington, D.C. 20531. Information on participating states and agency contacts may also be acquired by calling the Office of the Police Corps at 1-888-94CORPS or the U.S. Department of Justice Response Center at 1-800-421-6770 or by going to the OPCLEE Web site at www.ojp.usdoj.gov/opclee.

Index

A

Academies, police, 78–81
Accelerators, crime, 455
Accident investigation, 434–435
Accountability of police officers, 287–343. *See also* Brutality, police; Corruption, police; Ethics; Force and violence, use of; Liability
  alcohol and drug abuse, 315–316
  in China, 398
  complaints, dealing with, 317–320
  disciplinary policies and practices, 316–317
  misuse of firearms, 314–315
  moonlighting, 314
  religious practices of police officers, 312
  residency requirements, 313–314
  searches and seizures of police officers, 311–312
  self-incrimination, right against, 312
  sexual misconduct, 312–313
Accreditation of police agencies, 368–369
Active supervisors, 123
ADORE (Automated Daily Observation Report and Evaluation), 85–86
Adultery, 313
Affidavit, for arrest warrant, 264
AFISs (automated fingerprint identification systems), 437–438
African-Americans
  bias-based policing and, 302–304
  gangs, 244
  police officers, 363–365
Air Marshal Service, 44
Alarm calls, 167
Alcohol, future of policing and, 455
Alcohol and drug abuse, by police officers, 315–316
Alpert, Geoffrey, 85
American Arbitration Association, 353
American Bar Association, 132
American Federation of Labor (AFL), 349
American Federation of State, County, and Municipal Employees, 350
American Police Association, 372
Americans for Effective Law Enforcement, 333
Amparo, writ of, 408
Analysis, crime, 165–168
  definition of, 170
Angell, John, 100–101
Animal Liberation Front, 225
Animals, killing of, 315
Anthropometry, 189–191
Anti-Defamation League, 238
Arab-Americans and Muslims, 228–229, 236, 302
Arbitration, 353
Argersinger v. *Hamlin* (1973), 279
Arms. *See also* Firearms; Weapons
  carrying of, 18
Arrests, 199
  driving under the influence (DUI), 435
  false, 330–331, 336
  with and without a warrant, 264–265
Arther, Richard, 76
Ashcroft, John, 290
Assessment, in SARA process, 169

Astor, Saul, 365
ATF (Bureau of Alcohol, Tobacco, Firearms, and Explosives), 54–55
Atlanta Police Department, 196
  patrol allocation in, 135, 136
Augmented reality (AR), 447–448
Automated fingerprint identification systems (AFISs), 437–438
Automated Regional Justice Information System (ARJIS), 431

B

Background checks, 76
Badge, officer's, 80–81
Baldwin, Lola, 358
Baltimore, 17
  patrol allocation in, 135, 136
Bank Secrecy Act, 60
Bass, William III, 212
Bayley, David, 90, 141–142, 149
Beanbag, 427
Beanbag guns, 424
Beat culture, 140
Beat patrol (beat assignment; beat officers)
  future of, 452–453
  hazards of, 140–143
  influences of, 139–140
Belt, officer's, 80
Bender, Frank, 188
Berkeley, California, Police Department, 26–29, 153
Bertillon, Alphonse, 190
Bertillon system (anthropometry), 189–191
Beverly v. *Morris* (1972), 336–337
Bianchi, Kenneth, 209
Bias-based policing, 302–304
Bias crimes, 236–238
Bicycles, patrol on, 26–27
Biographical data inventories, 73
Bioterrorism, 230–235
Bittner, Egon, 149, 297
Bivens torts, 331
Bloods, the, 244
Blood typing, 194
Bobbies, 14–16
Bomb and Arson Tracking System, 55
Bonsignore v. *City of New York,* 335
Border and Transportation Security (BTS), 43–44
Borders, protecting, 249–251
Boredom, filling occasional hours of, 137
Boston Police Department, 17, 18, 437–438
Bouza, Anthony, 142–143
Bowman, Adrian, 421
Bow Street Runners, 195, 196
Boyd, Sandy, 449
Bradford, David, 79–80
Brandon v. *Allen* (1981), 338
Bratton, William, 117
Breed v. *Jones* (1975), 281–282
Brennan, William, Jr., 262
Bribery, 306–307
Broderick, John, 79, 87–88
Brutality, police, 295–300, 423
Brzeczek, Richard, 125
Bureaucracies, organizations as, 101
Bureau of Alcohol, Tobacco, Firearms and Explosives (ATF), 54–55, 236
Bureau of Narcotics, 57
Bureau of Narcotics and Dangerous Drugs, 57
Burkholder v. *City of Los Angeles* (1982), 335
Burns, William J., 365
Bush, George W., 229
Byrnes, Thomas, 196–197

C

CAD (computer-aided dispatching) system, 428, 429
CALEA (Commission on Accreditation for Law Enforcement Agencies), 368–369
CALGANG, 440
California, 23, 111
California Bureau of Criminal Identification, 197
California Personality Inventory (CPI), 74
Call for service analysis, 167
Calls for service, delay in responding to, 303
Captains, 118–120
Cardozo, Benjamin, 260, 261

Careers
in federal law enforcement, 460
in local policing, 461
with the state police, 460–461
Carmelo v. *Miller* (1978), 335
Carpenter, Bruce, 70
Carroll v. *United States* (1925), 270–271
Carter, David, 307
Case preparation, 199–200
Census Bureau, U.S., 429
Central Intelligence Agency (CIA), 59
Chain of command, 101, 105
Chapman, Samuel G., 340–341
Character investigations, 76
Charleston Police Department, 421
Charlotte-Mecklenburg, North Carolina, Police Department (CMPD), 178–179
Chemical weapons, 423
Chicago, University of, 28
Chicago Police Department, 17, 18, 23, 72, 81, 196, 309–310
patrol allocation in, 135, 136
Chief executive officers (CEOs), Mintzberg model of, 110, 114–116
Chiefs of police, 110–112
expectations of, 124–125
female, 355–357
Chimel v. *California* (1969), 267–268, 271
China, 395–398
Chiseling, 306
Cincinnati, 17
Cincinnati police, 289
Civil liability, 329–337, 340–341
legal foundation for, 329–332
of private police, 368
Civil Rights Act of 1871, 334
Civil Rights Act of 1964, 359
Civil service systems, 25
Cleveland, 21
CN gas, 423
Coffeyville, Kansas, 23
Cognitive tests, 73
Cold cases, 216–217
Collective bargaining, 350–355
chief executive officers (CEOs) and, 116
College education for police, 369–372
College system of academy training, 79
Colonial America
legacies of, 10–12
policing in, 8–10
sheriffs in, 3
Colquhoun, Patrick, 12
Combined DNA Index System (CODIS), 207
Commission on Accreditation for Law Enforcement Agencies (CALEA), 368–369
Communication, 101–105
barriers to effective, 104–105
chief executive officers (CEOs) as, 115–116
within police organizations, 103
written, 104
Communications skills, 88
Community-oriented policing (COP), 33–35
basic principles of, 161–162
Community-oriented policing and problem-solving. *See* COPPS
Community-Oriented Policing Services (COPS), Office of, 34–35
Community policing, 28
ethics and, 294–295
traditional *versus,* 163
Community surveys to analyze problems, 167–168
Complaints, dealing with, 317–320
Compstat, 116–117
Compstat program, 430
Computer-aided dispatching (CAD) system, 428, 429
Computer-assisted training, 439
Computer-based training (CBT), 84
Computer crimes, 214–215
Computer evidence, 342
Computers, investigations of police corruption and, 309–310
Confessions, 275–276. *See also* Self-incrimination, right against
Confidentiality, 293
Consent to search, 273–274
Constables, 3–4
Constitutional rights, of police officers, limitations on, 310
Continuing investigation, 198–199
Coolidge, Calvin, 29, 350

COPPS (community-oriented policing and problem solving), 34, 161, 169–181
basic principles of, 169–171
case studies, 178–181
crime prevention and, 175–176
ethics and, 294–295
evaluation of, 174–175
future of, 450–452
implementing, 171–173
three generations of, 35
Coroners, 5
Corpus delicti, 189
Corruption, police, 20–22, 27, 30, 305–310
code of silence and, 308–309
definition of, 305–306
in Mexico, 406
politics and, 124
possible solutions to, 309–310
types and causes of, 306–307
Counsel, right to, 278–279
Counseling, as disciplinary action, 321
County of Sacramento v. *Lewis* (1998), 341–342
Couper, David, 363
Courage, 89
Courts, 331
Covent Garden Journal, 195
Coyotes, 250
CPI, 87
Crank, John, 142
Creativity, 89
CR gas, 423
Crime accelerators, 455
Crime analysis, 165–168
definition of, 170
Crime clock, UCR, 53
Crime-control model of the exclusionary rule, 263
Crime mapping, 166–167, 429–430
Crime Mapping Research Center (CMRC), 430
Crime prevention, 14, 175–178
in colonial period, 10
Crime prevention through environmental design (CPTED), 176
Crime scene, linking a person to a, 189
Crime-scene investigations, 438–439
Criminal investigation(s), 185–217. *See also* Criminalistics
accident, 434–435
arrest and case preparation, 199–200
behavioral science in, 208–209
cold cases, 216–217
of complaints, 319
crimes against juveniles and missing youths, 215–216
crime-scene, 438–439
cybercrooks, 214–215
detectives and, 200–201
DNA analysis and, 203–207
English contribution to, 195–196
forensic entomology and, 211–213
hypnosis and, 209–210
interrogations and, 210–211
of police corruption, 309–310
polygraph examinations and, 202–203
psychics and, 209
stages and activities of, 197–199
stalking investigations, 213–214
undercover work and, 201–202
Criminal Investigation Division (CID; England), 196
Criminalistics, 186–197
anthropometry (Bertillon system), 189–191
contributions of Vollmer and others, 194
dactylography (fingerprint identification), 189–192
firearms identification, 192–194
origins of, 189–194
Criminal profiling, 208–209
Criminal prosecutions for police misconduct, 337–339
Crips, the, 244
CS gas, 423, 424
Curricula, recruit training, 78–80
Customs and Border Protection (CBP), 43, 249
CyberAngels, 215
Cybercrooks, 214–215
Cynicism, police, 87

D

Dactylography (fingerprint identification), 189–192
Dallas, Texas, Police Department, 370
Dalton Gang, 23–24
DARE (Drug Abuse Resistance and Education) program, 177–178
Databases, integrated, 428–429
Daubert v. *Merrell Dow Pharmaceuticals, Inc.,* 205
Davis, Kenneth Culp, 150, 152
Day, Frank, 299
Decision-maker role of chief executive officers (CEOs), 115–116
Decoding, 102
Defamation, 342–343
Defoe, Daniel, 8
DeForest, Peter, 189
De La Riva, Baltazar, 425
Democratizing the police abroad, 409–410
Demotion, 321
Department of Homeland Security (DHS), 42–48, 229
Department of Justice, 48
  investigation of allegations of racial bias in police departments, 289–290
  organizational structure of, 49
Deployment of patrol officers, 131
Detectives, 200–201
Detroit, patrol allocation in, 135, 136
Diallo, Amadou, 289
Diffusion generation of COPPS, 35
Directed patrol, 147
Discharging public employees, due process requirements for, 316–317
Disciplinary policies and practices, 316–317
  appealing disciplinary measures, 320
  level and nature of sanctions, 321
Discretion (discretionary use of police authority)
  patrol function and, 148–152
  understanding, 89
Disrespect, forms of, 304
Disturbance handlers, chief executive officers (CEOs) as, 116
DNA analysis, 203–207, 436–437
Documented oral counseling, as disciplinary action, 321
Dogs, search-and-rescue, 433
Domestic violence, 304–305
Domestic Violence Offender Gun Ban (Lautenberg Amendment), 304
Double marginality, 364
Driving under the influence (DUI), 154
  arrest process, 435
Drones (UAVs), 251
Drug abuse, by police officers, 315–316
Drug Abuse Resistance and Education (DARE) program, 177–178
Drug Enforcement Administration (DEA), 55–57
Drug or alcohol tests, 77, 315–316
Drugs
  future of policing and, 454–455
  police corruption related to, 307
Due process model of the exclusionary rule, 263
Due process requirements, for discharging public employees, 316–317
Duncan v. *Barnes* (1979), 336
Dunham, Roger, 85

E

Earp, Wyatt, 24
Earth Liberation Front (ELF), 225–226
Educational requirements for police officers, 369–372
Ego, 89
Einstein, Albert, 446
Electronic eavesdropping ("wiretapping"), 240
Electronic surveillance, 274
Eleventh Amendment, 332
ELF (Earth Liberation Front), 225–226
Emergency Preparedness and Response directorate, 45
Encoding, 102
Enforcers, 87
England
  criminal investigation in, 195–196
  in the nineteenth century, 19–20
  officers of the law in early, 2–7
  police reform in, 12–16
  system of policing in early, 7–8

Enthusiasm, 88
Entomology, forensic, 211–213
Entrapment, 277
Entrepreneurs, 115
Epithets, 304
Erotomanic stalkers, 214
Escobedo v. *Illinois* (1964), 276, 279
Ethics, 290–295
  community policing and, 294
  definition of, 294
  Law Enforcement Code of Ethics, 292–293
  types of, 294
Ethnic gangs, 244–245
Evidence. *See also* Exclusionary rule
  computer, 342
Exclusionary rule, 260–263
Exigent circumstances, for arrest without a warrant, 264
Extrasensory perception (ESP), 209

F

Fact-finding, 352–353
Fair Labor Standards Act (FLSA), 354–355
Fajardo, Robin, 369
False arrest, 330–331, 336
False statements made to FBI agents, 338
False victimization syndrome, 214
Fargo, William, 365
FATS (firearms training system), 439
Faulds, Henry, 191
Faurot, Joseph, 192
Favoritism, 306
Federal Bureau of Investigation (FBI), 28, 48–54, 197, 212, 337, 460
  ancillary investigative, training, and reporting services of, 51–54
  Bias Crimes Unit of, 236
  contemporary priorities and roles of, 50–51
  DNA analysis and, 204, 205, 207
  false statements made to FBI agents, 338
  Futures Working Group, 446
  organized crime (Mafia) and, 238–243
  terrorism and, 225–226, 229
Federal courts, 331
Federal Emergency Management Agency (FEMA), 45
Federal investigations, 289–290
Federal law enforcement agencies, 41–61
  careers in, 460
  Central Intelligence Agency (CIA), 59
  Department of Homeland Security (DHS), 42–48
  Department of Justice, 48–59
  Federal Law Enforcement Training Center (FLETC), 61
  Internal Revenue Service (IRS), 59–61
Federal Law Enforcement Training Center (FLETC), 61, 78
Federal marshals, 24
Feedback, 102, 103
Female police officers, 70, 72, 355–363
  academy training of, 360
  agency and chief executive representation, 355–357
  family and career of, 362–363
  field training of, 360
  harassment and discrimination of, 361
  key issues affecting, 357, 360–363
  mentoring of, 361
  preemployment physical testing of, 357
  promotions of, 361
  recruitment of, 357
  rookie's assignments, 360–361
Fielding, Henry, 11, 195
Fielding, John, 11
Field training, 85–86
Fifth Amendment, 275–278
  juveniles and, 281–282
Fingerprint identification (dactylography), 189–192
Fingerprints, 437–438
Firearms. *See also* Force and violence, use of
  developments relevant to, 439–440
  identification of, 192–194
  misuse of, 314–315
  private police and, 367–368
Firearms training system (FATS), 439

First-line supervisors (sergeants), 102, 120–123
Flint, Michigan, 147
Floyd, Chris, 421
Flynn, Robert, 421
FN 303 Launcher, 425
Focusing the investigation, 199
Foot patrol, 33
Force, use of, 18, 292
Force and violence, use of, 295–305
  excessive, against minority citizens, 304
  lethal use of force, 301
  prerogative to use force, 296–297
Foreign countries, policing in, 386–413
Forensic entomology, 211–213
Forensic science, 186
Fourteenth Amendment, juveniles and, 281
Fourth Amendment, 258–275, 301
  arrests with and without a warrant, 264–265
  exclusionary rule and, 260–263
  police officers and, 311–312
  probable cause and, 258–260
  searches and seizures. *See* Searches and seizures
Fox, Vicente, 406
Fraternal orders of police (FOPs), 350
Freedom of speech, of police officers, 310
Frisking. *See also* Stop and frisk
  of minority citizens, excessive, 304
Frye standard, 205
Fuld, Leonard, 131
Functions, policing, 91–92
Future of policing, 445–455
  augmented reality (AR), 447–448
  community-oriented policing and problem solving (COPPS), 450–452
  crime and violence and the influence of drugs and guns, 453–455
  unmanned aerial vehicles (UAVs), 449

G

Gaines, Larry, 100–101
Gallati, Robert, 299
Galton, Sir Francis, 191–192
Gang intelligence systems, 440
Gang intelligence units (GIUs), 246
GangNet, 440
Gang Resistance Education and Training (GREAT) program, 246–247
Gangs, street, 243–249
  ethnic and racial, 244–245
  organization and revenues of, 243–244
  terrorism and, 248–249
Garcia v. *San Antonio Transit Authority* (1985), 354–355
Garner, Joel H., 299
Garrity v. *New Jersey,* 312
General intelligence tests, 73–74
Geographic information system (GIS), 431
Geographic profiling, 430
George I, King, 8
Germann, A. C., 299
Gideon v. *Wainwright* (1963), 278–279
Gilliam v. *Falbo* (1982), 335
Global Positioning System (GPS), 433, 434
Goddard, Calvin, 194
Goldstein, Herman, 32, 35, 89, 164
Good Driver Recognition Program (Berkeley, California), 153
Good judgment, 89
Gottlieb, Steven, 170
GPS (Global Positioning System), 433, 434
Graffiti, 245
Grapevine, 103–104
Gratuities, 294–295
Greenberg, Sheldon, 446
Greenfeld, Lawrence, 298
Green River Killer, 206
Grievances, 349, 353
Griggs v. *Duke Power Company* (1971), 363
Gun "fingerprints," 439
Guns. *See* Firearms
Gunshot locator system, 432

H

Habeas corpus, 264
Hand signals, 245
Harassment, sexual, 313, 361
Harrington, Penny, 358–359

Harrison Narcotic Act (1914), 55–56
Harris v. *United States* (1968), 271
Hate crimes, 236–238
Haygood v. *City of Detroit* (1979), 335
Henry, Edward, 192
Heraux, Cedric, 299
Herschel, William, 191
Hickok, "Wild Bill," 24
Higher education for police, 369–372
High-speed pursuits, 337, 339–342
  preventing, 435–436
  searches and, 270–272
  simulation of, 86
Hispanic gangs, 244–245
Hit-and-run drivers, 154
HITS (homicide investigation and tracking system), 430
Hobbs Act (1970), 309
Holden, Richard, 119
Holmes, Oliver Wendell, 261
Homeland security, 225
Homeland Security, Department of, 42–48, 229
Homeland Security Act of 2002, 42, 55
Homicide investigation and tracking system (HITS), 430
Hoover, Herbert, 30
Hoover, J. Edgar, 28, 29, 48, 197, 239
Horne, Peter, 357
Houck, Max, 216
Houston, patrol allocation in, 135, 136
Human rights, 409–410
Hunter, Kenneth W., Jr., 231, 232–233
Hurdle process, 73
Hurrell, J. J., 378
Hypnosis, 209–210

I

Idealists, 87
Illinois v. *Caballes* (2005), 272
Illinois v. *Wardlow* (2000), 269
Immigration and Customs Enforcement, Bureau of (ICE), 42–44
Indoctrination, 103
"Inevitability of discovery exception" to the exclusionary rule, 261–262
Informants, 240–241
Informational role, 115
Informational role of chief executive officers (CEOs), 115
Information Analysis and Infrastructure Protection (IAIP), 46
In loco parentis, doctrine of, 280
Innovation generation of COPPS, 35
Innovative supervisors, 123
In Re Gault (1967), 281
In Re Winship (1970), 281
Insects, 211–213
Institute for Cold Case Evaluation, 216
Institutionalization, generation of COPPS, 35
Integrated databases, 428–429
Integrity, culture of, 291
Intelligence community, 230
Intelligence Reform and Terrorism Prevention Act of 2004 (Public Law 108-458), 230
Intelligence tests, 73–74
Intentional torts, 330
Interest inventories, 73
Internal Revenue Service (IRS), 59–61
International Brotherhood of Police Officers, 350
International Law Enforcement Educators and Trainers Association (ILEETA), 413
Interpersonal role of chief executive officers (CEOs), 114–115
Interpol (International Criminal Police Organization), 410–413
Interrogation(s), 210–211
  probable cause needed for, 265
  what constitutes, 279
Interviews, oral, 75–76
Investigation(s), criminal, 185–217. *See also* Criminalistics
  accident, 434–435
  arrest and case preparation, 199–200
  behavioral science in, 208–209
  cold cases, 216–217
  of complaints, 319
  crimes against juveniles and missing youths, 215–216
  crime-scene, 438–439
  cybercrooks, 214–215
  detectives and, 200–201
  DNA analysis and, 203–207
  English contribution to, 195–196

forensic entomology and, 211–213
hypnosis and, 209–210
interrogations and, 210–211
of police corruption, 309–310
polygraph examinations and, 202–203
psychics and, 209
stages and activities of, 197–199
stalking investigations, 213–214
undercover work and, 201–202
Investigative stages, 198–199
Iraq, 387–389
Irey, Elmer I., 60
Irish-Americans, 21
Irish Republican Army (IRA), 399–405
Islam, 391–395

J

James, Jesse, 24
Jeffreys, Alec, 203
Jennings v. *City of Detroit* (1979), 335
Job actions, 351, 353–354
Job hunting, preparing for, 459–460
Job instruction, 103
Job rationale, 103
Justice, Department of, 48
investigation of allegations of racial bias in police departments, 289–290
organizational structure of, 49
Juvenile delinquency, 281
Juveniles
investigating crimes against, 215–216
rights of, 280–282

K

Kansas City, Missouri, Police Department, 119, 147, 200
Kansas City Preventive Patrol Experiment, 146
Katz v. *United States* (1967), 274
Kelling, George L., 28, 35, 145–146, 148
Kelly, Raymond W., 231
Kent v. *United States* (1966), 281
Kirk, Paul, 188, 194
Knapp Commission, 305
Knowing the job and the system, 89
Knoxville, Tennessee, Police Department, 213
Kroes, W. H., 378
Ku Klux Klan Act of 1871, 332

L

Labor relations, 348–355
Larson, John, 194
Lattes, Leone, 194
Lautenberg Amendment, 304
Law enforcement agencies
federal. *See* Federal law enforcement agencies
state and local, 61–63
Law Enforcement Code of Ethics, 292
LEEP (Law Enforcement Education Program), 370
Lefkowitz, Joel, 70
Legalistic style, 92
Lethal use of force, 301
Letters of reprimand, 321
Liability civil. *See* Civil liability
new areas of potential, 339–343
Lieutenants, 118–120
Lindbergh, Charles, 60, 209
Lineups, 274–275
Listening, 104
Locard, Edmond, 194
London, 10–12
Metropolitan Police of, 14–16, 195–196
Los Angeles, California, gangs in, 247–248
Los Angeles Police Department (LAPD), 27, 30–31, 72
patrol allocation in, 135, 136
Rampart Division, 288–289
Rodney King case, 289
Lost persons, dogs and searches for, 433
Love obsessional stalkers, 214

M

McCabe, Kimberly, 369
McClelland v. *Facteau* (1979), 338
Mace, 423
McKeiver v. *Pennsylvania* (1971), 281
Madison, Connecticut, Police Department, 238
Mafia (Cosa Nostra), 239–243
Maggots, in forensic entomology, 211–212

Malibu, California, 118–119
Management directorate, 46
Mapping, crime, 166–167
Mapp v. *Ohio* (1961), 261–263, 269
Mara Salvatrucha 13 (MS-13), 248
Marshals, U.S., 58–59
Maryland v. *Wilson* (1997), 270
Masterson, William "Bat," 24
Maxwell, Christopher D., 299
Mayne, Richard, 14
Media for communication, 102
Mediation, 352
Medical examinations, 77
Mentoring, of female police officers, 361
Metropolitan Police Act of 1829 (England), 14
Mexico, 405–409
Middle managers, 118–120
Minnesota Multiphasic Personality Inventory (MMPI), 70, 74, 87
Minnesota v. *Dickerson* (1993), 269
Minorities, bias-based policing and, 302–304
Minority police officers, 363–365
Mintzberg, Henry, 114
Mintzberg model of chief executive officers, 110, 114–116
Miranda v. *Arizona* (1966; *Miranda* warning), 265, 275–277, 279
Misconduct, police, 316. *See also specific types of misconduct*
  complaints, dealing with, 317–320
  criminal prosecutions for, 337
  Section 1983 suits for, 333–337
Mitochondrial DNA, 206–207
Mobile data systems, 428
Modus operandi, 27, 189
Monell v. *Department of Social Services* (1978), 334
Monroe v. *Pape* (1961), 333
Mooching, 306
Moonlighting, 314
Moore, Mark, 28
Mothers Against Drunk Driving (MADD), 125
MS-13 (Mara Salvatrucha 13), 248
Mulberry Street Morning Parade, 196–197
Municipal police departments, 62–63
Murphy, Patrick V., 307, 308
Murray v. *City of Chicago* (1980), 336

N

Nanotechnology, 449
Naperville, Illinois, Police Department, 432
Narcotic Drugs Import and Export Act of 1922, 56
National Academy, 52, 197
National Advisory Commission on Criminal Justice Standards and Goals, 152, 370
National Association of Police Officers, 305
National Association of Police Organizations (NAPO), 71
National Black Police Association and the National Organization of Black Law Enforcement Executives (NOBLE), 363
National Center for Missing and Exploited Children (NCMEC), 216
National Commission on Law Observance and Enforcement (Wickersham Commission), 28–30
National Counterterrorism Center, 230
National Crime Commission (1925), 29
National Crime Information Center (NCIC), 52, 197
National DNA Index System (NDIS), 207
National Institute of Justice (NIJ), 85, 117, 309, 379
  Crime Mapping Research Center (CMRC), 430
  Less Than Lethal Program, 427
National Security Act of 1947, 59
National Treasury Employees Union v. *Von Raab* (1989), 315–316
NCMEC (National Center for Missing and Exploited Children), 216
Negligence by police officers, 330, 336–337
Negotiators, chief executive officers (CEOs) as, 116
Neighborhood Foot Patrol Program (Flint, Michigan), 147
Nelson, Scott, 392
Newark, New Jersey, 17, 33, 148

New Haven, Connecticut, Police Department, 147
New Orleans, 17
New technology in the training function, 85–86
New York City Police Department (NYPD), 87, 242
  Amadou Diallo killing, 289
  bioterrorism and, 231
  Compstat process, 116–117
  Compstat program, 430
  corruption in, 305
  investigative techniques, 196
  in the nineteenth century, 16–22
  patrol allocation in, 135, 136
  Section 1983 suits, 333
New York State Police (NYSP), 72
Niederhoffer, Arthur, 84, 87
911 calls, nonemergency, 133–134
9/11 Commission, 230
Nolan, Daniel, 192
Nonlethal weapons, 423
Northern Ireland, 399–405
North Tulsa, Oklahoma, 179–181
Nowicki, Dennis, 88
Nowicki, Ed, 413

O

O'Connor, 266
Office of Community-Oriented Policing Services (COPS), 450
Office of Personnel Management (OPM), 460
Oliver, Willard M., 35
Olmstead v. *United States* (1928), 261
Omerta (silence), 239
O'Neill, Francis, 23
Open-field searches, 272
OPM (Office of Personnel Management), 460
Optimists, 88
Oral interviews, 75–76
Organizational communication, 101–105
  barriers to effective, 104–105
  chief executive officers (CEOs) as, 115–116
  within police organizations, 103
  written, 104
Organizational policies and procedures, 109–110
Organizational structure, 106–107
Organizations, 100–101
  as bureaucracies, 101
  police agencies as, 105–109
Organized crime, 238–243
Osborn, Albert, 194
Oxnard, California, Police Department, 427

P

Palmer, Ron, 372
Paramilitary groups, in Northern Ireland, 401–403
Parens patriae, doctrine of, 280
Parker, William H., 27, 30–31, 33, 87
Parks, Bernard, 302
Patrol, 130–155
  on bicycles, 26–27
  directed, 147
  filling occasional hours of boredom, 137
  as a function of shift assignment, 137–139
  hazards of beat patrol, 140–143
  influences of beat assignment, 139–140
  job description, 134–135
  purposes and nature of, 131–135
  returning to patrol duties after undercover assignments, 202
  studies of, 145–148
  traffic control and, 152–154
Patrolmen's benevolent associations (PBAs), 350
Patrol vehicles, 143–145
Peace Officer Bill of Rights, 348–349
Peace Officers Standards and Training (POST) academy (California), 111
Peel, Sir Robert, 13–16, 33, 161
Peel's principles of policing, 16, 17
Pennsylvania State Police, 197
Pepper spray, 427
Perjury, 307, 309
Perkinje, John, 191
Personal appearance, of police officers, 311

Personality, police, 86–89
Personality-type tests, 73
Peterson, Scott, 206–207
PFI (Society of Police Futurists International), 446, 447, 449
Phantom drivers, 154
Philadelphia, 16–18
Photic driver, 424
Physical agility tests, 74–75
Physical testing, preemployment, of female police officers, 357
Pinkerton, Allan, 365
Pinkerton National Detective Agency, 365
Placa, 245
Plain-view searches, 272–273
Plastic bullets, 424–425
Plebe system (stress academy), 79
Poe, Edgar Allan, 17
Police academies, 78–81
Police brutality, 295–300, 423
Police chiefs, 110–112
  expectations of, 124–125
  female, 355–357
Police Corps, 372, 462–463
Police corruption, 20–22, 27, 30, 305–310
  code of silence and, 308–309
  definition of, 305–306
  in Mexico, 406
  politics and, 124
  possible solutions to, 309–310
  types and causes of, 306–307
Police cynicism, 87
Police Foundation, 145, 147
Police reform, 12–16
Police Service of Northern Ireland (PSNI), 401–403
Police subculture, 68–93
  integrity and, 291
  personality and, 86–89
  recruiting, 69–72
  roles, functions, and styles of policing, 89–93
  sixth sense (suspicion), 81–84
  testing new personnel and, 73–77
  training and, 78–86
Policies and procedures, 109–110
Policing functions, 91–92
Policing styles, 92–93
Political patronage, attempts to thwart, 25–26
Politicization of the office of sheriff, 112
Politics, 123–125
Polygraph examinations, 76–77, 194, 202–203, 349
Polymerase chain reaction (PCR), 204
POP (problem-oriented policing), 161–169
  broader role for the street officer and, 173–174
Popow v. *City of Margate* (1979), 336
Pornography, child, 215–216
Portland, Oregon, Police Bureau (PPB), 358–359
  organizational structure of, 107, 108
Posse comitatus, 3
Posse Comitatus Act of 1878, 228
Powell v. *Alabama* (1932), 278
Powe v. *City of Chicago* (1981), 336
Preemployment physical testing, of female police officers, 357
Prejudice
  investigation and prosecution. *See* Bias-based policing
  as police corruption, 306
Preliminary investigation, 198
President's Commission on Law Enforcement and the Administration of Justice (President's Crime Commission, 1967), 32–33
Preston v. *United States* (1964), 271
Pretrial identification procedures, 274–275
Prevention of crime, 14
  in colonial period, 10
Prior v. *Woods* (1981), 335
Privacy and Civil Liberties Board, 230
Private life of police officers, 293
Private police, 365–368
Probable cause, 258–260
  doctrine of, 264
Problem-analysis triangle, 166
Problem-oriented policing (POP), 161–169
  broader role for the street officer and, 173–174
Procedures and practice, 109
  communication about, 103

Professionalization, movement toward (professional era of policing), 25–31
Profiling, criminal, 208–209
on the basis of race, 302–304
Prohibition, 55
Promotions, of female police officers, 361
Psychics, 209
Psycholinguistics, 209
Psychological profiling, 208–209
Psychological screening tests, 74
Public information officers (PIOs), 342–343
Public trust, maintaining the, 316
Pursuits, high-speed, 337, 339–342
preventing, 435–436
searches and, 270–272
simulation of, 86
Pynes, Joan, 79–80

Q

Qualified immunity, 334
Quarantine, 234
Questioning, excessive, 304

R

Racial gangs, 244–245
Racketeer Influenced and Corrupt Organizations Act (RICO), 241–243
RAND Corporation, 200
Raza, Susan, 70
Realists, 88
Reception, 102
Reconstructing the crime, 199
Recruitment, 69–72
in China, 396–397
of female police officers, 357
Mexican police, 407
of private police, 367
problems and successes in, 71–72
Reform, police, 12–16
Regional community policing institutes (RCPIs), 35
Rehnquist, William, 261, 263, 265, 270
Reiser, Martin, 209
Reiss, Albert, 297
Religious practices of police officers, 312
Repeat victimization (RV), 177
Republicanism, 10
Residency requirements for police officers, 313
Resource allocators, chief executive officers (CEOs) as, 116
Respondeat superior, doctrine of, 331–332
Responses, in SARA process, 168
Response time, 147
Restriction fragment length polymorphism (RFLP), 203
Richards, Dennis D., 118–119
RICO (Racketeer Influenced and Corrupt Organizations Act), 241–243
Ridgway, Gary, 206
Rights of police officers, 348–349
Rogues' gallery, 196
Role conflicts, 90–91, 375
Roles of police, 89–93
Roosevelt, Theodore, 19, 22
Rowan, Charles, 14
Rubber bullets, 424
Rules and regulations, 109, 110
Rumors, 103

S

Sacramento, California, Police Department (SPD), 303
Sager v. *City of Woodlawn Park* (1982), 336
St. Valentine's Day Massacre (1929), 194
Salary, 72
San Diego County, Automated Regional Justice Information System (ARJIS) of, 431
Santa Ana, California, Police Department, 425
Sapp, Allen, 313
SARA (scanning, analysis, response and assessment) problem-solving process, 161, 164–169
Saudi Arabia, 389–395
Scanning, 164–165
Schneckloth v. *Bustamonte* (1973), 273–274
Science and Technology directorate, 45–46
Scientific theory of administration, 26
Scotland Yard, 196

Searches and seizures, 258, 265–274
 of automobiles, 270–272
 consent to search, 273–274
 electronic surveillance and, 274
 incidental to lawful arrest, 267–268
 plain-view and open-field searches, 272–273
 of police officers, 311
 Section 1983 suits, 336
 stop and frisk, 268–270
 with and without a warrant, 267
Seattle, patrol allocation in, 135, 136
Secret Service, U.S. (USSS), 46–48, 197
Section 242, 337
Section 1001, 338
Section 1983 suits, 331, 332–336
 police actions leading to, liability under, 334–337
 against police supervisors, 338–339
Section 1988 of the Civil Rights Act (1976), 333
Seedman, Al, 71, 201
Self-incrimination, right against, 275, 312
Self-motivation, 89
Selye, Hans, 373
Sense of humor, 89
Sergeants (first-line supervisors), 120–123
Serial killers, 208–209
Serial offenders, locating, 430–431
Service style, 92–93
Sex crimes
 against minors, 215–216
 by officers, 313
Sexual contacts, citizen-initiated, 313
Sexual discrimination, female police officers and, 361
Sexual harassment, 313, 361
Sexually motivated nonsexual contacts, 313
Sexual misconduct, by police officers, 312–313
Sexual shakedowns, 313
Shakedown, 307
Sheriffs, 2–3, 112
Sheriff's offices, 62
Sherlock Holmes, 208
Sherman, Lawrence, 151, 305
Shift assignments, 137–139
Shift work, 375
Simple obsessional stalkers, 214
Simpson, O. J., 203
Sixth Amendment, 278–280
Sixth sense (suspicion), 81–84
Skinheads, 245
Skolnick, Jerome, 86, 90, 141–142
Slaughter, John, 24
Slippery slope perspective, 294–295
Slowdowns, work, 353
Society of Police Futurists International (PFI), 446, 447, 449
Sound Curdler, 424
Southerland, Mittie, 100–101
Sovereign immunity, doctrine of, 332
Span of control, 109
Special Operations Group (SOG), USMS, 58
Speedups, work, 354
Squawk Box, 424
Stalking investigations, 213–214
Star Chamber, 275
Stare decisis, 329–330
State courts, 331
State police, 61–62
Stengel v. *Belcher* (1975), 335
Stoddard, Ellwyn, 306
Stop and frisk, 268–270
Stoppages, work, 354
Street gangs, 243–249
 ethnic and racial, 244–245
 organization and revenues of, 243–244
 terrorism and, 248–249
Stress, 373–379
 definition of, 373
 effects and management of, 377–379
 sources of, 373–377
Stress academies, 79
Stun guns, 425
Styles, policing, 92–93
Subculture, police, 68–93
 integrity and, 291
 personality and, 86–89
 recruiting, 69–72
 roles, functions, and styles of policing, 89–93
 sixth sense (suspicion), 81–84
 testing new personnel and, 73–77
 training and, 78–86

Suicide of police officers, 378
Supervisors, first-line (sergeants), 120–123
Supportive supervisors, 123
Supreme Court, U.S. *See specific decisions*
Surveys to analyze problems, 167–168
Suspension, 321
Swanson, Charles, 195

T

Tactical crime analysis, 170–171
Taser, 425, 426
Taylor, Frederick, 26
Team policing, 33–35, 146–147
Tear gas, 423
Technical training model, 79
Technology, 419–440
  augmented reality (AR), 447–448
  crime mapping, 429–430
  DNA, 436–437
  electronics in traffic functions, 434–436
  fingerprints and mug shots, 437–438
  gunshot locator system, 432–433
  less-lethal, 422–427
  locating serial offenders, 430–431
  nanotechnology, 449
  terrorism and, 422
  unmanned aerial vehicles (UAVs), 449
  wireless, 428–433
Tempe, Arizona, Police Department, Crime Analysis Unit, 170–171
Tenacity, 89
"Ten Most Wanted Fugitives" list, 52
Tennessee v. *Garner* (1985), 152, 301, 314
Termination, 321
Terrorism, 225–235
  bioterrorism, 230–235
  definition of, 225
  FBI and, 51
  gangs and, 248–249
  interrogations of terrorism suspects, 210–211
  law enforcement resources and, 229
  situations involving terrorists, 226–227
  technology and, 422
  terrorism and, 227–229
  types of terrorists, 226
Terry, W. Clinton III, 133
Terry v. *Ohio* (1968), 268–269
Testing new personnel, 73–77
Texas Border Patrol, 428–429
Thirst for knowledge, 89
Thomas, Timothy, 289–290
Three-dimensional computer-aided drafting (3-D CAD) software, 438
Title VII of the Civil Rights Act of 1964, 312
Togliatti, George, 240–241
Tort liability, 330
Torts, 330–331
Traditional supervisors, 121, 123
Traffic accident investigation (TAI), 153–154
Traffic control, 152–154
Traffic stop data, collecting, 303
Training, 52, 78–86
  in China, 396–397
  field, 85–86
  Mexican police, 407
  new technology in, 85–86
  of private police, 367
Train robbers, 24
Traits of good officers, 88–89
Transfer, disciplinary, 321
Transmission, 102
Transportation Security Administration (TSA), 43–44
Tucson, Arizona, 73
Tulsa, Oklahoma, Police Department, 372

U

Undercover work, 201–202
Uniform Crime Reports (UCR), 48, 52–53
Uniformed Division (UD), 47
Uniforms (uniformed police force), 18, 80
Unionization, 349–350
United States v. *Jakobetz,* 205
United States v. *Robinson* (1973), 267

Unity of command, 107, 109
University of California (Berkeley), 28
University of Tennessee in Knoxville, 212
Unmanned aerial vehicles (UAVs), 251, 449
U.S. Marshals Service (USMS), 58–59
U.S. Visitor and Immigrant Status Indicator Technology (US-VISIT), 249
USA PATRIOT Act, 227–229

V

Van Maanen, John, 79
Verbal abuse, 304
Vicarious liability, 331–332
Vidocq Society, 188
Vigilantes, 23–24
Violence, use of. *See* Force and violence, use of
Violent Crime Control and Law Enforcement Act of 1994 (Crime Act), 34, 35, 372
Vollmer, August, 26–28, 30, 69, 369
  criminalistics and, 194
Vote of confidence, 353
Voyeuristic contacts, 313
Vucetich, Juan, 192

W

Wackenhut, George R., 365
Wackenhut Corporation, 365
Walling, George, 22
"War on crime" concept, 29
Washington, George, 58
Washoe County, Nevada, Sheriff's Office, gratuity policy of, 310
Watchman style, 92
Wax, Ari, 421
Weapons. *See also* Firearms
  less-lethal, 422–427
WebShot, 427
Webster v. *City of Houston* (1994), 335
Weeks v. *United States* (1914), 260
Wells, Henry, 365
Wells, Kenneth, 198, 200
Wells Fargo, 365
West, Will, 192
Western Identification Network, 437
Western United States, 22–24
Westley, William, 69, 86, 308, 373
Weston, Paul, 198, 200
Wickersham, George W., 30
Wickersham Commission, 28–30
Wild, Jonathan, 8
Williams, Alexander "Clubber," 295–296
Wilmington, Delaware, 147
Wilson, James Q., 35, 91–92, 148
Wilson, O. W., 27, 28, 33, 152
Wilson v. *Arkansas,* 265–266
WINPHO, 437
Wireless technology, 428–433
Witness Protection Program, 58–59
Women police officers, 70, 72, 355–363
  academy training of, 360
  agency and chief executive representation, 355–357
  family and career of, 362–363
  field training of, 360
  harassment and discrimination of, 361
  key issues affecting, 357, 360–363
  mentoring of, 361
  preemployment physical testing of, 357
  promotions of, 361
  recruitment of, 357
  rookie's assignments, 360–361
Working personality, 86–89
Work slowdowns, 353
Work speedups, 354
Work stoppages, 354
Wrightsman, Lawrence, 70
Writ of *amparo,* 408
Written communication, 104
Written examinations, 73–74
Wrongful death suits, 335

Y

Youth gangs. *See* Street gangs